EXAMMATRIX
CPA REVIEW TEXTBOOK

FAR

Financial Accounting & Reporting

SECTIONS 2000–2500

YEAR 2011

Matrix Learning Systems CPA Review Production Staff
Vice President of Accounting & Editorial/Controller: Pearl Zeiler, MBA
Coordinating Editor: James O'Leary
Desktop Publishing: Kimberli Mullen

Software Development Group:
Vice President of IT: Delmur Mayhak, Jr., CISA
Testing Supervisor: Randy Morrow, MIS
Graphic Artist: Barry Schapiro

This book contains material copyrighted © 1953 through 2011 by the American Institute of Certified Public Accountants, Inc., and is used or adapted with permission.

Portions of various FAF documents, copyright © by the Financial Accounting Foundation, 401 Merritt 7, P.O. Box 5116, Norwalk, CT 06856-5116, are reprinted with permission. Complete copies of these documents are available from the FASB and GASB.

This book contains material from Freeman/Shoulders/Allison, *Governmental & Nonprofit Accounting: Theory & Practice.* Reprinted by permission of Prentice Hall, Inc., Englewood Cliffs, NJ.

Material from Uniform CPA Examination Questions and Unofficial Answers, copyright © 1976 through 2010, American Institute of Certified Public Accountants, Inc., is used or adapted with permission.

The databanks contain material from Welsch/Newman/Zlatkovich, *Intermediate Accounting.* Reprinted by permission of Richard D. Irwin, Inc., Homewood, IL.

The databanks and textbooks contain quotations from *Governmental Accounting, Auditing, and Financial Reporting,* copyright © 2005 Government Finance Officers Association of the United States and Canada. Reprinted with permission.

This book is written to provide accurate and authoritative information concerning the covered topics. It is not meant to take the place of professional advice. **The content of this book has been updated to reflect relevant legislative and governing body modifications as of January 2011.**

Software copyright 2011, Matrix Learning Systems, Inc.

No part of this work may be reproduced or transmitted in any form or by any means, electronic or mechanical, including photocopying and recording, or by any information storage or retrieval system, except as may be expressly permitted by the 1976 Copyright Act or in writing by the Publisher. Requests for permission should be addressed in writing to Editor, Matrix Learning Systems, Inc; 7991 Shaffer Parkway, #100, Littleton, CO 80127.

Printed in the United States of America.

Preface

Congratulations on purchasing the ExamMatrix CPA Review. This powerful course is a complete system for success. It will teach you what you need to know, validate your readiness, and allow you to face the CPA Exams with confidence. It will guide you efficiently through your studies and help you achieve what thousands of other ExamMatrix accounting students and professionals before you have achieved—passing scores on the CPA Examination.

We use the power of your computer and our software to do the following:

- Provide you with your own personal instructor, who guides your customized study program.
- Prepare you for what to expect on the examination so there is no guesswork about what you need to know to pass.
- Coach you on ways to be physically, emotionally, and intellectually ready for the examination.
- Provide full printed text of examination preparation materials for you to study.
- Simulate the examination for you, drilling you with thousands of questions, weighted in accordance with the most current examination outlines.
- Give you instant help and guidance on every question, every step of the way, referring you back to the printed study materials when you need remedial help.
- Provide you with an Editorial Support Line to answer any questions that may arise while studying—call 877-272-7277.
- Provide a Pass Update or Pass Refund guarantee.
- Validate your readiness to pass each part of your examination.

You will pass with confidence.

The ExamMatrix CPA Review system components will help you reach that goal. The software portion of the ExamMatrix CPA Review is composed of the following:

- A database of over 4,000 categorized objective questions with immediate feedback to teach and review the points covered in the CPA testing process generated by the published weights from the AICPA Content Specification Outlines.

- Questions in the task-based simulation format are contained in all four exam sections.

- The ExamMatrix CPA Review textbooks, which accompany your software, utilize a unique cross-referencing system to sections and paragraphs. The software targets your weak areas and, through the cross-referencing system, guides you directly to the section in the textbook that covers that material. Each Review textbook contains the following:

- Concise reviews of authoritative pronouncements needed to pass the CPA Examination in easy-to-understand paragraph form
- Learning aids such as charts, tables, and flowcharts to aid in remembering concepts and procedures

The Review textbooks are categorized as follows:

- Section 2000 Financial Accounting & Reporting (FAR)
- Section 3000 Auditing & Attestation (AUD)
- Section 4000 Regulation (REG)
- Section 5000 Business Environment & Concepts (BEC)

Our software and our CPA Review textbooks reflect all legislative changes and are in accordance with the AICPA Content Specification Outlines.

Thinking about achieving an additional designation? Matrix Learning Systems carries reviews for the following exams:

- Certified Management Accountant
- Certified Internal Auditor
- Certified Information Systems Auditor
- Chartered Financial Analyst
- Enrolled Agent

Matrix Learning Systems will be at your side throughout your professional career, meeting your educational needs every step of the way.

Acknowledgments

The ExamMatrix CPA Review was developed and written by a team of professionals who are experts in the fields of accounting, business law, and computer science, and are also experienced teachers in CPA Review programs and continuing professional education courses.

Matrix Learning Systems expresses its sincere appreciation to the many individual candidates, as well as accounting instructors, who took time to write to us about previous editions. The improvements in this edition are attributable to all of these individuals. Of course, any deficiencies are the responsibilities of the editors and authors. We very much appreciate and solicit your comments and suggestions about this year's edition.

The editors and authors are also indebted to the American Institute of Certified Public Accountants, the Financial Accounting Standards Board, and the Governmental Accounting Standards Board for permission to quote from their pronouncements. In addition, the AICPA granted us permission to use material from previous Uniform CPA Examination Questions and Answers. AICPA codification numbers are used throughout the Review to indicate the source of materials.

We recognize the work and dedication of our team of software designers and developers. Their vision has made this the best product possible. They contributed countless hours to deliver this package and are each fully dedicated to helping you pass the exam. Our thanks go out to the many individuals who have made contributions to both the software and textbook portions of the CPA Review. We extend our gratitude to our team of software testers who ensure that you receive only the highest quality product. Finally, we express appreciation to the editorial teams who have devoted their time to review this product. They have provided invaluable aid in the writing and production of the ExamMatrix CPA Review.

Good luck on the exam!

Matrix Learning Systems

ExamMatrix CPA Review Textbook Authors

Raymond J. Clay, Jr., DBA, CPA, holds the Internal Audit Professorship in Accounting at the University of North Texas. Prior to joining the University of North Texas, he served as Director of Professional Development at Union Pacific Corporation. Dr. Clay has held faculty positions in accounting at Indiana State University and Texas Tech University. He received his bachelor's and master's degrees from Northern Illinois University and his doctorate from the University of Kentucky. He has held significant committee appointments with professional organizations, including serving as a member of the AICPA Accounting and Review Services Committee for seven years. Dr. Clay is the author of 4 books, 10 continuing professional education courses, and numerous articles appearing in professional journals.

Ennis M. Hawkins, DBA, CPA, CMA, CIA, was a Professor of Accounting at Sam Houston State University in Huntsville, Texas. His teaching and research interests include environmental and cost accounting. Dr. Hawkins has served as the Program Co-Chairman and Vice President of the Southwest Region American Accounting Association. He is also a member of the AICPA, IMA, and IIA.

Jill Hazelbauer-Von der Ohe, MBA, CPA, CMA, CFM, CVA, has her MBA from Rockford College and is currently a professor at Keller University, where she teaches accounting. In addition to a CPA, she holds CMA and CFM certifications, having received the Gold Award for the CFM exam during the 1997-98 winter exam cycle. She also holds a CVA (Certified Valuation Analyst) through NACVA, a professional organization that focuses on the valuation of closely held business for tax, estate, and other purposes. She has worked on accounting projects in Uganda and Poland.

David G. Jaeger, JD, MST, MBA, is currently Associate Professor of Accounting and Taxation at the University of North Florida. He has taught numerous courses in taxation and business law at the undergraduate, MBA, Executive MBA, and Master of Accountancy levels, as well as in continuing education courses. His research has been published in such journals as *The Tax Advisor, TAXES, Tax Notes,* the *Journal of Accountancy,* and *Research in Accounting Regulation.* His work has also been cited by the U.S. Tax Court and several U.S. Federal Courts of Appeal.

Tabitha McCormick, CPA, CFE, is the owner of Cornerstone Accounting in Millville, Pennsylvania. Cornerstone Accounting concentrates on training small business owners and financial employees to keep accurate accounting records, create efficient and effective policies and procedures, and institute strong internal controls. Cornerstone also assists businesses with implementing accounting software packages. She is a Certified Advanced QuickBooks® and QuickBooks Point of Sale® ProAdvisor and enjoys teaching QuickBooks classes for Bloomsburg University's Magee Center and other training institutions. Tabitha is also the author of two CPE courses on Identity Theft for MicroMash. She is a member of the Pennsylvania Institute of Certified Public Accountants (PICPA) and the Association of Certified Fraud Examiners (ACFE).

Darlene A. Pulliam, PhD, CPA, joined the faculty of West Texas A&M in 1997. A native of eastern New Mexico, Dr. Pulliam received a BS in Mathematics in 1976 and an MBA in 1978 from Eastern New Mexico University and joined the accounting firm of Peat Marwick and Mitchell and Co. (now KPMG) in Albuquerque. After five years in public accounting, she completed her PhD at the University of North Texas and joined the faculty of the University of Tulsa in 1987. During her 10 years in Tulsa, she taught primarily in the University of Tulsa's Master of Taxation program. Her publications include many articles appearing in *Tax Advisor*; the *Journal of Accountancy; Practical Tax Strategies; Oil, Gas and Energy Quarterly*; and the *Journal of Forensic Accounting* as an author or coauthor.

Craig D. Shoulders, PhD, joined the faculty at the University of North Carolina at Pembroke in 2004 after serving over 20 years on the accounting faculty at Virginia Tech. Dr. Shoulders has received the Cornelius E. Tierney/Ernst & Young Research Award from the Association of Government Accountants and has been recognized twice by the AICPA as an Outstanding Discussion Leader. He has recently completed a major research study on the financial reporting entity for the Governmental Accounting Standards Board and coauthors a Prentice Hall textbook on state and local government accounting as well as several continuing education courses on governmental accounting and financial reporting. Dr. Shoulders received his bachelor's degree from Campbellsville University, his master's degree from the University of Missouri-Columbia, and his PhD from Texas Tech University.

Strategic Solutions for Business (SSB) is a management consulting firm based in Denver, Colorado, specializing in accounting and information technology. **Bryan Smith, CPA,** is a managing partner of SSB with over eleven years of experience assisting clients with business intelligence, data conversions, revenue/cost assurance, data and process analytics, internal audit, operational metrics, mergers and acquisitions, and financial and regulatory compliance. **Cary Lopez, CPA, PMP,** previously a staff accountant at one of the Big Four, has worked in consulting for over five years. She has worked in various industries including oil and gas, telecommunications, financial services, software, and healthcare. Cary's focus is on business analysis and project management with an emphasis on IT and accounting projects. She has written numerous training and certification guides.

Matrix Learning Systems

ExamMatrix CPA Review Question Database Contributors

Paul N. Brown, CPA, is the Director of Technical Services for the Florida Institute of CPAs (FICPA). One of his main duties is to serve as the technical reviewer in Florida for the AICPA Peer Review Program, which administers approximately 600 reviews annually in Florida. Paul has previously been an instructor for the AICPA Advanced Reviewers Training Course and writes and instructs his own course in Florida on peer review called Peer Review Forum for Reviewers, for which he has received several outstanding discussion leader and author awards. He has also served on the AICPA's Technical Reviewers Advisory Task Force to the Peer Review Board and serves as staff liaison to various committees of the Florida Institute of CPAs. Prior to joining the FICPA, Paul was an audit manager with a regional firm in Florida. He holds a BS in Accounting and Finance from Florida State University.

Annhenrie Campbell, PhD, CPA, CMA, CGFM, is a Professor of Accounting at California State University, Stanislaus. While working as a municipal accountant, Dr. Campbell taught governmental and not-for-profit accounting as an adjunct lecturer for several years. She completed her MBA at Humboldt State University in California and her PhD at the University of Colorado in Boulder. After earning a CPA and CMA and starting her university career, Dr. Campbell became a Certified Government Financial Manager at the start of the CGFM program. She has maintained her interest in students' professional preparation for governmental and not-for-profit careers, starting with her MBA thesis topic and a joint publication on the topic in the *Government Accountants' Journal,* and continuing now in teaching both graduate and undergraduate students. In addition to numerous presentations, Dr. Campbell and her colleagues have published additional articles on educational issues in the *Journal of Business and Management, The Accounting Educators' Journal, Accounting Perspectives,* and the *Journal of the Academy of Business Education* (forthcoming).

Anthony P. Curatola, PhD, is the Joseph F. Ford Professor of Accounting at Drexel University. He holds a BS in Accounting and an MBA in Finance from Drexel University, an MA in Accounting from the Wharton Graduate School of the University of Pennsylvania, and a PhD in Accounting from Texas A&M University. Dr. Curatola joined the faculty of Louisiana State University in 1981 and returned to Drexel University in 1989 by accepting the appointment to the Joseph F. Ford Professor of Accounting Chair. Dr. Curatola's findings have appeared in media such as *Forbes,* the *Washington Post, Money* magazine, the *Wall Street Journal,* and the *New York Times,* to name a few. Currently he serves on the Foundation of Academic Research. Most recently, he was awarded the R. Lee Brummet Award in Academic Excellence from the IMA.

Jill Hazelbauer-Von der Ohe, MBA, CPA, CMA, CFM, CVA, has her MBA from Rockford College and is currently a professor at Keller University, where she teaches accounting. In addition to a CPA, she holds CMA and CFM certifications, having received the Gold Award for the CFM exam during the 1997-98 winter exam cycle. She also holds a CVA (Certified Valuation Analyst) through NACVA, a professional organization that focuses on the valuation of closely held business for tax, estate, and other purposes. She has worked on accounting projects in Uganda and Poland.

Taylor S. Klett, CPA, JD, is of counsel for the firm of Havins & Associates, LLP. He is currently an Associate Professor at Sam Houston State University and was an administrator and on the adjunct faculty there. His teaching and research interests include taxation, estate planning, ethics, and business law. He is an attorney and CPA in Texas and a member of the American Bar Association, Texas Bar Association, and AICPA. He graduated from the University of Texas and attended law school at the University of Houston Law Center (JD, with honors).

Tabitha McCormick, CPA, CFE, is the owner of Cornerstone Accounting in Millville, Pennsylvania. Cornerstone Accounting concentrates on training small business owners and financial employees to keep accurate accounting records, create efficient and effective policies and procedures, and institute strong internal controls. Cornerstone also assists businesses with implementing accounting software packages. She is a Certified Advanced QuickBooks® and QuickBooks Point of Sale® ProAdvisor and enjoys teaching QuickBooks classes for Bloomsburg University's Magee Center and other training institutions. Tabitha is also the author of two CPE courses on Identity Theft for MicroMash. She is a member of the Pennsylvania Institute of Certified Public Accountants (PICPA) and the Association of Certified Fraud Examiners (ACFE).

Robert J. Nieschwietz, a Visiting Assistant Professor at Seattle University, received his PhD in Accountancy from Arizona State University in 2001. He received a BBA and MS in Accounting from Texas A&M University in 1991 and 1996, respectively. Dr. Nieschwietz's primary research and teaching interests are within the area of auditing. His research has been published in various journals, including the *Journal of Accounting Literature, International Journal of Accounting Information Systems, International Journal of Auditing, Journal of Accounting Education, Journal of Applied Business Research, Academy of Accounting and Financial Studies Journal,* and *Journal of Risk Research*.

Paul Pierson is Director of Technical Services for the Illinois CPA Society. In this capacity, he oversees the administration of the AICPA Peer Review Program for approximately 1,300 CPA firms in Illinois. Paul has served as a discussion leader at the AICPA's Annual Peer Review Conference and its Advanced Reviewer Training Course, and is editor for the Society's peer review newsletter. He is also responsible for monitoring the continuing professional education and licensing rules in the state and responding to member inquiries regarding those matters. He currently serves on the Technical Reviewers' Advisory Task Force of the AICPA, having previously served a three-year term, and is the staff liaison for the Illinois CPA Society's Peer Review Report Acceptance and Governmental Accounting Executive Committees. Paul graduated from Illinois State University with a BS in Accounting and was an audit manager with a large, local CPA firm in East Peoria, Illinois, prior to joining the Society.

Darlene A. Pulliam, PhD, CPA, joined the faculty of West Texas A&M in 1997. A native of eastern New Mexico, Dr. Pulliam received a BS in Mathematics in 1976 and an MBA in 1978 from Eastern New Mexico University and joined the accounting firm of Peat Marwick and Mitchell and Co. (now KPMG) in Albuquerque. After five years in public accounting, she completed her PhD at the University of North Texas and joined the faculty of the University of Tulsa in 1987. During her 10 years in Tulsa, she taught primarily in the University of Tulsa's Master of Taxation program. Her publications include many articles appearing in *Tax Advisor*; the *Journal of Accountancy; Practical Tax Strategies; Oil, Gas and Energy Quarterly*; and the *Journal of Forensic Accounting* as an author or coauthor.

Marianne Rexer, PhD, CPA, is currently an Associate Professor of Accounting at Wilkes University. She has also taught at Drexel University and Johnson & Wales University. She received her PhD in Accounting at Drexel in 1997, her MS in Taxation at Bryant College in 1989, and her BS in Accounting from Wilkes University in 1985. Dr. Rexer has worked at a national CPA firm. She is a member of the American Accounting Association, the AICPA, the AICPA Audit Division, and the Pennsylvania Institute of CPAs.

Reg Rezac, PhD, MS, BS, is a Professor of Accounting at Texas Woman's University. He received his bachelor's from Jamestown College, his master's degree from the University of North Dakota, and his doctorate from the University of Northern Colorado. He has written tax material for numerous continuing professional education courses, as well as CPA review courses and chapters of taxation texts. Rezac both developed and was the first director of the Master of Taxation program at the American University. He teaches an online tax research course at TWU for undergraduate, graduate, and continuing education credit.

Strategic Solutions for Business (SSB) is a management consulting firm based in Denver, Colorado, specializing in accounting and information technology. **Bryan Smith, CPA,** is a managing partner of SSB with over eleven years of experience assisting clients with business intelligence, data conversions, revenue/cost assurance, data and process analytics, internal audit, operational metrics, mergers and acquisitions, and financial and regulatory compliance. **Cary Lopez, CPA, PMP,** previously a staff accountant at one of the Big Four, has worked in consulting for over five years. She has worked in various industries including oil and gas, telecommunications, financial services, software, and healthcare. Cary's focus is on business analysis and project management with an emphasis on IT and accounting projects. She has written numerous training and certification guides.

Kevin D. Zeiler, JD, MBA, is an Assistant Professor of Health Care Management at the Metropolitan State College of Denver. Professor Zeiler holds a BS in Health Care Management from the Metropolitan State College of Denver, an MBA from Regis University, and a Juris Doctorate from the University of Denver College of Law. Prior to becoming a faculty member, he worked for several years as a Denver Paramedic and continues to maintain his certification in the State of Colorado. Professor Zeiler teaches upper-level management courses in finance, health disparities, management, and law.

Table of Contents

Financial Accounting & Reporting

Section 2000	Overview of the Financial Accounting and Reporting Examination	1
Section 2100	Conceptual Framework, Standards, Standard Setting, and Presentation of Financial Statements	5
Section 2200	Financial Statement Accounts: Recognition, Measurement, Valuation, Calculation, Presentation, and Disclosures	83
Section 2300	Specific Transactions, Events, and Disclosures: Recognition, Measurement, Valuation, Calculation, Presentation, and Disclosures	243
Section 2400	Governmental Accounting and Reporting	435
Section 2500	Not-for-Profit (Nongovernmental) Accounting and Reporting	539
	Index	553

This page intentionally left blank.

Section 2000
Overview of the Financial Accounting & Reporting Examination

2010 Purpose of the Examination
    2011 Examination Format
    2012 Pronouncements
    2013 Suggested Readings and References

2010 Purpose of the Examination

2011 Examination Format

2011.01 The Financial Accounting and Reporting section tests the candidate's knowledge of accounting principles generally accepted in the United States and standards accepted for international financial reporting (IFRS) for business enterprises, not-for-profit organizations, and governmental entities, and the skills needed to apply that knowledge. Content covered in this section includes financial accounting concepts and standards and their applications. To demonstrate such knowledge and skills, candidates will be required to:

- Identify and understand the differences between financial statements prepared on the basis of accounting principles generally accepted in the United States of America (U.S. GAAP) and International Financial Reporting Standards (IFRS).

- Prepare and/or review source documents, including account classification, and enter data into subsidiary and general ledgers

- Calculate amounts for financial statement components.

- Reconcile the general ledger to the subsidiary ledgers or underlying account details.

- Prepare account reconciliation and related schedules; analyze accounts for unusual fluctuations and make necessary adjustments.

- Prepare consolidating and eliminating entries for the period.

- Identify financial accounting and reporting methods and select those that are appropriate.

- Prepare consolidated financial statements, including balance sheets, income statements, and statements of retained earnings, equity, comprehensive income, and cash flows.

- Prepare appropriate notes to the financial statements.

- Analyze financial statements, including analysis of accounts, variances, trends, and ratios.

- Exercise judgment in the application of accounting principles.

- Apply judgment to evaluate assumptions and methods underlying estimates, including fair value measures of financial statement components.

- Produce required financial statement filings in order to meet regulatory or reporting requirements (e.g., Form 10-Q, 10-K, Annual Report).

- Determine appropriate accounting treatment for new or unusual transactions and evaluate the economic substance of transactions in making the determinations.
- Research relevant professional literature.

Source: *AICPA Content and Skill Specifications for the Uniform CPA Examination*, May 15, 2009

2012 Pronouncements

2012.01 As of September 15, 2009, the AICPA is using *The Financial Accounting Standards Board (FASB) Accounting Standards Codification*™ as the source of authoritative generally accepted accounting principles (GAAP) to be applied for only nongovernmental entities. Other authoritative standards being used are the rules and interpretive releases of the Securities and Exchange Commission (SEC) under authority of federal securities laws.

2013 Suggested Readings and References

2013.01 In addition to the careful reading and study of the ExamMatrix CPA Review, CPA candidates should also refer to other literature resources when necessary. The following references to suggested supplementary readings should be consulted when desirable:

a. **Textbooks:**

(1) **Intermediate accounting:**
- **Spiceland,** J. David, et al. *Intermediate Accounting.* New York: McGraw-Hill
- **Kieso,** Donald E. and Jerry J. Weygandt. *Intermediate Accounting.* New York: John Wiley & Sons.
- **Nikolai,** Loren A. and John D. Bazley. *Intermediate Accounting.* Mason, Ohio: Thomson South-Western
- **Stice,** James, et al. *Intermediate Accounting.* Mason, Ohio: Thomson South-Western.

(2) **Advanced accounting:**
- **Baker,** Richard E., et al. *Advanced Financial Accounting.* New York: McGraw-Hill.
- **Beams,** Floyd, A. et al. *Advanced Accounting.* Englewood Cliffs: Prentice Hall.
- **Hoyle,** Joe B. *Advanced Accounting.* New York: McGraw-Hill.
- **Jeter,** Debra, et al.. *Advanced Accounting.* New York: John Wiley & Sons.
- **Larsen,** E. John. *Modern Advanced Accounting.* New York: McGraw-Hill.
- **Pahler,** Arnold J., and Joseph E. Mori. *Advanced Accounting.* Mason, Ohio: Thomson South-Western.

(3) **Accounting theory:**
- **Hendriksen,** Eldon S. *Accounting Theory.* Homewood, IL: Richard D. Irwin.
- **Kam,** Vernon. *Accounting Theory.* New York: John Wiley & Sons.
- **Schroeder,** Richard G., et al. *Accounting Theory: Text and Readings.* New York: John Wiley & Sons.

— **Wolk,** Harry, et al. *Accounting Theory: Conceptual Issues in a Political and Economic Environment.* Mason, Ohio: Thomson South-Western.

    b. Other:

        (1) Journal articles, particularly in the *Journal of Accountancy* and *The CPA Journal*

        (2) Technical publications of CPA firms or private industries

This page intentionally left blank.

Section 2100
Conceptual Framework, Standards, Standard Setting, and Presentation of Financial Statements

2101 Basic Concepts and Financial Statement Overview

2110 Process by Which Accounting Standards Are Set and Roles of Accounting Standard-Setting Bodies
- 2111 U.S. Securities and Exchange Commission (SEC)
- 2112 Financial Accounting Standards Board (FASB)
- 2113 International Accounting Standards Board (IASB)
- 2114 Governmental Accounting Standards Board (GASB)

2120 Conceptual Framework
- 2121 Financial Reporting by Business Entities
- 2122 Financial Reporting by Not-for-Profit (Nongovernmental) Entities
- 2123 Financial Reporting by State and Local Governmental Entities

2130 Financial Reporting, Presentation, and Disclosures in General-Purpose Financial Statements
- 2131 Balance Sheet
- 2132 Income Statement
- 2133 Statement of Comprehensive Income
- 2134 Statement of Changes in Equity
- 2135 Statement of Cash Flows
- 2136 Notes to Financial Statements
- 2137 Consolidated and Combined Financial Statements
- 2138 First-Time Adoption of IFRS

2140 SEC Reporting Requirements (e.g., Form 10-Q, 10-K)

2150 Other Financial Statement Presentations, Including Other Comprehensive Bases of Accounting (OCBOA)
- 2151 Cash Basis
- 2152 Modified Cash Basis
- 2153 Income Tax Basis
- 2154 Personal Financial Statements
- 2155 Financial Statements of Employee Benefit Plans/Trusts

2101 Basic Concepts and Financial Statement Overview

2101.01 This section covers a number of topics related to the theory underlying financial statements and the form and content of financial statements under generally accepted accounting principles. Emphasis is placed on the preparation of the balance sheet, income statement, statement of cash flows, and the numerous disclosures that are an important part of these financial statements. Heavy reliance is placed on authoritative accounting pronouncements, primarily the FASB's conceptual framework and the FASB's *Accounting Standards Codification,* in those areas where they specify the form and content of financial statements.

In the following sections, much of the material is drawn from the authoritative accounting pronouncements. To assist in locating the various pronouncements where certain subjects are covered, the following abbreviations are used throughout these sections:

APBO	=	Accounting Principles Board Opinion
ARB	=	Accounting Research Bulletin (of the Committee on Accounting Procedure)
FASB ASC	=	FASB Accounting Standards Codification
FASBI	=	FASB Interpretation (may also be shown as FASBIN)
FASBTB	=	FASB Technical Bulletin
IAS	=	International Accounting Standard
IFRS	=	International Financial Reporting Standard
SFAS	=	(FASB) Statement of Financial Accounting Standards
SFAC	=	(FASB) Statement of Financial Accounting Concepts

2110 Process by Which Accounting Standards Are Set and Roles of Accounting Standard-Setting Bodies

2111 U.S. Securities and Exchange Commission (SEC)

2111.01 The Securities and Exchange Commission (SEC) is a governmental entity created to protect the interest of investors by ensuring full and adequate disclosure by publicly traded companies. Although the SEC has the authority to establish standards, it has generally deferred to the Financial Accounting Standards Board (FASB) or its predecessors to generate U.S. accounting standards.

2111.02 The SEC's website, **www.sec.gov,** includes a description of the rulemaking process within the SEC:

How the SEC Rulemaking Process Works

Rulemaking is the process by which federal agencies implement legislation passed by Congress and signed into law by the President. Major pieces of legislation, such as the Securities Act of 1933, the Securities Exchange Act of 1934, the Investment Company Act of 1940, and the Sarbanes-Oxley Act, provide the framework for the SEC's oversight of the securities markets. These statutes are broadly drafted, establishing basic principles and objectives. To ensure that the intent of Congress is carried out in specific circumstances—and as the securities markets evolve technologically, expand in size, and offer new products and services—the SEC engages in rulemaking.

Rulemaking can involve several steps: concept release, rule proposal, and rule adoption.

Concept Release: The rulemaking process usually begins with a rule proposal, but sometimes an issue is so unique and/or complicated that the Commission seeks out public input on which, if any, regulatory approach is appropriate. A concept release is issued describing the area of interest and the Commission's concerns and usually identifying different approaches to addressing the problem, followed by a series of questions that seek the views of the public on the issue. The public's feedback is taken into consideration as the Commission decides which approach, if any, is appropriate.

Rule Proposal: The Commission publishes a detailed formal rule proposal for public comment. Unlike a concept release, a rule proposal advances specific objectives and methods for achieving them. Typically the Commission provides between 30 and 60 days for review and comment. Just as with a concept release, the public comment is considered vital to the formulation of a final rule.

Rule Adoption: Finally, the Commissioners consider what they have learned from the public exposure of the proposed rule, and seek to agree on the specifics of a final rule. If a final measure is then adopted by vote of the full Commission, it becomes part of the official rules that govern the securities industry.

The SEC does issue its own rules in the form of Financial Reporting Releases, which generally agree with U.S. GAAP.

2112 Financial Accounting Standards Board (FASB)

Nature and Source of Authoritative Accounting Standards and Roles of Standard-Setting Bodies

2112.01 Specific measurement and reporting practices followed in the preparation of financial statements are based on several underlying concepts often are referred to as "principles" or "standards."

2112.02 Basic accounting principles or standards, commonly referred to as generally accepted accounting principles (GAAP), represent the most authoritative position at any point in time as to which economic resources and obligations should be recognized in financial statements as assets and liabilities, which changes in those assets and liabilities should be recognized, when those changes should be recognized, how those recognized changes should be measured, what information should be disclosed and how that information should be disclosed, and which financial statements should be prepared.

2112.03 Specific accounting principles are included in GAAP by virtue of having *substantial authoritative support.*

2112.04 For publicly held enterprises, such support comes primarily from the Securities and Exchange Commission (SEC). In Accounting Series Release (ASR) No. 150, the SEC specified that accounting principles followed in financial statements of SEC registrants must have substantial authoritative support. The SEC further noted in ASR 150 that "principles, standards, and practices promulgated by the FASB in its Statements and Interpretations will be considered by the Commission as having substantial authoritative support, and those contrary to such FASB promulgations will be considered to have no such support." The SEC also requires that SEC registrants follow any Accounting Research Bulletins (issued by the former Committee on Accounting Principles of the AICPA) and APB Opinions (issued by the former Accounting Principles Board of the AICPA) that have not been superseded by an FASB Statement or FASB Interpretation.

2112.05 Thus, the SEC, which is empowered by congress to regulate the securities markets, has chosen to follow the pronouncements of the FASB as long as they do not disagree with those pronouncements. However, if the SEC disagrees with those pronouncements, it has the power to overrule those pronouncements, as it has done on a few occasions.

2112.06　For publicly held enterprises, support for the FASB's pronouncements also comes from Rule 203 of the AICPA's Code of Professional Conduct, which specifies that an opinion that financial statements are in conformity with GAAP shall not be issued if such statements contain a departure from accounting principles promulgated by the body designated to establish accounting principles, unless the CPA can demonstrate that due to unusual circumstances the financial statements would otherwise be misleading. (If such a departure exists, the report should describe the departure, the approximate effects on the financial statements, and the reason(s) why compliance with the principle would result in a misleading statement.)

2112.07　For nonpublic enterprises, substantial authoritative support comes primarily from Rule 203 of the AICPA's Code of Professional Conduct since those enterprises are not SEC registrants.

2112.08　In addition, for both publicly held and nonpublic enterprises, support for the FASB's pronouncements comes from the various state boards of public accountancy, which generally require that practicing CPAs follow the pronouncements of the FASB, if applicable. In the absence of any specific FASB pronouncement, such state boards require that CPAs follow the recommendations (pronouncements) of the next most authoritative source.

Review of Underlying Principles

2112.09　The following list includes many of the underlying principles that support specific current accounting practices. The principle is identified to the left, an explanation of the principle appears in the middle column, and an example of the application of the principle appears to the right.

Underlying Principle	Explanation	Application
a. Historical cost	As a measurement basis, historical cost is the most objectively determinable and is the proper basis for the recording of many asset acquisitions, expenses, costs, creditor equities, and owner equities.	Plant assets are recorded at their historical cost and not current replacement value or some other basis in the primary financial statements.
b. Revenue recognition	Revenue is recognized when it is earned, measurable, and collectible. At this point, the earnings process is virtually complete. Although recognition through sale is the most consistently used test, circumstances may allow recognition at other points in the earning cycle.	Accrual accounting recognizes revenue at the point of sale and is generally accepted as opposed to the cash basis of accounting which records revenues in the period during which cash is received.
c. Matching	Net income or loss for an accounting period is determined by the process of associating realized revenues with those expenses and expired costs necessary to generate them. This often requires estimates and allocations.	The accrual basis of accounting correctly matches the revenue from the sale of goods with the historical cost of the inventory sold, the salesperson's salary, and other applicable costs and expenses.
d. Consistency	To enhance financial statement comparability, an entity employs the same accounting procedures from period to period. Changes within GAAP should be justified by more appropriate presentation of financial position and results of operations.	The LIFO inventory method, once adopted, is applied in following years.
e. Disclosure	Financial statements should include all information germane to the formation of valid business decisions. The user must neither be burdened with an information overload nor misled by the exclusion of material facts.	Notes to the financial statements are a common form of supplementary disclosure.
f. Objectivity/ verifiability	The economic activity which underlies financial statements must not only be substantive in fact but also presented without bias so as to be subject to similar determination by other technically competent individuals.	Plant assets are carried at cost, which is generally definite and determinable, and not at net present value based on subjective judgments.
g. Separate entity	A business enterprise is a discrete unit of accountability whose economic activities are kept separate from those of its owners and other business enterprises.	Personal business transactions of a major stockholder are not reported in the financial statements of a corporation.

h. Continuity/ going concern	In the absence of evidence to the contrary, an entity is assumed to have a life that is indefinite or sufficiently long for it to accomplish its objectives and fulfill its legal obligations.	Liquidation values of assets and liabilities are ordinarily not used in preparing a company's balance sheet.
i. Unit of measure	The common denominator upon which all financial data are based is the monetary unit. Further, it is assumed that the monetary unit remains stable in value (or changes are immaterial in amount) so that the impact of real changes in its purchasing power remain unadjusted-for in the primary financial statements.	The economic activity of a U.S. business enterprise is quantified in terms of the dollar. Inflationary trends are not reflected in the primary financial statements by adjustments to nonmonetary items.
j. Periodicity	The life of an enterprise is divided into artificial time periods to facilitate reporting and decision making.	Although the success or failure of an enterprise is subject to the most accurate determination when the enterprise discontinues operations, financial statements are prepared annually.

Modifying Conventions

2112.10 Strict adherence to the underlying principles as described in section **2112.09**, and to the specific practices that make up GAAP does not follow in all cases due to certain influences. These influences are identified here as modifying conventions and represent conceptual explanations for a departure from what might otherwise be thought of as generally accepted.

2112.11 In the same format used in presenting the underlying principles in section **2112.09**, the modifying conventions are presented as follows:

Modifying Convention	Explanation	Application
a. Conservatism	When confronted with alternative accounting procedures, the accountant follows that which has the least favorable impact on current income.	Losses may be anticipated while gains are normally not recognized in the accounts until they are realized.
b. Industry practices.	Departure from strict compliance with GAAP may exist in some cases due to the peculiar nature of the industry in which an enterprise operates.	Due primarily to allocation problems, the companies in the meat packing industry carry inventory at selling prices less costs of disposal, a departure from the principle of historical cost.
c. Substance over form	The economic substance of a transaction determines the accounting treatment, even though the legal form of the transaction may indicate a different treatment.	Under certain circumstances, leased property may be capitalized as a sale (by the lessor) and as an acquisition (by the lessee).
d. Application of judgment	In some cases, strict adherence to GAAP produces results that are unreasonable. A departure from GAAP may be made to render results that appear reasonable in the circumstances.	Disclosure of events which is not required by authoritative pronouncements may be considered necessary in specific circumstances by individual accountant(s) responsible for the content of financial statements.
e. Materiality	The accounting treatment of many items is dependent upon their resultant impact on users' decisions. Strict compliance with GAAP is necessary only when an item, due to its dollar size and/or nature, has a significant effect on financial statements and the accompanying investor decisions.	The purchase price of inexpensive long-lived assets might be expensed (rather than being capitalized and depreciated over their useful lives) if the dollar amounts involved are so small as to be insignificant.

Accounting Standards Codification

2112.12 Under FASB ASC 105-10-05-1, effective for financial statements issued for interim and annual periods ending after September 15, 2009, the *Accounting Standards Codification* is the single source of authoritative GAAP recognized by the FASB to be applied by nongovernmental entities. Rules and interpretive releases of the SEC under federal securities laws are also sources of authoritative GAAP for SEC registrants. All guidance contained in the Codification carries an equal level of authority.

2112.13 FASB ASC 105-10-05-2 requires that if the guidance for a transaction or event is not specified within a source of authoritative GAAP for that entity, an entity must first consider accounting principles for similar transactions or events within a source of authoritative GAAP for that entity and then consider nonauthoritative guidance from other sources. An entity cannot follow the accounting treatment specified in accounting guidance for similar transactions or events in cases in which those accounting principles either prohibit the application of the accounting treatment to the particular transaction or event or indicate that the accounting treatment should not be applied by analogy.

2112.14 FASB ASC 105-10-05-3 lists sources of nonauthoritative accounting guidance and literature that include, for example:

   a. practices that are widely recognized and prevalent either generally or in the industry,

   b. FASB Concepts Statements,

   c. American Institute of Certified Public Accountants (AICPA) Issues Papers,

   d. International Financial Reporting Standards of the International Accounting Standards Board (IASB),

   e. pronouncements of professional associations or regulatory agencies,

   f. Technical Information Service Inquiries and replies included in AICPA Technical Practice Aids, and

   g. accounting textbooks, handbooks, and articles.

   The appropriateness of other sources of accounting guidance depends on its relevance to particular circumstances, the specificity of the guidance, the general recognition of the issuer or author as an authority, and the extent of its use in practice.

2112.15 Accounting Standards Updates issued after the effective date of the Codification will not be considered authoritative in their own right. Instead, the Accounting Standards Updates will serve only to update the Codification, provide background information about the guidance, and provide the bases for conclusions on the change(s) in the Codification. After the effective date of the Codification, all nongrandfathered, non-SEC accounting literature not included in the Codification is superseded and deemed nonauthoritative. (FASB ASC 105-10-05-5)

2112.16 **Grandfathered guidance:** An entity that has followed, and continues to follow, an accounting treatment that was previously in category (c) or category (d) of that GAAP hierarchy as of March 15, 1992, need not change to an accounting treatment in a higher category ((b) or (c)) of that hierarchy (now included in the Codification in accordance with FASB ASC 105-10-70-1) if its effective date was before March 15, 1992. For standards whose effective date is after March 15, 1992, and for entities initially applying an accounting principle after March 15, 1992 (except for FASB Emerging Issues Task Force (EITF) consensus positions issued before March 16, 1992, which become effective in the hierarchy for initial application of an accounting principle after March 15, 1993), an entity shall follow the guidance in the Codification. (FASB ASC 105-10-70-1)

2112.17 Certain accounting standards, when issued, allowed for the continued application of superseded accounting standards for transactions that have an ongoing effect in an entity's financial statements. That superseded guidance has not been included in the Codification, is considered grandfathered, and remains authoritative for those transactions after the effective date of the Codification. The following are examples of such grandfathered items (FASB ASC 105-10-70-2):

   a. Pooling of interests in a business combination (originally addressed by APB Opinion 16, *Business Combinations*) described in paragraph B217 of SFAS 141, *Business Combinations*

   b. Pension transition assets or obligations described in paragraph 77 of SFAS 87, *Employers' Accounting for Pensions*

   c. Employee stock ownership plan shares (originally addressed by AICPA Statement of Position 76-3, *Accounting Practices for Certain Employee Stock Ownership Plans*) purchased by, and held as of December 31, 1992, as described in paragraphs 97 and 102 of AICPA Statement of Position 93-6, *Employers' Accounting for Employee Stock Ownership Plans*

   d. Loans restructured in a troubled debt restructuring before the effective date of SFAS 114, *Accounting by Creditors for Impairment of a Loan,* described in paragraph 24 of SFAS 118, *Accounting by Creditors for Impairment of a Loan—Income Recognition and Disclosures*

   e. Stock compensation for nonpublic and other entities (originally addressed by SFAS 123, *Accounting for Stock-Based Compensation,* or APB Opinion 25, *Accounting for Stock Issued to Employees*) described in paragraph 83 of SFAS 123 (revised 2004), *Share-Based Payment*

   f. For nonpublic entities electing the deferral of FASB Interpretation 48 *(Accounting for Uncertainty in Income Taxes),* SFAS 109 *(Accounting for Income Taxes),* and related standards

   g. For business combinations with an acquisition date before the first annual reporting period beginning on or after December 15, 2008, SFAS 141 and any other relevant standards

   h. For not-for-profit entities, pooling of interests as allowed for under APB Opinion 16, even though it has been superseded by SFAS 141 until SFAS 164, *Not-for-Profit Entities: Mergers and Acquisitions,* is effective

   i For goodwill and intangible assets arising from a combination between two or more not-for-profit entities or acquired in the acquisition of a for-profit business entity by a not-for-profit entity until SFAS 164 is effective, APB Opinion 16 and APB Opinion 17, *Intangible Assets*

Development of Accounting Standards

2112.18 The Financial Accounting Standards Board (FASB) is currently the body responsible for developing accounting standards in the United States. The FASB's primary functions are to study current issues and generate new accounting standards. The FASB describes its due process procedures on its website (**www.fasb.org**) as follows:

The FASB has established the following procedures for developing accounting standards. These procedures are used for major agenda projects. Not all of the steps may be necessary for application and implementation projects. Many other steps are followed during the course of the project that are not specifically required by the Board's Rules of Procedures.

   1. The Board identifies a financial reporting issue based on requests/recommendations from stakeholders or through other means.

2. The FASB Chairman decides whether to add a project to the technical agenda, after consultation with FASB Members and others as appropriate, and subject to oversight by the Foundation's Board of Trustees.

3. The Board deliberates at one or more public meetings the various reporting issues identified and analyzed by the staff.

4. The Board issues an Exposure Draft to solicit broad stakeholder input. (In some projects, the Board may issue a Discussion Paper to obtain input in the early stages of a project.)

5. The Board holds a public roundtable meeting on the Exposure Draft, if necessary

6. The staff analyzes comment letters, public roundtable discussion, and any other information and the Board redeliberates the proposed provisions at one or more public meetings.

7. The Board issues an Accounting Standards Update describing amendments to the *Accounting Standards Codification.*

2112.19 Accounting Standards Updates issued after September 2009 will not be considered authoritative in their own right. Instead, the Accounting Standards Updates will serve only to update the *Accounting Standards Codification,* provide background information about the guidance, and provide the bases for conclusions on the change(s) in the Codification.

2113 International Accounting Standards Board (IASB)

2113.01 The International Accounting Standards Board (IASB) is an international organization organized to develop international financial reporting standards (IFRSs). Additional goals of the organization are to promote the use of these standards and to work towards the convergence of the IFRSs and national accounting standards.

2113.02 The IASB has established the following steps for developing standards, as discussed on its website at **www.iasb.org:**

"International Financial Reporting Standards (IFRSs) are developed through an international consultation process, the 'due process,' which involves interested individuals and organizations from around the world. The due process comprises six stages, with the Trustees having the opportunity to ensure compliance at various points throughout:

1. Setting the agenda
2. Planning the project
3. Developing and publishing the discussion paper
4. Developing and publishing the exposure draft
5. Developing and publishing the standard
6. After the standard is issued"

2113.03 In addition to a conceptual framework very similar to the FASB conceptual framework, the IASB has currently issued:

a. International Financial Reporting Standards 1–9;

b. International Accounting Standards 1, 2, 7, 8, 10–12, 16–21, and 23;

c. IFRIC Interpretations 1-2, 4–7, 9–10, and 12-19; and

d. SIC Interpretations 7, 10, 12–13, 15, 21, 25, 27, 29, and 31–32.

2113.04 The IASB and the FASB are working together for the convergence of GAAP and IFRSs. The two organizations issued the following joint statement in June 2010:

Joint statement by the IASB and the FASB on their convergence work

In our November 2009 joint statement, we, the International Accounting Standards Board (IASB) and the US Financial Accounting Standards Board (FASB) again reaffirmed our commitment to improving International Financial Reporting Standards (IFRSs) and US generally accepted accounting principles (GAAP) and achieving their convergence. That Statement affirmed June 2011 as the target date for completing the major projects in the 2006 Memorandum of Understanding (MoU), as updated in 2008, described project-specific milestone targets, and acknowledged the need to intensify our standards-setting efforts to meet those targets.

We committed to providing transparency and accountability regarding those plans by reporting periodically on our progress. Our first report, dated 31 March 2010, described the progress we had made to date, explained some of the challenges we face in improving and converging our standards in certain areas, and reported changes made to certain project-specific milestone targets.

As noted in our March 2010 progress report, we recognise the challenges that arise from seeking effective global stakeholder engagement on a large number of projects. Since publishing the March progress report, stakeholders have voiced concerns about their ability to provide high-quality input on the large number of major Exposure Drafts planned for publication in the second quarter of this year.

The IASB and the FASB are in the process of developing a modified strategy to take account of these concerns that would:

- prioritise the major projects in the MoU to permit a sharper focus on issues and projects that we believe will bring about significant improvement and convergence between IFRS and U.S. GAAP.

- stagger the publication of Exposure Drafts and related consultations (such as public round table meetings) to enable the broad-based and effective stakeholder participation in due process that is critically important to the quality of their standards. We are limiting to four the number of significant or complex Exposure Drafts issued in any one quarter.

- issue a separate consultation document seeking stakeholder input about effective dates and transition methods.

The modified strategy retains the target completion date of June 2011 for many of the projects identified by the original MoU, including those projects, as well as other issues not in the MoU, where a converged solution is urgently required. The target completion dates for a few projects have extended into the second half of 2011. The nature of the comments received on the Exposure Drafts will determine the extent of the redeliberations necessary and the timeline required to arrive at high quality, converged standards.

The IASB and the FASB have begun discussions on this proposed strategy with their respective oversight bodies and regulators, including members of the IASC Foundation Monitoring Board.

—*IASB-FASB Joint Statement on Convergence Work, June 2010*

2114 Governmental Accounting Standards Board (GASB)

2114.01 When the Financial Accounting Foundation (FAF) established the GASB in a brother-sister relationship with the FASB, the FAF established the following jurisdiction policy.

   a. The GASB is to establish accounting and reporting standards for activities and transactions of *state and local governmental entities*—which include states, counties, cities, and towns; independent school districts; state and local government educational institutions (colleges and universities); hospitals and other health care organizations; and charitable and other not-for-profit organizations that are government organizations.

   b. The FASB is to establish accounting and reporting standards for activities and transactions of *all other entities*.

2114.02 **Definition of governmental organizations.** The GASB and the FASB agreed that the term "state and local governmental entities" should be defined as follows.

Governmental organizations are:

   a. public corporations and bodies corporate and politic and

   b. *other organizations* that have *one* or more of the following characteristics:

   (1) popular election of officers *or* appointment (or approval) of a controlling majority of the members of the organization's governing body *by officials of one or more state or local governments*,

   (2) the potential for unilateral dissolution by a government with the net assets reverting to a government,

   (3) the power to enact and enforce a tax levy, or

   (4) the ability to issue directly (rather than through a state or municipal authority) debt that pays interest exempt from federal taxation.

Entities meeting either part **a.** or part **b.** of this definition are under the GASB's jurisdiction; those not meeting this definition are under the FASB's jurisdiction.

2114.03 Consistent with the FAF jurisdiction agreement, the GASB has established a separate *state and local government* GAAP hierarchy with respect to the relative authoritativeness of the various standards, pronouncements, and other literature on financial accounting and reporting principles and procedures.

2114.04 In 2009, the GASB issued GASB Statement 55, *The Hierarchy of Generally Accepted Accounting Principles for State and Local Governments*. As outlined in GASB Statement 55, the sources of accounting principles that are generally accepted are categorized in descending order of authority as follows:

   a. Officially established accounting principles—Governmental Accounting Standards Board (GASB) Statements and Interpretations. GASB Statements and Interpretations are periodically incorporated in the Codification of Governmental Accounting and Financial Reporting Standards. Any AICPA or FASB pronouncements that have been made applicable by a GASB Statement or Interpretation are also a part of this level.

   b. GASB Technical Bulletins and, if specifically made applicable to state and local governmental entities by the American Institute of Certified Public Accountants (AICPA) and cleared by the GASB, AICPA Industry Audit and Accounting Guides, and AICPA Statements of Position

c. AICPA Practice Bulletins if specifically made applicable to state and local governmental entities and cleared by the GASB, as well as consensus positions of a group of accountants organized by the GASB that attempts to reach consensus positions on accounting issues applicable to state and local governmental entities

d. Implementation Guides ("Q&As") published by the GASB staff, as well as practices that are widely recognized and prevalent in state and local government

2114.05 If the accounting treatment for a transaction or other event is not specified by a pronouncement in category a., a governmental entity should consider whether the accounting treatment is specified by an accounting principle from a source in another category. In such cases, if categories b.–d. contain accounting principles that specify accounting treatments for a transaction or other event, the governmental entity should follow the accounting treatment specified by the accounting principle from the source in the highest category—for example, follow category b. treatment over category c. treatment.

2114.06 If the accounting treatment for a transaction or other event is not specified by a pronouncement or established in practice as described in categories a.–d., a governmental entity should consider accounting principles for similar transactions or other events within categories a.–d. and may consider other accounting literature. A governmental entity should not follow the accounting treatment specified in accounting principles for similar transactions or other events in cases in which those accounting principles either prohibit the application of the accounting treatment to the particular transaction or other event or indicate that the accounting treatment should not be applied by analogy.

2114.07 Other accounting literature includes GASB Concepts Statements; the pronouncements referred to in categories a.–d. of the GAAP hierarchy for nongovernmental entities if not specifically made applicable to state and local governmental entities by the GASB; Financial Accounting Standards Board Statements, Interpretations, Technical Bulletins, Staff Positions, and Concepts Statements; Federal Accounting Standards Advisory Board (FASAB) Statements, Interpretations, Technical Bulletins, and Concepts Statements; AICPA Issues Papers; International Public Sector Accounting Standards of the International Public Sector Accounting Standards Board or International Financial Reporting Standards of the International Accounting Standards Board, or pronouncements of other professional associations or regulatory agencies; Technical Information Service Inquiries and Replies included in AICPA Technical Practice Aids; and accounting textbooks, handbooks, and articles. The appropriateness of other accounting literature depends on its relevance to particular circumstances, the specificity of the guidance, and the general recognition of the issuer or author as an authority. For example, GASB Concepts Statements would normally be more influential than other sources in this category.

2114.08 The essence of this GAAP hierarchy for state and local governments is as follows:

a. **GASB Statements and Interpretations are the most authoritative sources** of GAAP applicable to state and local government entities—and supersede any guidance at levels b.–e.

b. If the GASB has not issued a statement or interpretation that addresses the issue directly or by recognizing an AICPA or FASB pronouncement that addresses the issue, the literature at levels b.–d. should be researched in sequential (hierarchical) order for guidance.

c. Finally, if guidance is not available at levels a.–d., determine if the principles found at those levels are applicable by analogy (if not prohibited) to the transaction being researched and consider other accounting literature (level e.), such as GASB Concepts Statements, textbooks, professional organization position papers, and other publications, journal articles, and speeches.

2114.09 Some not-for-profit organizations are government entities, but others are nongovernment.

    a. *Government* not-for-profit organizations follow the SLG government GAAP hierarchy in determining applicable GAAP. *These not-for-profit organizations are prohibited by GASB Statement 29 from applying FASB not-for-profit standards.*

    b. *Nongovernment* not-for-profit organizations should follow the business GAAP hierarchy and look to the FASB for primary guidance in determining applicable GAAP.

There are significant differences in GAAP applicable to *government* and *nongovernment not-for-profit organizations.*

2120 Conceptual Framework

2121 Financial Reporting by Business Entities

FASB Conceptual Framework

2121.01 **Note to candidates:** The need for a conceptual framework is generally recognized; such a framework serves as a theoretical structure for the establishment of authoritative guidance in new and emerging areas of practice and identifies and resolves inconsistencies in existing authoritative literature. The FASB indicates that the primary beneficiary of the conceptual framework is the FASB itself. The FASB often uses the conceptual framework to explain and justify positions it takes on issues. The framework is also used for educational purposes to explain the theoretical structure on which financial accounting practices rest.

The FASB's conceptual framework consists of seven statements identified as Statements of Financial Accounting Concepts (SFAC). In this section, we briefly summarize those statements that have relevance for financial reporting of business enterprises—SFAC 1, 2, 5, 6, and 7. SFAC 3 was superseded by SFAC 6, and SFAC 4 deals with nonbusiness organizations. Many of the ideas contained in the conceptual framework are normative in nature (i.e., they suggest what financial reporting should be rather than what it currently is) and, as a result, some of the ideas in this section are not consistent with current accounting practice. Material from the concepts statements is frequently included on the CPA Examination and, therefore, is relevant for the CPA Examination candidate.

2121.02 **IFRS:** In 1989, the IASC issued its conceptual framework.

Objectives of Financial Reporting by Business Enterprises

2121.03 Objectives of financial reporting are established in FASB Statement of Financial Accounting Concepts 1, *Objectives of Financial Reporting by Business Enterprises.*

2121.04 The statement identifies three major objectives and includes a significant amount of discussion expanding on these three objectives. The objectives are stated in terms of financial reporting and are not restricted to financial statements, in recognition of the fact that investors and creditors obtain financial information about the enterprise from a variety of sources. These objectives are summarized briefly in the following paragraphs.

2121.05 **Major Objective 1:** Financial reporting should provide information that is *useful* to present and potential investors and creditors and other users *in making rational investment, credit, and similar decisions.* The information should be comprehensible to those who have a reasonable understanding of business and economic activities and are willing to study the information with reasonable diligence (SFAC 1.34–.36).

    a. The terms *investors* and *creditors* include those financial statement users who deal directly with an enterprise as well as those who deal through intermediaries.

      b. While efforts should be made to increase the understandability of financial information, financial reporting should not exclude relevant information merely because it is difficult for some to understand or because some investors or creditors choose not to use it.

2121.06 **Major Objective 2:** Financial reporting should provide information to help present and potential investors and creditors and other users assess the *amounts, timing, and uncertainty of prospective cash receipts* from dividends or interest and the proceeds from the sale, redemption, or maturity of securities or loans (SFAC 1.37).

      a. People and business enterprises engage in investing, lending, and similar activities primarily to increase their cash resources. The test of success or failure of the operations of a business enterprise is the extent to which the cash returned exceeds the cash spent or invested over the long run.

      b. Since an enterprise's ability to bring in cash through its earning and financing activities affects both its ability to pay dividends and interest and the market prices of its securities, expected cash flows to investors and creditors are related to expected cash flows to the enterprise.

2121.07 **Major Objective 3:** Financial reporting should provide information about the *economic resources* of an enterprise, the *claims to those resources,* and the effects of transactions, events, and circumstances that *change resources and claims to those resources* (SFAC 1.40–.54).

      a. Direct indications should be provided of the cash flow potentials of some resources and of the cash needed to satisfy many, if not most, obligations.

      b. The primary focus is information about an enterprise's performance provided by measures of earnings and its components.

      c. Earnings information based on accrual accounting generally provides a better indication of enterprise performance than information about current cash receipts and payments.

      d. Information should be provided about how the enterprise obtains and spends cash, about its borrowing and repayment of borrowing, about its capital transactions, including cash dividends and other distributions of enterprise resources to owners, and about other factors that may affect an enterprise's liquidity or solvency.

      e. Information should be provided about how the management of an enterprise has discharged its stewardship responsibility to owners for the use of enterprise resources entrusted to it.

      f. Information should be provided that is useful to managers and directors in making decisions in the interests of owners.

      g. Information presented should include explanations and interpretations to help users understand the financial information presented.

2121.08 **IFRS:** The IFRS conceptual framework contains a similar "Objectives of Financial Statements" concept statement. While the FASB established the objectives of financial reporting, the IASB specifies the objectives of financial statements.

Qualitative Characteristics of Accounting Information (SFAC 2)

2121.09 The FASB's Statement of Financial Accounting Concept 2, *Qualitative Characteristics of Accounting Information,* examines those characteristics that make accounting information useful. These characteristics guide the selection of accounting policies from available alternatives.

2121.10 The primary qualitative characteristics of accounting information are relevance and reliability.

    a. **Relevance:** To be relevant to investors, creditors, and other users, accounting information must be capable of making a difference in a decision by helping users to form predictions about the outcomes of past, present, and future events or to confirm or correct expectations (SFAC 2.46).

    b. **Reliability:** To be reliable, investors, creditors, and other users must be able to depend on accounting information to represent the economic conditions or events that it purports to represent (SFAC 2.58).

2121.11 The primary characteristics of relevance and reliability relate closely to each other and are supported by several other concepts. These relationships are described in SFAC 2.32.

A Hierarchy of Accounting Qualities

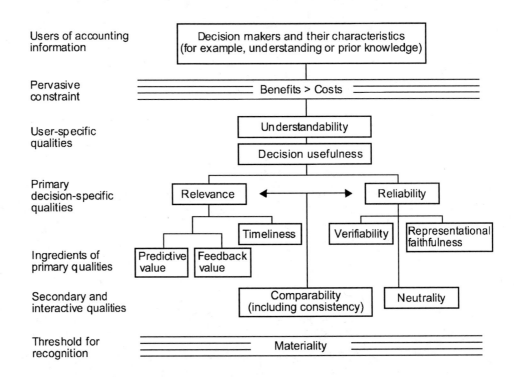

2121.12 Several of the concepts that are included in the hierarchy and are closely related to the primary concepts of relevance and reliability are described as follows:

    a. **Benefits/costs:** Unless the benefits to be derived from specific accounting information exceed the costs of providing that information, it should not be provided.

    b. **Understandability:** Financial information is a tool and is useful only if understood by its users. The FASB attempts to develop standards that relate to general purpose external financial reporting by considering the needs of broad classes of decision makers and their abilities to understand financial information.

    c. **Decision usefulness:** Financial reporting is concerned with decision making. The need for information on which to base investment, credit, and similar decisions underlies financial reporting.

d. **Relevance:**

   (1) **Predictive value/feedback value:** Information can make a difference in decisions by improving the decision makers' capacity to predict (predictive value) or by confirming or correcting earlier expectations (feedback value). These may be accomplished at the same time because knowledge of the past usually improves the ability to predict similar future events.

   (2) **Timeliness:** To be relevant, information must be available when it is needed (i.e., on a timely basis).

e. **Reliability:**

   (1) **Verifiability:** To be reliable, accounting information must be verifiable, meaning that several measurers making independent evaluations are likely to obtain the same measures.

   (2) **Representational faithfulness:** To be reliable, a correspondence must exist between a measure or description and the phenomenon it purports to represent.

   (3) **Neutrality** means that in either formulating or implementing accounting standards, the primary concerns are the relevance and reliability of information not the effect that a new standard would have on a particular financial interest.

f. **Comparability:** Information about an enterprise is more useful if it can be compared with similar information about other enterprises and with similar information about the same enterprise for other time periods or points in time (i.e., consistency).

g. **Materiality** deals with the omission or misstatement of an item on the basis that it is too small to be important. In essence, the omission or misstatement of an item is material if the magnitude of it is such that it is probable that the judgment of a reasonable person relying on the financial information would have been changed or influenced by the inclusion or correction of the item.

2121.13   **IFRS:** The IFRS conceptual framework contains a similar "Qualitative Characteristics" concept statement. The IASB does not prioritize the characteristics and does not refer to verifiability.

Elements of the Financial Statements

2121.14   Elements of financial statements are the building blocks with which financial statements are constructed. They are specified in Statement of Financial Accounting Concepts 6, *The Elements of the Financial Statements*.

2121.15   SFAC 6 defines 10 interrelated elements that are directly related to measuring the performance and status of an enterprise. These elements are defined as follows:

   a. **Assets** are probable future economic benefits obtained or controlled by a particular enterprise as a result of past transactions or events (SFAC 6.25).

   b. **Liabilities** are probable future sacrifices of economic benefits arising from present obligations of a particular enterprise to transfer assets or provide services to other enterprises as a result of past transactions or events (SFAC 6.35).

   c. **Equity** (or net assets) is the residual interest in the assets of an enterprise that remains after deducting its liabilities (SFAC 6.49). In a business enterprise, the equity is the ownership interest.

d. **Investments by owners** are increases in net assets of a particular enterprise resulting from transfers to it from other enterprises of something of value to obtain or increase ownership interests (or equity) in it. Assets are most commonly received as investments by owners, but what is received may also include services, satisfaction, or conversion of liabilities of the enterprise (SFAC 6.66).

e. **Distributions to owners** are decreases in net assets of a particular enterprise resulting from transferring assets or rendering services to the owner, or incurring liabilities by the enterprise on behalf of owners. Distributions to owners decrease ownership interests (or equity) in the enterprise (SFAC 6.67).

f. **Comprehensive income** is the change in equity (net assets) of an enterprise, during a period, from transactions and other events and circumstances from nonowner sources. It includes all changes in equity during a period, except those resulting from investments by owners and distributions to owners (SFAC 6.70).

g. **Revenues** are inflows or other enhancements of the assets of an enterprise or settlements of its liabilities (or a combination of both), during a period, from delivering or producing goods, rendering services, or other activities that constitute the enterprise's ongoing major or central operations (SFAC 6.78).

h. **Expenses** are outflows or other uses of assets or incurrences of liabilities (or a combination of both), during a period, from delivering or producing goods, rendering services, or carrying out other activities that constitute the enterprise's ongoing major or central operations (SFAC 6.80).

i. **Gains** are increases in equity (net assets) from peripheral or incidental transactions of an enterprise and from all other transactions and other events and circumstances affecting the enterprise during a period, except those that result from revenues or investments by owners (SFAC 6.82).

j. **Losses** are decreases in equity (net assets) from peripheral or incidental transactions of an enterprise and from all other transactions and other events and circumstances affecting the enterprise during a period, except those that result from expenses or distributions to owners (SFAC 6.83).

2121.16 The interrelationship of these elements of the financial statements is described in SFAC 6.64.

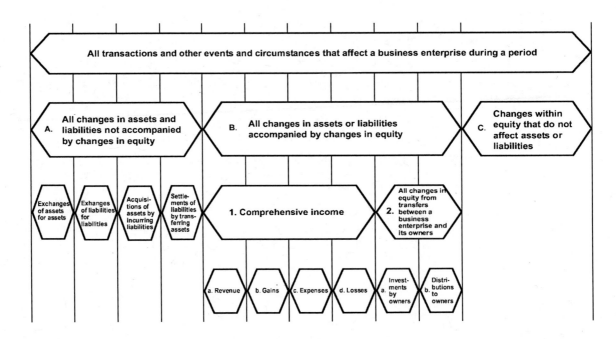

2121.17 "Articulation" is a term used to describe the interrelationship of the elements of the financial statements. Some elements are analogous to a still photograph in that they reflect aspects of the enterprise at a point in time—assets, liabilities, and equity. The remaining elements of the financial statements describe effects of transactions and other events and circumstances that occur over intervals of time. These two types of elements are related in such a way that (a) assets, liabilities, and equity are changed by elements of the other type and at any time are their cumulative result, and (b) an increase or decrease in an asset cannot occur without a corresponding increase or decrease in another asset, liability, or equity. The resulting financial statements are, fundamentally interrelated, even though they include different elements that reflect different characteristics of the enterprise and its activities (SFAC 6.20–.21).

2121.18 **IFRS:** The IFRS conceptual framework contains a similar "Elements of Financial Statements" concept statement. The IASB lists only five elements by including owner investments and distributions in equity, combining gains and revenues and combining expenses and losses. The IASB does not list comprehensive income, although comprehensive income is required elsewhere.

Recognition and Measurement in Financial Statements of Business Enterprises

2121.19 A full set of financial statements for a period shows the following (SFAC 5.13):

a. Financial position at the end of the period

b. Earnings for the period

c. Comprehensive income for the period

d. Cash flows during the period

e. Investments by and distributions to owners during the period

2121.20 Following are selected characteristics of financial statements identified and discussed in SFAC 5.

a. **General purpose financial statements:** General purpose financial statements are directed toward the common interests of various users and are feasible only because groups of users of financial information have similar needs (SFAC 5.15).

b. **Usefulness of financial statements:** Financial statements individually and collectively contribute to meeting the objectives of financial reporting. Each financial statement provides a different kind of information and, generally, various kinds of information cannot be combined into a smaller number of financial statements without unduly complicating the information (SFAC 5.17).

c. **Classification and aggregation:** Classification in financial statements facilitates analysis by grouping items with essentially similar characteristics and separating items with essentially different characteristics. Financial statements result from processing large amounts of data. Financial statements involve the need to simplify, condense, and aggregate information (SFAC 5.20–.21).

d. **Articulation of financial statements:** Financial statements interrelate, or articulate, because they reflect different aspects of the same transactions or other events affecting the entity (SFAC 5.23).

2121.21 A statement of financial position provides information about an enterprise's assets, liabilities, and equity and their relationships to one another at a point in time. The statement delineates the enterprise's resource structure (major classes and amounts of assets) and its financing structure (major classes and amounts of liabilities and equity). The statement does not purport to show the value of a business but may provide information that is useful to those who desire to make their own estimates of the enterprise's value (SFAC 5.26).

2121.22 **Earnings** is a measure of enterprise performance during a period and is similar to net income in present practice. It measures the extent to which asset inflows (revenues and gains) associated with cash-to-cash cycles substantially completed during the period exceed asset outflows (expenses and losses) associated with the same cycles. Comprehensive income is a broad measure of the effects of transactions and other events on an enterprise, comprising all recognized changes in equity of the enterprise, during the period, from all events and transactions other than those with owners. The statement of earnings and of comprehensive income together reflect the extent to which and the ways in which the equity of an enterprise increased or decreased from all sources other than transactions with owners during the period (SFAC 5.33).

2121.23 A statement of cash flows reflects an entity's cash receipts and cash payments classified by major uses (i.e., operating, investing, and financing activities). One important use of information about an entity's cash receipts and payments is to help to assess factors such as liquidity, financial flexibility, profitability, and risk. The statement of cash flows presents few recognition problems because receipts and payments are recognized when they occur (SFAC 5.52–.54).

2121.24 A statement of investment by and distributions to owners reflects the extent to which and ways in which the equity of an entity increases or decreases from transactions with owners during a period (SFAC 5.55).

2121.25 Financial statement items represent in words and numbers certain enterprise resources, claims to those resources, and the effects of transactions and other events and circumstances that result in changes in those resources and claims. An item and information about it should meet four fundamental recognition criteria to be recognized and should be recognized when the criteria are met, subject to cost-benefit and materiality thresholds (SFAC 5.63). These criteria are as follows:

    a. **Definition:** The item meets the definition of an element of financial statements.

    b. **Measurability:** The item has a relevant attribute measurable with sufficient reliability.

    c. **Relevance:** The information is capable of making a difference in user decisions.

    d. **Reliability:** The information is representationally faithful, verifiable, and neutral.

2121.26 Guidance for recognizing revenues and gains is based on their being realized or realizable as well as earned (SFAC 5.83).

    a. **Realized or realizable:** Revenues and gains are generally not recognized as components of earnings until realized or realizable.

    b. **Earned:** Revenues are not recognized until earned. Revenues are considered to have been earned when the entity has substantially accomplished what it must do to be entitled to the benefits represented by the revenues. For gains, being earned is generally less significant than being realized or realizable.

2121.27 Guidance for recognizing expenses and losses is as follows (SFAC 5.85):

    a. **Consumption of benefit:** Expenses are generally recognized when an enterprise's economic benefits are consumed in revenue-earning activities or otherwise.

    b. **Loss or lack of benefit:** Expenses or losses are recognized if it becomes evident that previously recognized future economic benefits of assets have been reduced or eliminated, or that liabilities have been incurred or increased, without associated economic benefits.

2121.28 IFRS: The IFRS conceptual framework contains a similar "Measurement of the Elements" concept statement. Financial capital maintenance is the basis for U.S. GAAP in SFAC 6. The IASB allows the enterprise to select financial or physical maintenance in its "Concepts of Capital and Capital Maintenance" concept statement.

Using Cash Flow Information and Present Value in Accounting Measurements

2121.29 Estimated cash flows have been used for years to value assets and liabilities when observable marketplace-determined amounts are not available. The measurement of these estimated cash flows raises many questions, including whether to use present value or not and, if so, the appropriate present value technique.

2121.30 Prior to the issuance of SFAC 7, *Using Cash Flow Information and Present Value in Accounting Measurements,* no official framework existed for the use of present value accounting measurements. SFAC 7 attempts to provide that framework.

2121.31 SFAC 7 is intended to provide the following:

    a. A common understanding of the objective of present value in accounting measurements

    b. A framework for using future cash flows as the basis for accounting measurements for the following:

        (1) Initial recognition of an asset or a liability

        (2) Fresh-start measurements

        (3) The interest method of amortization

    c. General principles that govern the use of present value, especially when the amount of future cash flows and/or their timing are uncertain

2121.32 SFAC 7 does not address issues related to asset or liability recognition or specify when fresh-start measurements should be made.

Objective of Present Value

2121.33 The measurement of many assets and liabilities can be based on an observable marketplace-determined price. In those cases, there is no need to use present value measurements. The market price already embodies the present value consideration. However, when an observable marketplace-determined price is not available, estimates of future cash flows may be used as a basis for measuring (or remeasuring) an asset or liability.

2121.34 The FASB specified that the objective of using present value in an accounting measurement is "to capture, to the extent possible, the economic difference between sets of future cash flows." For example, without present value, a $1,000 cash flow due tomorrow and a $1,000 cash flow due in 10 years appear the same. With present value, they do not appear the same.

2121.35 In the ideal case, a present value measurement that fully captures economic differences includes the following elements:

    a. An estimate of future cash flow(s)

    b. Expectations about possible variations in the amount or timing of those cash flows

    c. The time value of money, represented by the risk-free rate of interest

    d. The price for bearing the uncertainty inherent in the asset or liability (risk adjustment)

    e. Other (sometimes unidentifiable) factors including illiquidity and market imperfections

2121.36 Fair value captures all five of these elements. SFAC 7 specifies that a present value measurement "should capture the elements that taken together would comprise a market price if one existed, that is, fair value." Thus, the objective of present value is to **estimate fair value.**

Fair Value Should Be Based on Cash Transactions if Possible

2121.37 A cash transaction involving the enterprise in question (purchaser of an asset for cash or borrower of money) usually is the best measure of fair value. The absence of a cash transaction involving that enterprise requires the enterprise to turn to other techniques for the initial measurement of the asset acquired or liability incurred. However, the measurement objective remains the same—fair value.

2121.38 The absence of a cash transaction involving a particular enterprise means that the enterprise next should determine if others have bought or sold the same or similar items in recent cash transactions. If so, those transactions likely provide the best measure available to be used as an estimate of fair value to record the acquisition of the asset or the incurrence of the liability.

Absence of Observable Cash Transactions

2121.39 The absence of observable cash transactions for similar assets or liabilities may require the enterprise to use estimates of future cash flows in the measurement. However, the objective of the measurement still remains the same—fair value. Thus, the accounting measurement at initial recognition or fresh-start measurement should attempt to capture the elements that taken together would comprise a market price if one existed. In these cases, SFAC 7 takes the view that a present value measurement should be used because it "provides more relevant information than a measurement based on the undiscounted sum of those cash flows."

General Principles for Estimating Future Cash Flows and Interest Rates

2121.40 Paragraph 41 of SFAC 7 specifies that while the techniques used to estimate future cash flows and interest rates likely will vary from one situation to another depending on the circumstances surrounding the asset or liability, the following general principles should govern any application of present value techniques in measuring assets or liabilities:

- **a.** To the extent possible, estimated cash flows and interest rates should reflect assumptions about the future events and uncertainties that would be considered in deciding whether to acquire an asset or group of assets in an arm's-length transaction for cash.
- **b.** Interest rates used to discount cash flows should reflect assumptions that are consistent with those inherent in the estimated cash flows.
- **c.** Estimated cash flows and interest rates should be free from both bias and factors unrelated to the asset, liability, or group of assets or liabilities in question.
- **d.** Estimated cash flows and interest rates should reflect the range of possible outcomes rather than a single most likely, minimum, or maximum possible amount.

Traditional and Expected Cash Flow Approaches to Present Value

2121.41 Historically, accounting has tended to use a **traditional approach** to present value measurements. This approach tends to use a single set of estimated cash flows and a single interest rate. Thus, present value elements b–d listed in section **2121.35** are embedded in the discount rate (the rate used to compute the present value of the estimated cash flows) that is applied to the estimated cash flows (element a) to compute the present value of the estimated cash flows.

2121.42 In contrast, under the **expected cash flow approach,** only element c in section **2121.35** (the time value of money, represented by the risk-free rate of interest) is included in the discount rate. Elements b, d, and e in section **2121.35** cause adjustments in the determination of the risk-adjusted expected cash flows.

2121.43 The FASB indicates in SFAC 7 that it expects accountants will continue to use the traditional approach for some measurements, especially those in which comparable assets and liabilities can be observed in the marketplace. However, the FASB notes that the traditional approach "does not provide the tools needed to address some complex measurement problems including the measurement of nonfinancial assets and liabilities for which no market for the item or a comparable item exists." In these types of situations, the Board indicates that the expected cash flow approach is a more effective measurement tool.

2121.44 In that regard, the FASB emphasized that the expected cash flow approach uses all expectations about possible cash flows instead of the single most likely cash flow used by the traditional approach.

2121.45 To illustrate the difference between the two approaches when there is uncertainty as to the **amount** of estimated future cash flows, assume that a cash flow might be $100, $200, or $300 with probabilities of 10%, 60%, and 30%, respectively. The expected cash flow under the cash flow approach is $220 [($100 × .10) + ($200 × .60) + ($300 × .30)], whereas the estimated cash flow under the traditional approach is the most likely amount of $200.

2121.46 The two approaches also differ when there is uncertainty as to the **timing** of future cash flows. For example, a cash flow of $1,000 may be received in one year, two years, or three years with probabilities of 10%, 60%, and 30%, respectively. At an interest (discount) rate of 10%, the present value measurement would be as follows under the two approaches:

Traditional approach—present value (PV) of the best estimate:

PV of $1,000 in two years at 10%	$826.45

Expected cash flow approach-
expected present value:

PV of $1,000 in one year at 10%	$909.09	
Probability	10%	$ 90.91
PV of $1,000 in two years at 10%	$826.45	
Probability	60%	$495.87
PV of $1,000 in three years at 10%	$751.32	
Probability	30%	$225.40
Expected present value		$812.18

Consideration of Risk Adjustment

2121.47 Ideally an estimate of fair value should take into consideration the risk adjustment—the price that marketplace participants are able to receive for bearing the uncertainties in cash flows. However, the risk adjustment should be incorporated into the expected cash flow approach only if it is **identifiable, measurable, and significant.** Otherwise, the FASB takes the position that the present value of expected cash flows, discounted at a risk-free rate of interest, may be the best estimate of fair value (recall that the objective of any present value approach to measure assets and liabilities is to estimate fair value of the asset or liability).

2121.48 The FASB emphasized that the application of an expected cash flow approach is subject to a cost-benefit constraint. Thus, the cost of acquiring some data may exceed the expected benefits if that data were obtained.

Issues Unique to Measurement of Liabilities

2121.49 The concepts discussed previously apply to liabilities as well as to assets. However, the measurement of liabilities may involve some problems unique to liabilities.

2121.50 Paragraph 75 of SFAC specifies that "when using a present value measurement to estimate the fair value of a liability, the objective is to estimate the value of the assets required currently to (a) settle the liability with the holder or (b) transfer the liability to an entity of comparable credit standing." The most relevant measure of a liability always reflects the credit standing of the entity obligated to pay because such credit standing would be included in any valuation of the obligation by the marketplace.

2121.51 This "credit standing effect" is usually captured in an adjustment to the interest rate. In SFAC 7, the FASB indicates that in the case of contractual cash flows the traditional approach of measuring present value may be sufficient. (The "credit standing effect" is incorporated into the interest rate.) However, the Board pointed out that the expected cash flow approach may be more effective when measuring the effect of credit standing of other liabilities.

Interest Methods of Allocation

2121.52 Accounting allocations (e.g., depreciation) are planned (systematic and rational) approaches to reflect the "consumption" of assets or the reduction of liabilities. An interest method of allocation relates changes in reported amounts of assets or liabilities to changes in the present value of future cash inflows or outflows.

2121.53 While an interest method of allocation could be applied to any asset or liability, thus far it has tended to be applied to assets and liabilities that exhibit one or more of the following characteristics:

   a. The transaction giving rise to the asset or liability is commonly viewed as a borrowing and lending.

   b. Period-to-period allocation of similar assets and liabilities employs an interest method.

   c. A particular set of estimated future cash flows is closely associated with the asset or liability.

   d. The measurement at initial recognition was based on present value.

2121.54 Typically, the application of the interest method has been based on contractual cash flows and assumes a constant effective interest rate over the life of the cash flows (i.e., as it has been used to date, the interest method uses promised cash flows rather than expected cash flows and bases the interest rate on the single rate that equates the present value of the promised cash flows with the initial price of the asset or liability).

2121.55 To be consistent with the use of the expected cash flow approach used to measure the asset or liability at acquisition, changes in the timing or amount of the original estimated cash flows would need to be reflected in future allocations. These changes could be accommodated either (1) in the interest amortization scheme or (2) included in a fresh-start measurement of the asset or liability (i.e., remeasure the asset or liability). The FASB decided not to address in SFAC 7 the conditions that might govern the choice between these two approaches.

2121.56 If the changes in the estimated cash flows are to be reflected by a fresh-start (approach 2 in section **2121.55**), the guidance discussed to this point for measuring the present value of the asset or liability initially should be followed.

2121.57 On the other hand, if the changes in the estimated cash flows are to be reflected in the interest amortization scheme, three techniques have been used to reflect those changes.

    a. Prospective approach—a new effective interest rate is computed based on the carrying amount and remaining cash flows.

    b. Catch-up approach—the carrying amount is adjusted to the present value of the revised estimated cash flows, discounted at the original effective interest rate.

    c. Retrospective approach—a new effective interest rate is computed based on the original carrying amount, actual cash flows to date, and remaining estimated cash flows. The new effective interest rate is then used to adjust the carrying amount to the present value of the revised estimated cash flows, discounted at the new effective interest rate.

2121.58 The FASB indicated that the catch-up approach is preferable.

2121.59 The FASB decided that it will continue to decide whether to require an interest method of allocation on a project-by-project basis.

2121.60 **IFRS:** The IFRS conceptual framework does not contain a similar a concept statement regarding present value accounting, but allows it as one of the acceptable measurement bases.

2122 Financial Reporting by Not-for-Profit (Nongovernmental) Entities

Distinguishing Features of Nonbusiness Organizations

2122.01 All organizations other than business enterprises are known collectively as nonbusiness organizations. Thus, the term "nonbusiness organizations" encompasses all governments and all not-for-profit organizations, except those associated with businesses.

2122.02 FASB Statement of Financial Accounting Concepts (SFAC) 4, *Objectives of Financial Reporting by Nonbusiness Organizations,* observes that the major distinguishing characteristics of nonbusiness organizations include the following:

    a. Receipts of significant amounts of resources from resource providers who do not expect to receive either repayment or economic benefits proportionate to resources provided

    b. Operating purposes other than providing goods or services at a profit or profit equivalent

    c. Absence of defined ownership interests that can be sold, transferred, or redeemed, or that convey entitlement to a share of a residual distribution of resources in the event of liquidation of the organization

2122.03 SFAC 4 also states that the greatest dissimilarities between business and nonbusiness organizations arise principally in how they obtain resources.

    a. **Business enterprises** attempt to provide services and/or sell goods at prices that enable them to compensate all the parties providing resources, including owners. Thus, business enterprises must, in the long run, generate a profit as a return to the owners for their investment.

    b. **Nonbusiness organizations** obtain a significant portion of their resources from donors, grantors, members, taxpayers, and others who do not expect to receive an economic benefit proportional to the resources provided. Those resources are often provided for charitable, humanitarian, religious, or cultural reasons. These donated resources often are not monetary but consist of volunteer work and other contributed services and materials.

2122.04 Further, SFAC 4 notes that the performance of nonbusiness organizations is usually *not* subject to direct competition in markets as is that of business enterprises. Thus, other controls have been introduced to ensure efficient and effective operation (i.e., funds, budgets, donor restrictions).

2122.05 Finally, SFAC 4 observes that nonbusiness organizations generally have no single indicator of performance such as profit, net income, etc., and suggests two *performance indicators* for nonbusiness organizations:

1. Information about the nature and relationship between *inflows and outflows of resources*
2. Information about *service efforts and accomplishments*

Objectives of Nonbusiness Financial Reporting

2122.06 SFAC 4, *Objectives of Financial Reporting by Nonbusiness Organizations,* represents the most recent expression of the overall purposes and related objectives of financial reporting by nonbusiness organizations.

2122.07 The purposes and related accounting and reporting objectives set forth in SFAC 4 are *concepts*—not standards—and are designed to provide a basis for establishing detailed accounting and reporting standards.

2122.08 SFAC 4 indicates that financial reporting by nonbusiness organizations should provide information useful to present and potential resource providers (e.g., creditors, suppliers, employees, donors, taxpayers) and meet seven objectives:

Objective 1: Financial reporting by nonbusiness organizations should provide information that is useful to present and potential resource providers and other users in making rational decisions about the allocation of resources to those organizations.

Objective 2: Financial reporting should provide information to help present and potential resource providers and other users assess the services that a nonbusiness organization provides and its ability to continue to provide those services.

Objective 3: Financial reporting should provide information that is useful to present and potential resource providers and other users in assessing how managers of a nonbusiness organization have discharged their stewardship responsibilities and about other aspects of their performance.

Objective 4: Financial reporting should provide information about the economic resources, obligations, and net resources of an organization and the effects of transactions, events, and circumstances that change resources and interests in those resources.

Objective 5: Financial reporting should provide information about the performance of an organization during a period. Periodic measurement of the changes in the amount and nature of the net resources of a nonbusiness organization and information about the service efforts and accomplishments of an organization together represent the information most useful in assessing its performance.

Objective 6: Financial reporting should provide information about how an organization obtains and spends cash or other liquid resources, about its borrowings and repayment of borrowings, and about other factors that may affect an organization's liquidity.

Objective 7: Financial reporting should include explanations and interpretations to help users understand financial information provided.

Nonbusiness Accounting Standards-Setting

2122.09   The FASB is the predominant accounting standards-setter for nonbusiness organizations *other than governments.*

2122.10   In June 1993, the FASB issued two statements that significantly affect accounting and reporting for one major subset of nonbusiness organizations—those not-for-profit organizations that are *not* classified as governments. The FASB also issued three subsequent statements. The effective not-for-profit organization-specific guidance is now codified in FASB ASC 958 (*Not-for-Profit Entities*).

2122.11   GAAP applicable to *government* entities are established by the Governmental Accounting Standards Board (GASB). Currently effective GASB and predecessor body standards are published in the GASB *Codification of Governmental Accounting and Financial Reporting Standards.*

2122.12   GAAP applicable to nonbusiness organizations differ significantly from those applicable to business enterprises. Moreover, applicable GAAP differ significantly among the various types of nonbusiness organizations (e.g., between government hospitals and nongovernment hospitals and between government educational institutions and nongovernment educational institutions).

Financial Statements Issued by Nongovernmental, Nonprofit Entities

2122.13   The financial reports of nongovernmental, nonprofit entities resemble business financial statements more than governmental financial statements. A nongovernmental, nonprofit entity must issue three primary financial statements—a statement of position (balance sheet), a statement of activities (statement of revenues and expenses), and a statement of cash flows.

2122.14   Accounting for nongovernmental, nonprofit entities is discussed in detail in section **2500** of this reference book.

2123   Financial Reporting by State and Local Governmental Entities

2123.01   Background on governmental accounting concepts can be found in section **2410** of this book ("Governmental Accounting Concepts").

2123.02   GASB has developed its own concepts statements:

   a.   Concepts Statement 1, *Objectives of Financial Reporting*

   b.   Concepts Statement 2, *Service Efforts and Accomplishments Reporting*

   c.   Concepts Statement 3, *Communication Methods in General Purpose External Financial Reports That Contain Basic Financial Statements*

   d.   Concepts Statement 4, *Elements of Financial Statements*

   e.   Concepts Statement 5, *Service Efforts and Accomplishments Reporting (an amendment of GASB Concepts Statement No. 2)*

2123.03   The need for a separate conceptual framework is illustrated in GASB Concepts Statement 1. *Objectives of Financial Reporting* establishes the objectives of general purpose external financial reporting by state and local governmental entities and applies to both governmental-type and business-type activities.

2123.04 The significant characteristics of the governmental environment that affect financial reporting of governmental-type activities and that need to be considered when establishing financial reporting objectives are:

    a. Primary characteristics of government's structure and the services it provides:

        (1) The representative form of government and the separation of powers

        (2) The federal system of government and the prevalence of intergovernmental revenues

        (3) The relationship of taxpayers to services received

    b. Control characteristics resulting from government's structure:

        (1) The budget as an expression of public policy and financial intent and as a method of providing control

        (2) The use of fund accounting for control purposes

    c. Other characteristics:

        (1) The dissimilarities between similarly designated governments

        (2) The significant investment in non-revenue-producing capital assets

        (3) The nature of the political process

2123.05 Taking these characteristics of governmental entities into account, the GASB has established "accountability" as the cornerstone of financial reporting for governmental entities. Under GASB Concepts Statement 1, accountability consists of the following subobjectives:

    a. Interperiod equity: Financial reporting should provide information to determine whether current-year revenues were sufficient to pay for current-year services.

    b. Budgetary and fiscal compliance: Financial reporting should demonstrate whether resources were obtained and used in accordance with the entity's legally adopted budget; it should also demonstrate compliance with other finance-related legal or contractual requirements.

    c. Service efforts costs and accomplishments: Financial reporting should provide information to assist users in assessing the service efforts, costs, and accomplishments of the governmental entity.

2123.06 GASB Concepts Statement 1 also establishes two additional objectives:

    1. Financial reporting should assist users in evaluating the operating results of the governmental entity for the year.

    2. Financial reporting should assist the users in assessing the level of services that can be provided by the governmental entity and its ability to meet its obligations as they become due.

Financial Statements Issued by Governmental Entities

2123.07 Over time, the hierarchy that has developed between the FASB and the GASB results in governmental entities being under the standards developed by the GASB and nongovernmental, nonprofit entities reporting as required by the FASB.

2123.08 Budgetary compliance requires that governmental entities prepare a cash-basis budget. Interperiod compliance requires accrual-basis financial statements. GASB Statement 35 requires that governmental entities issue only two sets of financial statements:

    a. The statement of net assets (balance sheet)

    b. The statement of activities (statement of revenues and expenses)

2123.09 Various financial statements are required of the funds that make up the activities of the governmental accounting unit. The type of statement depends on the type of fund:

    a. **Governmental fund:** balance sheet, statement of revenues, and expenditures and changes in fund balances

    b. **Proprietary fund:** balance sheet, statement of revenues, expenses and changes in net assets, and statement of cash flows

    c. **Fiduciary funds:** statement of fiduciary net assets and statement of changes in fiduciary net assets

2123.10 Accounting for nongovernmental, nonprofit entities is discussed in detail in section **2500** of this reference book.

2130 Financial Reporting, Presentation, and Disclosures in General-Purpose Financial Statements

2131 Balance Sheet

Financial Statement Overview

2131.01 Under current generally accepted accounting principles, a complete set of financial statements for an annual period includes the following:

    a. A statement of financial position (balance sheet) as of the last day of the year

    b. An income statement for the year

    c. A statement of cash flows for the year

    d. A statement of changes in stockholders' equity (or retained earnings statement) for the year

    e. Supplemental and note disclosures

2131.02 GAAP does not require a statement of changes in stockholders' equity. However, GAAP requires that all material changes in equity be disclosed, either in a financial statement or in the notes to the financial statements. Many enterprises choose to report their material changes in a financial statement, which is usually identified as a statement of changes in stockholders' equity.

2131.03 GAAP also requires that changes in equity that are identified as "other comprehensive income" be reported in a financial statement rather than in the notes. These items of other comprehensive income are discussed more extensively in section **2133**.

2131.04 The relationship of the various financial statements and disclosures is described in the following diagram.

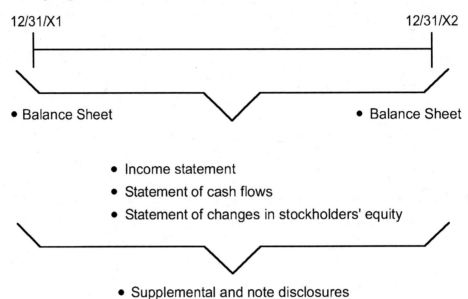

2131.05 The balance sheet represents the position of the enterprise at a point in time (e.g., the end of the year). The other statements explain the financial impact of various activities occurring throughout the year. The supplemental and note disclosures are designed to expand and supplement the information included in all of the financial statements.

2131.06 The content of these financial statements and disclosures is outlined in section **2130** with the exception of the statement of cash flows, which is covered in section **2135**.

2131.07 **IFRS:** IAS 1 requires the same set of financial statements.

Balance Sheet

2131.08 An example of the comparative balance sheet for Tiger Co., prepared in the *account form* (assets on the left, equities on the right), is presented as follows as of December 31, 20X1, and December 31, 20X2.

Tiger Co.
Comparative Balance Sheets
(Account Form)
At 12/31/X2 and 12/31/X1

Assets	20X2 (000s)	20X1 (000s)	Liabilities and Stockholders' Equity	20X2 (000s)	20X1 (000s)
Current assets			Current liabilities		
Cash	$ 290	$ 144	Accounts payable	$ 250	$ 375
Trading securities	150	200	Accrued taxes, interest, and		
Available-for-sale securities	45	25	other expenses	25	45
Notes and accounts receivable,			Dividends payable	20	30
net of allowance for doubtful			Current portion of obligations		
accounts of $100,000 in 20X2			under capital leases	36	23
and $150,000 in 20X1	900	950	Total current liabilities	$ 331	$ 473
Inventories carried at FIFO cost	670	500			
Prepayments and other current			Noncurrent liabilities		
Assets	50	30	Obligations under capital leases	$ 401	$ 437
Total current assets	$2,105	$1,849	9% bonds due in 20X5, net of		
			unamortized discount of		
Investments			$137,000 in 20X2 and		
Land held for resale	$10	$30	$150,000 in 20X1	863	850
Sinking fund for 9% bonds due			Total noncurrent liabilities	$1,264	$1,287
in 20X5	650	600	Total liabilities	$1,595	$1,760
Total investments	$ 660	$ 630			
			Stockholders' equity		
Property, plant, and equipment			7% convertible preferred stock		
Land	$1,150	$1,150	(noncumulative) authorized		
Plant facilities and fixtures	720	1,055	5,000 shares of $100 par		
Leased plant equipment under			value, issued and outstanding		
capital leases	500	500	3,000 shares in 20X1 and		
	$2,370	$2,705	2,500 shares in 20X2	$ 250	$ 300
Less accumulated			Common stock authorized		
Depreciation	267	400	100,000 shares of $25 par		
Net property, plant, and			value, issued 85,000 shares		
Equipment	$2,103	$2,305	in 20X1, 87,000 shares in 20X2	2,175	2,125
			Paid-in capital in excess of par		
Intangible assets			value on common stock	230	230
Patents	$190	$194	Paid-in capital in excess of cost	5	0
			of common treasury stock		
Other assets			Retained earnings	780	594
Unamortized			Treasury common stock at cost,		
organization costs	12	16	1,000 shares	0	(30)
Total assets	$5,070	$4,994	Accumulated other		
			comprehensive income	35	15
			Total stockholders' equity	$3,475	$3,234
			Total liabilities and stockholders'		
			equity	$5,070	$4,994

The following major categories typically appear on corporate balance sheets.

Item	Definition (SFAC 6)	Subcategories
Assets	Probable future economic benefits obtained or controlled by a particular entity as a result of past transactions or events.	Current assets Investments Property, plant, and equipment Intangible assets Other
Liabilities	Probable future sacrifices of economic benefits arising from present obligations to transfer assets or provide services to other entities as a result of past transactions.	Current Noncurrent

Equity	The residual interest in the assets of an entity that remains after deducting its liabilities. For a corporation, equity is the ownership interest (identified as "stockholders' equity").	Contributed capital
		  Par/stated value
		  Amounts in excess of par/stated value
		  Donated capital
		  Capital arising from asset revaluation
		Retained earnings
		Treasury stock
		Accumulated other comprehensive income

2131.09 Another form of the balance sheet, usually identified as the *report form,* includes the assets at the top of the statement and the equities at the bottom. An abbreviated example of this statement is as follows:

Tiger Co.
Comparative Balance Sheets
(Report Form)
At 12/31/X2 and 12/31/X1

	20X2	20X1
Assets		
Current assets	$2,105	$1,849
Investments	660	630
Property, plant, and equipment, net	2,103	2,305
Intangible assets	190	194
Other	12	16
Total assets	$5,070	$4,994
Liabilities		
Current liabilities	$ 331	$ 473
Noncurrent liabilities	1,264	1,287
Total liabilities	$1,595	$1,760
Stockholders' equity		
Contributed capital	$2,660	$2,655
Retained earnings	780	594
Treasury stock	0	(30)
Accumulated other comprehensive income	35	15
Total stockholders' equity	$3,475	$3,234
Total liabilities and stockholders' equity	$5,070	$4,994

2131.10 A third form of the balance sheet, usually identified as the *financial position form,* shows the net working capital (by deducting current liabilities from current assets), adds noncurrent assets, deducts noncurrent liabilities, and finally nets to the stockholders' equity, which is presented in detail in a balancing section. An abbreviated example of this balance sheet form for Tiger Co., which is encountered infrequently in practice, is illustrated as follows.

Tiger Co. Comparative Balance Sheet (Financial Position Form) At 12/31/X2 and 12/31/X1	20X2	20X1
Current assets	$2,105	$1,849
Less: Current liabilities	(331)	(473)
Net working capital	$1,774	$1,376
Noncurrent assets	2,965	3,145
Total net working capital and noncurrent assets	$4,739	$4,521
Less: Noncurrent liabilities	(1,264)	(1,287)
Total net assets	$3,475	$3,234
Stockholders' equity		
Contributed capital	$2,660	$2,655
Retained earnings	780	594
Accumulated other comprehensive income	35	15
Treasury stock	0	(30)
Total stockholders' equity	$3,475	$3,234

2131.11 A general principle of accounting is that the offsetting of assets and liabilities in the balance sheet is improper except where a right of setoff exists. This means, for example, that a debtor with a payable to an entity may not offset a receivable from that same entity and display only the difference as a net payable or receivable unless specified conditions are met. FASB ASC 210-20-45-1 specifies the following conditions that must be met for the right of setoff to exist:

   a. Each of the two parties owes the other determinable amounts.

   b. The reporting party has the right to set off the amount owed with the amount owed by the other party.

   c. The reporting entity intends to set off.

   d. The right of setoff is enforceable at law.

2131.12 **IFRS:** IAS 1 requires that the following categories be disclosed:

   a. Current assets

      (1) Receivables

      (2) Inventories

      (3) Cash and cash equivalents

      (4) Trade and other payables

   b. Noncurrent assets

      (1) Property, plant, and equipment

      (2) Investment property

      (3) Intangible assets

      (4) Financial assets

      (5) Equity method investments

      (6) Biological assets

c. Financial liabilities
d. Provisions
e. Current and deferred tax assets and liabilities
f. Equity capital and reserves
g. Minority interest
h. Parent's equity holder issued capital and reserves

2132 Income Statement

2132.01 An example of a comparative income statement for Tiger Co. for the years 20X2 and 20X1 is presented as follows.

Tiger Co.
Comparative Income Statements (in thousands)
For the Years 20X2 and 20X1

	12/31/X2	12/31/X1
Revenue from sales	$2,550	$2,000
Cost of goods sold	650	560
Gross profit	$1,900	$1,440
Selling and administrative expenses	1,210	1,040
Operating income	$ 690	$ 400
Other income:		
Gain on sale of land	$ 10	$ 0
Dividend income	5	4
Other expenses:		
Interest on long-term debt	(76)	(75)
Loss on trading securities	(50)	0
Income before taxes	$ 579	$ 329
Provision for income taxes	(279)	(160)
Income from continuing operations	$ 300	$ 169
Discontinued operations		
Loss from operations of discontinued component, net of applicable tax savings of $27,000 in 20X2 and $18,000 in 20X1 (including loss on disposal of $10,000 in 20X2)	(40)	(20)
Income before extraordinary items and cumulative effect of change in accounting principle	$ 260	$ 149
Extraordinary item—Gain on forced sale of assets to state municipality, net of applicable taxes of $45,000	0	50
Cumulative effect of FASB-mandated accounting change, net of applicable taxes of $28,000 (see section **2305.04–.23**)	30	0
Net income	$ 290	$ 199
Earnings per common share		
Income from continuing operations	$ 3.45	$ 1.99
Discontinued operations	(0.46)	(0.24)
Income before extraordinary items and cumulative effect of change in accounting principle	$ 2.99	$ 1.75
Extraordinary item	0.00	0.59
Cumulative effect of change in accounting principle (see section **2305.04–.23**)	0.34	0.00
Net income	$ 3.33	$ 2.34

2132.02 The income statement illustrated in section **2132.01** assumes that Tiger Co. elects to report items of other comprehensive income in a financial statement other than the income statement. As demonstrated in section **2132.03** Tiger Co. elects to report items of other comprehensive income in a separate comprehensive income statement. The reporting of other comprehensive income is discussed more extensively in section **2133**.

2132.03

Tiger Co. For the Years 20X2 and 20X1 (000's omitted)		
	20X1	**20X2**
Net income	$290	$199
Other comprehensive income:		
Unrealized gains (losses) on available-for-sale marketable securities	20	15
Comprehensive income	$310	$214

2132.04 As discussed in section **2133**, enterprises are required to report items of other comprehensive income in a formal financial statement. One of the acceptable alternative methods is that shown in section **2132.03** for Tiger Co. Another method that Tiger Co. could have chosen is to include another comprehensive income section at the bottom of its income statement following the caption "net income," with the final caption at the bottom of the statement being "comprehensive income." A third method that Tiger Co. could have chosen is to report the items of other comprehensive income in its statement of changes in stockholders' equity. These various methods of reporting other comprehensive income are demonstrated in section **2133**.

2132.05 Several definitions of the basic elements of an income statement, as presented in section **2132.01** are important and are described as follows (SFAC 6):

   a. **Revenue:** Inflows of assets or settlements of liabilities, during a period, from delivering or producing goods, rendering services, or other activities that constitute the entity's ongoing major or central operations.

   b. **Expenses:** Outflows of assets or incurrences of liabilities, during a period, from delivering or producing goods, rendering services, or other activities that constitute the entity's ongoing major or central operations.

   c. **Gains:** Increases in net assets other than from revenues or investments by owners.

   d. **Losses:** Decreases in net assets other than from expenses or withdrawals by owners.

   e. **Income:** The result of combining these four concepts for a specified period of time (sometimes referred to as *earnings*):

$$\text{Income} = \text{Revenues} - \text{Expenses} + \text{Gains} - \text{Losses}$$

2132.06 The concepts of gains and losses, as illustrated, relate to *peripheral or secondary activities* rather than to the major or central operations of the enterprise. While revenues and expenses are presented in *gross amounts* in the income statement, gains and losses are presented in the income statement in *net amounts* (i.e., they are measured by subtracting two or more other measures or they involve only an increase or decrease in an asset or liability with no offsetting decrease or increase in another asset or liability).

2132.07 The income statement may be presented in either of two formats—single step or multiple step.

    a. Single step: The single-step income statement is a simple and relatively straightforward presentation whereby all revenues and gains are combined at the top of the statement. From this subtotal, a total amount of all expenses and losses is deducted to render a net income figure. A popular variation of the single-step income statement is the separation of income taxes from the other expenses, resulting in an income figure before taxes (when revenues and gains are reduced by all other expenses and losses). Income tax is then deducted as a separate item, resulting in a net income figure.

    b. Multiple step: Under the multiple-step income statement, a distinction is made between operating and nonoperating items. The typical format is that illustrated previously in the example of Tiger Co., wherein cost of goods sold is deducted from revenues to yield gross profit; selling and administrative expenses are then deducted to yield operating income; other income and expense items are then added and deducted to yield net income (unless the enterprise is involved in some of the specialized gain and loss transactions described in section **2345**).

2133 Statement of Comprehensive Income

2133.01 In recent years, the FASB has required that various "gains" and "losses" be excluded from the income statement and reported as direct charges or credits to equity. Even though various pronouncements required specific disclosure of these items in the notes to the financial statements, they did not require them to be reported in the body of a financial statement. As a result of the increasing number of these items, the FASB decided to readdress the issue of how these direct charges and credits to equity should be reported. The FASB decided that these direct charges and credits to equity (other comprehensive income) should be reported in a formal financial statement rather than just disclosed in the notes.

2133.02 **Comprehensive income** is defined in SFAC 6 as "the change in equity (net assets) of a business enterprise during a period from transactions and other events and circumstances from nonowner sources. It includes all changes in equity during a period, except those resulting from investments by owners and distributions to owners." Thus, comprehensive income includes not only net income but also other components of comprehensive income that are not included in net income. This relationship is illustrated as follows:

Revenues and gains	$ XXX
Expenses and losses	XXX
Income before income taxes	XXX
Income taxes	XXX
Net income	XXX
Other comprehensive income	XXX
Comprehensive income	$ XXX

SFAC 6.71 includes a discussion of concepts of capital maintenance with its discussions of comprehensive income. A concept of maintenance of capital or recovery of cost is a prerequisite for separating return on capital from return of capital because only inflows in excess of the amount needed to maintain capital are a return on equity. Two major concepts of capital maintenance exist, both of which can be measured in units of either money or constant purchasing power: the financial capital concept and the physical capital concept (which is often expressed in terms of maintaining operating capability; that is, maintaining the capacity of an enterprise to provide a constant supply of goods or services). The major difference between them involves the effects of price changes on assets held and liabilities owed during a period. Under the financial capital concept, if the effects of those price changes are recognized, they are called "holding gains and losses" and are included in return on capital. Under the physical capital concept, those changes would be recognized but called "capital

maintenance adjustments" and would be included directly in equity and would not be included in return on capital. Under that concept, capital maintenance adjustments would be a separate element rather than gains and losses.

The financial capital concept is the traditional view and is generally the capital maintenance concept in present primary financial statements. Comprehensive income as defined in paragraph 70 of SFAC 6 is a return on financial capital.

2133.03 FASB ASC 220-10-45-4 defines **other comprehensive income** as "all revenues, expenses, gains, and losses that under generally accepted accounting principles are included in comprehensive income but excluded from net income." Currently, existing GAAP specifies that the following items should be reported as direct charges or credits to equity. Thus, the items that currently constitute other comprehensive income include the following:

  a. Foreign currency translation adjustments

  b. Gains and losses on foreign currency transactions that are designated as, and are effective as, economic hedges of a net investment in a foreign entity

  c. Gains and losses on intercompany foreign currency transactions that are of a long-term investment nature when the entities to the transaction are consolidated, combined, or accounted for by the equity method in the reporting entity's financial statements

  d. A change in the fair value of a derivative instrument that qualifies as the hedging instrument in a cash flow hedge

  e. Changes in (1) unrecognized prior service costs, (2) unrecognized gains and losses, and (3) unrecognized transition assets or obligations associated with defined benefit pension plans and defined benefit other postretirement benefit plans

  f. Unrealized holding gains and losses on available-for-sale securities

  g. Unrealized holding gains and losses that result from a debt security being transferred into the available-for-sale category from the held-to-maturity category

  h. Subsequent decreases (if not an other-than-temporary impairment) or increases in the fair value of available-for-sale securities previously written down as impaired

2133.04 **Reporting and Display of Comprehensive Income**

FASB ASC 220-10-45-5 requires that all components of comprehensive income be reported in the financial statements in the period in which they are recognized. An enterprise must display comprehensive income and its components in a financial statement that is displayed with the same prominence as other financial statements that constitute a full set of financial statements. FASB ASC 220-10-45-8 does not require a specific format for that financial statement but requires that an enterprise display net income as a component of comprehensive income in that financial statement.

2133.05 Although FASB ASC 220-10-45-2 does not require a specific format for displaying comprehensive income and its components, the FASB expresses a preference for displaying the components of other comprehensive income and total comprehensive income either (1) below the total for net income in a statement that reports results of operations (a one income-statement approach) or (2) in a separate statement of comprehensive income that begins with net income (a two-income-statement approach).

2133.06 Under the one-income-statement approach, the caption *net income* (including the components currently recognized under existing GAAP) is followed by a section for *other comprehensive income* items. This format is presented in section **2133.08**.

2133.07 Under the two-income-statement approach, the enterprise presents the income statement as it does now and also presents a separate statement that begins with net income and is followed by the components of other comprehensive income. This format is presented in section **2133.09**.

2133.08 **Format A: One-Statement Approach**

ABC Company
Statement of Income and Comprehensive Income
For the Year Ended December 31, 20X1

Revenues		$ 95,000
Expenses		(10,000)
Other gains and losses		6,000
Gain on sale of securities		2,000
Income from operations before income taxes		93,000
Income tax expense		23,250
Income before extraordinary items and cumulative effect of accounting change		69,750
Extraordinary item, net of tax		(10,000)
Cumulative effect of accounting change, net of tax (see section **2305.04–.23**)		3,000
Net income		62,750
Other comprehensive income, net of tax:		
Foreign currency translation adjustments[a]		9,000
Unrealized gains on securities:[b]		
Unrealized holding gains arising during period	$12,000	
Less: Reclassification adjustment for gain included in net income	(1,500)	10,500
Changes in unrecognized items related to pension and postretirement plans[c]		(3,000)
Other comprehensive income		16,500
Comprehensive income		$ 79,250

Alternatively, components of other comprehensive income could be displayed before tax with one amount shown for the aggregate income tax expense or benefit, as shown below:

Other comprehensive income, before income tax:		
Foreign currency translation adjustments[a]		$12,000
Unrealized gains on securities:[b]		
Unrealized holding gains arising during period	$16,000	
Less: Reclassification adjustment for gains included in net income	(2,000)	14,000
Changes in unrecognized items related to pension and postretirement plans[c]		(4,000)
Other comprehensive income, before income tax		22,000
Income tax expense related to items of other comprehensive income		(5,500)
Other comprehensive income, net of income tax		$16,500

[a] It is assumed that there was no sale of an investment in a foreign entity. Therefore, there is no reclassification adjustment for this period.

[b] This illustrates the gross display. Alternatively, a net display can be used, with disclosure of the gross amounts (current-period gain and reclassification adjustment) in the notes.

[c] This illustrates the required net display for this classification.

2133.09 Format B: Two-Statement Approach

ABC Company
Statement of Income
For the Year Ended December 31, 20X1

Revenues	$ 95,000
Expenses	(10,000)
Other gains and losses	6,000
Gain on sale of securities	2,000
Income from operations before income taxes	93,000
Income tax expense	(23,250)
Income before extraordinary items and cumulative effect of accounting change	69,750
Extraordinary item, net of tax	(10,000)
Cumulative effect of accounting change, net of tax	3,000
Net income	$ 62,750

ABC Company
Statement of Comprehensive Income
For the Year Ended December 31, 20X1

Net income		$62,750
Other comprehensive income, net of tax:		
Foreign currency translation adjustments		9,000
Unrealized gains on securities:		
Unrealized holding gains arising during period	12,000	
Less: Reclassification adjustment for gain included in net income	(1,500)	10,500
Changes in unrecognized items related to pension and postretirement plans		(3,000)
Other comprehensive income		16,500
Comprehensive income		$79,250

2133.10 Alternatively, comprehensive income (including the components of other comprehensive income) may be presented in a statement of changes in owners' equity (for a corporation, a statement of changes in stockholders' equity). An example of this type of presentation is shown in section **2133.12**.

2133.11 **IFRS:** Examples in IAS 1 refer to the income statement as the "Statement of Comprehensive Income."

2133.12 Format C: Statement of Changes in Stockholders' Equity Approach

ABC Company
Statement of Changes in Stockholders' Equity
For the Year Ended December 31, 20X1

	Total	Comprehensive Income	Retained Earnings	Accumulated Other Comprehensive Income	Common Stock	Paid-in Capital
Beginning balance	$570,000		$100,000	$20,000	$200,000	$250,000
Comprehensive income:						
Net income	62,750	$62,750	62,750			
Other comprehensive income, net of tax						
Unrealized gains on securities, net of reclassification adjustment	10,500	10,500				
Foreign currency translation adjustment	9,000	9,000				
Changes in unrecognized items related to pension and postretirement plans	(3,000)	(3,000)				
Other comprehensive income		16,500		16,500		
Comprehensive income		$79,250				
Common stock issued	150,000				50,000	100,000
Dividends declared on common stock	(10,000)		(10,000)			
Ending balance	$789,250		$152,750	$36,500	$250,000	$350,000

Alternatively, an enterprise can omit the separate column labeled "Comprehensive Income" by displaying an aggregate amount for comprehensive income, $79,250, in the "Total" column.

2133.13 It is important to note that comprehensive income is a change amount and not a cumulative amount. The amounts reported as direct charges or credits in the equity section of a balance sheet are cumulative amounts, similar to the way that retained earnings is a cumulative amount. Thus, merely showing the cumulative balances of these direct charges or credits to stockholders' equity, as was done prior to FASB ASC 220-10-45-8, will not satisfy the requirement to report other comprehensive income (i.e., the changes in these cumulative direct charges and credits to equity) in a primary financial statement.

2133.14 It is also important to note that whether comprehensive income is reported (1) under the one-statement format or the two-statement format for reporting comprehensive income or (2) in the statement of changes in stockholders' equity, comprehensive income must be reported in a primary financial statement. Mere disclosure in the notes is not acceptable.

2133.15 Recall that the FASB expressed a preference for enterprises to report comprehensive income in an income statement using either the one-statement format or the two-statement format. Accordingly, the remainder of the discussion in this section focuses on that type of approach for reporting comprehensive income.

Classifications within Net Income

2133.16 FASB ASC 220-10-45-7 does not change the manner in which the components of net income are classified and reported. Thus, the authoritative pronouncements that address the classifications of discontinued operations, extraordinary items, and the cumulative effect of changes in accounting principles remain in effect.

Classifications within Other Comprehensive Income

2133.17 Items included in other comprehensive income should be classified based on their nature. At any point in time, existing GAAP identify the items whose unrealized gains and losses must be reported as direct charges or credits to equity. Thus, existing GAAP would dictate what classifications within other comprehensive income are necessary.

2133.18 Under existing GAAP, an enterprise might separately classify other comprehensive income into foreign currency items, futures contracts items, changes in unrecognized items related to pension and postretirement plans, and unrealized gains and losses related to available-for-sale securities. Of course, additional classifications may result from future accounting standards.

Reclassifications Adjustments

2133.19 FASB ASC 220-10-45-15 specifies that enterprises must avoid double counting in comprehensive income items that are reported as part of net income for a period that also had been reported as part of other comprehensive income in that period or earlier periods. Reclassification adjustments arise from recognizing gains and losses in other comprehensive income when they are unrealized, but not recognizing them in net income until they are realized.

2133.20 To illustrate, assume that in 20X1, Alpha Company purchased 1,000 shares of Beta Company common stock for $10 per share and that these marketable equity securities qualify as available-for-sale (AFS) securities. Assume that at the end of 20X1 the fair value of the securities is $12 per share. In that case, the following entries are recorded in 20X1:

Investment in AFS Securities	$10,000	
Cash		$10,000
To record the purchase of the securities.		
Valuation Allowance—AFS Securities	$ 2,000	
Unrealized Gain—AFS Securities—OCI		$ 2,000
To record the unrealized holding gain that occurred in 20X1.		

OCI = other comprehensive income

2133.21 The $2,000 unrealized gain is reported as a component of other comprehensive income in 20X1.

2133.22 The "Unrealized gain—AFS securities—OCI" account (a temporary account) is closed at the end of 20X1 to the "Accumulated OCI—AFS securities" account (a permanent or balance sheet account) as follows:

Unrealized Gain—AFS Securities—OCI	$2,000	
Accumulated OCI—AFS Securities		$2,000

2133.23 Now assume that the Beta Company shares are sold in 20X2 for $13,000, meaning there was an additional $1,000 increase in their fair value in 20X2. The entries to record the additional increase in fair value and the sale of the Beta Company shares in 20X2 are:

Valuation Allowance—AFS Securities	$1,000	
Unrealized Gain—AFS Securities—OCI		$1,000

To record the additional unrealized holding gain that occurred in 20X2.

Cash	$13,000	
Investment in AFS Securities		$10,000
Realized Gain		3,000

To record the sale of the Beta shares, with the realized gain being the difference between the proceeds and the cost basis.

2133.24 The "Realized gain" and "Unrealized gain—AFS securities—OCI" accounts are closed at the end of 20X2, as follows:

Realized Gain	$3,000	
Net Income Summary		$3,000
Unrealized Gain—AFS Securities—OCI	$1,000	
Accumulated OCI—AFS Securities		$1,000

2133.25 The "Accumulated OCI—AFS Securities" account (a balance sheet account) has a $3,000 credit balance at the end of 20X2. This balance is the cumulative unrealized gain (loss) that has been included in other comprehensive income since the acquisition of the Beta Company shares. It is not coincidental that the balance in the "Valuation allowance—AFS securities" account is the same amount ($3,000) but of opposite direction (i.e., a debit balance instead of a credit balance). It is the recognition of the $3,000 increase in net assets (the $3,000 debit balance in the "Valuation allowance—AFS securities" account) for balance sheet purposes that resulted in the $3,000 direct credit to equity (the $3,000 credit balance in the "Accumulated OCI—AFS securities" account). In other words, the $3,000 unrealized gain was recognized for balance sheet purposes and for other comprehensive income purposes but not for net income purposes. (Recall that to *recognize* is to include the item in the column totals of a particular financial statement.)

2133.26 Since the reclassification adjustment is a required disclosure (either in the notes or on the face of the financial statement in which other comprehensive income is reported), it is helpful to set up a reclassification adjustment account for each category of other comprehensive income. In the case of available-for-sale securities, the reclassification adjustment recognized in a given period is the cumulative unrealized gain (loss) that has been recognized in the current or prior periods with respect to any available-for-sale securities sold during the current period. In the case of Alpha Company, since all of the Beta Company shares were sold in 20X2, the balance in the "valuation allowance—AFS securities" account represents the cumulative unrealized gains that were recognized through 20X2. Accordingly, the entry to set up the reclassification adjustment is as follows:

Reclassification Adjustment—AFS Securities	$3,000	
Valuation Allowance—AFS Securities		$3,000

To set up a reclassification adjustment for the AFS securities sold in the current period—20X2.

2133.27 The preceding entry results in the "valuation allowance—AFS securities" account now having a zero balance with respect to the securities sold. Note that the reclassification adjustment relates only to the securities sold. If Alpha had sold only a portion of the Beta shares, the reclassification adjustment would have been limited to the portion of the shares sold.

2133.28 The "Reclassification Adjustment—AFS securities" account is then closed as follows:

Accumulated OCI—AFS Securities	$3,000	
Reclassification Adjustment—AFS Securities		$3,000
To close the reclassification adjustment account.		

This entry also serves the purpose of "zeroing out" the balance in the "accumulated OCI—AFS securities" account with respect to the securities sold in 20X2.

2133.29 Assuming these securities transactions are the only components of comprehensive income (and ignoring income taxes) in 20X1 and 20X2, they would be reported as follows under the one-statement format:

20X1

Net income		$ 0
Other comprehensive income:		
Unrealized gain—AFS securities		2,000
Comprehensive income		$ 2,000

20X2

Realized gain		$ 3,000
Net income		3,000
Other comprehensive income:		
Unrealized gains/losses arising during the year	$ 1,000	
Less: Reclassification adjustment for gain included in net income	(3,000)	(2,000)
Comprehensive income		$ 1,000

2133.30 Note that with respect to the securities sold, the cumulative net income recognized in 20X1 and 20X2 is $3,000, which is the amount of cumulative realized gains recognized in those years (the difference between the $13,000 proceeds from sale and the $10,000 cost of the shares). In addition, the cumulative comprehensive income recognized in 20X1 and 20X2 is also $3,000. Therefore, with respect to the Beta shares sold in 20X2, the cumulative other comprehensive income recognized in 20X1 and 20X2 has to be zero. The essence of the amounts recognized is that the sale of the securities reclassified in 20X2 (the year of the sale) the cumulative unrealized gains recognized (in 20X1 and 20X2) from the "unrealized" category to the "realized" category.

Gross Display

2133.31 An enterprise must use a gross display for classifications related to items of other comprehensive income other than changes in unrecognized items related to pension and postretirement plans. Thus, reclassification adjustments must be displayed separately from other changes in the balances of those items so that the total change is displayed as two amounts. For a given category of other comprehensive income, an enterprise may choose to report in the body of the financial statement the gross unrealized gain or loss included in other comprehensive income and the reclassification adjustment on a separate line in that same financial statement, as Alpha Company did in section **2133.29**. Alternatively, the reclassification adjustment may be netted against the unrealized gain or loss in the body of the financial statement, with the gross unrealized gain or loss and the reclassification adjustment being disclosed in the notes to the financial statements.

Per-Share Reporting

2133.32 FASB ASC 260-10-45-1 does not require an earnings per share amount for comprehensive income.

Reporting Tax Effect of Other Comprehensive Income Items

2133.33 The components of other comprehensive income may be reported either (1) net of related tax effects, as shown for ABC Company in format A in section **2133.09**, or (2) before related tax effects with one amount shown for the aggregate income tax expense or benefit related to the total amount of other comprehensive income, as shown at the bottom of that same page.

2133.34 If the enterprise uses the type of presentation (such as that shown in section **2133.08** for ABC Company) in which it does not report in the body of a financial statement the tax effect of the components of other comprehensive income, it must disclose in the notes the amount of tax expense or benefit allocated to each component part of other comprehensive income.

2133.35 Thus, if the enterprise does not show the tax effect of each classification of other comprehensive income on the face of the financial statement in which other comprehensive income is reported, it must disclose the tax effect of each category in the notes to the financial statement.

Reporting Other Comprehensive Income in the Equity Section of the Balance Sheet

2133.36 The total of other comprehensive income for a period must be transferred to a separate component of equity in the balance sheet at the end of the accounting period. A descriptive title such as accumulated other comprehensive income should be used for that component of equity. An enterprise must disclose accumulated balances for each classification in that separate component of equity on the face of the balance sheet, in the statement of changes in equity, or in the accompanying notes. Those classifications should correspond to those used for components of other comprehensive income in the primary financial statement used to report other comprehensive income. Thus, if the enterprise does not report the accumulated amount separately for each classification (e.g., available-for-sale securities, pensions, foreign currency) on the face of a financial statement, it must do so in the notes.

2133.37 For example, an enterprise could report only the total accumulated amount on the balance sheet, with no breakdown for each classification, and disclose the separate breakdown of the accumulated amount in the notes. Alternatively, an enterprise might choose to report only the total accumulated amount on the balance sheet and show on the statement of changes in stockholders' equity a column for each classification of other comprehensive income. The ending balance (at the bottom of each column) would represent the accumulated other comprehensive income for that particular classification. Perhaps the easiest way to comply with GAAP with regard to disclosure of the accumulated balance for each classification is to show the breakdown in the equity section of the balance sheet, as demonstrated for ABC Company. You may wish to refer back to sections **2133.08, 2133.09,** and **2133.12** for illustrations of ABC Company's reporting of other comprehensive income.

ABC Company
Balance Sheet
December 31, 20X1

Assets:		
Cash		$ 180,000
Accounts receivable		200,000
Available-for-sale securities		145,000
Plant and equipment		940,250
Total assets		$ 1,465,250
Liabilities:		
Accounts payable		$ 150,000
Notes payable		386,000
Pension liability		140,000
Total Liabilities		676,000
Stockholders' equity:		
Common stock		$ 250,000
Additional paid-in capital		350,000
Retained earnings		152,750
Accumulated other comprehensive income:		
Foreign currency translation adjustments	$ 6,500	
Unrealized gains on securities	34,000	
Changes in unrecognized items related to pension and postretirement plans	(4,000)	36,500
Total stockholders' equity		789,250
Total liabilities and stockholders' equity		$ 1,465,250

2133.38   Alternatively, ABC Company could have chosen to (1) show on the balance sheet only the $36,500 total for the accumulated other comprehensive income and (2) show the accumulated amount for each classification of other comprehensive income (foreign currency, securities, and pensions) in the notes to the financial statements.

2134 Statement of Changes in Equity

2134.01 An example of a comparative statement of changes in stockholders' equity for Tiger Co. for 20X1 and 20X2 is presented as follows:

Tiger Co. Statement of Changes in Stockholders' Equity For the Years 20X2 and 20X1 (000's omitted)						
	7% Convertible Preferred Stock	Common Stock	Capital in Excess of Par Value	Capital from Treasury Stock Transactions	Treasury Stock at Cost	Retained Earnings
Balance at December 31, 20X0	$300	$1,375	$180	$0	$ 0	$500
Net income for the year 20X1						199
Cash dividends declared:						
7% convertible preferred stock						(21)
Common stock						(84)
Proceeds from sale of common stock, 30,000 shares		750	50			
Common share purchased and held in the treasury, 1,000 shares					(30)	
Balance at December 31, 20X1	$300	$2,125	$230	$0	$(30)	$594
Net income for the year 20X2						290
Cash dividends declared:						
7% convertible preferred stock						(18)
Common stock						(86)
Conversion of 500 shares of 7% convertible preferred stock to 2,000 shares of common stock	(50)	50				
Treasury common shares sold, 1,000 shares				5	30	
Balance at December 31, 20X2	$250	$2,175	$230	$5	$ 0	$780

2134.02 Tiger Co.'s statement of changes in stockholders' equity reveals the following:

    a. Column headings identify individual stockholders' equity accounts.

    b. Events changing stockholders' equity accounts are listed chronologically to the left.

    c. The body of the statement is presented in terms of the dollar impact of various transactions and events.

    d. The impact of the transactions on the number of shares of stock, if any, is presented in the descriptions to the left.

    e. The ending balances tie to the items presented in the stockholders' equity section of the balance sheet on the same dates (see section **2131.08**).

2134.03 **IFRS:** IAS 1 contains an example of a "Statement of Changes in Equity" very similar to the GAAP statement.

2135 Statement of Cash Flows

2135.01 In this section, the statement of cash flows is presented as part of the set of financial statements of Tiger Co. This statement omits some of the disclosures required by generally accepted accounting principles.

An example statement of cash flows for Tiger Co. for 20X1 and 20X2 is presented as follows:

Tiger Co. Statement of Cash Flows For the Years 20X1 and 20X2 (000's omitted)	20X2	20X1
Cash Flows from Operating Activities:		
Net Income	$290	$199
Adjustments to reconcile net income to cash provided by operating activities:		
Depreciation expense	50	75
Amortization expense	8	8
Accounts receivable—decr (incr)	50	(37)
Inventory—decr (incr)	(170)	(120)
Prepaid expenses—decr (incr)	(20)	(5)
Valuation of trading securities—loss (gain)	50	0
Accounts payable—incr (decr)	(125)	20
Accrued expenses—incr (decr)	(20)	10
Bond discount amortization	13	14
Change in depreciation method	(58)	0
Sale of land—loss (gain)	(10)	0
Sale of business segment—loss (gain)	19	0
Forced sale of assets—loss (gain)	0	(95)
Cash Flows From Operating Activities	$ 77	$ 69
Cash Flows from Investing Activities:		
Purchase of available-for-sale securities	0	$ (10)
Proceeds from forced sale of assets	0	145
Proceeds from sale of business segment	$191	0
Proceeds from sale of land	30	0
Sinking fund—decr (incr)	(50)	(50)
Cash Flows from Investing Activities	$171	$ 85
Cash Flows from Financing Activities:		
Retire bonds	0	($750)
Dividends paid	($114)	(100)
Capital leases payable—incr (decr)	(23)	(30)
Common stock—incr (decr)	0	800
Treasury stock—sale (purch)	35	(30)
Cash Flows from Financing Activities:	($102)	($110)
Net Change in Cash	$146	$ 44
Cash Balance—Beginning	144	100
Cash Balance—Ending	$290	$144

2135.02 The statement of cash flows is presented in three sections: cash flows from operating activities, from investing activities, and from financing activities. Each section presents both positive and negative cash flows from a specific aspect of the company's activities. The change in cash resulting from the total of these three sections reconciles the change in cash for the period.

2135.03 The operating activities section of the statement of cash flows presents the positive and negative cash flows from the company's primary operating activities. The most common method for presenting cash flows from operating activities is the indirect method, in which net income is adjusted for noncash items that have been included in its determination.

2135.04 The investing activities section of the statement of cash flows presents positive and negative cash flows for transactions involving assets that are not held for resale (i.e., inventories). The most significant investing activities involve investments in debt and equity securities, plant assets, and intangible assets.

2135.05 The financing activities section of the statement of cash flows presents positive and negative cash flows for transactions resulting from sources of financing for the company, primarily debt and equity financing.

Objectives and Purposes of Statement of Cash Flows

2135.06 The primary purpose of a statement of cash flows (SCF) is to provide information about the cash receipts and cash payments of an enterprise during a period of time.

2135.07 A business enterprise that provides a set of financial statements intended to report financial position and results of operations must provide an SCF for each period for which results of operations are presented.

2135.08 Cash flow information is considered useful to investors, creditors, and other financial statement users to assess the following:

    a. An enterprise's ability to generate positive future cash flows

    b. An enterprise's ability to meet obligations and pay dividends and its need for external financing

    c. The reasons for differences between net income and associated cash receipts and payments

    d. The effect on an enterprise's financial position of both its cash and noncash investing and financing transactions that took place during the period

2135.09 **IFRS:** IAS 7, *Cash Flow Statements,* is similar to the GAAP statement except that cash flows from extraordinary items are required to be disclosed separately under the categories. The cash flow from the acquisition or disposal of a subsidiary is presented separately as an investing activity.

Principles of Cash Flow Reporting

2135.10 The statement of cash flows (SCF) explains the change during the period in cash and cash equivalents.

2135.11 Cash equivalents are short-term, highly liquid investments that:

    a. are readily convertible to known amounts of cash and

    b. are so near maturity that they represent insignificant risk of changes in value due to changes in interest rates. (Generally, only investments with original maturities of three months or less qualify as cash equivalents, such as Treasury bills, commercial paper, money market funds, and federal funds sold.)

2135.12 Information about gross amounts of cash receipts and payments during a period is generally considered more relevant than information about net amounts. Therefore, gross cash flow information is usually presented in the statement of cash flows (SCF). Exceptions where net cash flow information is acceptable are when turnovers are quick, amounts are large, and maturities are short.

2135.13 The statement of cash flows (SCF) is presented in three primary sections: cash flows from operating activities, cash flows from investing activities, and cash flows from financing activities (in that order).

   a. **Cash flows from operating activities:** Cash flows from operating activities include those cash flows resulting from transactions included in the determination of net income, unless specifically classified by FASB ASC 230-10-05-2 as financing or investing activities.

   (1) Cash *inflows* from operating activities generally include the following:

   (a) Cash receipts from sales of goods or services

   (b) Cash receipts from interest and dividends on investments in another enterprise

   (c) All other cash receipts that are not classified as either investing or financing activities

   (2) Cash *outflows* classified as operating activities include the following:

   (a) Cash payments to acquire materials for manufacture or goods for resale

   (b) Cash payments to other suppliers and employees for goods and services

   (c) Cash payments to governments for taxes, duties, other fees, or penalties

   (d) Cash payments to lenders and other creditors for interest

   (e) All other cash payments that are not classified as investing or financing activities

   b. **Cash flows from investing activities:** Cash flows from investing activities involve asset transactions other than cash (and cash equivalents) and those assets related directly to the determination of operating results (e.g., inventories, receivables).

   (1) Specifically, the following are types of cash *inflows* from investing activities:

   (a) Cash receipts from collections or sales of loans made by the enterprise and of other debt instruments that are purchased by the enterprise

   (b) Cash receipts from sales of equity securities of other enterprises

   (c) Cash receipts from the sales of property, plant, and equipment and other productive assets

   (2) The following are categories of cash *outflows* from investing activities:

   (a) Cash payments for loans made by the enterprise and payments to acquire debt instruments of other entities

   (b) Cash payments to acquire equity instruments of other enterprises

   (c) Cash payments to purchase property, plant, as well as equipment and other productive assets

   c. **Cash flows from financing activities:** Cash flows from financing activities involve debt and equity financing.

   (1) Cash *inflows* from financing activities include the following:

   (a) Cash proceeds from issuing equity instruments

(b) Cash proceeds from issuing bonds, mortgages, notes, and other short- and long-term debt instruments

(2) Cash *outflows* classified as financing activities are as follows:

(a) Cash payments of dividends or other distributions to owners, including outlays to reacquire the enterprise's instruments

(b) Cash repayments of amounts borrowed

(c) Other principal cash payments to creditors who have extended long-term credit

2135.14 Several additional matters of form and content of the statement of cash flows (SCF) are as follows:

a. The SCF presents net cash flows from operating, investing, and financing activities to reconcile the change in cash (and cash equivalents) for the period.

b. In reporting cash flows from operating activities, enterprises are encouraged to use the *direct method,* with disclosure of at least the following:

(1) Cash collected from customers

(2) Interest and dividends received

(3) Other operating cash receipts

(4) Cash paid to employees and other suppliers of goods and services

(5) Interest paid

(6) Income taxes paid

(7) Other operating cash payments

c. Alternatively, the enterprise may use the *indirect method* of determining cash flows from operating activities, in which the calculation begins with net income and eliminates noncash amounts included in the determination of that figure as well as any transactions that are classified as investing or financing activities (e.g., gains or losses on sales of assets).

d. Regardless of whether the direct or indirect method is used to determine cash flows from operating activities, the following items are required to be disclosed in the SCF or related notes:

(1) Amount of income taxes paid during the period

(2) Amount of interest paid during the period

(3) Reconciliation of net income and net cash flows from operating activities (if the direct method is used, this is ordinarily done in a related note; if the indirect method is used, this is ordinarily part of the SCF section on operations)

e. Information about noncash investing and/or financing activities must be disclosed outside the main body of the SCF.

f. Cash-flow-per-share information shall *not* be presented.

g. FASB ASC 230-10-05-3 contains the following exceptions:

(1) The following organizations are exempt from the requirement to present an SCF—defined benefit pension plans and highly liquid investment companies that meet specified conditions.

(2) Cash receipts and payments of the following types are classified as operating cash flows in the SCF—securities specifically acquired for resale and carried in a trading account and loans that are acquired specifically for resale and are carried at the lower of cost or market value.

h. FASB ASC 942-230-45-1 and 230-10-45-14 include the following exceptions:

(1) Banks, savings institutions, and credit unions may report certain cash receipts and cash payments as net amounts rather than gross amounts. These receipts and payments include deposits placed with other financial institutions and withdrawals of deposits, time deposits accepted, and repayments of deposits, as well as loans made to customers and principal collections of loans.

(2) Cash flow results from future contracts, forward contracts, option contracts, or swap contracts that are accounted for as hedges of identifiable transactions or events may be classified in the same category as the cash flows from the items being hedged, provided that the accounting policy is disclosed.

2135.15 **Statement of Cash Flows Reporting:** The FASB decided not to amend SFAS 95, *Statement of Cash Flows* (FASB ASC 230-10-05-2). Thus, if the indirect method of reporting cash flow from operations is used, the statement of cash flows will still begin with net income (rather than comprehensive income) just as before the issuance of SFAS 130 (FASB ASC 230-10-45-1).

Example SCF Preparation

2135.16 In the following sections (section **2135.16–.19**), we consider a comprehensive example of the preparation of statement of cash flows (SCF), applying the direct method of determining cash flows from operating activities. As a basis for this example, we use the following comparative balance sheets for 20X1 and 20X2 for Wallace, Inc. along with the income statement for 20X2 and accompanying explanations.

Wallace, Inc.
Comparative Balance Sheet (in thousands)
At December 31, 20X2 and 20X1

	20X2	20X1
Assets:		
Cash	$ 22	$ 70
Accounts receivable	115	100
Inventories	170	180
Property, plant, and equipment	600	500
Accumulated depreciation	(130)	(100)
Intangible assets	58	50
Total assets	$835	$800
Liabilities and equities:		
Accounts payable	$ 60	$ 75
Accrued expenses	55	50
Taxes payable	30	25
Bonds payable	150	300
Common stock	215	100
Additional paid-in capital	85	50
Retained earnings	240	200
Total liabilities and equity	$835	$800

Wallace, Inc.
Income Statement (in thousands)
For Year Ended December 31, 20X2

Sales		$377
Expenses:		
Cost of sales	$120	
Selling and administrative	70	
Depreciation	40	
Amortization (of intangible assets)	2	
Interest	25	
Loss on sale of equipment	5	262
Income before income tax		$115
Income tax expense		(46)
Income before extraordinary gain		$ 69
Extraordinary gain—retirement of bonds, net of $4 income tax		6
Net income		$ 75

a. Property, plant, and equipment of $150,000 was purchased during the year; PPE costing $50,000, on which $10,000 of depreciation had been taken, was sold at a $5,000 loss.

b. Intangible assets costing $10,000 were purchased during 20X2.

c. Capital stock with a par value of $75,000 was sold for $100,000 during 20X2.

d. Dividends of $35,000 were declared and paid during 20X2.

e. Bonds of $100,000 were retired at a $10,000 gain, which was subject to income taxes at 40%.

f. Bonds of $50,000 were converted to common stock with par value of $40,000 during 20X2.

g. Accounts payable relate to inventory purchases; accrued expenses relate to selling and administrative expenses.

2135.17 The statement of cash flows (SCF) for Wallace, Inc. for 20X2, applying the direct method and disclosure of the reconciliation of net income to cash provided by operating activities, is presented here. An explanation of key amounts in the SCF follows the statement and the related disclosures.

Wallace, Inc.
Statement of Cash Flows (in thousands)
For Year Ended December 31, 20X2

Cash flows from operating activities:		
Cash received from customers	$ 362	
Cash paid to purchase inventory	(125)	
Cash paid for selling and administrative expenses	(65)	
Interest paid	(25)	
Income taxes paid	(45)	
Net cash provided by operating activities		$ 102
Cash flows from investing activities:		
Proceeds from sale of property, plant, and equipment	$ 35	
Payment for purchase of property, plant, and equipment	(150)	
Payment for purchase of intangible assets	(10)	
Net cash used by financing activities		(125)
Cash flows from financing activities:		
Payment for bond retirement	$ (90)	
Payment for dividends on common stock	(35)	
Proceeds from sale of common stock	100	
Net cash used by financing activities		(25)
Net decrease in cash		$ (48)
Cash, beginning of 20X2		70
Cash, end of 20X2		$ 22
Supplemental schedule of noncash financing activity:		
During 20X2, bonds of $50,000 were converted into common stock as follows:		
Common stock (at par value)		$ 40
Additional paid-in capital		10
		$ 50
Reconciliation of net income to net cash provided by operating activities:		
Net income		$ 75
Adjustments to reconcile net income to net cash provided by operating activities:		
Loss on sale of property, plant, and equipment	5	
Depreciation expense	40	
Amortization expense	2	
Accounts receivable increase	(15)	
Inventory decrease	10	
Accrued expenses increase	5	
Accounts payable decrease	(15)	
Taxes payable increase	5	
Extraordinary gain, gross	(10)	
Total adjustments		27
Net cash provided by operating activities		$ 102

2135.18 Calculations of key amounts included in the SCF are as follows:

Cash received from customers:		
Sales		$377
Increase in accounts receivable ($115 – $100)		(15)
		$362
Cash paid to purchase inventory:		
Cost of sales		$120
Decrease in inventory ($180 – $170)		(10)
Decrease in accounts payable ($75 – $60)		15
		$125
Cash paid for selling and administrative expenses:		
Selling and administrative expenses		$ 70
Increase in accrued expenses ($55 – $50)		(5)
		$ 65
Income taxes paid:		
Income tax expense, including tax on extraordinary gain ($46 + $4)		$ 50
Increase in taxes payable ($30 – $25)		(5)
		$ 45

2135.19 Several important summary observations can be made about the 20X2 SCF of Wallace, Inc.

  a. Net cash flows from operating activities ($102) are the same, whether computed by the direct method or the indirect method. If the direct method is used in the body of the SCF, the reconciliation of net income to net cash flows from operating activities must be included in related disclosures, as was done in the SCF of Wallace, Inc. Alternatively, the indirect method can be used in the primary statement by moving the reconciliation disclosure from the previous example into the statement.

  b. Interest and taxes paid are separately disclosed whether the direct method or the indirect method is used for determining cash flows from operating activities. In the case of Wallace, Inc., these were included in the SCF itself. Had the indirect method of determining operating cash flows been employed, these items would have been presented in related disclosures.

  c. Gains and losses included in the determination of net income on transactions that are classified as investing and/or financing activities are omitted from the operating activities section of the SCF. Examples from the Wallace, Inc. illustration are the extraordinary gain on debt retirement and the loss on the sale of property, plant, and equipment. These gains and losses are presented as adjustments to the amount of cash paid or received from the individual financing and investing activities.

  d. All income taxes are included in the operating activities section of the SCF, even if transactions with tax effects are reclassified as investing and/or financing activities. An example from the Wallace, Inc. illustration is the extraordinary gain on debt retirement, which was included in the financing activities section at the gross amount with the related income tax included in the operating activities section.

  e. Gross positive and negative cash flows are included in all categories in the SCF—operating, investing, and financing activities. These gross cash flows are then combined to determine a *net* figure for each major category in the SCF.

  f. The change in cash resulting from the combining of net cash flows from operating, investing, and financing activities is used to reconcile the change in the cash balance from the beginning to the end of the accounting period.

  g. Noncash transactions are separately disclosed outside the body of the SCF. An example in the Wallace, Inc. SCF is the conversion of outstanding bonds into common stock.

Preparation Tips for the SCF

2135.20 A good approach to the statement of cash flows (SCF) is to follow the following four steps:

Step 1: Determine the change in cash for the period, noting not only the *amount* of change but also the *direction* of change.

Step 2: Analyze all trial balance or balance sheet accounts to determine cash flows in operating, investing, and financing categories.

Step 3: Determine that the amounts of operating, investing, and financing cash flows reconcile the change in cash for the period. If they do not, reconsider changes in balance sheet accounts to identify incorrect or omitted items. Continue until the reconciliation can be made.

Step 4: Prepare the statement of cash flows, applying the form and content principles, including supplementary disclosures discussed earlier.

2135.21 A major concern in preparing the SCF is to ensure that all changes in financial position have been accounted for (see Steps 2 and 3 in section **2135.20**). This can be done in one of the following three ways:

    a. The problem will usually be presented in the form of a trial balance or a balance sheet. The quickest way to determine that all changes have been accounted for is to go through the trial balance or balance sheet accounts determining that the entire change (which may be a net of positive and negative elements) has been properly included in the SCF.

    b. Simple T-accounts can be set up for all accounts in the trial balance or balance sheet, and debit or credit entries can be made from those accounts into SCF T-accounts, preferably one each for operating, investing, and financing activities.

    c. A worksheet can be prepared with the following columnar headings: beginning balance, changes (debit/credit), and ending balance. Each account in the trial balance or balance sheet would then be entered in the worksheet. Debit and credit entries would be made to each account, with related amounts recorded in SCF accounts at the bottom of the worksheet.

Note: While this approach is frequently used in texts to teach the concepts underlying the preparation of the SCF, it may not be a practical approach on the CPA Examination due to the time required to prepare the worksheet.

2135.22 Reconciling net income to net cash provided by or used in operations involves adjusting for the effects of changes in current assets and current liabilities that relate directly to income statement items and for noncash items, such as depreciation and amortization. This reconciliation is required, either as a supplemental disclosure (if the operating section of the statement is prepared by the direct method) or as the primary presentation (if the statement is prepared by the indirect method).

Following are guidelines for the direction of the adjustment to net income for those items most frequently encountered in preparing this reconciliation.

Reconciling Item	Adjustment to Net Income Addition (+) Deduction (-)
Current Asset:	
Increase	-
Decrease	+
Current Liability:	
Increase	+
Decrease	-
Long-term Debt:	
Amortization of discount	+
Amortization of premium	-
Depreciation and amortization of long-lived assets	+

2135.23   If the problem calls for the direct method of calculating cash flows from operating activities, check your calculation by doing a quick indirect-method computation.

2135.24   Should you not be able to make the SCF balance (i.e., reconcile the beginning and ending cash balances), put an unexplained amount in the statement following cash flows from the three major categories of cash flows to get the number required to reconcile the change in cash. This will indicate to the grader that you know that the reconciliation is an important part of the statement even though you are unable to get the numbers to work out in the problem.

2136   Notes to Financial Statements

2136.01   The concept of adequate disclosure is firmly established as an underlying principle of financial reporting. The CPA's responsibility for disclosure extends to the inclusion of all information believed to be relevant to financial statement users who have a reasonable knowledge of accounting and business matters. The user must not be burdened with information that is irrelevant in terms of quantity and detail nor must the user be misled or left uninformed on important matters.

2136.02   Disclosure of financial information about an enterprise is accomplished through a variety of means, including the financial statements themselves, the auditor's report, discussions in the annual report other than the financial statements, press releases, and others. Of particular interest in the preparation of financial statements are the following types of disclosures:

    a. Form and content in the body of the financial statements (including parenthetical information, information shown "short," and classifications of information)

    b. Notes to the financial statement and supplemental information

Information presented in the body of the financial statements has been illustrated in the preceding example. Supplemental disclosures and notes to the financial statements are discussed in the following paragraphs.

2136.03   Notes to the financial statements and supplemental disclosures are difficult to categorize because appropriate disclosure in any particular set of circumstances is dependent on the particular characteristics of each financial reporting situation. The following chart shows the types of footnotes and supplemental disclosures that are frequently encountered.

	Supplemental and Note Disclosure Types	Examples
a.	Detail of information presented in the aggregate in the body of the financial statements	Disclosure of each of the next five years' lease payments for capitalized leases
b.	Accounting policies selected in the preparation of financial statements	Disclosure of inventory pricing methods, depreciation methods, etc.
c.	Qualitative information related to transactions included in the financial statements	Disclosure of various aspects of the company's pension plan
d.	Qualitative information related to events not quantified and included in the financial statements	Disclosure of contingencies for which accruals have not been made
e.	Other disclosures necessary in a particular situation to meet the objective of adequate disclosure	Disclosure of significant events occurring subsequent to the end of the reporting period

Accounting Policy Disclosure

2136.04 Information about accounting policies adopted by a reporting enterprise is an integral part of the financial statements and is necessary in interpreting other financial statement data. Accordingly, when financial statements are issued purporting to present fairly the financial position, cash flows, and results of operations in accordance with generally accepted accounting principles, a description of all significant accounting policies of the reporting enterprise is required. This reporting requirement extends to not-for-profit enterprises. It does not apply to unaudited financial statements issued between annual reporting dates if the reporting enterprise has not changed policies since the end of the latest fiscal year.

2136.05 The following statements describe the form and content of accounting policy disclosure:

  a. The disclosure encompasses important judgments as to appropriateness of principles relating to recognition of revenue and allocation of asset costs to current and future periods.

  b. The disclosure encompasses principles and methods that involve the selection from among existing acceptable alternatives.

  c. Principles and methods peculiar to the industry are disclosed, even if the principles and methods are predominantly followed in that industry.

  d. Unusual or innovative applications of generally accepted accounting principles are disclosed.

  e. Policy disclosure is particularly useful if presented in a separate summary schedule, preceding the notes to the financial statements or as the first note. This should be appropriately identified (e.g., "Summary of Significant Accounting Policies").

  f. Policy disclosure in a summary schedule should not duplicate information presented elsewhere in the financial statements.

  g. In some cases, policy disclosure may need to be cross-referenced to information disclosed in other parts of the financial statements (e.g., other notes).

2136.06 Examples of accounting principles and methods for which disclosure of policy is frequently made include, but are not limited to, the following:

  a. Depreciation methods

  b. Consolidation basis

c. Interperiod tax allocation

d. Inventory pricing

e. Revenue recognition methods

2136.07 **IFRS:** IFRS requires footnote disclosure of accounting policies.

2137 Consolidated and Combined Financial Statements

2137.01 Consolidated and combined financial statements are also discussed in sections **2315** ("Business Combinations") and **2320** ("Consolidation (Including Off-Balance-Sheet Transactions, Variable-Interest Entities, and Noncontrolling Interests)").

2137.02 The analysis and interpretation of financial statements is carried out in part through ratio analysis, which relates different financial statement elements in a meaningful way. Ratios are computed and analyzed on a comparative basis as follows:

a. Comparing operating characteristics of an enterprise over a series of successive years

b. Comparing operating characteristics of the enterprise with other similar enterprises, preestablished standards (target ratios), or legal requirements

2137.03 Many different ratios are computed and used to analyze the operating characteristics of enterprises, primarily by investors and creditors, both present and potential. Several of the frequently encountered ratios are presented in the next paragraph in the illustration of the Ratio Company, whose income statement (year 20X2) and comparative balance sheet (years 20X1 and 20X2) are presented as follows. The ratios are computed as of December 31, 20X2.

Ratio Company
Income Statement
For Year Ended December 31, 20X2

Net sales (all credit)	$1,000,000
Cost of goods sold ($25,000 depreciation)	600,000
Gross profit on sales	$ 400,000
Selling and administrative expenses	225,000
Income from operations	$ 175,000
Interest on long-term debt	50,000
Income before taxes	$ 125,000
Taxes, 40%	50,000
Net income	$ 75,000
Dividends declared on common stock	10,000
Dividends declared on preferred stock	15,000
Net income to retained earnings	$ 50,000
Net earnings per common share[a]	$ 3

[a] ($75,000 - 15,000)/20,000 shares = $3

Ratio Company
Comparative Balance Sheets
At December 31, 20X1 and 20X2

	12/31/X2	12/31/X1
Assets:		
Cash and marketable securities	$ 250,000	$ 200,000
Net accounts receivable	200,000	100,000
Inventories	100,000	150,000
Total current assets	550,000	450,000
Net plant and equipment	400,000	450,000
Goodwill	100,000	100,000
Total assets	$1,050,000	$1,000,000
Liabilities and equities:		
Accounts payable	$ 200,000	$ 150,000
Long-term debt	450,000	500,000
Preferred stock, $100 par	100,000	100,000
Common stock, $10 par (market price $17.00)	200,000	200,000
Retained earnings	100,000	50,000
Total liabilities and equity	$1,050,000	$1,000,000

Ratio Company
Statement of Cash Flows
For Year Ended December 31, 20X2

Cash flows from operating activities:		
Cash received from customers	$1,100,000	
Cash paid to purchase inventory	(675,000)	
Cash paid for selling and administrative expenses	(225,000)	
Cash paid for interest	(50,000)	
Cash paid for taxes	(50,000)	
Net cash provided by operating activities		$100,000
Cash from investing activities:		
Cash paid for plant and equipment		(75,000)
Cash from financing activities:		
Proceeds from long-term debt	$ 50,000	
Cash paid for dividends on common stock	(10,000)	
Cash paid for dividends on preferred stock	(15,000)	
Net cash provided by financing activities		25,000
Net increase in cash		$ 50,000
Cash, beginning of 20X2		$200,000
Cash, end of 20X2		$250,000

2137.04 These ratios should be understood in terms of the following:

    a. Definition (i.e., how is the ratio computed?)

    b. Significance (i.e., what does the ratio tell you?)

    c. Limitations (i.e., what care should be taken in the use of the ratio?)

Ratios Used in Financial Statement Analysis

Ratio	Definition	Significance	Computation	Limitations
a. Current ratio	$\dfrac{\text{Current assets}}{\text{Current liabilities}}$	Measures ability to discharge currently maturing obligations from existing current assets.	$\dfrac{\$550,000}{\$200,000} = 2.75$	Balance sheet account totals based on historical cost do not necessarily represent market values. A sizable amount of the current asset total might be tied up in inventory which is less liquid. Implies liquidation of assets and elimination of liabilities (neither of which is likely in a "going concern").
b. Quick (acid test) ratio	$\dfrac{\text{Current assets less inventories and prepaid assets}}{\text{Current liabilities}}$	Measures ability to discharge currently maturing obligations based on most liquid (quick) assets.	$\dfrac{\$550,000 - \$100,000}{\$200,000} = 2.25$	Receivables may be subject to a lengthy collection period and might have to be factored at less than carrying value if cash is needed immediately. Securities are subject to fluctuating market conditions which affect their liquidation amount.
c. Inventory turnover	$\dfrac{\text{Cost of goods sold}}{\text{Average inventory}}$	Measures relative control over inventory investment. May provide basis for determining the presence of obsolete inventory or pricing problems (in case of low turnover).	$\dfrac{\$600,000}{\left(\dfrac{\$150,000 + \$100,000}{2}\right)} = 4.80$	Different inventory cost flow assumptions can produce widely different inventory valuations and thus turnover ratios.
d. Receivables turnover	$\dfrac{\text{Net credit sales}}{\text{Average receivables}}$	Confirms the fairness of the receivable balance. May indicate presence of possible collection problems (in case of low turnover).	$\dfrac{\$1,000,000}{\left(\dfrac{\$200,000 + \$100,000}{2}\right)} = 6.67$	Affected by significant seasonal fluctuations unless denominator is a weighted average. Poor collection policy can understate this ratio by increasing average receivables.
e. Cash from operating activities to current liabilities	$\dfrac{\text{Net cash provided by operating activities}}{\text{Current liabilities}}$	Shows extent to which a company has covered its current liabilities by generating cash from normal operations.	$\dfrac{\$100,000}{\$200,000} = 0.50$	Current liabilities may understate short-term demands on cash.

Ratio	Definition	Significance	Computation	Limitations
f. Total asset turnover	$\dfrac{\text{Net sales}}{\text{Average total assets}}$	Measures how efficiently assets are used to produce sales.	$\dfrac{\$1{,}000{,}000}{\left(\dfrac{\$1{,}050{,}000 + \$1{,}000{,}000}{2}\right)} = 0.98$	Does not take into account that certain assets make no tangible contribution to sales. Assumes that an asset's participation in generating sales is relative to its recorded amount. Rate of return is based on historical asset cost which does not reflect current values.
g. Rate of return on total assets	$\dfrac{\text{Net income plus interest expense (net-of-tax effect)}}{\text{Average total assets}}$	Measures the productivity of assets in terms of producing income.	$\dfrac{\$75{,}000 + (\$50{,}000 - \$20{,}000)}{\left(\dfrac{\$1{,}050{,}000 + \$1{,}000{,}000}{2}\right)} = 0.10$	Similar to total asset turnover ratio. Accrual net income subject to estimates and does not reflect actual cash return. Rate of return is based on historical asset cost which does not reflect current values.
h. Return on common stock-holders' equity	$\dfrac{\text{Net income less preferred dividends}}{\text{Average common stockholders' equity}}$	Measures return to common stockholders in aggregate.	$\dfrac{\$75{,}000 - \$15{,}000}{\left(\dfrac{\$300{,}000 + \$250{,}000}{2}\right)} = 0.22$	Book value of common stockholders' equity reflects historical cost and not current value. Accrual net income involves estimates and does not reflect actual cash return.
i.(1) Debt ratio	$\dfrac{\text{Total liabilities}}{\text{Total assets}}$	Indicates extent of leverage used and creditor protection in case of insolvency.	$\dfrac{\$200{,}000 + \$450{,}000}{\$1{,}050{,}000} = 0.62$	Denominator reflects historical costs and not current values.
i.(2) Debt/equity ratio	$\dfrac{\text{Total liabilities}}{\text{Shareholder's equity}}$	Determines the equity's long-term debt-paying ability.	$\dfrac{\$200{,}000 + \$450{,}000}{\$100{,}000 + \$200{,}000 + \$100{,}000} = 1.62$	There is a lack of uniformity in calculating this ratio.
j. Equity ratio	$\dfrac{\text{Total stockholders' equity}}{\text{Total assets}}$	Measures total asset investment provided by stockholders.	$\dfrac{\$100{,}000 + \$200{,}000 + \$100{,}000}{\$1{,}050{,}000} = 0.38$	Assets are recorded at historical cost and not at current value.
k. Times interest earned	$\dfrac{\text{Income before interest expenses and taxes}}{\text{Interest expense}}$	Measures ability to cover interest charges.	$\dfrac{\$175{,}000}{\$50{,}000} = 3.50$	Accrual income does not necessarily indicate availability of cash to pay interest charges.
l. Price-earnings ratio	$\dfrac{\text{Market price per common share}}{\text{Earnings per share}}$	Indicates relationship of common stock to net earnings.	$\dfrac{\$17.00}{\$3.00} = 5.67$	Earnings per share computation subject to arbitrary assumptions and accrual income. EPS is not the only factor affecting market prices.

Ratio	Definition	Significance	Computation	Limitations
m. Dividend yield	$\dfrac{\text{Dividend per common share}}{\text{Market price per common share}}$	Shows return to stockholders based on current market price of stock.	$\dfrac{\$10,000 \div 20,000 \text{ shares}}{\$17.00/\text{share}}$ $= 0.029$ $= 2.9\%$	Dividend payments to stockholders are subject to many variables. The relationship between dividends paid and market prices is a reciprocal one.
n. Profit margin on sales	$\dfrac{\text{Net income}}{\text{Sales}}$	Measures efficiency of earning income from sales.	$\dfrac{\$75,000}{\$1,000,000}$ $= 0.075$ $= 7.5\%$	Accrual income includes estimates. Income includes costs over which management has little or no control (e.g., taxes).
o. Book value per common share	$\dfrac{\text{Common stockholder's equity}}{\text{Common shares outstanding}}$	Measures net assets applicable to each common share.	$\dfrac{\$200,000 + \$100,000}{20,000 \text{ shares}}$ $= \$15.00 \text{ per share}$	Assets are recorded at historical cost and not at current value.
p. Cash flow per common share	$\dfrac{\text{Income plus noncash adjustments}}{\text{Common shares outstanding}}$	Measures resources (i.e., cash) generated per common share.	$\dfrac{\$75,000 + \$25,000}{20,000 \text{ shares}}$ $= \$5.00 \text{ per share}$	This ratio is the least understood and therefore the most likely to mislead an investor. FASB ASC 230-10-45-3 strongly recommends against the isolated disclosure of this ratio.
q. Payout ratio to common shareholders	$\dfrac{\text{Common dividends}}{\text{Net income less preferred dividends}}$	Measures portion of net income to common shareholders paid out in dividends.	$\dfrac{\$10,000}{\$75,000 - \$15,000}$ $= 0.17$ $= 17\%$	Income does not necessarily measure cash available for dividend payment. Heavily influenced by management policy, nature of business, and stage of development—all of which diminish comparability.
r. Cash from operating activities to net income	$\dfrac{\text{Net cash provided by operating activities}}{\text{Net income}}$	Shows cash flow effects of the company's net income for the period.	$\dfrac{\$100,000}{\$75,000}$ $= 1.33$	Net income includes noncash revenues and expenses recognized by accrual accounting principles.

2137.05 For analytical purposes, the ratios presented in this table can be grouped as follows:

  a. Measures of liquidity (i.e., ability to meet current debt):

  (1) Current ratio

  (2) Quick ratio

  (3) Inventory turnover

  (4) Receivables turnover

  (5) Cash from operating activities to current liabilities

  b. Measures of return on investment:

  (1) Total asset turnover

  (2) Rate of return on total assets

  (3) Return on common stockholders' equity

(4) Price-earnings ratio

(5) Dividend yield

(6) Profit margin on sales

(7) Payout ratio to common

c. Measures of solvency (i.e., long-term financing and debt-paying ability):

(1) Debt to equity ratio

(2) Equity ratio

(3) Times interest earned

(4) Book value per common share

(5) Cash flow per common share

(6) Cash from operating activities to net income

2137.06 Care must be taken in the use of ratios such as those described for several reasons, as can be seen by the specific limitations stated. In summary, several of the critical considerations of which you must be continually mindful of in ratio analysis include the following:

a. Accounting methods used to state assets, liabilities, stockholders' equity, revenues, and expenses are not necessarily designed to produce the most useful numbers for the purposes for which the ratios are intended.

b. Differences in the underlying economic events, the types of enterprises involved, the stage of development of enterprises, and other factors affect comparability between enterprises.

c. Several ratios include the use of external market values of stock which are influenced by numerous variables over which management has little influence or control.

d. Management policy may influence many ratios.

2138 First-Time Adoption of IFRS

2138.01 IFRS 1, *First-time Adoption of International Financial Reporting Standards (IFRS),* was developed by the International Accounting Standards Board (IASB) to help entities in their transition to using IFRS as their basis for their financial statements. The stated objectives of this IFRS are to ensure that an entity's first IFRS financial statements, and its interim financial reports for part of the period covered by those financial statements, contain high-quality information that is transparent for users and comparable over all periods presented, provides a suitable starting point for accounting in accordance with IFRSs, and can be generated at a cost that does not exceed the benefits.

2138.02 The entity's first IFRS financial statements must contain an explicit and unreserved statement that the financial statements are in compliance with IFRSs.

2138.03 The first balance sheet must recognize all assets and liabilities as required by the IFRSs and not recognize assets or liabilities not permitted by the IFRSs. These asset and liabilities must be measured as required by the IFRSs. These assets and liabilities must be classified as required by the IFRSs. Disclosure must be made to explain how the transition from GAAP to the IFRSs affects the financial statements. Where the compliance cost exceeds the benefit to the financial statement users, there are limited exceptions to these requirements.

2138.04 Differences in the application of GAAP and IFRSs must be recognized as adjustments directly to retained earnings (or, if appropriate, another category of equity) at the date of transition to IFRSs.

2138.05 The IASB published IFRS 1 to provide guidance for entities upon their initial adoption of IFRS. The standard outlines the method to be used in preparing the entity's first financials after adopting IFRS. The balance sheet is the starting point. As of the beginning of the first year the entity adopts IFRS—the date of transition—all assets, liabilities, and equity accounts must be reported under IFRS. IFRS 1, paragraph 8, presents the following example to explain this first set of financials:

"**Example: Consistent application of latest version of IFRSs**

Background

The end of entity A's first IFRS reporting period is 31 December 20X5. Entity A decides to present comparative information in those financial statements for one year only (see paragraph 21). Therefore, its date of transition to IFRSs is the beginning of business on 1 January 20X4 (or, equivalently, close of business on 31 December 20X3). Entity A presented financial statements in accordance with its previous GAAP annually to 31 December each year up to, and including, 31 December 20X4.

Application of requirements

Entity A is required to apply the IFRSs effective for periods ending on 31 December 20X5 in:

(a) preparing and presenting its opening IFRS statement of financial position at 1 January 20X4; and (b) preparing and presenting its statement of financial position for 31 December 20X5 (including comparative amounts for 20X4), statement of comprehensive income, statement of changes in equity and statement of cash flows for the year to 31 December 20X5 (including comparative amounts for 20X4) and disclosures (including comparative information for 20X4).

If a new IFRS is not yet mandatory but permits early application, entity A is permitted, but not required, to apply that IFRS in its first IFRS financial statements."

2138.06 The entity's first IFRS financial statements must include at least three statements of financial position, two statements of comprehensive income, two separate income statements (if presented), two statements of cash flows, and two statements of changes in equity and related notes.

2138.07 The entity must explain how the transition to IFRSs affects its financial statements. This must be done with reconciliations of equity, comprehensive income, and any impairment losses recognized or reversed in preparing the statement of financial position.

2138.08 The entity may designate previously recognized financial assets or liabilities as financial assets or liabilities measured at fair value. A profit or loss is recognized for the difference in the asset or liability's fair value and the amount reported on the prior GAAP financial statements.

2138.09 An entity has the option to measure an item of property, plant, and equipment; intangible asset; or investment property at fair value at the date of transition.

2140 SEC Reporting Requirements (e.g., Form 10-Q, 10-K)

2140.01 Under federal securities laws, publicly traded companies are required to file forms with the SEC periodically. The forms are available to anyone using the EDGAR database at **www.sec.gov**. The most common forms are the 10-K and the 10-Q. These forms must be filed electronically on EDGAR unless this filing causes hardship on the filing company.

2140.02 Form 10-K is the required annual report. It provides a comprehensive report of a company's business and financial condition, including audited financial statements. This form must be filed with the SEC based on the following schedule:

Category of Filer	Revised Deadlines for Filing Periodic Reports	
	Form 10-K Deadline	Form 10-Q Deadline
Large Accelerated Filer ($700MM or more)	75 days for fiscal years ending before December 15, 2006, and 60 days for fiscal years ending on or after December 15, 2006	40 days
Accelerated Filer ($75MM or more and less than $700MM)	75 days	40 days
Non-accelerated Filer (less than $75MM)	90 days	45 days

Source: http://www.sec.gov/answers/form10k.htm

The form must also be available on the company's website. A blank copy of the form can be found on the SEC website (www.sec.gov). A sample first page follows. A typical complete document is over 100 pages.

UNITED STATES
SECURITIES AND EXCHANGE COMMISSION
Washington, D.C. 20549
FORM 10-K

(Mark One)

  x   ANNUAL REPORT PURSUANT TO SECTION 13 OR 15(d) OF THE SECURITIES EXCHANGE ACT OF 1934
For the fiscal year ended December 31, 2008
OR

  ___   TRANSITION REPORT PURSUANT TO SECTION 13 OR 15(d) OF THE SECURITIES EXCHANGE ACT OF 1934
Commission file number: 000-50726

ABC Company
(Exact name of registrant as specified in its charter)

Delaware   66-239581
(State or other jurisdiction of incorporation or organization)   (IRS Employer Identification Number)

1000 Main Parkway
Your City, CA 94045
(Address of principal executive offices)

(650) 555-0000
(Registrant's telephone number, including area code)

Securities registered pursuant to Section 12(b) of the Act:

Title of Each Class	Name of Exchange on Which Registered (Nasdaq Global Select Market)
Class A Common Stock, $0.001 par value	(Nasdaq Global Select Market) The Nasdaq Stock Market LLC

Securities registered pursuant to Section 12(g) of the Act:
Title of Each Class
Class B Common Stock, $0.001 par value
Options to purchase Class A Common Stock

Indicate by check mark if the Registrant is a well-known seasoned issuer as defined in Rule 405 of the Securities Act.   Yes x   No

Indicate by check mark if the Registrant is not required to file reports pursuant to Section 13 or Section 15(d) of the Act.   Yes   No x

Indicate by check mark whether the Registrant (1) has filed all reports required to be filed by Section 13 or 15(d) of the Securities Exchange Act of 1934 during the preceding 12 months (or for such shorter period that the registrant was required to file such reports), and (2) has been subject to such filing requirements for the past 90 days.   Yes x   No

Indicate by check mark if disclosure of delinquent filers pursuant to Item 405 of Regulation S-K is not contained herein, and will not be contained, to the best of the Registrant's knowledge, in definitive proxy or information statements incorporated by reference in Part III of this Form 10-K or any amendment to this Form 10-K.

Indicate by check mark whether the Registrant is a large accelerated filer, an accelerated filer, a non-accelerated filer or a smaller reporting company. See definitions of "large accelerated filer," "accelerated filer" and "smaller reporting company" in Rule 12b-2 of the Exchange Act. (Check one):

Large accelerated filer x   Accelerated filer   Non-accelerated filer   Smaller reporting company

Indicate by check mark whether the Registrant is a shell company (as defined in Rule 12b-2 of the Exchange Act).   Yes   No x

At June 30, 2008, the aggregate market value of shares held by non-affiliates of the Registrant (based upon the closing sale price of such shares on The Nasdaq Global Select Market on June 30, 2008) was $116,684,274,176.

At January 31, 2009, there were 240,289,354 shares of the Registrant's Class A common stock outstanding and 75,004,353 shares of the Registrant's Class B common stock outstanding.

DOCUMENTS INCORPORATED BY REFERENCE

Portions of the Registrant's Proxy Statement for the 2008 Annual Meeting of Stockholders are incorporated herein by reference in Part III of this Annual Report on Form 10-K to the extent stated herein. Such proxy statement will be filed with the Securities and Exchange Commission within 120 days of the Registrant's fiscal year ended December 31, 2008.

Table of Contents

Form 10-K
For the Fiscal Year Ended December 31, 2008
INDEX
TABLE OF CONTENTS

		Page
PART I		
Item 1.	Business	1
Item 1A.	Risk Factors	17
Item 1B.	Unresolved Staff Comments	31
Item 2.	Properties	31
Item 3.	Legal Proceedings	31
Item 4.	Submission of Matters to a Vote of Security Holders	32
PART II		
Item 5.	Market for Registrant's Common Equity, Related Stockholder Matters and Issuer Purchases of Equity Securities	33

Item 6.	Selected Financial Data	36
Item 7.	Management's Discussion and Analysis of Financial Condition and Results of Operation	37
Item 7A.	Quantitative and Qualitative Disclosures About Market Risk	59
Item 8.	Financial Statements and Supplementary Data	61
Item 9.	Changes in and Disagreements with Accountants on Accounting and Financial Disclosure	96
Item 9A.	Controls and Procedures	96
Item 9B.	Other Information	96

PART III

Item 10.	Directors, Executive Officers and Corporate Governance	97
Item 11.	Executive Compensation	98
Item 12.	Security Ownership of Certain Beneficial Owners and Management and Related Stockholder Matters	99
Item 13.	Certain Relationships and Related Transactions, and Director Independence	99
Item 14.	Principal Accounting Fees and Services	99

PART IV

Item 15.	Exhibits and Financial Statement Schedules	100

2140.03 Form 10-1Q is the quarterly report. The filing schedule can be found at section **2140.02**. A blank copy of the form can be found on the SEC website at (www.sec.gov) and is duplicated below:

UNITED STATES SECURITIES AND EXCHANGE COMMISSION
Washington, D.C. 20549
FORM 10-Q

(Mark One)

___ QUARTERLY REPORT PURSUANT TO SECTION 13 OR 15(d) OF THE SECURITIES EXCHANGE ACT OF 1934
For the quarterly period ended or

___ TRANSITION REPORT PURSUANT TO SECTION 13 OR 15(d) OF THE SECURITIES EXCHANGE ACT OF 1934
For the transition period from to Commission File Number:
(Exact name of registrant as specified in its charter)
(State or other jurisdiction of incorporation or organization) (I.R.S. Employer Identification No.)
(Address of principal executive offices) (Zip Code)
(Registrant's telephone number, including area code)
(Former name, former address and former fiscal year, if changed since last report)

Indicate by check mark whether the registrant (1) has filed all reports required to be filed by Section 13 or 15(d) of the Securities Exchange Act of 1934 during the preceding 12 months (or for such shorter period that the registrant was required to file such reports), and (2) has been subject to such filing requirements for the past 90 days. Yes ___ No ___

Indicate by check mark whether the registrant has submitted electronically and posted on its corporate Web site, if any, every Interactive Data File required to be submitted and posted pursuant to Rule 405 of Regulation S-T (§232.405 of this chapter) during the preceding 12 months (or for such shorter period that the registrant was required to submit and post such files). Yes ___ No ___

Indicate by check mark whether the registrant is a large accelerated filer, an accelerated filer, a non-accelerated filer, or a smaller reporting company. See the definitions of "large accelerated filer," "accelerated filer" and "smaller reporting company" in Rule 12b-2 of the Exchange Act.

Large accelerated filer ___ Accelerated filer ___ Non-accelerated filer ___ Smaller reporting company ___

SEC 1296 (03-10) **Potential persons who are to respond to the collection of information contained in this form are not required to respond unless the form displays a currently valid OMB control number.**

Indicate by check mark whether the Registrant is a shell company (as defined in Rule 12b-2 of the Exchange Act). Yes   No

APPLICABLE ONLY TO ISSUERS INVOLVED IN BANKRUPTCY PROCEEDINGS DURING THE PRECEDING FIVE YEARS: Indicate by check mark whether the registrant has filed all documents and reports required to be filed by Sections 12, 13 or 15(d) of the Securities Exchange Act of 1934 subsequent to the distribution of securities under a plan confirmed by a court.
Yes_____   No_____

APPLICABLE ONLY TO CORPORATE ISSUERS:
Indicate the number of shares outstanding of each of the issuer's classes of common stock, as of the latest practicable date.

PART I—FINANCIAL INFORMATION

Item 1. Financial Statements.
Provide the information required by Rule 10-01 of Regulation S-X (17 CFR Part 210).A smaller reporting company, defined in Rule 12b-2 (§ 240.12b-2 of this chapter) may provide the information required by Article 8-03 of Regulation S-X (§ 210.8-03 of this chapter).

Item 2. Management's Discussion and Analysis of Financial Condition and Results of Operations.
Furnish the information required by Item 303 of Regulation S-K (§ 229.303 of this chapter).

Item 3. Quantitative and Qualitative Disclosures About Market Risk.
Furnish the information required by Item 305 of Regulation S-K (§ 229.305 of this chapter).

Item 4. Controls and Procedures.
Furnish the information required by Item 307 of Regulation S-K (§ 229.307 of this chapter) and Item 308(c) of Regulation S-K (§229.308(c) of this chapter).

Item 4T. Controls and Procedures.
(a) If the registrant is neither a large accelerated filer nor an accelerated filer as those terms are defined in §240.12b-2 of this chapter, furnish the information required by Items 307 and 308T(b) of Regulation S-K (17 CFR 229.307 and 229.308T(b)) with respect to a quarterly report that the registrant is required to file for a fiscal year ending on or after December 15, 2007 but before December 15, 2009.

(b)This temporary Item 4T will expire on June 30, 2010.

PART II—OTHER INFORMATION

Instruction. The report shall contain the item numbers and captions of all applicable items of Part II, but the text of such items may be omitted provided the responses clearly indicate the coverage of the item. Any item which is inapplicable or to which the answer is negative may be omitted and no reference thereto need be made in the report. If substantially the same information has been previously reported by the registrant, an additional report of the information on this form need not be made. The term "previously reported" is defined in Rule 12b-2 (17 CFR 240. 12b-2). A separate response need not be presented in Part II where information called for is already disclosed in the financial information provided in Part I and is incorporated by reference into Part II of the report by means of a statement to that effect in Part II which specifically identifies the incorporated information.

Item 1. Legal Proceedings.
Furnish the information required by Item 103 of Regulation S-K (§ 229.103 of this chapter). As to such proceedings which have been terminated during the period covered by the report, provide similar information, including the date of termination and a description of the disposition thereof with respect to the registrant and its subsidiaries.

Instruction. A legal proceeding need only be reported in the 10-Q filed for the quarter in which it first became a reportable event and in subsequent quarters in which there have been material developments. Subsequent Form 10-Q filings in the same fiscal year in which a legal proceeding or a material development is reported should reference any previous reports in that year.

Item 1A. Risk Factors.
Set forth any material changes from risk factors as previously disclosed in the registrant's Form 10-K

(§249.310) in response to Item 1A. to Part 1 of Form 10-K. Smaller reporting companies are not required to provide the information required by this item.

Item 2. Unregistered Sales of Equity Securities and Use of Proceeds.
(a) Furnish the information required by Item 701 of Regulation S-K (17 CFR 229.701) as to all equity securities of the registrant sold by the registrant during the period covered by the report that were not registered under the Securities Act. If the Item 701 information previously has been included in a Current Report on Form 8-K (17 CFR 249.308), however, it need not be furnished.

(b) If required pursuant to Rule 463 (17 CFR 230.463) of the Securities Act of 1933, furnish the information required by Item 701(f) of Regulation S-K (§ 229.701(f) of this chapter).

(c) Furnish the information required by Item 703 of Regulation S-K (§ 229.703 of this chapter) for any purchase made in the quarter covered by the report. Provide disclosures covering repurchases made on a monthly basis. For example, if the quarter began on January 16 and ended on April 15, the chart would show repurchases for the months from January 16 through February 15, February 16 through March 15, and March 16 through April 15.

Instruction. Working capital restrictions and other limitations upon the payment of dividends are to be reported hereunder.

Item 3. Defaults Upon Senior Securities.
(a) If there has been any material default in the payment of principal, interest, a sinking or purchase fund installment, or any other material default not cured within 30 days, with respect to any indebtedness of the registrant or any of its significant subsidiaries exceeding 5 percent of the total assets of the registrant and its consolidated subsidiaries, identify the indebtedness and state the nature of the default. In the case of such a default in the payment of principal, interest, or a sinking or purchase fund installment, state the amount of the default and the total arrearage on the date of filing this report.

Instruction. This paragraph refers only to events which have become defaults under the governing instruments, i.e., after the expiration of any period of grace and compliance with any notice requirements.

(b) If any material arrearage in the payment of dividends has occurred or if there has been any other material delinquency not cured within 30 days, with respect to any class of preferred stock of the registrant which is registered or which ranks prior to any class of registered securities, or with respect to any class of preferred stock of any significant subsidiary of the registrant, give the title of the class and state the nature of the arrearage or delinquency. In the case of an arrearage in the payment of dividends, state the amount and the total arrearage on the date of filing this report.

Instructions to Item 3.
1. Item 3 need not be answered as to any default or arrearage with respect to any class of securities all of which is held by, or for the account of, the registrant or its totally held subsidiaries.

2. The information required by Item 3 need not be made if previously disclosed on a report on Form 8-K (17 CFR 249.308).

Item 4. (Removed and Reserved).

Item 5. Other Information.
(a) The registrant must disclose under this item any information required to be disclosed in a report on Form 8-K during the period covered by this Form 10-Q, but not reported, whether or not otherwise required by this Form 10-Q. If disclosure of such information is made under this item, it need not be repeated in a report on Form 8-K which would otherwise be required to be filed with respect to such information or in a subsequent report on Form 10-Q; and

(b) Furnish the information required by Item 407(c)(3) of Regulation S-K (§229.407 of this chapter).

Item 6. Exhibits.
Furnish the exhibits required by Item 601 of Regulation S-K (§ 229.601 of this chapter).

SIGNATURES*
Pursuant to the requirements of the Securities Exchange Act of 1934, the registrant has duly caused this report to be signed on its behalf by the undersigned thereunto duly authorized.

Date (Signature) **

Typical completed Form 10-Qs can be found on a company's website. Following is a sample of the form's first pages:

UNITED STATES SECURITIES AND EXCHANGE COMMISSION
Washington, D.C. 20549
FORM 10-Q

(Mark One)

__X__ QUARTERLY REPORT PURSUANT TO SECTION 13 OR 15(d) OF THE SECURITIES EXCHANGE ACT OF 1934

For the quarterly period ended June 30, 2007

OR

____ TRANSITION REPORT PURSUANT TO SECTION 13 OR 15(d) OF THE SECURITIES EXCHANGE ACT OF 1934

For the transition period from to
Commission file number 001-14905

XYZ COMPANY INC.
(Exact name of registrant as specified in its charter)

Delaware   22-3334444
(State or other jurisdiction of incorporation or   (IRS Employer Identification Number)
organization)

1240 Main Plaza, Your City, Nebraska 68132
(Address of principal executive offices)
(401) 555-1400
(Registrant's telephone number, including area code)
(Former name, former address and former fiscal year, if changed since last report)

Indicate by check mark whether the registrant (1) has filed all reports required to be filed by Section 13 or 15(d) of the Securities Exchange Act of 1934 during the preceding 12 months (or for such shorter period that the registrant was required to file such reports), and (2) has been subject to such filing requirements for the past 90 days.   Yes X   No

Indicate by check mark whether the registrant has submitted electronically and posted on its corporate Web site, if any, every Interactive Data File required to be submitted and posted pursuant to Rule 405 of Regulation S-T (§232.405 of this chapter) during the preceding 12 months (or for such shorter period that the registrant was required to submit and post such files).   Yes   No

Indicate by check mark whether the registrant is a large accelerated filer, an accelerated filer, a non-accelerated filer, or a smaller reporting company. See the definitions of "large accelerated filer," "accelerated filer" and "smaller reporting company" in Rule 12b-2 of the Exchange Act.

Large accelerated filer   X   Accelerated filer   Non-accelerated filer   Smaller reporting company

Indicate by check mark whether the Registrant is a shell company (as defined in Rule 12b-2 of the Exchange Act).   Yes   No X

Number of shares of common stock outstanding as of July 27, 2007:
Class A—1,088,878
Class B—13,753,590

FORM 10-Q   Q/E 6/30/07   1
XYZ COMPANY INC.
PART I—FINANCIAL INFORMATION

Item 1. Financial Statements.
Consolidated Balance Sheets —

June 30, 2007 and December 31, 2006
Consolidated Statements of Earnings —
Second Quarter and First Six Months 2007 and 2006
Condensed Consolidated Statements of Cash Flows —
First Six Months 2007 and 2006
Notes to Interim Consolidated Financial Statements

Item 2. Management's Discussion and Analysis of Financial Condition and Results of Operations.
Item 3. Quantitative and Qualitative Disclosures About Market Risk.
Item 4. Controls and Procedures.
         PART II—OTHER INFORMATION
Item 1. Legal Proceedings.
Item 1A. Risk Factors.
Item 4. Submission of Matters to a Vote of Security Holders.
Item 6. Exhibits.

Signature

Exhibit 31 Rule 13a-14(a)/15d-14(a) Certifications
Exhibit 32 Section 1350 Certifications

2140.04   A list of other forms required to be filed may be found on EDGAR at the SEC's website (**www.sec.gov**).

2150 Other Financial Statement Presentations, Including Other Comprehensive Bases of Accounting (OCBOA)

2151 Cash Basis

2151.01   Under the cash basis of accounting, revenue is recognized when cash is received and expenses are recognized when cash is disbursed. No income or expense is accrued.

2151.02   The cash basis method of accounting is not an allowable method under GAAP unless there is no material difference from the accrual method. However, cash-basis financial statements are sometimes provided for investors or creditors. Cash basis accounting results in a measure similar to net income called net operating cash flow. Net operating cash flow is the difference between cash receipts and cash disbursements.

2151.03   The cash basis is an acceptable method for the preparation of tax returns. This basis of accounting is discussed at section **2153**.

2152 Modified Cash Basis

2152.01   The modified cash basis is a hybrid method that combines features of both the cash basis and the accrual basis. Modifications to the cash basis accounting include such items as the capitalization of assets and the accrual of income taxes. If these modifications are made, the resulting balance sheet would include long-term assets, accumulated depreciation, and a liability for income taxes. The income statement would report depreciation expense and income tax expense. Modified cash basis financial statements are intended to provide more information to users than cash basis statements while continuing to avoid the complexities of GAAP. ("A Look at the Modified Cash Basis," Kenneth M. Hiltebeitel. Reprinted from *The CPA Journal,* February 1992, with permission from the New York State Society of Certified Public Accountants.)

2152.02 The modified cash basis does not comply with GAAP unless there are no material differences in this method and GAAP.

2153 Income Tax Basis

2153.01 There are three acceptable methods to report taxable income: cash basis, accrual basis, and the hybrid method. (IRC Section 44)

2153.02 Under the cash basis—or cash receipts method—property or services received are included in gross income when actually or constructively received. Cash or checks received are considered gross income. Accounts receivable are not included in gross income. The value of any other property that is received, including a note receivable, is included in gross income.

2153.03 Income that is constructively received is included in gross income. An example is interest income credited to an account by a financial institution. Income is constructively received if:

    a. it is readily available to the taxpayer and

    b. actual receipt is not subject to substantial limitations or restrictions.

2153.04 Under the cash basis of accounting, expenses are deductible only when actually paid with cash or other property. There is no current deduction for capital expenditures. The expense for capital expenditures will be recognized in the form of depreciation, amortization, or depletion.

2153.05 The accrual method for tax purposes is, for the most part, the same as the accrual method required by GAAP. An item is included in gross income for the year in which it is earned. A deduction can be recognized when:

    a. all the events have occurred to create the liability and

    b. the amount of the liability can be determined with reasonable accuracy.

2153.06 The hybrid method is a combination of the cash and accrual methods. Generally, a company using the cash method must use the accrual method for the accounts involved in computing cost of goods sold and gross profit if inventory is a material income-producing factor. The cash method can be used for all other accounts.

2154 Personal Financial Statements

Source of GAAP for Personal Financial Statements

2154.01 The FASB indicated in SFAS 83, *Designation of AICPA Guides and Statements of Position on Accounting by Brokers and Dealers in Securities, by Employee Benefit Plans, and by Banks as Preferable for Purposes of Applying APB Opinion 20 (rescinded by SFAS 111),* that it has no plans to include financial reporting for personal financial statements within the scope of its activities.

2154.02 There is, however, a section entitled "Personal Financial Statements" in the FASB *Accounting Standards Codification.* (FASB ASC 274-10-05)

Statement of Financial Condition

2154.03 Personal financial statements may be prepared for an individual, a husband and wife, or a family.

2154.04 The statement of financial condition is the basic personal financial statement. It presents the following:

    a. Estimated current values of assets

    b. Estimated current liabilities

    c. Estimated income taxes on the difference between the estimated values of assets and liabilities and their tax bases

    d. Net worth

2154.05 Net worth is the difference between total assets and total liabilities after deducting estimated income taxes on the difference between the estimated values of assets and liabilities and their tax bases.

2154.06 Assets should be presented in the order of their liquidity and liabilities in the order of their maturity. They should not be classified as current or noncurrent.

2154.07 Assets and liabilities should be recognized on the accrual basis rather than on the cash basis.

2154.08 If personal financial statements are prepared for one of a group of joint owners, the statements should include only that person's interest as a beneficial owner.

2154.09 If business interests constitute a large part of a person's total assets, they should be shown separately from other investments. The estimated current value of an investment in a separate entity (e.g., closely held corporation, partnership, or sole proprietorship) should be shown in one amount as an investment. Assets and liabilities of the separate entity should not be combined with similar personal assets and liabilities.

Statement of Changes in Net Worth

2154.10 The statement of changes in net worth presents the major sources of increases and decreases in net worth.

2154.11 The major sources of increases in net worth are the following:

    a. Income

    b. Increases in the estimated current values of assets

    c. Decreases in the estimated current amounts of liabilities

    d. Decreases in estimated income taxes on the differences between the estimated current values of assets and liabilities and their tax bases

2154.12 The major sources of decreases in net worth are the following:

    a. Expenses

    b. Decreases in the estimated current values of assets

    c. Increases in the estimated current amounts of liabilities

    d. Increases in estimated income taxes on the differences between the estimated current values of assets and liabilities and their tax bases

2154.13 The presentation of a statement of changes in net worth is optional.

Guidelines for Determining Estimated Values

2154.14 Estimated Current Value of Assets

The estimated current value of an asset in personal financial statements is the amount at which the item could be exchanged between an informed and willing buyer and an informed and willing seller, neither of whom is compelled to buy or sell. Costs of disposal (e.g., commissions), if material, should be considered in determining estimated current values. (FASB ASC 274-10-20)

2154.15 For some assets, the determination of current value poses few, if any, problems. For others, however, the difficulty in determining current value is more pronounced. In light of this difficulty, FASB ASC 274-10-35 provides guidelines for determining the current value of assets. These guidelines are summarized as follows:

a. **Receivables** are valued at discounted amounts of cash the person estimates will be collected.

b. **Marketable securities** (both debt and equity) are valued at their quoted market prices if traded on the date of the statement of financial condition. If not traded on that date, the value assigned should be within the range of bid and ask prices.

c. **Options** are valued at published prices if available; otherwise, on the basis of the values of assets subject to option (considering such factors as exercise price and length of option period).

d. **Investments in life insurance** are valued at the cash value of the policy less the amounts of any loans against it. (The face amount of the policy should be disclosed.)

e. **Investments in closely held businesses** are valued as a single-line net investment at estimated current value. There is no single generally accepted method of valuing investments in closely held businesses. The method used should approximate the amount at which the investment could be exchanged between willing and informed parties, neither of whom is compelled to buy or sell.

f. **Real estate (including leaseholds)** is valued at estimated current value. Various factors may be helpful in estimating current value including, for example, sales of similar property and appraisal values.

g. **Intangible assets** are valued at the discounted amount of projected cash flows from the planned use or sale of the asset if both the amounts and timing of the cash flows can be reasonably estimated. Otherwise, cost should be used.

h. **Future interests and similar nonforfeitable rights** are valued at their discounted amounts. Examples of such assets are the following:

  (1) Guaranteed minimum portions of pensions

  (2) Vested interests in pensions or profit sharing plans

  (3) Deferred compensation contracts

  (4) Remainder interests in property subject to life estates

  (5) Annuities

  (6) Fixed amounts of alimony for a definite future period

Estimated Current Amount of Liabilities

2154.16 The estimated amount of a liability is the discounted amount of cash to be paid. The discount rate should be the rate implicit in the transaction giving rise to the liability. However, if the debtor is able to discharge the liability currently at a lower amount, the liability should be presented at the lower amount.

2154.17 Noncancelable commitments to pay future sums should be presented as liabilities at their discounted amounts.

2154.18 The liability for income taxes payable should include unpaid income taxes for completed tax years and any unpaid estimated income taxes payable for the elapsed portion of the current year up to the date of the financial statements.

Estimated Income Taxes on the Differences Between Estimated Current Values and Tax Bases

2154.19 An estimate must be made of the amount of income taxes on the differences between the estimated current values of assets and the estimated current amounts of liabilities and their tax bases.

2154.20 This estimated tax on *appreciation* should be presented on the statement of financial condition between liabilities and net worth. Changes in the estimated tax on *appreciation* represent increases or decreases in net worth to be disclosed on the statement of changes in net worth.

2154.21 The estimated tax on *appreciation* should be computed as if the estimated current values of all assets had been realized and the estimated current amounts of liabilities had been liquidated on the financial statement date, using applicable income tax laws and regulations.

Illustrative Financial Statements

2154.22 Illustrative personal financial statements are presented for James and Jane Person. They are adapted from FASB ASC 274-10-55-9. The notes to the financial statements would be an integral part of the financial statements. However, for the sake of brevity, the notes to the financial statements of James and Jane Person have not been reproduced here.

James and Jane Person
Statements of Financial Condition
December 31, 20X2 and 20X1

	12/31/X2	12/31/X1
Assets		
Cash	$ 3,700	$ 15,600
Bonus receivable	20,000	10,000
Investments		
Marketable securities (Note 2)	160,500	140,700
Stock options (Note 3)	28,000	24,000
Kenbruce Associates (Note 4)	48,000	42,000
Davekar Company, Inc. (Note 5)	550,000	475,000
Vested interest in deferred profit sharing plan	111,400	98,900
Remainder interest in testamentary trust (Note 6)	171,900	128,800
Cash value of life insurance ($43,600 and $42,900), less loans payable to insurance companies ($38,100 and $37,700) (Note 7)	5,500	5,200
Residence (Note 8)	190,000	180,000
Personal effects (excluding jewelry) (Note 9)	55,000	50,000
Jewelry (Note 9)	40,000	36,500
	$1,384,000	$1,206,700
Liabilities		
Income taxes—current year balance	$ 8,800	$ 400
Demand 10.5% note payable to bank	25,000	26,000
Mortgage payable (Note 10)	98,200	99,000
Contingent liabilities (Note 11)	0	0
Total liabilities	$ 132,000	$ 125,400
Estimated income taxes on the differences between the estimated current values of assets and the estimated current amounts of liabilities and their tax bases (Note 12)	239,000	160,000
Net worth	1,013,000	921,300
	$1,384,000	$1,206,700

The notes to the financial statements are an integral part of these statements. *Source:* Adapted from FASB ASC 274-10-55-9.

James and Jane Person
Statements of Changes in Net Worth
For the Years Ended December 31, 20X2 and 20X1

	Years ended December 31	
	20X2	**20X1**
Realized increases in net worth		
Salary and bonus	$ 95,000	$ 85,000
Dividends and interest income	2,300	1,800
Distribution from limited partnership	5,000	4,000
Gains on sales of marketable securities	1,000	500
	$ 103,300	$ 91,300
Realized decreases in net worth		
Income taxes	26,000	22,000
Interest expense	13,000	14,000
Real estate taxes	4,000	3,000
Personal expenditures	36,700	32,500
	$ 79,700	$ 71,500
Net realized increase in net worth	$ 23,600	$ 19,800
Unrealized increases in net worth		
Marketable securities		
(net of realized gains on securities sold)	$ 3,000	$ 500
Stock options	4,000	500
Davekar Company, Inc.	75,000	25,000
Kenbruce Associates	6,000	
Deferred profit sharing plan	12,500	9,500
Remainder interest in testamentary trust	43,100	25,000
Jewelry	3,500	
	$ 147,100	$ 60,500
Unrealized decreases in net worth		
Estimated income taxes on the differences between the estimated current values of assets and the estimated amounts of liabilities and their tax bases	$ 79,000	$ 22,000
Net unrealized increase in net worth	$ 68,100	$ 38,500
Net increase in net worth	$ 91,700	$ 58,300
Net worth at the beginning of year	921,300	863,000
Net worth at the end of year	$1,013,000	$921,300

2155 Financial Statements of Employee Benefit Plans/Trusts

2155.01 Employee benefit plans and trusts must prepare two financial statements according to GAAP (FASB ASC 962-205-45-1):

1. A statement of net assets available for benefits of the plan as of the end of the plan year

2. A statement of changes in net assets available for benefits of the plan for the year then ended

2155.02 The statement of net assets available for benefits of the plan must include the following (FASB ASC 962-205-45-2):

  a. Total assets

  b. Total liabilities

  c. Net assets reflecting all investments at fair value

  d. Net assets available for benefits

2155.03 The statement of changes in net assets available for benefits of the plan must include the following (FASB ASC 962-205-45-7):

  a. The change in fair value (or estimated fair value) of each significant type of investment, including participant-directed and self-directed investments held in brokerage accounts. Gains and losses from investments sold need not be segregated from unrealized gains and losses relating to investments held at year-end. Realized gains and losses on investments that were both bought and sold during the period should be included. This information may be presented in the accompanying footnotes.

  b. Investment income, exclusive of changes in fair value described in (a)

  c. Contributions from employers, segregated between cash and noncash contributions (a noncash contribution shall be recorded at fair value; the nature of noncash contributions shall be described either parenthetically or in a note)

  d. Contributions from participants, including those transmitted by the sponsor

  e. Contributions from other identified sources (for example, state subsidies or federal grants)

  f. Benefits paid to participants

  g. Payments to insurance entities to purchase contracts that are excluded from plan assets

  h. Administrative expenses

2155.04 Required disclosure includes the following:

  a. A brief, general description of the plan agreement including, but not limited to, vesting and allocation provisions and the disposition of forfeitures. If a plan agreement or a description providing this information is otherwise published and made available, this description may be omitted from the financial statements provided that reference to the other source is made.

  b. A description of significant plan amendments adopted during the period, and the effects of such amendments on net assets if significant either individually or in the aggregate

  c. The amount of unallocated assets, as well as the basis used to allocate asset values to participants' accounts if that basis differs from the one used to record assets in the financial statements

  d. The basis for determining contributions by employers and, for a contributory plan, the method of determining participants' contributions. Plans subject to the minimum funding requirements of the Employee Retirement Income Security Act, such as money purchase pension plans, shall disclose whether those requirements have been met. If a minimum funding waiver has been granted by the Internal Revenue Service (IRS), or if a request for waiver is pending before the IRS, that fact shall be disclosed.

  e. If significant costs of plan administration are being absorbed by the employers, that fact shall be disclosed in the notes to financial statements.

  f. The policy regarding the purchase of contracts with insurance entities that are excluded from plan assets

g. The federal income tax status of the plan if a favorable determination letter has not been obtained or maintained. Note that reports filed in accordance with the requirements of the Employee Retirement Income Security Act (ERISA) must include disclosure of information concerning whether a tax ruling or determination letter has been obtained, which is more than is required by FASB ASC 960-10. (FASB ASC 962-205-50-1)

h. Guarantees by others of debt of the plan

i. Amounts allocated to accounts of persons who have elected to withdraw from the plan but have not yet been paid. These amounts shall not be reported as a liability on the statement of net assets available for benefits in financial statements prepared in conformity with generally accepted accounting principles (GAAP). A footnote to reconcile the audited financial statements to IRS Form 5500 may be necessary to comply with the Employee Retirement Income Security Act (ERISA).

j. The amount and disposition of forfeited nonvested accounts. Specifically, identification of those amounts that are used to reduce future employer contributions, expenses, or reallocated to participant's accounts, in accordance with plan documents.

This page intentionally left blank.

Section 2200
Financial Statement Accounts: Recognition, Measurement, Valuation, Calculation, Presentation, and Disclosures

2210 Cash and Cash Equivalents

2211 Receivables

2212 Inventory

2213 Property, Plant, and Equipment

2220 Investments
- 2221 Financial Assets at Fair Value Through Profit or Loss
- 2222 Available for Sale Financial Assets
- 2223 Held-to-Maturity Investments
- 2224 Joint Ventures
- 2225 Equity Method Investments (Investments in Associates)
- 2226 Investment Property

2230 Intangible Assets – Goodwill and Other

2231 Payables and Accrued Liabilities

2232 Deferred Revenue

2240 Long-Term Debt (Financial Liabilities)
- 2241 Notes Payable
- 2242 Bonds Payable
- 2243 Debt with Conversion Features and Other Options
- 2244 Modifications and Extinguishments
- 2245 Troubled Debt Restructurings by Debtors
- 2246 Debt Covenant Compliance

2250 Equity

2251 Revenue Recognition

2252 Costs and Expenses

2260 Compensation and Benefits
- 2261 Compensated Absences
- 2262 Deferred Compensation Arrangements
- 2263 Nonretirement Postemployment Benefits
- 2264 Retirement Benefits
- 2265 Stock Compensation (Share-Based Payments)

2270 Income Taxes

2210 Cash and Cash Equivalents

Working Capital Defined

2210.01 **Working capital** is the excess of current assets over current liabilities.

2210.02 Current assets consist of cash and other assets reasonably expected to be realized in cash or sold or consumed in operations within one year or an operating cycle, whichever is longer. Examples of typical current assets are as follows:

    a. Cash (unrestricted)

    b. Marketable debt and equity securities

    c. Other short-term investments

    d. Accounts and notes receivable

    e. Trade installment receivables

    f. Inventories

    g. Other short-term receivables

    h. Prepaid expenses

Prepaid expenses (e.g., prepaid insurance, prepaid taxes) are traditionally included in current assets because, without the prepayment, the acquisition of the "benefit" (e.g., insurance coverage) would require the use of cash or other current assets during the next year or operating cycle.

2210.03 Current liabilities represent obligations whose liquidation is expected to require the use of current assets or the creation of other current liabilities. The emphasis on the use of current assets closely aligns the definition of current liabilities with that of current assets. Both definitions draw heavily on the concept of the operating cycle, which is the average length of time necessary to complete the cycle of cash to inventories to receivables to cash.

Cash

2210.04 Cash may be categorized as unrestricted and restricted. **Unrestricted cash** is cash available for current operations. It is the most liquid asset; accordingly, it is listed first in the current assets section. **Restricted cash** is all cash not designated or available for use in current operations. Examples are special cash funds set aside for the acquisition of noncurrent assets or the retirement of long-term debt and cash in banks of foreign countries that place restrictions on its transfer. Restricted cash for use in other than current operations should be classified as long-term investments rather than as current assets.

2210.05 Imprest cash funds (e.g., petty cash) are normally included with unrestricted cash. Accounting for petty cash consists of the following types of entries:

    a. Increases in the size of the fund, including initial establishment of the fund:

Petty Cash	XXX	
Cash		XXX

    b. Replenishment of the fund:

Expenses	XXX	
Miscellaneous Other Accounts	XXX	
Cash		XXX

c. Decreases in the size of the fund:

    Cash   XXX
        Petty Cash   XXX

d. End of the period adjustments necessary if the petty cash fund is not replenished:

    Expenses   XXX
        Petty Cash   XXX

2210.06 **Bank Reconciliations**

The accounting and physical control of cash is very important. One widely used control procedure is a bank reconciliation. The objective of the reconciliation is to compare the cash balance per the company's books with the cash balance per the bank statement for purposes of detecting any errors and identifying any needed adjustments to the cash account. Bank reconciliations are normally prepared at the end of each month on receipt of the bank statement.

2210.07 The bank reconciliation consists of a schedule identifying the differences between the cash balance per the bank statement and the cash balance per the company's books. These differences can be categorized into the following four types:

a. Bank errors (EBA)

b. Time lag differences (TLBA) (i.e., the company's cash account properly reflects the item but the bank statement does not because of the time lag in the item reaching the bank)

c. Book errors (EBO)

d. Time lag differences (TLBO) (i.e., the bank statement properly reflects the item but the company's cash account does not because of the time lag in the item reaching the company). EBO and TLBO differences require adjustments to the cash account. Obviously, the company would notify the bank of any bank errors (EBA differences); however, these differences do not require any adjustments on the company's books. TLBA differences also require no adjustments.

2210.08 Two general forms of bank reconciliations are used. The basic format of these two forms is presented as follows:

Form A		Form B	
Balance per bank statement	$XXX	Balance per bank statement	$XXX
+ or - EBA	XXX	+ or - EBA	XXX
+ or - TLBA	XXX	+ or - TLBA	XXX
Corrected cash balance	$XXX	+ or - TLBO	XXX
Balance per depositor's books	$XXX	Balance per depositor's books	$XXX
+ or - TLBO	XXX		
Corrected cash balance	$XXX		

Both forms identify all differences between the bank balance and the book balance. Form A is generally preferred for the following reasons:

a. It reconciles to the corrected cash balance. This is the cash balance if all outstanding items were cleared and all errors were corrected.

b. The required adjustments are easily identified. All differences between the book balance and the corrected cash balance (EBO and TLBO) require adjusting entries. The differences between the bank balance and the corrected cash balance (EBA and TLBA) do not require adjusting entries on the depositor's books.

2210.09 The following data for Alpha Company is used to demonstrate both forms of bank reconciliations:

a. Balance per bank statement June 30, $6,451.11

b. Balance per Alpha Company's books June 30, $7,218.44

c. Cash receipts of $1,533.55 for the day of June 30 were placed in the bank's night depository. The bank recorded the deposit the next day.

d. Checks outstanding as of June 30:

#103, dated May 24	$175.00
#152, dated June 29	222.00
#168, dated June 30	110.98
	$507.98

e. Bank service charges, $18 (unrecorded by Alpha at June 30)

f. Note receivable from Omega Company collected for Alpha by the bank (principal $500, interest $25) (unrecorded by Alpha at June 30)

g. Check #117, dated June 16, included in the canceled checks (meaning it had cleared the bank) was made out to Beta Company as payment on account in the amount of $180; however, Alpha recorded the check as $130.

h. The bank incorrectly charged Alpha's account with a $198.76 check written by Alfred Company.

2210.10 The advantages of Form A over Form B are reflected in the reconciliations prepared for Alpha Company. First, Form A shows that the corrected cash balance as of June 30, 20XX, is $7,675.44; Form B does not identify the corrected balance. The corrected balance is the amount that would be shown on the June 30 balance sheet. Second, the adjusting entries necessary are easily identified on Form A, but not on Form B. On Form A, each difference between the balance per books and the corrected cash balance requires an adjusting entry on Alpha's books. The required adjusting entries are:

Cash	$525.00	
Notes Receivable/Omega Company		$500.00
Interest Earned		25.00
Miscellaneous Expense	18.00	
Accounts Payable/Beta Company	50.00	
Cash		68.00

Form A
Alpha Company Bank Reconciliation
First National Bank, June 30, 20XX

Balance per bank statement, June 30, 20XX		$6,451.11
Add:		
Deposit in transit (June 30 cash receipts placed in night depository)	$1,533.55	
Bank error (Alfred Company check charged against account of Alpha Company)	198.76	1,732.31
		8,183.42
Deduct:		
Outstanding checks:		
#103	175.00	
#152	222.00	
#168	110.98	507.98
Corrected cash balance, June 30, 20XX		$7,675.44
Balance per Alpha Company's books, June 30, 20XX		$7,218.44
Add:		
Note receivable from Omega Company collected by bank		
Principal	500.00	
Interest	25.00	525.00
		7,743.44
Deduct:		
Bank service charges	18.00	
Book error (check #117 to Beta Company as payment on account correctly made out for $180 but recorded as $130)	50.00	68.00
Corrected cash balance, June 30, 20XX		$7,675.44

Form B
Alpha Company Bank Reconciliation
First National Bank, June 30, 20XX

Balance per bank statement, June 30, 20XX			$6,451.11
Add:			
Deposit in transit (June 30 cash receipts placed in night depository)		$1,533.55	
Bank error (Alfred Company check charged against account of Alpha Company)		198.76	
Bank service charges		18.00	
Book error (check #117 to Beta Company as payment on account correctly made out for $180 but recorded as $130)		50.00	1,800.31
			$8,251.42
Deduct:			
Outstanding checks:			
#103	$175.00		
#152	222.00		
#168	110.98	507.98	
Note receivable from Omega Company Collected by bank			
Principal	500.00		
Interest	25.00	525.00	1,032.98
Balance per Alpha Company's books, June 30, 20XX			$7,218.44

2210.11 **Proof of cash:** Either of the forms of bank reconciliation can be expanded into a four-column bank reconciliation, also known as a "proof of cash." The four-column reconciliation not only reconciles the cash balances at a point in time (e.g., at the end of the month) but also reconciles the receipts and disbursements during a period of time (e.g., during the month). To demonstrate, the data for Alpha Company (see section **2210.09**) will be used, along with the following additional information necessary for a four-column reconciliation:

Total credits to Alpha's account recorded by the bank during June, 20XX, per bank statement (deposits and other credits, such as the note receivable collected for Alpha by the bank)	$26,296.98
Total charges to Alpha's account recorded by the bank during June, 20XX, per bank statement (canceled checks and other charges, such as the bank service charges)	$22,385.16
Total cash payments during June, 20XX, per Alpha's cash payments journal	$22,465.38
Total cash receipts during June, 20XX, per Alpha's cash receipts journal	$26,318.00

2210.12 A four-column reconciliation also requires the information from the bank reconciliation prepared at the end of the preceding month. Alpha Company's May 31 reconciliation information is provided in the first column of the four-column reconciliation.

Expanded Form A

		June		
	Balance May 31	Receipts	Disbursements	Balance June 30
Balance per bank statement	$2,539.29	$26,296.98	$22,385.16	$6,451.11
Deposits in transit:				
May 31	987.53	(987.53)		
June 30		1,533.55		1,533.55
Bank error			(198.76)	198.76
Outstanding checks:				
May 31	(175.00)		(175.00)	
June 30			507.98	(507.98)
Corrected balance	$3,351.82	$26,843.00	$22,519.38	$7,675.44
Balance per books	$3,365.82	$26,318.00	$22,465.38	$7,218.44
Note collected by bank		525.00		525.00
Bank service charges:				
May 31	(14.00)		(14.00)	
June 30			18.00	(18.00)
Book error			50.00	(50.00)
Corrected balance	$3,351.82	$26,843.00	$22,519.38	$7,675.44

Expanded Form B

	Balance May 31	June Receipts	June Disbursements	Balance June 30
Balance per bank statement	$2,539.29	$26,296.98	$22,385.16	$6,451.11
Deposits in transit:				
May 31	987.53	(987.53)		
June 30		1,533.55		1,533.55
Bank error			(198.76)	198.76
Bank service charges:				
May 31	14.00		14.00	
June 30			(18.00)	18.00
Book error			(50.00)	50.00
Outstanding checks:				
May 31	(175.00)		(175.00)	
June 30			507.98	(507.98)
Note collected by bank		(525.00)		(525.00)
Balance per books	$3,365.82	$26,318.00	$22,465.38	$7,218.44

2210.13 Note that the last column of the four-column bank reconciliation (proof of cash) is the same as the shorter form of bank reconciliation prepared for Alpha Company. The first column is the shorter form of reconciliation prepared at the end of the previous month. The second column reconciles the receipts per the bank statement with the receipts per the company's books. The third column reconciles the disbursements per the bank statement with the disbursements per the company's books. These additional reconciliations make the four-column form of bank reconciliation a stronger control measure. For example, the four-column bank reconciliation should disclose unrecorded disbursements and receipts, which would not be detected by the shorter form of bank reconciliation.

2211 Receivables

2211.01 Receivables represent claims against others for money, goods, or services. They should be classified as current assets if they are expected to be collected or otherwise realized within one year or an operating cycle, whichever is longer. Receivables may be categorized as (a) trade receivables and (b) nontrade, or other, receivables. Trade receivables arise from the sale of goods and services. The two principal types of trade receivables are accounts receivable and notes receivable. Nontrade receivables arise from various types of transactions. Nontrade receivables should be reported on the balance sheet separately from trade receivables. Additionally, receivables from officers, employees, and affiliated companies should be shown separately from other receivables.

2211.02 Receivables classified as current assets should be reported at net realizable value, which is the amount expected to be collected. Accordingly, various valuation (contra) accounts may be necessary. The most common valuation account is the allowance for uncollectible accounts.

Accounts Receivable – Trade

2211.03 The term "accounts receivable" is normally used to represent receivables arising from the sale of goods and services on open account. Accounts receivable are recorded at the point at which goods are delivered or services performed. The amount is usually the gross amount billed.

2211.04 The amount collected on accounts receivable is often less than the amount billed. Some of the factors responsible for this difference are cash discounts, sales returns and allowances, and uncollectible accounts.

Accounting for Sales Discounts

2211.05 Sales discounts (also called cash discounts) are sometimes offered to trade debtors as an inducement for prompt payment. For example, goods may be sold on account for $1,000 with the terms stated as 2/10, n/30. A 2% discount is allowed if the account is paid within 10 days; otherwise, the full $1,000 is due within 30 days. Two methods of recording sales discounts are described as follows:

	Method 1 (Net)		Method 2 (Gross)	
Entry at time of sale:				
Accounts Receivable	$ 980		$1,000	
Sales		$980		$1,000
Entry if cash received within discount period:				
Cash	$ 980		$ 980	
Sales Discounts			20	
Accounts Receivable		$980		$1,000
Entry if cash received after discount period:				
Cash	$1,000		$1,000	
Accounts Receivable		$980		$1,000
Sales Discounts Not Taken		20		

Method 1 records both the receivable and sales at the net amount. The Sales Discounts Not Taken account is viewed as a type of financing income and is included on the income statement as *other income*. Method 2, the most commonly used method, records the receivable and sales at the gross amount. The Sales Discounts account preferably should be shown as a deduction from (contra to) sales on the income statement. A less desirable alternative is to include it in the *other expenses* classification.

2211.06 One may need to evaluate the accounts receivable account at the end of the year with regard to cash discounts arising from current-year sales that will be taken after the end of the year. In theory, the matching principle requires such discounts to be recognized in the year of sale. If the amount of sales discounts included in year-end receivables remains relatively constant or is immaterial, theoretical considerations can be ignored. Otherwise, the amount of cash discounts embodied in the year-end receivables should be estimated and recorded as follows:

Sales Discounts	XXX	
Allowance for Sales Discounts		XXX

The Allowance for Sales Discounts account should be shown as a deduction from accounts receivable on the balance sheet. It is one of the contra or valuation accounts that results in accounts receivable being reflected at net realizable value.

Accounting for Sales Returns and Allowances

2211.07 Sales returns and allowances are normally recorded as they occur. The entry is:

Sales Returns and Allowances	XXX	
Accounts Receivable		XXX

Similar to the case of sales discounts, it may be necessary at the end of the year to estimate the amount of sales returns and allowances associated with the year-end accounts receivable. In such cases, the following entry would be recorded:

Sales Returns and Allowances	XXX	
Allowance for Sales Returns and Allowances		XXX

Sales returns and allowances is a contra account to sales. Allowance for sales returns and allowances is a contra account to accounts receivable. If sales returns and allowances are accrued at year end as shown, in theory, an additional entry should be recorded to estimate the cost of the goods expected to be returned, as follows:

Inventory	XXX	
Cost of Goods Sold		XXX

Accounting for Uncollectible Accounts

2211.08 Enterprises make sales on accounts fully aware that some of the accounts may prove to be uncollectible. The expectation is that net income will be greater than if only cash sales were made. The matching principle suggests the uncollectible accounts should be charged to the accounting period in which the sale was made that gave rise to the uncollectible accounts. Whether a given sale will give rise to an uncollectible account may not be known by the end of the period in which the sale is made. As a result, it is usually necessary at the end of the period to estimate the amount of receivables that will prove to be uncollectible. The approaches to estimating uncollectible accounts may be categorized as follows:

    a. The income statement approach

    b. The balance sheet approach

2211.09 **Income statement approach:** This approach attempts to relate the amount of losses from uncollectible accounts to the amount of credit sales. The term "income statement approach" stems from the fact that primary attention is focused on uncollectible accounts expense (an income statement account) rather than on the net realizable value of the year-end accounts receivable. It attempts to match the cost (uncollectible accounts expense) with the related revenue (credit sales). If credit sales are not separately identified, the uncollectible accounts expense may be based on a percentage of total sales (cash and credit).

2211.10 **Balance sheet approach:** This approach emphasizes the net realizable value of accounts receivable at the end of the period rather than the amount of uncollectible accounts expense. The two most common forms of the balance sheet approach are as follows:

    a. Percentage of outstanding accounts receivable

    b. Aging of accounts receivable

The first form bases the accounting for uncollectible accounts on an estimate of the percentage of year-end accounts receivable that will prove to be uncollectible. The percentage is based on previous experience. The second form, aging of accounts receivable, requires the enterprise to set up an aging schedule. The aging schedule identifies how long each account has been outstanding and relates the likelihood of collection to the age of the receivable.

2211.11 To illustrate the methods involved, assume the following data for Delta Company:

Sales:	
Credit sales	$300,000
Cash sales	200,000
	$500,000
Accounts receivable, end of year:	$60,000
Allowance for uncollectible accounts, before adjusting entry (credit)	800

The adjusting entry at the end of the year under the various methods, given the assumptions stated, is presented as follows:

a. **Income statement approach.** Past experience indicates that 1% of credit sales will prove to be uncollectible.

Uncollectible Accounts Expense	$3,000	
Allowance for Uncollectible Accounts		$3,000

The entry is based on 1% of credit sales of $300,000.

b. **Balance sheet approach—percentage of receivables.** Past experience indicates that 6% of the year-end accounts receivable will prove to be uncollectible.

Uncollectible Accounts Expense	$2,800	
Allowance for Uncollectible Accounts		$2,800

The amount is computed as follows:

Desired credit balance in allowance (6% of $60,000)	$(3,600)
Less: Credit balance in allowance before adjustment	(800)
Debit (credit) to allowance needed	$(2,800)

c. **Balance sheet approach—aging of receivables.** First, each individual account is aged to determine how long it has been outstanding. Second, an estimated loss percentage is developed for each age category based on past experience and the advice of credit department personnel. The summarized information for Delta Company is presented as follows:

	Receivable Balance Dec. 31	Under 30 Days	31-60 Days	61-90 Days	Over 90 Days
Aaron	$ 1,000		$ 1,000		
Blue	500				$ 500
Farley	2,000	$ 2,000			
Jacobs	3,000	3,000			
..	..	..	..	..	..
..	..	..	..	..	..
Zebo	900			$ 900	
Totals	$60,000	$45,000	$10,000	$4,000	$1,000
Percentage estimated uncollected		4%	7%	15%	40%
Estimated uncollectible	$ 3,500	$ 1,800	$ 700	$ 600	$ 400

The adjusting entry is:

Uncollectible Accounts Expense	$2,700	
Allowance for Uncollectible Accounts		$ 2,700

The amount is computed as follows:

Desired credit balance in allowance	$(3,500)
Less: Credit balance in allowance before adjustment	(800)
Debit (credit) to allowance needed	$(2,700)

Transfer of Receivables

2211.12 Accounts receivable are sometimes used to obtain short-term financing. In some cases, the accounts receivable are merely pledged. In other cases, they are transferred to a third party either with recourse or without recourse.

2211.13 **Pledging:** A process by which receivables are pledged as collateral for a loan. The borrower continues to collect the receivables and applies the collections against the loan. Disclosure should be made in the balance sheet or in the notes to the financial statements of the amounts of receivables pledged.

2211.14 **Transfers of receivables to third parties:** See the discussion at section **2393** ("Transfers and Servicing of Financial Assets and Derecognition").

Notes Receivable

2211.15 A note receivable represents a contractual right to receive money on fixed or determinable dates. It is an unconditional written promise of the maker of the note to pay the payee or holder a specific amount. In form, a note may be interest bearing or noninterest bearing. In substance, many if not most noninterest-bearing notes have an interest element included in the face amount of the note. In this case, proper accounting requires that the interest element be accounted for as interest rather than as a part of the transaction price.

2211.16 The basic entries involved in accounting for each of the identified types of notes receivable are demonstrated as follows for ABC Company:

    a. Case facts: ABC Company sold merchandise on credit for $10,000 on October 1, 20X1, and received a note receivable due September 30, 20X2. The representative interest rate is 10%. ABC Company uses the calendar year as its accounting year.

    b. Assumption 1: The note is interest bearing, with a face amount of $10,000 and a stated interest rate of 10%.

    c. Assumption 2: The note is noninterest bearing, with a face amount of $11,000. (The face amount includes 10% interest on the sales price.)

The entries for ABC Company under each of the assumptions described are presented:

		Assumption 1 (Interest Bearing)		Assumption 2 (Noninterest Bearing)	
Oct. 1, 20X1	Notes receivable Discount on notes receivable Sales (To record sale.)	$10,000	$10,000	$11,000	$ 1,000 10,000
Dec. 31, 20X1	Interest receivable Discount on notes receivable Interest income (Adjusting entry at end of year: $10,000 \times 0.10 \times 3/12$)	$ 250	$ 250	$ 250	$ 250
Sept. 30, 20X2	Cash Discount on notes receivable Interest receivable Interest income Notes receivable (To record collection of note.)	$11,000	$ 250 750 10,000	$11,000 750	$ 750 11,000

Discounting Notes Receivable

2211.17 Most notes receivable qualify as negotiable instruments. As such, they may be sold (discounted) to another entity (payee) before the maturity date of the note. The new payee becomes a holder in due course.

2211.18 Notes may be discounted with or without recourse. If a note is discounted *without recourse*, the transaction is accounted for as a sale of the note receivable. The difference between the proceeds received and the carrying value of the note is recognized as a gain or loss.

2211.19 Most notes are discounted on a *with recourse* basis. Accordingly, if the three criteria listed in section **2392.02** are met, the discounting (transfer of the note) is accounted for as a sale, with the difference between the "sales price" of the note and the net receivable transferred being recognized as a gain or loss. If the discounting of the note does not qualify as a sale, the transaction is accounted for as a borrowing.

2211.20 **Discounting qualifies as a sale.** Assume that ABC Company (original payee) discounts a 10%, 1-year, $100,000 note receivable at First National Bank (new payee or holder in due course) nine months before maturity of the note at a discount rate of 14%. If the transfer of the note qualifies as a sale, the entries and related computations would be as follows:

Interest receivable	$ 2,500	
Interest income ($100,000 × 0.10 × 3/12 = $2,500)		$ 2,500
To record interest accrued to date of discounting.		
Cash	$ 98,450	
Loss on sale of note	4,050	
Notes receivable		$100,000
Interest receivable		2,500
To record transfer of note.		

The relevant amounts are computed as follows:

Maturity value of note:
Face amount		$100,000
Interest to maturity ($100,000 × 0.10 × 12/12)		10,000
		$110,000

Amount of discount:
Maturity value × discount rate × discount period	$ 11,550
($110,000 × 0.14 × 9/12)	

Proceeds at date of discounting:
Maturity value of note	$110,000
Amount of discount	(11,550)
Proceeds	$ 98,450

Gain (loss) on sale of note:
Sales price of note (proceeds)		$ 98,450
Net receivable transferred:		
Face amount	$100,000	
Accrued interest receivable	2,500	102,500
Loss on sale		$ (4,050)

2211.21 If the maker of the note pays First National Bank when the note is due, no entry is necessary on ABC Company's books at that time. However, if the maker defaults and ABC has to pay the note, ABC would record the following entry on the maturity date of the note:

Dishonored Notes Receivable	$110,000	
Cash		$110,000

2211.22 **Discounting does not qualify as a sale.** If the discounting (transfer) of the note does not qualify as a sale, the transfer should be accounted for as a borrowing as follows:

Cash	$ 98,450	
Interest Expense (or financing expense)	4,050	
Payable to Bank		$100,000
Interest Receivable		2,500

2211.23 Theoretically, any note receivable should be recorded at its present value at the time of the exchange. Strict application of this present value requirement may be relaxed for notes "arising from transactions with customers or suppliers in the normal course of business which are due in customary terms not exceeding approximately one year" (FASB ASC 310-10-30-1). Other notes receivable should be recorded at present value. The accounting for these other notes receivable is discussed in section **2252.05–.11**, which combines the discussion of other notes receivable with that of notes payable.

Impairment of a Loan

2211.24 FASB ASC 310-10-35-2 specifies that when a loan is impaired, a creditor shall recognize the impairment in the period in which it becomes probable that the creditor will be unable to collect all amounts due (both principal and interest) according to the contractual terms of the loan agreement. Depending on the circumstances, including when the loan is expected to be collected, the investment in the loan (the loan receivable) may qualify for classification as a current asset or as a noncurrent asset. Since it is more likely that an impaired loan would be classified as a noncurrent asset, the detailed discussion of impairment of a loan is presented in section **2225.49**.

2212 Inventory

2212.01 The inventory of a merchandising concern consists of goods on hand acquired for resale. A manufacturing concern usually has the following three types of inventories:

1. Finished goods (completed goods awaiting sale)
2. Work-in-process (goods in the course of production)
3. Raw materials and supplies (items to be consumed or used directly or indirectly in production)

2212.02 **Basis of accounting—general rule:** The primary basis of accounting for inventories is cost, which is the cash equivalent of the expenditures necessarily incurred to bring the items to the condition and location necessary for their intended use. Cost may be determined under any one of several assumptions as to cost flow such as first-in, first-out; average; and last-in, first-out.

2212.03 In theory, the inventory of a merchandising concern should include the net purchase price plus the indirect acquisition costs such as freight-in and handling. FASB ASC 330-10-30-7 specifies that abnormal amounts of freight in and handling must be treated as period changes rather than as inventory costs.

2212.04 As a practical matter, even the normal portion of indirect costs such as freight in and handling are often treated as period charges (expenses) rather than as inventory costs.

2212.05 The work-in-process and finished-goods inventories of a manufacturing concern include the applicable materials and labor costs and a representative share of the manufacturing overhead costs. FASB ASC 330-10-30-3 specifies that the allocation of fixed manufacturing overhead to inventory cost should be based on the normal capacity of the production facilities.

2212.06 Inventory cost should not include any general and administrative expenses, except for those clearly related to production. Selling expense should never be included in inventory costs; they are period charges (expenses).

2212.07 FASB ASC 835-20-15-3 specifies that the cost of assets intended for sale (inventory items) that are constructed or otherwise produced as *discrete projects* and whose construction or production requires a "period of time," should include the interest cost incurred during the "acquisition period" (i.e., construction or production period) as a result of expenditures for the asset. The amount of such interest capitalized should be determined by applying an interest rate (the rate applicable to borrowings outstanding during the period or, if applicable, the rate associated with any necessary specific new borrowing) to the average amount of accumulated expenditures for the asset. The capitalization period should begin when the following three conditions are present:

1. Expenditures for the asset have been made.
2. Activities that are necessary to get the asset ready for its intended use are in progress.
3. Interest cost is being incurred.

Interest capitalization should continue as long as the listed three conditions are present. The capitalization period ends when the asset is substantially complete and ready for its intended use.

2212.08 Interest cost should not be capitalized for inventories that are routinely manufactured or otherwise produced in large quantities on a repetitive basis.

2212.09 **Exceptions to the general rule—inventories stated at lower of cost or market:** A departure from the cost basis is required when the utility of goods is no longer as great as cost. In such cases, the loss should be recognized in the period in which the decline takes place. This is accomplished by stating inventories at the lower of cost or market. The application of lower of cost or market is illustrated in sections **2212.34–.41**.

2212.10 **Exceptions to the general rule—inventories stated above cost:** In rare cases, inventories may be stated above cost. For example, precious metals may be stated at selling price *if* there is an effective government-controlled market at a fixed monetary value. Any other exception (i.e., inventories stated above cost) must be justified by:

   a. inability to determine appropriate approximate costs,
   b. immediate marketability at quoted prices, and
   c. the characteristic of unit interchangeability.

2212.11 Standard costs may be used for inventory pricing if they are adjusted at reasonable intervals to reflect current conditions. Inventory costs so determined must reasonably approximate costs computed under one of the recognized cost flow methods (e.g., FIFO, LIFO, average cost).

2212.12 Inventory should include all goods to which the enterprise holds legal title. As a practical matter, inventory is often accounted for on a when-received and when-shipped basis. However, such practical conveniences should not be allowed to result in misstated financial statements.

2212.13 **Goods in transit:** At the balance sheet date, goods in transit that were shipped F.O.B. shipping point should be included in the inventory of the buyer. Goods in transit shipped F.O.B. destination should be included in the inventory of the seller.

2212.14 **Consigned goods:** Goods out on consignment should be included in the inventory of the consignor. The consignee should include none of these goods in its inventory.

2212.15 **Inventory systems:** Various inventory systems are used to account for the physical flow of units and the flow of costs. In general, these systems can be summarized as follows:

   a. Periodic: Units and costs (ending inventory and costs of goods sold) are determined at the end of the period based on a physical count of inventory.
   b. Perpetual:
      (1) Units and costs are accounted for on a perpetual basis. The inventory subsidiary ledger is kept in agreement with the controlling inventory general ledger account on a continuous basis.
      (2) Units only are accounted for on a perpetual basis, but costs (ending inventory and cost of goods sold) are determined only at the end of the period.

Cost Flow Methods

2212.16 Several cost flow assumptions are used for purposes of determining inventory cost. Among the most commonly used methods are the following:

    a. First-in, first-out (FIFO)

    b. Last-in, first-out (LIFO)

    c. Average

    d. Specific identification

2212.17 The first three of these methods are demonstrated as follows for both a periodic and a perpetual (units and costs) inventory system.

Facts:

	Units		Price		Cost
June 1 inventory	200	at	$10	=	$2,000
Purchases (June):					
June 9	400	at	$11	=	$4,400
June 22	100	at	$14	=	$1,400
June 29	300	at	$12	=	$3,600
	800				$9,400
Sold (June):					
June 6	100				
June 12	200				
June 25	300				
	600				

The information can be further summarized as follows:

	Units	Cost
Inventory, June 1	200	$ 2,000
Purchases	800	9,400
Cost of goods available for sale	1,000	11,400
Inventory, June 30	400	??
Cost of goods sold	600	??

The objective is to determine the cost of the June 30 inventory. The amount determined will also dictate the amount of cost of goods sold.

2212.18 Periodic inventory system.

    a.   FIFO

June 30 inventory:	
300 units at $12	$ 3,600
100 units at $14	1,400
	$ 5,000
Cost of goods sold:	
Cost of goods available for sale	$11,400
Less June 30 inventory	5,000
	$ 6,400

    b.   LIFO

June 30 inventory:	
200 units at $10	$ 2,000
200 units at $11	2,200
	$ 4,200
Cost of goods sold:	
Cost of goods available for sale	$11,400
Less June 30 inventory	4,200
	$ 7,200

    c.   Average (weighted-average)

Computation of average cost per unit:	
Total cost of goods available for sale	$11,400
divided by total units for sale	1,000
= average cost per unit	$ 11.40
June 30 inventory:	
400 units at $11.40	$ 4,560
Cost of goods sold:	
Cost of goods available for sale	$11,400
Less June 30 inventory	4,560
	$ 6,840

2212.19 Perpetual inventory system.

    a. FIFO

Note that the June 30 inventory (and cost of goods sold for June) is the same as FIFO under the periodic inventory system. This will always be true for FIFO but not for the other cost flow methods.

Date	Purchased	Sold	Balance
June 1			200 @ $10 = $2,000
June 6		100 @ $10 = $1,000	100 @ 10 = 1,000
June 9	400 @ $11 = $4,400		100 @ 10 = 1,000 400 @ 11 = 4,400
June 12		100 @ 10 = 1,000 100 @ 11 = 1,100	300 @ 11 = 3,300
June 22	100 @ 14 = 1,400		300 @ 11 = 3,300 100 @ 14 = 1,400
June 25		300 @ 11 = 3,300	100 @ 14 = 1,400
June 29	300 @ 12 = 3,600		100 @ 14 = 1,400 300 @ 12 = 3,600
Totals June 30	800 $9,400	600 $6,400	400 $5,000

b. LIFO

Note that the June 30 inventory under LIFO-perpetual is not the same as under LIFO-periodic. The application of LIFO procedures at the time of each individual sale under the perpetual inventory system resulted in a partial depletion of the June 1 inventory layer; whereas under the periodic inventory system, the entire beginning inventory layer of costs is assumed to be still on hand at June 30. Thus, LIFO-perpetual may result in the ending inventory being comprised of different layers of cost than would be the case under LIFO-periodic.

Date	Purchased	Sold	Balance
June 1			200 @ $10 = $2,000
June 6		100 @ $10 = $1,000	100 @ 10 = 1,000
June 9	400 @ $11 = $4,400		100 @ 10 = 1,000 400 @ 11 = 4,400
June 12		200 @ 11 = 2,200	100 @ 10 = 1,000 200 @ 11 = 2,200
June 22	100 @ 14 = 1,400		100 @ 10 = 1,000 200 @ 11 = 2,200 100 @ 14 = 1,400
June 25		100 @ 14 = 1,400 200 @ 11 = 2,200	100 @ 10 = 1,000
June 29	300 @ 12 = 3,600		100 @ 10 = 1,000 300 @ 12 = 3,600
Totals June 30	800 $9,400	600 $6,800	400 $4,600

IFRS: Under IAS 2, the use of LIFO is not allowed.

c. Average (moving-average)

The average cost method under a perpetual system utilizes a "moving average" unit cost. It requires that a new unit cost be computed after each acquisition.

Date	Purchased	Sold	Balance
June 1			200 @ $10.00 = $2,000
June 6		100 @ $10.00 = $1,000	100 @ 10.00 = 1,000
June 9	400 @ $11 = $4,400		500 @ 10.80 = 5,400
June 12		200 @ 10.80 = 2,160	300 @ 10.80 = 3,240
June 22	100 @ 14 = 1,400		400 @ 11.60 = 4,640
June 25		300 @ 11.60 = 3,480	100 @ 11.60 = 1,160
June 29	300 @ 12 = 3,600		400 @ 11.90 = 4,760
Totals June 30	800 $9,400	600 $6,640	400 $4,760

2212.20 **Comparison of FIFO and LIFO:** If prices remain unchanged, FIFO and LIFO will yield similar results. In periods of rising prices, LIFO will result in smaller inventory costs and larger cost of goods sold than FIFO. The reverse is true in periods of price declines. Of the two methods, LIFO comes closest to matching current costs against current revenues. However, LIFO also results in inventory being stated in terms of the oldest costs.

Modifications of LIFO

2212.21 The application of LIFO can prove to be quite burdensome. To alleviate some of this burden but at the same time enable the taxpayer to retain some of the benefits associated with the use of LIFO for tax purposes, the Internal Revenue Service allows various modifications of LIFO for tax purposes. Frequently, when an enterprise uses a given modification of LIFO for tax purposes, it also uses the same modification for financial reporting purposes. However, the enterprise is not necessarily required to use the same modification for financial purposes. The IRS allows certain variations between the application of LIFO for tax purposes and its application for financial reporting purposes. For example, an enterprise may use a combination of LIFO and the weighted-average cost method demonstrated as follows. In this particular case, the current period's purchases are treated as if they were all acquired at the average cost of all goods purchased during the period. To illustrate, using the data presented previously, the June 30 inventory would be determined as follows:

Weighted-average cost/unit for June purchases:	
Cost of June purchases	$9,400
divided by units purchased in June	800
= weighted-average cost/unit	$11.75
June 30 inventory:	
June 1 inventory (200 at $10)	$2,000
Increase in June (200 at $11.75)	2,350
	$4,350

Any decrease in the number of units in subsequent periods would be regarded as a reduction in the most recent layer, then in successively older layers, and finally in the original layer. Once a specific layer is reduced or eliminated, it may not be restored later. This particular modification of LIFO is sometimes referred to as the "unit LIFO" method. Alternatively, it may be referred to as the "LIFO/average cost" method. Other similar modifications, such as "LIFO/FIFO" (current period *increases* priced at actual cost of *latest* acquisitions during the period) and "LIFO/LIFO" (current period *increases* priced at actual cost of *earliest* acquisitions during the period), are acceptable for tax purposes and, as a result, may also be encountered in financial statements as well as on tax returns. However, these latter modifications ("LIFO/FIFO" and "LIFO/LIFO") thus far have not been directly addressed on the CPA Examination. Their mention here is to emphasize that various modifications of LIFO may be acceptable for financial reporting purposes as well as for tax purposes.

Dollar-Value LIFO

2212.22 The objective of the dollar-value LIFO method is to state inventory on a LIFO cost basis. The dollar-value aspect of the name of the method stems from the *procedure* used to arrive at LIFO cost. The procedure is essentially one of measuring inventory layers in terms of dollar values rather than physical units. Dollar-value LIFO requires the use of a price index and the concept of a base year, the year in which dollar-value LIFO is adopted. (The price index may be an acceptable external index or an internally developed index.) The process involves the following steps:

    a. Ending inventory is priced at current costs.

    b. Ending inventory is restated to base-year costs by use of the year-end price index.

    c. Beginning inventory is restated to base-year costs by use of the appropriate price index. (Information regarding the beginning-of-year inventory at base-year prices should be available from computations made at the end of the preceding year.)

    d. Compare (b) and (c) to determine the "physical" increase or decrease in inventory.

102

  e. The inventory increase or decrease in (d), stated in terms of base-year costs, is then priced in terms of LIFO cost by using the appropriate price index.

   (1) Inventory increases are priced in terms of prices at the end of the current year.

   (2) Inventory decreases are priced in terms of prices prevailing when the most recent inventory layers were added.

2212.23 **Example:** Raider Company manufactures one product. On December 31, 20X1, Raider adopted the dollar-value LIFO method. Inventory on December 31, 20X1, using the dollar-value LIFO method, was $100,000. The price index on that date was 100. Inventory data for the next three years are as follows:

Year	Inventory at Year-End Prices	Price Index at Year-End
20X2	$114,400	104
20X3	137,500	110
20X4	126,000	120

Inventory at December 31, 20X2, would be determined as follows:

December 31, 20X2

12/31/20X2 inventory at 20X2 year-end prices	$114,400
12/31/20X2 inventory at base-year prices ($114,400 ÷ 1.04)	110,000
01/01/20X2 inventory at base-year prices	100,000
20X2 inventory increase at base-year prices	10,000
20X2 inventory increase—LIFO cost ($10,000 × 1.04)	10,400
01/01/20X2 inventory at LIFO cost (from 12/31/20X1 data)	100,000
12/31/20X2 inventory at LIFO cost ($100,000 + $10,400)	110,400

Composition of December 31, 20X2, inventory:

	Base-Year Prices	Price Index	LIFO Cost
20X1 layer	$100,000	100	$100,000
20X2 layer	10,000	104	10,400
	$110,000		$110,400

Retaining the type of information presented regarding the composition of the inventory in terms of both base-year prices and LIFO cost will prove valuable in computations for subsequent years.

December 31, 20X3

12/31/20X3 inventory at 20X3 year-end prices	$137,500
12/31/20X3 inventory at base-year prices ($137,500 ÷ 1.10)	125,000
01/01/20X3 inventory at base-year prices (see 20X2 computations)	110,000
20X3 inventory increase at base-year prices	15,000
20X3 inventory increase—LIFO cost ($15,000 × 1.10)	16,500
01/01/20X3 inventory at LIFO cost (see 20X2 computations)	110,400
12/31/20X3 inventory at LIFO cost ($16,500 + $110,400)	126,900

Composition of December 31, 20X3, inventory:

	Base-Year Price	Price Index	LIFO Cost
20X1 layer	$100,000	100	$100,000
20X2 layer	10,000	104	10,400
20X3 layer	15,000	110	16,500
	$125,000		$126,900

The December 31, 20X3, inventory consists of three layers, each at a different price level (price index). Any subsequent reduction in inventory would first come from the 20X3 layer, then from the 20X2 layer, and finally from the 20X1 (base year) layer.

December 31, 20X4

12/31/20X4 inventory at 20X4 year-end prices	$126,000
12/31/20X4 inventory at base-year prices ($126,000 ÷ 1.20)	105,000
01/01/20X4 inventory at base-year prices (see 20X3 computations)	125,000
20X4 inventory decrease at base-year prices	20,000

20X4 inventory decrease—LIFO cost:

From 20X3 layer	$15,000	× 1.10	$ 16,500
From 20X2 layer	5,000	× 1.04	5,200
	$20,000		$ 21,700

01/01/20X4 inventory at LIFO cost (see 20X3 computation)	$126,900
12/31/20X4 inventory at LIFO cost ($126,900 - $21,700)	105,200

Composition of December 31, 20X4, inventory:

	Base-Year Prices	Price Index	LIFO Cost
20X1 layer	$100,000	100	$100,000
20X2 layer	5,000	104	5,200
	$105,000		$105,200

The reductions in the 20X2 and 20X3 layers would not be "restored" in the event of inventory increases in subsequent years. For example, if inventory increased in 20X5, the December 31, 20X5, inventory would consist of the 20X1 layer, the remaining 20X2 layer ($5,000 in terms of base-year prices), and a 20X5 layer.

Retail Method

2212.24 The retail method is actually a "system" for determining inventory at retail prices. The inventory at retail is then converted to cost (FIFO, LIFO, or average) or to the lower of cost or market based on the cost-to-retail ratio. Application of the retail method requires a system that provides the following information *in addition* to that normally available in the typical cost system:

a. Beginning inventory and purchases at retail (a cost system normally provides information about beginning inventory and purchases only in terms of cost)

b. Adjustments to original sales price, such as additional markups, markup cancellations, markdowns, and markdown cancellations

In certain cases, information in addition to that listed may be required.

2212.25 **Example:** The basic idea of the retail method is illustrated as follows:

	Cost	Retail	Cost-to-Retail Ratio
Beginning inventory	$8,000	$12,000	
Plus: Purchases	27,000	38,000	
Goods available for sale	$35,000	50,000	70%
Less: Sales		(43,000)	
Ending inventory, at retail		$7,000	
Ending inventory, at cost ($7,000 × 0.70)	$4,900		

As reflected in the illustration, the retail method consists of the following two basic steps:

1. Determining the ending inventory at retail
2. Converting the ending inventory from retail to cost by applying the appropriate cost-to-retail ratio

2212.26 The presence of additional markups and markdowns complicates the use of the retail method. The key issue is whether or not to include markups and/or markdowns in the computation of the cost-to-retail ratio.

2212.27 **Average cost:** The retail method can be used to state the ending inventory at approximate cost (FIFO, LIFO, or average). In this case, both net additional markups (additional markups less markup cancellations) and net markdowns (markdowns less markdown cancellations) are included in the cost-to-retail ratio. To illustrate, assume the following data:

	Cost	Retail
Beginning inventory	$35,000	$50,000
Purchases	45,000	80,000
Additional markups		12,000
Markup cancellations		3,000
Markdowns		8,000
Markdown cancellations		1,000
Sales		72,000

The ending inventory at approximate average cost would be determined as follows:

	Cost	Retail	Cost-to-Retail Ratio
Beginning inventory	$35,000	$50,000	
Plus: Purchases	45,000	80,000	
Net additional markups ($12,000 - $3,000)		9,000	
Net markdowns ($8,000 - $1,000)		(7,000)	
Total goods available	$80,000	132,000	60.6%
Less: Sales		(72,000)	
Ending inventory, at retail		$60,000	
Ending inventory, at approximate average cost ($60,000 × 0.606)	$36,360		

The inclusion of both net additional markups and net markdowns in the determination of the cost-to-retail ratio results in the ending inventory being converted to some form of cost basis. In the illustration, the particular form of cost is average cost because the cost-to-retail ratio is based on all goods available for sale (i.e., the ratio represents an "average" for the total goods available).

2212.28 **FIFO and LIFO cost:** The retail method can also be used to approximate FIFO or LIFO cost. To do so, total goods available is viewed as consisting of two layers—the beginning inventory layer and the current period acquisitions layer. A cost-to-retail ratio is computed for each layer. Using the data presented, inventory would be determined as follows:

	Cost	Retail	Cost-to-Retail Ratio
Beginning inventory	$35,000	$ 50,000	70.0%
Plus: Purchases	45,000	80,000	
Net additional markups		9,000	
Net markdowns		(7,000)	
Current year acquisition	45,000	82,000	54.9%
Total goods available	$80,000	132,000	60.6%
Less: Sales		(72,000)	
Ending inventory, at retail		$ 60,000	
Ending inventory, at FIFO cost:			
$60,000 × 0.549	$32,940		
Ending inventory, at LIFO cost:			
$50,000 × 0.70	$35,000		
$10,000 × 0.549	5,490		
	$40,490		

The computation of separate cost-to-retail ratios for the beginning inventory and the current year acquisitions facilitates the use of FIFO or LIFO cost. FIFO assumes that the ending inventory is composed of the most recent purchases; consequently, the ending inventory at retail is converted using the current year acquisitions (i.e., the most recent layer) cost-to-retail ratio. On the other hand, LIFO assumes the ending inventory consists of the oldest acquisitions. Therefore, the LIFO inventory is based first on the beginning inventory (oldest acquisitions) cost-to-retail ratio with the current year's inventory increase (based on retail prices) converted on the basis of the next-oldest layer (i.e., the current year's layer).

2212.29 **Conventional retail (lower of average cost or market):** As pointed out, the inclusion of both net additional markups and net markdowns in the computation of the cost-to-retail ratio results in ending inventory being stated at cost. The exclusion of *net markdowns* from the cost-to-retail ratio results in a lower cost-to-retail ratio and, therefore, an ending inventory lower than cost. The inventory is said to be stated at the *lower of average cost or market.* This approach is referred to as the conventional retail method. Continuing the example presented, the ending inventory would be determined as follows:

	Cost	Retail	Cost-to-Retail Ratio
Beginning inventory	$35,000	$ 50,000	
Plus: Purchases	45,000	80,000	
Net additional markups		9,000	
Total goods available	$80,000	$139,000	57.6%
Less:			
Sales		72,000	
Net markdowns		7,000	
Total		79,000	
Ending inventory, at retail		$ 60,000	
Ending inventory, at lower of average cost or market ($60,000 × 0.576)	$34,560		

The differences resulting from the alternative treatments of net markdowns are highlighted in the following summary of the average cost results (see section 2212.23) and of the lower of average cost or market results:

	Average Cost (Net Markdowns Included in Ratio)	Lower of Average Cost or Market (Net Markdowns Excluded from Ratio)
Ending inventory, at retail	$60,000	$60,000
Cost-to-retail ratio	60.6%	57.6%
Ending inventory	$36,360	$34,560

Notice that the ending inventory at retail is the same in both cases. The only issue is the inclusion or exclusion of net markdowns in the determination of the cost-to-retail ratio. Including net markdowns in the computation of the ratio assumes that they apply to all goods available for sale. Excluding them assumes that they apply only to goods sold.

2212.30 **Other items:** Other specific items may be encountered in the application of the retail method. In general, they should be incorporated into the computations according to their underlying nature. Listed as follows are some specific items and how they should be included in the computations:

Item	Treatment
Special discounts (such as employee discounts) and estimated losses from spoilage and theft	Included with sales in the total deducted from total goods available at retail
Sales returns and allowances	Deducted from sales
Freight-in and purchase discounts	Adjustments to purchases at cost
Purchase returns and allowances	Adjustments to purchases at both cost and retail
Sales discount (cash discount)	Excluded from computations unless sales are recorded at "net"

Gross Profit Method

2212.31 The gross profit method can be used to estimate inventory cost when a physical inventory is impossible or impractical. It can also be used to test the reasonableness of a physical inventory. The gross profit method is based on an assumed relationship between sales and gross profit. This assumed relationship is usually based on previous experience. The basic steps in the application of the gross profit method are as follows.

Step 1: Determine the cost of goods available for sale (based on the balances in the inventory and purchases accounts in the accounting records).

Step 2: Compute the amount of gross profit by multiplying sales by the gross profit percentage.

Step 3: Calculate cost of goods sold (i.e., sales on a cost basis) by deducting gross profit from sales.

Step 4: Determine the ending inventory at cost by deducting cost of goods sold from the cost of goods available for sale.

2212.32 The following data is used to demonstrate the steps involved in applying the gross profit method.

Facts:	Sales	$300,000
	Beginning inventory	40,000
	Purchases (net)	220,000
	Gross profit as a percentage of sales	25%
Step 1.	Determine cost of goods available for sale.	
	Beginning inventory	$ 40,000
	Plus: Purchases (net)	220,000
	Cost of goods available for sale	$260,000
Step 2.	Compute the amount of gross profit.	
	Sales	$300,000
	Gross profit as a percentage of sales	.25
	Gross profit	$ 75,000
Step 3.	Calculate cost of goods sold.	
	Sales	$300,000
	Less: Gross profit	75,000
	Cost of goods sold	$225,000
Step 4.	Determine ending inventory at cost.	
	Cost of goods available for sale	$260,000
	Less: Cost of goods sold	225,000
	Ending inventory	$ 35,000

The four steps are illustrated in the following table:

Beginning inventory		$ 40,000
Plus: Purchases (net)		220,000
Cost of goods available for sale		260,000
Less: Cost of goods sold (sales at cost):		
Sales	$300,000	
Less: Gross profit (0.25 × $300,000)	75,000	225,000
Ending inventory		$ 35,000

2212.33 Gross profit may be expressed as a percentage of cost rather than sales. In that case, the simplest approach is to convert from a percentage based on cost to a percentage based on sales. For example, if gross profit is expressed as 25% of cost, the conversion would be as follows:

$$\text{Gross profit as a percentage of sales} = \frac{\text{Gross profit as a percentage of cost}}{1 + \text{Gross profit as a percentage of cost}} = \frac{0.25}{1.25} = 0.20 = 20\%$$

The conversion is based on the relationship among sales, cost of goods sold, and gross profit, as demonstrated:

Sales	125%C
Cost of goods sold (C)	100%C
Gross profit	25%C

$$\frac{\text{Gross Profit}}{\text{Sales}} = \frac{0.25C}{1.25C} = 0.20 = 20\%$$

The gross profit expressed as a percentage of sales, in this case 20%, would then be used as demonstrated in the illustration presented in section **2212.32**.

Lower of Cost or Market

2212.34 As mentioned previously, a departure from the cost basis is required when the utility of the goods is no longer as great as cost. The decline in utility is recognized by stating inventory at the lower of cost or market.

2212.35 A key issue in applying the lower of cost or market rule is determination of market. Market will be replacement cost unless:

    a. Replacement cost exceeds net realizable value (estimated selling price less costs of completion and disposal), in which case market will be net realizable value (the "ceiling") or

    b. Replacement cost is less than net realizable value reduced by a normal profit margin (the "floor"), in which case market will be the "floor."

2212.36 Example:

Item	Cost	Replacement Cost	Net Realizable Value (ceiling)	Net Realizable Value Less Normal Profit (floor)
A	$20	$25	$28	$22
B	12	10	13	8
C	30	33	27	21
D	17	12	19	14

The application of the lower of cost or market rule to these four items of inventory is summarized as follows:

Item	Cost	Market	Description of Market	Lower of Cost or Market
A	$20	$25	replacement cost	$20
B	12	10	replacement cost	10
C	30	27	ceiling	27
D	17	14	floor	14

2212.37 The lower of cost or market rule may be applied to individual items, major categories, or inventory as a whole. The most conservative approach (i.e., the smallest inventory and largest loss) is to apply the rule to individual items.

2212.38 Cost, as used in the lower of cost or market (LCM) rule, is cost determined under one of the acceptable cost flow methods, such as FIFO, LIFO, or average cost. Currently, the LCM rule cannot be used *for tax purposes* if cost is determined by using the LIFO method. However, it is acceptable to use LCM in such cases (i.e., when cost is determined by using LIFO) *for financial reporting purposes* as well as in cases in which cost is determined under FIFO, average cost, or some other acceptable cost flow method.

2212.39 **Recording lower of cost or market in the accounts:** There are various ways in which the application of the lower of cost or market rule can be reflected in the accounts. Two such approaches are summarized as follows:

    a. Direct method:

        (1) Beginning and ending inventories are reflected in the accounts at the lower of cost or market (LCM).

        (2) The loss from price decline is included in cost of goods sold.

b. **Allowance method:**

(1) Ending inventory is reflected at cost. An allowance account is used to reflect any writedowns.

(2) Beginning inventory is reflected at the lower of cost or market.

(3) The loss from price decline is reported separately.

2212.40 The following data are used to illustrate these two approaches:

	20X1	20X2
Beginning inventory (BI):		
Cost	$10,000	$30,000
Market	15,000	22,000
Purchases	60,000	55,000
Ending inventory (EI):		
Cost	30,000	20,000
Market	22,000	17,000
Sales	80,000	90,000
Operating expenses	13,000	10,000

Assuming the use of a periodic inventory system, the two approaches would be reflected in the accounts and in the income statement presented as follows:

Entries December 31, 20X1

Direct Method			Allowance Method		
Income summary	$10,000		Income summary	$10,000	
Inventory (BI)		$10,000	Inventory (BI)		$10,000
Inventory (EI)	$22,000		Inventory (EI)	$30,000	
Income summary		$22,000	Loss from decline	8,000	
			Income summary		$30,000
			Allowance for decline		8,000

Income Statement, 20X1

Direct Method			Allowance Method		
Sales		$80,000	Sales		$80,000
Cost of goods sold:			Cost of goods sold:		
BI (at LCM)	$10,000		BI (at LCM)	$10,000	
Purchases	60,000		Purchases	60,000	
Total available	70,000		Total available	70,000	
EI (at LCM)	22,000	48,000	EI (at cost)	30,000	40,000
Gross profit		32,000	Gross profit		40,000
Operating expenses		13,000	Loss from decline		8,000
Net income		$19,000			32,000
			Operating expenses		13,000
			Net income		$19,000

Entries January 1, 20X2

Direct Method			Allowance Method		
(none)			Allowance for decline	$8,000	
			Inventory		$8,000

Entries December 31, 20X2

Direct Method			Allowance Method		
Income summary	$22,000		Income summary	$22,000	
Inventory (BI)		$22,000	Inventory (BI)		$22,000
Inventory (EI)	$17,000		Inventory (EI)	$20,000	
Income summary		$17,000	Loss from decline	3,000	
			Income summary		$20,000
			Allowance for decline		3,000

Income Statement, 20X2

Direct Method			Allowance Method		
Sales		$90,000	Sales		$90,000
Cost of goods sold:			Cost of goods sold:		
BI (at LCM)	$22,000		BI (at LCM)	$22,000	
Purchases	55,000		Purchases	55,000	
Total available	77,000		Total available	77,000	
EI (at LCM)	17,000	60,000	EI (at cost)	20,000	57,000
Gross profit		30,000	Gross profit		33,000
Operating expenses		10,000	Loss from decline		3,000
Net income		$20,000			30,000
			Operating expenses		10,000
			Net income		$20,000

2212.41 One should note that the amount of net income reported is the same under both methods. However, the allowance method separates the loss from inventory price declines from cost of goods sold, whereas the direct method does not. Both methods are consistent with the requirement that, once inventory has been written down below cost, such reduced amount is to be considered as cost in the subsequent accounting period.

2213 Property, Plant, and Equipment

Overview

2213.01 **Nature and classification:** Plant and equipment includes those tangible, long-lived assets used in the operations of the enterprise.

2213.02 Various terms are often used as being synonymous with plant and equipment, some of which are plant assets; property, plant, and equipment; and fixed assets.

Accounting Basis – General Rule

2213.03 **At acquisition:** The general rule for recording the acquisition of plant and equipment is the same as that for other asset acquisitions (i.e., plant and equipment should be recorded at historical cost, which includes the costs necessarily incurred to bring them to the condition and location necessary for their intended use). Cost should be measured at the fair value of the consideration given or the fair value of the asset acquired, whichever is more clearly evident.

2213.04 **Subsequent to acquisition:** Plant and equipment represents *bundles of services* acquired by the enterprise. Accordingly, the cost of plant and equipment should be charged to the accounting periods receiving the benefits of these bundles of services. In theory, each period would be charged according to the quantity of benefits that it received. In practice, various depreciation methods are used to allocate the cost of a plant asset over its useful life. Subsequent to acquisition, plant and equipment other than land are reflected at cost less accumulated depreciation. Land is shown at cost.

2213.05 Plant and equipment should not be written up by an enterprise to reflect appraisal, market, or current values which are above cost. However, a permanent decline in the value of a plant asset below cost should be recognized by writing down the plant asset to its net realizable value.

Cost at Acquisition

2213.06 Cost of a plant asset includes all expenditures necessary to acquire the asset and prepare it for its intended use. These expenditures are referred to as capital expenditures. The related benefits extend beyond the current period; hence, the expenditure is capitalized as part of the asset account. Expenditures are identified as revenue expenditures if all the related benefits will be realized in the current period. Revenue expenditures are recognized as expenses in the period in which incurred.

2213.07 Land costs include the following:

a. The purchase price

b. Costs incidental to acquisition, such as legal fees, commissions, and title insurance

c. Costs of preparing the land for use, such as the costs of surveying, grading, filling, draining, and clearing

Land improvement costs may also be charged to the land account if the improvements have an indefinite service life. Improvements that have limited lives should be set up in a separate account and depreciated over their useful lives.

2213.08 **Buildings, machinery, and equipment** costs similarly include the expenditures necessary to purchase or construct the asset and prepare it for its intended use. Preparation costs include those costs incurred in testing the asset (e.g., machinery) to ensure that it will operate as desired.

2213.09 The cost of tearing down an existing building should not be included as part of the cost of the new building to be erected on that site. These costs are included in land costs as preparing the land for use. However, costs of excavating for the foundation of the new building should be included as part of the cost of the new building.

2213.10 Other problem areas in determining the cost of plant and equipment are examined in the discussion that follows.

Special Problems in Determining Cost

2213.11 **Cash discounts:** Cost of a plant asset should be net of any cash discount allowed. For example, if equipment is purchased for $1,000 with terms stated as 2/10, n/30, the equipment should be recorded at $980 whether or not the discount is taken. If payment is not made within the discount period, the $20 discount not taken should be treated as a financing expense.

2213.12 **Deferred payment contracts:** The basic principle involved in determining the cost of a plant asset acquired under a deferred payment contract is the same as that for determining the cost of any other asset under such a contract. Cost is the fair value (cash equivalent) of the asset acquired or the fair value of the debt, whichever is more clearly evident. For example, if a machine that normally sells for $10,000 cash is purchased under an agreement calling for payments of $2,638 at the end of each of the next five years, the entry is:

Machinery	$10,000	
Discount on Notes Payable	3,190	
Notes Payable		$13,190

In this case, the asset is recorded at the fair value of the asset acquired. The fair value of the debt would be used if it were more clearly evident than the fair value of the asset. In the absence of an established exchange price for the asset or evidence of the fair value of the debt, the asset is recorded by discounting the future payments using a representative imputed rate of interest. An example of the procedures involved when it is necessary to use an imputed rate of interest is presented in section **2252.05–.11**.

2213.13 **Overhead costs:** There is general agreement that the materials, labor, and variable overhead costs associated with constructing a plant asset should be capitalized as part of the cost of the asset. There is less agreement as to the treatment of fixed overhead costs. The following three views have surfaced regarding the amount of fixed overhead that should be allocated to the plant asset being constructed:

1. Allocate no fixed overhead
2. Allocate only the incremental fixed overhead
3. Allocate a portion of all fixed overhead

The first view (no fixed overhead) has little, if any, merit. The second view (incremental fixed overhead) holds that the incremental or additional overhead represents the cost on which the enterprise based its decision to construct rather than purchase the asset; accordingly, it represents the relevant cost to be capitalized.

2213.14 The third view (a portion of all fixed overhead) emphasizes the production effort rather than the items produced. Thus, plant assets being constructed are treated no differently than items of inventory being produced for sale.

2213.15 **Lump-sum acquisitions:** A group of assets may be acquired in a single transaction for a lump sum. In the absence of evidence that portions of the total price apply to particular individual assets, the lump-sum cost should be allocated to the individual assets based on the best indicator of their relative fair values. To illustrate, assume that land and a building were acquired for a lump-sum price of $100,000. Assuming an independent appraisal showed the appraised values of the land and building to be $30,000 and $90,000, respectively, the $100,000 cost would be allocated as follows:

Asset	Appraised Value	Allocation of Cost	
Land	$ 30,000	($30,000 ÷ $120,000) × $100,000 =	$ 25,000
Building	90,000	($90,000 ÷ $120,000) × $100,000 =	$ 75,000
	$120,000		$100,000

2213.16 **Issuance of equity securities:** Plant and equipment acquired by issuing equity securities should be recorded at the fair value of the securities issued or the fair value of the assets received, whichever is more clearly evident. The par or stated value of stock issued should not be used as a measure of the fair value of stock issued or of the cost of the asset acquired. In the absence of exchange transactions to indicate the fair value of the stock issued or the asset received, the asset acquired should be recorded based on the best measure of cost available, such as independent appraised values.

2213.17 **Donated assets:** Plant assets are occasionally donated to an enterprise by a city or other municipality as an inducement for the enterprise to locate a plant in the area. If the donation is of the "no strings attached" type, it is a nonreciprocal transfer; accordingly, the asset should be recorded at fair value at the time of the transfer (FASB ASC 840-10-30-1). If the donation has "strings attached," the substance of the transaction must be carefully examined. For example, the asset may represent a contingent asset, which normally would not be reflected in the accounts until the conditions have been met. On the other hand, clear title to the asset may have been transferred to the enterprise, but at the same time, the enterprise agreed to fulfill certain conditions in the future. In this case, a careful assessment must be made of whether the enterprise has a loss contingency (per FASB ASC 450-10-05-1) that should be disclosed or possibly even recorded.

2213.18 **Interest:** Historically, interest generally has been regarded as a cost of financing and not as a part of the cost (acquisition or construction) of a fixed asset. However, some enterprises have capitalized interest on debt incurred during construction as a part of the cost of the fixed asset. Additionally, regulatory agencies have allowed public utilities to capitalize not only the interest on debt but also an implicit interest charge for internal funds used. This diversity in practice in accounting for interest costs led to the issuance of SFAS 34, *Capitalization of Interest Cost,* now found in FASB ASC 835-20.

Capitalization of Interest (FASB ASC 835-20-15-3)

2213.19 If specified conditions are met, interest shall be capitalized for the following qualifying assets:

    a. Assets that are constructed or otherwise produced for an enterprise's own use (including assets constructed or produced for the enterprise by others for which deposits or progress payments have been made)

    b. Assets intended for sale or lease that are constructed or otherwise produced as discrete projects (e.g., ships or real estate developments)

    c. Investments (equity, loans, and advances) accounted for by the equity method while the investee has activities in progress necessary to commence its planned principal operations (i.e., while the investee is a development stage enterprise per FASB ASC 915-10) provided that the investee's activities include the use of the funds to acquire qualifying assets for its own operations

2213.20 Interest cost specifically shall not be capitalized for the following:

    a. Inventories that are routinely manufactured or otherwise produced in large quantities on a repetitive basis

    b. Assets that are in use or ready for their intended use in the earning activities of the enterprise

c. Assets that are not being used in the earning activities of the enterprise and that are not undergoing the activities necessary to get them ready for use

d. Assets that are not included in the consolidated balance sheet of the parent company and consolidated subsidiaries

e. Investments accounted for by the equity method after the planned principal operations of the investee begin (i.e., after the investee no longer qualifies as a development stage enterprise)

f. Investments in regulated investees that are capitalizing both the cost of the debt and equity capital

2213.21 For qualifying assets (see section **2213.19**), the interest cost incurred during the period of time required to carry out activities necessary to bring the asset to the condition and location necessary for its intended use is a part of the historical cost of acquiring the asset. The amount of interest to be capitalized *during a given accounting period* is determined by applying the appropriate capitalization rate to the average amount of accumulated expenditures for the asset during that period. *Expenditures* for this purpose are capitalized expenditures for the qualifying asset that have required the payment of cash, the transfer of other assets, or the incurring of a liability on which interest is recognized.

2213.22 In general, the capitalization rate shall be a weighted average of the rates applicable to borrowings (debt) outstanding during the accounting period for which the capitalizable interest is being calculated. However, if an enterprise associates a specific new borrowing with a qualifying asset, the enterprise *may* use the rate on that specific borrowing as the capitalization rate to be applied to that portion of the average accumulated expenditures for the asset that does not exceed the amount of the specific borrowing. If the average accumulated expenditures for the qualifying asset exceed the amount of that specific borrowing, the capitalization rate to be used on the *excess* is the weighted average of the rates applicable to *other* borrowings of the enterprise.

2213.23 The capitalization period normally begins when all of the following three conditions are present:

a. Expenditures for the asset have been made.

b. Activities that are necessary to get the asset ready for its intended use are in progress.

c. Interest cost is being incurred.

Interest capitalization shall continue as long as these conditions continue. The capitalization period ends when the qualifying asset is substantially complete and ready for its intended use.

2213.24 Since the capitalized interest becomes a part of the cost of the qualifying asset, its disposition should be the same as that of other components of the asset's cost (e.g., depreciation, depletion, amortization, and cost of goods sold).

2213.25 In an accounting period in which no interest cost is capitalized, the total interest incurred and charged to expense during the period should be disclosed. In an accounting period in which some interest cost is capitalized, disclosure should be made of the total interest cost incurred, the amount capitalized, and the amount charged to expense.

2213.26 **Example:** In 20X1, Alpha Company decided to construct an additional warehouse to be used for storage of its raw materials. The following data, transactions, and events relate to this undertaking:

a. April 1, 20X1—Alpha borrowed $1 million on a 20% note maturing in 20X4 to help finance the following:

(1) The acquisition of land on which to build the warehouse

(2) The construction of the warehouse

Note: Alpha already has outstanding a 16%, $1 million note that was issued at face amount in 20X0 and matures in 20X5.

b. April 1, 20X1—Alpha purchased the land for the warehouse for $500,000. On this date, Alpha also contracted with Beta Company for construction of the warehouse. Beta began construction immediately, with completion scheduled for 20X2.

c. June 1, 20X1—Alpha paid Beta progress payments of $1.5 million.

d. April 1, 20X2—Alpha paid Beta progress payments of $1 million.

e. September 1, 20X2—Alpha paid Beta progress payments of $900,000.

f. December 31, 20X2—Alpha made the final payment to Beta in the amount of $600,000. The warehouse was accepted by Alpha on this date and is now ready for use.

2213.27 The qualifying assets for interest capitalization purposes are the warehouse being constructed and the related land. However, any interest capitalized will be debited to the warehouse under construction account, because FASB ASC 835-20-15-8 requires that "if the resulting asset is a structure, such as a plant or a shopping center, interest capitalized on the land expenditures is part of the acquisition cost of the structure."

2213.28 The capitalization period begins April 1, 20X1, and ends December 31, 20X2.

2213.29 The average accumulated expenditures (AAE) for 20X1 is calculated as follows:

Date of Expenditure	Amount	Weighting Factor	AAE
04/01/X1	$ 500,000	9/12	$ 375,000
06/01/X1	1,500,000	7/12	875,000
			$1,250,000

2213.30 The $1.25 million AAE means that the actual expenditures made during 20X1 were the equivalent of an expenditure of $1.25 million made at the beginning of the accounting year, January 1. Since the AAE ($1.25 million) exceeds the amount of the specific borrowing ($1 million), the interest associated with the first $1 million of AAE is capitalized at the interest rate of the specific borrowing (20%), and the interest associated with the $250,000 excess AAE is capitalized at the weighted-average interest rate of the other outstanding debt (16%), shown as follows:

	AAE	Capitalization Rate
Total AAE for 20X1	$1,250,000	
Amount of specific borrowing	1,000,000	20%
Excess of AAE over specific borrowing	$ 250,000	16%

2213.31 Therefore, the interest to be capitalized in 20X1 based on AAE is:

AAE related to specific borrowing ($1,000,000 × 0.20)	$200,000
AAE related to other debt ($250,000 × 0.16)	40,000
Interest to be capitalized in 20X1 based on AAE	$240,000

2213.32 The interest to be capitalized in 20X1 *based* on AAE is $240,000. However, the amount of interest capitalized may not exceed the actual interest incurred. More specifically, the amount of interest capitalized in an *accounting period* may not exceed the interest incurred during the portion of the *capitalization period* included in that accounting period. In Alpha's case, the interest capitalized in the accounting period 20X1 may not exceed the interest incurred from April 1, 20X1, (the earliest date of the capitalization period included in 20X1) to December 31, 20X1 (the latest date of the capitalization period included in 20X1), shown as follows:

Interest incurred in 20X1:	
Prior to capitalization period:	
$1,000,000 × 0.16 × 3/12	$ 40,000
During the portion of the capitalization period included in 20X1 (April 1-Dec. 31):	
On specific borrowing ($1,000,000 × 0.20 × 9/12)	$150,000
On other debit ($1,000,000 × 0.16 × 9/12)	120,000
	$270,000

2213.33 Since the interest to be capitalized in 20X1 based on AAE ($240,000) does not exceed the interest incurred April 1–December 31, 20X1 ($270,000), the amount of interest to be capitalized in 20X1 is $240,000.

2213.34 Therefore, the $310,000 interest incurred in 20X1 (i.e., $40,000 incurred prior to April 1 plus $270,000 incurred after April 1) should be accounted for as follows:

Capitalized as part of the acquisition cost of the warehouse under construction	$240,000
Recognized as interest expense in 20X1	70,000
	$310,000

2213.35 The relevant computations for 20X2 are as follows:

Average accumulated expenditures (AAE):

Date of Expenditure	Amount	Weighting Factor	AAE
04/01/X1	$ 500,000	12/12	$ 500,000
06/01/X1	1,500,000	12/12	1,500,000
12/31/X1	240,000*	12/12	240,000
04/01/X2	1,000,000	9/12	750,000
09/01/X2	900,000	4/12	300,000
12/31/X2	600,000	0/12	0
			$3,290,000

* Interest capitalized in 20X1.

Interest to be capitalized in 20X2 based on AAE:

	AAE	Capitalization Rate	Interest to be Capitalized
Total AAE	$3,290,000	—	—
Specific borrowing (SB)	1,000,000	20%	$200,000
Excess of AAE over SB	$2,290,000	16%	366,400
			$566,400

Interest incurred during the portion of the capitalization period included in 20X2 (January 1, 20X2–December 31, 20X2):

On specific borrowing	$1,000,000 × 0.20 × 12/12 =	$200,000
On other debt	1,000,000 × 0.16 × 12/12 =	160,000
		$360,000

2213.36 Since the interest to be capitalized in 20X2 based on AAE ($566,400) exceeds the interest incurred ($360,000), the amount of interest that should be capitalized in 20X2 is $360,000. The entire $360,000 should be capitalized as part of the cost of the warehouse.

2213.37 The capitalization period ended on December 31, 20X2, the date on which the asset was completed and ready for use. Therefore, no additional interest may be capitalized after that date.

2213.38 Additional aspects of capitalization of interest that the CPA Examination candidate should be familiar with are as follows:

    a. There is a lack of agreement as to whether the interest capitalized in a given accounting period constitutes an expenditure for purposes of calculating the interest to be capitalized in subsequent accounting periods (i.e., whether capitalized interest should be compounded). In this regard, FASB ASC 835-20-35-3 states that "the Board concluded that compounding is conceptually consistent with its conclusion that interest on expenditures for the asset is a cost of acquiring the asset." The authors have interpreted the FASB's position as being that capitalized interest should be compounded, as shown in section **2213.35**. (For Alpha, if capitalized interest is not compounded, the AAE for 20X2 would be $3,290,000 − $240,000, or $3,050,000.)

    b. Interest earned shall not be offset against interest cost in determining the amount of interest cost to be capitalized, *except* in situations involving acquisition of qualifying assets financed with the proceeds of tax-exempt borrowings, and even then only if those funds are externally restricted to finance acquisition of specified qualifying assets or to service the related debt. In the latter case (which arises principally in the case of governmental entities), the interest capitalized shall be all interest cost of the borrowing less any interest earned with proceeds of the tax-exempt borrowing from the date of the borrowing (i.e., the capitalization period begins on the date of the borrowing) until the assets are ready for their intended use. (FASB ASC 835-20-30-10)

Post-Acquisition Costs

2213.39 Various expenditures relating to plant and equipment will normally be incurred during the useful lives of those assets. The proper accounting treatment of these post-acquisition expenditures is often a difficult issue. Conceptually, all post-acquisition expenditures and the preferred accounting treatment can be summarized as follows:

Purpose, Impact, or Type of Expenditure	Accounting Treatment
1. To maintain asset in good working order consistent with original desires and expectations. Examples: ordinary repairs and maintenance.	1. Charge to expense in period in which incurred.
2. To restore asset to predamage condition. Examples: Repairs resulting from fire, Flood, accident, and other similar events.	2. Charge portion not reimbursable from insurance to loss account in period in which event occurred.

3. To enhance the service potential of the asset by increasing its efficiency or capability. Examples: additions, improvements, and appropriate portion of other asset modifications, overhauls, and rearrangements.	3. Capitalize by debiting the asset account. Carrying amount of assets or parts of assets replaced should be removed from accounts and gain or loss recognized.
4. To increase the service potential of the asset by extending its useful life. Examples: replacements and appropriate portion of other asset modifications, overhauls, and rearrangements.	4. Capitalize by debiting the accumulated depreciation account. Remove carrying amount of any assets replaced and recognize gain or loss.

2213.40 In practice, identifying the portions of an expenditure that are applicable to the different categories listed is often difficult at best. For example, it may not be practical to distinguish between the amount of an expenditure applicable to the extension of an asset's life and the amount applicable to an increase in the asset's efficiency. From a financial accounting standpoint, the most critical distinction is that between expensing and capitalizing.

Depreciation

2213.41 Depreciation accounting is the process of allocating the cost of plant and equipment to the accounting periods in which the benefits (bundles of services) are received. It is a process of cost allocation, not of valuation.

2213.42 Ideally, depreciation should be matched with the periods benefited on a cause-and-effect basis. However, such an ideal matching is usually not practical. As a result, a depreciation method is deemed to be acceptable if it results in a *systematic* and *rational* allocation of the cost of an asset over the asset's useful life.

2213.43 Determining the amount of depreciation expense requires that the following items be identified:

   a. Cost

   b. Estimated useful life

   c. Estimated residual (salvage) value

   d. Depreciation method

2213.44 Estimation of the useful life should take into consideration the various factors that limit the service life of an asset. These limiting factors can be categorized as follows:

   a. Physical factors, such as normal deterioration and wear and tear from usage

   b. Functional factors, such as obsolescence and inadequacy

2213.45 The estimated useful life relates to the period of time over which that particular enterprise expects to use the asset. For example, if management plans to trade the asset at the end of three years, the estimated useful life for depreciation purposes would be three years, even though the asset might have a physical life of five years.

2213.46 Similarly, the estimated residual value is the amount expected to be realized at the end of the estimated useful life. This amount may differ from the scrap value of the asset at the end of its physical life.

2213.47 The following data for Munter Company is used to demonstrate some of the most common depreciation methods:

a. Cost (C): $10,000

b. Estimated salvage value (S): $1,000

c. Estimated useful life (N): four years

2213.48 Straight-line method.

$$\text{Depreciation (D)} = \frac{\text{Depreciation Base}}{\text{Life}} = \frac{C - S}{N}$$

$$(D) = \frac{\$10{,}000 - \$1{,}000}{4} = \$2{,}250$$

Year	Depreciation Expense	Accumulated Depreciation	Book Value
0			$10,000
1	$2,250	$2,250	7,750
2	2,250	4,500	5,500
3	2,250	6,750	3,250
4	2,250	9,000	1,000
	$9,000		

The annual rate (r) is:

$$r = \frac{1}{N}$$

$$r = \frac{1}{4} = 25\%$$

The straight-line method results in a constant annual rate (25%) and amount ($2,250). The book value at the end of the useful life (four years) is the estimated salvage value ($1,000).

2213.49 Fixed-percentage-of-declining-balance method. The fixed percentage is:

$$r = 1 - \sqrt[N]{\frac{S}{C}}$$

$$= 1 - \sqrt[4]{\frac{\$1{,}000}{\$10{,}000}}$$

$$= 1 - 56.23\% = 43.77\%$$

Year	Depreciation Expense		Accumulated Depreciation	Book Value
0				$10,000
1	0.4377 × $10,000 =	$4,377	$4,377	5,623
2	0.4377 × 5,623 =	2,461	6,838	3,162
3	0.4377 × 3,162 =	1,384	8,222	1,778
4	0.4377 × 1,778 =	778	9,000	1,000
		$9,000		

When the fixed percentage is calculated by using the formula presented, the book value at the end of the useful life will be equal to the estimated salvage value.

2213.50 **Double-declining-balance method.** The results obtained by using the fixed-percentage method discussed can be approximated by using the double-declining-balance method. The double-declining-balance method also applies a constant rate to the declining book value, but the rate is simply twice the straight-line rate, shown as follows for Munter Company:

$$r = \frac{2}{N}$$

$$r = \frac{2}{4} = 50\%$$

Year	Depreciation Expense		Accumulated Depreciation	Book Value
0				$10,000
1	0.50 × $10,000 =	$5,000	$5,000	5,000
2	0.50 × 5,000 =	2,500	7,500	2,500
3	0.50 × 2,500 =	1,250	8,750	1,250
4	($1,250 - $1,000)=	250[a]	9,000	1,000
		$9,000		

[a]Using the formula, depreciation in Year 4 would be 0.50 × $1,250 = $625. The $250 depreciation shown results in a book value at the end of Year 4 equal to the estimated salvage value.

Salvage value is ignored under the double-declining-balance method, except that the asset cannot be depreciated below the salvage value. Thus, it will usually be necessary to plug the last year's depreciation to result in a book value equal to salvage value.

2213.51 If the asset had been acquired on April 1, Year 1, the depreciation for Years 1 and 2 would be computed as follows:

Year 1:	0.50 × $10,000 × (9/12) =	$3,750
Year 2:	0.50 × ($10,000 - $3,750) × (12/12) =	$3,125

2213.52 **Sum-of-the-years'-digits method.** Under this method, the depreciable base is multiplied by a fraction, the denominator of which is the sum of the years' digits in the asset's life, and the numerator is the remaining life at the beginning of the year. The formula for the denominator is:

$$\frac{N(N + 1)}{2}$$

The denominator for Munter Company is:

$$\frac{4(4 + 1)}{2} = 10$$

The depreciation for Munter would be determined as follows:

Year	Depreciation Expense		Accumulated Depreciation	Book Value
0				$10,000
1	4/10 × $9,000 =	$3,600	$3,600	6,400
2	3/10 × 9,000 =	2,700	6,300	3,700
3	2/10 × 9,000 =	1,800	8,100	1,900
4	1/10 × 9,000 =	900	9,000	1,000
		$9,000		

Note that the numerators of the fractions for the four years are simply the years' digits in reverse order.

2213.53 If the asset had been acquired on April 1, Year 1, the depreciation for Years 1 and 2 would be computed as follows:

Year 1:

$$\frac{4}{10} \times \$9{,}000 \times \frac{9}{12} = \underline{\$2{,}700}$$

Year 2:

$$\frac{4}{10} \times \$9{,}000 \times \frac{3}{12} = \underline{\$\ 900}$$

$$\frac{3}{10} \times \$9{,}000 \times \frac{9}{12} = \underline{\$2{,}025}$$

$$\$900 + \$2{,}025 = \underline{\$2{,}925}$$

2213.54 **Units-of-production (service life).** The units-of-production method relates depreciation expense to some activity base, such as units of output or service hours. To illustrate, assume that Munter Company estimated the asset (a machine) would be used a total of 20,000 hours during its useful life. The depreciation rate per machine hour would be:

($10,000 - $1,000) ÷ 20,000 hours = $0.45 per hour

If Munter used the machine 6,000 hours in Year 1, the amount of depreciation would be $2,700 (i.e., 6,000 hours × $0.45 per hour).

2213.55 **Group-or-composite depreciation:** Many companies compute depreciation by using the group-or-composite-depreciation method rather than calculating depreciation for each asset separately. The term "group" refers to a collection of similar assets. The term "composite" refers to a collection of dissimilar assets. The procedural aspects of the two methods are essentially the same. The composite method is demonstrated as follows:

Asset	Cost	Salvage Value	Depreciable Base	Estimated Life (Years)	Annual Depreciation
A	$20,000	$ 2,000	$18,000	4	$ 4,500
B	30,000	5,000	25,000	5	5,000
C	10,000	1,000	9,000	3	3,000
D	20,000	4,000	16,000	8	2,000
	$80,000	$12,000	$68,000		$14,500

Composite depreciation rate on cost: $14,500 ÷ $80,000 = 18.125%
Composite life: $68,000 ÷ $14,500 = 4.69 years

2213.56 The composite rate is applied to the balance in the asset account at the beginning of the year. If the balance in the asset account does not change, the group of assets will be depreciated to the estimated salvage value at the end of the composite life. Thus, in the example, if the balance in the asset account remains at $80,000, the group of assets will be depreciated to the $12,000 salvage value in 4.69 years.

2213.57 One of the underlying assumptions of the group-or-composite method is that assets in the group are regularly replaced with other assets similar to the ones being replaced. As an asset is retired or replaced, an entry is made to remove the original cost from the asset account, with the difference between original cost and the proceeds received being debited to accumulated depreciation. Thus, under normal conditions, no gain or loss is recognized on the retirement of a specific asset included in the group.

2213.58 For example, if asset C in the example is replaced at the end of Year 3 with asset E, costing $11,000, the related entries would be as follows:

```
Dec. 31, Yr. 3
    Cash                                    $   800
    Accumulated Depreciation                  9,200
        Asset (C)                                        $10,000
To record the disposal of asset C assuming proceeds from disposal of $800.

Dec. 31, Yr. 3
    Asset (E)                               $11,000
        Cash                                             $11,000
To record the acquisition of asset E.

Dec. 31, Yr. 3
    Depreciation Expense                    $14,500
        Accumulated Depreciation                         $14,500
To record depreciation for Year 3, computed as
    follows:

    Balance in asset account Jan. 1, Year 3           $80,000
    Composite rate                                    ×0.18125
        Depreciation—Year 3                            $14,500

Dec. 31, Yr. 4
    Depreciation Expense                    $14,681
        Accumulated Depreciation                         $14,681
To record depreciation for Year 4, computed as
    follows:

    Balance in asset account Jan. 1, Year 4           $81,000
    Composite rate                                    ×0.18125
        Depreciation—Year 4                            $14,681
```

Required Disclosures

2213.59 The following disclosures related to fixed assets and depreciation should be made in the financial statements or in the footnotes:

    a. Depreciation expense for the period

    b. Balances of major classes of depreciable assets, by nature or function, at the balance sheet date

    c. Accumulated depreciation, either by major classes of depreciable assets or in total, at the balance sheet date

    d. A general description of the method or methods used in computing depreciation with respect to major classes of depreciable assets

IFRS: Property, Plant and Equipment (IAS 16)

2213.60 According to IAS 16, the cost of an item of property, plant, and equipment comprises:

    (a) its purchase price, including import duties and non-refundable purchase taxes, after deducting trade discounts and rebates.

    (b) any costs directly attributable to bringing the asset to the location and condition necessary for it to be capable of operating in the manner intended by management.

(c) the initial estimate of the costs of dismantling and removing the item and restoring the site on which it is located, the obligation for which an entity incurs either when the item is acquired or as a consequence of having used the item during a particular period for purposes other than to produce inventories during that period.

IAS 16.31:

"**Measurement after recognition:** An entity shall choose either the cost model or the revaluation model as its accounting policy and shall apply that policy to an entire class of property, plant and equipment.

"**Revaluation model:** After recognition as an asset, an item of property, plant and equipment whose fair value can be measured reliably shall be carried at a revalued amount, being its fair value at the date of the revaluation less any subsequent accumulated depreciation and subsequent accumulated impairment losses. Revaluations shall be made with sufficient regularity to ensure that the carrying amount does not differ materially from that which would be determined using fair value at the end of the reporting period.

"If an asset's carrying amount is increased as a result of a revaluation, the increase shall be recognised in other comprehensive income and accumulated in equity under the heading of revaluation surplus. However, the increase shall be recognised in profit or loss to the extent that it reverses a revaluation decrease of the same asset previously recognised in profit or loss. If an asset's carrying amount is decreased as a result of a revaluation, the decrease shall be recognised in profit or loss. However, the decrease shall be recognised in other comprehensive income to the extent of any credit balance existing in the revaluation surplus in respect of that asset."

2220 Investments

Nature and Classification

2220.01 Long-term investments are shown in the balance sheet as a separate classification. Included in this classification are investments in stocks, bonds, and special-purpose funds that do not qualify as current assets. Normally, it is management's intent to hold these investments for an extended period of time.

2220.02 The accounting issues related to the various types of long-term investments are described in the remaining portion of this section.

Investments in Debt and Equity Securities

2220.03 FASB ASC 320-10-05-1 governs the accounting for all investments in debt securities and investments in equity securities that have readily determinable fair values except for the following:

 a. Investments in equity securities accounted for under the equity method

 b. Investments in consolidated subsidiaries

 c. Not-for-profit organizations

  However, it does apply to cooperatives and mutual enterprises, including credit unions and mutual insurance companies.

 d. Enterprises with specialized accounting practices relating to investments in debt and equity securities (e.g., brokers and dealers in securities)

2220.04 Investments in equity securities that do not have readily determinable fair values, such as investments in closely held corporations, are to be reported at cost. Even though the fair value of these securities may not be readily determinable, if there is evidence of an other-than-temporary decline in the value of the investment, the investment should be written down to a reasonable estimate of its fair value.

2220.05 Unless stated otherwise, the remaining discussion in this section focuses on investments in debt and equity securities accounted for under FASB ASC 320-10-05-1.

2220.06 **Debt securities** include all securities representing a *creditor* relationship with an enterprise (e.g., U.S. Treasury securities, U.S. government agency securities, municipal securities, corporate bonds, convertible debt, and commercial paper). Debt securities also include preferred stock that, by its terms, either must be redeemed by the issuing enterprise or is redeemable at the option of the investor.

2220.07 **Equity securities** include all securities representing an *ownership* interest in an enterprise (e.g., common, preferred, or other capital stock or the right to acquire (put options) an ownership interest in an enterprise at fixed or determinable prices). However, they do not include preferred stock that, by its terms, either must be redeemed by the issuing enterprise or is redeemable at the option of the investor.

2220.08 All investments in debt securities will be classified on the balance sheet in one of the following three categories:

   a. Held-to-maturity securities
   b. Trading securities
   c. Available-for-sale securities

Investments in equity securities that have a readily determinable fair value will be classified as either trading securities or available-for-sale securities.

2221 Financial Assets at Fair Value Through Profit or Loss

2221.01 Trading Securities

Trading securities include debt securities and readily marketable equity securities that are bought and held principally for the purpose of selling them in the near term. They generally reflect active and frequent buying and selling.

2221.02 Trading securities are recognized in the balance sheet at fair value. Unrealized holding gains and losses for trading securities are included in earnings.

2221.03 Example—Trading Securities

Assume that Beta Company began operations on January 1, 20X1. During 20X1, Beta purchased various marketable equity securities and on December 31, 20X1, purchased a debt security at face amount. The cost and fair value of these securities at the end of 20X1 were as follows:

	Shares or Face	Cost	Market	Unrealized Loss	Unrealized Gain
Red Co. stock	100 sh	$2,000	$2,500		$500
Blue Co. stock	100 sh	3,000	2,600	$400	
White Co. stock	100 sh	1,000	1,200		200
Pink Co. stock	100 sh	1,500	1,350	150	
Gold Co. debt	$1,000	1,000	1,060		60
		$8,500	$8,710	$550	$760

2221.04 Assume that Beta incurred the following transactions during 20X2:

a. Received dividends of $1 per share on the Red Co. stock.

b. Sold the White Co. stock for $1,250.

c. Sold the Pink Co. stock for $1,400.

d. Purchased 100 shares of Green Co. stock for $10 per share.

e. Received interest of $80 on the investment in Gold Co. debt.

2221.05 Assume that the cost and fair value of Beta's investments in securities at December 31, 20X2, were as follows:

	Shares or Face	Cost	Market	Unrealized Loss	Unrealized Gain
Red Co. stock	100 sh	$2,000	$2,200		$200
Blue Co. stock	100 sh	3,000	2,400	$600	
Green Co. stock	100 sh	1,000	1,150		150
Gold Co. debt	$1,000	1,000	1,080		80
		$7,000	$6,830	$600	$430

2221.06 Assuming all of the securities qualify as trading securities, the adjusting entry at the end of 20X1 is:

Valuation Allowance	$210	
Net Unrealized Holding Gain/Loss—Earnings		$210

2221.07 The *valuation allowance* account represents the difference between cost and fair value. A debit balance indicates that fair value is larger than cost, and a credit balance means that fair value is less than cost. Thus, the balance in the trading securities account plus any debit balance or less any credit balance in the valuation allowance account is equal to fair value, shown as follows for Beta Company at December 31, 20X1.

	Dr. (Cr.)
Trading securities account (cost)	$8,500
Valuation allowance	210
Trading securities, at fair value	$8,710

2221.08 Beta's trading securities would be reported on its December 31, 20X1, balance sheet in the current assets section at their fair value of $8,710.

2221.09 Since market of $8,710 is larger than cost of $8,500, Beta has experienced an unrealized holding gain of $210. Further, since these securities qualify as trading securities, the unrealized holding gain is included in net income. Thus, the *net unrealized holding gain or loss—net income* account is a temporary account (i.e., it is an income statement account) that reflects the change in the net unrealized gain or loss during the current period.

2221.10 The 20X2 transactions are recorded as follows:

Cash	$ 100	
Dividend Revenue		$ 100
Cash	$1,250	
Trading Securities (White Co.)		$1,000
Realized Gain		250
Cash	$1,400	
Realized Loss	100	
Trading Securities (Pink Co.)		$1,500
Trading Securities (Green Co.)	$1,000	
Cash		$1,000
Cash	$ 80	
Interest Revenue		$ 80

2221.11 The realized gain or loss is the difference between the sales price and the cost basis of the particular security. For example, the realized loss of $100 on the sale of the Pink Co. stock is the excess of the cost basis of $1,500 over the sales price of $1,400.

2221.12 The adjusting entry at December 31, 20X2, is:

Net Unrealized Holding Gain/Loss—Earnings	$380	
Valuation Allowance		$380

The $380 change in the valuation allowance account is determined as follows:

Valuation allowance balance needed at 12/31/X2:

	Dr. (Cr.)
Cost	$ 7,000
Market	6,830
Balance needed	(170)
Less valuation allowance balance at 01/01/X2	210
Change in valuation allowance in 20X2	$ (380)

2221.13 Beta's 20X2 income statement would include the following items related to its investment in trading securities:

Dividend revenue	$100
Interest revenue	80
Net realized gain (loss) ($250 - $100)	150
Net unrealized holding gain(loss)	(380)

2221.14 Beta's trading securities would be reported on its December 31, 20X2, balance sheet in the current assets section at their fair value of $6,830.

Financial Instruments

2221.15 A financial instrument is cash, evidence of an ownership interest in an entity, or a contract that both:

   a. imposes on one entity a contractual obligation to deliver cash or another financial instrument to a second entity or to exchange financial instruments on potentially unfavorable terms with the second entity and

   b. conveys to that second entity a contractual right to receive cash or another financial instrument from the first entity or to exchange other financial instruments on potentially favorable terms with the first entity.

2221.16 Some financial instruments are currently recognized as assets, and the amount recognized reflects the risk of accounting loss to the entity. Other financial instruments that are recognized as assets may expose the entity to a risk of accounting loss that exceeds the amount currently recognized in the balance sheet. The latter have off-balance-sheet risk.

2221.17 Some financial instruments are currently recognized as liabilities, and the amount needed to settle the obligation cannot exceed the amount recognized in the balance sheet. Other financial instruments that are recognized as liabilities expose the entity to a risk of accounting loss that exceeds the amount recognized in the balance sheet. The latter have off-balance-sheet risk.

2221.18 As discussed in section **2355,** derivative financial instruments must be recognized on the balance sheet as assets or liabilities at fair value. Other financial instruments currently may not be recognized as assets or liabilities but may expose the entity to a risk of accounting loss. These latter financial instruments have off-balance-sheet risk.

Information About Fair Value

2221.19 An entity must disclose, either in the body of the financial statements or in the notes, the fair value of financial instruments for which it is practicable to estimate that value. The fair value disclosed must be presented, together with the related carrying amount, in a form that makes it clear whether the fair value and carrying amount represent assets or liabilities and how the carrying amounts relate to what is reported in the balance sheet. The method or methods and significant assumptions used to estimate the fair value must also be disclosed.

2221.20 Quoted market prices, if available, are the best evidence of the fair value of financial instruments. If quoted market prices are not available, management's best estimate of fair value may be based on the quoted market price of a financial instrument with similar characteristics or on appropriate valuation techniques.

2221.21 *Practicable* means that an estimate of fair value can be made without incurring excessive costs. It is a dynamic concept. What is practicable for one entity might not be for another.

2221.22 If it is not practicable to estimate the fair value of a financial instrument or class of financial instruments, the following must be disclosed:

   a. Information pertinent to estimating the fair value of that instrument or class of instruments, such as the carrying amount, effective interest rate, and maturity

   b. The reasons why it is not practicable to estimate fair value

2221.23 No disclosure about fair value is required for trade receivables and payables as their carrying amount approximates their fair value.

Disclosures About Concentrations of Credit Risk of Financial Instruments

2221.24 An entity must disclose the following for all significant concentrations of *credit risk* arising from all financial instruments:

    a. Information about the (shared) activity, region, or economic characteristics that identifies the concentration

    b. The maximum amount of loss due to credit risk that, based on the gross fair value of the financial instrument, the entity would incur if parties to the financial instruments that make up the concentration failed completely to perform according to the terms of the contracts and collateral or other security, if any, for the amount due proved to be no value to the entity

    c. The entity's policy of requiring collateral or other security to support financial instruments subject to credit risk, information about the entity's access to that collateral or other security, and the nature and a brief description of the collateral or the other security supporting those financial instruments

    d. The entity's policy of entering into master netting arrangements to mitigate the credit risk of financial instruments, information about the arrangements for which the entity is a party, and a brief description of the terms of those arrangements, including the extent to which they would reduce the entity's maximum amount of loss due to credit risk

Disclosure About Market Risk of Financial Instruments

2221.25 An entity is encouraged, but not required, to disclose quantitative information about the *market risks* of financial instruments.

Derivative Financial Instruments

2221.26 Derivatives represent a particular subset of financial instruments. This complex subset is discussed in section **2355**.

2221.27 Some financial instruments have characteristics of both liabilities and equity. The classification of these financial instruments has been somewhat controversial. The FASB issued FASB ASC 480-10, *Distinguishing Liabilities from Equity*, which reduces at least some of the controversy. See section **2385** for a discussion of FASB ASC 480-10-10 as it relates to these issues.

2222 Available for Sale Financial Assets

2222.01 **Available-for-Sale Securities**

Available-for-sale securities are investments in debt securities and readily marketable equity securities that are not classified as held-to-maturity securities or as trading securities.

2222.02 These securities are recognized in the balance sheet at fair value. However, any related unrealized holding gains and losses are excluded from net income and reported as other comprehensive income. See section **2365** for a discussion of when an available-for-sale security is hedged by a derivative instrument.

2222.03 Dividend and Interest Income and Realized Gains or Losses

Dividend and interest income, including amortization of the premium or discount arising at acquisition, for all three categories of investments in securities shall continue to be included in earnings. In addition, realized gains and losses for securities classified as either available-for-sale securities or held-to-maturity securities shall continue to be reported in earnings.

2222.04 Transfers Between Categories of Investments

Transfers between categories shall be accounted for at fair value. Any unrealized holding gain or loss at the time of transfer shall be accounted for as follows:

a. Transfers from trading securities to either of the other two categories—the unrealized holding gain or loss will already have been recognized in earnings and shall not be reversed

b. Transfers into the trading securities category—the unrealized holding gain or loss shall be recognized in earnings immediately

c. Transfers into the available-for-sale category from the held-to-maturity category—the unrealized holding gain or loss shall be recognized as other comprehensive income

d. Transfers into the held-to-maturity category from the available-for-sale category—the unrealized holding gain or loss at the time of transfer shall continue to be reported as accumulated other comprehensive income in stockholders' equity but shall be amortized over the remaining life of the security as an adjustment of yield in a manner consistent with the amortization of any premium or discount

2222.05 Impairment of Securities

Individual securities classified as either available-for-sale or held-to-maturity shall be evaluated to determine whether a decline in fair value below the amortized cost basis is other than temporary. If so, the cost basis of the individual security should be written down to fair value and the amount of the write-down included in earnings.

2222.06 Financial Statement Presentation

If an enterprise presents a classified balance sheet, it should include trading securities in the current assets section. It should list individual held-to-maturity securities and individual available-for-sale securities as either current or noncurrent per FASB ASC 210-10-45. Accordingly, those held-to-maturity securities and available-for-sale securities that the enterprise expects to sell or that are scheduled to mature within the next year (or operating cycle, if longer) shall be classified as current assets; all others should be classified as noncurrent assets.

2222.07 Cash flows from purchases, sales, and maturity of available-for-sale securities and held-to-maturity securities shall be classified as cash flows from investing activities and reported gross for each security classification. Cash flows from purchases, sales, and maturity of trading securities shall be classified as cash flows from operating activities.

2222.08 Example—Available-for-Sale Securities

Assume the same information as that shown in sections **2221.03–.05** except assume that the securities qualify as available-for-sale securities rather than trading securities.

2222.09 The adjusting entry at the end of 20X1 (the first year) is as follows:

Valuation Allowance (Red Co.)	$500	
Valuation Allowance (White Co.)	200	
Valuation Allowance (Gold Co.)	60	
Valuation Allowance (Blue Co.)		$400
Valuation Allowance (Pink Co.)		150
Net Unrealized Holding Gain/Loss—OCI		210

OCI = other comprehensive income

This entry is quite similar to that shown before in section **2221.06** when the securities were assumed to be trading securities. However, notice the designation "OCI" (other comprehensive income) has been substituted for the words "net income" in the account credited. This difference in account title emphasizes that the balance in this account is included in other comprehensive income rather than in net income. In addition, for convenience, a separate valuation account has been set up for each security. Setting up a separate valuation account for each security makes it easier to identify the reclassification adjustments for each security at the end of the year. (A detailed discussion of other comprehensive income, including reclassification adjustments, is included in section **2133**) If separate valuation accounts are not maintained for each security, the adjusting entry at December 31, 20X1, is as follows:

Valuation Allowance	$210	
Net Unrealized Holding Gain/Loss—OCI		$210

2222.10 The balance in the net unrealized holding gain/loss—OCI account (a temporary account) is closed into the balance sheet account Accumulated OCI—AFS Securities as follows:

Net Unrealized Holding Gain/Loss—OCI	$210	
Accumulated OCI—AFS Securities		$210

2222.11 The accumulated OCI—AFS securities account has a credit balance of $210 and is included in the stockholders' equity section of the balance sheet.

2222.12 Beta's available-for-sale securities would be reported on its December 31, 20X1, balance sheet at their fair value of $8,710. Each security would be evaluated to determine whether it should be classified in current assets or in noncurrent assets. Those that are expected to be sold within the next year should be included in current assets. The others should be included in noncurrent assets.

2222.13 The entries to record the 20X2 transactions are as follows:

Cash	$ 100	
Dividend Revenue		$ 100
Cash	$1,250	
Available-for-Sale Securities (White Co.)		$1,000
Realized Gain		250
Cash	$1,400	
Realized Loss	100	
Available-for-Sale Securities (Pink Co.)		$1,500
Available-for-Sale Securities (Green Co.)	$1,000	
Cash		$1,000
Cash	$ 80	
Interest Revenue		$ 80

2222.14 Notice that the entries are the same as those shown in section **2221.10** for trading securities, except for the substitution of the account title "available-for-sale securities" for that of "trading securities."

2222.15 The adjusting entries necessary at December 31, 20X2, to record the *unrealized* gains and losses that occurred in 20X2 are as follows:

Net Unrealized Holding Gain/Loss—OCI $300
    Valuation Allowance (Red Co.) $300
To adjust the valuation allowance for the Red Co. shares for the decrease in fair value in 20X2 ($2,500 - $2,200) and recognize the $300 unrealized loss in other comprehensive income.

Net Unrealized Holding Gain/Loss—OCI $200
    Valuation Allowance (Blue Co.) $200
To adjust the valuation allowance for the Blue Co. shares for the decrease in fair value in 20X2 ($2,600 - $2,400) and recognize the $200 unrealized loss in other comprehensive income.

Valuation Allowance (White Co.) $ 50
    Net Unrealized Holding Gain/Loss—OCI $ 50
To adjust the valuation allowance for the White Co. shares to the fair value on the date they were sold, $1,250, and recognize this additional $50 unrealized gain ($1,250 selling price - $1,200 fair value at 12/31/X1) in other comprehensive income.

Valuation Allowance (Pink Co.) $ 50
    Net Unrealized Gain/Loss—OCI $ 50
To adjust the valuation allowance for the Pink Co. shares to the fair value on the date they were sold, $1,400, and recognize this additional $50 unrealized gain ($1,400 selling price - $1,350 fair value at 12/31/X1) in other comprehensive income.

Valuation Allowance (Gold Co.) $ 20
    Net Unrealized Gain/Loss—OCI $ 20
To adjust the valuation allowance for the Gold Co. investment for the increase in fair value in 20X2 ($1,080 - $1,060) and recognize the $20 unrealized gain in other comprehensive income.

Valuation Allowance (Green Co.) $150
    Net Unrealized Gain/Loss—OCI $150
To adjust the valuation allowance for the Green Co. shares purchased in 20X2 for the increase in fair value in 20X2 since their acquisition and recognize the $150 unrealized gain in other comprehensive income.

2222.16 For each security, the balance in the valuation account represents (at the balance sheet date or the date the securities were sold) the difference between the fair value of the securities and their cost. The balances for the individual securities are as follows:

	Cost	Fair Value	Valuation Allowance Dr. (Cr.)
Securities on hand at 12/31/X2:			
Red Co.	$2,000	$2,200	$ 200
Blue Co.	3,000	2,400	(600)
Green Co.	1,000	1,150	150
Gold Co.	1,000	1,080	80
	$7,000	$6,830	$(170)
Securities sold in 20X2:			
White Co.	$1,000	$1,250	$ 250
Pink Co.	1,500	1,400	(100)
	$2,500	$2,650	$ 150

2222.17 If valuation allowance accounts are not maintained for each security, the following summary entry would be recorded instead of the individual entries presented in section **2222.15**:

Net Unrealized Holding Gain/Loss—OCI	$380	
Valuation Allowance		$380

2222.18 At December 31, 20X2, the Net Unrealized Holding Gain/Loss – OCI account would be closed as follows:

Accumulated OCI-AFS Securities	$230	
Net Unrealized Holding Gain/Loss—OCI		$230

2222.19 FASB ASC 320-10-35-1 requires that unrealized gains and losses occurring during the year related to available-for-sale securities be recognized in other comprehensive income. It also requires that reclassification adjustments be recognized in other comprehensive income. For a given security, the reclassification adjustment is the cumulative net unrealized gain or loss that has been reported in other comprehensive income. It includes the unrealized gains and losses included in other comprehensive income in prior years plus the unrealized gain or loss included in other comprehensive income in the year in which the individual security is sold.

2222.20 Since Beta sold the White Co. and Pink Co. stock in 20X2, it must recognize in 20X2 the reclassification adjustments related to those shares. The entries could be made at the time of sale of the securities or, as a matter of convenience, at the end of the year. These entries that Beta records in 20X2 are:

Reclassification Adjustment (White Co.)—OCI	$250	
Valuation Allowance (White Co.)		$250

Entry used to transfer the balance in the valuation allowance related to the White Co. shares, at the time of sale of those shares (see section **2222.16**), to the reclassification adjustment. The balance is the difference between the sales price of the shares sold ($1,250) and the cost of those shares ($1,500).

Valuation Allowance (Pink Co.)	$100	
Reclassification Adjustment (Pink Co.)—OCI		$100

Entry used to transfer the balance in the validation allowance related to the Pink Co. shares, at the time of sale of those shares (see section **2222.16**), to the reclassification adjustment. The balance is the difference between the sales price of the shares sold ($1,400) and the cost of those shares ($1,500). The reclassification adjustment accounts now have a net $150 debit balance, as shown:

	Dr. (Cr.)
Reclassification adjustment related to White Co.	$250
Reclassification adjustment related to Pink Co.	(100)
Net balance at 12/31/20X2	$150

2222.21 The reclassification adjustment accounts are closed at the end of 20X2 as follows:

Accumulated OCI—AFS Securities	$150	
Reclassification Adjustment (Pink Co.)	100	
Reclassification Adjustment (White Co.)		$250

For both Pink Co. and White Co., this entry "zeroes out" the balances in their valuation allowance and reclassification adjustment accounts. In addition, the portion of the accumulated OCI—AFS securities account related to Pink and White is also eliminated. These zero balances are consistent with the fact that, as of the end of 20X2, there are no Pink Co. or White Co. shares left. Therefore, after closing entries, all balances related to those securities should be zero.

2222.22 The use of the reclassification adjustment account is a matter of convenience (just as the use of a dividends-declared account is to capture the amount of dividends declared during the year—instead of debiting the retained earnings account directly). If a reclassification adjustment account is not used, the entry to eliminate the valuation allowance accounts of White Co. and Pink Co. would be as follows:

Accumulated OCI—AFS Securities	$150	
Valuation Allowance (Pink Co.)	100	
Valuation Allowance (White Co.)		$250

2222.23 In 20X2, Beta would report the following items related to its investment in available-for-sale securities:

In net income:		
Dividend revenue	$100	
Interest revenue	80	
Net realized gain (loss) ($250 - $100)	150	
In other comprehensive income:		
Net unrealized gain (loss)	$(230)	
Less reclassification adjustment gain (loss)	(150)	$(380)

2222.24 Notice that the unrealized holding gain or loss is not included in Beta's income statement. Rather the $(170) balance at December 31, 20X2, is included in Beta's stockholders' equity section as follows:

Stockholder's equity:	
Common stock	$XXX
Retained earnings	XXX
Net unrealized holding gain (loss)	(170)
Total stockholders' equity	$XXX

Disclosure Requirements

2222.25 FASB ASC 320-10-50 also requires several specific disclosures. For debt securities classified as available-for-sale and separately for all securities classified as held-to-maturity, an enterprise must disclose the aggregate fair value, gross unrealized holding gains, gross unrealized holding losses, and amortized cost basis by major security type as of each date for which a balance sheet is presented.

2222.26 For investments in debt securities classified as available-for-sale and separately for all securities classified as held-to-maturity, an enterprise must disclose information about the contractual maturities of those securities as of the date of the most recent balance sheet presented. It must disclose the fair value and the amortized cost of debt securities based on at least four maturity groupings: (a) within one year, (b) after one year through five years, (c) after five years through 10 years, and (d) after 10 years.

2222.27 For each period for which the results of operations are presented, an enterprise must disclose the following:

    a. The proceeds from sales of available-for-sale securities and the gross realized gains and gross realized losses on those sales

    b. The basis on which cost was determined in computing realized gain or loss (e.g., specific identification, average cost, or other method)

    c. The gross gains and gross losses included in earnings from transfers of securities from the available-for-sale category into the trading category

    d. The change in net unrealized holding gain or loss on available-for-sale securities that has been included in the separate component of shareholders' equity during the period

e. The change in net unrealized holding gain or loss on trading securities that has been included in earnings during the period

2222.28 In addition, for any sales of or transfers from securities classified as held-to-maturity, the amortized cost amount of the sold or transferred security, the related realized or unrealized gain or loss, and the circumstances leading to the decision to sell or transfer the security must be disclosed.

2223 Held-to-Maturity Investments

2223.01 Only investments in debt securities will be classified in the held-to-maturity securities category since equity securities have no maturity date. Further, for the investment in the debt security to be included in this category, the reporting enterprise must have the positive intent and ability to hold the debt security to maturity. An investment in a debt security should not be included in this category if the enterprise has the intent to hold the security for an indefinite period.

2223.02 Investments classified as held-to-maturity securities are to be measured at amortized cost. Amortized cost is the acquisition cost adjusted for any amortized premium or discount. (The application of the amortized cost approach is demonstrated in detail in section **2225.39–.48**.)

2223.03 Most investments in debt securities included in the held-to-maturity category will be classified as noncurrent assets in the long-term investments section. However, those within one year of maturity should be classified as current assets.

2224 Joint Ventures

Joint Venture Accounting

2224.01 A joint venture is a legal arrangement between two or more companies to enter into an economic activity together. The goal is to share resources and/or expertise to accomplish a specific purpose. The joint venturers contribute assets or expertise to the joint venture and share in revenues, expenses, and control of the joint venture.

2224.02 In most cases, each joint venturer owns a specified equity interest in the joint venture and does not own any type of interest in the other joint venturers.

2224.03 Investments in joint ventures apply the equity method to account for their investment. This assumes that the company has significant influence but not control over the joint venture.

General Partnership Concepts

2224.04 A *partnership* is an association of two or more persons to carry on as co-owners a business for profit. While the partners are ordinarily natural persons, other partnerships and in some cases corporations can be partners in a partnership. While a formal partnership agreement is desirable, no formal written contract of any type is necessary to create a partnership. (UPA part 2, para. 6)

2224.05 As a form of business organization, the partnership can be characterized as follows:

a. **Limited life:** The death, retirement, bankruptcy, or incapacity of any partner results in the termination of the partnership.

b. **Ease of formation:** The lack of legal involvement (when contrasted to other forms of organization) makes the partnership one of the simplest forms of business organization to start in terms of both cost and time.

c. **Mutual agency:** Each partner has authority to act for the partnership and thus to obligate the other partners.

d. **Unlimited liability:** All partners are responsible for the debts of the organization, such responsibility extending to the personal assets of the partners. In a special form—the limited partnership—one or more partners is limited in liability to their investment in the firm.

e. **Organization not taxed:** The partnership pays no income taxes. Rather, the partners must claim their share of the partnership profits as individual income.

2224.06 While the partnership can be formed without legal approval, a written partnership agreement (i.e., articles of co-partnership) is desirable to specifically establish a variety of details concerning the organization. Examples of items that typically appear in the partnership agreement include the following:

a. Name, address, and nature of partnership

b. Names and addresses of partners

c. Authority, rights, and duties of partners

d. Date of inception of the partnership and duration of agreement

e. Procedures governing valuation of assets invested by partners, admission of new partners, withdrawal of partners, distribution of profits and losses, salaries of partners, and so on

f. Matters requiring the consent of partners and methods of arbitrating disputes

Partnership Accounts

2224.07 Partnership accounts typically consist of capital accounts, drawings accounts, and in some cases loans to and from partners.

2224.08 The capital and drawings accounts, kept separately for each partner, increase and decrease as a result of various activities, such as the following:

Capital Account

Decrease:	Increase:
Disinvestment by partner	Investments of assets by partners
Partner's share of net loss	Partner's share of net income
Close of drawings into capital account	

Drawings Account

Increase:	Decrease:
Withdrawal of assets by partner	Drawings closed into capital account

Numerous other situations, such as admission and retirement of partners and liquidation, also result in changes in the capital accounts. These are illustrated in examples that follow.

Distribution of Partnership Income/Loss

2224.09 If there is no statement in the partnership agreement concerning profit or loss distribution, all partners share equally in both profits and losses. Several factors, however, are frequently considered in establishing an agreement on profit or loss division.

a. Relative asset investment of partners

b. Relative time (service) investment of partners

c. Relative experience, expertise, and education of partners

2224.10 Agreements on the distribution of income or loss typically include some combination of the following: salaries to some or all partners, interest on capital balances, bonus to managing partner, and distribution of any residual in a fixed or determinable ratio.

2224.11 Example: H and J are partners who agree to share all profits and losses according to the following plan:

a. 5% bonus on income (after bonus) to H as managing partner (not applicable in net loss situations)

b. 10% interest to each on the average capital balance

c. Salaries of $20,000 to H and $15,000 to J

d. Remainder divided equally

Average capital balances during the year 20X1 for H and J were $50,000 and $75,000, respectively. In Case A, income before bonus is $100,000; in Case B, net loss is $25,000.

Case A

	Partner H	Partner J	Balance to Distribute
Step 1: Bonus to H B = 5% ($100,000 - B) = 4,762	$ 4,762	$ 0	$100,000 (4,762) $ 95,238
Step 2: Interest on capital to H: 10% ($50,000) = $5,000 to J: 10% ($75,000) = $7,500	5,000	7,500	(12,500) $ 82,738
Step 3: Salaries to H: $20,000 to J: $15,000	20,000	15,000	(35,000) $ 47,738
Step 4: Remainder	23,869 $53,631	23,869 $46,369	(47,738) $ 0
Allocation to H Allocation to J Total			$ 53,631 46,369 $100,000

Case B

	Partner H	Partner J	Balance to Distribute
Step 1: Bonus Not applicable	$ 0	$ 0	$(25,000) 0 $(25,000)
Step 2: Interest on capital. See case A	$ 5,000	$ 7,500	(12,500) $(37,500)
Step 3: Salaries. See case A	20,000	15,000	(35,000) $(72,500)
Step 4: Remainder ($72,500)/2 = ($36,250)	(36,250) $(11,250)	(36,250) $(13,750)	72,500 $ 0
Allocation to H			$(11,250)
Allocation to J			(13,750)
Total			$(25,000)

2224.12 The basis for allocation may include numerous steps; the cases mentioned previously are included here for illustrative purposes. It can be seen that the step-by-step procedure should be followed in cases of net income as well as net loss. In some cases, the balance to distribute might start as positive and become negative as you move through the steps. This would be the case in the previous example if net income were not large enough to absorb the bonus of step 1, the interest of step 2, and/or the salaries of step 3. The same procedure, however, should be followed with any residual negative balance distributed to the partners' capital accounts, as was done in case B.

Changes in Partners

2224.13 The admission or retirement of a partner results in the dissolution of the former partnership and the formation of a new partnership. The conditions under which partners are admitted or retired and the appropriate accounting that should be followed vary with the circumstances. In the following paragraphs, a number of situations are illustrated whereby changes in partners are recorded in the appropriate accounts. In each example, assume that H and J share profits and losses equally prior to any changes in partners.

2224.14 **Example: New Partner Buys Prior Partner's Interest**

	Capital Balances		Other Accounts	
	H	J		
	Dr(Cr)	Dr(Cr)	Dr(Cr)	Accounts
Balances before	$(100,000)	$(120,000)		
New partner M buys J's interest for $150,000 (with H's approval)		120,000	$(120,000)	M capital
Balances after	$(100,000)	0		

The amount that M pays J for the partnership interest is not recorded by the business itself but represents a personal transaction of the two partners. The $120,000 interest acquired is simply transferred from J to M as the entry indicates. This will result in M having an "outside basis" for personal tax purposes of $150,000, but an "inside basis" for partnership purposes of $120,000.

2224.15 Example: New Partner Added by Investment Other Than Cash

Capital Balances

	H Dr(Cr)	J Dr(Cr)	Other Accounts Dr(Cr)	Accounts
Balances before	$(100,000)	$(120,000)		
New partner Z admitted with investment of land valued at $75,000			$75,000 (75,000)	Land Z capital
Balances after	$(100,000)	$(120,000)		

Here Z's capital account is set up at the value of his investment, and the accounts of H and J are not changed.

2224.16 Example: Bonus Method to Previous Partner(s)

Capital Balances

	H Dr(Cr)	J Dr(Cr)	Other Accounts Dr(Cr)	Accounts
Balances before	$(100,000)	$(100,000)		
New partner X admitted with $130,000 for one-third interest with bonus divided equally	(10,000)	(10,000)	$(110,000) 130,000	X capital Cash
Balances after	$(110,000)	$(110,000)		

Partner X pays a premium price for the one-third interest. Assuming that the bonus method is used, the $20,000 premium ($130,000 - $110,000) is allocated to the existing partners according to their P & L ratio (50%:50%). The fact that X will pay the premium price indicates an undervaluation of the capital accounts of H and J. Under the bonus method, which is indicated here, the excess accrues to the existing partners on the basis that the increased value was created by H and J prior to X's admission to the partnership.

2224.17 Example: Goodwill Method to Previous Partner(s)

Capital Balances

	H Dr(Cr)	J Dr(Cr)	Other Accounts Dr(Cr)	Accounts
Balances before	$(100,000)	$(100,000)		
Same as 0.04 case with implied goodwill to be recognized	(30,000)	(30,000)	$(130,000) 130,000 60,000	X capital Cash Goodwill
Balances after	$(130,000)	$(130,000)		

Assume the same facts as those in section **2224.16**, except that the goodwill method will be used instead of the bonus method.

In that case, the fact that new partner X pays $130,000 implies that partnership net assets are worth $390,000 (i.e., $130,000 × 3). Goodwill of $60,000 is recognized and allocated to existing partners H and J in their P & L ratio (50%:50%).

2224.18 Example: Bonus Method to New Partner

	Capital Balances		Other Accounts	
	H Dr(Cr)	**J** Dr(Cr)	Dr(Cr)	Accounts
Balances before	$(100,000)	$(100,000)		
New partner A receives one-third interest for $70,000 with bonus to A deducted from H and J	10,000	10,000	$(90,000) 70,000	A capital Cash
Balances after	$ (90,000)	$ (90,000)		

Assuming the bonus method is used, new partner A is credited with one-third of total capital of $270,000 ($200,000 net assets of old partnership plus $70,000 contributed by A). The $20,000 excess of the $90,000 credited to A over the $70,000 contributed by A is deducted from the capital accounts of H and J in their P & L ratio (50%:50%).

2224.19 Example: Goodwill Method to New Partner

	Capital Balances		Other Accounts	
	H Dr(Cr)	**J** Dr(Cr)	Dr(Cr)	Accounts
Balances before	$(100,000)	$(100,000)		
New partner K receives one-third interest for $70,000 with goodwill to be recognized			$(100,000) 70,000 30,000	K capital Cash Goodwill
Balances after	$(100,000)	$(100,000)		

If goodwill were not recorded (i.e., if the bonus method is used), the new partner would be credited with one-third of the total capital of the new partnership, or $90,000, shown as follows (and in section **2224.18**):

New assets (capital) of old partnership	$200,000
New partner's contribution	70,000
Net assets (capital) of new partnership without goodwill	$270,000

The new partner's share would be one-third of $270,000, or $90,000. The main point is that the new partner (K) is being credited with more than the net assets the new partner is contributing. Accordingly, if goodwill is to be recorded, it will be credited to the new partner. In this case, the computation of the goodwill is based on the old partners' *existing* capital balances and on their combined P & L ratio *after* the admission of K as illustrated:

Implied value of new partnership:		
$200,000 divided by two-thirds		$300,000
Less: Net assets of new partnership excluding goodwill:		
Net assets of old partnership	$200,000	
New partner's contribution	70,000	270,000
Implied goodwill of new partnership		$ 30,000

2224.20 Example: Retiring Partner Receives More Than Capital Balance

Capital Balances

	H	J	Y	Other Accounts	
	Dr(Cr)	Dr(Cr)	Dr(Cr)	Dr(Cr)	Accounts
Balances before	$(100,000)	$(100,000)	$(100,000)		
Partner Y retires, receiving $115,000	7,500	7,500	100,000	$(115,000)	Cash
Balances after	$(92,500)	$(92,500)	0		

While the $15,000 excess over the capital balance of Y implies the existence of goodwill, it normally should not be recognized since it has not been purchased.

2224.21 Example: Retiring Partner Receives Less Than Capital Balance

Capital Balances

	H	J	Y	Other Accounts	
	Dr(Cr)	Dr(Cr)	Dr(Cr)	Dr(Cr)	Accounts
Balances before	$(100,000)	$(100,000)	$(100,000)		
Partner Y retires, receiving $90,000	(5,000)	(5,000)	100,000	$(90,000)	Cash
Balances after	$(105,000)	$(105,000)	0		

The fact that Y retires and receives less than Y's capital account results in a positive adjustment to the accounts of H and J.

2224.22 In several of the preceding cases, the goodwill method and the bonus method are both illustrated (e.g., sections **2224.16–2224.19**). Generally, the bonus method is preferable where the new partner pays an amount greater than book value on the basis that it adheres more closely to the historical cost concept and does not result in the recording of "implied" goodwill.

Partnership Liquidation

2224.23 The steps in the liquidation of a partnership are summarized as follows:

Step 1: Sale of assets with recognition of gains or losses in partners' capital accounts

Step 2: Payment of liabilities

Step 3: If a partner's account is negative, either (a) absorption of deficit by other partners or (b) additional asset contribution by partner

Step 4: Final distribution to partners

2224.24 **Example:** An example of the steps that would be followed is illustrated. While the specifics of the circumstances will vary from case to case, this is generally indicative of the process to be followed:

Statement of Liquidation

Description	Assets Cash	Assets Other	Liabilities	Partners' Capital H(1/3)	Partners' Capital J(1/3)	Partners' Capital Y(1/3)
Beginning balances	$ 20,000	$ 50,000	$50,000	$ 10,000	$ 5,000	$ 5,000
Step 1: Sales of assets for $32,000	32,000	(50,000)	—	(6,000)	(6,000)	(6,000)
	$ 52,000	0	$50,000	$ 4,000	$(1,000)	$(1,000)
Step 2: Payment of liabilities	(50,000)	—	(50,000)	—	—	—
	$ 2,000	—	—	$ 4,000	$(1,000)	$(1,000)
Step 3a: Absorption of Y deficit	—	—	—	(500)	(500)	1,000
	$ 2,000	—	—	$ 3,500	$(1,500)	—
Step 3b: Cash contribution by J	1,500	—	—	—	1,500	—
	$ 3,500	—	—	$ 3,500	—	—
Step 4: Cash distribution to H	$ (3,500)	—	—	$(3,500)	—	—

2224.25 Several variations in the illustration may emerge, depending on the particulars of the situation. The following situations are frequently encountered:

Situation	Appropriate Accounting
Creditors proceed against one partner's personal assets for satisfaction of claim against partnership	Reduce liabilities; increase partner's capital account for amount of liabilities paid
Capital account of one partner positive and other partner negative; partner with negative balance pays partner with positive balance directly	Reduce capital of partner with positive balance; increase capital of partner with negative balance for amount paid
A partner has a loan as well as a capital balance	Combine loan and capital balances before preparing liquidation statement

2224.26 The liquidation process may take place over a long period of time. Distributions that can be safely made to partners can be determined in advance by establishing priority among partners to receive cash as it becomes available. Such a schedule will avoid problem situations, such as a partner receiving cash and then later having a negative capital balance that requires a reinvestment by the same partner.

2224.27 **Example:** Partners H, J, and Y share profits and losses in the ratio of 5:3:2, respectively. Their capital balances prior to liquidation are $100,000, $90,000, and $25,000, respectively. A sample cash distribution schedule is prepared as follows:

Cash Distribution Schedule

	Partners		
	H (5/10)	J (3/10)	Y (2/10)
Capital balances	$100,000	$90,000	$25,000
P & L ratio	÷ 5	÷ 3	÷ 2
Capital balance / P & L ratio	$20,000	$30,000	$12,500
Priority 1:			
To reduce J to H		(10,000)	
	$20,000	$20,000	$12,500
Priority 2:			
To reduce H and J to Y	(7,500)	(7,500)	
	$12,500	$12,500	$12,500

Priorities in cash distribution after satisfaction of liabilities:

1. To J: $10,000 × 3 — $30,000
2. To H and J in 5:3 ratio as distributed:
   - H - $7,500 × 5 — $37,500
   - J - $7,500 × 3 — 22,500
3. Remainder in P & L ratio — 5/10, 3/10, 2/10

2224.28 It can be seen that no cash should be distributed to partner Y until J is paid $52,500 ($30,000 + $22,500) and H is paid $37,500. This distribution schedule should be applied after all liabilities are paid or sufficient cash is withheld for their satisfaction.

Fiduciary Accounting

2224.29 The term "fiduciary" refers to one who holds something in trust for another. In an accounting context, the term "fiduciary" is normally used to refer to the reporting done in cases of estates and trusts and insolvency or bankruptcy situations. In this section, a cursory overview is provided of the primary types of financial statements the CPA may encounter in dealing with the situations mentioned.

Estates/Trusts

2224.30 Accounting for estates and trusts is designed primarily for purposes of reporting to a court the accountability of the fiduciary or trustee. The responsibility of the fiduciary is increased by asset inflows to the fiduciary and decreased by asset outflows from the fiduciary.

2224.31 An important distinction in estate and trust accounting is that of principal and income. Inflows and outflows of assets to and from the fiduciary are separated into these two categories, since the fiduciary's responsibilities for the two types of assets typically vary. The principal includes assets received by the fiduciary, including interest earned and dividends declared prior to that time.

2224.32 The statement prepared periodically to report on the responsibility of the fiduciary is identified as the *Charge and Discharge Statement.* An example of such a statement, prepared on a pro forma basis, is presented here:

Estate of William X
Joseph Y, Executor
Charge and Discharge Statement
for the Period January 1, 20X1, to May 31, 20X1

As to Principal

I charge myself with		
Assets originally received	$XXX	
Assets subsequently discovered	XXX	
Gains on realization of principal assets	XXX	$XXX
I credit myself with		
Funeral and administrative expenses	$XXX	
Debts paid	XXX	XXX
Balance of estate principal		
Cash	$XXX	
Land	XXX	
Bonds in Co. M	XXX	$XXX

As to Interest

I charge myself with		
Estate income		$XXX
I credit myself with		
Expense charged to estate income	$XXX	
Distributions of income to beneficiaries	XXX	XXX
Balance of estate income		
Cash		$XXX

2224.33 It can be seen in the example statement that the inventory of principal assets must equal the difference between the charges and credits to the executor for principal assets. The same is true of income, wherein the balance of the income assets must equal the difference between charges and credits to the executor for income assets.

Insolvency/Bankruptcy

2224.34 *Insolvency* is a term used to describe a situation whereby an enterprise is incapable of paying currently maturing debt. *Bankruptcy* is a legal concept wherein the aggregate value of an enterprise's assets is not sufficient to pay its debts. An enterprise could be insolvent but not in bankruptcy (i.e., it might be unable to pay currently maturing debt, but if all assets were liquidated it would be capable of satisfying debt requirements).

2224.35 *A Statement of Affairs* (S of A) is prepared when an enterprise is exhibiting signs of financial difficulty and parties with a financial interest in the enterprise are attempting to make decisions on the appropriate course of action to take. The concept of the S of A is to measure assets at estimated realizable values and to show how the amounts expected to be generated from liquidation would be distributed to creditors and stockholders. While the traditional balance sheet is based on the concept of a going concern and assets are measured primarily at historical cost, the S of A is a listing of balance sheet items based on the assumption of liquidation and assets are measured at exit values (i.e., amounts expected to be realized on sale).

2224.36 An example of an S of A is presented as follows, based on assumed numbers for illustrative purposes:

Dollarless Corporation
Statement of Affairs
March 31, 20X1
(000 omitted)

Assets

| | Book Value | Valuation Adjustment | Net Realizable Value | Distribution | | | Net Unsecured |
				Fully Secured	Partially Secured	Unsecured	
Cash	$ 10	0	$ 10			$10	
Receivables	150	$(120)	30			30	
Machinery	100	(75)	25		$25		
Land	250	200	450	$425		25	
Other	300	(300)	0				
	$810	$(295)	$515	$425	$25		$65

Claims on Assets

| | Carrying Amount | Status of Claims | | |
		Fully Secured	Partially Secured	Unsecured
Liabilities				
Accounts payable	$ 35		$25	$10
Accrued expenses	25			25
Taxes payable	75			75
Interest accrued on bonds	25	$ 25		
Bonds payable	400	400		
	$560	$425	$25	$110
Deficiency to unsecured creditors				$(45)

Estimated payment to unsecured creditors ($65/$110)   59 cents per $1.00

Stockholders' equity	
Common stock (200 shares)	$200
Additional paid-in capital	100
Retained earnings (deficit)	(50)
	$250
Total liabilities & stockholders' equity	$810

2224.37 The following points provide insight into the S of A and refinements in the preparation of the statement not illustrated:

    a. The valuation adjustment represents the amount needed to adjust assets to reflect the current fair value as opposed to the carrying value in the accounting system.

    b. Fully secured claims are matched with assets against which claims are held; any excess expected to be available is allocated to unsecured claims (e.g., bonds payable matched with land in the example).

    c. Partially secured claims are matched with assets against which claims are held; excess payables become part of unsecured claims (e.g., accounts payable—machinery in example S of A).

d. Some unsecured claims have legal priority over others. Examples of priority items are costs of administering bankruptcy, wages to employees (subject to specified limitations), and taxes (subject to specified limitations). Among unsecured claims, these are covered before distributions are made to other unsecured claims.

e. Residual amounts available for unsecured creditors are compared with unsecured claims to determine the status of unsecured creditors and stockholders. In the example S of A, amounts available ($65) were insufficient to cover unsecured claims ($110), resulting in a deficiency ($45). If amounts available had been $235, however, the S of A would appear as follows:

Amount available to unsecured claims		$235
Unsecured claims		110
Available for stockholders		$125
Stockholders' equity		
Common stock	$200	
Additional paid-in capital	100	
Retained earnings (deficit)	(50)	250
Deficiency to stockholders		$125
Estimated payments to stockholders ($125/200 shares)	$0.625	per share

2224.38 After an enterprise declares bankruptcy and a receiver or trustee (i.e., fiduciary) is appointed, periodic reports on the activities of the fiduciary are prepared. Such a report is called a *statement of realization and liquidation* (S of R/L).

2224.39 A pro forma S of R/L is presented as follows, illustrating the format of the statement and its major categories: assets, liabilities, and revenues and expenses.

Folding Company
Statement of Realization and Liquidation
for the Period January 1, 20X1, to June 30, 20X1
Submitted by Fred Dollar, Trustee

Assets

Assets to be realized:			Assets realized:			
Accounts receivable	$XX		Accounts receivable	$XX		
Inventory	XX		Inventory	XX		
Investments	XX		Investments	XX	$ XX	
Land	XX	$XX				
Assets acquired:			Assets not realized:			
Accounts receivable	$XX		Accounts receivable	$XX		
Notes receivable	XX	XX	Inventory	XX		
			Land	XX		
			Notes receivable	XX	XX	

Liabilities

Liabilities liquidated:			Liabilities to be liquidated:		
Accounts payable	$XX		Accounts payable	$XX	
Interest payable	XX	XX	Interest payable	XX	
			Mortgage payable	XX	XX
Liabilities not liquidated:			Liabilities added:		
Mortgage payable	$XX		Taxes payable	$XX	
Taxes payable	XX		Trustee fee payable	XX	XX
Trustee fee payable	XX	XX			

Revenues and Expenses

Expenses:			Revenue:		
Taxes	$XX		Sales		XX
Trustee fee	XX	XX			$XX
			Net loss		XX
		$XX			$XX

2224.40 The following observations are helpful in understanding the S of R/L:

a. *Assets to be realized* and *assets acquired* constitute the total group of assets available to the trustee. *Assets realized* are the assets converted to cash during the period. *Assets not realized* are those that have not been converted at the end of the period.

b. *Liabilities to be liquidated* are liabilities to be paid from available assets at the beginning of the period and *liabilities added* are those that were incurred during the period. *Liabilities liquidated* are those which were paid during the period and *liabilities not liquidated* are those that remain unpaid at the end of the period.

c. *Revenues* and *expenses* represent a continuation of the income-producing activities of the enterprise during bankruptcy. The net loss for the period is shown at the bottom of the statement. If there had been a net income for the period, it would be added on the left side of the statement.

d. It should be observed that cash is omitted from the S of R/L. Since the statement is prepared on the basis of realization of cash, cash itself (which has already been realized) is omitted. The court would receive a detailed account of the cash flow activities during the period along with the S of R/L.

2225 Equity Method Investments (Investments in Associates)

Investment in Stocks

2225.01 An enterprise that acquires shares of stock of another entity is referred to as an *investor*. The entity whose stock the investor acquires is an *investee*.

2225.02 The accounting method that should be used by an investor to account for the investment in an investee depends on the following:

a. The nature of the stock of the investee

b. The degree of influence or control the investor exercises over the investee

The decisions involved in selecting the appropriate accounting method are summarized in the following flowchart.

Accounting for Investment in Stocks

```
                    ┌─────────────────┐
                    │ Investor owns   │
                    │ stock of        │
                    │ investee        │
                    └────────┬────────┘
                             │
              No      ┌──────▼──────┐
        ┌────────────│   Common    │
        │            │    stock?   │
        │            └──────┬──────┘
        │                   │ Yes
        │            ┌──────▼──────┐
        │            │    Does     │
        │            │ investor own│    Yes    ┌──────────────┐
        │            │ over 50% of ├──────────▶│  Parent-sub  │
        │            │   voting    │           │ relationship │
        │            │  stock of   │           │    exists    │
        │            │  investee?  │           └──────┬───────┘
        │            └──────┬──────┘                  │
        │                   │ No                      ▼
        │            ┌──────▼──────┐           ┌─────────────┐
        │     No     │    Does     │    No     │    Are      │
        │   ┌────────│  investor   │◀──────────│ statements  │
        │   │        │   have      │           │to be consol-│
        │   │        │ability to   │           │   idated    │
        │   │        │ influence   │           │ statements? │
        │   │        │  investee?  │           └──────┬──────┘
        │   │        └──────┬──────┘                  │ Yes
        │   │               │ Yes                     ▼
        │   │               │                  ┌─────────────┐
        │   ▼               │           No     │ Appropriate │
        │ ┌──────────┐      │        ┌─────────│ to include  │
        │ │ Is stock │      │        │         │    sub in   │
        │ │marketable│      │        │         │consolidated │
        │ │  equity  │      │        │         │ statements? │
        │ │ security?│      │        │         └──────┬──────┘
        │ └─┬──────┬─┘      │        │                │ Yes
        │No │      │ Yes    │        │                ▼
        ▼   │      ▼        ▼        ▼         ┌──────────────┐
 ┌────────┐ │ ┌────────┐ ┌────────┐            │ Include sub's│
 │Use cost│ │ │  Use   │ │  Use   │            │ accounts in  │
 │method  │ │ │ fair   │ │ equity │            │ consolidated │
 │or LCM  │ │ │ value  │ │ method │            │  statements  │
 │if other│ │ │ method │ │        │            └──────────────┘
 │than    │ │ └────────┘ └────────┘
 │temp.   │ │
 │decline │ │
 │in value│ │
 │below   │ │
 │ cost   │ │
 └────────┘ │
```

2225.03 As the flowchart indicates, long-term investments in *stocks* other than common stock (e.g., preferred stock) are accounted for at fair value if the stock qualifies as a marketable equity security; otherwise, the cost method should be used. However, investments for which the cost method (as described in section **2225.08–.12**) is used should be written down to market value if there has been an other-than-temporary decline in market value below cost. Accounting for marketable equity securities (both current and noncurrent) is described in section **2220**.

2225.04 If an investor owns a controlling interest in the voting stock of an investee, normally the investor (parent) should prepare consolidated financial statements and include the accounts of the investee (subsidiary) in those statements.

Ability to Exercise Significant Influence

2225.05 Other investments in voting stock of the investee (i.e., if the investor does not own a controlling interest) should be accounted for by the equity method if the investor has the ability to exercise significant influence over the operating and financial policies of the investee. If the investor does not have the ability to exercise significant influence, the fair value, the cost method, or the lower of cost or market method should be used, whichever is appropriate.

2225.06 As a general rule, ownership of less than 20% (direct or indirect) of the voting stock of the investee leads to the presumption that an investor does not have the ability to exercise significant influence. This presumption can be overcome, however, if the ability to exercise significant influence can be demonstrated in other ways. Examples of circumstances that may indicate the investor has the ability to exercise significant influence over the investee even though it owns less than 20% of the voting shares of the investee include the following:

   a. Representation on the investee's board of directors,
   b. Participation in the investee's policy-making processes
   c. Material intercompany transactions with the investee
   d. Interchange of managerial personnel
   e. Technological dependency of the investee on the investor

2225.07 As a general rule, the ownership of 20% or more of the voting stock of the investee leads to the presumption that, in the absence of evidence to the contrary, the investor has the ability to exercise significant influence over the investee. Examples of possible evidence to the contrary which might cause this presumption to be overcome include the following:

   a. Opposition by the investee, such as litigation, challenges the investor's ability to exercise significant influence.
   b. The investor and investee sign an agreement under which the investor surrenders significant rights as a shareholder.
   c. Majority ownership of the investee is concentrated among a small group of shareholders who operate the investee without regard to the views of the investor.
   d. The investor needs or wants more financial information to apply the equity method than is available to the investee's other shareholders, tries to obtain that information, and fails.
   e. The investor tries and fails to obtain representation on the investee's board of directors.

Fundamentals of Cost and Equity Methods

2225.08 **Cost method:** The investor records and maintains the investment account at cost. Earnings of the investee are recognized as income by the investor only as received by the investor in the form of dividends.

2225.09 **Equity method:** The investor initially records the investment at cost. Subsequent to acquisition, the investor adjusts the carrying amount of the investment to recognize the investor's share of the earnings or losses of the investee after the date of acquisition.

2225.10 The amount of the adjustment is included in the net income of the investor and reflects adjustments similar to those made in preparing consolidated statements. The types of adjustments include those necessary to:

    a. recognize the investor's share of the investee's reported earnings or losses,

    b. eliminate intercompany gains and losses, and

    c. amortize any difference between cost of the investment and the investor's equity in the net assets of the investee. (However, any difference that is attributable may not be amortized.)

2225.11 Dividends received from an investee reduce the carrying amount of the investment but are not included in the income of the investor.

2225.12 The general types of entries for the two methods are illustrated as follows:

Cost Method	Equity Method
a. Acquisition of 40% of stock of investee at a cost of $48,000; book value of stockholders' equity of investee is $100,000.	

Inv. in investee $48,000
  Cash $48,000
	Inv. in investee $48,000
	  Cash $48,000

b. Cash dividends of $5,000 are declared and paid by investee during the year.	

Cash $2,000
  Income from investee $2,000
	Cash $2,000
	  Inv. in investee $2,000

c. Investee reports net income of $10,000 during the year.	
(no entry)	Inv. in investee $4,000 Income from investee $4,000
d. Amortization of $8,000 excess of cost over 40% of book value of investee; assume attributable to depreciable assets that have a remaining life of 10 years.	
(no entry)	Inv. from investee $800 Income in investee $800
e. Elimination of 40% of $3,000 intercompany profit included in investee's inventory at year-end.	
(no entry)	Income from investee $1,200 Inv. in investee $1,200

Additional Consideration When Equity Method Is Used

2225.13 The investor's ownership percentage is based on voting stock, whether common or preferred. However, the investor's share of the investee's earnings or losses is based on *common* stock.

2225.14 The investment should be shown in the investor's balance sheet as a single amount. The investor's share of earnings or losses from continuing operations of an investee should be shown in the income statement as a single amount. The investor's share of special items (extraordinary items, discontinued operations, cumulative effect of a change in accounting principle, and prior-period adjustments) should be classified in the same manner as the special item is classified by the investee, unless the investor's share of the special item is immaterial in the income statement of the investor.

2225.15 The investor should ordinarily discontinue applying the equity method when the investment account is reduced to zero unless the imminent return to profitable operations by the investee appears to be assured. If the investee subsequently reports net income, the investor should resume applying the equity method only after its share of that net income equals the share of net losses not recognized during the period the equity method was suspended.

2225.16 The investor's ownership percentage may decrease below the level required for the equity method to be used. In such a case, the investor should switch to the cost method (or LCM if a marketable equity security) on a prospective basis. The balance in the investment account at the time of the switch would be considered to be cost for purposes of applying the cost method.

2225.17 On the other hand, an investment that was previously accounted for by other than the equity method may become qualified for use of the equity method by an increase in the investor's ownership percentage. When this occurs, the investor should switch to the equity method on a retroactive basis. The investment, results of operations (current and prior periods), and retained earnings of the investor should be adjusted retroactively. (The retroactive application of the equity method is demonstrated in sections **2328.14–2438.22**.)

Special Problems in Accounting for Investments in Stocks

2225.18 The appropriate treatment of stock dividends, stock splits, and stock rights is discussed in this section.

Stock Dividends and Splits

2225.19 Stock dividends do not constitute income to the investor. A stock dividend takes nothing from the property of the corporation and adds nothing to the interests of the stockholders; that is, the corporation's property is not diminished and the interests of the stockholders are not increased. The proportional interest of each shareholder remains the same. However, the carrying amount per share is affected by the stock dividend, as demonstrated in the following example.

2225.20 **Example:** Before receipt of a 10% stock dividend (one additional share for each 10 shares owned), Investor Company owns 100 shares of common stock of Investee Company. The balance in the Investee Company account is $6,600.

	Before 10% Stock Dividend	After 10% Stock Dividend
Balance in investment account	$6,600	$6,600
Divided by numbers of shares owned	÷ 100	÷ 110
Carrying amount per share	$ 66	$ 60

2225.21 Stock splits are treated by the investor in the same manner as stock dividends.

Stock Rights

2225.22 Corporations sometimes issue certificates, known as warrants, that give the holder of the warrant the right to purchase a specified number of shares of stock at a specified price within a specified time period. In some cases, these warrants are issued to existing stockholders as a means of either:

  a. complying with any preemptive right associated with that class of stock or

  b. aiding the sale of additional shares of stock.

In such cases, the stockholder is entitled to one right for each new share of stock owned but more than one right may be required to purchase one new share of stock. For example, the purchase of one share of stock may require two rights plus $60.

2225.23 If the rights enable the holder to purchase stock below the market price, the rights have a value themselves. After their issuance, they may be purchased and sold like any other security.

2225.24 After the corporation declares the intention to issue stock rights, the stock will sell "rights on" until the date of record. The stock will then sell "ex-rights."

2225.25 The recipient of stock rights has the following three alternative courses of action:

    a. Exercise the right in purchasing shares of stock.

    b. Sell the right.

    c. Allow the right to expire.

2225.26 Since the corporation issuing the stock rights has not distributed any assets, the recipient of the rights should treat the rights in a manner similar to stock dividends. Accordingly, the investor (recipient) should allocate the carrying amount of the stock already owned between the stock and the rights. The allocation should be on the basis of relative fair values.

2225.27 As noted in section **2220.07** stock rights are included in the definition of equity securities. Since the stock rights are equity securities, they should be accounted for in the same manner as investments in other equity securities (per FASB ASC 320-10-20). Accordingly, they must be classified as either trading securities or available-for-sale securities and accounted for as described in section **2220.**

2225.28 You may wish to review section **2220** for the discussion of the accounting for investment in equity securities. This section focuses on the accounting problems that are unique to investments in stock rights.

2225.29 You are to assume in the discussion in sections **2225.30–.36** that the shares of stock already held and the stock rights received are both properly classified as available-for-sale (AFS) securities.

2225.30 Assume that Investor Company holds shares of Investee Company and in 20X1 receives one stock right for each share of stock held. Assume the following information:

Shares owned by Investor Company before receipt of rights	1,000
Carrying amount of investment (balance of available-for-sale (AFS) account)	$105,000
Rights received in 20X1 (one right for each share of stock owned)	1,000
Terms of exercise of rights: Two rights plus $170 for each new share of stock purchased	
Market value (FMV): Common stock (per share):	
Rights on	$200
Ex-rights	190
Stock rights (per right)	$ 10

2225.31 The $105,000 carrying value of the Investee Company stock held by Investor Company should be allocated between the shares held and the stock rights being received, as follows:

Allocation of carrying amount:

To rights:

$$\frac{\text{MV of one right}}{\text{MV of one share of stock ex-rights + MV of one right}} \times \begin{array}{c}\text{Carrying amount}\\ \text{of stock before}\\ \text{rights received}\end{array}$$

$$\frac{\$10}{\$190 + \$10} \times \$105,000 = \$5,250$$

To "old" shares of stock:

$$\frac{\text{MV of one share of stock ex-rights}}{\text{MV of one share of stock ex-rights + MV of one right}} \times \begin{array}{c}\text{Carrying amount}\\ \text{of stock before}\\ \text{rights received}\end{array}$$

$$\frac{\$190}{\$190 + 10} \times \$105,000 = \underline{\$\ 99,750}$$

$$\underline{\$105,000}$$

Total allocated

Carrying amount per unit:

Rights	$5,250 / 1,000	= $ 5.25	
Stock	$99,750 / 1,000	= $99.75	

2225.32 The entry on receipt of the stock rights is:

AFS Securities (Stock Rights)	$5,250	
AFS Securities		$5,250

(See calculation of amount in section **2225.31**.)

2225.33 If the investor (the recipient of the rights) immediately sold the rights for the market price of $10 each, the entry would be:

Cash	$10,000	
AFS Securities (Stock Rights)		$5,250
Realized Gain		4,750

2225.34 Assume, on the other hand, that the investor held the rights and sold them during the next year (20X2) for $9,300 and that the rights had a market price of $9,400 at the end of the year in which the investor received the rights (20X1). The related entries would be:

Valuation Allowance	$4,150	
Net Unrealized Holding Gain/Loss—Equity		$4,150

To recognize, for balance sheet purposes, the difference at 12/31/X1 between fair market value of $9,400 and cost basis (carrying value) of $5,250.

Cash	$9,300	
AFS Securities (Stock Rights)		$5,250
Realized Gain		4,050

To record realized gain or loss on sale of stock rights—the difference between sale price of the rights and the cost basis of the rights.

Assuming these were the only rights held by Investor Company, since the rights were sold the following adjusting entry would be required at the end of 20X2:

Net Unrealized Holding Gain/Loss—Equity	$4,150	
Valuation Allowance		$4,150
To reverse out at 12/31/X2 the balances in these accounts since Investor Company no longer owns the rights.		

2225.35 Assume that instead of selling the rights, Investor Company, on receipt of the 1,000 rights, immediately exercised them, receiving 500 shares of stock (1,000 rights ÷ 2 rights per new share). The entry to record their exercise would be:

Investment in Investee Stock (500 shares)	$90,250	
Cash ((1,000 ÷ 2) × $170)		$85,000
AFS Securities (Stock Rights)		5,250

2225.36 If Investor Company should allow the rights to expire instead of selling or exercising them, a realized loss equal to the carrying value of the rights would be recognized at the expiration date as shown:

Realized Loss from Expired Stock Rights	$5,250	
AFS Securities (Stock Rights)		$5,250

2225.37 The CPA Examination candidate may be asked to allocate the carrying amount of the old stock without the market value of the rights being given. In such cases, the allocation can be made by using one of the following formulas, depending on whether the market value (MV) of stock is given as rights on or as ex-rights:

$$\text{Theoretical MV of one right} = \frac{\text{MV of one share of stock ex-rights} - \text{Exercise price per share for new stock}}{\text{Number of rights to buy one share}}$$

$$\text{Theoretical MV of one right} = \frac{\text{MV of one share of stock rights on} - \text{Exercise price per share for new stock}}{\text{Number of rights to buy one share} + 1}$$

2225.38 **Example:** Using the facts presented in section **2225.30** where the stock was selling ex-rights at $190 per share, the theoretical market value of each right would be:

$$\frac{\$190 - \$170}{2} = \$10$$

If the market value had been stated as $200 rights on, the theoretical market value would be:

$$\frac{\$200 - \$170}{2 + 1} = \$10$$

Investments in Debt Securities

2225.39 The accounting for investments in debt securities is specified by FASB ASC 320-10. Investments in debt securities shall be classified as held-to-maturity securities if the enterprise has the positive intent and ability to hold those securities to maturity. Otherwise, the investments should be classified as trading securities or as available-for-sale securities and reported on the balance sheet at fair value. (See section **2220** for a discussion of the reporting of debt securities and marketable equity securities classified as trading securities or as available-for-sale securities.)

2225.40 Held-to-maturity securities are accounted for using the amortized cost method. They are carried at original cost adjusted for the amortization of any discount or premium. A single account is more of a tradition than a requirement; the discount or premium could be set up in a separate account.

2225.41 Amortization of Discount or Premium

The discount or premium should be amortized by using the interest method. Other methods, such as the straight-line method, may be used if the results obtained are not materially different from those that would result from the interest method.

2225.42 The various computations and entries associated with long-term investments in bonds are illustrated in the following example:

Facts: On January 1, Year 1, Alpha Company purchased $100,000 face value, 3-year, 8% bonds of Beta Company for $94,924, which provides an effective interest rate of 10%. The bonds pay interest semi-annually on June 30 and December 31.

2225.43 The amount of the discount is $5,076, determined as follows:

Face value of bonds	$100,000
Price paid	94,924
Discount	$ 5,076

2225.44 Since candidates may be required to solve problems using either method, the amortization of discount is presented as follows under both the interest method and the straight-line method.

2225.45 It is helpful to set up an amortization schedule first, such as the ones presented as follows:

Amortization Schedule—Interest Method				
Date	Cash Interest (4% Semi-annual)	Effective Interest (5% Semi-annual)	Discount Amortization	Carrying Value of Bonds
01/01/Yr. 1				$ 94,924
06/30/Yr. 1	$4,000^a	$4,746^b	$746^c	95,670^d
12/31/Yr. 1	4,000	4,784	784	96,454
06/30/Yr. 2	4,000	4,823	823	97,277
12/31/Yr. 2	4,000	4,864	864	98,141
06/30/Yr. 3	4,000	4,907	907	99,048
12/31/Yr. 3	4,000	4,952	952	100,000

^{a} $0.04 \times \$100,000$
^{b} $0.05 \times \$94,924$
^{c} $\$4,746 - \$4,000$
^{d} $\$94,924 + \$746$

Amortization Schedule—Straight-Line Method				
Date	Cash Interest (4% Semi-annual)	Effective Interest (5% Semi-annual)	Discount Amortization	Carrying Value of Bonds
01/01/Yr. 1				$ 94,924
06/30/Yr. 1	$4,000	$4,846[b]	$846[a]	95,770[c]
12/31/Yr. 1	4,000	4,846	846	96,616
06/30/Yr. 2	4,000	4,846	846	97,462
12/31/Yr. 2	4,000	4,846	846	98,308
06/30/Yr. 3	4,000	4,846	846	99,154
12/31/Yr. 3	4,000	4,846	846	100,000

[a] $5,076 discount × (6 months ÷ 36 months) = amortization per 6-month period
[b] $4,000 + $846
[c] $94,924 + $846

2225.46 Entries for the first year and at the maturity date under the two methods would be:

	Interest Method		S-L Method	
01/01/Yr. 1				
Investment in Bonds	$ 94,924		$ 94,924	
Cash		$ 94,924		$ 94,924
06/30/Yr. 1				
Cash	$ 4,000		$ 4,000	
Investment in Bonds	746		846	
Interest Income		$ 4,746		$ 4,846
12/31/Yr. 1				
Cash	$ 4,000		$ 4,000	
Investment in Bonds	784		846	
Interest Income		$ 4,784		$ 4,846
12/31/Yr. 3				
Cash	$ 4,000		$ 4,000	
Investment in Bonds	952		846	
Interest Income		$ 4,952		$ 4,846
Cash	$100,000		$100,000	
Investment in Bonds		$100,000		$100,000

2225.47 The last entry assumes the bonds are held to maturity. If the bonds are sold before maturity, any difference between the carrying value of the bonds at the date of sale and the proceeds received would be recognized as a gain or loss. For example, assume that the bonds are sold on December 31, Year 2, after receiving the interest payment, for $98,000. The sale would be recorded as follows:

	Interest Method		S-L Method	
12/31/Yr. 2				
Cash	$98,000		$98,000	
Loss on Sale of Bonds	141		308	
Investment in Bonds		$98,141		$98,308

2225.48 The accounting for bond investments becomes slightly more complicated if the bonds are purchased between interest payment dates or if the end of the accounting year does not coincide with an interest payment date. To illustrate, assume the 3-year bonds in the example were originally issued on April 30, Year 1, and were purchased on August 31, Year 1, for $94,924 plus accrued interest, with the bonds paying interest semi-annually on April 30 and October 31. Entries through October 31, Year 2, under the straight-line method would be:

Purchase of Bonds

08/31/Yr. 1
Investment in Bonds	$94,924	
Interest Receivable[a]	2,667	
Cash		$97,591

[a] $\$100,000 \times 0.08 \times 4/12 = \$2,667$

Receipt of Interest Payment and Amortization of Discount

10/31/Yr. 1
Cash	$4,000	
Interest Receivable (4 months)		$2,667
Interest Income (2 months)		1,333
Investment in Bonds[b]	$ 318	
Interest Income		$ 318

[b]
Amount of discount	$5,076
÷ Number of months to maturity	32
Amortization per month (rounded to nearest $1)	$ 159
$159 × 2 months (September and October)	$ 318

Year-End Adjusting Entries

12/31/Yr. 1
Interest Receivable[c]	$1,333	
Interest Income		$1,333
Investment in Bonds[d]	$ 318	
Interest Income		$ 318

[c] $\$100,000 \times 0.08 \times 2/12 = \$1,333$
[d] Amortization for November and December ($159 × 2)

Receipt of Interest Payment and Amortization of Discount

04/30/Yr. 2
Cash	$4,000	
Interest Receivable		$1,333
Interest Income		2,667
Investment in Bonds[e]	$ 636	
Interest Income		$ 636

[e] Amortization for first four months of Year 2 ($159 × 4)

Receipt of Interest Payment and Amortization of Discount

10/31/Yr. 2
Cash	$4,000	
Interest Income		$4,000
Investment in Bonds ($159 × 6)	$ 954	
Interest Income		$ 954

Impairment of a Loan

2225.49 FASB ASC 310-10-35-16 specifies that a loan is impaired when, based on current information and events, it is probable that a creditor will be unable to collect all amounts due (both principal and interest) according to the contractual terms of the loan agreement. For purposes of applying FASB ASC 310-10-20, a loan is a contractual right to receive money on demand or on fixed or determinable dates recognized as an asset in the creditor's balance sheet. Examples include accounts receivable with terms exceeding one year and notes receivable.

2225.50 FASB ASC 310-10-35-13 applies to all loans, uncollateralized as well as collateralized, except the following:

a. Large groups of smaller-balance homogeneous loans that are collectively evaluated for impairment, such as credit cards, residential mortgages, and consumer installment loans

b. Loans that are measured at fair value or at lower of cost or fair value

c. Leases

d. Debt securities as defined in FASB ASC 320-10

2225.51 When a loan is impaired, a creditor shall measure the impairment based on the present value of expected future cash flows discounted at the loan's effective interest rate, except that as a practical matter, a creditor may measure impairment based on a loan's observable market price or the fair value of the collateral if the loan is collateral dependent. (A loan is collateral dependent if the repayment of the loan is expected to be provided solely by the underlying collateral.)

2225.52 If the measure of the impaired loan is less than the recorded investment in the loan, a creditor shall recognize an impairment by creating a valuation allowance with a corresponding charge to bad-debt expense or by adjusting an existing valuation allowance for the impaired loan with a corresponding charge or credit to bad-debt expense.

2225.53 Subsequently, if there is a significant change (increase or decrease) in the amount or timing of an impaired loan's expected future cash flows, or if actual cash flows are significantly different from those previously projected, a creditor shall recalculate the impairment. The net carrying amount of the loan shall at no time exceed the recorded investment in the loan.

Illustrative Example

2225.54 Assume that on December 31, 20X1, Baker Company issued a $200,000, 10%, 4-year, unsecured note to Third National Bank. Interest payments are to be made annually on December 31 of each year, with the principal amount due on December 31, 20X5. The note was issued to yield 10% annual interest. Since the stated and effective interest rates are each 10%, the note was issued at the face amount of $200,000 with no discount or premium. Therefore, Baker Company received, and Third National Bank paid, $200,000 on December 31, 20X1.

2225.55 The entries to record this transaction on the books of Third National Bank (creditor) and Baker Company (debtor) are:

Third National Bank (creditor):
12/31/X1   Notes Receivable $200,000
                  Cash $200,000

Baker Company (debtor):
12/31/X1   Cash $200,000
                  Notes Payable $200,000

2225.56 If the interest and principal payments are paid when due, Third National Bank will recognize interest revenue of $20,000 in each of the years 20X2–20X5.

2225.57 Baker made the interest payment due on December 31, 20X2. However, early in 20X3 (after Third National Bank's 20X2 financial statements had been issued) Baker's business took a sudden downturn. As a result, Third National Bank reevaluated Baker's loan and concluded that it is probable that Baker will be able to pay only 60% of the interest and principal payments due. Thus, Third National Bank expects Baker to make interest payments of $12,000 on December 31, 20X3, December 31, 20X4, and December 31, 20X5, and a principal payment of $120,000 on December 31, 20X5.

2225.58 The following present value table for $1 at 10% will prove helpful in the discussion that follows.

Periods	Present Value Factor
1	0.90909
2	0.82645
3	0.75132
4	0.68301

2225.59 Since Third National Bank concluded that it is probable that Baker will be unable to pay all of the interest and principal payments due, it must recognize an impairment loss in 20X3 as follows:

Recorded investment in the note		$200,000
Present value of estimated future payments discounted to 01/01/X3 at the historical effective interest rate of 10% (see present value table in section **2225.58**):		
Principal ($120,000 × 0.75132)	$90,158	
Interest due 12/31/X3 ($12,000 × 0.90909)	10,909	
Interest due 12/31/X4 ($12,000 × 0.82645)	9,917	
Interest due 12/31/X5 ($12,000 × 0.75132)	9,016	120,000
Impairment loss		$ 80,000

2225.60 Assuming that Third National Bank has not previously recognized any bad-debts expense related to Baker Company's note, the entry to record the impairment loss is:

01/01/X3	Bad Debts Expense	$80,000	
	Allowance for Uncollectible Accounts		$80,000

2225.61 If Third National Bank had previously recognized bad-debts expense related to Baker Company's note, the impairment loss recognized on January 1, 20X3, would be adjusted accordingly. For example, if Third National Bank had previously recognized bad-debts expense related to Baker Company's note of $5,000, the entry in section **2225.60** would be for $75,000 rather than $80,000.

2225.62 Assuming that Third National Bank's estimate of the interest payment to be made by Baker on December 31, 20X3, is correct, the entry to record the interest payment is:

12/31/X3	Cash	$12,000	
	Interest Revenue		$12,000

Subsequent Reevaluation

2225.63 Assume that early in 20X4 (after Third National Bank issued its 20X3 financial statements), Third National Bank reevaluates Baker Company's loan and now concludes that it is probable that Baker Company will pay 80% (instead of the 60% estimated one year ago) of the principal amount due December 31, 20X5, and 80% of the interest payments due on December 31, 20X4, and December 31, 20X5. In that event, Third National Bank must remeasure the impairment as follows:

Recorded investment in the note		$200,000
Present value of estimated future payments discounted to 01/01/X4 at the historical effective interest rate of 10% (see present value table in section **2225.58**):		
Principal ($160,000 × 0.82645)	$132,232	
Interest due 12/31/X4 ($16,000 × 0.90909)	14,545	
Interest due 12/31/X5 ($16,000 × 0.82645)	13,223	160,000
Revised impairment loss		$ 40,000

2225.64 The revised impairment loss is the balance now needed in the allowance for bad debts account. Therefore, the allowance for bad debts account and bad debts expense (the impairment loss) must be adjusted as shown:

	Dr. (Cr.)
Current balance in Allowance for Bad Debts	$(80,000)
Balance needed in allowance account 01/01/X4	(40,000)
Adjustment on 01/01/X4	$ 40,000

The entry to record the adjustment on 01/01/X4 is:		
Allowance for Bad Debts	$40,000	
Bad Debts Expense		$40,000

2225.65 FASB ASC 310-10-35-40 requires that one of two alternative income recognition methods be used to account for changes in the net carrying amount of an impaired loan subsequent to the initial measure of impairment. Under the first method, a creditor would accrue interest on the net carrying amount of the impaired loan and report other changes in the net carrying amount of the loan as an adjustment to bad-debts expense. Under the second method, a creditor would recognize all changes in the net carrying amount of the loan as an adjustment to bad-debts expense.

2225.66 FASB ASC 310-10-35-37 specifies that methods other than those described in section **2225.65** may be used to account for changes in the net carrying amount of an impaired loan subsequent to the initial measure of impairment. Thus, under FASB ASC 310-10-35-37, the creditor may use either of the methods in section **2225.65** or may use some other reasonable method.

Accounting for Convertible Bonds

2225.67 **Convertible bonds:** Bonds that may be converted at the option of the holder into other securities (usually common stock) of the issuing company. The conversion usually must take place within a specified time period and is based on a stated conversion ratio. The conversion ratio is the number of shares of common stock or other security the bondholder is entitled to receive for each bond converted.

Recording Issuance

2225.68 Theoretically, the conversion feature has an economic value in that the bond should sell at a higher price with the conversion feature than without it. However, primarily because of the inseparability of the debt and the conversion option, FASB ASC 470-20-25-12 requires that no part of the proceeds from the issuance of convertible debt should be accounted for as attributable to the conversion feature. Accordingly, the issuance of convertible debt is accounted for in the same manner as the issuance of straight debt.

Recording Conversion

2225.69 The conversion of debt into common stock by the holder poses a problem to the issuer of which basis to use to record the conversion. The following two alternative methods or bases are currently acceptable:

1. The carrying amount of the debt converted (book value method)
2. The fair value of the stock issued (fair value method)

2225.70 To illustrate, assume that bonds with a face amount of $100,000 and a carrying amount of $104,000 are converted into common stock at the ratio of 10 shares of $10 par common stock for each $1,000 bond. The market price of the stock is $116 per share.

2225.71 The entry under each method is presented as follows:

Carrying Amount of Bonds Used as Basis for Recording

Bonds Payable	$100,000	
Bond Premium	4,000	
Common Stock (1,000 × $10 par)		$10,000
Capital in Excess of Par		94,000

Computations:
$100,000 ÷ $1,000 face per bond = 100 bonds converted
100 bonds × 10 shares per bond = 1,000 shares of stock

Fair Value of Stock Used as Basis for Recording

Bonds Payable	$100,000	
Bond Premium	4,000	
Loss on Conversion of Bonds	12,000	
Common Stock		$ 10,000
Capital in Excess of Par		106,000

Computations:
Fair value of stock = 1,000 shares × $116 price per share
Loss on conversion:

Fair value of stock issued	$116,000
Carrying amount of bonds	104,000
	$ 12,000

2225.72 Use of the fair value of the stock, with the recognition of gain or loss, is consistent with the accounting treatment required for early extinguishment of debt. It is also consistent with the idea that an exchange has taken place; therefore, fair value should be used.

2225.73 One of the chief arguments in favor of using book value as the basis for recording the conversion is that it is not appropriate to recognize gains and losses arising from transactions in a company's own stock. It is further argued that the substance of the transaction is the substitution of one form of security for another. It is not an exchange in the sense that this term is normally used.

2225.74 The book value method is used most widely in practice.

Induced Conversions of Convertible Debt

2225.75 An induced conversion of debt is one in which the issuer of the debt either:

    a. changes the conversion privileges in a convertible debt instrument or

    b. pays additional consideration to convertible debt holders for the purpose of inducing prompt conversion of the debt to equity securities.

In such cases, the question arises as to whether the induced conversion should be accounted for as other conversions (with no gain or loss recognized) or as an extinguishment of debt (with gain or loss recognized).

2225.76 FASB ASC 470-20-40-15 specifies that the debtor enterprise should recognize an expense equal to the fair value of all securities and other consideration transferred in the transaction in excess of the fair value of securities issuable pursuant to the original conversion terms.

2225.77 The expense recognized should not be reported as an extraordinary item.

2225.78 **Example:** Assume that on January 1, 20X1, ABC Company issues at par a $1,000 face amount, 10% convertible bond maturing in 20 years on December 31. The bond is convertible into common stock of ABC at a conversion price of $25 per share. On January 1, 20X4, the convertible bond has a market value of $1,700. To induce convertible bondholders to convert their bonds promptly, ABC reduces the conversion price to $20 for bondholders who convert prior to February 28, 20X4. The market price of ABC's $10 par common stock on the date of conversion is $40 per share.

2225.79 The fair value of the securities issuable pursuant to the original terms is:

Face amount of bond	$1,000	
divided by original conversion price	÷ $ 25	per share
= Number of common shares issuable pursuant to original conversion terms	40	shares
times price per common share	× $ 40	per share
= Fair value of securities issuable pursuant to original conversion terms	$1,600	

2225.80 The fair value of the securities issued to debt holders under the revised conversion term is:

Face amount of bonds	$1,000	
divided by new conversion price	÷ $ 20	per share
= Number of common shares issued upon conversion	50	shares
times price per common share	× $ 40	
= Fair value of securities issued	$2,000	

2225.81 Therefore, the fair value of the incremental consideration is:

Fair value of securities issued (see section **2225.80**)	$2,000
Fair value of securities issuable pursuant to original conversion terms (see section **2225.79**)	1,600
Fair value of incremental consideration	$ 400

2225.82 The entry to record the conversion of the bond is:

Convertible Debt	$1,000	
Debt Conversion Expense	400	
Common Stock (50 shares × $10 par)		$ 500
Additional Paid-in Capital		900

Disclosure of Long-Term Obligations

Unconditional Purchase Obligations

2225.83 The accounting for unconditional obligations associated with certain project financing arrangements currently presents some unsettled measurement problems. Some argue that such unconditional purchase obligations result in participants acquiring ownership interests and obligations that should be recognized on their balance sheets. On the other hand, others argue that these obligations merely result in commitments that should be disclosed but not recorded.

2225.84 An example of such an unconditional purchase obligation would be a company entering into a take-or-pay contract with a refinery to purchase 40% of the planned capacity production of certain types of gasoline each period while the debt used to finance the refinery is outstanding. The monthly payments might include, for example, 40% of raw material (crude oil) costs, operating expenses, depreciation, interest on the debt used to finance the refinery, and a return on the owners' equity investment. The arrangement assures the purchaser a supply of gasoline but, at the same time, obligates the purchaser to pay for the specified quantity even if the purchaser should voluntarily take a lesser quantity.

2225.85 Currently, the FASB has elected to delay consideration of the accounting measurement issues related to unconditional purchase obligations related to project financing arrangements until further work is completed on the project. However, the FASB has addressed the *disclosure* requirements related to such unconditional purchase obligations.

2225.86 The specific unconditional purchase obligations addressed by the FASB are those that have all of the following characteristics:

    a. Is noncancelable or cancelable only:

        (1) on the occurrence of some remote contingency

        (2) with the permission of the other party

        (3) if a replacement agreement is signed between the same parties

        (4) on payment of a penalty in an amount such that continuation of the agreement appears reasonably assured

    b. Was negotiated as part of arranging financing for the facilities that will provide the contracted goods or services or for costs related to those goods or services

    c. Has a remaining term in excess of one year

Unrecorded Unconditional Purchase Obligations

2225.87 If unconditional purchase obligations that have all of the listed characteristics have not been recognized (recorded) as a liability on the balance sheet, the purchaser must disclose the following:

    a. The nature and term of the obligation(s)

      b. The amount of the fixed and determinable portion of the obligation(s) as of the date of the latest balance sheet presented in the aggregate and, if determinable, for each of the five succeeding fiscal years

      c. The amount of any variable components of the obligation(s)

      d. The amounts purchased under the obligation(s) for each period for which an income statement is presented

2225.88 Disclosure of the present value of these *unrecorded* unconditional purchase obligations is encouraged but not required. If present value is disclosed, the appropriate discount rate is the initial interest rate of the borrowing that financed the facility that will provide the contracted goods or services, if known by the purchaser. If that rate is unknown to the purchaser, the purchaser's incremental borrowing rate should be used.

Recorded Unconditional Purchase Obligations

2225.89 In some cases, unconditional purchase obligations having the characteristics set forth in section **2225.86** are recorded (rather than merely disclosed) by the purchaser as an asset and a related liability. In such cases, the purchaser should also disclose the aggregate amount of payments for such unconditional purchase obligations for each of the five years following the date of the latest balance sheet presented.

Disclosures of Other Long-Term Obligations

2225.90 Whether they have unconditional purchase obligations or not, enterprises are required to make the following disclosures related to long-term obligations for each of the five years following the date of the latest balance sheet presented:

      a. The combined aggregate amount of maturities and sinking fund requirements for all long-term borrowings

      b. The amount of redemption requirements for all issues of capital stock that are redeemable at fixed or determinable prices on fixed or determinable dates, separately by issue or combined

2226 Investment Property

Cash Surrender Value of Life Insurance

2226.01 Enterprises often carry life insurance policies on the lives of key officers and employees. If the enterprise is the beneficiary, the cash surrender value of the policy is an asset of the enterprise. The amount to be charged to expense is the amount of such premiums paid less the increase in cash surrender value during the period. For example, if Company X pays an annual premium of $3,000 on a policy covering its president, the entry during a year when the cash surrender value increased by $600 would be:

Insurance Expense	$2,400	
Cash Surrender Value	600	
Cash		$3,000

2226.02 At the time of death of an insured officer or employee, a gain would be recognized equal to the excess of the face amount of the policy over the cash surrender value at the time, as presented:

Cash	XXX	
Cash Surrender Value		XXX
Gain from Proceeds of Life Insurance		XXX

Special-Purpose Funds

2226.03 Enterprises will sometimes set aside cash for special purposes, such as a sinking fund for the retirement of bonds. Some of these funds are placed under the control of an external trustee, whereas others are managed by internal personnel.

2226.04 Funds set aside to meet specific current obligations arising from operations are usually classified as current assets. Other special-purpose funds are classified as long-term investments.

2226.05 In general, the types of entries associated with special funds are those presented as follows:

```
Establishment of the fund:
    Special Fund Cash                              XXX
        Cash                                             XXX

Investment of special fund cash in investments:
    Special Fund Investments                       XXX
        Special Fund Cash                                XXX

Earnings (losses) of the fund:
    Special Fund Cash                              XXX
    Special Fund Expenses                          XXX
        Special Fund Revenues                            XXX

Use of fund for specified purpose:
    Bonds Payable, Building, etc.                  XXX
        Special Fund Cash                                XXX
```

2230 Intangible Assets – Goodwill and Other

2230.01 Goodwill represents the reputation, business contacts, staff relationships, and industry experience that make a business more than a collection of assets.

2230.02 Goodwill is a residual number. It is recognized when it is purchased as part of the acquisition of another company. The amount recognized is the excess of the purchase price over the aggregate fair value of the identifiable assets acquired.

2230.03 Goodwill is discussed below at section **2230.16–.22** ("Nature of Intangible Assets") and in detail at section **2315.12–.32** as part of "The Acquisition Method."

Casualty Insurance (Coinsurance)

2230.04 Most companies carry some type of casualty insurance on their fixed assets as well as on other assets. Many insurance companies include a coinsurance clause in these policies. A coinsurance requirement provides that if the property is insured for less than a certain percentage of the fair market value at the time of loss, the insurance company will be liable for only a portion of the loss; the insured in effect becomes a coinsurer with the insurance company.

2230.05 When an insurance policy contains a coinsurance clause, the amount recoverable from the insurance company is limited to the lesser of the following three amounts:

1. Face of the policy
2. Amount of the loss (based on fair market value)
3. Amount of loss adjusted for coinsurance requirement

2230.06 When only a single insurance policy is involved, the coinsurance limitation is:

$$\frac{\text{Face of policy}}{\text{Coinsurance percentage} \times \text{FMV of asset}} \times \text{Loss}$$

2230.07 The impact of the coinsurance requirement is demonstrated in the following independent cases, in which a building with a fair market value of $50,000 is damaged by fire.

Case	Coinsurance Percentage	Face of Policy	Amount of Loss	Coinsurance Limitation	Amount Recoverable
1	None	$20,000	$40,000	None	$20,000
2	90%	20,000	40,000	$17,778^a	17,778
3	60%	20,000	40,000	26,667^b	20,000
4	50%	30,000	10,000	12,000^c	10,000

^{a}($20,000 \div (0.90 \times \$50,000)) \times \$40,000 = \$17,778$
^{b}($20,000 \div (0.60 \times \$50,000)) \times \$40,000 = \$26,667$
^{c}($30,000 \div (0.50 \times \$50,000)) \times \$10,000 = \$12,000$

2230.08 If an asset is insured under two or more policies, the amount recoverable is still limited to the lesser of the three amounts identified in section **2230.05** except that item (2) the fair market value of loss is prorated among the policies in the ratio of the face amount of the individual policy to the face amount of all policies.

2230.09 To illustrate, assume a building with a fair market value of $100,000 suffers a $30,000 loss and is insured under the four policies identified as follows:

Policy Number	Coinsurance Percentage	Face of Policy	Prorated Amount of Loss$^{(a)}$	Coinsurance Limitation	Amount Recoverable
1	None	$10,000	$ 5,000	None	$ 5,000
2	50%	20,000	10,000	$12,000$^{(b)}$	10,000
3	80%	10,000	5,000	3,750$^{(c)}$	3,750
4	90%	20,000	10,000	6,667$^{(d)}$	6,667
		$60,000	$30,000		$25,417

$^{(a)}$(Face of policy ÷ Total face of all policies) × Loss
$^{(b)}$($20,000 \div (0.50 \times \$100,000)) \times \$30,000 = \$12,000$
$^{(c)}$($10,000 \div (0.80 \times \$100,000)) \times \$30,000 = \$3,750$
$^{(d)}$($20,000 \div (0.90 \times \$100,000)) \times \$30,000 = \$6,667$

Natural Resources/Depletion

2230.10 Natural resources include timber, oil, gas, coal, and other types of wasting assets. In general, the accounting issues associated with extraction and sale of natural resources are similar to those encountered in the manufacture and sale of products. For example, the following accounting problems, among others, are common to both types of operations:

   a. Distinguishing between capitalizable costs and expenses

   b. Determining inventory quantities and costs

   c. Matching expired costs with the appropriate revenue or time periods

2230.11 The type of costs incurred and the specific accounting methods followed will vary somewhat according to the type of natural resource. The accounting methods used may also vary among enterprises involved in the extraction and sale of the same type of natural resource (e.g., oil or gas) because more than one accounting method is recognized as being generally accepted.

2230.12 Notwithstanding these possible variations in types of costs and accounting methods, the accounting for a natural resource involves the determination of the cost of the natural resource and the allocation of that cost to revenue. The allocation of the cost of the natural resource is known as *depletion*.

2230.13 The depletion charge is usually determined by using the unit-of-production method. The depletion charge per unit is computed as follows:

$$\frac{\text{Capitalized natural resource costs}}{\text{Total estimated units economically recoverable}} = \text{Depletion charge per unit}$$

The depletion charge per unit is revised as the numerator and/or denominator changes. Thus, the depletion charge is accounted for prospectively based on the revised amounts of unamortized cost and estimated recoverable units; past depletion charges are not revised.

2229.14 The depletion charge is determined by multiplying the number of units produced during the accounting period by the depletion charge per unit. The depletion charge becomes a part of cost of goods sold in the period in which the natural resource is sold.

2230.15 For income tax purposes, the depletion charge allowed for certain natural resources may be based on a specified percentage of revenue with certain restrictions as to the total depreciation charge. This method of determining the depletion charge (for income tax purposes) is known as *percentage depletion*.

Intangible Assets Other Than Goodwill

Nature of Intangible Assets

2230.16 Intangible assets are assets other than financial assets that lack physical substance. Their value stems from the rights their ownership confers. They may be categorized according to several different bases, four of which are the following:

    a. Identifiability—separately identifiable or lacking specific identification

    b. Manner of acquisition—acquired singly, in groups, in business combinations, or developed internally

    c. Expected period of benefit—limited by law or contract, related to human or economic factors, or indefinite or indeterminate duration

    d. Separability from an entire enterprise—rights transferable without title, saleable, or inseparable from the enterprise or a substantial part of it

2230.17 Some of the most common types of intangible assets are patents, copyrights, trademarks or trade names, franchises, licenses, and goodwill.

2230.18 Intangible assets do not include financial assets such as bank deposits, accounts receivable, and long-term investments in bonds and stocks. Financial assets lack physical substance, but they are not classified as intangible assets.

2230.19 An intangible asset should be recognized as an asset apart from goodwill if it arises from *contractual* or other *legal* rights. Otherwise, it should be recognized as an asset apart from goodwill only if it is *separable* (i.e., it is capable of being separated or divided from the acquired entity and sold, transferred, licensed, rented, or exchanged).

2230.20 The following are examples of intangible assets that meet the criteria for recognition apart from goodwill because they meet the contractual-legal criterion:

    a. Trademarks or trade names

    b. Internet domain names

    c. Noncompetition agreements

    d. Royalty agreements

    e. Franchise agreements

    f. Patented technology

    g. Computer software

    h. Trade secrets

2230.21 The following are examples of intangible assets that do not arise from contractual or other legal rights, but nonetheless should be recognized as assets apart from goodwill because they meet the separability criterion:

    a. Customer lists

    b. Unpatented technology

    c. Databases

2230.22 This section addressed the accounting for intangible assets other than goodwill. Thus, unless stated otherwise, the use of the term "intangible assets" in this section (section **2230**) will refer to all intangible assets other than goodwill. The accounting for goodwill is addressed in section **2315**.

Accounting for Costs at Acquisition: Purchased Intangibles

2230.23 **Acquired singly:** Intangible assets acquired separately should be recorded at cost at the date of acquisition. As in the case of the acquisition of other assets, cost is the fair value of the consideration given or the fair value of the asset received, whichever is more clearly evident.

2230.24 **Acquired as part of a group and is identifiable:** Specifically identifiable assets acquired as part of a group of assets should also be recorded at cost at the date of acquisition. The particular accounting problem involved is the allocation of the total cost of the group of assets to the individual assets acquired. The problem is just another example of a lump-sum acquisition. As in the case of other lump-sum acquisitions, the individual assets acquired are assigned part of the total cost of the group of assets based on their relative fair values.

2230.25 **Acquired as part of a group and is unidentifiable:** The acquisition of a major part or all of another enterprise may result in the recognition of the intangible asset known as "goodwill." The amount assigned to goodwill is the excess of the cost of the group of assets or enterprise acquired over the sum of the fair values of the identifiable net assets acquired. A more detailed discussion of the accounting for goodwill is presented in section **2315.12–.55**.

Accounting for Costs at Acquisition: Internally Developed Intangibles

2230.26 Costs of developing, maintaining, or restoring intangible assets generally should be expensed as incurred. Most costs incurred internally to develop "intangible assets" (such as patents and formulas) are research and development costs, which are expensed as incurred. (The accounting for research and development costs is discussed in section **2388**.)

Determining the Useful Life of an Intangible Asset

2230.27 Determining the useful life of an intangible asset is important because the accounting for an intangible asset is based on whether it has a finite or indefinite life. An intangible asset with a finite life is amortized over its useful life. An intangible asset with an indefinite life is not amortized but is reviewed annually for impairment.

2230.28 The useful life of an intangible asset is defined in FASB ASC 350-30-20 as "the period over which the asset is expected to contribute directly or indirectly to future cash flows of that entity." All relevant information should be considered when estimating the useful life of an intangible asset. FASB ASC 350-30-35-3 lists the following as specific items that should be considered:

    a. The expected use of the asset by the entity

    b. The expected useful life of another asset or group of assets to which the useful life of the intangible asset may relate (such as mineral rights to depleting assets)

    c. Any legal, regulatory, or contractual provisions that may limit the useful life

    d. Any legal, regulatory, or contractual provisions that enable renewal or extension of the asset's legal or contractual life without substantial cost (provided there is evidence to support renewal or extension and renewal or extension can be accomplished without material modifications of the existing terms and conditions)

    e. The effects of obsolescence, demand, competition, and other economic factors (such as the stability of the industry, known technological advances, legislative action that results in an uncertain or changing regulatory environment, and expected changes in distribution channels)

    f. The level of maintenance expenditures required to obtain the expected future cash flows from the asset (e.g., a material level of required maintenance in relation to the carrying amount of the asset may suggest a very limited useful life)

2230.29 If there are no legal, regulatory, contractual, competitive, economic, or other factors that limit the useful life of an intangible asset to the entity, the useful life of the asset is considered to be indefinite. The term "indefinite" does not mean infinite, but that the life extends beyond the foreseeable horizon (i.e., there is no foreseeable limit to the period of time over which the intangible asset is expected to contribute to the cash flows of the entity).

2230.30 Some intangible assets are based on legal rights that are conveyed in perpetuity or are indefinitely renewable. Those assets may result in cash flows for many years or even indefinitely. If the cash flows are expected to continue for a finite time, the useful life of an intangible asset is limited to that finite period. If the cash flows are expected to continue indefinitely, the useful life of the intangible asset is indefinite rather than finite.

Intangible Assets with Indefinite Useful Lives

2230.31 An intangible asset that has an indefinite life should not be amortized until its useful life is determined to no longer be indefinite.

2230.32 The useful life of the asset should be evaluated annually to determine whether it should be revised. If the asset should be determined to no longer have an indefinite life, it should be amortized from that point on a prospective basis.

2230.33 After acquisition, it may be necessary to evaluate the intangible asset to determine if it is impaired. The impairment of long-lived assets is discussed in section **2370.01–.27**.

Intangible Assets with Finite Useful Lives

2230.34 An intangible asset with a finite useful life should be amortized over its useful life to the reporting entity. There is no arbitrary maximum amortization period. (The 40-year maximum amortization period previously prescribed by APB Opinion 17 was deleted by FASB ASC 350-30-35-14.)

2230.35 It is possible that the intangible asset's life may be finite but the precise length of that life may not be known. In that case, the intangible asset should be amortized over the best estimate of its useful life.

2230.36 The useful life should be evaluated annually to determine whether it should be revised. If the useful life is changed, the remaining carrying value is amortized prospectively over the revised remaining useful life.

2230.37 The amortization method should reflect the pattern in which the economic benefits of the intangible asset are consumed or are otherwise used up. The straight-line amortization method should be used if that pattern cannot be reliably determined.

2230.38 The amount of an intangible asset to be amortized is the amount initially assigned to that asset less any residual value. The residual value is the estimated fair value of the intangible asset at the end of its useful life to the reporting entity less any disposal costs. The residual value should be assumed to be zero unless at the end of its useful life the asset is expected to continue to have a useful life to another entity and:

    a. the reporting entity has a commitment from a third party to purchase the asset at the end of its useful life or

    b. the residual value can be determined by reference to an exchange transaction in an existing market for that asset and that market is expected to exist at the end of the asset's useful life.

2230.39 If an intangible asset that is being amortized is subsequently determined to have an indefinite useful life, amortization of that intangible asset should cease and it should be tested for impairment. It should then be accounted for as an intangible asset not subject to amortization.

2230.40 As in the case of those not subject to amortization, intangible assets subject to amortization may need to be tested for impairment. The impairment of long-lived assets is discussed in section **2370.01–.27**.

Financial Statement Presentation

2230.41 All intangible assets (other than goodwill, which is discussed in section **2315**) should be aggregated and presented as a separate line item in the balance sheet.

2230.42 The amortization expense and impairment losses for intangible assets (other than goodwill, which is discussed in section **2315**) should be presented in the income statement within income from continuing operations. The amount of each impairment loss related to an intangible asset must be identified, but generally that disclosure would be in the notes to the financial statements.

2230.43 **IFRS:** IAS 38 applies to purchased and internally developed intangible assets.

Recognize an intangible asset only if:

    a. the asset is identifiable and

  b. the future economic benefits specifically attributable to the asset will flow to the enterprise, and cost is reliably measurable.

Recognition criteria apply to both purchased and internally generated intangibles.

After initial recognition in the financial statements, an intangible asset should be measured under one of the following two treatments:

1. Benchmark treatment: historical cost less any amortization and impairment losses; or
2. Allowed alternative treatment: revalued amount (based on fair value) less any subsequent amortization and impairment losses.

Revaluations for intangible assets are permitted only if fair value can be determined by reference to an active market. Active markets are expected to be rare for intangible assets.

The statement requires intangible assets to be amortized over the best estimate of their useful life.

2231 Payables and Accrued Liabilities

Nature and Definition of Liabilities

2231.01 **Liabilities** are defined in SFAC 6 as "probable future sacrifices of economic benefits arising from present obligations of a particular entity to transfer assets or provide services to other entities in the future as a result of past transactions or events" (SFAC 6.35).

2231.02 For a liability to be recognized (recorded), it must arise from the occurrence of some critical *event* in the *past* from which a benefit (which may be negative, as in the case of a liability for injuries suffered by a customer on the enterprise's premises) has been received (i.e., at least one critical event has already occurred and the benefit received).

2231.03 A second critical event may be necessary in some cases for a liability to be recognized. For example, in the case of product warranties, the first critical event is the issuance of the product warranty at the time of sale. The benefit received in the past (as of the time of sale) is the excess of sales over what they would have been without the warranty. The second critical event is the product proving to be defective, for without this event the enterprise will not experience any outlay of cash or other resources. The *amount* may or may not be subject to reasonable estimation.

2231.04 In other cases, there may be no second critical event. For example, when employees have earned wages (i.e., the enterprise has received the *benefit* of their work), no future critical event is necessary for a liability to be recognized. The amount in this case is usually known.

2231.05 The concept of a second critical event is drawn from the underlying theme of FASB ASC 450-10.

2231.06 For a liability to be recognized, a critical event must have occurred in the past and the enterprise must have received a benefit (though perhaps negative). Liabilities and the appropriate accounting treatment can be categorized as follows by drawing on FASB ASC 450-10 and focusing on the event and amounts involved. (See also section **2330.01–.09** on contingencies.)

Current Status of Second Critical Event	Current Status of Amount	Accounting Treatment
Not necessary (first critical event was determining)	Known or estimable (amount should at least be estimable if second critical event is not necessary)	Recorded as liability at known or estimated amount
Occurred	Known	Recorded as liability at known amount
Occurred	Unknown but estimable	Recorded as liability at estimated amount
Probable future occurrence	Known	Recorded as liability at known amount
Probable future occurrence	Unknown but estimable	Recorded as liability at estimated amount

Current Liabilities Defined

2231.07 As presented in section **2210.03**, current liabilities represent "obligations whose liquidation is expected to require the use of current assets or the creation of other current liabilities." Current liabilities include the following:

   a. Obligations for items that have entered into the operating cycle

   b. Collections received in advance of the delivery of goods or performance of services

   c. Debts arising from operations directly related to the operating cycle (e.g., accruals for wages, salaries, commissions, rentals, royalties, and income and other taxes)

   d. Other liabilities whose regular and ordinary liquidation is expected to occur within one year or less (FASB ASC 210-10-45-9)

Classification of Obligations That Are Callable by the Creditor

2231.08 In addition to the liabilities defined as current in section **2231.07**, current liabilities also include obligations that are due on demand or will be due on demand within one year (or operating cycle, if longer) from the balance sheet date. Current liabilities may also include long-term obligations that are or will be callable by the creditor because the debtor has violated a covenant in the debt agreement that either:

   a. makes the obligation callable or

   b. will make the obligation callable if the violation is not cured within a specified grace period.

If such a violation exists, the related debt must be classified as current unless either:

   a. the creditor has waived or, subsequent to the violation, has lost the right to demand payment (e.g., because the violation has been cured) for more than one year (or operating cycle, if longer) from the balance sheet date or

   b. it is probable that the violation will be cured within the specified grace period, if one exists.

Short-Term Obligations Expected to Be Refinanced

2231.09 Short-term obligations arising from transactions in the normal course of business that are due in customary terms (see items (a), (b), and (c) in section **2231.07**) must be classified as current liabilities. Other short-term obligations (see item (d) in section **2231.07**), may be excluded from current liabilities, but only if the enterprise:

   a. intends to refinance the obligation on a long-term basis *and*

   b. demonstrates the ability to consummate the refinancing.

2231.10 Refinancing a short-term obligation on a long-term basis means:

   a. replacing it with a long-term obligation or equity securities *or*

   b. renewing, extending, or replacing it with short-term obligations for an uninterrupted period extending beyond one year (or the operating cycle, if applicable) from the date of an enterprise's balance sheet.

2231.11 The ability to consummate the refinancing may be demonstrated in either of the following two ways:

   a. By actual issuance of a long-term obligation or equity security after the balance sheet date, but before the balance sheet is issued, for the purpose of refinancing the short-term obligation

   b. By entering into a financing agreement, before the balance sheet is issued, that clearly permits the enterprise to refinance the short-term obligation on a long-term basis on terms that are readily determinable

   In the latter case (financing agreement), the following conditions must also be met:

   a. The agreement does not expire within one year (or operating cycle, if applicable) from the enterprise's balance sheet date, and during that period the agreement is not cancelable by the lender except for violation of a provision with which compliance is objectively determinable or measurable.

   b. No violation of any provision in the agreement exists prior to the issuance of the balance sheet or, if one exists, a waiver has been obtained.

   c. The lender is expected to be financially capable of honoring the agreement.

2231.12 The amount of the short-term obligation to be excluded from current liabilities is the lesser of the amount of the short-term obligation or:

   a. the proceeds of the new long-term obligation or the equity security issued where the ability to refinance is demonstrated by actual issuance *or*

   b. the minimum amount expected to be available at any date from the scheduled maturity of the short-term obligation to the end of the fiscal year where the ability to refinance is demonstrated by entering into a financing agreement.

2231.13 FASB ASC 470-10-45-15 specifies that the repayment of a short-term obligation before funds are obtained through long-term financing requires that the short-term obligation be classified as a current liability. For example, assuming a balance sheet date of December 31, 20X1, and a financial statement issuance date of April 1, 20X2, the payment of a short-term obligation (i.e., one that existed as of the balance sheet date) on February 1, 20X2, would require that the short-term obligation be classified on the December 31, 20X1, balance sheet as a current liability unless it were refinanced on a long-term basis and the proceeds from the long-term financing were received on or before February 1, 20X2.

2232 Deferred Revenue

2232.01 In some cases, revenue is received in advance of earning and delivering the product or service. Examples are magazine subscriptions and assets constructed to the buyer's specifications where an advance is received. The revenue received in advance is a liability representing an obligation to provide goods or services in the future. When the agreed-upon activity is completed, the revenue is recognized.

2232.02 **Example:** Blue Company agrees to produce a special type of machinery for the Purple Company, with 10% of the purchase price to be received in advance. The price of the asset is $100,000. Entries to record the transactions on the books of the Blue Company are as follows:

Cash	$10,000	
Customer Advance		$ 10,000
To record receipt of the 10% advance.		
Cash	$90,000	
Customer Advance	10,000	
Sales		$100,000
To record transfer of machinery on completion.		

2240 Long-Term Debt (Financial Liabilities)

2240.01 Long-term liabilities are those liabilities scheduled to mature beyond one year (or the operating cycle, if applicable) from the date of an enterprise's balance sheet.

2240.02 Long-term liabilities are initially recorded on a present-value basis, which is the sum of the future payments discounted at an appropriate rate of interest. Any related discount or premium should be amortized using the interest method. The unamortized discount or premium should be reported in the balance sheet as a direct deduction from or addition to the face amount of the liability.

2240.03 Issue costs are included in the cost of the bonds and are therefore amortized over the life of the debt.

2241 Notes Payable

2241.01 Notes payable are liabilities that are formally recognized by a written promissory note. These notes most often occur when the company cannot pay short-term accounts payable or obligations for items that have entered into the operating cycle discussed under section **2231** ("Payables and Accrued Liabilities"). In those instances, the company may sign an interest-bearing note to defer payment for a short time. These notes payable are usually short-term liabilities.

2241.02 **Short-term bank loan**: A common way for a company to acquire temporary financing is to arrange a short-term bank loan. The company signs an interest-bearing promissory note.

Example: On February 1, 20X1, ABC Corp. borrows $500,000 for United Bank by signing a six-month 8% promissory note. Interest is due upon maturity of the note.

February 1, 20X1:

Cash	$500,000	
Notes payable		$500,000

August 1, 20X1:

Interest expense ($500,000 × 8% × 6/12)	$ 20,000	
Notes payable	500,000	
Cash		$520,000

2241.03 **Credit limit:** A common method of acquiring short-term notes payable is a credit line. A credit line allows a company to borrow up to an arranged limit without using formal loan paperwork.

2241.04 **Commercial paper:** Another type of note payable is commercial paper. Commercial paper is an unsecured note generally sold in minimum amounts of $25,000 with maturities of 30 to 270 days. Commercial paper is issued directly to the buyer.

2242 Bonds Payable

Computation of Issue Price

2242.01 When a bond is issued, the bond contract (indenture) specifies the amount and timing of payments the issuer is obligated to pay. The issuer will pay the following:

  a. The face or principal amount at the maturity date of the bonds

  b. Interest at specified intervals, usually semi-annually, during the life of the bond based on a stated percentage of the face amount

The interest rate stated in the bond contract is known variously as the stated, coupon, contract, or nominal rate.

2242.02 The effective interest the issuer will pay is determined in the marketplace, not in the bond contract. At any given time, a market rate of interest exists. This is the rate that the investor (purchaser of a bond) can command in the marketplace for the particular type of bond and risk level. Accordingly, the investor is not willing to accept a return on the investment that is less than the market rate. Alternatively, the market rate of interest can be viewed as the rate that the issuer of the bonds can command in the marketplace. The issuer is not willing to pay any more for the use of the investor's money than the market requires.

2242.03 The salient point of the preceding discussion is that the issuer of the bonds will effectively pay the market rate of interest, regardless of the coupon or contract rate. If the coupon rate is greater than the market (or effective) rate, the bonds will sell at a premium (i.e., at an amount greater than the face amount of the bonds). If the coupon rate is less than the market rate, the bonds will sell at a discount. The issue price is determined by discounting the payments (principal and interest) to the present using the effective or market rate of interest.

2242.04 **Example:** To illustrate, assume that the issuance of 3-year bonds with a face amount of $100,000, which pay interest semi-annually at a contract rate of 8% per year. The issue price of the bonds is computed as follows under three different assumptions as to the market or effective interest rate.

	Effective Annual Rate (Compounded Semi-Annually)		
	6%	8%	10%
Present value of payment of face amount of $100,000 at the end of three years (discounted for six periods at one-half of the effective annual rate):			
(0.83748[a] × $100,000)	$ 83,748		
(0.79031 × $100,000)		$ 79,031	
(0.74622 × $100,000)			$74,622
Present value of semi-annual interest payments of $4,000 (discounted for six periods at one-half of the effective annual rate):			
(5.41719[b] × $4,000)	21,669		
(5.24214 × $4,000)		20,969	
(5.07569 × $4,000)			20,303
Bond issue price	$105,417	$100,000	$94,925

[a] *Present value of $1 for six periods at 3%*
[b] *Present value of annuity of $1 for six periods at 3%*

Amortization of Premium or Discount

2242.05 Any discount or premium should be amortized by using the interest method, which results in a constant *rate* of interest. Other methods, such as the straight-line method (a constant *amount* per period) may be used if the results are not materially different.

Illustrative Entries

2242.06 Assume that the bonds described in section **2242.04** were issued on January 1, 20X1, when the market rate of interest was 6%, and that the bonds pay interest semi-annually on June 30 and December 31. Amortization schedules for the interest method and the straight-line method are presented.

Amortization Schedule—Interest Method					
Date	Interest Paid (4% Semi-annual)	Debit to Interest Expense (3% Semi-annual)	Premium Amortized	Unamortized Premium	Carrying Value of Bonds
01/01/X1				$5,417	$105,417
06/30/X1	$4,000[a]	$3,163[b]	$ 837[c]	4,580[d]	104,580[e]
12/31/X1	4,000	3,137	863	3,717	103,717
06/30/X2	4,000	3,112	888	2,829	102,829
12/31/X2	4,000	3,085	915	1,914	101,914
06/30/X3	4,000	3,057	943	971	100,971
12/31/X3	4,000	3,029	971	0	100,000
	$24,000	$18,583	$5,417		

[a] *$100,000 × 0.04*
[b] *$105,417 × 0.03*
[c] *$4,000 - $3,163*
[d] *$5,417 - $837*
[e] *($105,417 - $837) or ($100,000 + $4,580)*

	Amortization Schedule—Straight-Line Method				
Date	Interest Paid (4% Semi-annual)	Debit to Interest Expense (3% Semi-annual)	Premium Amortized	Unamortized Premium	Carrying Value of Bonds
01/01/X1				$5,417	$105,417
06/30/X1	$ 4,000	$ 3,097[b]	$ 903[a]	4,514[c]	104,514[d]
12/31/X1	4,000	3,097	903	3,611	103,611
06/30/X2	4,000	3,097	903	2,708	102,708
12/31/X2	4,000	3,097	903	1,805	101,805
06/30/X3	4,000	3,097	903	902	100,902
12/31/X3	4,000	3,098	902	0	100,000
	$24,000	$18,583	$5,417		

[a] $5,417 premium × (6/36)
[b] $4,000 - $903
[c] $5,417 - $903
[d] ($105,417 - $903) or ($100,000 + $4,514)

2242.07 Assuming that the bonds were issued on January 1, 20X1, entries for 20X1 are presented as follows for the interest method and the straight-line method:

	Interest Method		S-L Method	
01/01/X1				
Cash	$105,417		$105,417	
Bonds Payable		$100,000		$100,000
Bond Premium		5,417		5,417
To record issuance of bonds.				
06/30/X1				
Interest Expense	$ 4,000		$ 4,000	
Cash		$ 4,000		$ 4,000
To record payment of interest at 06/30/X1.				
06/30/X1				
Bond Premium	$ 837		$ 903	
Interest Expense		$ 837		$ 903
To record amortization of premium at 06/30/X1.				
12/31/X1				
Interest Expense	$ 4,000		$ 4,000	
Cash		$ 4,000		$ 4,000
To record payment of interest at 12/31/X1.				
12/31/X1				
Bond Premium	$ 863		$ 903	
Interest Expense		$ 863		$ 903
To record amortization of premium at 12/31/X1.				

2242.08 Assuming that the bonds were sold on April 30, 20X1, for $105,417 plus accrued interest, entries through December 31, 20X1, under the straight-line method would be:

04/30/X1	Cash		$108,084	
	Bonds Payable			$100,000
	Bond Premium			5,417
	Interest Payable ($4,000 × 4/6)			2,667
	To record issuance of bonds on 04/30/X1.			
06/30/X1	Interest Payable (four months)		$ 2,667	
	Interest Expense (two months)		1,333	
	Cash			$ 4,000
	To record payment of interest on 06/30/X1.			
06/30/X1	Bond Premium[a]		$ 338	
	Interest Expense			$ 338
	To record amortization of premium at 06/30/X1.			

[a] Amount of premium	$ 5,417
÷ number of months to maturity	32
Amortization per month	$ 169
$169 × 2 months (May and June)	$ 338

12/31/X1	Interest Expense		$ 4,000	
	Cash			$ 4,000
	To record payment of interest on 12/31/X1.			
12/31/X1	Bond Premium (6 × $169)		$ 1,014	
	Interest Expense			$ 1,014
	To record amortization of premium at 12/31/X1.			

Serial Bonds

2242.09 Some bond issues provide for the payment of the principal in periodic installments. These bonds are known as serial bonds. The bond issue is, in essence, a series of separate bond issues that mature at different dates.

2242.10 If the effective interest rate for each series is known, each series can be accounted for as a separate bond issue. Alternatively, the serial bonds can be accounted for on a group basis.

2242.11 Any premium or discount associated with serial bonds should be amortized by using the interest method. The straight-line method may be used if it does not produce materially different results. The bonds outstanding method is a variation of the straight-line method that is often used.

2242.12 The following example is used to demonstrate the amortization of discount on serial bonds under both the interest method and the bonds outstanding method.

2242.13 **Example:** Assume that a serial bond issued in the amount of $30,000, dated January 1, 20X1, is sold on that date for $28,952, which represents an effective yield of 10% compounded semi-annually. The bonds mature in the amount of $10,000 on December 31 of each year, beginning on December 31, 20X1, and pay interest semi-annually at a rate of 8% per annum.

2242.14 The discount to be amortized is $1,048, determined as follows:

Face amount of bonds	$30,000
Issue price	28,952
Discount	$ 1,048

2242.15 Amortization schedules are presented for both the interest method and the bonds outstanding method.

Discount Amortization—Interest Method						
Date	Interest Paid (4% Semi-annual)	Debit to Expense (5% Semi-annual)	Discount Amortized	Unamortized Discount	Bonds Matured (Face)	Carrying Value of Bonds
01/01/X1				$1,048		$28,952
06/30/X1	$1,200[a]	$1,448[b]	$ 248[c]	800		29,200
12/31/X1	1,200	1,460	260	540	$10,000	19,460[d]
06/30/X2	800	973	173	367		19,633
12/31/X2	800	981	181	186	10,000	9,814
06/30/X3	400	491	91	95		9,905
12/31/X3	400	495	95	0	10,000	0
	$4,800	$5,848	$1,048		$30,000	

[a] $0.04 \times \$30,000$ bonds outstanding during period
[b] $0.05 \times \$28,952$ (effective rate × carrying value at beginning of period)
[c] $1,448 - $1,200
[d] $29,200 (CV of bonds at 06/30/20X1) + $260 (discount amortized) - $10,000 (bonds matured at 12/31/20X1) = $19,460. Alternatively, $20,000 bonds outstanding - $540 unamortized discount.

Discount Amortization—Bonds Outstanding Method					
Year	Bonds Outstanding (Face Amount)	Fraction of Total of Bonds Outstanding	Amortization of Discount ($1,048 × Fraction)	Interest Payments (8% of Bonds Outstanding)	Interest Expense
20X1	$30,000	30/60	$ 524	$2,400	$2,924
20X2	20,000	20/60	349	1,600	1,949
20X3	10,000	10/60	175	800	975
	$60,000	60/60	$1,048	$4,800	$5,848

2242.16 The entries for 20X1 are:

		Interest Method		Bonds Outstanding Method	
Jan. 1	Cash	$28,952		$28,952	
	Bond discount	1,048		1,048	
	Serial Bonds Payable		$30,000		$30,000
June 30	Interest expense	$ 1,448		$ 1,462	
	Cash		$ 1,200		$ 1,200
	Bond Discount		248		262
Dec. 31	Interest expense	$ 1,460		$ 1,462	
	Cash		$ 1,200		$ 1,200
	Bond Discount		260		262
Dec. 31	Serial Bonds Payable	$10,000		$10,000	
	Cash		$10,000		$10,000

2242.17 Under the bonds outstanding method, the amounts recorded for the interest payments and amortization represent one-half of the annual amounts shown in the amortization schedule in section **2242.15**.

2243 Debt with Conversion Features and Other Options

Convertible Bonds

2243.01 Convertible bonds are bonds that can be exchanged for stock at the option of the bondholder. These bonds have features of both debt and equity. The bondholder has an interest-bearing security that can become equity. The convertible feature is not recorded as such on the books of the issuing company.

Example: ABC Corp. issues $100,000 of convertible bonds at 102. The bonds would be worth $98,000 without the conversion feature.

Cash	$102,000	
Bonds payable		$100,000
Premium on bonds payable		2,000

Before any premium amortization, the bondholders convert the bonds into 10,000 shares of $1 par value common stock.

Bonds payable	$100,000	
Premium on bonds payable	2,000	
Common stock		$10,000
Additional paid-in capital—common stock		92,000

Debt Issued with Detachable Stock Purchase Warrants

2243.02 Debt securities are sometimes issued in combination with stock purchase warrants. The warrant gives the debt holder the right to purchase a specified number of shares of stock at a specified price.

2243.03 If the warrants are detachable, the proceeds from the bond issue must be allocated between the debt and the warrants on the basis of their relative fair values. The amount allocated to the warrants is accounted for as additional paid-in capital.

2243.04 **Example:** Blade Company sold 8%, 10-year, $100,000 face amount bonds with detachable 3-year stock purchase warrants for $102,000. The warrant attached to each $1,000 bond provides its holder the right to purchase five shares of Blade's $10 par value common stock at $27 per share. At the date of issuance, the market value of the bonds, without the detachable warrant, was quoted at 97½. The market value of each detachable warrant was quoted at $25. Blade's common stock had a market value of $30 per share on the date the bonds were issued.

Allocation of proceeds:
Total proceeds (issue price of bonds with warrants) $102,000

Allocated to bonds:

$$\frac{\text{Value of bonds without warrants}}{\text{Value of bonds without warrants} + \text{Value of warrants}} \times \$102{,}000$$

$$\frac{\$97{,}500^a}{\$97{,}500 + \$2{,}500^b} \times \$102{,}000 = \$99{,}450$$

^{a} 97½% of $100,000
^{b} 100 warrants × $25 market value per warrant

Allocated to warrants:

$$\frac{\text{Value of warrants}}{\text{Value of bonds without warrants} + \text{Value of warrants}} \times \$102{,}000$$

$$\frac{\$2{,}500}{\$97{,}500 + \$2{,}500} \times \$102{,}000 = \$2{,}550$$

To record issuance of bonds with warrants

Cash	$102,000	
Bond discount ($100,000 face - $99,450)	550	
Bonds payable		$100,000
Paid-in capital—stock warrants		2,550

Entry if warrants are exercised when market price of common stock is $33 per share

Cash (500 shares × $27 exercise price)	$ 13,500	
Paid-in capital—stock warrants	2,550	
Common stock (500 × $10 par)		$ 5,000
Paid-in capital—common stock		11,050

2243.05 If the warrants are not detachable, the proceeds should be allocated totally to the debt.

2244 Modifications and Extinguishments

Modification of Debt

2244.01 FASB ASC 470-50-40-6 states, "An exchange of debt instruments with substantially different terms is a debt extinguishment and shall be accounted for in accordance with paragraph 405-20-40-1. A debtor could achieve the same economic effect as an exchange of a debt instrument by making a substantial modification of terms of an existing debt instrument. Accordingly, a substantial modification of terms shall be accounted for like an extinguishment."

2244.02 FASB ASC 470-50-40-14 states, "If it is determined that the original and new debt instruments are not substantially different, then a new effective interest rate shall be determined based on the carrying amount of the original debt instrument, adjusted for an increase (but not a decrease) in the fair value of an embedded conversion option (calculated as the difference between the fair value of the embedded conversion option immediately before and after the modification or exchange) resulting from the modification, and the revised cash flows."

Extinguishment of Debt

2244.03 The FASB has concluded that all extinguishments of debt are fundamentally alike and should, therefore, be accounted for alike. The conversion of convertible debt by the holder of the debt is not deemed to be an extinguishment of debt. (FASB ASC 470-40-15-3)

2244.04 FASB ASC 405-20-40-1 specifies that debt is extinguished if either of the following conditions is met:

    a. The debtor pays the creditor and is relieved of its obligation for the liability. (Paying the creditor includes delivery of cash, other financial assets, goods or services, or reacquisition by the debtor of its outstanding debt securities whether the securities are canceled or held as so-called treasury bonds.)

    b. The debtor is legally released from being the primary obligor under the liability, either judicially or by the creditor.

2244.05 Any difference between the reacquisition price and the net carrying amount of the extinguished debt should be included in income in the period of extinguishment. Such gain or loss is a gain or loss on extinguishment of debt and, accordingly, should be classified as to whether ordinary or extraordinary as any other gain or loss (see section **2345.15–.19**).

2244.06 The reacquisition price is the amount paid, including any call premium and other costs incidental to reacquisition. If the extinguishment is achieved by issuing new securities (debt or equity), the reacquisition price is the total present value of the new securities.

2244.07 The net carrying amount is the carrying value of the debt, as discussed previously, less any unamortized issue costs.

Example: Extinguishment of Debt with Proceeds from Sale of Stock

2244.08 Assume that outstanding bonds with a face amount of $100,000 and a carrying amount of $95,000 are called by the issuer at 102 prior to the maturity date of the bonds. The extinguishment was made possible by the sale of 1,000 shares of $10 par common stock for $108,000.

2244.09 Even though the proceeds from the sale of the stock were used to reacquire the bonds, this extinguishment is not a direct exchange of stock for bonds. Therefore, the reacquisition price is the amount paid for the bonds, not the amount for which the stock was sold. The loss from extinguishment is $7,000, computed as follows:

Reacquisition price (call price)	$102,000
Net carrying amount of bonds	95,000
Loss from extinguishment	$ 7,000

2244.10 The entries to record the extinguishment of the debt and the issuance of the stock are:

Extinguishment of debt:		
Bonds Payable	$100,000	
Loss on Extinguishment of Debt	7,000	
Bond Discount		$ 5,000
Cash		102,000
Issuance of stock:		
Cash	$108,000	
Common Stock (1,000 × $10 par)		$10,000
Capital in Excess of Par		98,000

Example: Extinguishment by Direct Exchange of New Debt

2244.11 Keith Company has outstanding 8% nonconvertible bonds with a face amount of $100,000 and unamortized bond premium of $5,000. There are also unexpired bond issue costs of $1,200. Keith issues new 7% convertible bonds, $100,000 face amount, in direct exchange for the 8% bonds. The new bonds have a market value of $98,000.

Net carrying amount of 8% bonds:		
Face amount	$100,000	
Unamortized bond premium	5,000	
Unamortized bond issue costs	(1,200)	$103,800
Reacquisition price (FMV of 7% bonds)		98,000
Gain from extinguishment of debt		$ 5,800
Journal entries:		
8% bonds payable	$100,000	
Bond premium (8% bonds)	5,000	
Bond discount (7% bonds)	2,000	
Unamortized bond issue costs		$ 1,200
7% bonds payable		100,000
Gain from extinguishment of debt		5,800
To record the extinguishment.		

Classification of Gains and Losses from Extinguishment of Debt

2244.12 Gains and losses on extinguishment of debt are to be classified on the same basis as other gains and losses. Thus, gains and losses on extinguishment of debt are to be classified as extraordinary only if they meet the criteria established for extraordinary gains and losses (see section **2345.15–.19**). If such gains and losses fail to meet those criteria, they must be classified as ordinary gains and losses and included in the determination of income from continuing operations.

2245 Troubled Debt Restructurings by Debtors

2245.01 A restructuring of debt constitutes a troubled debt restructuring (TDR) if the creditor, for economic or legal reasons related to the debtor's financial difficulties, grants a concession to the debtor that it would not otherwise consider. This concession may stem from an agreement between the creditor and the debtor, or it may be imposed by law or a court.

2245.02 FASB ASC 310-40 establishes accounting standards for TDR situations. For purposes of applying the statement, debt is any contractual right to receive money or a contractual obligation to pay money on demand or on fixed or determinable dates that is already included as an asset or liability in the creditor's or debtor's balance sheet at the time of the TDR. Examples are accounts receivable or payable, notes, debentures, bonds, and related accrued interest.

2245.03 A troubled debt restructuring is normally accomplished by one or a combination of the following:

    a. Transfer from the debtor to the creditor of assets (e.g., real estate, receivables) to satisfy fully or partially the debt

    b. Issuance of an equity interest to the creditor by the debtor to satisfy fully or partially the debt

    c. Modification of terms of the debt, such as:

        (1) reduction in the interest rate for the remainder of the life of the debt

        (2) extension of maturity date(s) at an interest rate less than the current rate for new debt

        (3) reduction of the face amount or maturity amount of the debt

        (4) reduction of accrued interest

2245.04 Several examples are developed in the following paragraphs to illustrate the proper accounting for TDR under various plans. In each case, the creditor is identified as Co. C and the debtor is identified as Co. D.

Transfer of Assets

2245.05 In a transfer of assets to satisfy debt in a TDR, proper accounting by the debtor and the creditor is as follows:

Debtor	Creditor
Recognize a gain or loss on the transfer of assets (equal to the difference between the fair and recorded values of the asset transferred).	Account for the asset received at fair value, recognizing a loss equal to the difference between the fair value of the asset and the recorded investment in the receivable.
Recognize a gain on the restructuring of a debt (equal to the difference between the fair value of the asset and the carrying value of the debt).	

2245.06 **Example:** Co. C holds a $100,000 note from Co. D. Land costing $35,000 and currently appraised at $75,000 is transferred from Co. D to Co. C in full settlement of the debt. The TDR is recorded as follows:

Co. D			Co. C		
Note payable	$100,000		Land	$75,000	
Gain—transfer of land		$40,000	Loss—		
Gain—restructure of debt		25,000	restructuring of		
Land		35,000	receivable	25,000	
			Note receivable		$100,000

2245.07 Granting of Equity Interest

In a granting of equity interest to satisfy debt in a TDR, proper accounting by the debtor and the creditor is as follows:

Debtor	Creditor
Recognize the distribution of the stock at fair value.	Account for the asset received (i.e., investment) at fair value, recognizing a loss equal to the difference between the fair value of the asset and the recorded investment in the receivable.
Recognize a gain on the restructuring of a debt (equal to the difference between the fair value of the equity interest and the carrying value of the debt).	

2245.08

Example: Co. C holds a $100,000 note from Co. D. Common stock in Co. D is transferred to Co. C in full settlement of the debt. The par value of the stock is $50,000, and the fair value at the date of transfer is $85,000. The TDR is recorded as follows:

Co. D			Co. C		
Note Payable	$100,000		Investment in Co. D.	$85,000	
Common Stock		$50,000	Loss—		
Additional Paid-in Capital		35,000	Restructuring of		
Gain—Restructuring of			Receivable	15,000	
Debt		15,000			
			Note Receivable		$100,000

2245.09 Modification of Terms

In a modification of terms, if the total scheduled cash payments *exceed* or *equal* the carrying value of the debt, the TDR is accounted for by the debtor as follows:

a. Change in payments handled on a prospective basis

b. Interest expense recognized at reduced amount

2245.10

Example: Co. C holds a $100,000 note from Co. D, bearing a 10% interest rate. An agreement is reached whereby the interest rate is reduced to 5%, payable semi-annually. The TDR is recorded by the debtor as follows:

No entry at time of agreement
At each interest payment:
  Interest Expense $2,500
    Cash $2,500

2245.11

In a modification of terms, if the total scheduled cash payments *are less than* the carrying value of the debt, the TDR is recorded by the debtor as follows:

a. Reduce carrying value of debt to total scheduled cash payments.

b. Recognize gain (equal to the difference between the carrying value of the debt and the total scheduled cash payments).

c. Recognize all future payments—whether designated as principal or interest—as principal, reducing payable.

2245.12 Example: Co. C holds a $100,000 note from Co. D, bearing a 10% interest rate. An agreement is reached whereby the face value of the note is reduced to $60,000, and the interest rate is reduced to 8% (payable semi-annually). The life of the restructured note is two years. The total future cash to be exchanged is $69,600 and the gain to be recognized is $30,400:

Face value of note		$100,000
Scheduled cash payments:		
Revised face value	$60,000	
Interest ($60,000 × 0.08 × 2 years)	9,600	69,600
Gain to be recognized		$30,400
The TDR is recorded by the debtor (Co. D) as follows:		
Note payable	$30,400	
Gain—Restructuring of Debt		$30,400
At each interest payment date:		
Notes Payable	$ 2,400	
Cash		$ 2,400

2245.13 FASB ASC 310-10-35-22 requires the creditor to account for a restructured loan at its present value, computed at the original contractual interest rate. Calculating the loss in the example from the previous paragraph for the creditor, Co. C, results in the following:

Recorded investment in note		$100,000
Present value of restructured agreement:		
Face value ($60,000 × 0.82270*)	$49,362	
Interest payments ($60,000 × 0.04 × 3.54595**)	8,510	57,872
Loss		$ 42,128

*Present value of 1, 5%, 4 periods
**Present value of annuity, 5%, 4 periods

Because FASB ASC 470-60-35-2 requires the debtor to compute its gain based on absolute amounts, and FASB ASC 310-10-35-22 requires the creditor to compute its loss based on present values, the two amounts will differ, as indicated in this example.

Co. C, the creditor, records the loss on restructuring as follows:

Loss—Restructuring of Receivable	$42,128	
Note Receivable		$42,128

2245.14 Combination of Types

In a TDR accomplished by a combination of the types of restructuring described previously, the note receivable or payable is first reduced by the fair value of the assets or equity interest transferred. For the remainder of the debt, the rules for the modification of terms are followed.

2245.15 Financial Statement Disclosure

A debtor discloses, either in the body or in the notes to the financial statements, the following information about TDR:

a. For each TDR, a description of the principal change in terms and/or the major features of the settlement

b. The aggregate gain on restructuring of payables and the related income tax effect

c. The aggregate net gain or loss on transfers of assets recognized during the period

  d. Per-share amount of the aggregate gain on restructuring of payables, net of related income tax effects

  e. Contingent amounts payable, if any, and the condition under which amounts become payable

2245.16 A creditor discloses, either in the body or in the notes to the financial statements, the following information about TDR:

  a. For outstanding receivables whose terms have been modified in TDR, by major category:

   (1) The aggregate recorded investment

   (2) The gross interest income that would have been recorded in the period if terms had not been changed

   (3) The amount of interest income on those receivables that was included in income

  b. The amount of commitments, if any, to lend additional funds to debtors owing receivables whose terms have been modified in TDR

Accounting by Creditors for Impairment of a Loan

2245.17 FASB ASC 310-10-35-2 addresses how allowances for credit losses related to certain loans should be determined. According to this statement, a loan is a contractual right to receive money on demand or on fixed or determinable dates that is recognized as an asset in the creditor's statement of financial position. FASB ASC 310-10-35-2 applies to all creditors.

2245.18 A loan is impaired when, based on current information, it is probable that a creditor will be unable to collect all amounts due according to the contractual terms of the loan agreement, including both the contractual interest payments and the contractual principal payments. FASB ASC 310-10-35-17 provides the following guidance for implementing this general principle:

  a. Creditors should apply their normal loan review procedures in making the judgment of collectibility.

  b. An insignificant delay or insignificant shortfall in the amount of payments does not require application of FASB ASC 310-10-35-2.

  c. A loan is not considered impaired during a period of delay in payment if the creditor expects to collect all amounts due, including interest accrued at the contractual interest rate, for the period of delay.

  d. The term "probable" in the general principle is consistent with its use in FASB ASC 450-20-20. This means future events (i.e., collection of the loan) are likely to occur. (FASB ASC 310-10-35-18)

2245.19 Measuring impaired loans requires judgment and estimation. Impairment is generally based on the present value of expected future cash flows discounted at the loan's effective interest rate. For a loan restructured in a troubled debt restructuring, present value is based on the original contractual interest rate rather than on the rate specified in the restructuring agreement. As a practical matter, a creditor may measure the amount of impairment based on the loan's recoverable market price or on the fair value of collateral, if the loan is collateral dependent.

2245.20 FASB ASC 310-10-35-38 indicates that the issue of how a creditor should recognize, measure, or display interest income on an impaired loan is not addressed in these pronouncements and is a matter of management choice.

2245.21 FASB ASC 310-10-50-15 requires the following information be disclosed when the impairment of a loan has been recognized:

  a. As of the date of each statement of financial position, the total recorded investment in the impaired loans at the end of each period, the amount of that recorded investment for which there is a related allowance for credit losses and the amount of that allowance, and the amount of that recorded investment for which there is no related allowance for credit losses

  b. The creditor's policy for recognizing interest income on impaired loans, including how cash receipts are recorded

  c. For each period for which results of operations are presented, the average recorded investment in the impaired loans during each period, the related amount of interest income recognized during the time within that period that the loans were impaired and, unless not practicable, the amount of interest income recognized using a cash-basis method of accounting during the time within that period that the loans were impaired

  d. For each period for which results of operations are presented, the activity in the allowance for credit losses, including the beginning and ending balances, additions charged to operations, direct write-downs charged against the allowance, and recoveries of amounts previously written off

2246 Debt Covenant Compliance

2246.01 Long-term debt often has covenants in the debt contract. Debt covenants are standards for the financial strength and performance of the borrower. These covenants are intended to protect the interest of the lending institution. Common ratios used to define debt covenants are the current ratio and the interest coverage ratio. Other covenants could include such requirements as maintaining a specific debt/equity ratio, having enough cash flow to cover interest expense, or acquiring an unqualified audit opinion. (FASB ASC 470-10-45-1)

2246.02 A covenant violation could result in the bonds becoming callable—giving the lending institution the right to receive the maturity value of the bonds prematurely or the right to convert the debt. Such debt would no longer be classified as long term, but would be considered a short-term liability. (FASB ASC 470-10-45-1)

2250 Equity

Classification of Stockholders' Equity

2250.01 **Stockholders' equity** is the excess of total assets over total liabilities of a corporation. It represents the sources of the net assets of the corporation. This emphasis on source is evidenced in the stockholders' equity classifications used in the balance sheet.

2250.02 Stockholders' equity is classified into the major categories presented.

Contributed capital:		
Paid-in capital:		
Capital stock, at par or stated value		$XXX
Additional paid-in capital:		
Capital in excess of par	$XXX	
Other additional paid-in capital	XXX	XXX
Donated capital		XXX
Retained earnings:		
Appropriated	$XXX	
Unappropriated	XXX	XXX
Unrealized capital		XXX
Accumulated other comprehensive income		XXX
		$XXX
Less: Treasury stock		XXX
Total stockholders' equity		$XXX

2250.03 **Capital stock** includes the par or stated value of preferred and common stock. It is sometimes referred to as legal capital.

2250.04 **Additional paid-in capital** represents increases in capital (net assets) in excess of par or stated value arising from transactions involving the enterprise's own stock. Some corporations show only the total of additional paid-in capital in the balance sheet. Others provide a breakdown of the total, such as between the amount identified with preferred stock and the amount identified with common stock. The extent to which additional paid-in capital is detailed in a corporation's records (as opposed to the financial statements) will be influenced by the requirements of state laws regarding the identification of capital by class of stock.

2250.05 **Donated capital** arises from gifts or donations of assets to the corporation. Some include all donated capital in this section of stockholders' equity. Others restrict this category to donations from outsiders; donated capital from owners would be included as a subcategory of additional paid-in capital.

2250.06 **Retained earnings** is the increase in net assets arising from operations that have been retained in the business. Restrictions on the use of retained earnings are sometimes formally acknowledged by an appropriation of retained earnings. Such appropriated retained earnings are shown separately from unappropriated retained earnings. However, all restrictions on retained earnings should be disclosed whether formally appropriated or not.

2250.07 **Unrealized capital** results from the write-up of assets above cost. Except in limited situations, such write-ups are not in accordance with GAAP; accordingly, they are seldom found in financial statements. The "unrealized loss from decline in value" for noncurrent marketable equity securities is an example of negative unrealized capital that may be found in the stockholders' equity section.

2250.08 **Accumulated other comprehensive income** represents the accumulated balance of other comprehensive income recognized over the years (technically, since the beginning of the entity). This is the accumulated balance of changes in net assets that have not been included in net income and do not represent transactions with owners as owners.

2250.09 **Treasury stock** reflects the reduction in total stockholders' equity resulting from the corporation reacquiring its own shares of stock.

Issuance of Stock

2250.10 A corporation may have various classes of stock outstanding. In such cases, each class has one or more characteristics or rights that distinguish it from the other classes of stock. *Capital stock* is generally considered to be either preferred stock or common stock.

2250.11 **Preferred stock** is so designated because it has a preference or priority over common stock in one or more areas. The most common areas are those relating to dividends and participation in the distribution of assets on liquidation of the corporation.

2250.12 **Common stock** is a residual equity security. Common stockholders have the right to vote in certain corporate matters, whereas preferred stockholders usually do not.

Par Value Stock

2250.13 **Par value** is a fixed per-share amount printed on each stock certificate of par value stock. Traditionally, par value has represented the amount of capital that must be retained in the corporation (i.e., owners could not be paid a dividend if to do so would impair legal capital).

2250.14 A stockholder may be contingently liable if the stock is sold at a discount (i.e., below par). Many states do not allow the issuance of stock below par value.

2250.15 Because most states now allow the establishment of par value at a nominal amount or the issuance of no-par stock, the legal capital aspect of par value has less practical significance today.

No-Par Stock

2250.16 The laws of most states now allow the issuance of no-par stock. Many states, however, either authorize or require that a stated value be assigned to the stock. From an accounting standpoint, the stated value assigned serves essentially the same role as par value.

2250.17 Both preferred stock and common stock may be no-par; however, most preferred stock is par value stock.

2250.18 **Example:** Assume that 1,000 shares of common stock are issued at a price of $17 per share. The entries to record the issuance under various assumptions as to the type of stock issued are presented as follows:

Assuming the stock has a par value of $10 per share:

Cash	$17,000	
Common Stock (1,000 × $10)		$10,000
Capital in Excess of Par—Common		7,000

Assuming the stock is no-par, with a stated value of $5 per share:

Cash	$17,000	
Common Stock (1,000 × $5)		$ 5,000
Capital in Excess of Stated Value—Common		12,000

Assuming the stock is pure no-par:

Cash	$17,000	
Common Stock (1,000 × $17)		$17,000

Stock Subscriptions

2250.19 Stock may be sold on a subscription basis. In such cases, the shares of stock are not issued until the full subscription price is received. However, the subscriber usually has all the rights and privileges of a stockholder unless the subscription contract specifies otherwise.

2250.20 The entries associated with stock subscriptions are illustrated in the following example:

Subscriptions received for 1,000 shares of $1 par common at $14:

Stock Subscriptions Receivable	$14,000	
Common Stock Subscribed		$ 1,000
Capital in Excess of Par—Common		13,000
One-half of subscription price is received:		
Cash	$ 7,000	
Stock Subscriptions Receivable		$ 7,000
Remainder of subscription price received and stock issued:		
Cash	$ 7,000	
Stock Subscriptions Receivable		$ 7,000
Common Stock Subscribed	$ 1,000	
Common Stock		$ 1,000

2250.21 Stock Subscriptions Receivable would normally be included in the current assets section of the balance sheet. Common Stock Subscribed is included in the paid-in capital section in a manner similar to Common Stock.

2250.22 If a subscriber defaults on the subscription contract after paying a portion of the subscription price, the action taken by the corporation will usually depend on the requirements of the applicable state laws. Three such possible actions are shown as follows, assuming that the subscribers in the preceding example defaulted after making the first payment:

   a. The stock is forfeited; subscribers receive nothing:

Common Stock Subscribed	$ 1,000	
Capital in Excess of Par—Common	13,000	
Stock Subscriptions Receivable		$ 7,000
Paid-in Capital—Defaulted Subscriptions		7,000

b. The amount previously paid is returned to subscribers:

Common Stock Subscribed	$ 1,000	
Capital in Excess of Par—Common	13,000	
Stock Subscriptions Receivable		$ 7,000
Cash		7,000

c. The subscribed shares are sold to others for $11 per share. The amount previously paid by subscribers is returned less the excess of subscription price over the price at which the shares were subsequently sold:

Cash	$11,000	
Common Stock		$ 1,000
Capital in Excess of Par—Common		10,000
Common Stock Subscribed	$ 1,000	
Capital in Excess of Par—Common	13,000	
Stock Subscriptions Receivable		$ 7,000
Cash ($7,000 - ($14,000 - $11,000))		4,000
Paid-in Capital—Defaulted Subscriptions		3,000

Treasury Stock Transactions

2250.23 Treasury stock is a corporation's own previously issued and outstanding stock that is reacquired but not retired. After being reacquired, the shares are still considered to be issued but not outstanding.

2250.24 Two methods are used to account for transactions involving treasury stock—the cost method and the par value method. Both methods are considered to be GAAP.

2250.25 The primary difference in the two methods is that the cost method subscribes to a single transaction concept, whereas the par value method adheres to a "two transactions" concept. The cost method views the reacquisition of the outstanding shares and their subsequent sale as a single transaction. The treasury stock account is carried at cost pending the outcome of the subsequent sale of the treasury shares. The par value method views the reacquisition of the shares and their subsequent sale as two separate transactions. The reacquired shares are accounted for in much the same manner as retired shares. The subsequent sale of the shares is accounted for essentially as if the shares were unissued shares.

2250.26 **Example:** Assume that the stockholders' equity section of Delphi Company's balance sheet at December 31, 20X1, appears as follows:

Common stock, $10 par (1,000 shares authorized, issued, and outstanding)	$10,000
Additional paid-in capital (capital in excess of par)	4,000
Total paid-in capital	14,000
Retained earnings	60,000
Total stockholders' equity	$74,000

Assume also that Delphi had the following treasury stock transactions:

January 10: Reacquired 100 shares of its outstanding common stock at $17 per share.
January 16: Sold 40 shares of treasury stock at $19 per share.
January 23: Sold 50 shares of treasury stock at $11 per share.

2250.27 The cost method is illustrated as follows for Delphi Company under two different assumptions as to additional paid-in capital:

1. Additional paid-in capital is treated as a homogeneous category with no distinction made among the various sources of additional paid-in capital.

2. Additional paid-in capital is accounted for as a heterogeneous category with distinction made among the various sources of additional paid-in capital.

The abbreviation PIC is henceforth used for the term "additional paid-in capital."

		(Assumption 1) Assuming a Single PIC Account		(Assumption 2) Assuming Detailed PIC	
Jan. 10	Treasury Stock (at cost)	$1,700		$1,700	
	Cash		$1,700		$1,700
Jan. 16	Cash	$760		$760	
	Treasury Stock (40 × $17)		$680		$680
	PIC		80		
	PIC—Treasury Stock				80
Jan. 23	Cash	$550		$550	
	PIC[a]	300			
	PIC—Treasury Stock[b]			80	
	Retained Earnings			220	
	Treasury Stock (50 × $17)		$850		$850

[a] *Maximum debit at this time is $4,080, which is the original balance of $4,000 plus the increase on January 16.*

[b] *Maximum debit is $80, which is the balance in the account (from January 16 treasury stock transaction).*

2250.28 The Treasury Stock account is carried at cost under both of the assumptions regarding additional paid-in capital. Under assumption 2, the sale of treasury stock below cost can reduce additional paid-in capital only to the extent of any balance in the PIC—Treasury Stock account arising from previous treasury stock transactions.

2250.29 **Par value method:** The par value method views the acquisition of treasury stock as the constructive retirement of those shares. The entries for the described treasury stock transactions are:

Jan. 10	Treasury Stock (at par)	$1,000	
	PIC (capital in excess of par)[a]	400	
	Retained Earnings (100 x ($17 – $14))	300	
	Cash		$1,700
Jan. 16	Cash (40 × $19)	$ 760	
	Treasury Stock (40 × $10)		$ 400
	PIC (capital in excess of par) (40 x ($19 – $10))		360
Jan. 23	Cash (50 × $11)	$ 550	
	Treasury Stock (50 × $10)		$ 500
	PIC (capital in excess of par) ($50 x ($11 – $10)		50

[a] *Pro rata share of account (10% of $4,000)*

Common stock, $10 par (1,000 shares authorized, issued, and outstanding) $10,000
Additional paid-in capital (capital in excess of par)   4,000
Total paid-in capital $14,000
$14,000 ÷ 1,000 shares = $14 per share issue price
100 shares x ($14 issue price per share - $10 par value per share)
   = 100 shares x $4 per share = $400
OR
(100 shares ÷ 1,000 shares) x $4,000 APIC = .10 x $4,000 = $400

Balance Sheet Presentation

2250.30   Delphi Company's balance sheet on January 10, immediately after acquiring the treasury shares, would appear as follows under the cost method:

Common stock $10 par (1,000 shares authorized and issued, of which 100 are in the treasury)	$10,000
Additional paid-in capital	4,000
Total paid-in capital	$14,000
Retained earnings	60,000
	74,000
Less: Treasury stock, at cost	1,700
Total stockholders' equity	$72,300

2250.31   Delphi would prepare the following stockholders' equity section on that date if the par value method is used:

Common stock, $10 par (1,000 shares authorized and issued)		$10,000
Less: Treasury stock, at par (100 shares)	1,000	$ 9,000
Additional paid-in capital		3,600
Total paid-in capital		$12,600
Retained earnings		59,700
Total stockholders' equity		$72,300

2250.32   Note that total stockholders' equity is the same under the two methods (cost and par value). The difference lies in the manner in which treasury stock is accounted for and disclosed.

Dividends and Stock Splits

2250.33   The following three dates are important as they relate to dividends:

1. Date of declaration
2. Date of record
3. Date of payment

2250.34   The *date of declaration* is the date the dividend is declared by the board of directors and becomes a liability, if other than a stock dividend.

2250.35   The *date of record* is the date on which the stockholders whose names appear on the corporation's records are entitled to receive the dividend.

2250.36   The *date of payment* is the date the dividend is paid or issued.

Types of Dividends

2250.37   Dividends may take any of various forms, such as the following:

a. Cash dividends

b. Property dividends

c. Scrip dividends

d. Liquidating dividends

e. Stock dividends

2250.38 **Cash dividends** are declared on the basis of a specified amount for each share of outstanding stock. The entries would be:

    At date of declaration:
        Retained Earnings   XXX
            Dividends Payable   XXX

    At date of payment:
        Dividends Payable   XXX
            Cash   XXX

2250.39 **Property dividends** are rare. They are paid in the form of some noncash asset, such as merchandise, investments, or fixed assets. A property dividend is a nonreciprocal transfer of nonmonetary assets to the owners. Accordingly, it should be accounted for on the basis of the fair value of the assets transferred.

2250.40 **Scrip dividends** occur when a corporation declares a dividend, but because it is unable to pay the dividend now, obligates itself to pay the dividend at a later date. The scrip issued to the stockholders is a special form of liability.

2250.41 **Liquidating dividends** occur when the corporation uses paid-in capital, rather than retained earnings, as a basis for dividends. Liquidating dividends are returns *of* capital rather than returns *on* capital. The appropriate additional paid-in capital account, rather than retained earnings, should be debited when a liquidating dividend is declared.

2250.42 **Stock dividends** occur when a corporation issues shares of its own stock in the form of a dividend.

Stock Dividends vs. Stock Split

2250.43 A stock dividend changes neither the par value of the stock nor the total stockholders' equity. However, the number of shares issued and outstanding is increased.

2250.44 A stock split also involves an increase in the number of shares issued and outstanding. A stock split involves a change in the par or stated value of the stock.

2250.45 Accounting for a stock dividend (par value is not changed) depends on whether it is considered to be a small stock dividend or a large stock dividend.

2250.46 Stock dividends resulting in the issuance of additional shares representing less than 20%–25% of the outstanding shares are considered to be small stock dividends. Stock dividends involving the issuance of more than 20%–25% of the outstanding stock are deemed to be large stock dividends.

2250.47 **Small stock dividends** are accounted for on the basis of fair value of the shares issued in the form of a stock dividend. For example, assume that Company X has outstanding 1,000 shares of $10 par common stock. A 10% stock dividend is declared, meaning the current stockholders will receive one share of new stock for each 10 shares of the company's stock presently held. Assuming the fair value of the shares issued as a stock dividend is $23 per share, the entries to record the stock dividend are:

Date of declaration:		
Retained Earnings (100 × $23)	$2,300	
Stock Dividends Distributable (100 × $10)		$1,000
PIC—Stock Dividends		1,300
Date of payment:		
Stock Dividends Distributable	$1,000	
Common Stock		$1,000

2250.48 Stock dividends distributable should be shown in the capital stock section of the balance sheet and not as a liability.

2250.49 **Large stock dividends** are usually accounted for on the basis of the par or stated value of the stock rather than on the basis of fair value. To illustrate, assume that Company Y has outstanding 1,000 shares of $10 par common stock. The entry to record the declaration of a 40% stock dividend is:

Retained Earnings (400 × $10 par)	$ 4,000	
Stock Dividends Distributable		$ 4,000

2250.50 **Stock splits** involve an increase in the number of shares outstanding and a corresponding decrease in the par or stated value of each share. (A "reverse" stock split, such as a 1-for-2 split, *decreases* the shares outstanding and increases the par or stated value per share.) Stock splits have no impact on retained earnings or total stockholders' equity. No entry is required for a stock split. However, a formality entry might be used to acknowledge a stock split. For example, a 2-for-1 stock split involving the issuance of 2,000 shares of $5 par stock to replace 1,000 shares of $10 par stock could be reflected in the accounts by the following entry:

Common Stock, $10 par	$10,000	
Common Stock, $5 par		$10,000

Dividends on Preferred Stock

2250.51 Preferred stock usually has a priority over common stock with regard to dividends. The preferred stockholders must be paid their stated preference amount before common stockholders can be paid anything.

2250.52 Preferred stock may be cumulative or noncumulative. If cumulative, any preferred dividends not paid in prior years (dividends in arrears) plus the current year's preferred dividend must be paid before any dividends can be paid to common stockholders. Noncumulative preferred stock has a preference right only with respect to the current year's dividends. Prior years' undeclared dividends are gone forever.

2250.53 Preferred stock may be participating or nonparticipating. Participating preferred stock participates with common stock in dividend distributions in excess of specified amounts for preferred and common.

2250.54 **Example:** Assume that Marcelle Company has both preferred and common stock outstanding as shown:

6% preferred stock, $100 par (1,000 shares)	$100,000
Common stock, $10 par (20,000 shares)	200,000

Assuming dividends were not paid on preferred stock during the two previous years, the declaration of total cash dividends of $42,000 in the current year would be distributed as shown under each of the assumptions given:

a. Preferred stock is noncumulative and nonparticipating:

	Preferred	Common	Total
Preference rate (6% of $100,000)	$6,000		$ 6,000
Remainder to common		$36,000	36,000
	$6,000	$36,000	$42,000

b. Preferred stock is cumulative and nonparticipating:

	Preferred	Common	Total
Dividends in arrears (2 × $6,000)	$12,000		$12,000
Preference rate (6% of $100,000)	6,000		6,000
Remainder to common		$24,000	24,000
	$18,000	$24,000	$42,000

c. Preferred stock is cumulative and fully participating:

	Preferred	Common	Total
Dividends in arrears	$12,000		$12,000
Preference rate (6% of $100,000)	6,000		6,000
Similar rate to common (6% of $200,000)		$12,000	12,000
Participation	4,000	8,000	12,000
	$22,000	$20,000	$42,000

2250.55 The participation amounts may be determined in either of two ways:

1. $$\frac{\text{Total par value of preferred}}{\text{Total par value of preferred and common}} \times \text{Participation amount} =$$

   ($100,000 ÷ ($100,000 + $200,000)) × $12,000

   = $4,000 to preferred and ($12,000 - $4,000) to common

2.
Participation amount	$ 12,000
Total par value of all stock participating	300,000
Participation rate ($12,000 × $300,000)	4%
To preferred: 4% of $100,000	4,000
To common: 4% of $200,000	8,000

Miscellaneous Issues

Book Value per Share

2250.56 When only one class of stock is outstanding, book value per share of common stock is determined as follows:

$$\frac{\text{Total stockholders' equity}}{\text{Common shares outstanding}} = \text{Book value per share}$$

2250.57 If both preferred stock and common stock are outstanding, the computation of book value per share requires that the amount of total stockholders' equity applicable to each class of stock first be determined.

2250.58 To illustrate, assume that the stockholders' equity section of ABC Company appears as follows:

Preferred stock, $100 par (1,000 shares authorized, issued, and outstanding), callable at $105		$100,000
Common stock, $10 par (20,000 shares authorized and issued, of which 1,000 shares are in the treasury)		200,000
		300,000
Additional paid-in capital:		
Preferred	$18,000	
Common	40,000	58,000
		358,000
Retained earnings		200,000
		558,000
Less: Treasury stock (common), at cost (1,000 shares)		32,000
Total stockholders' equity		$526,000

2250.59 Assuming that the preferred stock is cumulative and has dividends in arrears of $12,000, book value per share of common stock is determined as follows:

Total stockholders' equity		$526,000
Applicable to preferred:		
Call price of preferred (1,000 × $105)	$105,000	
Dividends in arrears	12,000	117,000
Stockholders' equity applicable to common		$409,000
Book value per share of common:		
Stockholders' equity applicable to common		$409,000
Divided by number of common shares outstanding		÷ 19,000
Book value per share of common		$ 21.53

Conversion of Preferred Stock

2250.60 The conversion of convertible preferred stock into common stock is recorded on the basis of the book value of the convertible preferred.

2250.61 To illustrate, assume that 1,000 shares of $100 par convertible preferred stock, which were originally issued at $105 per share, are converted into 3,000 shares of $10 par common stock at a time when common stock is selling for $120 per share. The entry to record the conversion is:

Preferred Stock	$100,000	
Capital in Excess of Par—Preferred	5,000	
Common Stock (3,000 × $10 par)		$30,000
Capital in Excess of Par—Common		75,000

Disclosure of Information About Capital Structure

2250.62 All enterprises, public and nonpublic, that have issued securities are required to make certain disclosures about their capital structure. The FASB ASC Glossary defines securities as "the evidence of debt or ownership of a related right."

Information About Securities

2250.63 An enterprise must explain, in summary form within its financial statements, the pertinent rights and privileges of the various securities outstanding. Examples of this type of information include the following:

    a. Dividend and liquidation preferences

    b. Participation rights

    c. Call prices and dates

    d. Conversion or exercise prices or rates and pertinent dates

    e. Sinking-fund requirements

    f. Unusual voting rights

    g. Significant terms of contracts to issue additional shares

2250.64 An enterprise must disclose within its financial statements the number of shares issued on conversion, exercise, or satisfaction of required conditions during at least the most recent annual fiscal period and any subsequent interim period presented.

Liquidation Preference of Preferred Stock

2250.65 If an enterprise issues preferred stock (or other senior stock) that has a preference in involuntary liquidation significantly in excess of the par or stated value of the shares, it must disclose the liquidation preference of the stock (i.e., the relationship between the preference in liquidation and the par or stated value of the shares). That disclosure must be made in the equity section of the balance sheet in the aggregate, either parenthetically or "in short." Disclosure on a per-share basis or through disclosure in the notes will not satisfy this disclosure requirement.

2250.66 An enterprise must also disclose within its financial statements (either on the face of the balance sheet or in the notes) the following:

    a. The aggregate or per-share amounts at which preferred stock may be called or is subject to redemption through sinking fund operations or otherwise

    b. The aggregate and per-share amounts of arrearages in cumulative preferred stock dividends

2250.67 An enterprise that issues redeemable stock must disclose the amount of redemption requirements, separately by issue or combined, for all issues of capital stock that are redeemable at fixed or determinable prices on fixed or determinable dates in each of the five years following the date of the latest balance sheet presented.

2251 Revenue Recognition

General Revenue Recognition Concepts

2251.01 Revenue is generally considered to be realized when the following conditions are met:

    a. The earning process is complete.

    b. An exchange has taken place.

If these conditions are met, the realization should be evidenced by the recognition of revenue in the income statement.

2251.02 In most situations, revenue is recognized at the point of sale because it is generally felt that the sale transaction provides evidence that realization (i.e., earning) is complete or virtually complete. Prior to the point of sale, significant uncertainties may exist concerning realization.

    a. Will the product being held or manufactured be completed?

    b. What will the total cost of manufactured inventory be?

    c. Will existing inventory be sold?

    d. At what price will the inventory sell?

    e. Will the sales price be collectible (in the case of a credit sale)?

    f. Will costs arise after the sale (e.g., warranties) and if so, how much?

While the sales transaction does not resolve all these questions, it does represent a strong indication that the conditions for revenue realization have been met and that it is appropriate to formally recognize the revenue in the income statement. Typically, the physical flow of the products sold closely parallels the sales transaction.

2251.03 Revenues recognized at the point of sale result in the recognition of an asset (e.g., cash or receivables) and a credit to a revenue account. Allowances for various unresolved items at the point of sale must be made to complete the matching process for the income statement. These estimates are based on prior experience with similar items: uncollectible receivables, warranty costs, and merchandise returns.

2251.04 A number of situations arise in which there are difficulties in applying these general principles of revenue recognition. For example, in some cases, it may not be possible to accurately estimate costs that will be incurred after the point of sale. In other cases, the physical flow of merchandise may not indicate that a sale transaction has taken place. In some cases, the transaction covers a number of accounting periods rather than being culminated at a single point in time or over a short period of time. In the following sections, a number of unique problems of revenue recognition are reviewed.

Revenue on Long-Term Contracts

2251.05 Long-term contracts pose an interesting revenue recognition problem because they typically span two or more accounting periods. Two methods are used in accounting for revenues under long-term contracts—the percentage-of-completion method (PC) and the completed-contracts method (CC). These two methods are described in the following analysis:

Method	Description	Circumstances Where Appropriate
PC	Partial revenue is recognized on an estimated basis in each period covered by the contract.	Reliable estimates of the degree of completion can be made based on costs incurred to date or other bases (e.g., engineering estimates).
CC	All revenue is deferred and recognized in the period when the contract is completed.	Reliable estimates of the degree of completion cannot be made at intermediate points in the contract period.

2251.06 **Example:** Contract Co. is engaged in a long-term contract to construct a building. The amount to be received on the contract is $400,000. The contractor can bill the customer for 80% of expenses incurred to date periodically and receive payment for that amount. The remainder of the contract price is to be billed when the project is complete. Data for the three years over which the contract spans are as follows:

	20X1	20X2	20X3
Accumulated costs incurred to year end	$ 50,000	$175,000	$272,000
Estimated costs to complete	200,000	90,000	0
Estimated total costs	$250,000	$265,000	$272,000
Collections to date	$ 35,000	$135,000	$400,000

The contract was completed and final payments made in 20X3. Percentage-of-completion is estimated based on costs incurred to date over total estimated costs. An analysis of the contract is as follows:

	20X1	20X2	20X3
Contract price	$400,000	$400,000	$400,000
Costs incurred to year end	$ 50,000	$175,000	$272,000
Expected costs to complete	200,000	90,000	0
Total estimated costs	$250,000	$265,000	$272,000
Estimated profit	$150,000	$135,000	$128,000
Percentage-of-completion based on costs to date:			
$50,000/$250,000	20%		
$175,000/$265,000		66%	
$272,000/$272,000			100%
Progress billings to date[a]	$ 40,000	$140,000	$400,000
Collections to date	$ 35,000	$135,000	$400,000
Estimated income earned each year:			
$150,000 × 0.20	$ 30,000		
($135,000 × 0.66) - $30,000		$ 59,100	
($128,000 - ($30,000 + $59,100))			$ 38,900

[a] *80% of costs incurred to date in 20X1 and 20X2; total contract price ($400,000) in 20X3*

Entries for the year 20X1 and the financial statement presentation at December 31, 20X1, (which are indicative of all years) are presented as follows:

Construction in Progress	$50,000	
Materials, Cash, Payables, etc.		$50,000
To record the construction costs incurred.		
Accounts Receivable—Construction Contract	$40,000	
Billings on Construction in Progress		$40,000
To record progress billings.		
Cash	$35,000	
Accounts Receivable—Construction Contract		$35,000
To record collections of billings.		
Construction in Progress	$30,000	
Estimated Income on Long-term Contract		$30,000
To recognize income.		

Income Statement
    Estimated income on long-term contract $30,000

Balance Sheet
Current assets
Accounts receivable—construction contract		$ 5,000
Inventory—construction in progress	$80,000	
Less billings on construction in progress	40,000	$40,000

Similar entries are made under the PC method for the other years. Under the CC method, all entries are the same—except the last one (to recognize income) is not made and all income is recognized in the year of the completion of the contract. The inventory item on the previous page is reduced by the amount of income that was recognized under the PC method in the previous example.

2251.07 Where reasonably dependable estimates of the percentage-of-completion can be made, the PC method should be used; otherwise, the CC method is used. Disclosure of the method used must be made in the financial statements (in the summary of significant accounting policies).

2251.08 Where total billings on construction in process exceed the total cost of construction in process, the difference is presented as a current liability (the opposite of the situation demonstrated in the previous example in which the excess of costs incurred over amounts billed was presented as an asset).

2251.09 A departure from the procedures outlined is necessary where a loss becomes apparent on a long-term contract. Under both the percentage-of-completion method and the completed-contracts method, the estimated total loss on the contract is recognized in the period in which the loss becomes apparent and estimable.

Installment Sales

2251.10 Under the installment sales method of recognizing revenue, recognition is deferred beyond the point of sale and is associated with the subsequent collection of payments. The rationale underlying the method is that the length of the installment contract and the nature of the contract itself impose degrees of uncertainty concerning collection such that reasonably dependable estimates of uncollectibles are not possible. Where these conditions exist, the seller typically retains the right to repossess the property involved in the sale.

2251.11 Under the installment sales method, the gross profit on sales is deferred and recognized as cash is actually collected. Each payment is divided into two parts—a recovery of cost and a recognition of gross profit. Since gross profit margins may vary from period to period, it is necessary to identify receivables and deferred gross profit accounts by year, as illustrated in the following example.

2251.12 **Example:** The Ice Cold Company sells refrigerators and other appliances on an installment basis. Data for a 2-year period is as follows:

	20X1	20X2
Sales on installment basis	$500,000	$600,000
Costs of sales	400,000	475,000
Gross profit	$100,000	$125,000
Gross profit percentage	20%	21%
Collections:		
20X1 sales	$175,000	$200,000
20X2 sales	0	250,000

Partial entries to record these events are as follows:

Installment Accounts Receivable (20X1)	$500,000	
Installment Sales		$500,000
Cost of Installment Sales	$400,000	
Inventory		$400,000

To record 20X1 installment sales and cost of sales.

Cash	$175,000	
Installment Accounts Receivable (20X1)		$175,000

To record collections on 20X1 installment sales.

Installment Sales	$500,000	
Cost of Installment Sales		$400,000
Deferred Gross Profit (20X1)		100,000

To close nominal accounts.

Deferred Gross Profit (20X1)	$ 35,000	
Realized Gross Profit (20X1)		$ 35,000
($175,000 × 0.20 = $35,000)		

To recognize gross profit on 20X1 collections.

Gross profit deferred as installment sales are made in 20X2 is $125,000, recorded in a manner similar to 20X1. Deferred gross profit recognized, as realized in 20X2, is as follows:

    For 20X1 sales: $200,000 × 0.20 = $40,000
    For 20X2 sales: $250,000 × 0.21 = $52,500

2251.13 For the protection of the seller, legal title to the property and/or the right to repossess the property on nonpayment by the customer typically resides with the seller. In the case of a default, an entry similar to the following pro forma entry is made to reestablish the inventory and to eliminate the deferred gross profit and account receivable on the defaulted contract.

Repossessed Inventory	XXX	
Deferred Gross Profit (20XX)	XXX	
Installment Accounts Receivable (20XX)		XXX

The repossessed inventory is debited for the fair value of the asset received. It will be necessary to recognize a gain or loss on repossession if the fair value of the asset is greater or less than the excess of the receivable balance over the deferred gross profit on the deferred contract at the time of repossession.

2251.14 When installment sales contracts include the payment of interest, the interest and gross profit portions of payments are separated and accounted for as distinctly different elements of income.

2251.15 The installment sales method is more conservative than the usual policy of revenue recognition at the point of sale, because it defers recognition until cash is received. As the previous example indicates, a portion of the total gross profit on the sale is recognized each time a cash payment is received. The *cost recovery method* is an even more conservative approach in that the early payments are considered entirely a recovery of cost, and not until the cost is completely recovered is any gross profit recognized. This method is rarely encountered in practice.

2251.16 Under generally accepted accounting principles, profit is deemed to be realized at the point of sale unless circumstances are such that the collection of the sales price is not reasonably assured. Only in exceptional cases—where receivables are collectible over an extended period of time and, because of the terms of the transaction or other uncertainties, there is no reasonable basis for estimating the degree of collectibility—are the installment sales and cost recovery methods acceptable in the preparation of general purpose financial statements.

Consignment Sales

2251.17 Under a consignment arrangement, the consignor (owner) transfers merchandise to the consignee, who attempts to sell the merchandise for the consignor. Typically, the consignor retains ownership of the property and reimburses the consignee for costs of selling, including a commission on the sale.

2251.18 **Example:** R Company transfers goods to E Company on consignment as follows: 100 units at a cost of $10 each are to be sold for $18 each; freight paid by R Company is $70; expenses incurred by E Company are $75 plus 20% commission on all units sold based on the selling price. The goods are transferred on November 15, 20X1, and by December 31, 20X1, 65 units have been sold. An accounting from E Company was made to R Company at this point. Special accounts used by the consignor and consignee are demonstrated as follows:

Consignor

Consignment Out Account Ledger			
Shipment: 100 at $10	$1,000.00	$1,170.00	Sales: 65 at $18
Freight	70.00	400.75	Inventory at 12/31[a]
Consignee expenses			
Miscellaneous	75.00		
Commissions (0.20 × $18 × 65)	234.00		
Gross profit on consignment sales[a,b]	191.75		
	$1,570.75	$1,570.75	
Inventory at 01/01 (brought forward)[b]	$ 400.75		

[a] *Gross profit on consignment sales:*

Selling price		$1,170.00
Commissions	$ 234.00	
Inventoriable costs	744.25	978.25
		$ 191.75

[b] *Inventoriable costs related to all 100 items are:*

		Allocated to:	
Unit cost	$1,000.00		
Freight	70.00	Items sold (65%)	$ 744.25
Miscellaneous (by consignee)	75.00	Items in inventory (35%)	400.75
	$1,145.00		$1,145.00

The balance in the consignment out account represents inventory to the consignor. Until sales are reported to the consignor by the consignee, no income is recognized by the consignor.

Consignee

Consignment In			
Miscellaneous (consignee)	$ 75.00	$1,170.00	Sales: 65 at $18
Commissions (0.20 × $18 × 65)	234.00		
Cash transferred to consignor	861.00		
	$1,170.00	$1,170.00	

At this point, the consignment in account balance is zero because a reporting has just been made. When a balance does exist, a debit balance represents a receivable to the consignee from the consignor. A credit balance represents a payable from the consignee to the consignor.

Franchise Fee Revenue

2251.19   Franchise fee revenue is recognized when all material services or conditions relating to the sale have been substantially performed or satisfied by the franchisor. In addition, an appropriate provision is made for estimated uncollectible amounts. Substantial performance means that the franchisor has no remaining obligations, virtually all services required of the franchisor have been performed, and no other material obligations of the franchisor remain.

2251.20 If a portion of the initial franchise fee is designated to compensate the franchisor for continuing services to be rendered during the franchise period, a portion of the fee is deferred and recognized over the franchise period.

2251.21 If the conditions necessary for recognition of franchise fee revenue are not met, direct costs relating to franchise sales are deferred until the related revenue is recognized. Any costs deferred in this manner, however, should not exceed anticipated revenue less estimated additional related costs to be incurred.

2251.22 The following information is disclosed in the financial statements and related notes concerning franchises:

    a. The nature of all significant commitments and obligations from franchises

    b. The details of deferred franchise fees

    c. The separation of initial franchise fees from other franchise fee revenues

    d. Revenues and costs related to franchise-owned outlets, separate from revenues and costs related to franchise outlet, if practicable

Revenue Recognition When Right of Return Exists

2251.23 When the right of return exists, revenue is recognized by the seller when the following conditions are met:

    a. The seller's price is substantially fixed or determinable at the date of the sale.

    b. The buyer has paid the seller; or the buyer is obligated to pay the seller, and this obligation is not contingent on the resale of the products.

    c. The buyer's obligation is not changed in the event of theft or destruction of the products.

    d. The buyer has economic substance apart from the seller.

    e. The seller does not have significant obligations for future performance to directly bring about resale of the products.

    f. The amount of future returns can be estimated.

2251.24 Where these criteria are met, revenue is recognized with an appropriate allowance for estimated returns and the cost of those returns. Where one (or more) of these criteria is not met, both the revenue and the related cost are deferred and recognized only when all six criteria are met.

Accounting for Product Financing Arrangements

2251.25 Product financing arrangements include agreements in which a sponsor (the enterprise seeking to finance a product, pending future resale or use) does the following:

    a. Sells the product to another entity and, in a related transaction, agrees to repurchase the product

    b. Arranges for another entity to purchase the product on the sponsor's behalf and, in a related transaction, agrees to purchase the product from the other entity

    c. Controls the disposition of the product that has been purchased by another entity in accordance with either of the arrangements described previously

2251.26 Product financing arrangements are accounted for as follows by the sponsor:

    a. If a sponsor sells a product to another entity, agreeing to repurchase the product in the future, the sponsor records a liability at the time the proceeds are received. The sponsor does not record a sale and does not remove the product from its balance sheet.

    b. If the sponsor is a party to an arrangement whereby another entity purchases a product on the sponsor's behalf, the sponsor records the asset and the related liability when the product is purchased from the other entity.

2251.27 Costs of the product, excluding processing costs, in excess of the sponsor's original production or purchase costs or the other entity's purchase costs represent financing and holding costs to be recorded by the sponsor.

Accounting for Sales of Real Estate

2251.28 Profit is recognized in full when real estate is sold, provided:

    a. the profit is determinable (i.e., collectibility is reasonably assured or the amount that will not be collectible can be estimated) and

    b. the earnings process is virtually complete (i.e., the seller has no further obligations to earn the profit).

2251.29 In accounting for sales of real estate, the collectibility of the sales price is demonstrated by the buyer's commitment to pay, which in turn is supported by substantial initial and continuing investments that give the buyer a stake in the property sufficient that the risk of loss through default motivates the buyer to honor its obligation to the seller. Collectibility can also be assessed by considering factors such as the credit standing of the buyer, age and location of the property, and adequacy of the cash flow from the property.

2251.30 Profit on real estate sale transactions is not recognized until all of the following criteria are met:

    a. A sale is consummated.

    b. The buyer's initial and continuing investments are adequate to demonstrate a commitment to pay for the property.

    c. The seller's receivable is not subject to future subordination.

    d. The seller has transferred to the buyer the usual risks and rewards of ownership in a transaction that is in substance a sale, and the seller does not have a substantial continuing involvement with the property.

2251.31 FASB ASC 978-10-05-4 specifies that real estate time-sharing transactions should be accounted for as nonretail land sales. FASB ASC 978-10-05 provides additional guidance on the accounting for those types of transactions.

Milestone Method

2251.32 Research and development revenue involving deliverables or units of account must be accounted for under the milestone method of revenue recognition. This method applies to research or development deliverables or units of accounting under which a vendor satisfies its performance obligations over a period of time, and when a portion or all of the consideration is contingent upon uncertain future events or circumstances.

2251.33 Recognition is contingent upon the achievement of a substantive milestone in its entirety in the period in which the milestone is achieved.

2251.34 Determining whether a milestone is substantive is a matter of judgment; that assessment shall be performed only at the inception of the arrangement. The consideration earned from the achievement of a milestone shall meet all of the following for the milestone to be considered substantive (FASB ASC 605-28-25-2):

    a. It is commensurate with either of the following:

        (1) The vendor's performance to achieve the milestone

        (2) The enhancement of the value of the delivered item or items as a result of a specific outcome resulting from the vendor's performance to achieve the milestone

    b. It relates solely to past performance.

    c. It is reasonable relative to all of the deliverables and payment terms (including other potential milestone consideration) within the arrangement.

2251.35 A milestone is not substantive if any portion of the associated milestone consideration relates to the remaining deliverables in the unit of accounting (that is, it does not relate solely to past performance). To recognize the milestone consideration in its entirety as revenue in the period in which the milestone is achieved, the milestone shall be substantive in its entirety. Milestone consideration shall not be divided into substantive and nonsubstantive components. In addition, if a portion of the consideration earned from achieving a milestone may be refunded or adjusted based on future performance (for example, through a penalty or clawback), the contingent consideration is not considered to relate solely to past performance and, thus, the related milestone cannot be considered substantive. If the consideration from an individual milestone is not considered to relate solely to past performance, the vendor is not precluded from using the milestone method for other milestones in the arrangement. (FASB ASC 605-28-25-3)

2252 Costs and Expenses

2252.01 As discussed in section **2121.27**, guidance for recognizing expenses and losses is as follows (SFAC 5.85):

    a. **Consumption of benefit:** Expenses are generally recognized when an enterprise's economic benefits are consumed in revenue-earning activities or otherwise.

    b. **Loss or lack of benefit:** Expenses or losses are recognized if it becomes evident that previously recognized future economic benefits of assets have been reduced or eliminated, or that liabilities have been incurred or increased, without associated economic benefits.

2252.02 Stated differently in section **2132.05**, expenses are outflows of assets or incurrences of liabilities, during a period, from delivering or producing goods, rendering services, or other activities that constitute the entity's ongoing major or central operations. Losses are decreases in net assets other than from expenses or withdrawals by owners.

2252.03 Expenses are accrued (expensed) based on the matching principle. As discussed in section **2112.09(c)**, the matching principle states that the accrual basis of accounting correctly matches the revenue from the sale of goods with the historical cost of the inventory sold, the salesperson's salary, and other applicable costs and expenses. Net income or loss for an accounting period is determined by the process of associating realized revenues with those expenses and expired costs necessary to generate them. This often requires estimates and allocations.

2252.04 Following are some of the most common expenses and costs:

    a. Cost of goods sold (discussed at section **2212**, "Inventory")

    b. Depreciation (discussed at section **2213**, "Property, Plant, and Equipment")

    c. Interest (discussed at section **2241**, "Notes Payable," and section **2242**, "Bonds Payable")

    d. Uncollectible accounts (discussed at section **2211.08**, "Accounting for Uncollectible Accounts")

    e. Post-acquisition costs (discussed at section **2213.39**, "Post-Acquisition Costs")

    f. Amortization and impairment (discussed at section **2230**, "Intangible Assets – Goodwill and Other")

Imputed Interest on Receivables and Payables

2252.05 Debt instruments representing contractual rights or obligations to receive or pay money on fixed or determinable dates are generally recorded at the present value of the instrument at the issuance date. The difference between the face and present value is recognized as interest income or expensed over the life of the instrument in such a way as to result in a constant rate of interest.

2252.06 Types of consideration typically exchanged for notes and the proper accounting are as follows:

	Consideration Exchanged	**Accounting Treatment**
a.	Cash alone	The note is presumed to have a present value at issuance equal to the cash proceeds exchanged.
b.	Cash with unstated or stated rights or privileges	Rights or privileges are given accounting recognition by establishing a note discount or premium account. The effective rate differs from the stated rate.
c.	Property, goods, or services	The face value of the note is presumed to represent the bargained purchase price unless: (1) interest is not stated, (2) the stated interest is unreasonable, or (3) the face value of the note varies significantly from the cash sales price of the property or the market value of the note.

2252.07 Where the present value of the note must be established (as in (b) and (c)), the following should be considered:

    a. The fair value of the consideration exchanged

    b. The market value of the note

    c. The present value of all future payments (imputed by estimating the incremental borrowing rate of the debtor)

2252.08 **Example:** Co. S (seller) sells merchandise to Co. P (purchaser) in exchange for a $2,000 noninterest-bearing note due in two years. The merchandise cost Co. S $1,200 and typically sells for $1,640. Co. S will record the sale and Co. P will record the purchase as follows:

Co. S			Co. P		
Note Receivable (N/R)	$2,000		Inventory	$1,640	
Discount on N/R		$ 360	Discount on N/P	360	
Sale		1,640	Note Payable (N/P)		$2,000

The discount is recognized as interest income by Co. S and as interest expense by Co. P over the 2-year life of the note at a constant rate.

2252.09 **Example:** Co. B (borrower) issues a noninterest-bearing note to Co. L (lender) in exchange for $1,000 cash and the promise to sell Co. L inventory at a reduced price during the credit period. The present value of the note is estimated at $900. Co. B and Co. L will record the transaction as follows:

Co. B			Co. L		
Cash	$1,000		Note Receivable	$1,000	
			Inventory	100	
Discount on N/P	100				
Note Payable (N/P)		$1,000	Discount on N/R		$ 100
Sales (or Deferred Revenue)		100	Cash		1,000

The discounts are recognized as interest over the life of the note at a constant rate.

2252.10 **Example:** Co. S (seller) sells used equipment with no determinable market value to Co. P (purchaser) in exchange for a $10,000, 3-year, noninterest-bearing note. Co. P's incremental borrowing rate is estimated at 10%. Co. S originally paid $20,000 for the asset and has recognized $15,000 depreciation. The present value of the note is determined as follows:

($10,000) × (0.7513)[a] = $7,513
[a] Present value of $1, 3 periods, 10%

The note is recorded at its present value of $7,513 with a discount of $2,487 established and recognized over the 3-year period according to the following schedule:

	Annual Interest[a]	Balances		
		Face	Discount	Net
01/01/Year 1	$ 0	$10,000	$2,487	$ 7,513
12/31/Year 1	751	10,000	1,736	8,264
12/31/Year 2	826	10,000	910	9,090
12/31/Year 3	910	10,000	0	10,000
	$2,487			

[a] 10% of the carrying value of the note, rounded in last year to eliminate the remaining discount

Entries to record the note and interest are as follows:

Co. S			Co. P		
Note Receivable (N/R)	$10,000		Equipment	$ 7,513	
			Discount on N/P	2,487	
Accumulated Depreciation	15,000		Note Payable		$10,000
Equipment		$20,000			
Discount on N/R		2,487			
Gain on Sale		2,513			
Discount on N/R	$ 751		Interest Expense	$ 751	
Interest Income		$ 751	Discount on N/P		$ 751
(Year 1 interest)			(Year 1 interest)		
Discount on N/R	$ 826		Interest Expense	$ 826	
Interest Income		$ 826	Discount on N/P		$ 826
(Year 2 interest)			(Year 2 interest)		
Discount on N/R	$ 910		Interest Expense	$ 910	
Interest Income		$ 910	Discount on N/P		$ 910
(Year 3 interest)			(Year 3 interest)		
Cash	$10,000		Note Payable	$10,000	
Note Receivable		$10,000	Cash		$10,000

2252.11   As indicated in the previous examples, the difference between the present value and the face value of a note is treated as a discount or premium and amortized as interest expense or income over the life of the note in such a way that it results in a constant rate of interest when applied to the amount outstanding at the beginning of the period. Other methods may be used if the results obtained are not materially different from those obtained using the interest method described. Any unamortized discount or premium existing when a balance sheet is prepared is presented as a deduction from or addition to the face amount of the note. Amortization of the premium or discount is reported as interest in the income statement. Issue costs are included in the cost of the bonds and are therefore amortized over the life of the note.

2260 Compensation and Benefits

2261 Compensated Absences

2261.01   Compensated absences are employees' absences, such as for vacations, illness, and holidays, for which it is expected that the employees will be paid.

2261.02   In general, the employer should accrue a liability for such future absences if *all* the following conditions are met:

    a.   The employer's obligation relating to employees' rights to receive compensation for future absences is attributable to employees' services already rendered.

    b.   The obligation relates to rights that vest or accumulate.

    c.   Payment of the compensation is probable.

    d.   The amount can be reasonably estimated.

2261.03 The rights *vest* if the employer is obligated to make payment, even if the employee terminates (i.e., the right to compensated absences is not contingent on the employee's future service). The rights *accumulate* if earned, but unused rights to compensated absences may be carried forward to one or more periods subsequent to that in which they are earned.

2261.04 Notwithstanding, the general rule presented in section **2261.02**, FASB ASC 710-10-25-1 does *not* require an employer to accrue a liability for *nonvesting* accumulating rights to receive sick pay benefits. However, FASB ASC 710-10-25-2 notes that benefits that, in substance, are not sick pay benefits even though they may be called sick pay benefits should not be treated as sick pay benefits for accounting purposes. An example would be a situation in which employees are customarily paid sick benefits even though their absences are not actually the result of illness. The fact that these benefits are not to be considered sick pay benefits means that the criteria listed in section **2261.02** are applicable to such sick pay benefits.

2261.05 **Example:** Assume that in its first year of operation (20X1), Blue Company determines that its employees have earned 100 days of vacation, the right to which is vested. In addition, the employees have accumulated 50 days of nonvested sick pay. Wages and other fringe benefits, other than vacation and sick pay, average $200 per day. During 20X2, Blue paid its employees 80 days of vacation pay and 15 days of sick pay, all of which were earned in 20X1. The related entries are:

End of 20X1:
Wages Expense $20,000
    Estimated Liability for Compensated Absences $20,000
To record the estimated vacation pay earned in 20X1, 100 days × $200 wages per day = $20,000.

During 20X2:
Estimated Liability For Compensated Absences $16,000
    Cash $16,000
To record payment of wages related to vacation days taken in 20X2 but earned in 20X1 80 days × $200 wages per day = $16,000.

Wages Expense $ 3,000
    Cash $ 3,000
To record payment of wages related to sick pay days taken in 20X2 but earned in 20X1 15 days × $200 wages per day = $3,000.

2261.06 Note that the accrual at the end of 20X1 is only for vacation pay. Blue is not required to accrue the compensation related to sick pay. (However, even though FASB ASC 710-10-25-3 does not require Blue to accrue the sick pay, it does *permit* the accrual of sick pay if the enterprise so chooses and if the criteria in section **2261.02** are met.)

2261.07 The estimated liability for compensated absences would normally be disclosed as a current liability. However, any portion of the liability related to payments expected to be made beyond one year (or operating cycle, if longer) should be classified as a long-term liability.

2261.08 The discussion in sections **2261.01–.07** relates to compensated absences (benefits provided) during the employee's term of employment. Employees also may be granted benefits that will be provided after the term of employment, but before retirement. If the conditions in section **2261.02** are met for these postemployment benefits, the employer should accrue a liability for these postemployment benefits during the employee's term of employment. The accounting should be consistent with that described in sections **2261.03–.07**. However, the only portion of the estimated liability for postemployment benefits that should be classified as a current liability is the amount expected to be paid or provided within the next year (or operating cycle, if longer) (FASB ASC 712-10).

2262 Deferred Compensation Arrangements

2262.01 Companies arrange various types of deferred compensation. The most common is referred to as a **rabbi trust.** This term is in reference to a tax arrangement allowed by a private letter ruling involving a rabbi. A grantor trust is set up to fund compensation for a group of managers or executives. The goal is to provide a benefit that is not taxable to the recipients until some later date when they actually receive compensation. To qualify for no current taxation, the trust agreement must explicitly state that the assets of the trust are available to satisfy the claims of general creditors in the event of bankruptcy of the employer.

2262.02 To the extent the cost of deferred compensation benefits is attributable to an employee's service in a specified year, these costs must be expensed in that year. If the benefits are for services of more than one year, the cost must be allocated and expensed in a rational and systematic way over those years. (FASB ASC 710-10-25-11)

2263 Nonretirement Postemployment Benefits

Accounting for Postretirement Benefits Other Than Pensions

2263.01 FASB ASC 712-10 was issued to address the accounting and reporting problems associated with postretirement benefits other than pensions. These benefits include, for example, postretirement health care, life insurance, tuition assistance, day care, legal services, and housing subsidies. The most frequent type of plan is for health care.

2263.02 FASB ASC 715-60-35-3 requires that the accumulated benefit obligation is the measurement of future benefits for the projected benefit obligation required to be recognized. The accumulated benefit obligation utilized current compensation levels whereas the projected benefit obligation is based on future compensation levels.

2263.03 Except for the use of the accumulated benefit obligation in place of the projected benefit obligation, the accounting and reporting requirements of FASB ASC 715-60-50-3 for defined benefit postretirement plans other than those for pensions is essentially the same as those for pensions. Thus, a sponsor of a defined benefit postretirement plan must recognize an underfunded plan in its balance sheet as an asset or an underfunded plan as a liability. The discussion in section **2264.06–.41** related to defined benefit pension plans is equally applicable to defined benefit other postretirement plans except for the substitution of accumulated benefit obligation for projected benefit obligation.

Accounting for Postemployment Benefits

2263.04 FASB ASC 715-60 establishes standards of accounting and reporting for postemployment benefits provided to former or inactive employees, their beneficiaries, or covered dependents after employment but before retirement. Examples of postemployment benefits are salary continuation, supplemental unemployment benefits, severance benefits, disability-related benefits, job training, counseling, and continuation of benefits in effect during active employment (such as health care and life insurance benefits). Postemployment benefits may be paid immediately on cessation of active employment or over a specified period of time.

2263.05 Postemployment benefits that meet the conditions for recognition of compensated absences as prescribed in FASB ASC 710-10-25 are required to be recognized as expense and related liability in accordance with FASB ASC 710-10. FASB ASC 710-10-25-1 criteria for recognition include all of the following:

    a. The employer's obligation relates to employee benefits that are attributed to services already rendered.

b. The obligation relates to rights that vest or accumulate.

   c. Payment of the compensation is probable.

   d. The amount can be reasonably estimated.

2263.06 If the criteria specified in FASB ASC 710-10-25 are not met, postemployment benefits are accounted for in accordance with the criteria for loss contingencies as specified in FASB ASC 450-10. Those criteria require recognition of expense and liability if the following conditions are met:

   a. Information available prior to issuance of the financial statements indicates that it is probable that an asset had been impaired or a liability had been incurred at a date of the financial statements.

   b. The amount of loss can be reasonably estimated.

2263.07 If an obligation for postemployment benefits is not recognized in accordance with either FASB ASC 710-10 or FASB ASC 450-10 because the amount cannot be reasonably estimated, the financial statements must disclose the fact.

2264 Retirement Benefits

Basic Concepts Underlying Pension Accounting

2264.01 A *pension plan* is an arrangement whereby a company provides benefits that can be determined or estimated in advance to its retired employees. A pension plan is best thought of as *deferred compensation* in which employees receive a portion of their earned compensation after retirement. The determination (by estimation) of amounts to be paid results from provisions of the plan and from established company practices.

2264.02 Pension plans typically have three parties:

   1. **Employer (sponsor):** The company establishing the plan for the benefit of its employees

   2. **Employees:** Those individuals who qualify to receive benefits under the pension plan

   3. **Trustee:** A financial institution (e.g., bank or insurance company) that accepts contributions from the employer, invests those funds, and administers payments to employees

2264.03 Under current generally accepted accounting principles, pension plans are accounted for by accrual accounting (i.e., the expense recognized is related to the estimated future benefits earned by employees during an accounting period, and the expense for that period may not relate directly to either the funding of the pension plan by the employer or the receipt of cash benefits by the employees that occur during that period). One way to understand the significance of accrual accounting in the area of pensions is to realize that pension benefits are simply portions of the total compensation earned by employees for their services to the employer. A designated portion of that compensation is delayed or deferred and paid after the period of active employment. From a matching/accrual perspective, however, the expense of those benefits must be recognized when the benefits are earned by the employees, not when they are paid. This may result in the recognition of a liability by the employer company, as we will see in the following sections.

2264.04 Two general types of pension plans exist:

1. **Defined contribution plans:** Payments to employees are based on the amounts contributed into the plan that, in turn, are based on an agreed-upon formula between the employer and the employees. Few difficult accounting problems exist for this type of plan because the periodic expense of the employer is the amount funded (or obligated to be funded) to the trustee as a result of employee services rendered during the year. The employees assume the investment risk on the plan, and the employer's obligation is satisfied on funding the specified amount of contribution.

2. **Defined benefit plans:** Benefits to be received by employees in the future are defined, rather than the contribution the employer must make as in the case of the defined contribution plans. Benefits to be paid are the result of many estimates and assumptions about salary levels, retirement ages, employee turnover, etc. Accounting for defined benefit pension plans is more difficult than for defined contribution plans, because the expense is based on an estimate of future benefits rather than on a required contribution. The employer bears the risk of return on plan assets because the employer's obligation is to provide funds sufficient to pay a defined level of benefit rather than to contribute a specified amount into the pension fund.

Defined Benefit Pension Plan Definitions

2264.05 Several definitions are important in accounting for defined benefit pension plans, the basis for the remainder of this section on pension accounting.

a. **Actuarial assumptions:** Estimates of future events affecting pension costs, such as mortality, withdrawal from workforce, disablement and retirement, changes in compensation, and discount (interest) rates to reflect the time value of money.

b. **Projected benefit obligation:** The actuarial present value as of a date of all benefits attributed by the pension benefit formula to employee services rendered to that date. The PBO is measured using assumptions as to future compensation levels if the pension benefit formula is based on those future compensation levels.

c. **Accumulated benefit obligation:** The actuarial present value as of a specified date of the benefits attributed by the pension benefit formula to employee services rendered before that date and based on compensation prior to that date. The ABO differs from the PBO in that it includes no assumption concerning future compensation levels.

d. **Fair value of plan assets:** The amount that a pension plan could reasonably expect to receive for an investment in a current sale between a willing buyer and a willing seller.

e. **Prior service cost:** The cost of granting the benefits of a plan amendment retroactively to employees who provided services before the plan amendment.

Recognition of Pension Expense and Other Changes in Plan Assets and Obligations

2264.06 FASB ASC 715-20-45-2 requires an entity to recognize on its balance sheet the full overfunded or underfunded status of its defined benefit pension plans. The overfunded or underfunded status is the difference between the fair value of the plan assets and the projected benefit obligation. Thus, from a balance sheet standpoint, the requirements of FASB ASC 715-20-45-2 are a significant step in the direction of requiring an entity to recognize defined benefit pension plans on a fair value basis.

Nature and Composition of Pension Expense

2264.07 Pension expense represents the amount of pension expense recognized during a period under current GAAP. That expense is made up of five components that either increase or decrease the amount of pension expense recognized during the period. These components are:

1. **Service cost:** The portion of pension expense that represents an estimate of the increase in pension benefits payable (specifically, the increase in the projected benefit obligation) as a result of employee services rendered during the current period.

2. **Interest cost:** The portion of pension expense that represents the increase in the projected benefit obligation as a result of the passage of time. The fact that at the end of the year the payment of the pension benefits is closer in time than it was at the beginning of the year causes the present value of the pension benefit obligation to increase. The interest cost component causes an increase in pension expense.

3. **Return on plan assets:** An increase in the plan assets (for example, from dividends received and increases in the fair value of investments held by the plan) causes the net cost of the pension plan to the employer to be less than it otherwise would be. The amount recognized in the current period as a reduction of pension expense is the estimated return on plan assets, not the actual return (i.e., not the actual dividends, etc. received and actual changes in the fair value of the plan assets). The estimated return on plan assets that is credited to pension expense during the period is calculated by multiplying the expected rate of return times the fair value of the plan assets at the beginning of the year. The actual return, which may be different than the estimated return, is recognized as a component of other comprehensive income, as will be demonstrated later. (See also the discussion of "gain or loss recognition" immediately below.)

4. **Gain or loss recognition:** The unrealized gains and losses associated with changes in the fair value of the plan assets and with changes in the projected benefit obligation are recognized as components of other comprehensive income. In certain cases, however, GAAP may require the recognition of a portion of these gains and losses as a component of pension expense. The recognition of a gain would decrease pension expense, whereas the recognition of a loss would increase pension expense. The amount of the gain or loss included in pension expense would also be reflected as a reduction of the remaining unrecognized gain or loss included in accumulated other comprehensive income.

5. **Prior service cost amortization:** When plan amendments are made, additional benefits are sometimes applied retroactively to employees for service rendered in prior years. This increase in the benefits to be paid to employees represents a cost to the employer. GAAP requires that this cost be recognized as a component of pension expense over the remaining service years of the affected employees. FASB ASC 715-20-50-1 requires that the unrecognized prior service cost be recognized as a component of other comprehensive income. The amortization of the unrecognized prior service cost is recognized as an increase in pension expense and as a reduction of the unrecognized amount remaining in accumulated other comprehensive income.

2264.08 In addition to these five components of pension expense (section **2264.07**), a component representing the amortization of a transition asset or obligation may be encountered. The transition asset or obligation is the unrecognized asset or obligation stemming from the initial application of FASB ASC 715-30-35-4, which requires that any remaining unrecognized transition asset or obligation be recognized as an adjustment of accumulated other comprehensive income. For example, a remaining transition obligation would be recognized for balance sheet purposes as a credit to the projected benefit obligation and a debit to accumulated other comprehensive income. Any subsequent amortization of the transition obligation would be recognized by debiting pension expense and crediting other comprehensive income.

2264.09 The measurement and recognition of pension expense and the accounting for other changes in pension assets and obligations of a defined benefit pension plan are demonstrated in the following paragraphs.

Micro Company Facts – 20X4

2264.10 Micro Company adopted a defined benefit plan for its employees effective January 1, 20X1. At January 1, 20X4, the current year, the plan assets and the projected benefit obligation each showed a balance of $10,000. Micro Company had no unrecognized gains or losses, prior service costs, or transition asset or obligation as of January 1, 20X4. The changes in the plan assets (PA) and projected benefit obligation (PBO) during 20X4 were as follows:

	PA	PBO
(a) Balance 1/1/X4	$10,000	$10,000
(b) Service cost		5,000
(c) Interest cost (10% of 1/1/X4 PBO)		1,000
(d) Contributions by Micro to the plan	2,000	
(e) Benefits paid by the plan to employees	(1,100)	(1,100)
(f) 12/31/X4 balances if no further changes	$10,900	$14,900
(g) Unrealized gain (losses) associated with plan assets	8,000	
(h) Unrealized (gains) losses associated with PBO	0	0
(i) 12/31/X4 actual balances	$18,900	$14,900

2264.11 Micro Company is the sponsor of this pension plan. The pension fund is actually under the control of a separate entity, a funding agency. It is a separate legal and accounting entity. The funding agency receives payments from Micro Company, invests the fund assets, and makes pension benefit payments to Micro's employees. The funding agency has a separate set of books and accounts for the plan under FASB ASC 960-10-15.

2264.12 The entries demonstrated below (sections **2264.13–.21**) are those of Micro Company, the sponsor of the plan. Even though the individual assets and liabilities of the plan will appear on the funding agency's books, since FASB ASC 715-20-45-3 requires Micro Company to recognize on its balance sheet the overfunded or underfunded balance of its pension plan, it will prove convenient if Micro Company maintains a Plan Assets account and a Projected Benefit Obligation (PBO) account on its own books to reflect the balances and summary changes in these two accounts. Under this approach, Micro Company would record a summary entry for each type of change in either the Plan Asset account or the Projected Benefit Obligation account. The overfunded or underfunded amount to be reported on Micro Company's balance sheet can easily be determined as the difference between the Plan Asset account and the Projected Benefit Obligation account.

2264.13 Except for contributions by Micro Company to the plan (item (d) in section **2264.10**) and benefits paid by the plan to employees (item (e)), each change in the Plan Assets account or the Projected Benefits Obligation account must be either (a) included in pension expense or (b) recognized in other comprehensive income (i.e., remain unrecognized for net income purposes but recognized for other comprehensive income and balance sheet purposes).

2264.14 Micro Company's entries in 20X4 are:

1. Plan assets   2,000
      Cash   2,000
   (To record the contributions Micro made to the plan in 20X4 – see item (d))

2. PBO   1,100
      Plan assets   1,100
   (To record the benefit payments made by the funding agency to Micro's employees during the period – see item (e))

3. Plan assets   8,000
      Other comprehensive income (unrecognized gains/losses)   8,000
   (To recognize the increase in plan assets resulting from unrealized gains on the plan assets during 20X4 – see item (g))

4. Other comprehensive income (unrealized gains/losses)   1,200
      Pension expense   1,200
   (To recognize the estimated return on assets based on a 12% estimated return rate and the plan assets balance at 1/1/X4.)

5. Pension expense   5,000
      PBO   5,000
   (To recognize the service cost component of pension expense – see item (b))

6. Pension expense   1,000
      PBO   1,000
   (To recognize the interest cost component of pension expense – see item (c))

2264.15 Micro Company's pension expense for 20X4 can be summarized as follows:

Service cost (entry 5)	$5,000
Interest cost (entry 6)	1,000
Expected return on assets (entry 4)	(1,200)
Net pension expense	$4,800

2264.16 Some might prefer to recognize pension expense as one entry. In that case, entries 4, 5, and 6 could be combined as follows:

Pension Expense   4,800
Other comprehensive income (unrecognized gains/losses)   1,200
   PBO   6,000

2264.17 Note that the actual return on assets during the year (i.e., the increase in the plan assets from dividends and interest on investments held by the plan and increases or decreases in the fair value of the plan assets) is recognized in other comprehensive income (entry 3), whereas the amount credited to pension expense is based on a calculated amount based on an estimated rate applied to the plan asset balance at the beginning of the current period. Entries 3 and 4, of course, could be combined as follows:

Plan assets	8,000	
Pension Expense		1,200
Other comprehensive income (unrecognized gains/losses)		6,800

They are shown as separate entries in section **2264.14** to emphasize that they are separate determinations. Entry 3 reflects the actual return on plan assets during the current period, whereas entry 4 reflects the return that is actually included in the determination of pension expense during the current period (but which is based on an expected rate of return rather than on the actual return).

2264.18 The entries in section **2264.14** resulted in a net credit to other comprehensive income (unrealized gains/losses) of $6,800. Thus, as of 1/1/X5, accumulated other comprehensive income (a balance sheet account) has a credit balance of $6,800 reflecting the net unrealized gains that have been recognized for balance sheet purposes but have not yet been recognized for income statement purposes; that is, they have not yet been included in the determination of pension expense.

2264.19 In 20X4 there were no unrealized gains or losses associated with the projected benefit obligation (PBO). Such unrealized gains or losses could occur, however, from events such as a change in an actuarial assumption that could cause the PBO to change. If such unrealized gains or losses did occur, they would be recognized in other comprehensive income just as are unrealized gains or losses associated with plan assets.

2264.20 As reflected in section **2264.10**, the fair value of the plan assets and the projected benefit obligation at 12/31/X4 are as follows:

Plan assets (fair value)	$18,900
Projected benefit obligation (PBO)	14,900
Excess of plan assets over PBO	$ 4,000

GAAP requires that Micro Company recognized this excess as an asset in its 12/31/X4 balance sheet. The entire amount ($4,000) must be reported as a noncurrent asset. No part of an overfunded pension plan may be classified as current.

If the PBO had exceeded the plan assets, the difference would have been reported as a liability. In that case, the amount that would be reported as a current liability would be the amount by which the actuarial present value of benefits included in the benefit obligation payable in the next 12 months (or operating cycle, if longer) exceeds the fair value of the plan assets. Thus, in Micro Company's case, if the pension plan had been underfunded rather than overfunded, the "current portion" would have to be larger than $18,900 for any of the underfunded balance to be reported as a current liability. Any remaining part of the underfunded balance would be reported as a noncurrent liability.

2264.21 In addition, Micro Company will report a $6,800 credit balance in its accumulated other comprehensive income in the equity section of its 12/31/X4 balance sheet. In summary, Micro Company's defined benefit pension plan will be reported in its 12/31/X4 balance sheet as follows:

Noncurrent assets:	
Excess of fair value of plan assets over benefit obligations	$4,000
Stockholders' equity:	
Accumulated other comprehensive income (unrecognized gains/losses)	$6,800

Micro Company Facts – 20X5

2264.22 In 20X5 Micro Company amended its pension plan by increasing the amount of pension benefit that would be paid for each year of service. As a result, annual service cost will increase in the future. However, Micro Company also decided to apply this higher benefit rate retroactive to January 1, 20X1. Micro Company determined that the present value at January 1, 20X5, of this retroactive application of the higher benefit rate is $12,000. This $12,000 unrecognized prior service cost will be amortized over the estimated remaining service period of 8 years.

2264.23 The changes in the plan assets and the projected benefit obligation during 20X5 were as follows:

	PA	PBO
(a) Balance 1/1/X5 (See section **2264.10** 12/31/X4 balances.)	$18,900	$14,900
(b) Service cost		6,000
(c) Interest cost (10% of ($14,900 1/1/X5 PBO + $12,000 increase in PBO 1/1/X5 due to increase in unrecognized prior service cost))		2,690
(d) Unrecognized prior service cost		12,000
(e) Contributions by Micro to the plan	2,500	
(f) Benefits paid by the plan to employees	(1,400)	(1,400)
(g) 12/31/X5 balances if no further changes	$20,000	$34,190
(h) Unrealized (gains) losses	15,000	0
(i) 12/31/X5 actual balances	$35,000	$34,190

2264.24 Micro Company's entries in 20X5 are:

1. Plan assets   2,500
       Cash   2,500
   (To record the contributions Micro made to the plan in 20X5 – see item (f) in section **2264.23**)

2. PBO   1,400
       Plan assets   1,400
   (To record the benefit payments made by the funding agency to Micro's employees during the period – see item (f))

3. Plan assets   15,000
       Other comprehensive income (unrecognized gains/losses)   15,000
   (To recognize the increase in plan assets resulting from unrealized gains on the plan assets during 20X5 – see item (h))

4. Other comprehensive income – unrecognized PSC   12,000
       PBO   12,000
   (To recognize the increase in PBO at 1/1/X5 due to the unrecognized prior service cost – see item (d))

5. Other comprehensive income (unrecognized gains/losses)   2,268
       Pension expense   2,268
   (To recognize the estimated return on assets based on a 12% estimated return rate and the $18,900 plan assets balance at 1/1/X5)

6. Pension expense   1,500
       Other comprehensive income – unrecognized PSC   1,500

7.	Pension expense		6,000	
	PBO			6,000
	(To recognize the service cost component of pension expense – see item (b))			
8.	Pension expense		2,690	
	PBO			2,690
	(To recognize the interest cost component of pension expense – see item (c)) [10% of ($14,900 PBO at 1/1/X5 + $12,000 increase in PBO 1/1/X5 due to increase in prior service cost)]			
9.	Other comprehensive income (unrecognized gains/losses)		614	
	Pension expense			614

2264.25 As explained in section **2264.18**, the remaining unrecognized gain/loss at 12/31/X4 (and thus at 1/1/X5) was a net unrecognized gain of $6,800, resulting in a $6,800 credit balance in the Accumulated Other Comprehensive Income (unrealized gains/losses) account. Current GAAP indicates that unrecognized gains/losses remaining at the beginning of the year do not have to be included in the determination of pension expense as long as those unrecognized gains/losses are not too large.

Corridor for Unrecognized Gains/Losses

2264.26 To prevent the accumulated other comprehensive income related to unrealized gains and losses from getting too large, current GAAP utilizes a corridor approach. Under this approach, the accumulated other comprehensive income (AOCI) related to unrealized gains and losses does not have to be amortized (i.e., included in the determination of pension expense) as long as the balance in that particular AOCI does not exceed the larger of the beginning-of-year balances in the projected benefit obligation or the market-related value of the plan assets. (The market-related value of plan assets can be either fair market value or a calculated value that recognizes changes in fair value in a systematic and rational manner over not more than five years. The market-related value of plan assets is herein assumed to be the same as fair value.) If it does exceed this limit, the excess must be amortized over the average remaining service period of active employees who are expected to receive benefits under the plan.

2264.27 Thus, Micro Company must determine if its AOCI balance at 1/1/X5 related to unrealized gains/losses is "too large." Micro Company computes the limit (corridor) as follows:

    A.   10% of market-related value of plan assets (fair value) at 1/1/X5:
            (10% of $18,900) $1,890

    B.   10% of projected benefit obligation (PBO) at 1/1/X5:
            (10% of $14,900) $1,490

2264.28 Since Micro Company's AOCI related to unrecognized gains/losses at 1/1/X5, $6,800, is larger than $1,890, the excess must be amortized. The amortization amount is determined as follows:

Unrecognized gains/losses at 1/1/X5:	
Credit balance in AOCI related to gains/losses	$6,800
Limit (corridor) at 1/1/X5 (See section **2264.27**.)	1,890
Excess	4,910
Amortization period (8 years)	÷ 8
Amortization for 20X5	$ 614

2264.29 Since the AOCI related to unrecognized gains/losses has a credit balance at 1/1/X5, there is an unrecognized net gain (as opposed to an unrecognized net loss). Therefore, the amortization will result in a decrease in pension expense. The amortization is reflected in entry 9 in section **2264.24**.

2264.30 Micro Company's pension expense for 20X5 can be summarized as follows:

Service cost (entry 7)	$6,000
Interest cost (entry 8)	2,690
Expected return on assets (entry 5)	(2,268)
Amortization of prior service cost (entry 6)	1,500
Amortization of unrecognized gain/loss (entry 9)	(614)
Net pension expense	$7,308

2264.31 If one prefers to recognize pension expense as one entry, it may be recorded as follows:

Pension Expense	7,308	
Other comprehensive income (unrecognized gains/losses) [$2,268 + $614]	2,882	
PBO		8,690
Other comprehensive income (unrecognized PSC)		1,500

2264.32 The AOCI related to unrecognized gains/losses that will be reported on Micro Company's 12/31/X5 balance sheet is determined as follows:

	Dr. (Cr.)
Balance 1/1/X5 (See section **2264.25**.)	$ (6,800)
Unrealized gain/loss occurring in 20X5 (See item (h) in section **2264.23**.)	(15,000)
Expected return on assets recognized in pension expense in 20X5 (See entry 5 in section **2264.24**.)	2,268
Amortization of unrecognized gain/loss in 20X5 (See entry 9 in section **2264.24**.)	614
Balance 12/31/X5	$(18,918)

2264.33 Micro Company will also report on its 12/31/X5 balance sheet the AOCI related to the unrecognized prior service cost, computed as shown below:

	Dr. (Cr.)
Balance 1/1/X5	$ 0
Increase 1/1/X5 resulting from plan amendment	12,000
Amortization of prior service cost in 20X5	(1,500)
Balance 12/31/X5	$10,500

2264.34 As reflected in section **2264.23**, the fair value of the plan assets and the projected benefit obligation at 12/31/X5 are as follows:

Plan assets (fair value)	$35,000
Projected benefit obligation (PBO)	34,190
Excess of Plan assets over PBO	$ 810

Micro Company will report this $810 excess as an asset (noncurrent asset) in its 12/31/X5 balance sheet.

2264.35 Thus, Micro Company's 12/31/X5 balance sheet will report the following items related to its defined benefit pension plan:

Noncurrent assets:	
Excess of fair value of plan assets over benefit obligations	$ 810
Stockholders' equity:	
Accumulated other comprehensive income related to unrecognized pension gains	18,918
Accumulated other comprehensive income related to unrecognized prior service costs of pension plan	(10,500)

2264.36 As the entries for Micro Company for 20X4 and 20X5 show, except for contributions by Micro Company to the plan and benefits paid by the plan to employees, each change in the Plan Assets account or the Projected Benefits Obligation account must be either (a) included in pension expense or (b) recognized in other comprehensive income (i.e., remain unrecognized for net income purposes but recognized for other comprehensive income and balance sheet purposes).

2264.37 In summary, except for contributions and benefits paid, the changes in the plan assets and/or projected benefit obligation fall into three categories:

1. Changes due to unrecognized gains and losses (e.g., increases in plan assets from dividends, interest, etc. received and increases in the fair value of plan assets and changes in the projected benefit obligation due to events other than the payment of pension benefits to employees)

2. Changes due to prior service cost

3. Changes associated with a transition asset or obligation

2264.38 In all three categories, the initial event or occurrence is reflected as a change in the plan asset/PBO with an offsetting change in other comprehensive income. The subsequent allocation or amortization of that category's unrecognized amount is recognized as an increase or decrease in pension expense and an offsetting change in other comprehensive income (AOCI from a balance sheet standpoint). That is, the item (category) initially is recognized for other comprehensive and balance sheet purposes but not for net income purposes; that is, it is not initially included in the determination of pension expense.

2264.39 For example, increases in plan assets resulting from actual returns (increases from dividends, interest, etc. received and increases in the fair value of the plan assets) and the inclusion of those unrecognized gains are recorded as follows:

Plan assets	XXX	
Other comprehensive income (unrecognized gains/losses)		XXX
(Recognition of actual return on plan assets)		
Other comprehensive income (unrecognized gains/losses)	XXX	
Pension expense		XXX
(Recognition of expected return on plan assets)		
Other comprehensive income (unrecognized gains/losses)	XXX	
Pension expense		XXX
(Recognition of amortization of unrecognized net gains)		

2264.40 The changes and entries related to prior service costs are:

Other comprehensive income (unrecognized PSC)	XXX	
PBO		XXX
(Recognition initially of the total prior service cost)		
Pension expense	XXX	
Other comprehensive income (unrecognized PSC)		XXX
(Recognition of amortization of prior service cost)		

2264.41 Any remaining unrecognized transition asset or obligation (remaining from the initial application of FASB ASC 715-30-35-4) should be recognized at the time FASB ASC 715-30-35-4 is adopted by including it in other comprehensive income (AOCI from a balance sheet standpoint). Thus, the following entry would be made for an existing unrecognized transition obligation:

Other comprehensive income (unrecognized transition obligation)	XXX	
PBO		XXX
(Recognize unrecognized transition obligation when FASB ASC 715-30-35-4 is adopted)		

The unrecognized transition obligation would then be amortized over the remaining estimated service period as follows:

Pension expense	XXX	
Other comprehensive income (unrecognized transition obligation)		XXX

Settlement and Curtailment of Defined Benefit Pension Plans

2264.42 A *settlement* of a pension plan is defined as an irrevocable action that relieves the employer (or the plan) of primary responsibility for an obligation and eliminates significant risks related to the obligation and the assets used to effect the settlement. A *curtailment* is defined as a significant reduction in, or elimination of, defined benefit accruals for present employees' future services.

2264.43 Amounts resulting from the settlement or curtailment of defined benefit pension plans are generally required to be recognized immediately rather than being delayed.

Accounting and Reporting by Defined Benefit Pension Plans

2264.44 FASB ASC 960-205 establishes standards of accounting and reporting for the separate financial statements of pension plans. This is in contrast to those standards already discussed that apply to the presentation of pension information in the financial statements of the employer corporation sponsoring the pension plan.

2264.45 The financial statements of defined benefit pension plans must include the following information:

    a. The net assets available for benefits as of the end of the plan year

    b. The changes in net assets during the plan year

    c. The actuarial present value of accumulated plan benefits as of either the beginning or end of the plan year

    d. The effects, if significant, of certain factors affecting the year-to-year change in the actuarial present value of accumulated plan benefits

2264.46 Miscellaneous additional provisions of this statement are as follows:

    a. Information regarding net assets is to be prepared on the accrual basis.

    b. Plan investments (excluding contracts with insurance companies) are to be presented at fair value. Contracts with insurance companies are to be presented in the same way as in the plan's annual report to certain governmental agencies pursuant to the Employee Retirement Income Security Act of 1974 (ERISA). Plans not subject to ERISA are to account for their contracts with insurance companies as if they also filed that annual report.

    c. Participants' accumulated plan benefits are those future benefit payments that are attributable under the plan's provisions to employee services rendered to the benefit information date. The primary information regarding participants' accumulated plan benefits reported in plan financial statements is their actuarial present value.

2264.47 FASB ASC 962-325-55-1 requires a defined benefit pension plan to report an investment contract issued by either an insurance enterprise or other entity at fair value. It permits a defined benefit pension plan to report only contracts that incorporate mortality or morbidity risk at contract value.

2265 Stock Compensation (Share-Based Payments)

2265.01 Corporations often provide various types of stock options and other equity plans for their officers and key employees. FASB ASC 718-10-30 requires enterprises to use the fair value method.

Intrinsic Value Method

2265.02 Under the intrinsic value method, the amount of compensation cost is the excess of the market price of the stock at the measurement date (usually the grant date) over the exercise price (the amount the employee must pay for the stock at the date of exercise).

    a. Substantially all full-time employees meeting limited employment qualifications may participate.

    b. Stock is offered to eligible employees equally or based on a uniform percentage of salary or wages.

    c. The time permitted for exercise of an option or purchase right is limited to a reasonable period.

    d. The discount from the market price of the stock is no greater than would be reasonable in an offer of stock to stockholders or others.

2265.03 The compensation cost, if any, is allocated to the periods in which the employee performs the related services.

Example – Intrinsic Value Method

2265.04 On January 1, 20X1, Company X grants options to key employees that may be exercised after December 31, 20X3, to purchase 10,000 shares of $10 par common stock at an exercise price of $30 per share. The stock is selling at $45 per share on January 1, 20X1. The options are granted for services to be performed during the period 20X1-20X3.

2265.05 The total compensation cost is $150,000, computed as follows:

Market price per share	$ 45
Exercise price per share of stock	− 30
Excess of market price over exercise price	15
Number of shares of stock that the options allow the employees to acquire	× 10,000
Total compensation cost	$ 150,000

2265.06 The total compensation cost of $150,000 should be recognized in the amount of $50,000 in each of the three years in the service period (20X1, 20X2, and 20X3). The entries to recognize the compensation expense are:

Dec. 31, 20X1, 20X2, and 20X3 – to accrue compensation expense:

Compensation Expense	$50,000	
Additional Paid-in Capital – Stock Options		$50,000

2265.07 Assuming all of the options are exercised on January 1, 20X4, when the market price of Company X's stock is $58 per share, the entry to record the exercise is:

Jan. 1, 20X4 – all options exercised when market price of stock is $58:

Cash (10,000 x $30)	$300,000	
Additional Paid-in Capital – Stock Options	150,000	
Common Stock (10,000 shares x $10 par)		$100,000
Capital in Excess of Par – Common		350,000

2265.08 Notice that the total amount credited to equity (Common Stock and Capital in Excess of Par – Common) is $450,000 or $45 per share ($450,000 ÷ 10,000 shares), which is based on the $45 market price of the stock on the measurement date (January 1, 20X1) rather than the $58 market price of the stock on the exercise date. Stated differently, the $450,000 represents the exercise price of the stock (10,000 x $30 = $300,000) plus the total compensation cost recognized over the 3-year service period ($150,000).

Fair Value Method

2265.09 FASB ASC 718-10-30 requires the fair value method. It applies to all share-based payment plans except equity instruments held by an employee stock ownership plan (ESOP), which is covered by FASB ASC 718-40-25.

2265.10 The fair value method recognizes the cost of consideration received for employee services at the fair value of the equity instruments issued. The objective of the measurement process is to estimate the fair value at the grant date of the stock options and other equity instruments to which employees are entitled when they have rendered the required services and satisfied all other conditions necessary to earn the right to benefit from the instruments.

Example – Fair Value Method

2265.11 On January 1, 20X1, Company F grants 10,000 stock options to employees in which the $50 exercise price is equal to the market price of the stock on the grant date. Each option entitles its holder to acquire one share of stock at the exercise price provided the employee is still employed by Company F at the close of business December 31, 20X3. Applying an appropriate option pricing model, a fair value of $18 per option is determined. Company F expects 5% of the options to be forfeited each year during the 3-year vesting period.

2265.12 The number of stock options expected to be exercised is determined as follows, applying the assumption of 5% forfeitures each year:

$10,000 \times 0.95 \times 0.95 \times 0.95 = 8,574$

2265.13 The estimated compensation cost for the 3-year vesting period is $154,332 (8,574 options × $18 fair value per option). The servicing period is the 3-year vesting period. The total compensation expense of $154,332 should be recognized in the amount of $51,444 in each of the three years in the service period. The entries to recognize compensation expense are:

Dec. 31, 20X1, 20X2, and 20X3 – to accrue compensation expense:

Compensation Expense	$51,444	
Additional Paid-in Capital – Stock Options		$51,444

2265.14 Assuming all of the options remaining at January 1, 20X4 (i.e., those not forfeited), when the market price of Company F's stock is $65 per share, the entry to record the exercise is:

Jan. 1, 20X4 – 8,574 options remaining exercised when market price of stock is $65:

Cash (8,574 x $50 exercise price)	$428,700	
Additional Paid-in Capital – Stock Options		
(8,574 x $18 fair value 1/1/X1)	154,322	
Common Stock (8,574 shares x $10 par)		$85,740
Capital in Excess of Par – Common		497,292

2265.15 Notice that the $583,032 total amount credited to equity (i.e., $85,740 to Common Stock and $497,292 to Capital in Excess of Par – Common) is the $428,700 exercise price plus the $154,322 fair value of the options that were exercise on January 1, 20X4. It is not based on the $65 market price of the stock on the date of exercise. In other words, the total amount credited to equity is the sum of the exercise price and the fair value at the January 1, 20X1, grant date of the options that were not later forfeited.

2265.16 If the forfeiture rate used to estimate the number of options that will be exercised is determined to be inaccurate, a revised estimate of the amount of compensation expense is made on a prospective basis. For example, if on December 31, 20X2, the forfeiture rate is changed to 7% per year over the 3-year period, compensation expense for 20X2 and 20X3 would be as follows:

Total compensation cost estimate under the 7% forfeiture assumption:	
(10,000 × .93 × .93 × .93 = 8,044 options; 8,044 options × $18)	$144,792
Compensation cost recognized in 20X1 (see section **2265.13**)	51,444
Total compensation cost to be recognized in 20X2 and 20X3	$ 93,348
Annual compensation expense, 20X2 and 20X3:	
($93,348 ÷ 2 years)	$ 46,674

2265.17 Entries to reflect this change in estimate are as follows:

Dec. 31, 20X2 and 209X3 – to accrue compensation expense:

Compensation Expense	$ 46,674	
Additional Paid-in Capital – Stock Options		$ 46,674

2265.18 If all of the remaining 8,044 options were exercised on January 1, 20X4, the entry to record their exercise is:

Jan. 1, 20X4 – 8,044 remaining options exercised:

Cash (8,044 x $50)	$402,200	
Additional Paid-in Capital – Stock Options (8,044 x $18)	144,792	
Common Stock (8,044 x $10 par)		$80,440
Capital in Excess of Par – Common		466,552

Determining Fair Value

2265.19 The fair value of an equity share (for example, a stock option) should be based on the observable market price of a share with the same or similar terms and conditions, if one is available. If an observable market price is not available, which is the usual case, the fair value should be estimated using an acceptable valuation technique. FASB ASC 718-10-30-6 specifies that the valuation technique should be one that:

    a. is applied in a manner consistent with the fair value measurement objective of FASB ASC 718-10-30-6,

    b. is based on established principles of financial economic theory and generally applied in that field, and

    c. reflects all substantive characteristics of the instruments.

2265.20 The FASB notes that a lattice model and a closed-form model are among the valuation techniques that meet the criteria specified in FASB ASC 718-10-20. A lattice model is one that produces an estimated fair value based on the assumed changes in prices of a financial instrument over successive periods of time. The binomial model is an example of a lattice model. A closed-form model is one that uses an equation to produce an estimated fair value. The Black-Scholes-Merton formula is an example of a closed-form model.

2265.21 For a share option or similar instrument, the valuation technique or model must meet the criteria specified in section **2265.20** above and must take into account, at a minimum, the following six items:

1. Exercise price of the option
2. Expected term of the option
3. Current price of the underlying share
4. Expected volatility of the price of the underlying share for the expected term of the option
5. Expected dividends on the underlying share for the expected term of the option
6. Risk-free interest rate for the expected term of the option

Liability Awards

2265.22 Some awards of share-based compensation necessitate the recognition of a liability by the issuing entity because the employees can require the entity to settle the award by transferring assets (e.g., cash) to employees rather than by issuing equity instruments. For example, a share-based compensation plan may require the entity to pay an employee, either on demand or at a specified date, an amount to be determined by the increase in the entity's share price from a specified level. In this case, the entity needs to recognize the related liability.

2265.23 Compensation cost for plans including share appreciation rights or other variable plan awards are measured according to the terms the employee is most likely to choose based on the information available each period.

2265.24 The entity measures the amount of the liability each period based on the current fair value of the award at the end of the period. The effects of changes in the liability during the service period are recognized as compensation cost over the service period. Changes in the amount of the liability due to changes in the fair value of the award after the service period are compensation costs of the period in which the changes occur.

2265.25 **Example:** On January 1, 20X1, Alpha Company grants its employees 10,000 share appreciation rights (SARs). Each SAR entitles the employee to receive cash equal to the difference between $10 and the market price of Alpha's common stock on the date each SAR is exercised. The service period is 20X1 through 20X3, and the SARs are exercisable as of January 1, 20X4, and must be exercised no later than December 31, 20X5. The fair value of the SARs was $6 on December 31, 20X1; $9 on December 31, 20X2; and $11 on December 31, 20X3.

2265.26 Alpha would record the following entry at December 31, 20X1:

Compensation expense	$20,000	
Liability under SARs		$20,000

The $20,000 amount is computed as follows:

Total compensation cost at 12/31/X1 (10,000 SARs x $6 fair value)	$60,000
Portion of service period to 12/31/X1	x 1/3
Compensation cost to-date as of 12/31/X1	$20,000
Less compensation expense recognized in prior years	– 0
Compensation expense – 20X1	$20,000

2265.27 Alpha would record the following entry at December 31, 20X2:

Compensation expense	$40,000	
Liability under SARs		$40,000

The $40,000 amount is computed as follows:

Total compensation cost at 12/31/X2 (10,000 SARs x $9 fair value)	$90,000
Portion of service period to 12/31/X2	x 2/3
Compensation cost to-date as of 12/31/X2	$60,000
Less compensation expense recognized in 12/31/X1	– 20,000
Compensation expense – 20X2	$40,000

2265.28 As shown in section **2265.27**, the compensation to-date is calculated first. It is based on the fair value of the award (the SARs in this case) at the current date, December 31, 20X2, which is $90,000. The portion of this $90,000 total that is to be recognized to-date is a proportionate part based on the portion of the service period to-date (two-thirds (2/3) in this case). Thus, $60,000 should be recognized through 20X2. The amount to be recognized in the current period, 20X2, is actually a "plug" figure, which is the difference in the compensation cost to be recognized to-date, $60,000, and the amount recognized in prior years (20X1 in this case).

2265.29 The $60,000 compensation cost to-date is also the amount to be recognized as a liability on Alpha's balance sheet at December 31, 20X2. It is the balance in the Liability under SARs account after the entries recorded at December 31, 20X1, and December 31, 20X2.

2265.30 Alpha would record the following entry at December 31, 20X3:

Compensation expense	$50,000	
Liability under SARs		$50,000

The $50,000 amount is computed as follows:

Total compensation cost at 12/31/X3 (10,000 SARs x $11 fair value)	$110,000
Portion of service period to 12/31/X3	× 3/3
Compensation cost to-date as of 12/31/X3	$110,000
Less compensation expense recognized in prior years (20X1 and 20X2)	− 60,000
Compensation expense – 20X3	$ 50,000

2265.31 Assuming that all of the SARs are exercised on July 1, 20X4, when the market price of Alpha's common stock is $24 and the fair value of the SARs is $14, Alpha would make the following entry to record compensation expense in 20X4:

Compensation expense	$30,000	
Liability under SARs		$30,000

The $30,000 amount is computed as follows:

Total compensation cost at 7/1/X4 (10,000 SARs x $14 fair value)	$140,000
Portion of service period to 7/1/X4	× 3/3
Compensation cost to-date as of 7/1/X4	$140,000
Less compensation expense recognized in prior years (20X1-20X3)	−110,000
Compensation expense – 20X4	$ 30,000

2265.32 Even though the service period ended December 31, 20X3, compensation expense continues to be recognized until the SARs are settled (exercised).

2265.33 Alpha would make the following entry on July 1, 20X4, to recognize the settlement of the SARs:

Liability under SARs	$140,000	
Cash (($24 market price less $10) x 10,000 SARs)		$140,000

2270 Income Taxes

Accounting for Deferred Tax Assets and Liabilities

2270.01 Income taxes represent a unique feature of financial reporting because of the influence of income tax laws on the elements of the financial statements. The current amount of income taxes paid or payable is calculated on the basis of a company's income tax return, which indicates the required payment of taxes to the government for the current period. Different accounting procedures are frequently employed, however, in the preparation of financial statements. These differences, along with certain other unique aspects of income tax law and generally accepted accounting principles, require the recognition of deferred tax assets and liabilities in the financial statements.

2270.02 Accounting for income taxes under FASB ASC 740-10-05-5 is based on the "liability method." Under the liability method as required by FASB ASC 740-10-10-1, accounting for income taxes has two primary objectives—to recognize the amount of taxes currently payable or refundable and to recognize deferred tax liabilities and assets for the future tax consequences of temporary differences. (FASB ASC 740-10-10-1)

2270.03 Temporary differences arise when items are treated differently in the financial statements and the income tax return with the expectation that those differences will offset in the future. The following are examples of typical temporary differences:

   a. Installment sales and the related asset recognized under GAAP at the time of the sale but deferred for income tax purposes until collected

   b. Warranty expense and the related liability recognized under GAAP at the time of sale but deferred for income tax purposes until paid

   c. Liability recognized for an advance payment that is taxable on receipt of cash but deferred under GAAP until earned

   d. Depreciation recognized more rapidly for income tax purposes than under GAAP

2270.04 Other differences in the determination of financial and taxable income are *permanent* in nature in that they are not expected to reverse in the future. Examples are items that are included in either taxable or financial income, but which will never enter into the determination of the other, such as the following:

   a. Interest received on investments in municipal securities that is included in the determination of financial income but is not taxable

   b. Insurance premiums paid on policies for which the company is beneficiary that are not deductible for tax purposes

   c. Depletion in excess of cost that is deductible for income tax purposes but is not included in the determination of financial income

2270.05 The term "liability method" employed by FASB ASC 740-10-10-3 in recognizing deferred tax liabilities and assets comes from the fact that the balance sheet elements are calculated first and, from those figures, the amount of income tax expense is derived. For example, if a company determined that its current income tax payable was $100,000 and that its deferred tax liability balance resulting from temporary differences increased during the year by $30,000, the entry to record income taxes for the year would be:

Income Tax Expense	$130,000	
Income Tax Payable		$100,000
Deferred Income Tax Liability		30,000

The elements of the balance sheet—in this case liabilities—are first determined and they become the basis for determining the amount of income tax expense.

2270.06 The following basic principles are applied in accounting for income taxes at the date of the financial statements (FASB ASC 740-10-05-7):

   a. A current tax liability or asset is recognized for the estimated taxes payable or refundable on tax returns for the current year.

   b. A deferred tax liability or asset is recognized for the estimated future tax effects attributable to temporary differences and carryforwards.

   c. The measurement of current and deferred tax liabilities and assets is based on provisions of the enacted tax law, the effects of future changes in tax laws or rates are not anticipated.

   d. The measurement of deferred tax assets is reduced by a valuation allowance if, based on available evidence, some or all of the deferred tax asset balance is not expected to be realized.

2270.07 The annual computation of deferred taxes results from applying the following steps (FASB ASC 740-10-10-3):

    a. Identify all cumulative temporary differences and operating and tax credit carryforwards.

    b. Measure the total deferred tax liability for taxable temporary differences.

    c. Measure the total deferred tax asset for deductible temporary differences and loss carryforwards.

    d. Measure deferred tax assets for each type of tax credit carryforward.

    e. Reduce deferred tax assets by a valuation allowance if, based on available evidence, it is more likely than not that some or all of the deferred tax asset will not be realized.

2270.08 The measurement of deferred tax liabilities and assets is done using the enacted tax rate or rates expected to apply to taxable income in the periods in which the deferred tax liability or asset is expected to be settled or realized (FASB ASC 740-10-10-3).

2270.09 Current and noncurrent classifications of deferred taxes are based on the classification of the asset or liability giving rise to the temporary difference, unless no underlying asset or liability exists, in which case the expected timing of reversal governs the classification (FASB ASC 740-10-10-3).

2270.10 **Example:** Phillips Co. had the following pretax financial income, permanent and temporary differences, taxable income, and income tax rates for 20X1–20X4:

	20X1	20X2	20X3	20X4
Pretax financial income (loss)	$125,000	$78,000	$25,000	$(205,000)
Permanent differences:				
Nontaxable interest income on municipal securities	(10,000)	(8,000)	(3,000)	(10,000)
Nondeductible insurance expense	15,000	15,000	15,000	15,000
	$130,000	$85,000	$37,000	$(200,000)
Temporary differences:				
Depreciation expense	(50,000)	(60,000)	(75,000)	(80,000)
Warranty expense	30,000	35,000	32,000	26,000
Taxable income	$110,000	$60,000	$(6,000)	$(254,000)
Income tax rate	35%	38%	38%	40%

Depreciation expense is a noncurrent taxable temporary difference (related to plant assets, which are noncurrent), and warranty expense is a current deductible temporary difference (related to warranty payable, which is current). The loss carryforward in 20X4 is considered noncurrent based on the assumption that it will be several years before the company again becomes profitable.

The amount of deferred tax assets (liabilities) on cumulative temporary differences (20X1–20X4) and carryforward (20X4) are computed as follows:

			Current (Warranty)	Noncurrent (Depreciation and Carryforward)
20X1				
Warr:	$ 30,000	× 0.35	$10,500	
Depr:	$ (50,000)	× 0.35		$(17,500)
Less: Previous balance			0	0
20X1 change			$10,500	(17,500)
20X2				
Warr:	$ 30,000			
	35,000			
	$ 65,000	× 0.38	$24,700	
Depr:	$ (50,000)			
	(60,000)			
	$(110,000)	× 0.38		$(41,800)
Less: Previous balance			10,500	(17,500)
20X2 change			$14,200	$(24,300)
20X3				
Warr:	$ 65,000			
	32,000			
	$ 97,000	× 0.38	$36,860	
Depr:	$(110,000)			
	(75,000)			
	$(185,000)	× 0.38		$(70,300)
Less: Previous balance			24,700	(41,800)
20X3 change			$12,160	$(28,500)
			Current (Warranty)	**Noncurrent (Depreciation and Carryforward)**
20X4				
Warr:	$ 97,000			
	26,000			
	$ 123,000	× 0.40	$49,200	
Depr:	$(185,000)			
	(80,000)			
	$(265,000)	× 0.40		$(106,000)
Carryforward:	$ 90,000	× 0.40		$ 36,000
Current balance			49,200	$ (70,000)
Less: Previous balance			36,860	(70,300)
20X4 change			$12,340	$ 300

An analysis of each year, including the income tax accrual and the tax-related items presented in the financial statements, follows. Each year the adjustment required to bring current and noncurrent deferred taxes to the desired balance is made, income tax payable or receivable is computed, and the amount of income tax expense or benefit is forced to balance the entry. An assumption is made that no valuation allowance is required for the deferred tax asset resulting from the deductible temporary difference for warranty expense.

20X1

The income tax accrual for 20X1 is as follows:

Income Tax Expense	$45,500	
Deferred Tax/Current	10,500	
Deferred Tax/Noncurrent		$17,500
Income Tax Payable ($110,000 × 0.35)		38,500

Financial statement presentation is as follows:

Income statement: Income tax expense	$45,500
Balance sheet: Income tax payable (current liability)	38,500
Deferred taxes:	
Current asset	$10,500
Noncurrent liability	17,500

20X2

In 20X2, deferred taxes are measured by applying the new tax rate of 38%.
The income tax accrual for 20X2 is as follows:

Income Tax Expense	$32,900	
Deferred Tax/Current	14,200	
Deferred Tax/Noncurrent		$24,300
Income Tax Payable ($60,000 × 0.38)		22,800

Financial statement presentation is as follows:

Income statement: Income tax expense	$32,900
Balance sheet: Income tax payable (current liability)	22,800
Deferred taxes:	
Current asset	$24,700
Noncurrent liability	41,800

20X3

The income tax accrual for 20X3 is as follows:

Income Tax Receivable ($6,000 × 0.35)	$ 2,100	
Income Tax Expense	14,240	
Deferred Tax/Current	12,160	
Deferred Tax/Noncurrent		$28,500

Note: The receivable represents the 20X3 loss that is carried back to 20X1 and is computed at the 20X1 tax rate of 35%.

Financial statement presentation is as follows:

Income statement: Income tax expense	$14,240
Balance sheet: Income tax receivable (current asset)	2,100
Deferred taxes:	
Current asset	$36,860
Noncurrent liability	70,300

20X4

In 20X4, deferred taxes are measured by applying the new tax rate of 40%.
The income tax accrual for 20X4 is as follows:

Income Tax Receivable*	$59,200	
Deferred Tax/Current	12,340	
Deferred Tax/Noncurrent	300	
Income Tax Benefit		$71,840

*20X1: ($110,000 - $6,000) × 0.35 =	*$36,400*
20X2: $60,000 × 0.38 =	*22,800*
	$59,200

The $90,000 carryforward, included in the computation of the deferred tax assets and liabilities, is computed as follows:

20X4 loss	$254,000
Carried back to:	
20X1	(104,000)
20X2	(60,000)
Carried forward	$ 90,000

The assumption is made that the 40% enacted income tax rate for 20X4 also applies to future years. This results in a deferred tax asset for the carryforward of $36,000 ($90,000 × 0.40). Assuming further that management determines that half of the deferred tax assets from the carryforward should be written off via valuation allowance, the following entry is required:

Income Tax Expense (benefit)	$18,000	
Deferred Tax/Noncurrent		$18,000

Financial statement presentation is as follows:

Income statement: Income tax benefit ($71,840 - $18,000)	$53,840
Balance sheet: Income tax receivable	59,200
Deferred tax:	
Current asset	49,200
Noncurrent liability	70,000

Intraperiod Income Tax Allocation

2270.11 The term "intraperiod tax allocation" refers to the distribution of the tax expense for the period to the various categories of income as presented in the income statement and, on occasion, to items resulting in the direct adjustment of retained earnings. The need for intraperiod tax allocation thus arises from the categorization of various elements of income as one or more of the following in addition to normal, recurring operations:

    a. Discontinued operations

    b. Extraordinary items

    c. Cumulative effects of accounting changes

    d. Prior-period adjustments

    e. Direct adjustments to capital accounts

Items treated in any of these ways must include the tax effect to maintain the proper relationship among the various income captions on the income statement.

2270.12 **Example:** The concept of intraperiod tax allocation is illustrated in the following situation:

Facts:

    a. Income before taxes and "special" items, $200,000

    b. "Special" items include:

        (1) An extraordinary gain of $70,000

        (2) A prior-period adjustment (loss) resulting from the correction of an error in previously issued financial statements, $150,000

    c. The income tax rate is 40%.

Solution:

Computation of Tax Expense		
Item	Amount	Tax (at 40%)
Income before special items	$200,000	$80,000
Extraordinary gain	70,000	28,000
Correction of error	(150,000)	(60,000)
Total	$120,000	$48,000

Partial Income Statement Presentation	
Income before taxes	$200,000
Provision for income taxes	80,000
Income before extraordinary item	120,000
Extraordinary gain, net of $28,000 applicable tax	42,000
Net income	$162,000

Partial Retained Earnings Statement	
Retained earnings, 01/01 as previously stated (assumed amount)	$500,000
Correction of error in previously issued financial statements, net of $60,000 applicable tax savings	(90,000)
Retained earnings, 01/01 as restated	$410,000

2270.13 The total tax expense ($48,000) does not appear in the financial statements as a single figure. To present this number as the provision for income taxes in the income statement would result in a distortion of the extraordinary item, the income figures, and the correction of error in previously issued financial statements. The net effect of the tax figures that are presented in the appropriate places in the financial statements is, however, the total net tax of $48,000:

Provision for income taxes	$80,000
Tax expense offset against extraordinary gain	28,000
Tax savings offset against correction of error (loss)	(60,000)
Total income tax recognized	$48,000

2270.14 It should also be observed—though not apparent from the illustration—that no items appearing in the income statement prior to the provision for income taxes are presented net-of-tax. The provision represents the accumulated tax effect of all items included in the income before tax amount.

Accounting for the Investment Tax Credit

2270.15 The investment tax credit (ITC) is a reduction in taxes payable, equal to a specified percentage of the cost of certain assets, subject to various limitations and restrictions. While there is general agreement that the ITC is an element in the determination of income of the enterprise acquiring assets that qualify, disagreement as to the timing of the impact of income has led to two generally accepted methods of accounting for the ITC. The ITC is not currently included in income tax laws. Because it is a recurring feature of the law, however, a brief summary is included.

2270.16 The two methods are the *deferred* and the *flow-through* methods. These are described in the following table:

Method	Interpretation of ITC	Accounting Treatment
Deferred	ITC is a reduction in the net cost of assets acquired. Benefit of the ITC is created through the use of the related asset.	ITC is deferred and recognized as a reduction in tax expense over the periods benefiting from the use of the asset.
Flow-through	ITC is a reduction of taxes resulting from the investment in the acquired asset rather than from the asset's use.	ITC is recognized as a reduction in tax expense in the period of asset acquisition.

2270.17 **Example:** During 20X1, Alex Company acquires an asset for $125,000 that qualifies for the 10% investment credit. Thus, the tax payable in the year of acquisition is reduced by $12,500 ($125,000 × 0.10). Accounting for the ITC under the two methods outlined is illustrated as follows, assuming a 10-year asset life and net income in 20X1 of $70,000. The appropriate tax rate is 40%.

Deferred Method	Description	Flow-Through Method

Asset $125,000
  Cash $125,000
	Entry to record asset acquisition	Asset $125,000
		  Cash $125,000

Tax Expense $28,000
  Deferred ITC $12,500
  Tax Payable 15,500
($70,000 × 0.40 = $28,000)
	Entry to for accrue taxes 20X1	Tax Expense $15,500
		  Tax Payable $15,500
		[($70,000 × 0.40) – $12,500 = $15,500]

Deferred ITC $1,250 Tax Expense $1,250 ($12,500 / 10 yrs. = $1,250)	Entry to amortize ITC—20X1	None

Tax Payable $15,500
  Cash $15,500
	Entry to pay tax liability	Tax Payable $15,500
		  Cash $15,500

Income Statement
  Income tax expense $26,750
Balance Sheet
  Deferred ITC $11,250
	Financial statement presentation	**Income Statement**
		  Income tax expense $15,500
		Balance Sheet
		  None

2270.18 This example illustrates that under the deferred method the reduction in tax expense is recognized on a pro rata basis over the asset life. Under the flow-through method, the full effect (i.e., reduction in tax expense) is recognized in the initial year. Under both methods, the tax liability is reduced for the full amount of the ITC in the period of acquisition of the asset.

2270.19 While both the deferred and flow-through methods are acceptable under generally accepted accounting principles, the method selected must be followed consistently from period to period. Disclosure of the method being used is required.

Accounting for Uncertainty in Income Taxes

2270.20 The accounting for income taxes is influenced by the tax positions an entity takes in its tax returns. In some cases, there may be some degree of uncertainty about the amounts included in the entity's tax return. For example, there may be some degree of uncertainty as to whether the taxing authority will allow the full amount of a particular deduction the entity took on its tax return.

2270.21 FASB ASC 740-10-20 defines a tax position as "a position in a previously filed tax return or a position expected to be taken in a future tax return that is reflected in measuring current or deferred income tax assets and liabilities for interim or annual periods." It also encompasses the following:

   a. A decision not to file a tax return

   b. An allocation or a shift of income between jurisdictions

   c. The characterization of income or a decision to exclude reporting taxable income in a tax return

   d. A decision to classify a transaction, entity, or other position in a tax return as tax exempt

   e. An entity's status, including its status as a pass-through entity or a tax-exempt not-for-profit entity

Recognition

2270.22 FASB ASC 740-10-25-6 requires that an entity must initially recognize the effects of a tax position when it is **more likely than not,** based on the technical merits, that the position will be sustained upon examination. That is, there must be a greater than 50% chance that the taxing authority will agree with the entity taking the tax position (e.g., allowing a particular deduction in the entity's tax return). If there is only a 50% or less chance that a particular deduction will be allowed, the tax position fails the more-likely-than-not requirement. Accordingly, the entity's financial statements must reflect that fact; usually this would mean reflecting the additional tax liability in the financial statements.

2270.23 The entity must presume that the tax position will be examined by the relevant taxing authority that has full knowledge of all relevant information. Thus, whether the tax position meets the more-likely-than-not requirement must be based on the technical merits of the tax position and not on whether or not the taxing authority is likely to examine that tax position. The entity must therefore assume that the taxing authority will have full knowledge of the tax position that the entity has taken.

2270.24 Each tax position must be considered separately; it may not be combined or aggregated with other tax positions.

Measurement

2270.25 Many entities will measure the benefit of the tax position based on an overall assessment of whether or not a given tax position meets the more-likely-than-not requirement. If the tax position meets the more-likely-than-not requirement, the entity will reflect benefits of that tax position in its financial statements. For example, an entity may have taken a deduction on the tax return and there may be some uncertainty as to whether the taxing authority will allow that particular deduction. If the entity concludes that there is a greater than 50% chance that the taxing authority will allow the deduction, the entity will recognize a smaller tax liability (or greater tax benefit) than it would have if it had concluded that there is a 50% or less chance that the deduction would be allowed.

2270.26 If a tax position fails the more-likely-than-not requirement, an entity will reflect that conclusion in its financial statement. This "failure" normally would require the entity to recognize either a larger tax liability or a smaller tax benefit.

2270.27 If it meets the more-likely-than-not recognition threshold, a tax position should be measured as the largest amount of tax benefit that is greater than 50% likely of being realized upon settlement. FASB ASC 740-10-30-7 requires that this measurement must "consider the amounts and probabilities of the outcomes that could be realized upon settlement using the facts, circumstances, and information available at the reporting date."

2270.28 To illustrate the issue of considering the amounts and probabilities of the outcomes, the FASB presented the following illustration in FASB ASC 740-10-55-117.

2270.29 An entity has determined that a tax position resulting in a benefit of $100 qualifies for recognition and now should be measured. The entity has determined the following amounts and probabilities of the possible outcomes:

Possible Estimated Outcomes	Individual Probability of Occurring (%)	Cumulative Probability of Occurring (%)
$100	5	5
80	25	30
60	25	55
50	20	75
40	10	85
20	10	95
0	5	100

2270.30 The entity should recognize a tax benefit of $60 in its financial statements. This is the largest amount of benefit that is greater than 50% likely of being realized upon settlement.

Subsequent Recognition, Derecognition, and Measurement

2270.31 If an entity deems that the more-likely-than-not-threshold is not met in the period in which a tax position is taken, it should recognize the benefit of the tax position in the first subsequent period in which any of the following three conditions are met:

1. The more-likely-than-not recognition threshold is met by the reporting date.

2. The tax position is effectively settled through examination, negotiation, or litigation.

3. The statute of limitation of the relevant taxing authority to examine and challenge the tax position has expired.

2270.32 An enterprise shall evaluate all of the following conditions when determining when a tax position has been effectively settled:

a. The taxing authority has completed its examination procedures, including all appeals and administrative reviews that the taxing authority is required and expected to perform for the tax position.

b. The enterprise does not intend to appeal or litigate any aspect of the tax position included in the completed examination.

c. It is remote that the taxing authority would examine or reexamine any aspect of the tax position. In making this assessment, management shall consider the taxing authority's policy on reopening closed examinations and the specific facts and circumstances of the tax position. Management shall presume the relevant taxing authority has full knowledge of all relevant information in making the assessment on whether the taxing authority would reopen a previously closed examination.

2270.33 In the tax years under examination, a tax position does not need to be specifically reviewed or examined by the taxing authority to be considered effectively settled through examination. Effective settlement of a position subject to an examination does not result in effective settlement of similar or identical tax positions in periods that have not been examined.

2270.34 If an enterprise that had previously considered a tax position effectively settled becomes aware that the taxing authority may examine or reexamine the tax position or intends to appeal or litigate any aspect of the tax position, the tax position is no longer considered effectively settled and the enterprise shall reevaluate the tax position in accordance with FASB ASC 740-10-55-117.

2270.35 An enterprise may obtain information during the examination process that enables that enterprise to change its assessment of the technical merits of a tax position or of similar tax positions taken in other periods. However, the effectively settled conditions discussed above do not provide any basis for the enterprise to change its assessment of the technical merits of any tax position in other periods.

2270.36 Conversely, an entity should derecognize a previously recognized tax position in the first subsequent period in which it is no longer more likely than not that the tax position would be sustained upon examination.

2270.37 Subsequent recognition, derecognition, and measurement should be based on management's best judgment at the reporting date. Subsequent changes in judgment that lead to changes in recognition, derecognition, and measurement should be as a result of new information and not from a new evaluation by management of information that was available in a previous financial reporting period. Thus, unless there is new information, there is no basis for changes in recognition, derecognition, or measurement.

Interest and Penalties

2270.38 In cases in which tax law requires interest to be paid on an underpayment of income taxes, an entity should begin recognizing interest expense in the first period the interest would begin accruing according to the provisions of the relevant tax law. The amount to be recognized is determined by applying the applicable statutory interest rate to the difference between the tax position recognized and the amount previously taken or expected to be taken in a tax return.

2270.39 If a tax position does not meet the minimum statutory threshold to avoid payment of penalties, an entity should recognize an expense for the amount of the penalty in the period in which the entity claims or expects to claim the position in the tax return.

Classification

2270.40 It is possible that interest and/or penalties may have been recognized in one or more prior periods and in a subsequent period the tax position first meets the more-likely-than-not criterion. In that case, the previously recognized interest and penalties should be derecognized in the period in which the more-likely-than-not criterion is met.

2270.41 The application of FASB ASC 740-10-45-11 may result in the amount of benefit recognized in the balance sheet being different from the amount taken in a tax return for the current year. In that case, a liability should be recognized for these unrecognized tax benefits. This liability should be classified as a current liability to the extent the entity anticipates payment (or receipt) of cash within one year or the operating cycle, if longer. It should not be combined with deferred tax liabilities or deferred tax assets. A liability recognized as a result of applying FASB ASC 740-10-45-11 should not be classified as a deferred tax liability unless it arises from a taxable temporary difference.

2270.42 Interest recognized as a result of applying FASB ASC 740-10-45-24 may be classified as either income taxes or interest expense, based on the accounting policy election of the entity. Penalties recognized in FASB ASC 740-10-45-24 may be classified as either income taxes or another expense classification, based on the accounting policy election of the entity. These elections should be applied consistently.

Disclosure

2270.43 Public entities shall disclose both of the following at the end of each annual reporting period presented (FASB ASC 740-10-50-15A):

    a. A tabular reconciliation of the total amounts of unrecognized tax benefits at the beginning and end of the period, which shall include at a minimum the following:

        (1) The gross amounts of the increases and decreases in unrecognized tax benefits as a result of tax positions taken during a prior period

        (2) The gross amounts of increases and decreases in unrecognized tax benefits as a result of tax positions taken during the current period

        (3) The amounts of decreases in the unrecognized tax benefits relating to settlements with taxing authorities

        (4) Reductions to unrecognized tax benefits as a result of a lapse of the applicable statute of limitations

    b. The total amount of unrecognized tax benefits that, if recognized, would affect the effective tax rate

Miscellaneous Tax Allocation Topics

2270.44 Various situations have emerged that require careful analysis and consideration to determine the appropriate applications of the basic concepts of tax allocation. Several of these have been specifically considered by authoritative accounting bodies and are briefly discussed in this section.

Undistributed Earnings of Subsidiary

2270.45 The APB took the position that all undistributed earnings of a subsidiary are assumed to result in temporary differences except to the extent that the indefinite reversal criteria apply. The problem of measuring and recognizing the effects of temporary differences does not justify ignoring the tax effects of such differences.

2270.46 **Indefinite reversal criteria:** The presumption that all undistributed earnings will be transferred to the parent company may be overcome, and no income taxes need be accrued by the parent company, if sufficient evidence shows that the subsidiary has invested or will invest the undistributed earnings indefinitely or that the earnings will be remitted in a tax-free liquidation. A parent company must have evidence of specific plans for reinvestment of undistributed earnings of a subsidiary which demonstrate that remittance of the earnings will be postponed indefinitely. If circumstances change and it becomes apparent that some or all of the undistributed earnings of a subsidiary will be remitted in the foreseeable future, but income taxes have not been recognized by the parent company, it should accrue as an expense of the current period income taxes attributable to that remittance. Income tax expense of such undistributed earnings is not to be accounted for as an extraordinary item.

Bad-Debt Reserves of Savings and Loan Associations

2270.47   Regulatory authorities require both stock and mutual savings and loan associations to appropriate a portion of earnings to general reserves and to retain the reserves as a protection for depositors. Provisions of the U.S. Internal Revenue Code permit a savings and loan association to deduct an annual addition to a reserve for bad debts in determining taxable income, subject to certain limitations. This permitted annual addition generally differs significantly from the bad-debt experience on which determination of pretax accounting income is based. Thus, taxable income and pretax accounting income of an association usually will differ.

2270.48   The APB concluded that a difference between taxable income and pretax accounting income attributable to a bad-debt reserve that is accounted for as part of the general reserves and undivided profits of a savings and loan association may not reverse until indefinite future periods, or it may never reverse. The association controls the events that create the tax consequence, and the association is required to take specific action before the initial difference reverses. Therefore, a savings and loan association should not provide income taxes on this difference. However, if circumstances indicate that the association is likely to pay income taxes, either currently or in later years, because of known or expected reductions in the bad-debt reserve, the income taxes attributable to that reduction must be accrued as a tax expense of the current period. The accrual of those income taxes is not accounted for as an extraordinary item.

Policyholders' Surplus of Life Insurance Companies

2270.49   The FASB concluded that a difference between taxable income and pretax accounting income attributable to amounts designated as policyholders' surplus of a life insurance company may not reverse until indefinite future periods or may never reverse. The insurance company controls the events that create the tax consequences, and the company is generally required to take specific actions before the initial difference reverses. Therefore, a life insurance company does not accrue income taxes on the difference between taxable income and pretax accounting income attributable to amounts designated as policyholders' surplus. If circumstances change and it appears that the company is likely to pay income taxes on the amounts in policyholders' surplus, income taxes attributable to that reduction are accrued as a tax expense of the current period. The accrual of those taxes is not accounted for as an extraordinary item.

This page intentionally left blank.

Section 2300
Specific Transactions, Events, and Disclosures: Recognition, Measurement, Valuation, Calculation, Presentation, and Disclosures

2305 Accounting Changes and Error Corrections

2310 Asset Retirement and Environmental Obligations

2315 Business Combinations

2320 Consolidation (Including Off-Balance-Sheet Transactions, Variable-Interest Entities, and Noncontrolling Interests)
- 2321 Introduction and Overview
- 2322 Fundamentals of Consolidated Worksheets (Acquisition Method)
- 2323 Emphasis on Adjusting and Eliminating Entries (Acquisition Method)
- 2324 Elimination of Intercompany Profits and Losses (Acquisition Method)
- 2325 Fundamentals of Consolidated Worksheets (Purchase Method)
- 2326 Emphasis on Adjusting and Eliminating Entries (Purchase Method)
- 2327 Elimination of Intercompany Profits and Losses (Purchase Method)
- 2328 Miscellaneous Problem Areas

2330 Contingencies, Commitments, and Guarantees (Provisions)

2335 Earnings per Share

2340 Exit or Disposal Activities and Discontinued Operations

2345 Extraordinary and Unusual Items

2350 Fair Value Measurements, Disclosures, and Reporting

2355 Derivatives and Hedge Accounting

2360 Foreign Currency Transactions and Translation
- 2361 General Concepts
- 2362 Foreign Currency Transactions Other Than Forward Contracts
- 2363 Hedges of Foreign Currency Exposures That Do Not Qualify for Hedge Accounting
- 2364 Foreign Currency Fair Value Hedges
- 2365 Foreign Currency Cash Flow Hedges
- 2366 Foreign Currency Net Investment in a Foreign Entity Hedge
- 2367 Translation of Foreign Currency Financial Statements

2370 Impairment

2375 Interim Financial Reporting

2380 Leases
- 2381 General Lease Accounting Concepts
- 2382 Cases—Treatment of Leases Under Varying Circumstances
- 2383 Miscellaneous Lease Considerations
- 2384 Other FASB Codification on Leases

2385 Distinguishing Liabilities from Equity

2386 Nonmonetary Transactions (Barter Transactions)

2387 Related Parties and Related Party Transactions

2388 Research and Development Costs

2389 Risks and Uncertainties

2390 Segment Reporting

2391 Software Costs

2392 Subsequent Events

2393 Transfers and Servicing of Financial Assets and Derecognition

2305 Accounting Changes and Error Corrections

Overview of Accounting Changes and Error Correction

2305.01 Accounting changes are classified into the following three general categories for purposes of financial statement presentation:

1. Changes in accounting principle
2. Changes in accounting estimate
3. Changes in reporting entity

These three types of accounting changes, along with the corrections of errors, require special disclosure in the financial statements to enhance comparability among accounting periods.

2305.02 Definitions of the three types of accounting changes and correction of errors and examples of each are given as follows:

Event	Description	Examples
Changes in accounting principle	The adoption of a generally accepted principle different from one used previously for reporting purposes. The term "principle" includes methods of applying principles.	Change in inventory method
Changes in accounting estimate	The preparation of financial statements requires estimation. Future events and their effect cannot be determined in advance with certainty. Accounting estimates change as new events occur, as more experience is acquired, or as additional information becomes available.	Estimation of service lives of assets Estimation of uncollectible accounts receivable Changes in depreciation, amortization, and depletion methods
Changes in reporting entity	Changes in reporting entity result as the combination of companies making up a reporting enterprise differ between periods.	Presenting consolidated statements in place of individual company statements Change of specific subsidiaries making up the reporting entity
Corrections of error	Not an accounting change but includes some of the same characteristics. Distinguishable from a change in estimate because an estimate results from new information or subsequent developments leading to new and better insight and judgment.	Correcting for mathematical errors Corrections for oversight or misuses of fact Change from an accounting principle not generally accepted to one that is generally accepted

2305.03 A series of examples follows which demonstrates the proper accounting and reporting for each of the types of accounting changes and corrections of errors.

Changes in Accounting Principle: Retrospective Approach

2305.04 FASB ASC 250-10-2 requires that in the absence of a specific statement by the FASB to the contrary, accounting changes should be accounted for using the **retrospective approach**. Under this approach, all prior years' financial statements presented should be restated and the cumulative effect of the change should be reported in the retained earnings statement (or in the statement of changes in stockholders' equity) as an adjustment of the beginning-of-period balance of retained earnings of the earliest year presented.

2305.05 **Example**: Beta Company, which began operations in 20X1, appropriately reported income under the completed-contract method in years 20X1–20X3. Beta justifiably changed to the percentage-of-completion method in 20X4. Assume a 40% tax rate for all years. Comparative amounts for the four years are as follows:

	Completed Contract	Percentage of Completion	Annual Difference Before Tax	Cumulative Difference Before Tax	Cumulative Difference After Tax
20X1	$80,000	$95,000	$15,000	$15,000	$9,000
20X2	110,000	100,000	(10,000)	5,000	3,000
20X3	90,000	125,000	35,000	40,000	24,000
20X4	85,000	105,000	20,000		

Throughout 20X1–20X4 Beta had 10,000 shares of common stock outstanding and paid dividends of $5,000 in each of those years.

2305.06 Assume that Beta had no other revenues or gains and that its operating expenses (before tax) were as follows:

20X1	$30,000
20X2	45,000
20X3	35,000
20X4	30,000

2305.07 Beta reported income statement information in its 20X1–20X3 financial statements as follows:

	20X3	20X2	20X1
Construction income	$90,000	$110,000	$80,000
Operating expenses	35,000	45,000	30,000
Income before income taxes	$55,000	$65,000	$50,000
Income taxes (40%)	22,000	26,000	20,000
Net income	$33,000	$39,000	$30,000
Earnings per share	$3.30	$3.90	$3.00

Note that the construction income amounts are those under the completed-contract method (the old method).

2305.08 Beta's retained earnings statements for those same years were as follows:

	20X3	20X2	20X1
Retained Earnings, January 1	$59,000	$25,000	$ 0
Net Income	33,000	39,000	30,000
	$92,000	$64,000	$30,000
Dividends	5,000	5,000	5,000
Retained Earnings, December 31	$87,000	$59,000	$25,000

2305.09 The change in method of accounting for long-term construction contracts took place in 20X4. FASB ASC 250-10-45-5 requires, for annual financial statements, changes in accounting principle to be reported as if they were made at the beginning of the earliest year presented in the current year's financial report. Thus, if Beta Company includes financial statements for 20X4 and 20X3 in its 20X4 financial report, it should report this change in accounting principle as if it took place at January 1, 20X3, which is the earliest year presented in the 20X4 financial report. Accordingly, the 20X4 and 20X3 income statements would be presented in Beta's 20X4 financial report as follows:

	20X4	20X3 As Adjusted
Construction Income	$105,000	$125,000
Operating expenses	30,000	35,000
Income before taxes	$75,000	$90,000
Income taxes (40%)	30,000	36,000
Net income	$45,000	$54,000

2305.10 Construction income is reported under the new method (percentage-of-completion method) in Beta's 20X4 financial report for the current year (20X4) and all prior years presented (20X3 in Beta's case). Thus, the current year is presented based on the new method and all prior years presented are reported as if the new method had been used in each of those prior years as well.

2305.11 The cumulative effect of changing to the new method is reported as an adjustment of the beginning-of-year retained earnings balance of 20X3, which is the earliest year presented in Beta's 20X4 financial report. The amount shown as the adjustment of the January 1, 20X3, retained earnings is the cumulative effect of the change up to January 1, 20X3. As shown in section **2305.05**, it is the cumulative effect, net-of-tax effect, of the change on all years prior to 20X3. This cumulative effect must be reported on a net-of-tax basis. Beta's comparative years' retained earnings statements included in its 20X4 financial report should be presented as follows:

	20X4	20X3 As Adjusted
Retained earnings, January 1		$59,000
Retrospective application of percentage-of-completion method (net of applicable income taxes of $2,000)		3,000
As adjusted	$111,000	$62,000
Net Income	45,000	54,000
Dividends	(5,000)	(5,000)
Retained earnings, December 31	$151,000	$111,000

2305.12 The "As Adjusted" January 1, 20X3, retained earnings amount, $62,000, is what the retained earnings balance would have been at that date if Beta Company had been using the percentage-of-completion method rather than the completed-contract method. The 20X3 net income amount, $54,000, is the amount under the new method, the percentage-of-completion method. All of the amounts shown for 20X4 are based on the new method, including the January 1, 20X4, retained earnings amount.

2305.13 The January 1, 20X4, adjusted retained earnings presented in section **2305.11** is $111,000, which is $24,000 larger than the January 1, 20X4, $87,000 unadjusted balance at that date under the old method. This $24,000 difference (i.e., $111,000 - $87,000) is the cumulative effect of the change in accounting methods at January 1, 20X4. The $87,000 January 1, 20X4, unadjusted balance is the same as the December 31, 20X3, unadjusted balance shown in section **2305.08**.

2305.14 If Beta Company had included the financial statements of 20X4, 20X3, and 20X2 in its 20X4 financial report, its comparative years' retained earnings statements would be presented as follows:

	20X4	20X3 As Adjusted	20X2 As Adjusted
Retained Earnings, January 1			$25,000
Retrospective application of percentage-of-completion method (net of income taxes of $6,000)			9,000
As adjusted	$111,000	$62,000	$34,000
Net Income	45,000	54,000	33,000
Dividends	(5,000)	(5,000)	(5,000)
Retained earnings, December 31	$151,000	$111,000	$62,000

2305.15 As previously mentioned, the cumulative effect is reported as an adjustment of the beginning balance of retained earnings of the earliest year presented, which is 20X2 under the assumptions presented in section **2305.14**. The income statements of 20X2 and 20X3 would be shown "As Adjusted" because the financial statement amounts shown in the 20X4 financial report are different than the amounts reported in prior years' financial reports. It is not necessary to report the 20X4 financial statement "As Adjusted" because it has not been presented previously.

2305.16 Regardless of how many prior years' financial statements are presented in its 20X4 financial report, Beta Company would record the following entry at January 1, 20X4 (the beginning of the year in which the accounting change is made):

Construction-in-process	$40,000	
Income taxes payable		$16,000
Retained Earnings		24,000

2305.17 The credit to the Retained Earnings account is the cumulative effect of the change in accounting methods as of the beginning of the year in which the accounting change is made, 20X4. (See section **2305.05** for the computation of the amount.) The credit to the Income Taxes Payable account assumes that the same change is made for tax purposes. If the change is not made for tax purposes, the $16,000 credit would be to the Deferred Tax Liability account. The debit to the Construction-in-Process account is the cumulative effect before income taxes as of the beginning of the year in which the accounting change is made, 20X4.

2305.18 Under the retrospective approach, all financial statements are restated for all prior years presented. For example, assuming that Beta includes the 20X4 and 20X3 financial statements in its 20X4 financial report, it will restate its 20X3 income statement, 20X3 statement of cash flows, and December 31, 20X3, balance sheet.

2305.19 Its December 31, 20X3, restated balance sheet will report all assets, liabilities, and stockholders' equity amounts as if the new method (the percentage-of-completion method) had been used since Beta began operations on January 1, 20X1. The three balance sheet items that would be reported on a restated basis are construction-in-process, income taxes payable, and retained earnings.

2305.20 Beta's 20X3 restated statement of cash flows would show the restated cash provided by or used in operating activities. The 20X3 restated net income would cause the cash provided by or used in operating activities to be different than the amount shown in the 20X3 unadjusted statement of cash flows presented in the 20X3 financial report.

2305.21 FASB ASC 250-10-45-8 specifies that retrospective application should include only the "direct effects" of a change in accounting principle. In Beta's case, the direct effects are the changes in construction-in-process, income taxes payable, and retained earnings associated with the change in method of accounting for long-term construction contracts, as reflected at January 1, 20X4, in the entry in section **2305.16**.

2305.22 "Indirect effects" should not be included in the retrospective application. An example of an indirect effect is a change in a nondiscretionary profit-sharing payment that is based on a reported amount such as revenue or net income. For example, in Beta's case, if a portion of compensation expense is based on a percentage of profits, a change in the method of accounting for long-term construction could change the amount of compensation expense reported in each of the years affected. If indirect effects are actually incurred and recognized, they should be reported in the accounting period in which the accounting change is made. Thus, if Beta will actually pay more compensation cost as a result of this change in the method of accounting for long-term construction, the additional compensation cost should be recognized in 20X4, the year of the accounting change. Years prior to 20X4 would not be restated with respect to this indirect cost.

2305.23 FASB ASC 250-10-45-7 specifies that an entity should report a change in accounting principle using the retrospective approach unless it is impracticable to do so. FASB ASC 250-10-45-9 holds that it should be deemed impracticable to apply the effects of a change in accounting principle using the retrospective approach only if any of the following conditions exist:

    a. After making every reasonable effort to do so, the entity is unable to apply the requirement.

    b. Retrospective application requires assumptions about management's intent in a prior period that cannot be independently substantiated.

    c. Retrospective application requires significant estimates of amounts, and it is impossible to distinguish objectively information about those estimates that:

        (1) provides evidence of circumstances that existed on the date(s) at which those amounts would be recognized, measured, or disclosed under retrospective application, and

        (2) would have been available when the financial statements for that prior period were issued.

Changes in Accounting Principle: Current Approach

2305.24 Prior to the issuance of FASB ASC 250-10-45, authoritative standards required most changes in accounting principle to be measured and reported under the **current approach**. Under this approach, the cumulative effect of the change would be reported net of any related income tax effect in net income of the year of change, with prior years not being restated.

2305.25 Under the current approach, using the same data as presented in sections **2305.04–.23**, Beta's change in method of accounting for long-term construction contracts would be accounted for by including the cumulative effect of the change as of January 1, 20X4 (the year of the change), in net income of 20X4. Beta's comparative years' income statements for 20X4 and 20X3 included in its 20X4 financial report would be reported as follows:

	20X4	20X3
Construction income	$105,000	$90,000
Operating expenses	30,000	35,000
Income before change in accounting principle before income taxes	$75,000	$55,000
Income taxes (40%)	30,000	22,000
Income before change in accounting principle	$45,000	$33,000
Change in accounting principle (less income taxes of $16,000)	24,000	
Net income	$69,000	$33,000
Earnings per share	$6.90	$3.30

Under this approach, the 20X4 financial statements would be reported based on the **new** method (percentage-of-completion method) and all prior years presented would be reported under the **old** method (completed-contract method). The cumulative effect as of January 1, 20X4, the beginning of the year of change, would be included in net income of 20X4 on a net-of-tax basis as shown. The $24,000 cumulative effect was computed in section **2305.05**.

2305.26 The current approach can be used only for changes made pursuant to a specific authoritative pronouncement in which the authoritative body specifies that the current approach must be used. It would be used, for example, if the FASB issues a new FASB Statement and specifies in that Statement that the current approach must be used for accounting changes made to comply with that particular FASB Statement.

Changes in Accounting Estimates

2305.27 Changes in accounting estimates are handled on a prospective basis—in the current year and future years. The issue of retroactive application is not encountered. Note disclosure includes an explanation and justification for the change and the impact on current income and EPS.

2305.28 **Example:** Alpha Company reported income figures for 20X3 and 20X4 of $72,000 and $96,000, respectively. An asset acquired at the beginning of 20X1 for $75,000 was being depreciated over a 10-year life until 20X4, when the decision was made that the remaining life beyond 20X4 was only three years. This change is not reflected, however, in the income figures. The company has had 100,000 shares of common stock outstanding throughout its existence.

2305.29 The analysis necessary to account for this change is as follows:

Book value at 12/31/X3:	
Cost	$75,000
Accumulated depreciation ($75,000 ÷ 10) × 3	(22,500)
	$52,500
Depreciation over remaining 3 years (including 20X4): $52,500 ÷ 3	$17,500

2305.30 The presentation for this change in a 20X3/20X4 comparative income statement is as follows:

	20X4	20X3
Depreciation expense	$17,500	$ 7,500
Net income	$86,000[a]	$72,000
Earnings per share	$ 0.86	$ 0.72

[a] *Adjustment of 20X4 income ($96,000 - ($17,500 - $7,500)) = $86,000*
Note: Original depreciation of $7,500 is already included in 20X4 net income.

2305.31 Note disclosure includes the following:

a. Explanation and justification of the change

b. Impact on income and EPS of 20X4—income reduced by difference in depreciation expense of $10,000 ($0.10 per share)

2305.32 Estimates that recur annually in the normal course of business activities (e.g., bad-debt and inventory-obsolescence estimation) do not require any special disclosure. However, if their effects in a given year are so material that disclosure is deemed desirable, the appropriate disclosure is that presented for a change in estimate affecting several periods.

2305.33 After the effective date of FASB ASC 250-10-45-17, any change in a depreciation, amortization, and depletion method must be reported as a change in accounting estimate. Prior to FASB ASC 250-10-45-17, such changes would have been reported as changes in accounting principles.

2305.34 **Example**: Assume that Park Company has only one machine, which it acquired for $100,000 at the beginning of 20X1, Park's first year of operations. The machine has no estimated residual value and is being depreciated over its 10-year estimated life under the straight-line depreciation method. The annual depreciation expense is $10,000 (i.e., $100,000 ÷ 10 years).

2305.35 Assume that on January 1, 20X5, Park appropriately switches to the double-declining-balance depreciation method. This change in depreciation method must be recognized as a change in accounting estimate. The carrying amount (book value) of the machine at January 1, 20X5, would be depreciated over the estimated remaining life of the asset using the double-declining-balance method. The machine's carrying amount at January 1, 20X5, is $60,000, as shown below:

Acquisition cost of machine at 1/1/X1	$100,000
Accumulated depreciation at 1/1/X5 ($10,000 x 4 years)	40,000
Carrying amount (book value) of machine at 1/1/X5	$60,000

2305.36 The double-declining-balance depreciation rate would be twice the straight-line rate for the remaining life of the asset. Since the estimated remaining life is six years, the straight-line rate would be 1/6 and the double-declining-balance rate would be 2 x 1/6 = 1/3 (or 33⅓%). The depreciation for 20X5 would be $20,000, as computed below:

$60,000 carrying amount at 1/1/X5 x 33⅓% = $20,000

2305.37 The depreciation recognized over the 10 years of the asset's life would be:

Year	Depreciation	Computation
20X1	$10,000	$100,000 ÷ 10 years (SL depr.)
20X2	10,000	$100,000 ÷ 10 years (SL depr.)
20X3	10,000	$100,000 ÷ 10 years (SL depr.)
20X4	10,000	$100,000 ÷ 10 years (SL depr.)
20X5	20,000	($60,000 x 33⅓%) (DDB depr.)
20X6	13,333	($60,000 − $20,000 = $40,000) x 33⅓% (DDB depr.)
20X7	8,889	($40,000 − $13,333 = $26,667) x 33⅓% (DDB depr.)
20X8	5,926	($26,667 − $8,889 = $17,778) x 33⅓% (DDB depr.)
20X9	3,951	($17,778 − $5,926 = $11,852) x 33⅓% (DDB depr.)
20X10	7,901	(DDB depr. − amount necessary for depreciation to total $100,000)
	$100,000	

2305.38 It was necessary to "plug" the amount of depreciation in 20X10 in order for the total depreciation in years' 20X5–20X10 to be $60,000, the carrying amount of the machine at January 1, 20X5, the beginning of the year in which the change in depreciation methods took place. Alternatively, the $7,901 is the amount necessary for the total depreciation over the life of the asset to be $100,000. The total depreciation recognized over the machine's 10-year life is $100,000, which is the acquisition cost of the machine. If the machine had an estimated residual value, the total depreciation would have been the $100,000 acquisition cost less the estimated residual value.

2305.39 Prior years' financial statements (20X1–20X4) would not be restated. In addition, the cumulative effect of the change in depreciation method would not be recognized in either the income statement or the retained earnings statement.

2305.40 Park Company would have to report in the notes to the 20X5 financial statement its justification for the change in depreciation method and the effect that the change had on earnings and earnings per share of 20X5.

Changes in Reporting Entity

2305.41 Consolidated financial statements normally are prepared when the parent company (or controlling entity) has control over another entity(ies). The reporting entity in that case is the consolidated entity. For example, if Company P (the parent company) controls Company S (a subsidiary), consolidated financial statements normally would be prepared. The reporting entity would be the consolidated entity as opposed to Company P or Company S.

2305.42 Changes or events may occur that cause the financial statements to be those of a different reporting entity. For example, events may occur that result in Company P having control over Company T even though Company P did not acquire any additional shares of Company T. In that event, Company T should now be included in the consolidated financial statements.

2305.43 A change in reporting entity is reported by restating all prior years' financial statements presented as if the new reporting entity existed during all of those years. In addition, the cumulative effect of the change up to the beginning of the first year presented is shown as an adjustment of the beginning retained earnings of the earliest year presented. Thus, a change in reporting entity is accounted for and reported by using the retrospective approach discussed in section **2305.04–.23**.

Corrections of Errors

2305.44 A correction of an error in prior years' financial statements is reported in the year of correction by restating all prior years affected by the error. The cumulative effect of the error on periods prior to those presented must be reflected in the carrying amounts of the assets and liabilities as of the beginning of the earliest year presented in the current period's financial report. In addition, the offsetting amount of this cumulative effect must be reported as an adjustment to the opening balance of retained earnings of the earliest year presented in the current period's financial report.

2305.45 The FASB chose to describe this method of accounting for and reporting corrections of errors as restatements rather than as retrospective application. he Board chose to use the term "retrospective application" to describe the manner of reporting a change in accounting principle (as discussed in section **2305.04–.23**) or a change in reporting entity (as discussed in section **2305.41–.43**) and to use the term "restatement" only to refer to the correction of an error. Actually, the computation and manner of presenting the two (retrospective application and restatement) are essentially the same except for the different terms used.

2305.46 **Example**: Omega Company inadvertently expensed a plant asset in 20X1 purchased at the beginning of 20X1. This is Omega's only plant asset. The asset cost $70,000 and has a 10-year life with no residual value. Omega Company uses the straight-line depreciation method and is subject to a 40% income tax rate. The error was discovered in 20X4. Retained earnings at the beginning of 20X3 and 20X4 previously were reported as $150,000 and $230,000, respectively. Dividends of $10,000 have been declared annually, including 20X3 and 20X4. Omega has had 100,000 shares of common stock outstanding throughout its existence. Omega reported net income of $90,000 in 20X3 (before the error was discovered) and would have reported net income of $100,000 in 20X4 if the error had not been discovered.

2305.47 Depreciation of $7,000 (i.e., $70,000 ÷ 10 years) should have been recognized in each of the three years 20X1–20X3, as well as in 20X4 and each of the remaining six years of the asset's life after 20X4. However, no depreciation was recorded in any of the years up to January 1, 20X4; rather, an expense of $70,000 was recognized in 20X1.

2305.48 The analysis necessary to correct this error is as follows:

	(A) Overstatement (Understatement) of Income Before Tax	(B) Cumulative Effect of Error (Before Tax)	(C) Cumulative Effect of Error (After Tax)
20X1	$(63,000)	$(63,000)	$(37,800)
20X2	7,000	(56,000)	(33,600)
20X3	7,000	(49,000)	(29,400)

2305.49 The net effect of the error on income before income tax in 20X1 was a $(70,000) understatement because of the inappropriate expensing of the $70,000 cost of the plant asset and a $7,000 overstatement because of the failure to record depreciation of $7,000. The effect on income before income taxes in 20X2 and 20X3, an overstatement of $7,000 in each year, was limited to the failure to record depreciation of $7,000 in each of those years. The $(56,000) net understatement through the end of 20X2 is due to the $(63,000) understatement in 20X1 and the $7,000 overstatement in 20X2. Similarly, the $(49,000) net understatement through the end of 20X3 is due to the $(63,000) understatement in 20X1 and the $7,000 overstatements in each of the years 20X2 and 20X3.

2305.50 Column C in section **2305.48** is the same as Column B except for the tax effect. For example, the $(37,800) amount shown for 20X1 is the $(63,000) cumulative effect before tax shown in Column B less the 40% tax effect of $(25,200) [i.e., $(63,000) x .40].

2305.51 The presentation of this correction of an error in the income statements in the 20X4 financial report (which contains financial statements for 20X4 and 20X3) is as follows:

	20X4	20X3 (As Restated)
Depreciation expense	$7,000	$7,000
	...	...
Net income	$95,800[a]	$85,800[b]
Earnings per share	$.96	$.86

[a] $100,000 - $7,000 depreciation + $2,800 tax effect of depreciation ($7,000 x .40)

[b] $90,000 - $7,000 depreciation + $2,800 tax effect of depreciation

2305.52 Note that the depreciation expense is reported correctly in all years presented in the 20X4 financial report (i.e., in the 20X4 and 20X3 income statements presented). In addition, the net income amounts presented are the corrected amounts.

2305.53 The 20X4 and 20X3 retained earnings statements included in the 20X4 financial report should be presented as follows:

	20X4	20X3 As Restated
Retained earnings, January 1		$150,000
Cumulative effect of correction of error in prior years' financial statements (net of applicable income taxes of $22,400)		
As corrected	$259,400	$183,600
Net income	95,800	85,800
Dividends	(10,000)	(10,000)
Retained earnings, December 31	$345,200	$259,400

2305.54 The cumulative effect of the error correction is reported as an adjustment to the beginning-of-year retained earnings of the earliest year presented (20X3 in Omega's case). The $33,600 amount is the cumulative effect of the correction of the error as of January 1, 20X3 (see section **2305.48**).

2305.55 Omega should record the following entry on January 1, 20X4:

Machinery	$70,000	
Accumulated depreciation ($7,000 × 3 years)		$21,000
Income taxes payable (($70,000 − $21,000) × .40)		19,600
Retained earnings		29,400

2305.56 This entry results in these four balance sheet accounts being corrected as of January 1, 20X4. The $29,600 credit to the Retained Earnings account is the cumulative effect of the error after income taxes as of January 1, 20X4 (see section **2305.49**). Omega would record the correct amount of depreciation, $7,000, in 20X4 and in each of the future years over the remaining life of the asset.

2310 Asset Retirement and Environmental Obligations

2310.01 Initially, the FASB considered addressing the accounting for the costs of nuclear decommissioning. Later, the Board decided to expand the scope of the project to include similar closure or removal-type costs in other industries.

2310.02 As a result, FASB ASC 410-20-40-1 establishes accounting standards for recognition and measurement of a liability for an *asset retirement obligation* and the associated *asset retirement cost.*

2310.03 An asset retirement obligation refers to an obligation associated with the retirement of a tangible, long-lived asset, such as a nuclear power plant.

2310.04 The term "asset retirement cost" refers to the amount capitalized that increases the carrying amount of the long-lived asset when a liability for an asset retirement obligation is recognized.

2310.05 Within the context of FASB ASC 410-10-20, the term "retirement" is defined as the other-than-temporary removal of a long-lived asset from service. It includes the sale, abandonment, recycling, or disposal in some other manner, but does not encompass the temporary idling of a long-lived asset.

Initial Recognition of Asset Retirement Obligation

2310.06 An entity should recognize the fair value of an asset retirement obligation in the period in which it is incurred if a reasonable estimate of fair value can be made. Otherwise, the liability should be recognized in the first period in which a reasonable estimate of fair value can be made.

2310.07 The fair value of a liability for an asset retirement obligation is the amount at which that liability could be settled in a current transaction between willing parties. If quoted market prices are not available, the best estimate of fair value should be used.

2310.08 FASB ASC 410-20-25-6 explains that an asset retirement obligation is reasonably estimable if (a) it is evident that the fair value of the obligation is embodied in the acquisition price of the asset, (b) an active market exists for the transfer of the obligation, or (c) sufficient information exists to apply an expected present value technique.

2310.09 FASB ASC 410-20-25-8 specifies that an entity has sufficient information to apply an expected value technique if either of the following conditions exists:

    a. The settlement date and method of settlement of the obligation have been specified by others.

    b. The information is available to reasonably estimate (1) the settlement date or the range of potential dates, (2) the method of settlement or potential methods of settlement, and (3) the probabilities associated with the potential settlement dates and potential methods of settlement.

2310.10 When an asset retirement obligation is recognized, an entity should capitalize an asset retirement cost by increasing the carrying amount of the related long-lived asset by the same amount as the asset retirement obligation. Subsequently, the entity should amortize the asset retirement cost to expense using a systematic and rational method over its useful life.

Changes Subsequent to Initial Recognition

2310.11 If the related asset is tested for impairment, the carrying amount of the asset being tested for impairment should include amounts capitalized as asset retirement costs.

2310.12 After the initial measurement, an entity should recognize period-to-period changes in the liability for an asset retirement obligation resulting from (a) the passage of time and (b) revisions to either the timing or the amount of the original estimate of undiscounted cash flows.

2310.13 An entity should measure changes in the asset retirement obligation due to the passage of time by applying the interest method based on an interest rate equal to the credit-adjusted, risk-free rate that existed when the liability was initially measured. That amount should be recognized as *accretion expense* on the income statement. (Accretion expense should not be considered to be interest cost for purposes of applying FASB ASC 835-20-25.)

2310.14 On settlement of the asset retirement obligation, an entity recognizes a gain or loss for the difference between the settlement amount and the carrying amount of the asset retirement obligation at the date of settlement.

Disclosures Required

2310.15 The following disclosures must be made about an entity's asset retirement obligations:

    a. A general description of the asset retirement obligations and the associated long-lived assets

    b. The fair value of assets that are legally restricted for purposes of settling asset retirement obligations

    c. A reconciliation of the beginning and ending aggregate carrying amount of asset retirement obligations showing separately the changes attributable to (1) liabilities incurred in the current period, (2) liabilities settled in the current period, (3) accretion expense, and (4) revisions in estimated cash flows, whenever there is a significant change in one or more of those four components during the reporting period.

2315 Business Combinations

Overview of Business Combinations

2315.01 A business combination occurs when two or more business enterprises are brought under common control and into one accounting entity. Business combinations traditionally have been classified as mergers, consolidations, or acquisitions.

Forms of Business Combinations

2315.02 A statutory *merger* is of the form "A + B = A" in which one enterprise (A) acquires another enterprise (B) with the latter (B) ceasing to exist after the combination.

2315.03 A statutory *consolidation* is of the form "A + B = C" in which a new enterprise (C) is created to acquire the net assets of other enterprises (A and B). Enterprises A and B cease to exist after the combination.

2315.04 An *acquisition* is of the form "A + B = A + B" in which one enterprise (A) acquires a majority share of the stock of another enterprise (B), but both entities continue their legal existence after the combination in a parent-subsidiary relationship.

2315.05 The statutory merger and statutory consolidation forms of business combinations may be categorized as *fusions*. In both forms, the acquired enterprise ceases to exist as a legal entity; thus, it is *fused* into the surviving enterprise.

2315.06 The acquisition form of business combination may be described as an *affiliation*, since the combining enterprises continue to exist as affiliated entities.

2315.07 In the remaining discussion, business combinations are identified as being either a fusion or an affiliation.

Methods of Accounting

2315.08 Prior to the issuance of FASB ASC 805-10, a business combination had to be accounted for under the pooling of interest method if it met the 12 criteria for a pooling of interests specified in APBO 16, *Business Combinations*. Otherwise, the combination had to be accounted for under the purchase method.

2315.09 Combinations after the effective date for FASB ASC 805-10-05 must be accounted for under the acquisition method. Combinations before the effective date of FASB ASC 805-10-05 but after the effective date of SFAS 141 must be accounted for under the purchase method. Pre-SFAS 141 combinations still must be accounted for by the pooling of interests method if they were appropriately being accounted for under the pooling of interests method prior to SFAS 141.

2315.10 The acquisition of all or part of a financial institution that meets the definition of a business combination also should be accounted for by the acquisition method.

2315.11 A summary overview of the combination forms and accounting methods is presented in the following illustration. The numbered lines at the top of the illustration identify the various situations that might exist. For example, line 1 identifies the possible situation of a fusion for which the acquisition method of accounting is required. Similarly, line 3 identifies the possibility of an affiliation for which the acquisition method is required. The methods of accounting are explained in more detail in the discussion that follows.

Overview of Form of Combination and Methods of Accounting

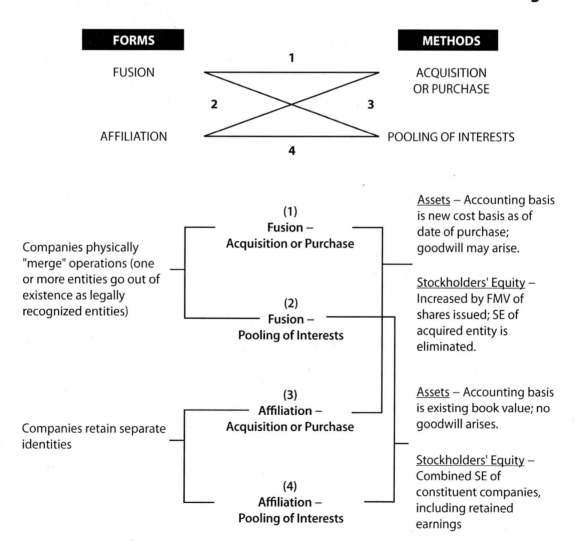

The Acquisition Method

2315.12 Under the acquisition method, a business combination is deemed to be the acquisition of one entity by another. Accordingly, the accounting for the combination follows the historical cost principle related to acquisitions. The accounting basis is the fair value of the consideration given or the fair value of the consideration (net assets) received, whichever is more clearly determinable. The acquirer is the entity that obtains control of one or more businesses in the business combination. The acquisition date is the date that the acquirer achieves control.

If the acquiring corporation gains control with smaller noncontrolling purchases eventually culminating in a purchase that achieves control, the assets and liabilities acquired in the series of purchases must all be marked to fair value as of the date control is achieved. Gains and losses from revaluing these former purchases must be included in current financial statements.

2315.13 The acquiring corporation must recognize the assets acquired, the liabilities assumed, and any noncontrolling interest in the acquiree at the acquisition date, measured at their fair values as of that date. The acquirer must then recognize goodwill as of the acquisition date equal to the excess of the consideration transferred plus the fair value of any noncontrolling interest in the acquiree over the fair values of all identifiable net assets acquired (all assets other than goodwill). The tax basis of an asset or liability should not be a factor in determining its fair value. However, a deferred tax asset or liability should be recognized for any difference between the fair value and the tax basis of an asset or liability if the difference represents a temporary difference.

Contingent assets and liabilities should be included when:

a. a contractual contingency exists or

b. a noncontractual contingency is more likely than not to give rise to an asset or a liability.

In-process research and development results are classified as intangible assets with indefinite lives until the research and development phase is complete or the project is abandoned. These assets are originally recorded at fair value and will be subject to impairment tests.

Acquisition costs must be recognized separately from the acquisition. Restructuring costs are also recognized separately from the business combination. These costs must be recognized in the acquirer's postcombination financial statements in accordance with generally accepted accounting principles—usually expensed.

2315.14 In an acquisition-method business combination, the consideration given (paid) by the acquiring corporation may be assets, debt (payable by acquirer to acquired), stock, or combinations thereof. Any stock issued is recorded at fair value. Any difference between par (stated) value and fair value (FV) is recognized as additional paid-in capital.

Excess of Cost Over Book Value of Identifiable Net Assets Acquired

2315.15 If the fair value of the consideration plus the fair value of a noncontrolling interest in the acquiree exceeds the fair value of the identifiable net assets acquired, this "excess" should be recognized as goodwill. The acquisition entry in that situation may be summarized as follows:

Fusion:
Individual Identifiable Assets Acquired (at FV)	$XXX	
Goodwill (excess of cost over FV of identifiable net assets acquired)	XXX	
Individual Liabilities Assumed (at FV)		$XXX
Common Stock (par value of stock issued)		XXX
Additional Paid-in Capital		XXX
Noncontrolling Interest in Acquiree		XXX

Affiliation:
    Investment in Subsidiary (cost of acquired enterprise) $XXX
        Common Stock (par value of stock issued) $XXX
        Additional Paid-in Capital   XXX

In the case of an affiliation, goodwill and the fair value of the individual identifiable net assets acquired would surface on the consolidated worksheet. Consolidated worksheets are discussed in section **2320**.

2315.16 Two examples of the acquisition entries to be recorded when the cost of the acquired enterprise exceeds the fair value of the identifiable net assets acquired are presented immediately following. Example 1 represents a situation in which the acquiring enterprise acquires 100% of the stock of the acquired enterprise. Example 2 relates to the acquiring enterprise's acquisition of less than 100% of the acquired enterprise's stock.

2315.17 **Example 1:** Acquisition of 100% of acquired company's stock. The balance sheet of S Company (the acquired company) immediately before the combination appears as follows:

S Company
Balance Sheet
Prior to Combination

Current assets	$ 15	Liabilities	$ 10
Plant assets	95	Common stock, par $1	20
		Retained earnings	80
	$110		$110

2315.18 P Company issues 10 shares of $1 par stock for 100% of the common stock of S Company. The fair value of the P Company stock issued is $200. Fair values of S Company's net identifiable assets are the same as their book values, except for plant assets, which have a fair value of $100. The $200 fair value of P Company's stock issued exceeds P's equity (100%) in the book value (BV) of the net assets of S. This excess of cost over book value is allocated as follows:

Cost of investment (FV of P stock issued)	$200
Less 100% of BV of identifiable net assets of S	100
Differential (excess of cost over book value of identifiable net assets)	100
Adjustments for P's share of differences between FV and BV of identifiable assets and liabilities of S:	
Plant assets ($100 – $95)	(5)
Adjusted differential (excess of cost over FV of identifiable net assets)—goodwill	$ 95

2315.19 The entries to record the acquisition are presented for both a fusion and an affiliation:

Fusion:
Current Assets	$ 15	
Plant Assets	100	
Goodwill	95	
Liabilities		$ 10
Common Stock		10
Capital in Excess of Par		190

Affiliation:
Investment in Subsidiary	$200	
Common Stock		$ 10
Capital in Excess of Par		190

2315.20 **Example 2:** Acquisition of less than 100% of stock. Assume the same facts as presented in Example 1, except that P acquires only 80% of the stock of S for 8 shares of P. Thus, the $160 fair value of P Company's stock issued exceeds P's equity (80%) in the net assets of S. This excess of cost over book value (goodwill) is computed as follows:

Value of controlling interest (FV of P stock issued)	$160
Value of noncontrolling interest	40
Total acquisition-date fair value of S Company	200
Identifiable net assets	105
Goodwill	$ 95

2315.21 The acquisition entry is:

Fusion: No fusion since less than 100% of S stock acquired.
Affiliation:

Investment in Subsidiary	$160	
Common Stock		$ 8
Capital in Excess of Par		152

The $5 increment in plant assets and the $95 of goodwill would surface on the consolidated worksheet and would be included in the consolidated financial statements. Consolidated worksheets are discussed in section **2320**.

Excess of Book Value of Identifiable Net Assets Acquired Over Cost

2315.22 If the values assigned to the identifiable net assets exceed the cost of the acquired company, such "excess" must be recognized as a gain in earnings of the acquisition date.

2315.23 Thus, the fair values of the "eligible" assets would be recognized on the acquisition date. Under FASB ASC 805-10-05-2, any excess should be recognized as an extraordinary gain.

2315.24 The following example (Example 3) demonstrates the entries involved if the values assigned to the identifiable net assets exceed the cost of the acquired company. In Example 3, the "excess" (the credit differential) is less than the assigned amount of the "eligible" assets. In that case, the "excess" is recognized as an extraordinary gain.

2315.25 **Example 3:** Excess of book value over cost. Assume the same facts as presented in Example 1 (P acquired 100% of S), except that the fair value of the P stock issued is $80 instead of $200. Thus, the fair value of P's stock ($80) is less than P's equity ($100) in the net assets of S. This difference is determined and allocated as follows:

Cost of investment (FV of P stock issued)	$ 80
Less 100% of BV of net assets of S	100
Differential (excess of book value over cost)	(20)
100% of excess of FV of plant assets over BV ($100 – $95)	(5)
Extraordinary gain (excess of fair value of identifiable net assets over cost)	$(25)

2315.26 The acquisition entries are:

Fusion:

Current Assets	$15	
Plant Assets	100	
Liabilities		$10
Common Stock		10
Capital in Excess of Par		70
Extraordinary Gain on Acquisition		25

Affiliation:
Investment in Subsidiary $80
Common Stock $10
Capital in Excess of Par 70

The recognition of the extraordinary gain would surface on the consolidated worksheet and would be reflected on the consolidated financial statements.

2315.27 The steps involved in determining and allocating any difference between cost and the acquiring company's (P's) equity in the net assets of the acquired company (S) are as follows:

a. **Step 1:** Subtract P's equity in the book value of S from the cost of the investment.

b. **Step 2:** Adjust the differential computed in Step 1 for P's share of any difference between the fair value and book value of the identifiable net assets of S. (This differential will be amortized on the consolidated worksheet in an affiliation. Consolidated worksheets are discussed in section **2320**.)

c. **Step 3:** Allocate the adjusted differential from Step 2. If positive, allocate to goodwill. If negative, recognize an extraordinary gain.

2315.28 In a fusion, the acquiring company records on its books the individual assets and liabilities of the acquired company at their fair value. Any goodwill resulting from the combination is also recorded on the books at that time.

2315.29 In an affiliation, the acquiring company debits the investment in the subsidiary account for the fair value of the consideration given. The individual assets and liabilities of the acquired company are not recorded on the books of the acquiring company. The individual assets and liabilities, the parent's share of any differences between their fair values and book values, and any goodwill arising from the business combination surface only at the time consolidated workpapers are prepared by the parent (acquiring) company.

2315.30 In an acquisition business combination, the acquiring company's share of the net income of the acquired company should be included with that of the acquiring company only after the date of the business combination. In the case of consolidated financial statements, the consolidated net income in the period of a purchase business combination should include the parent's net income for the entire year and the parent's share of the subsidiary's net income after the combination. The consolidated net income also should reflect the effect of any differential amortization (e.g., amortization of any differential associated with plant assets whose fair values at the date of the combination exceeded their book values) and the elimination of any intercompany transactions.

2315.31 FASB ASC 805-10-50 includes a great deal of specific disclosure. These disclosures include that management will have to describe the economic factors that validate the recorded goodwill, other unrecognized intangibles, and synergies expected from the combination. It also contains a reference to "whatever additional information is necessary to meet those objectives." This is a move toward principles-based accounting.

2315.32 FASB ASC 805-10 applies prospectively to business combinations for which the acquisition date is on or after the beginning of the first annual reporting period beginning on or after December 15, 2008. Assets and liabilities that arose from business combinations whose acquisition dates preceded the application of the statement are not to be adjusted upon application of the statement.

The Purchase Method

2315.33 Under the purchase method, a business combination is deemed to be the acquisition of one entity by another. Accordingly, the accounting for the combination follows the historical cost principle related to acquisitions. The accounting basis is the fair value of the consideration given or the fair value of the consideration (net assets) received, whichever is more clearly determinable.

2315.34 The acquiring corporation should allocate the cost of the acquired company to the assets acquired and liabilities assumed. First, all identifiable net assets acquired (all assets other than goodwill) should be assigned a portion of the cost equal to their fair values at the date of acquisition. The tax basis of an asset or liability should not be a factor in determining its fair value. However, a deferred tax asset or liability should be recognized for any difference between the fair value and the tax basis of an asset or liability if the difference represents a temporary difference. Contingent assets and liabilities should be included when:

   a. the fair value of the preacquisition contingency can be determined during the allocation period or

   b. information available prior to the end of the allocation period indicates that it is probable that an asset existed, a liability had been incurred, or an asset had been impaired, and the amount of the asset or liability can be reasonably estimated.

2315.35 In a purchase-method business combination, the consideration given (paid) by the acquiring corporation may be assets, debt (payable by acquirer to acquired), stock, or combinations thereof. Any stock issued is recorded at fair value. Any difference between par (stated) value and fair value (FV) is recognized as additional paid-in capital.

Excess of Cost Over Book Value of Identifiable Net Assets Acquired

2315.36 If the fair value of the consideration (the cost of the acquired enterprise) exceeds the fair value of the identifiable net assets acquired, this "excess" should be recognized as goodwill. The acquisition entry in that situation may be summarized as follows:

Fusion:		
Individual Identifiable Assets Acquired (at FV)	$XXX	
Goodwill (excess of cost over FV of identifiable net assets acquired)	XXX	
Individual Liabilities Assumed (at FV)		$XXX
Common Stock (par value of stock issued)		XXX
Additional Paid-in Capital		XXX
Affiliation:		
Investment in Subsidiary (cost of acquired enterprise)	$XXX	
Common Stock (par value of stock issued)		$XXX
Additional Paid-in Capital		XXX

In the case of an affiliation, goodwill and the fair value of the individual identifiable net assets acquired would surface on the consolidated worksheet. Consolidated worksheets are discussed in section **2320**.

2315.37 Two examples of the acquisition entries to be recorded when the cost of the acquired enterprise exceeds the fair value of the identifiable net assets acquired are presented immediately following. Example 1 represents a situation in which the acquiring enterprise acquires 100% of the stock of the acquired enterprise. Example 2 relates to the acquiring enterprise's acquisition of less than 100% of the acquired enterprise's stock.

2315.38 **Example 1:** Acquisition of 100% of acquired company's stock. The balance sheet of S Company (the acquired company) immediately before the combination appears as follows:

S Company
Balance Sheet
Prior to Combination

Current assets	$ 15	Liabilities	$ 10
Plant assets	95	Common stock, par $1	20
		Retained earnings	80
	$110		$110

2315.39 P Company issues 10 shares of $1 par stock for 100% of the common stock of S Company. The fair value of the P Company stock issued is $200. Fair values of S Company's net identifiable assets are the same as their book values, except for plant assets, which have a fair value of $100. The $200 fair value of P Company's stock issued exceeds P's equity (100%) in the book value (BV) of the net assets of S. This excess of cost over book value is allocated as follows:

Cost of investment (FV of P stock issued)	$200
Less 100% of BV of identifiable net assets of S	100
Differential (excess of cost over book value of identifiable net assets)	100
Adjustments for P's share of differences between FV and BV of identifiable assets and liabilities of S:	
Plant assets ($100 - $95)	(5)
Adjusted differential (excess of cost over FV of identifiable net assets)—goodwill	$ 95

2315.40 The entries to record the acquisition are presented for both a fusion and an affiliation:

Fusion:		
Current Assets	$ 15	
Plant Assets	100	
Goodwill	95	
Liabilities		$ 10
Common Stock		10
Capital in Excess of Par		190
Affiliation:		
Investment in Subsidiary	$200	
Common Stock		$ 10
Capital in Excess of Par		190

2315.41 **Example 2:** Acquisition of less than 100% of stock. Assume the same facts as presented in Example 1, except that P acquires only 80% of the stock of S. Thus, the $200 fair value of P Company's stock issued exceeds P's equity (80%) in the net assets of S. This excess of cost over book value is allocated as follows:

Cost of investment (FV of P stock issued)	$200
Less 80% of BV of identifiable net assets of S (0.80 × $100)	80
Differential (excess of cost over BV of identifiable net assets)	120
Adjustments for P's share of differences between FV and BV of identifiable assets and liabilities of S:	
Plant assets 0.80 × ($100 - $95)	(4)
Adjusted differential (excess of cost over FV of identifiable net assets)—goodwill	$116

2315.42 The acquisition entry is:

Fusion: No fusion since less than 100% of S stock acquired.
Affiliation:

Investment in Subsidiary	$200	
Common Stock		$ 10
Capital in Excess of Par		190

The $4 increment in plant assets and the $116 of goodwill would surface on the consolidated worksheet and would be included in the consolidated financial statements.

Excess of Book Value of Identifiable Net Assets Acquired Over Cost

2315.43 If the values assigned to the identifiable net assets exceed the cost of the acquired company, such "excess" should be allocated as a pro rata deduction of the amount that otherwise would have been assigned to all of the assets acquired except for the following:

a. Financial assets other than investments accounted for by the equity method

b. Assets to be disposed of by sale

c. Deferred tax assets

d. Prepaid assets relating to pension or other postretirement benefit plans

e. Any other current assets

2315.44 Thus, the fair values of the "eligible" assets (the assets acquired excluding those listed in section **2315.43**) would be reduced pro rata. If any "excess" remains after reducing the "eligible" assets to zero, that "excess" should be recognized as an extraordinary gain.

2315.45 The following two examples (Example 3 and Example 4) demonstrate the entries involved if the values assigned to the identifiable net assets exceed the cost of the acquired company. In Example 3, the "excess" (the credit differential) is less than the assigned amount of the "eligible" assets. In that case, the "excess" is eliminated without reducing the "eligible" assets to zero. In Example 4, the "excess" is larger than the assigned amounts of the "eligible" assets, which results in the "eligible" assets being reduced to zero and an extraordinary gain being recognized.

2315.46 **Example 3:** Excess of book value over cost. Assume the same facts as presented in Example 1 (P acquired 100% of S), except that the fair value of the P stock issued is $80 instead of $200. Thus, the fair value of P's stock ($80) is less than P's equity ($100) in the net assets of S. This difference is determined and allocated as follows:

Cost of investment (FV of P stock issued)	$ 80
Less 100% of BV of net assets of S	100
Differential (excess of book value over cost)	(20)
100% of excess of FV of plant assets over BV ($100 - $95)	(5)
Adjusted differential (excess of fair value of identifiable net assets over cost)	$(25)
Allocated to "eligible" assets:	
Plant assets	$(25)

2315.47 The acquisition entries are:

Fusion:

Current Assets	$15	
Plant Assets ($95 + $5 – $25)	75	
Liabilities		$10
Common Stock		10
Capital in Excess of Par		70

Affiliation:
Investment in Subsidiary	$80	
Common Stock		$10
Capital in Excess of Par		70

2315.48 **Example 4:** Excess of book value over cost with extraordinary gain recognized. Assume that the balance sheet of S Company immediately before the combination appears as follows:

S Company
Balance Sheet
Prior to Combination

Current assets	$ 95	Liabilities	$ 10
Plant assets	15	Common stock, $1 par	20
		Retained earnings	80
	$110		$110

Assume that Company P acquires 100% of S by issuing Company P stock whose fair value is $70. The fair value (FV) of the plant assets of Company S is $20. The credit differential would be determined and allocated as follows:

Cost of investment (FV of P stock issued)	$ 70
Less 100% of BV of identifiable net assets of S	100
Differential (excess of book value over cost)	(30)
100% of excess of FV of plant assets over BV ($20 – $15)	(5)
Adjusted differential (excess of fair value of identifiable net assets over cost)	(35)
Allocation of credit differential to "eligible" assets:	
Plant assets	20
Extraordinary gain	$(15)

2315.49 The acquisition entries for a fusion are:

Current Assets	$95	
Plant Assets ($15 + $5 – $20)	0	
Liabilities		$10
Common Stock		10
Capital in Excess of Par		60
Extraordinary Gain		15

2315.50 The adjusted differential (credit differential) of $(35) is larger than the amounts that would have been assigned to the "eligible" assets ($20 fair value of plant assets). Therefore, the "eligible" assets would be reduced to zero and an extraordinary gain recognized.

2315.51 The acquisition entries for Example 4 for an affiliation are:

Investment in Subsidiary	$70	
Common Stock		$10
Capital in Excess of Par		60

The reduction in the "eligible" assets and the recognition of the extraordinary gain would surface on the consolidated worksheet and would be reflected on the consolidated financial statements.

2315.52 The steps involved in determining and allocating any difference between cost and the acquiring company's (P's) equity in the net assets of the acquired company (S) are as follows:

a. **Step 1:** Subtract P's equity in the book value of S from the cost of the investment.

b. **Step 2:** Adjust the differential computed in Step 1 for P's share of any difference between the fair value and book value of the identifiable net assets of S.

    c. Step 3: Allocate the adjusted differential from Step 2. If positive, allocate to goodwill. If negative, reduce the amounts assigned to noncurrent assets (except for long-term investments in marketable securities) on a proportionate basis.

    d. Step 4: Any adjusted credit differential balance remaining after Step 3 should be recognized as a deferred credit and amortized.

2315.53 In a fusion, the acquiring company records on its books the individual assets and liabilities of the acquired company at their fair values (except for the "eligible" assets in the case of a credit differential). Any goodwill resulting from the combination is also recorded on the books at that time.

2315.54 In an affiliation, the acquiring company debits the investment in the subsidiary account for the fair value of the consideration given. The individual assets and liabilities of the acquired company are not recorded on the books of the acquiring company. The individual assets and liabilities, the parent's share of any differences between their fair values and book values, and any goodwill arising from the business combination (or any reductions in the "eligible" assets and any extraordinary gain resulting from a credit differential) surface only at the time consolidated workpapers are prepared by the parent (acquiring) company.

2315.55 In a purchase business combination, the acquiring company's share of the net income of the acquired company should be included with that of the acquiring company only after the date of the business combination. In the case of consolidated financial statements, the consolidated net income in the period of a purchase business combination should include the parent's net income for the entire year and the parent's share of the subsidiary's net income after the combination. The consolidated net income also should reflect the effect of any differential amortization (e.g., amortization of any differential associated with plant assets whose fair values at the date of the combination exceeded their book values) and the elimination of any intercompany transactions.

The Pooling of Interests Method

2315.56 A *pooling of interests* is a combination of two or more corporations (combining companies) in which the holders of substantially all of the ownership interests in the constituent corporations become owners of a single corporation (combined or survivor company), which owns the assets and liabilities of the constituent corporations. The surviving company may be one of the combining companies, or it may be a newly formed entity. The combined (or surviving) company is also sometimes identified as the issuing company, with the combining corporations known as the nonissuer companies.

2315.57 For accounting purposes, a new basis of accountability does not arise in a pooling of interests. The combination is accounted for as the uniting of the ownership interests of two or more companies by exchange of equity securities. The assets and liabilities of the constituent companies are carried forward into the surviving entity at precombination book values. However, adjustments prior to combination specifically to attain uniform accounting methods are allowed and recommended but not required.

2315.58 When a pooling of interests combination occurs, the issuing or combined corporation makes the appropriate one of the following entries:

Fusion:
Individual Assets (at book value)	$XXX	
Individual Liabilities (at book value)		$XXX
Common Stock (par value of stock issued)		XXX
Retained Earnings (of combining company)		XXX
Additional Paid-in Capital (to balance)		XXX

Affiliation:
    Investment in Subsidiary (BV of net assets of combining company) $XXX
        Common Stock (par value of stock issued) $XXX
        Retained Earnings (RE of combining company)   XXX
        Additional Paid-in Capital (to balance)   XXX

2315.59 Under pooling, the balance in the surviving (combined) entity's capital accounts after the combination is equal to the sum of the capital balances of the constituents (combining companies) immediately prior to the combination. Common stock issued by the issuing (surviving or combined) company to effect the combination is recorded at its par or stated value. If the total par value of the stock issued by the issuing company is less than the total par value of the combining (nonissuing) company or companies, the difference is credited to the additional paid-in capital of the issuing company. All the retained earnings of the combining company or companies are carried forward.

2315.60 If the total par value of the stock issued by the issuing company is greater than that of the combining company or companies, the excess is first charged against the additional paid-in capital of the issuer (combined) corporation. Any additional charges needed are made against the retained earnings of the combining company or companies.

2315.61 This results in retained earnings of the surviving corporation being equal to or less than the retained earnings of the constituent (combining) companies. However, the surviving retained earnings could not be greater than the aggregate retained earnings of the combining corporations prior to the combination.

2315.62 The entries to record a business combination accounted for as a pooling of interests are demonstrated in the following four examples.

2315.63 **Example 1:** This example demonstrates the type of entry recorded when the total par value of the combined (or issuer) corporation is *less than* the *total* par value of the combining (or nonissuer) corporation.

Nonissuer Corporation S
Balance Sheet
Prior to Combination

Current assets	$ 15	Liabilities	$ 10
Plant assets	95	Common stock, par $1	20
		Retained earnings	80
	$110		$110

P Company issued 10 shares (par value $1 per share) for 100% of stock of S.

Fusion:
    Current Assets $ 15
    Plant Assets   95
        Liabilities $10
        Common Stock—P (10 × $1)   10
        Retained Earnings—P   80
        Additional Paid-in Capital—P   10

Affiliation:
    Investment in Subsidiary $100
        Common Stock—P (10 × $1) $10
        Retained Earnings—P   80
        Additional Paid-in Capital—P   10

2315.64 **Example 2:** In this example, the total par value of the issuer corporation is *more than* the total par value of the nonissuer corporation.

P company issues 10 shares (par value $1 per share) for 100% of stock of S.

Nonissuer Corporation S
Balance Sheet
Prior to Combination

Current assets	$ 15	Liabilities	$ 10
Plant assets	95	Common stock, par $1	6
		Retained earnings	94
	$110		$110

2315.65 If the issuer (combined) corporation had additional paid-in capital of at least $4, which is the amount of the excess of the total par value of the P stock being issued ($10) over the total par value of the S stock ($6), the entry would be:

Fusion:
Current Assets	$ 15	
Plant Assets	95	
Additional Paid-in Capital—P	4	
Current Liabilities		$10
Common Stock—P (10 × $1)		10
Retained Earnings—P		94

Affiliation:
Investment in Subsidiary	$100	
Additional Paid-in Capital—P	4	
Common Stock—P (10 × $1)		$10
Retained Earnings—P		94

2315.66 **Example 3:** Assume the same facts as presented in Example 2, except that the issuer corporation had additional paid-in capital of only $3. As a result, the amount of retained earnings of S Company that can be carried forward will be less than the balance shown on S Company's books. The amount of the reduction is determined as follows:

Total par value of P stock being issued	$10
Total par value of S stock	6
Excess of par value of P stock over S stock	$ 4
P Company's additional paid-in capital balance	3
Reduction in amount of retained earnings of S Company that can be carried forward	$ 1

The entries to record the combination would be:

Fusion:
Current Assets	$ 15	
Plant Assets	95	
Additional Paid-in Capital—P	3	
Current Liabilities		$10
Common Stock—P (10 × $1)		10
Retained Earnings—P ($94 − $1)		93

Affiliation:
Investment in Subsidiary	$100	
Additional Paid-in Capital—P	3	
Common Stock—P (10 × $1)		$10
Retained Earnings—P ($94 − $1)		93

2315.67 **Example 4:** This example demonstrates the entry necessary when *less than 100%* of the stock is acquired:

S Company
Balance Sheet
Prior to Combination

Current assets	$ 15	Current liabilities	$ 10
Plant assets	95	Common stock, par $1	20
		Additional paid-in capital	10
		Retained earnings	70
	$110		$110

2315.68 Company P issues 10 shares of $1 par stock for 18 shares (90%) of the outstanding stock of Company S. The entry under pooling of interests is:

Affiliation:		
Investment in Subsidiary (90% of $100)	$90	
Common Stock—P (10 × $1)		$10
Retained Earnings—P (90% of $70)		63
Additional Paid-in Capital—P (to balance)		17

Reporting Results of Operations

2315.69 The combined (issuer) corporation should report results of operations for the period in which the combination occurs as though the companies had been combined as of the beginning of the earliest year presented. The effects of intercompany transactions should be eliminated.

2315.70 Expenses of effecting the combination should be deducted in determining net income of the combined corporation.

2315.71 Gains or losses on normal asset dispositions after the combination are included in income before extraordinary items. Gains or losses on abnormal asset dispositions within two years after the combination are included as extraordinary gains or losses.

Pooling of Interests Criteria

2315.72 To qualify as a pooling of interests, a business combination had to meet *all* of the following 12 criteria:

1. Each of the combining companies is autonomous and has not been a subsidiary or division of another corporation within two years before the plan of combination is initiated.

2. Each of the combining companies is independent of the other combining companies.

3. The combination is effected in a single transaction or completed in accordance with a specific plan within one year after the plan is initiated.

4. A corporation offers and issues only common stock with rights identical to those of the majority of its outstanding voting common stock in exchange for *substantially all* of the voting common stock interest of another company at the date the plan of combination is consummated.

5. None of the combining companies changes the equity interest of the voting common stock in contemplation of effecting the combination either within two years before the plan of combination is initiated or between the dates the combination is initiated and consummated.

6. Each of the combining companies reacquires shares of voting stock only for purposes other than business combinations, and no company reacquires more than a normal number of shares between the dates the plan of combination is initiated and consummated.

7. The ratio of the interest of an individual common stockholder to those of other common stockholders in a combining company remains the same as a result of the exchange of stock to effect the combination.

8. The voting rights to which the common stock ownership interests in the resulting combined corporation are entitled are exercisable by the stockholders; the stockholders are neither deprived nor restricted in exercising those rights for a period.

9. The combination is resolved at the date the plan is consummated, and no provisions of the plan relating to the issue of securities or other considerations are pending.

10. The combined corporation does not agree directly or indirectly to retire or reacquire all or part of the common stock issued to effect the combination.

11. The combined corporation does not enter into other financial arrangements for the benefit of the former stockholders of a combining company, such as the guarantee of loans secured by stock issued in the combination, which in effect negates the exchange of equity securities.

12. The combined corporation does not intend or plan to dispose of a significant part of the assets of the combining companies within two years after the combination other than disposals in the ordinary course of business of the formerly separate companies and to eliminate duplicate facilities or excess capacity.

2315.73 A business combination occurring after the effective date of FASB ASC 805-10 may not be accounted for as a pooling of interests. However, a pre-SFAS 141 business combination that appropriately was accounted for as a pooling of interests must continue to be accounted for as a pooling of interests.

2315.74 **IFRS:** GAAP requires the full goodwill method of accounting, while revised IFRS 3 provides this as an option.

    a. Subsequent measurement and recognition of gains or losses of contingent consideration may result since, under GAAP, all contingent consideration classified as a liability is remeasured at fair value through earnings unless it is a hedging instrument recognized through other comprehensive income. Under IFRS, contingent consideration classified as a liability is remeasured based on the applicable IFRS standards, such as IAS 37 or IAS 39.

    b. Different definitions of fair value could lead to different amounts for assets or liabilities initially recognized at fair value.

    c. Accounting for some assets and liabilities occurs according to other standards and, as a result, creates differences applicable to assets and liabilities not initially measured at fair value, such as taxes, employee benefits, and share-based payments.

    d. If bargain purchase (excess of fair value of net assets over purchase price) amounts remain after reducing certain assets, U.S. GAAP requires and IFRS prohibits recognition as an extraordinary gain.

    e. Revised IFRS 3 includes and FASB ASC 805-10-15-4 excludes from its scope combinations of not-for-profit organizations.

    f. Accounting for restructuring costs is similar except for consequential differences in measurement attributes in IAS 37 versus FASB ASC 420-10-25-1.

2320 Consolidation (Including Off-Balance-Sheet Transactions, Variable-Interest Entities, and Noncontrolling Interests)

2321 Introduction and Overview

2321.01 The ownership by one entity of a controlling interest in another entity presents a situation of the two entities being separate legal entities but in substance a single economic or accounting entity. In such cases, there is a presumption under current GAAP that consolidated financial statements are more meaningful than separate financial statements.

2321.02 As a general rule, current GAAP requires that consolidated financial statements be prepared when one of the entities in the group directly or indirectly has a controlling financial interest in the other entities. FASB ASC 810-10-15-9 specifies that the usual condition for consolidated financial statements is ownership (direct or indirect) of a majority voting interest (i.e., at least one share in excess of 50%).

2321.03 However, in part, due to the attention devoted to the Enron case, the FASB became concerned that strict application of the "majority voting interest requirement" could result in a particular entity not being consolidated because the entity does not own more than 50% of the voting interests even though it has a controlling financial interest through arrangements that do not involve voting interests. As a result, FASB ASC 810-10-30-1 deals with certain specialized issues related to those types of situations. FASB ASC 810-10-30-1 addresses specialized situations that generally should be beyond the scope of the CPA Examination. Nevertheless, see the discussion beginning at section **2328.47** for a summary of the fundamental issues of FASB ASC 810-10-30-1 as they relate to the issue of when to prepare consolidated financial statements.

2321.04 Consolidated financial statements present the results of operations, financial position, and cash flows of a parent company and its subsidiaries as if they were a single company. All intercompany balances and transactions should be eliminated when consolidated statements are prepared.

2321.05 All majority-owned subsidiaries should be consolidated unless control does not rest with the majority owner (e.g., if the subsidiary is in legal reorganization or in bankruptcy).

2321.06 Unconsolidated subsidiaries should be accounted for by the parent under the cost method or the equity method, whichever is appropriate. The equity method should be used if the parent (investor) has the ability to significantly influence the operating and financial policies of the unconsolidated subsidiary (investee); otherwise, the cost method should be used.

2321.07 A parent company may own less than 100% of the voting stock of a subsidiary. In such cases, there is a noncontrolling (minority) interest in the net assets of the subsidiary as well as a controlling interest. The amount of equity identified with the noncontrolling (minority) interest must be disclosed in the consolidated financial statements prepared for the parent company and its subsidiaries.

2321.08 The noncontrolling (minority) interest represents a subset of total stockholders' equity, as demonstrated for a consolidated balance sheet:

Stockholders' equity:	
Controlling interest	$XXX
Noncontrolling interest	XXX
Total stockholders' equity	$XXX

2321.09 Under FASB ASC 810-10-45-16, the noncontrolling interest is reported in the consolidated statement of financial position within equity, separately from the parent's equity.

Overview of Section 2320

2321.10 The remainder of this section focuses on the various issues related to the preparation of consolidated worksheets and consolidated financial statements. The major areas of discussion are the following:

   a. Fundamentals of consolidated worksheets

   b. Adjusting and eliminating entries

   c. Elimination of intercompany profits and losses

   d. Various miscellaneous problem areas associated with consolidated worksheets and financial statements

2322 Fundamentals of Consolidated Worksheets (Acquisition Method)

2322.01 A *consolidated worksheet* is the vehicle by which data from the various entities involved in a consolidation are combined, adjusted, and summarized in a form suitable to serve as a basis for the preparation of consolidated financial statements. A consolidated worksheet includes columns for the following:

   a. The trial balance of each of the entities

   b. Adjustments and eliminations

   c. The consolidated balances for the financial statement(s) to be prepared

2322.02 The particular adjusting or eliminating entries to be reflected on the worksheet are a function of the following three factors:

   1. The actual transactions or economic events that have occurred

   2. How the transactions or events have been recorded in the accounts

   3. What constitutes GAAP for presentation in the consolidated financial statements

2322.03 Some enterprises may choose to maintain their books during the year in strict accordance with GAAP. In such cases, financial statements can be prepared without making any adjustments to the balances shown in the ledger accounts.

2322.04 Other enterprises may elect to maintain their books during the year in a more *convenient manner*, with the awareness that the accounts will have to be adjusted at the end of the period before financial statements can be prepared. During the year, the books are merely *unadjusted* rather than wrong.

2322.05 The essence of the preceding discussion is that the CPA Examination candidate should not take for granted that an enterprise's books are kept in strict accordance with GAAP. The candidate must first determine what GAAP require for the financial statements and how the transaction or event has been recorded in the accounts. Only then is the candidate in a position to determine what adjusting or eliminating entries are required.

2322.06 For example, GAAP require that the excess of the cost of an investment over the investor's share of the underlying net assets be amortized. A parent company may, in general, be using the equity method to account for its investment in a subsidiary but may not have reflected such amortization on its own books. In that event, the adjusting and eliminating entries required are different than if the parent had recorded the amortization on its own books.

The equity method requires that the amortization be for the parent's percentage ownership in the subsidiary. FASB ASC 810-10-45-19 requires that both the excess of the cost of an investment over the total (not the investor's share) of the underlying net assets and the amortization be presented in the consolidated financial statements at their gross amounts. This is different from the purchase method, which presents the assets at the book value plus the parent's percentage ownership of the excess and only the parent's percentage ownership of the amortization.

Types of Consolidated Worksheets

2322.07 Under the current CPA Examination method, candidates will not be asked to prepare either:

a. a worksheet for a consolidated balance sheet only or

b. a comprehensive worksheet for a consolidated income statement, retained earnings statement, and balance sheet.

However, a thorough understanding of these worksheets will provide the basis to answer short, objective questions that will be encountered on the exam. The basic use of these two types of worksheets is demonstrated in the following illustrations.

Worksheet for Consolidated Balance Sheet

2322.08 On December 31, 20X1, P Corporation acquired 800 shares (80%) of S Corporation's $10 par common stock *at book value* of $20 per share. The adjusted trial balance of each company at December 31, 20X1, after the acquisition, is shown in the first two columns of the following worksheet. To conserve space, current assets and liabilities are shown as totals only; in practice, the accounts would be listed individually.

	Worksheet for Consolidated Balance Sheet December 31, 20X1					
	Adjusted Trial Balance		**Adjustments and Eliminations**		**Noncontrolling Interest**	**Consolidated Balance Sheet**
	P	**S**	**Dr**	**Cr**		
Current assets	$ 94,000	$17,000				$111,000
Land	40,000	13,000				53,000
Investment in S	16,000			(1) $16,000		0
	$150,000	$30,000				$164,000
Liabilities	$50,000	$10,000				$60,000
Common stock	50,000	10,000	(1) $10,000			50,000
Capital in excess of par	20,000	3,000	(1) 3,000			20,000
Retained earnings	30,000	7,000	(1) 7,000			30,000
Noncontrolling interest				4,000	$4,000	4,000
	$150,000	$30,000	$20,000	$20,000		$164,000

2322.09 Since P acquired 80% of the stock of S, the balances in the stockholders' equity accounts of the subsidiary (S Corporation) are eliminated and 20% of the stockholders' equity accounts is extended to the noncontrolling interest account in the worksheet.

2322.10 Revenues, expenses, gains, losses, net income or loss, and other comprehensive income are reported in the consolidated financial statements at the consolidated amounts, which include the amounts attributable to the owners of the parent and the noncontrolling interest. Net income or loss and *comprehensive income* or loss, as described in FASB ASC 810-10-45-20, are attributed to the parent and the noncontrolling interest.

Losses attributable to the parent and the noncontrolling interest in a subsidiary may exceed their interests in the subsidiary's equity. The excess, and any further losses attributable to the parent and the noncontrolling interest, is attributed to those interests. That is, the noncontrolling interest will continue to be attributed its share of losses even if that attribution results in a deficit noncontrolling interest balance (FASB ASC 810-10-45-21).

2322.11 The noncontrolling interest is shown as a subset of stockholders' equity, as follows:

Liabilities		$ 60,000
Stockholders' equity:		
Controlling interest:		
Common stock	$ 50,000	
Capital in excess of par	20,000	
	$ 70,000	
Retained earnings	30,000	
	100,000	
Noncontrolling interest	4,000	
Total stockholders' equity		104,000
		$164,000

Comprehensive Worksheet

2322.12 Assume that P Corporation in the example maintained its 80% investment in S Corporation during all of 20X2. Assume further that S Corporation reported net income during 20X2 of $4,000 and declared dividends of $1,000, as reflected in the adjusted trial balance columns of the comprehensive worksheet presented as follows:

	Comprehensive Worksheet For the Year Ended December 31, 20X2					
	Trial Balance		Adjustments and Eliminations		Noncontrolling Interest	Consolidated
	P	S	Dr	Cr		
Income Statement						
Revenues	$ 50,000	$ 12,000				$62,000
Expenses	30,000	8,000				38,000
Income from Operations	20,000	4,000				24,000
Sub income	3,200		(1) $ 3,200			
NC share of sub NI					$ 800	(800)
Net income	$ 23,200	$ 4,000	$ 3,200	$ 0	$ 800	$ 23,200
Retained Earnings Statement						
Retained earnings, Jan. 1	$ 30,000	$ 7,000	(3) $ 7,000			$ 30,000
Net income	23,200	4,000	3,200	$ 0	800	23,200
Dividends	(10,000)	(1,000)		(2) 800	(200)	(10,000)
Retained earnings, Dec. 31	$ 43,200	$10,000	$10,200	$ 800	600	$ 43,200
Balance Sheet						
Current assets	$115,800	$22,000				$137,800
Land	40,000	13,000				53,000
Investment in S	18,400		(2) $ 800	(1) $ 3,200		
				(3) 16,000		
	$174,200	$35,000				$190,800
Liabilities	$61,000	$12,000				$73,000
Common stock	50,000	10,000	(3) 10,000			50,000
Capital in excess of par	20,000	3,000	(3) 3,000			20,000
Retained earnings	43,200	10,000				43,200
Noncontrolling interest, Jan. 1				(3) 4,000	4,000	
Noncontrolling interest – Dec. 31					$4,600	4,600
	$174,200	$35,000	$24,000	$24,000		$190,800

2322.13 Format of worksheet. The comprehensive worksheet format illustrated for P Corporation is one with which candidates should be familiar. The following points should be noted about the worksheet format:

a. The worksheet contains a section for each financial statement in the order in which the statements are normally prepared.

b. The entire net income line in the income statement section is carried forward to the net income line in the retained earnings section.

c. The end-of-year retained earnings line is carried forward to the retained earnings line in the balance sheet section.

d. The noncontrolling interest's share of the subsidiary's net income is shown as a deduction in the consolidated balances column and as an addition to the noncontrolling interest column.

2322.14 Explanation of eliminating entries. The general approach followed for the eliminating entries is to eliminate the following:

a. All transactions affecting the investment account *during* the year

b. The balance in the investment account as of the *beginning* of the year

The beginning balance and the changes in the investment account are:

Investment in S

| Jan. 1, 20X2, balance | $16,000 | 20X2 sub dividends (80%) | $800 |
| 20X2 sub income (80%) | 3,200 | | |

2322.15 The eliminating entries in journal form are:

(1) Sub income $ 3,200
      Investment in S $ 3,200

(2) Investment in S $ 800
      Dividends[a] $ 800

(3) Common stock—S $10,000
    Capital in excess of par—S   3,000
    Retained earnings—S (Jan. 1)   7,000
      Investment in S (Jan. 1 balance) $16,000
      Noncontrolling interest (Jan. 1 balance)   4,000

[a] *Retained earnings (sub) is credited if a dividends account is not used.*

2322.16 One should pay special attention to the debit to retained earnings. The debit is to the beginning-of-year retained earnings, which is included in the retained earnings section of the comprehensive worksheet. Following this approach, the retained earnings shown in the balance sheet section are *never* debited or credited in an eliminating entry on a comprehensive worksheet.

2322.17 If a worksheet were prepared at the end of 20X2 for a consolidated balance sheet *only*, the investment elimination would be:

Common Stock—S $10,000
Capital in Excess of Par—S   3,000
Retained Earnings—S (Dec. 31)   10,000
    Investment in S (Dec. 31 balance) $18,400
    Noncontrolling Interest (Dec. 31 balance)   4,600

2323 Emphasis on Adjusting and Eliminating Entries (Acquisition Method)

2323.01 The worksheets illustrated in section **2322** provide a framework for identifying the various types of adjusting and eliminating entries. The types of eliminations may be categorized as those related to the following:

a. The investment account

b. Current year changes in the investment account

c. Year-end reciprocal balance sheet accounts

d. Reciprocal income statement accounts

e. Intercompany profits and losses

2323.02 The first two types of eliminations were illustrated in section **2322**, in which the cost of the investment was equal to the book value of the parent's share of the net assets of the subsidiary. Consideration is now given to situations in which the cost of the investment is not equal to book value.

Excess of Cost Over Book Value

2323.03 **Example:** Assume that on December 31, 20X1, P Company acquires 80% of the stock of S Company at a cost of $170,000. The stockholders' equity of S Company on December 31, 20X1, is as follows:

Common stock ($10 par)	$100,000
Retained earnings	50,000
	$150,000

S Company has a building that at December 31, 20X1, has a book value (BV) of $60,000 and a fair value (FV) of $90,000. In addition, S Company's inventory has a book value of $10,000 and a fair value of $15,000. The fair values of all other identifiable assets and liabilities are the same as their book values. It is assumed that the fair value of the noncontrolling interest is $42,500. (Total value of S Company = $170,000 ÷ 0.80 = $212,500. Value of noncontrolling interest = $212,500 – $170,000.)

2323.04 The excess of the cost of P's investment in S is allocated as follows:

S's acquisition-day fair value		$212,500
BV of S Company at 12/31/20X1		150,000
Excess of cost over book value		62,500
Excess of fair value over book value of identifiable net assets:		
Inventory	$ 5,000	
Building	30,000	35,000
Goodwill		$ 27,500

2323.05 The eliminating entry at December 31, 20X1, is:

Common Stock—S	$100,000	
Retained Earnings—S	50,000	
Inventory	5,000	
Building (net)	30,000	
Goodwill	27,500	
Investment in S		$170,000
Noncontrolling Interest		42,500

2323.06 The $5,000 increase in inventory, $30,000 increase in building, and $27,500 goodwill are reflected only on the consolidated financial statements and not on the books of either company. The only entry recorded in 20X1 on the books of P Company on December 31, 20X1, with regard to this business combination is:

Investment in S	$170,000	
Cash		$170,000

2323.07 Continuing the example into 20X2, assume that S Company reports net income in 20X2 of $30,000. Assume also that (a) S Company uses the FIFO inventory method, (b) the building has an estimated remaining life of 10 years as of December 31, 20X1, and (c) goodwill was not impaired in 20X2. Accordingly, the amortization of the excess of cost over book value is as follows:

Inventory	$5,000 ÷ 1 year (FIFO method) =	$5,000	per year for 1 year
Building	$30,000 ÷ 10 years =	3,000	per year for 10 years
		$8,000	

2323.08 The eliminating entries at the end of 20X2 will be influenced by whether or not P Company (the parent) has recorded the current-year's amortization on its own books. Both assumptions are illustrated as follows:

	Assuming P Records Amortization of Differential on Its Books		Assuming P Does Not Record Amortization of Differential on Its Books	
Entries on P Company's books (20X2):				
Investment in S	$ 24,000		$ 24,000	
Sub Income (0.80 × $30,000)		$ 24,000		$ 24,000
(To record P's share of net income of S.)				
Sub Income	$ 6,400		(no entry)	
Investment in S		$ 6,400		
(To record amortization of "excess.")				
Eliminating entries for comprehensive worksheet for 20X2:				
(1) Sub Income	$ 24,000		$ 24,000	
Investment in S		$ 24,000		$ 24,000
(2) Investment in S	$ 6,400		(no entry)	
Sub Income		$ 6,400		
(3) Common Stock—S	$100,000		$100,000	
Retained Earnings—S (Jan. 1)	50,000		50,000	
Inventory	5,000		5,000	
Building	30,000		30,000	
Goodwill	27,500		27,500	
Investment in S		$170,000		$170,000
Noncontrolling Interest in S		42,500		42,500
(4) Cost of Goods Sold	$ 5,000		$ 5,000	
Inventory		$ 5,000		$ 5,000
(5) Depreciation Expense	$ 3,000		$ 3,000	
Building (or Acc. depr.)		$ 3,000		$ 3,000

2323.09 Note that entry (2) is the only eliminating entry that is different under the two assumptions regarding P Company's recording the current-year's amortization of the "excess" on its own books. As one will note, such an eliminating entry (entry 2) is necessary only if P Company has recorded the current-year's amortization. Another way of stating it is that one does not have to eliminate (or "reverse out") what was not recorded in the first place. The consolidated financial statements are the same under both assumptions.

2323.10 The eliminating entries for a worksheet for a consolidated balance sheet (only) at December 31, 20X2, are:

	Assuming P Has Recorded Current-Year's Amortization	Assuming P Has Not Recorded Current-Year's Amortization
Retained Earnings—P Investment in S	(no entry)	$ 8,000 $ 8,000
Common Stock—S	$100,000	$100,000
Retained Earnings—S (Dec. 31)	80,000	80,000
Building (net) ($30,000 − $3,000)	27,000	27,000
Goodwill	27,500	27,500
Investment in S	$187,600	$187,600
Noncontrolling Interest in S	46,900	46,900

2323.11 Entry (1) is necessary because P Company's failure to record the current-year's amortization on its own books results in P's retained earnings being overstated. P Company should record a similar entry on its own books to avoid its retained earnings and investment in S accounts from being overstated at the beginning of 20X3.

2323.12 Assuming S Company reported net income of $40,000 in 20X3 and that goodwill was not impaired in 20X3, the journal entries on P Company's books and the eliminating entries for a comprehensive worksheet for 20X3 would be as follows:

	Assuming P Records Amortization of Differential on Its Books		Assuming P Does Not Record Amortization of Differential on Its Books	
Entries on P Company's books (20X3): 　Investment in S 　　Sub income (0.80 × $40,000) 　　(To record P's share of net income of S) 　Sub income 　　Investment in S 　　(To record amortization of "excess")	$ 32,000 $ 2,400	$ 32,000 $ 2,400	$ 32,000 (no entry)	$ 32,000
Eliminating entries for comprehensive worksheet for 20X3:				
(1) Sub income 　　Investment in S	$ 32,000	$ 32,000	$ 32,000	$ 32,000
(2) Investment in S 　　Sub income	$ 2,400	$ 2,400	(no entry)	
(3) Investment in S 　　Retained earnings — P (Jan. 1)			$ 6,400	$ 6,400
(4) Common stock — S 　Retained earnings — S (Jan. 1) 　Building (net) ($27,000 balance 01/01/X2 less $3,000 amortized in 20X2) 　Goodwill 　　Investment in S 　　Noncontrolling interest in S	$100,000 80,000 24,000 27,500	 $185,200 46,300	$100,000 80,000 24,000 27,500	 $185,200 46,300
(5) Depreciation expense 　　Building (net) (or Acc. depr.)	$ 3,000	$ 3,000	$ 3,000	$ 3,000

2323.13 Note that eliminating entry (2) is for $2,400 rather than the $6,400 shown in section **2323.08** for 20X2. The amortization of the differential in 20X2 was attributable to two things—the $4,000 increase in cost of goods sold because of the $4,000 parent's share of the excess of the fair value of inventory over its books value *and* the $2,400 increase in depreciation expense due to the recognition for consolidated financial statement purposes of the excess of the fair value of the plant assets over their book value. Since S Company uses the FIFO method of inventory costing, all of the differential attributable to inventory was amortized or "flowed out" in 20X2. Therefore, the amortization of the differential in 20X3 relates only to the $2,400 increase in depreciation expense recognized for consolidated financial statement purposes.

2323.14 If P Company does not record on its own books the amortization of the differential, an eliminating entry such as entry (3) must be made on the worksheet to update the Investment in S account and the Retained Earnings—P account for the cumulative amount of such amortization that P Company has not recorded on its own books in prior years. The entry is made for the cumulative amount of such amortization not recorded as of the beginning of the current year. As of January 1, 20X3, with respect to prior years, P Company has not recorded the amortization in only one year, 20X2. The comparable entry for the 20X4 worksheet will be for $8,800, which would be for the $6,400 amortization not recorded in 20X2 and the $2,400 not recorded in 20X3.

2323.15 Eliminating entry (4) eliminates P Company's share of the stockholders' equity of S Company as of January 1, 20X3 (i.e., the beginning of the current year). The $80,000 debit to retained earnings—S is for S Company's retained earnings balance at January 1, 20X2 ($50,000 balance at January 1, 20X2, plus S Company's 20X2 net income of $30,000). The $21,600 debit to building (net) is for the unamortized portion of the differential attributable to the building as of January 1, 20X3 (i.e., the beginning of the current year). If P Company records amortization of the differential on its own books, the $185,200 credit to the investment in S account is for the balance in the investment in S account as of January 1, 20X3. If P Company does not record amortization of the differential on its own books, the $185,200 credit to the investment in S account is for the $194,000 balance in the investment in S account on P Company's books as of January 1, 20X3 ($170,000 balance January 1, 20X2, plus the $24,000 P Company's share of S Company's net income in 20X2) plus the adjustment in entry (3) for the amortization of the differential that P Company has not recorded on its own books.

Excess of Book Value Over Cost

2323.16 **Example:** Assume that on December 31, 20X1, Parent Company pays $120,000 for 100% of the stock of Sub Company. Sub has common stock of $100,000 and retained earnings of $40,000. The fair values of Sub's identifiable assets and liabilities are the same as their book values.

2323.17 The identifiable net assets exceed the cost of the acquired company. The "excess" (the credit differential) is less than the assigned amount of the "eligible" assets. In that case, FASB ASC 805-10-05-2 requires that the "excess" is recognized as an extraordinary gain. The eliminating entry at December 31, 20X1, would be:

Common Stock—Sub	$100,000	
Retained Earnings—Sub	40,000	
Extraordinary gain (excess of fair value of identifiable net assets over cost)		$ 20,000
Investment in Sub		120,000

Elimination of Year-End Reciprocal Balance Sheet Accounts

2323.18 Another type of eliminating entry the candidate should look for is that relating to year-end reciprocal balance sheet accounts. The following are examples of such accounts:

a. Accounts receivable or accounts payable

b. Notes receivable or notes payable

c. Advance to sub (parent) or advance from parent (sub)

2323.19 The receivable and payable must be associated with another entity included in the consolidation. For example, the accounts receivable must be receivable from one of the affiliated entities.

Elimination of Reciprocal Income Statement Accounts

2323.20 All reciprocal income statement accounts must also be eliminated. For example, if the parent company sells merchandise to the sub, sales and purchases of that amount must be eliminated. Interest income and interest expense are another set of reciprocal income statement accounts often found in consolidation worksheet problems.

Elimination of Intercompany Profits and Losses

2323.21 The elimination of intercompany profits and losses is usually a major aspect of any CPA Examination problem involving consolidated worksheets. Accordingly, one should be quite familiar with the issues and procedures related to these eliminations.

2323.22 At this point, discussion will be restricted to the elimination of intercompany profit on the sale of land. This discussion will facilitate the demonstration of the treatment of intercompany profits on the worksheets in the remaining part of this section, including their impact on the computation of noncontrolling interest, without the candidate becoming bogged down in excess detail. A detailed discussion of the various types of intercompany profit eliminations is presented in section **2324**.

2323.23 **Example:** Assume that on December 31, 20X1, Ply Company acquires 80% of Sly Company's outstanding 10,000 shares of $10 par common stock at their book value of $15 per share. Sly Company on this date has retained earnings of $50,000.

2323.24 The eliminating entry at December 31, 20X1, is:

Common Stock—Sly	$100,000	
Retained Earnings—Sly	50,000	
Investment in Sly		$120,000
Noncontrolling Interest in Sly		30,000

2323.25 Assume further that Sly reports net income in 20X2 of $70,000. Included in net income is a $15,000 gain on sale of land to Ply Company on September 1, 20X2; the land had a book value of $48,000 at the time of the sale.

2323.26 The following transaction entries were recorded on September 1, 20X2:

On Ply's books:		
Land	$63,000	
Cash		$63,000
On Sly's books:		
Cash	$63,000	
Land		$48,000
Gain on Sale of Land		15,000

2323.27 From a consolidated entity standpoint, the gain is unrealized and the land is overstated by the amount of the gain. Therefore, the consolidated worksheet should reflect the elimination of this unrealized gain. The gain will be considered as realized only if Ply sells the land to an "outsider."

2323.28 The elimination entries for 20X2 are:

For a comprehensive worksheet:

(1)	Sub Income (0.80 × $70,000)	$ 56,000	
	Investment in Sly		$ 56,000
(2)	Gain on Sale of Land	$ 15,000	
	Land		$ 15,000
(3)	Common Stock—Sly	$100,000	
	Retained Earnings—Sly (Jan. 1, 20X2)	50,000	
	Investment in Sly		$120,000
	Noncontrolling Interest in Sly		30,000

For a worksheet for a consolidated balance sheet only:

(1)	Retained Earnings—Ply (0.80 × $15,000)	$ 12,000	
	Retained Earnings—Sly (0.20 × $15,000)	3,000	
	Land		$ 15,000
(2)	Common Stock—Sly	$100,000	
	Retained Earnings—Sly (Dec. 31)	120,000	
	Investment in Sly		$176,000
	Noncontrolling Interest in Sly		44,000

2323.29 Special attention should be directed to the eliminating entries for a consolidated balance sheet (section **2323.28**). Since the worksheet is for a consolidated balance sheet, the only accounts still open are balance sheet accounts. The $15,000 gain was closed into the retained earnings account of Sly. However, since Ply is using the equity method, Ply picked up 80% or $12,000 of the gain when it recorded its share of Sly's net income. Therefore, the elimination of the gain involves a debit of $12,000 to Ply's retained earnings and a debit of $3,000 to Sly's retained earnings. Entry (2) is the normal investment eliminating entry.

2323.30 The noncontrolling interest's share of Sly's 20X2 net income is determined as follows:

Net income reported by Sly	$70,000
Unrealized gain included in Sly's net income	15,000
Confirmed (or realized) net income of Sly	55,000
Noncontrolling interest percentage	× .20
Noncontrolling interest's share of net income	$11,000

2323.31 Ply's share of Sly's net income then is:

Confirmed net income of Sly	$55,000
Controlling interest percentage	× .80
Ply's share of Sly's net income	$44,000

2323.32 If Ply had sold the land to Sly (instead of the reverse), the unrealized gain would not have affected the computation of the noncontrolling interest's share of Sly's net income (i.e., reported net income and confirmed net income of Sly would have been the same). Only intercompany gains or losses associated with the subsidiary affect the determination of the noncontrolling interest's share of net income.

2323.33 The concept of confirmed (or realized) earnings also applies to retained earnings. This is illustrated by examining the retained earnings line on a worksheet for a consolidated balance sheet at December 31, 20X2, for Ply Company and its subsidiary, Sly Company. Assume that Ply's retained earnings at December 31, 20X2, is $56,000 (its share of Sly's 20X2 reported net income). (Refer to entries (1) and (2) in the latter part of section **2323.28**)

	Ply	Sly	Eliminations Dr	Eliminations Cr	Noncontrolling Interest	Consolidated
Retained earnings:						
Ply	$56,000		(1) $12,000			
Sly		$120,000	(2) 3,000		$21,000[a]	$44,000
			(3) 96,000			

[a] Sly's reported retained earnings, Dec 31, 20X2 .... $120,000
Less unrealized profit in Sly's retained earnings 15,000
Confirmed retained earnings $105,000
Noncontrolling interest percentage .... .20
Noncontrolling interest's share of Sky's retained earnings $21,000

Example: Comprehensive Worksheet

2323.34 The comprehensive worksheet illustrated in section **2322.12** included only a limited number of eliminating entries; attention was focused primarily on the worksheet format. The following comprehensive worksheet incorporates the various types of eliminating entries.

2323.35 The following assumptions are made for P Corporation and S Corporation:

a. On January 1, 20X1, P Corporation acquired 80% of the 5,000 outstanding shares of S Corporation's $10 par common stock for $76,000.

b. S Corporation's stockholders' equity on January 1, 20X1, consisted of common stock, $50,000, and retained earnings, $20,000.

c. P Corporation uses the equity method but does not record the amortization of any differential or the impairment of any goodwill after the consolidated financial statements are prepared. Thus, with regard to its investment in S Corporation, in 20X1 P Corporation recorded on its own books its initial investment in the stock of S, its share of the net income of S, and its share of the dividends of S.

d. The fair values of S Corporation's identifiable assets and liabilities on January 1, 20X1, were the same as their book values, except for buildings which had a book value of $30,000 and a fair value of $40,000. Thus, $10,000 of the excess of cost over book value was attributable to undervalued buildings and $15,000 to goodwill, as shown:

Cost of investment	$76,000
Fair value of noncontrolling interest	19,000
S Corporation's acquisition-date fair value	$95,000
Less the book value of S	70,000
Excess of cost over book value	$25,000
Allocated to building	10,000
Goodwill	$15,000

e. S Corporation's buildings have an estimated remaining life of 10 years. (The portion of the differential that is attributable to undervalued buildings is to be amortized over 10 years.)

f. P Corporation determined at the end of 20X1 that goodwill related to its investment in S Corporation had been impaired in the amount of $2,000.

g. During 20X1, S Corporation sold land with a book value of $30,000 to P Corporation for $40,000. P Corporation still owns the land at December 31, 20X1.

h. At December 31, 20X1, S Corporation owes P Corporation $5,000 on open account.

i. During 20X1, P Corporation sold merchandise to S Corporation at cost for $8,000.

Comprehensive Worksheet
For the Year Ended December 31, 20X1

	Trial Balance		Adjustments and Eliminations				Noncontrolling Interest	Consolidated
	P	S		Dr		Cr	Dr (Cr)	Dr (Cr)
Sales	$ 80,000	$20,000	(6)	$ 8,000				$ 92,000
Cost of goods sold	(50,000)	(12,000)			(6)	$ 8,000		(54,000)
Gross margin	30,000	8,000						38,000
Expenses	(10,000)	(2,000)	(4)	1,000				(13,000)
Gain on sale of land		10,000	(8)	10,000				0
Goodwill impairment			(5)	2,000				(2,000)
Income from operations	20,000	16,000						23,000
Sub income	12,800		(1)	12,800				
NI share of S net income							$ 1,200	(1,200)
Net income	$ 32,800	$16,000		$ 33,800		$ 8,000	$ 1,200	$ 21,800
Retained earnings, Jan. 1	$ 40,000	$20,000	(3)	$ 20,000				$ 40,000
Net income	32,800	16,000		33,600		$ 8,000	1,200	21,800
Dividends	(10,000)	(5,000)			(2)	4,000	(1,000)	(10,000)
Retained earnings, Dec. 31	$ 62,800	$31,000		$ 53,800		$ 12,000	$ 200	$ 51,800
Current assets	$ 50,200	$56,000			(7)	$ 5,000		$101,200
Building (net)	45,000	30,000	(3)	$ 10,000	(4)	1,000		84,000
Land	40,000	10,000			(8)	10,000		40,000
Investment in S	84,800		(2)	4,000	(1)	12,800		0
					(3)	76,000		
Goodwill			(3)	15,000	(5)	2,000		13,000
	$220,000	$96,000						$238,200
Current liabilities	$ 57,200	$15,000	(7)	$ 5,000				$ 67,200
Common stock	100,000	50,000	(3)	50,000				100,000
Retained earnings	62,800	31,000		53,800		$ 12,000	200	51,800
Noncontrolling interest, Jan. 1					(3)	19,000	19,000	
Noncontrolling interest, Dec. 31							19,200	19,200
	$220,000	$96,000		$137,800		$137,800		$238,200

2323.36 Each of the eliminating entries is explained as follows:

(1) Sub Income (0.80 × $16,000) $12,800
     Investment in S $12,800
To eliminate the accrual of P's share of net income of S Corporation.

(2) Investment in S $ 4,000
     Dividend—S (0.80 × $5,000) $ 4,000
To eliminate intercompany dividends.

(3) Common Stock—S $50,000
     Retained Earnings—S (Jan. 1)   20,000
     Buildings (net)   10,000
     Goodwill   15,000
       Investment in S $76,000
       Noncontrolling Interest in S   19,000

(4) Expenses (depreciation) $ 1,000
     Buildings (net) (or Acc. Depr.) $ 1,000

To recognize depreciation related to P's share of the excess of the fair value of the building over its book value ($10,000 excess ÷ 10 years).

(5) Goodwill Impairment Loss $ 2,000
     Goodwill $ 2,000
To recognize the 20X1 impairment of goodwill.

(6) Sales $ 8,000
     Cost of Goods Sold $ 8,000
To eliminate intercompany sales.

(7) Current Liabilities (Accounts Payable) $ 5,000
     Current Assets $ 5,000
To eliminate intercompany receivables and payables.

(8) Gain on Sale of Land $10,000
     Land $10,000
To eliminate unrealized intercompany gain on sale of land.

2323.37 The noncontrolling interest's share of net income, shown as a deduction in the consolidated column and as an addition in the noncontrolling interest column, is determined as follows:

Reported net income of S	$16,000
Less: Unrealized gain on sale of land	10,000
Confirmed net income of S	$ 6,000
Noncontrolling interest percentage	× .20
Noncontrolling interest's share of net income	$ 1,200

The noncontrolling interest, shown as part of the stockholders' equity section, is determined as follows:

Noncontrolling interest, Jan. 1	$19,000
Noncontrolling interest's share of net income	1,200
Dividends paid to noncontrolling interest (20% of $5,000)	1,000
Noncontrolling interest, Dec. 31	$19,200

Alternative Format for Comprehensive Worksheet

2323.38 A detailed discussion of the issues associated with goodwill impairment is presented in section **2227**.

2323.39 The CPA Examination candidate should be familiar with other formats for comprehensive worksheets. One such format is illustrated as follows. The data presented in the comprehensive worksheet is the same as that presented previously; the only difference is in the format of the worksheet.

Comprehensive Worksheet

For the Year Ended December 31, 20X1

	P	S	Adjustments and Eliminations				Noncontrolling Interest	Consolidated
	Dr(Cr)	Dr(Cr)	Dr		Cr		Dr(Cr)	Dr(Cr)
Current assets	$ 50,200	$ 56,000			(7)	$ 5,000		$ 101,200
Building (net)	45,000	30,000	(3)	$ 10,000	(4)	1,000		84,000
Land	40,000	10,000			(8)	10,000		40,000
Investment in S	84,800		(2)	4,000	(1)	12,800		0
					(3)	76,000		
Goodwill			(3)	15,000	(5)	2,000		13,000
Current liabilities	(57,200)	(15,000)	(7)	5,000				(67,200)
Common stock	(100,000)	(50,000)	(3)	50,000				(100,000)
Retained earnings, Jan. 1	(40,000)	(20,000)	(3)	20,000				(40,000)
Dividends	10,000	5,000			(2)	4,000	1,000	10,000
Sales	(80,000)	(20,000)	(6)	8,000				(92,000)
Gain on sale of land		(10,000)	(8)	10,000				0
Sub income	(12,800)		(1)	12,800				0
Cost of goods sold	50,000	12,000			(6)	8,000		54,000
Expenses	10,000	2,000	(4)	1,000				13,000
Goodwill impairment			(5)	2,000				2,000
	$ 0	$ 0		$118,600		$118,600		
Noncontrolling interest, Jan. 1					(3)	19,000	19,000	
NI share of net income							$ (1,200)	1,200
Total noncontrolling interest							$(19,200)	(19,200)
								$ 0

2324 Elimination of Intercompany Profits and Losses (Acquisition Method)

2324.01 Discussion relating to the elimination of unrealized intercompany profits and losses was first introduced in section **2323**. The situation illustrated in that section was the intercompany profit on sale of land. This section contains a detailed discussion of the three major areas in which intercompany profits and losses are usually found:

1. Inventories

2. Plant assets

3. Intercorporate bond investments

2324.02 Unrealized intercompany profits and losses must be eliminated in preparing consolidated financial statements so that the resulting statements will present the operations as if the separate legal entities are one operating entity.

2324.03 The entire amount (100%) of any unrealized intercompany profit or loss should be eliminated for consolidation purposes, rather than just the parent company's ownership percentage. Unrealized intercompany profits and losses arising from sales by the subsidiary to the parent (upstream) should be allocated between the majority and noncontrolling interests in accordance with their respective ownership percentages. Unrealized intercompany profits and losses arising from parent to subsidiary (downstream) sales are allocated totally to the controlling (majority) interest.

2324.04 The determination of the noncontrolling interest's share of net income and retained earnings is affected only by unrealized intercompany profits and losses arising from upstream transactions.

2324.05 In cases where unrealized intercompany profits or losses exist in recorded account balances, the diagram following is helpful in establishing where the profit resides. The location of the profit in recorded account balances depends on the following:

   a. Whether the profit or loss is associated with the current period (i.e., located in a nominal account) or with a prior period (i.e., located in a balance sheet account)

   b. Whether the parent sells to the subsidiary or vice versa

   c. Whether the parent uses the equity method or the cost method during the period

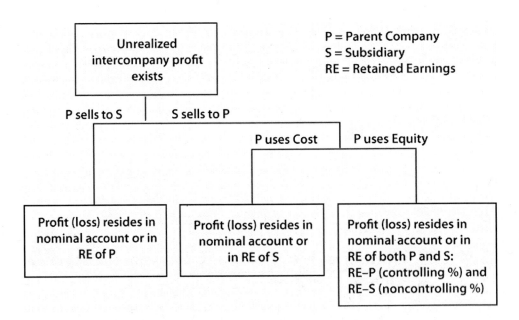

2324.06 In the discussion of intercompany profits and losses in the remaining parts of this section, the following assumptions are made unless otherwise indicated:

   a. Company P (parent) owns 80% of the common stock of Company S (subsidiary).

   b. Company P uses the equity method during the year to the extent that it records its share of the subsidiary's net income and dividends. However, Company P does not record on its own books the elimination of unrealized or unconfirmed intercompany profits.

2324.07 The elimination entries illustrated are those related to intercompany transactions and unrealized profits or losses. The other types of eliminating entries were discussed in section **2323**. The following abbreviations are used in the ensuing discussion.

    CW = comprehensive worksheet
    BSW = balance sheet only worksheet

Intercompany Inventory Profits and Losses

2324.08 **Example 1:** During 20X1, Company P sells merchandise which costs $20,000 to Company S for $30,000. The merchandise is still in the inventory of Company S at December 31, 20X1 (the entries assume that both companies use a perpetual inventory system).

CW entries—20X1:
    Sales $30,000
        Cost of Goods Sold $30,000
    To eliminate intercompany sales.

    Cost of Goods Sold $10,000
        Inventory $10,000
    To eliminate unrealized profit in ending inventory.

BSW entries—12/31/X1:
    Retained Earnings—P $10,000
        Inventory $10,000
    P sold to S; therefore 100% of unrealized profit charged against P.

CW entries—20X2:
    Retained Earnings—P $10,000
        Cost of Goods Sold $10,000
    To eliminate unrealized profit in 20X2 beginning inventory (inventory overstated).

2324.09 **Example 2:** Assume the same facts as in Example 1, except that Company S sold the merchandise to Company P (instead of the reverse):

CW entries—20X1:
    Sales $30,000
        Cost of Goods Sold $30,000
    To eliminate intercompany sales.

    Cost of Goods Sold $10,000
        Inventory $10,000
    To eliminate unrealized profit in ending inventory.

BSW entries—12/31/X1:
    Retained Earnings—P (0.80 × $10,000) $ 8,000
    Retained Earnings—S (0.20 × $10,000)   2,000
        Inventory $10,000
    S sold to P; therefore profit resides in retained earnings of P (80%) and S (20%).

CW entries—20X2:
    Retained Earnings—P (0.80 × $10,000) $8,000
    Retained Earnings—S (0.20 × $10,000)   2,000
        Cost of Goods Sold $10,000
    To eliminate unrealized profit in 20X2 beginning inventory.

2324.10 **Example 3:** Assume the same facts as in Example 2 (S sells to P), except that at December 31, 20X1, only one-half of the merchandise is still in Company P's inventory:

CW entries—20X1:
Sales $30,000
    Cost of Goods Sold $30,000
To eliminate intercompany sales.

Cost of Goods Sold $ 5,000
    Inventory $ 5,000
To eliminate unrealized profit (0.50 × $10,000) in ending inventory.

BSW entries—12/31/X1:
Retained Earnings—P (0.80 × $5,000) $ 4,000
Retained Earnings—S (0.20 × $5,000) 1,000
    Inventory $ 5,000
Elimination of unrealized profit residing in retained earnings of P (80%) and S (20%).

CW entries—20X2:
Retained Earnings—P $ 4,000
Retained Earnings—S 1,000
    Cost of Goods Sold $ 5,000
To eliminate unrealized profit in 20X2 inventory (inventory overstated).

Intercompany Profit in Plant Assets

2324.11 **Example 4:** On January 1, 20X1, Company P sells equipment to Company S for $100,000. The equipment has a book value of $80,000 (original cost of $88,000 and accumulated depreciation of $8,000) and an estimated remaining life of 10 years as of January 1, 20X1.

2324.12 The following transaction entries were recorded by P and S on January 1, 20X1:

	Company P			**Company S**	
Cash	$100,000		Equipment	$100,000	
Accumulated Depreciation	8,000		Cash		$100,000
Equipment		$88,000			
Gain on Sale of Equipment		20,000			

2324.13 Company S will record depreciation expense of $10,000 per year. Without the sale, Company P would have recorded depreciation of $8,000 per year.

2324.14 The consolidated worksheet eliminating entries are:

CW entries—20X1:
Gain on Sale of Equipment $20,000
    Equipment $12,000
    Accumulated Depreciation 8,000
To eliminate unrealized gain and restore the equipment and accumulated depreciation accounts to their presale balances.

Accumulated Depreciation $ 2,000
    Depreciation Expense $ 2,000
To eliminate excess depreciation recorded in 20X1 after the sale.

BSW entries—12/31/X1:
    Retained Earnings—P $18,000
        Equipment $12,000
        Accumulated Depreciation   6,000
To eliminate remaining unconfirmed profit; $20,000 unconfirmed gain less $2,000 confirmed during 20X1 through excess depreciation.

CW entries—20X2:
    Retained Earnings—P $18,000
        Equipment $12,000
        Accumulated Depreciation   6,000
To eliminate intercompany profit residing in 01/01/20X2 retained earnings of P ($20,000 gain in 20X1 less $2,000 excess depreciation in 20X1).

    Accumulated Depreciation $ 2,000
        Depreciation Expense $ 2,000
To eliminate excess depreciation in 20X2.

BSW entries—12/31/X2:
    Retained Earnings—P $16,000
        Equipment $12,000
        Accumulated Depreciation   4,000
To eliminate remaining unconfirmed profit; $20,000 unconfirmed gain less $4,000 confirmed in 20X1 and 20X2 through excess depreciation.

2324.15 The original unconfirmed profit of $20,000 arising from the sale of the equipment will continue to be confirmed each year to the extent of the $2,000 excess depreciation recognized. The total $20,000 profit will be confirmed by the end of 10 years.

2324.16 The eliminating entry for a consolidated balance sheet worksheet at the end of the ninth year (20X9) would be:

Retained Earnings—P ($20,000 − $18,000) $ 2,000
Accumulated Depreciation   10,000
    Equipment $12,000

The accounts can be verified as follows:

	Balance if Sale Not Made	Balance on S Books	Adjustment Necessary
Equipment	$88,000	$100,000	$12,000 credit
Accumulated depr.	80,000[a]	90,000[b]	10,000 debit

[a] Jan. 1, 20X1, balance ($8,000) + Years 1–9 (9 × $8,000) = $80,000
[b] Years 1–9 (9 × $10,000) = $90,000

2324.17 **Example 5:** Assume the same facts as in Example 4, except assume that Company S sold the equipment to Company P (instead of the reverse).

CW entries—20X1:
    Gain on Sale of Equipment $20,000
        Equipment $12,000
        Accumulated Depreciation   8,000
To eliminate unrealized gain and restore the equipment and accumulated depreciation accounts to their presale balances.

    Accumulated Depreciation $ 2,000
        Depreciation Expense $ 2,000
To eliminate excess depreciation recorded in 20X1 after the sale.

BSW entries—12/31/X1:
Retained Earnings—P (0.80($20,000 - $2,000)) $14,400
Retained Earnings—S (0.20($20,000 - $2,000))   3,600
  Equipment $12,000
  Accumulated Depreciation   6,000
To eliminate remaining unconfirmed profit ($20,000 - $2,000) in ratio of 80% P and 20% S.

BSW entries—12/31/X2:
Retained Earnings—P (0.80($20,000 - $4,000)) $12,800
Retained Earnings—S (0.20($20,000 - $4,000))   3,200
  Equipment $12,000
  Accumulated Depreciation   4,000
To eliminate remaining unconfirmed profit ($20,000 - $4,000) in ratio of 80% P and 20% S.

Intercompany Bond Investments

2324.18 The acquisition by one entity of another unrelated (unaffiliated) entity's outstanding bonds presents no special problems. The issuer must account for its bonds payable, whereas the acquiring entity must account for its investments in bonds. No gain or loss is recognized by the issuer when the bonds are sold nor by the acquirer when the outstanding bonds are purchased.

2324.19 The same is true from the standpoint of the separate entities if the two entities are affiliates of each other. However, from a consolidated entity standpoint the acquisition of an affiliate's outstanding bonds constitutes the consolidated entity's *reacquisition* of its own bonds. Accordingly, any difference between the carrying amount of the bonds and their acquisition price should be recognized as a gain or loss for consolidation purposes.

2324.20 Eliminations related to inventory and fixed assets involve the elimination of *recorded but unrealized* gains and losses. On the other hand, eliminations related to bonds involve the recognition of *realized but unrecorded* gains and losses.

2324.21 **Example 6:** On December 31, 20X0, the carrying value of Company P's outstanding 10% bonds is $110,000 (face amount $100,000, premium on bonds payable $10,000). The bonds pay interest annually on each December 31 and mature in 10 years. On December 31, 20X0, Company S acquired from existing bondholders all the outstanding bonds for $106,000 after interest had been paid for 20X0.

2324.22 The eliminating entry for purposes of consolidation on December 31, 20X0, is:

CW entries—20X0:
Bonds Payable (P) $100,000
Premium on Bonds Payable (P)   10,000
  Investment in P Bonds (S) $106,000
  Gain on Reacquisition of Bonds (P)   4,000

BSW entries—20X0:
Bonds Payable (P) $100,000
Premium on Bonds Payable (P)   10,000
  Investment in P Bonds (S) $106,000
  Retained Earnings (P)   4,000

2324.23 The gain on reacquisition is determined as follows:

Carrying value of bonds:		
Bonds payable	$100,000	
Premium on bonds payable	10,000	$110,000
Acquisition price		106,000
Gain on reacquisition of bonds		$ 4,000

2324.24 The gain or loss on reacquisition is identified with the *issuer* of the bonds (Company P in this case).

2324.25 Assuming that the straight-line amortization method is used, Company P and Company S would record the following transaction entries on their books during 20X1:

Company P:
Interest Expense	$10,000	
Cash (10% of $100,000)		$10,000
To record payment of contractual interest.		
Premium on Bonds Payable ($10,000 ÷ 10)	$ 1,000	
Interest Expense		$ 1,000
To record amortization of premium.		

Company S:
Cash (10% of $100,000)	$10,000	
Interest Income		$10,000
To record receipt of contractual interest.		
Interest Income	$ 600	
Investment in P Bonds ($6,000 ÷ 10)		$ 600
To record amortization of premium.		

2324.26 The 20X1 eliminating entries must, on the worksheet, zero-out all accounts related to the bonds. These accounts and their balances at December 3, 20X1, are:

On P books:	
Bonds payable	$100,000
Premium on bonds payable ($10,000 - $1,000)	9,000
Interest expense ($10,000 - $1,000)	9,000
On S books:	
Investment in P bonds ($106,000 - $600)	$105,400
Interest income ($10,000 - $600)	9,400

2324.27 The eliminating entries on the 20X1 consolidated worksheet are:

CW entries—20X1:

(1)
Bonds Payable	$100,000	
Premium on Bonds Payable	10,000	
Investment in P Bonds		$106,000
Retained Earnings—P		4,000

To eliminate the related accounts as of January 1, 20X1, and to credit the 20X0 gain to retained earnings of P (the issuer).

(2)
Interest Income	$ 10,000	
Interest Expense		$ 10,000

To eliminate the contractual interest recorded in 20X1.

(3) Interest Expense $1,000
    Premium on Bonds Payable $1,000
To eliminate the amortization of premium on bonds payable during 20X1.

(4) Investment in P Bonds $600
    Interest Income $600
To eliminate the amortization of premium on the bond investment during 20X1.

2324.28 As a check on the eliminating entries, the balances in the accounts related to the bonds should be examined to see if they have zero balances after the eliminating entries:

Accounts	12/31/20X1 Balance per Trial Balance	Entry #	Effect of Worksheet Eliminating Entries	Balance Extended to Consolidated Column
Bonds payable	$100,000	(1)	$(100,000)	0
Premium on bonds payable	9,000	(1)	(10,000)	0
		(3)	1,000	
Interest expense	9,000	(2)	(10,000)	0
		(3)	1,000	
Investment in P bonds	105,400	(1)	(106,000)	0
		(4)	600	
Interest income	9,400	(2)	(10,000)	0
		(4)	600	

2324.29 The eliminating entry for a worksheet for a consolidated balance sheet at December 31, 20X1, is:

BSW entry—12/31/X1:
  Bonds Payable $100,000
  Premium on Bonds Payable ($10,000 - $1,000) 9,000
    Investment in P Bonds ($106,000 - $600) $105,400
    Retained Earnings—P ($4,000 - $1,000 + $600) 3,600
To eliminate balances in bond accounts at December 31, 20X1, and credit retained earnings of issuer with realized but unrecorded gain at this point in time, as shown:

Carrying amount of bonds, December 31, 20X0	$110,000	
Face amount of bonds	100,000	
Gain (loss) if bonds acquired at face		$10,000
Face amount of bonds	$100,000	
Acquisition price, Dec. 31, 20X0	106,000	
Gain (loss) if bonds issued at face		(6,000)
Net gain (loss) on reacquisition		$4,000
Gain recorded in retained earnings as a result of amortization of premium on bonds payable (reduction of interest expense) in 20X1		(1,000)
Loss recorded in retained earnings as a result of amortization of premium on bond investment (reduction of interest income) in 20X1		600
Realized but unrecorded gain, Dec. 31, 20X1		$3,600

2324.30 The eliminating entries for 20X2 are:

CW entries—20X2:
Bonds Payable	$100,000	
Premium on Bonds Payable	9,000	
Investment in P Bonds		$105,400
Retained Earnings—P		3,600

To eliminate balance in bond accounts as of January 1, 20X2, and credit retained earnings of issuer with realized but unrecognized gain as of January 1, 20X2.

Interest Income	$ 10,000	
Interest Expense		$ 10,000

To eliminate the contractual interest recorded in 20X2.

Interest Expense	$ 1,000	
Premium on Bonds Payable		$ 1,000

To eliminate the amortization of premium on bonds payable recorded in 20X2.

Investment in P Bonds	$ 600	
Interest Income		$ 600

To eliminate the amortization of premium on bond investment recorded in 20X2.

BSW entries—12/31/X2:
Bonds Payable	$100,000	
Premium on Bonds Payable ($10,000 - $2,000)	8,000	
Investment in P Bonds ($106,000 - $1,200)		$104,800
Retained Earnings—P ($4,000 - $2,000 + $1,200)		3,200

2324.31 Each year, $400 of the gain is being recognized in the accounts because of the amortization of the net premium ($1,000 - $600). Therefore, the amount of *realized but unrecognized* gain declines by $400 each year, as reflected in the decreasing amounts credited to the retained earnings of P each year.

2324.32 If S had been the issuer of the bonds (instead of P) and P had acquired the bonds, the only change in the eliminating entries illustrated would be that the credit to retained earnings would be allocated 80% to P and 20% to S instead of 100% to P. For example, the eliminating entry for a worksheet for a consolidated balance sheet at December 31, 20X2, would be (compare with the comparable entry shown in section **2324.30**):

Bonds Payable	$100,000	
Premium on Bonds Payable	8,000	
Investment in P Bonds		$104,800
Retained Earnings—P (0.80 × $3,200)		2,560
Retained Earnings—S (0.20 × $3,200)		640

2324.33 As mentioned previously, intercompany profits and losses affect the computation of the noncontrolling interest's share of net income only if the subsidiary is the seller of the asset or issuer of the bonds. The types of adjustments to be made to the reported net income of the subsidiary are summarized as follows:

Computation of Noncontrolling Interest's Share of Sub's Net Income	
$ XXX	Reported net income of subsidiary
	Intercompany profit in inventory (where sub is seller):
+ XXX	In beginning inventory
− XXX	In ending inventory
	Fixed assets sold by sub at a gain:
− XXX	Gain on sale (if sale in current year)
+ XXX	Excess depreciation (whether sale in current year or in a prior year)
	Fixed assets sold by sub at a loss:
+ XXX	Loss on sale (if sale in current year)
− XXX	Deficient depreciation (whether sale in current year or in a prior year)
	Intercompany bonds where sub is issuer:
+ XXX	Gain on reacquisition (if in current year)
− XXX	Amortization during current year of premium on bonds payable (by sub) and of discount on bond investment (by parent), whether bonds acquired in current year or in a prior year.
− XXX	Loss on reacquisition (if in current year)
+ XXX	Amortization during current year of discount on bonds payable (by sub) and of premium on bond investment (by parent), whether bonds acquired in current year or in a prior year.
$ XXX	Confirmed net income of subsidiary
MI%	Noncontrolling interest percentage
$ XXX	Noncontrolling interest's share of subsidiary's net income

2325 Fundamentals of Consolidated Worksheets (Purchase Method)

2325.01 A *consolidated worksheet* is the vehicle by which data from the various entities involved in a consolidation are combined, adjusted, and summarized in a form suitable to serve as a basis for the preparation of consolidated financial statements. A consolidated worksheet includes columns for the following:

　　a. The trial balance of each of the entities

　　b. Adjustments and eliminations

　　c. The consolidated balances for the financial statement(s) to be prepared

2325.02 The particular adjusting or eliminating entries to be reflected on the worksheet are a function of the following three factors:

　　1. The actual transactions or economic events that have occurred

　　2. How the transactions or events have been recorded in the accounts

　　3. What constitutes GAAP for presentation in the consolidated financial statements

2325.03 Some enterprises may choose to maintain their books during the year in strict accordance with GAAP. In such cases, financial statements can be prepared without making any adjustments to the balances shown in the ledger accounts.

2325.04 Other enterprises may elect to maintain their books during the year in a more *convenient manner,* with the awareness that the accounts will have to be adjusted at the end of the period before financial statements can be prepared. During the year, the books are merely *unadjusted* rather than wrong.

2325.05 The essence of the preceding discussion is that the CPA Examination candidate should not take for granted that an enterprise's books are kept in strict accordance with GAAP. The candidate must first determine what GAAP require for the financial statements and how the transaction or event has been recorded in the accounts. Only then is the candidate in a position to determine what adjusting or eliminating entries are required.

2325.06 For example, GAAP require that the excess of the cost of an investment over the investor's share of the underlying net assets be amortized. A parent company may, in general, be using the equity method to account for its investment in a subsidiary but may not have reflected such amortization on its own books. In that event, the adjusting and eliminating entries required are different than if the parent had recorded the amortization on its own books.

Types of Consolidated Worksheets

2325.07 Under the current CPA Examination method, candidates will not be asked to prepare either:

    a. a worksheet for a consolidated balance sheet only or

    b. a comprehensive worksheet for a consolidated income statement, retained earnings statement, and balance sheet.

However, a thorough understanding of these worksheets will provide the basis to answer short, objective questions that will be encountered on the exam. The basic use of these two types of worksheets is demonstrated in the following illustrations.

Worksheet for Consolidated Balance Sheet

2325.08 On December 31, 20X1, P Corporation acquired 800 shares (80%) of S Corporation's $10 par common stock *at book value* of $20 per share. The adjusted trial balance of each company at December 31, 20X1, after the acquisition, is shown in the first two columns of the following worksheet. To conserve space, current assets and liabilities are shown as totals only; in practice, the accounts would be listed individually.

Worksheet for Consolidated Balance Sheet
December 31, 20X1

	Adjusted Trial Balance		Adjustments and Eliminations		Noncontrolling Interest	Consolidated Balance Sheet
	P	S	Dr	Cr		
Current assets	$ 94,000	$17,000				$111,000
Land	40,000	13,000				53,000
Investment in S	16,000			(1) $16,000		0
	$150,000	$30,000				$164,000
Liabilities	$50,000	$10,000				$60,000
Common stock	50,000	10,000	(1) $8,000		$2,000	50,000
Capital in excess of par	20,000	3,000	(1) 2,400		600	20,000
Retained earnings	30,000	7,000	(1) 5,600		1,400	30,000
Noncontrolling interest					$4,000	4,000
	$150,000	$30,000	$16,000	$16,000		$164,000

2325.09 Since P acquired 80% of the stock of S, only 80% of the balances in the stockholders' equity accounts of the subsidiary (S Corporation) are eliminated. The remaining 20% is extended to the noncontrolling interest column in the worksheet.

2325.10 Revenues, expenses, gains, losses, net income or loss, and other comprehensive income are reported in the consolidated financial statements at the consolidated amounts, which include the amounts attributable to the owners of the parent and the noncontrolling interest. Net income or loss and *comprehensive income* or loss, as described in FASB ASC 810-10-45-20, are attributed to the parent and the noncontrolling interest.

Losses attributable to the parent and the noncontrolling interest in a subsidiary may exceed their interests in the subsidiary's equity. The excess, and any further losses attributable to the parent and the noncontrolling interest, is attributed to those interests. That is, the noncontrolling interest will continue to be attributed its share of losses even if that attribution results in a deficit noncontrolling interest balance (FASB ASC 810-10-45-21).

2325.11 The noncontrolling interest is shown as a subset of stockholders' equity, as follows:

Liabilities		$ 60,000
Stockholders' equity:		
Controlling interest:		
Common stock	$ 50,000	
Capital in excess of par	20,000	
	$ 70,000	
Retained earnings	30,000	
	100,000	
Noncontrolling interest	4,000	
Total stockholders' equity		104,000
		$164,000

Comprehensive Worksheet

2325.12 Assume that P Corporation in the example maintained its 80% investment in S Corporation during all of 20X2. Assume further that S Corporation reported net income during 20X2 of $4,000 and declared dividends of $1,000, as reflected in the adjusted trial balance columns of the comprehensive worksheet presented as follows:

	Comprehensive Worksheet For the Year Ended December 31, 20X2					
	Trial Balance		Adjustments and Eliminations		Noncontrolling Interest	Consolidated
	P	S	Dr	Cr		
Income Statement						
Revenues	$ 50,000	$ 12,000				$62,000
Expenses	30,000	8,000				38,000
Income from Operations	20,000	4,000				24,000
Sub income	3,200		(1) $ 3,200			
NC share of sub NI					$ 800	(800)
Net income	$ 23,200	$ 4,000	$ 3,200	$0	$ 800	$ 23,200
Retained Earnings Statement						
Retained earnings, Jan. 1	$ 30,000	$ 7,000	(3) $ 5,600		$1,400	$ 30,000
Net income	23,200	4,000	3,200	$ 0	800	23,200
Dividends	(10,000)	(1,000)		(2) 800	(200)	(10,000)
Retained earnings, Dec. 31	$ 43,200	$10,000	$ 8,800	$ 800	$2,000	$ 43,200
Balance Sheet						
Current assets	$115,800	$22,000				$137,800
Land	40,000	13,000				53,000
Investment in S	18,400		(2) $800	(1) $ 3,200		
				(3) 16,000		
	$174,200	$35,000				$190,800
Liabilities	$61,000	$12,000				$73,000
Common stock	50,000	10,000	(3) 8,000		$2,000	50,000
Capital in excess of par	20,000	3,000	(3) 2,400		600	20,000
Retained earnings	43,200	10,000	8,800	800	2,000	43,200
Noncontrolling interest					$4,600	4,600
	$174,200	$35,000	$20,000	$20,000		$190,800

2325.13 **Format of worksheet.** The comprehensive worksheet format illustrated for P Corporation is one with which candidates should be familiar. The following points should be noted about the worksheet format:

a. The worksheet contains a section for each financial statement in the order in which the statements are normally prepared.

b. The entire net income line in the income statement section is carried forward to the net income line in the retained earnings section.

c. The end-of-year retained earnings line is carried forward to the retained earnings line in the balance sheet section.

d. The noncontrolling interest's share of the subsidiary's net income is shown as a deduction in the consolidated balances column and as an addition to the noncontrolling interest column.

2325.14 **Explanation of eliminating entries.** The general approach followed for the eliminating entries is to eliminate the following:

    a. All transactions affecting the investment account *during* the year

    b. The balance in the investment account as of the *beginning* of the year

The beginning balance and the changes in the investment account are:

	Investment in S		
Jan. 1, 20X2, balance	$16,000	20X2 sub dividends (80%)	$800
20X2 sub income (80%)	3,200		

2325.15 The eliminating entries in journal form are:

    (1) Sub income $3,200
            Investment in S $3,200

    (2) Investment in S $800
            Dividends[a] $800

    (3) Common stock—S (0.80 × $10,000) $8,000
         Capital in excess of par—S (0.80 × $3,000)   2,400
         Retained earnings—S (Jan. 1) (0.80 × $7,000)   5,600
            Investment in S (Jan. 1 balance) $16,000

[a] *Retained earnings (sub) is credited if a dividends account is not used.*

2325.16 One should pay special attention to the debit to retained earnings. The debit is to the beginning-of-year retained earnings, which is included in the retained earnings section of the comprehensive worksheet. Following this approach, the retained earnings shown in the balance sheet section are *never* debited or credited in an eliminating entry on a comprehensive worksheet.

2325.17 If a worksheet were prepared at the end of 20X2 for a consolidated balance sheet *only*, the investment elimination would be:

     Common Stock—S (0.80 × $10,000) $8,000
     Capital in Excess of Par—S (0.80 × $3,000)   2,400
     Retained Earnings—S (Dec. 31) (0.80 × $10,000)   8,000
         Investment in S (Dec. 31 balance) $18,400

2326 Emphasis on Adjusting and Eliminating Entries (Purchase Method)

2326.01 The worksheets illustrated in section **2325** provide a framework for identifying the various types of adjusting and eliminating entries. The types of eliminations may be categorized as those related to the following:

    a. The investment account

    b. Current year changes in the investment account

    c. Year-end reciprocal balance sheet accounts

    d. Reciprocal income statement accounts

    e. Intercompany profits and losses

2326.02 The first two types of eliminations were illustrated in section **2325**, in which the cost of the investment was equal to the book value of the parent's share of the net assets of the subsidiary. Consideration is now given to situations in which the cost of the investment is not equal to book value.

Excess of Cost Over Book Value

2326.03 **Example:** Assume that on December 31, 20X1, P Company acquires 80% of the stock of S Company at a cost of $170,000. The stockholders' equity of S Company on December 31, 20X1, is as follows:

Common stock ($10 par)	$100,000
Retained earnings	50,000
	$150,000

S Company has a building that at December 31, 20X1, has a book value (BV) of $60,000 and a fair value (FV) of $90,000. In addition, S Company's inventory has a book value of $10,000 and a fair value of $15,000. The fair values of all other identifiable assets and liabilities are the same as their book values.

2326.04 The excess of the cost of P's investment in S is allocated as follows:

Cost of investment		$170,000
Less 80% of BV of S Company at 12/31/20X1		120,000
Excess of cost over book value		50,000
P's share of excess of fair value over book value of identifiable net assets:		
Inventory (0.80 × $5,000)	$ 4,000	
Building (0.80 × $30,000)	24,000	28,000
Goodwill		$ 22,000

2326.05 The eliminating entry at December 31, 20X1, is:

Common Stock—S (0.80 × $100,000)	$80,000	
Retained Earnings—S (0.80 × $50,000)	40,000	
Inventory	4,000	
Building (net)	24,000	
Goodwill	22,000	
Investment in S		$170,000

2326.06 The $4,000 increase in inventory, $24,000 increase in building, and the $22,000 goodwill are reflected only on the consolidated financial statements and not on the books of either company. The only entry recorded in 20X1 on the books of P Company on December 31, 20X1, with regard to this business combination is:

Investment in S	$170,000	
Cash		$170,000

2326.07 Continuing the example into 20X2, assume that S Company reports net income in 20X2 of $30,000. Assume also that (a) S Company uses the FIFO inventory method, (b) the building has an estimated remaining life of 10 years as of December 31, 20X1, and (c) goodwill was not impaired in 20X2. Accordingly, the amortization of the excess of cost over book value is as follows:

Inventory	$4,000 ÷ 1 year (FIFO method) =	$4,000	per year for 1 year
Building	$24,000 ÷ 10 years =	2,400	per year for 10 years
		$6,400	

2326.08 The eliminating entries at the end of 20X2 will be influenced by whether or not P Company (the parent) has recorded the current-year's amortization on its own books. Both assumptions are illustrated as follows:

	Assuming P Records Amortization of Differential on Its Books		Assuming P Does Not Record Amortization of Differential on Its Books	
Entries on P Company's books (20X2): Investment in S	$24,000		$24,000	
Sub Income (0.80 × $30,000)		$24,000		$24,000
(To record P's share of net income of S.)				
Sub Income	$6,400		(no entry)	
Investment in S		$6,400		
(To record amortization of "excess.")				
Eliminating entries for comprehensive worksheet for 20X2:				
(1) Sub Income	$24,000		$24,000	
Investment in S		$24,000		$24,000
(2) Investment in S	$6,400		(no entry)	
Sub Income		$6,400		
(3) Common Stock—S (0.80 × $100,000)	$80,000		$80,000	
Retained Earnings—S (Jan. 1) (0.80 × $50,000)	40,000		40,000	
Inventory	4,000		4,000	
Building	24,000		24,000	
Goodwill	22,000		22,000	
Investment in S		$170,000		$170,000
(4) Cost of Goods Sold	$4,000		$4,000	
Inventory		$4,000		$4,000
(5) Depreciation Expense	$2,400		$2,400	
Building (or Acc. depr.)		2,400		$2,400

2326.09 Note that entry (2) is the only eliminating entry that is different under the two assumptions regarding P Company's recording the current-year's amortization of the "excess" on its own books. As one will note, such an eliminating entry (entry 2) is necessary only if P Company has recorded the current-year's amortization. Another way of stating it is that one does not have to eliminate (or "reverse out") what was not recorded in the first place. The consolidated financial statements are the same under both assumptions.

2326.10 The eliminating entries for a worksheet for a consolidated balance sheet (only) at December 31, 20X2, are:

	Assuming P Has Recorded Current-Year's Amortization	Assuming P Has Not Recorded Current-Year's Amortization
Retained Earnings—P	(no entry)	$ 6,400
Investment in S		$ 6,400
Common Stock—S (0.80 × $100,000)	$80,000	$80,000
Retained Earnings—S (Dec. 31) (0.80 × $80,000)	64,000	64,000
Building (net) ($24,000 - 2,400)	21,600	21,600
Goodwill	22,000	22,000
Investment in S	$187,000	$187,000

2326.11 Entry (1) is necessary because P Company's failure to record the current-year's amortization on its own books results in P's retained earnings being overstated. P Company should record a similar entry on its own books to avoid its retained earnings and investment in S accounts from being overstated at the beginning of 20X3.

2326.12 Assuming S Company reported net income of $40,000 in 20X3 and that goodwill was not impaired in 20X3, the journal entries on P Company's books and the eliminating entries for a comprehensive worksheet for 20X3 would be as follows:

	Assuming P Records Amortization of Differential on Its Books		Assuming P Does Not Record Amortization of Differential on Its Books	

Entries on P Company's books (20X3):
Investment in S
    Sub income (0.80 × $40,000)
    (To record P's share of net income of S)
Sub income
    Investment in S
    (To record amortization of "excess")
	$32,000
	
	$ 2,400
		
		$ 32,000
		
		$ 2,400
			$32,000
			
			(no entry)
				
				$ 32,000

Eliminating entries for comprehensive worksheet for 20X3:				
(1) Sub income Investment in S	$32,000	 $ 32,000	$32,000	 $ 32,000
(2) Investment in S Sub income	$ 2,400	 $ 2,400	(no entry)	
(3) Investment in S Retained earnings — P (Jan. 1)			$ 6,400	 $ 6,400

(4) Common stock — S (0.80 × $100,000)
Retained earnings — S (Jan. 1)
    (0.80 × $80,000)
Building (net) ($24,000 balance 01/01/X2 less $2,400 amortized in 20X2)
Goodwill
    Investment in S
	$80,000
	
	64,000
	
	21,600
	22,000
		
		$187,600
			$80,000
			
			64,000
			
			21,600
			22,000
				
				$187,600

(5) Depreciation expense Building (net) (or Acc. depr.)	$ 2,400	 $ 2,400	$ 2,400	 $ 2,400

2326.13 Note that eliminating entry (2) is for $2,400 rather than the $6,400 shown in section **2326.08** for 20X2. The amortization of the differential in 20X2 was attributable to two things—the $4,000 increase in cost of goods sold because of the $4,000 parent's share of the excess of the fair value of inventory over its books value *and* the $2,400 increase in depreciation expense due to the recognition for consolidated financial statement purposes of the excess of the fair value of the plant assets over their book value. Since S Company uses the FIFO method of inventory costing, all of the differential attributable to inventory was amortized or "flowed out" in 20X2. Therefore, the amortization of the differential in 20X3 relates only to the $2,400 increase in depreciation expense recognized for consolidated financial statement purposes.

2326.14 If P Company does not record on its own books the amortization of the differential, an eliminating entry such as entry (3) must be made on the worksheet to update the Investment in S account and the Retained Earnings—P account for the cumulative amount of such amortization that P Company has not recorded on its own books in prior years. The entry is made for the cumulative amount of such amortization not recorded as of the beginning of the current year. As of January 1, 20X3, with respect to prior years, P Company has not recorded the amortization in only one year, 20X2. The comparable entry for the 20X4 worksheet will be for $8,800, which would be for the $6,400 amortization not recorded in 20X2 and the $2,400 not recorded in 20X3.

2326.15 Eliminating entry (4) eliminates P Company's share of the stockholders' equity of S Company as of January 1, 20X3 (i.e., the beginning of the current year). The $64,000 debit to retained earnings—S is for 80% of S Company's $80,000 retained earnings balance at January 1, 20X2 ($50,000 balance at January 1, 20X2, plus S Company's 20X2 net income of $30,000). The $21,600 debit to building (net) is for the unamortized portion of the differential attributable to the building as of January 1, 20X3 (i.e., the beginning of the current year). If P Company records amortization of the differential on its own books, the $187,600 credit to the investment in S account is for the balance in the investment in S account as of January 1, 20X3. If P Company does not record amortization of the differential on its own books, the $187,600 credit to the investment in S account is for the $194,000 balance in the investment in S account on P Company's books as of January 1, 20X3 ($170,000 balance January 1, 20X2, plus the $24,000 P Company's share of S Company's net income in 20X2) plus the adjustment in entry (3) for the amortization of the differential that P Company has not recorded on its own books.

Excess of Book Value Over Cost

2326.16 **Example:** Assume that on December 31, 20X1, Parent Company pays $120,000 for 100% of the stock of Sub Company. Sub has common stock of $100,000 and retained earnings of $40,000. The fair values of Sub's identifiable assets and liabilities are the same as their book values.

2326.17 Assuming the only "eligible" asset Sub Company has is land with a book value and fair value of $75,000, the eliminating entry at December 31, 20X1, would be:

Common Stock—Sub	$100,000	
Retained Earnings—Sub	40,000	
Land (allocation of credit differential)		$ 20,000
Investment in Sub		120,000

2326.18 If Sub's "eligible" asset had been a depreciable asset, depreciation would also have to be adjusted on the worksheet. For example, if the only noncurrent asset is a building with a 10-year remaining life, the eliminating entries for a comprehensive worksheet at the end of 20X2 (ignoring any net income reported by Sub) would be:

Common Stock—Sub	$100,000	
Retained Earnings—Sub (Jan. 1, 20X2)	40,000	
Building (net)		$ 20,000
Investment in Sub		120,000
Building (or Accumulated Depreciation)	$ 2,000	
Depreciation Expense ($20,000 ÷ 10)		$ 2,000

Elimination of Year-End Reciprocal Balance Sheet Accounts

2326.19 Another type of eliminating entry the candidate should look for is that relating to year end reciprocal balance sheet accounts. The following are examples of such accounts:

    a. Accounts receivable or accounts payable

    b. Notes receivable or notes payable

    c. Advance to sub (parent) or advance from parent (sub)

2326.20 The receivable and payable must be associated with another entity included in the consolidation. For example, the accounts receivable must be receivable from one of the affiliated entities.

Elimination of Reciprocal Income Statement Accounts

2326.21 All reciprocal income statement accounts must also be eliminated. For example, if the parent company sells merchandise to the sub, sales and purchases of that amount must be eliminated. Interest income and interest expense are another set of reciprocal income statement accounts often found in consolidation worksheet problems.

Elimination of Intercompany Profits and Losses

2326.22 The elimination of intercompany profits and losses is usually a major aspect of any CPA Examination problem involving consolidated worksheets. Accordingly, one should be quite familiar with the issues and procedures related to these eliminations.

2326.23 At this point, discussion will be restricted to the elimination of intercompany profit on the sale of land. This discussion will facilitate the demonstration of the treatment of intercompany profits on the worksheets in the remaining part of this section, including their impact on the computation of noncontrolling interest, without the candidate becoming bogged down in excess detail. A detailed discussion of the various types of intercompany profit eliminations is presented in section **2327**.

2326.24 **Example:** Assume that on December 31, 20X1, Ply Company acquires 80% of Sly Company's outstanding 10,000 shares of $10 par common stock at their book value of $15 per share. Sly Company on this date has retained earnings of $50,000.

2326.25 The eliminating entry at December 31, 20X1, is:

Common Stock—Sly (0.80 × $100,000)	$80,000	
Retained Earnings—Sly (0.80 × $50,000)	40,000	
Investment in Sly		$120,000

2326.26 Assume further that Sly reports net income in 20X2 of $70,000. Included in net income is a $15,000 gain on sale of land to Ply Company on September 1, 20X2; the land had a book value of $48,000 at the time of the sale.

2326.27 The following transaction entries were recorded on September 1, 20X2:

On Ply's books:		
Land	$63,000	
Cash		$63,000
On Sly's books:		
Cash	$63,000	
Land		$48,000
Gain on Sale of Land		15,000

2326.28 From a consolidated entity standpoint, the gain is unrealized and the land is overstated by the amount of the gain. Therefore, the consolidated worksheet should reflect the elimination of this unrealized gain. The gain will be considered as realized only if Ply sells the land to an "outsider."

2326.29 The elimination entries for 20X2 are:

For a comprehensive worksheet:

(1)	Sub Income (0.80 × $70,000)	$56,000	
	Investment in Sly		$ 56,000
(2)	Gain on Sale of Land	$15,000	
	Land		$ 15,000
(3)	Common Stock—Sly (0.80 × $100,000)	$80,000	
	Retained Earnings—Sly (Jan. 1, 20X2) (0.80 × $50,000)	40,000	
	Investment in Sly		$120,000

For a worksheet for a consolidated balance sheet only:

(1)	Retained Earnings—Ply (0.80 × $15,000)	$12,000	
	Retained Earnings—Sly (0.20 × $15,000)	3,000	
	Land		$ 15,000
(2)	Common Stock—Sly (0.80 × $100,000)	$80,000	
	Retained Earnings—Sly (Dec. 31) (0.80 × $120,000)	96,000	
	Investment in Sly		$176,000

2326.30 Special attention should be directed to the eliminating entries for a consolidated balance sheet (section **2326.29**). Since the worksheet is for a consolidated balance sheet, the only accounts still open are balance sheet accounts. The $15,000 gain was closed into the retained earnings account of Sly. However, since Ply is using the equity method, Ply picked up 80% or $12,000 of the gain when it recorded its share of Sly's net income. Therefore, the elimination of the gain involves a debit of $12,000 to Ply's retained earnings and a debit of $3,000 to Sly's retained earnings. Entry (2) is the normal investment eliminating entry.

2326.31 The noncontrolling interest's share of Sly's 20X2 net income is determined as follows:

Net income reported by Sly	$70,000
Unrealized gain included in Sly's net income	15,000
Confirmed (or realized) net income of Sly	55,000
Noncontrolling interest percentage	× .20
Noncontrolling interest's share of net income	$11,000

2326.32 Ply's share of Sly's net income then is:

Confirmed net income of Sly	$55,000
Controlling interest percentage	× .80
Ply's share of Sly's net income	$44,000

2326.33 If Ply had sold the land to Sly (instead of the reverse), the unrealized gain would not have affected the computation of the noncontrolling interest's share of Sly's net income (i.e., reported net income and confirmed net income of Sly would have been the same). Only intercompany gains or losses associated with the subsidiary affect the determination of the noncontrolling interest's share of net income.

2326.34 The concept of confirmed (or realized) earnings also applies to retained earnings. This is illustrated by examining the retained earnings line on a worksheet for a consolidated balance sheet at December 31, 20X2, for Ply Company and its subsidiary, Sly Company. Assume that Ply's retained earnings at December 31, 20X2, is $56,000 (its share of Sly's 20X2 reported net income). (Refer to entries (1) and (2) in the latter part of section **2326.29**)

	Ply	Sly	Eliminations Dr	Eliminations Cr	Noncontrolling Interest	Consolidated
Retained earnings:						
Ply	$56,000		(1) $12,000			
Sly		$120,000	(2) 3,000		$21,000[a]	$44,000
			(3) 96,000			

[a]
Sly's reported retained earnings, Dec 31, 20X2	$ 120,000
Less unrealized profit in Sly's retained earnings	15,000
Confirmed retained earnings	$ 105,000
Noncontrolling interest percentage	.20
Noncontrolling interest's share of Sky's retained earnings	$ 21,000

Example: Comprehensive Worksheet

2326.35 The comprehensive worksheet illustrated in section **2325.12** included only a limited number of eliminating entries; attention was focused primarily on the worksheet format. The following comprehensive worksheet incorporates the various types of eliminating entries.

2326.36 The following assumptions are made for P Corporation and S Corporation:

a. On January 1, 20X1, P Corporation acquired 80% of the 5,000 outstanding shares of S Corporation's $10 par common stock for $76,000.

b. S Corporation's stockholders' equity on January 1, 20X1, consisted of common stock, $50,000, and retained earnings, $20,000.

c. P Corporation uses the equity method but does not record the amortization of any differential or the impairment of any goodwill after the consolidated financial statements are prepared. Thus, with regard to its investment in S Corporation, in 20X1 P Corporation recorded on its own books its initial investment in the stock of S, its share of the net income of S, and its share of the dividends of S.

d. The fair values of S Corporation's identifiable assets and liabilities on January 1, 20X1, were the same as their book values, except for buildings which had a book value of $30,000 and a fair value of $40,000. Thus, $8,000 of the excess of cost over book value was attributable to undervalued buildings and $12,000 to goodwill, as shown:

Cost of investment	$76,000
Less 80% of the book value of S (0.80 × $70,000)	56,000
Excess of cost over book value	20,000
Allocated to building (0.80 × $10,000)	8,000
Goodwill	$12,000

e. S Corporation's buildings have an estimated remaining life of 10 years. (The portion of the differential that is attributable to undervalued buildings is to be amortized over 10 years.)

f. P Corporation determined at the end of 20X1 that goodwill related to its investment in S Corporation had been impaired in the amount of $2,000.

g. During 20X1, S Corporation sold land with a book value of $30,000 to P Corporation for $40,000. P Corporation still owns the land at December 31, 20X1.

h. At December 31, 20X1, S Corporation owes P Corporation $5,000 on open account.

i. During 20X1, P Corporation sold merchandise to S Corporation at cost for $8,000.

	Comprehensive Worksheet For the Year Ended December 31, 20X1						
	Trial Balance		Adjustments and Eliminations			Noncontrolling Interest	Consolidated
	P	S	Dr		Cr	Dr (Cr)	Dr (Cr)
Sales	$ 80,000	$20,000	(6)	$ 8,000			$ 92,000
Cost of goods sold	(50,000)	(12,000)			(6) $ 8,000		(54,000)
Gross margin	30,000	8,000					38,000
Expenses	(10,000)	(2,000)	(4)	800			(12,800)
Gain on sale of land		10,000	(8)	10,000			0
Goodwill impairment			(5)	2,000			(2,000)
Income from operations	20,000	16,000					23,200
Sub income	12,800		(1)	12,800			
MI share of S net income						$ 1,200	(1,200)
Net income	$ 32,800	$16,000		$ 33,600	$ 8,000	$ 1,200	$ 22,000
Retained earnings, Jan. 1	$ 40,000	$20,000	(3)	$ 16,000		$ 4,000	$ 40,000
Net income	32,800	16,000		33,600	$ 8,000	1,200	22,000
Dividends	(10,000)	(5,000)			(2) 4,000		(11,000)
Retained earnings, Dec. 31	$ 62,800	$31,000		$ 49,600	$ 12,000	$ 5,200	$ 51,000
Current assets	$ 50,200	$56,000			(7) $ 5,000		$101,200
Building (net)	45,000	30,000	(3)	$ 8,000	(4) 800		82,200
Land	40,000	10,000			(8) 10,000		40,000
Investment in S	84,800		(2)	4,000	(1) 12,800		0
					(3) 76,000		
Goodwill			(3)	12,000	(5) 2,000		10,000
	$220,000	$96,000					$233,400
Current liabilities	$ 57,200	$15,000	(7)	$ 5,000			$ 67,200
Common stock	100,000	50,000	(3)	40,000		$10,000	100,000
Retained earnings	62,800	31,000		49,600	$ 12,000	5,200	51,000
Noncontrolling interest						15,200	15,200
	$220,000	$96,000		$118,600	$118,600		$233,400

2326.37 Each of the eliminating entries is explained as follows:

(1) Sub Income (0.80 × $16,000) $12,800
    Investment in S $12,800
To eliminate the accrual of P's share of net income of S Corporation.

(2) Investment in S $ 4,000
    Dividend—S (0.80 × $5,000) $ 4,000
To eliminate intercompany dividends.

(3) Common Stock—S (0.80 × $50,000) $40,000
    Retained Earnings—S (Jan. 1) (0.80 × $20,000) 16,000
    Buildings (net) 8,000
    Goodwill 12,000
        Investment in S $76,000

(4) Expenses (depreciation) $ 800
    Buildings (net) (or Acc. Depr.) $ 800
To recognize depreciation related to P's share of the excess of the fair value of the building over its book value ($8,000 excess ÷ 10 years).

(5) Goodwill Impairment Loss $ 2,000
    Goodwill $ 2,000
To recognize the 20X1 impairment of goodwill.

(6) Sales $ 8,000
    Cost of Goods Sold $ 8,000
To eliminate intercompany sales.

(7) Current Liabilities (Accounts Payable) $ 5,000
    Current Assets $ 5,000
To eliminate intercompany receivables and payables.

(8) Gain on Sale of Land $10,000
    Land $10,000
To eliminate unrealized intercompany gain on sale of land.

2326.38 The noncontrolling interest's share of net income, shown as a deduction in the consolidated column and as an addition in the noncontrolling interest column, is determined as follows:

Reported net income of S	$16,000
Less: Unrealized gain on sale of land	10,000
Confirmed net income of S	$ 6,000
Noncontrolling interest percentage	× .20
Noncontrolling interest's share of net income	$ 1,200

Alternative Format for Comprehensive Worksheet

2326.39 A detailed discussion of the issues associated with goodwill impairment is presented in section **2227**.

2326.40 The CPA Examination candidate should be familiar with other formats for comprehensive worksheets. One such format is illustrated as follows. The data presented in the comprehensive worksheet is the same as that presented previously; the only difference is in the format of the worksheet.

Comprehensive Worksheet

For the Year Ended December 31, 20X1

	P	S	Adjustments and Eliminations				Noncontrolling Interest	Consolidated
	Dr(Cr)	Dr(Cr)	Dr		Cr		Dr(Cr)	Dr(Cr)
Current assets	$ 50,200	$ 56,000			(7)	$ 5,000		$ 101,200
Building (net)	45,000	30,000	(3)	$ 8,000	(4)	800		82,200
Land	40,000	10,000			(8)	10,000		40,000
Investment in S	84,800		(2)	4,000	(1)	12,800		0
					(3)	76,000		
Goodwill			(3)	12,000	(5)	2,000		10,000
Current liabilities	(57,200)	(15,000)	(7)	5,000				(67,200)
Common stock	(100,000)	(50,000)	(3)	40,000			(10,000)	(100,000)
Retained earnings, Jan. 1	(40,000)	(20,000)	(3)	16,000			(4,000)	(40,000)
Dividends	10,000	5,000			(2)	4,000	1,000	10,000
Sales	(80,000)	(20,000)	(6)	8,000				(92,000)
Gain on sale of land		(10,000)	(8)	10,000				0
Sub income	(12,800)		(1)	12,800				0
Cost of goods sold	50,000	12,000			(6)	8,000		54,000
Expenses	10,000	2,000	(4)	800				12,800
Goodwill impairment			(5)	2,000				2,000
	$ 0	$ 0		$118,600		$118,600		
MI share of net income							$(1,200)	1,200
Total noncontrolling interest							$(14,200)	(14,200)
								$ 0

2327 Elimination of Intercompany Profits and Losses (Purchase Method)

2327.01 Discussion relating to the elimination of unrealized intercompany profits and losses was first introduced in section **2326**. The situation illustrated in that section was the intercompany profit on sale of land. This section contains a detailed discussion of the three major areas in which intercompany profits and losses are usually found:

1. Inventories

2. Plant assets

3. Intercorporate bond investments

2327.02 Unrealized intercompany profits and losses must be eliminated in preparing consolidated financial statements so that the resulting statements will present the operations as if the separate legal entities are one operating entity.

2327.03 The entire amount (100%) of any unrealized intercompany profit or loss should be eliminated for consolidation purposes, rather than just the parent company's ownership percentage. Unrealized intercompany profits and losses arising from sales by the subsidiary to the parent (upstream) should be allocated between the majority and noncontrolling interests in accordance with their respective ownership percentages. Unrealized intercompany profits and losses arising from parent to subsidiary (downstream) sales are allocated totally to the controlling (majority) interest.

2327.04 The determination of the noncontrolling interest's share of net income and retained earnings is affected only by unrealized intercompany profits and losses arising from upstream transactions.

2327.05 In cases where unrealized intercompany profits or losses exist in recorded account balances, the diagram following is helpful in establishing where the profit resides. The location of the profit in recorded account balances depends on the following:

a. Whether the profit or loss is associated with the current period (i.e., located in a nominal account) or with a prior period (i.e., located in a balance sheet account)

b. Whether the parent sells to the subsidiary or vice versa

c. Whether the parent uses the equity method or the cost method during the period

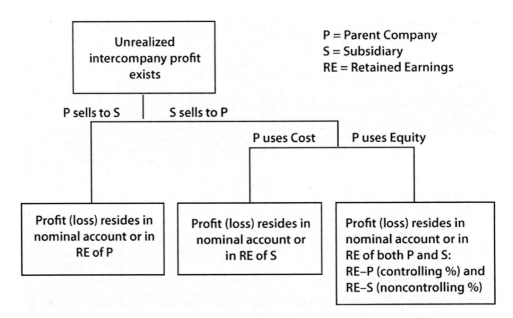

2327.06 In the discussion of intercompany profits and losses in the remaining parts of this section, the following assumptions are made unless otherwise indicated:

a. Company P (parent) owns 80% of the common stock of Company S (subsidiary).

b. Company P uses the equity method during the year to the extent that it records its share of the subsidiary's net income and dividends. However, Company P does not record on its own books the elimination of unrealized or unconfirmed intercompany profits.

2327.07 The elimination entries illustrated are those related to intercompany transactions and unrealized profits or losses. The other types of eliminating entries were discussed in section 2326. The following abbreviations are used in the ensuing discussion.

CW = comprehensive worksheet
BSW = balance sheet only worksheet

Intercompany Inventory Profits and Losses

2327.08 **Example 1:** During 20X1, Company P sells merchandise which costs $20,000 to Company S for $30,000. The merchandise is still in the inventory of Company S at December 31, 20X1 (the entries assume that both companies use a perpetual inventory system).

    CW entries—20X1:
Sales	$30,000	
Cost of Goods Sold		$30,000

To eliminate intercompany sales.

Cost of Goods Sold	$10,000	
Inventory		$10,000

To eliminate unrealized profit in ending inventory.

    BSW entries—12/31/X1:
Retained Earnings—P	$10,000	
Inventory		$10,000

P sold to S; therefore 100% of unrealized profit charged against P.

    CW entries—20X2:
Retained Earnings—P	$10,000	
Cost of Goods Sold		$10,000

To eliminate unrealized profit in 20X2 beginning inventory (inventory overstated).

2327.09 **Example 2:** Assume the same facts as in Example 1, except that Company S sold the merchandise to Company P (instead of the reverse):

    CW entries—20X1:
Sales	$30,000	
Cost of Goods Sold		$30,000

To eliminate intercompany sales.

Cost of Goods Sold	$10,000	
Inventory		$10,000

To eliminate unrealized profit in ending inventory.

    BSW entries—12/31/X1:
Retained Earnings—P (0.80 × $10,000)	$ 8,000	
Retained Earnings—S (0.20 × $10,000)	2,000	
Inventory		$10,000

S sold to P; therefore profit resides in retained earnings of P (80%) and S (20%).

    CW entries—20X2:
Retained Earnings—P (0.80 × $10,000)	$8,000	
Retained Earnings—S (0.20 × $10,000)	2,000	
Cost of Goods Sold		$10,000

To eliminate unrealized profit in 20X2 beginning inventory.

2327.10 **Example 3:** Assume the same facts as in Example 2 (S sells to P), except that at December 31, 20X1, only one-half of the merchandise is still in Company P's inventory:

CW entries—20X1:
Sales $30,000
    Cost of Goods Sold $30,000
To eliminate intercompany sales.

Cost of Goods Sold $ 5,000
    Inventory $ 5,000
To eliminate unrealized profit (0.50 × $10,000) in ending inventory.

BSW entries—12/31/X1:
Retained Earnings—P (0.80 × $5,000) $ 4,000
Retained Earnings—S (0.20 × $5,000) 1,000
    Inventory $ 5,000
Elimination of unrealized profit residing in retained earnings of P (80%) and S (20%).

CW entries—20X2:
Retained Earnings—P $ 4,000
Retained Earnings—S 1,000
    Cost of Goods Sold $ 5,000
To eliminate unrealized profit in 20X2 inventory (inventory overstated).

Intercompany Profit in Plant Assets

2327.11 **Example 4:** On January 1, 20X1, Company P sells equipment to Company S for $100,000. The equipment has a book value of $80,000 (original cost of $88,000 and accumulated depreciation of $8,000) and an estimated remaining life of 10 years as of January 1, 20X1.

2327.12 The following transaction entries were recorded by P and S on January 1, 20X1:

Company P			Company S		
Cash	$100,000		Equipment	$100,000	
Accumulated Depreciation	8,000		Cash		$100,000
Equipment		$88,000			
Gain on Sale of Equipment		20,000			

2327.13 Company S will record depreciation expense of $10,000 per year. Without the sale, Company P would have recorded depreciation of $8,000 per year.

2327.14 The consolidated worksheet eliminating entries are:

CW entries—20X1:
Gain on Sale of Equipment $20,000
    Equipment $12,000
    Accumulated Depreciation 8,000
To eliminate unrealized gain and restore the equipment and accumulated depreciation accounts to their presale balances.

Accumulated Depreciation $ 2,000
    Depreciation Expense $ 2,000
To eliminate excess depreciation recorded in 20X1 after the sale.

BSW entries—12/31/X1:
    Retained Earnings—P $18,000
        Equipment $12,000
        Accumulated Depreciation   6,000
To eliminate remaining unconfirmed profit; $20,000 unconfirmed gain less $2,000 confirmed during 20X1 through excess depreciation.

CW entries—20X2:
    Retained Earnings—P $18,000
        Equipment $12,000
        Accumulated Depreciation   6,000
To eliminate intercompany profit residing in 01/01/20X2 retained earnings of P ($20,000 gain in 20X1 less $2,000 excess depreciation in 20X1).

    Accumulated Depreciation $ 2,000
        Depreciation Expense $ 2,000
To eliminate excess depreciation in 20X2.

BSW entries—12/31/X2:
    Retained Earnings—P $16,000
        Equipment $12,000
        Accumulated Depreciation   4,000
To eliminate remaining unconfirmed profit; $20,000 unconfirmed gain less $4,000 confirmed in 20X1 and 20X2 through excess depreciation.

2327.15 The original unconfirmed profit of $20,000 arising from the sale of the equipment will continue to be confirmed each year to the extent of the $2,000 excess depreciation recognized. The total $20,000 profit will be confirmed by the end of 10 years.

2327.16 The eliminating entry for a consolidated balance sheet worksheet at the end of the ninth year (20X9) would be:

Retained Earnings—P ($20,000 − $18,000) $ 2,000
Accumulated Depreciation   10,000
    Equipment $12,000

The accounts can be verified as follows:

	Balance if Sale Not Made	Balance on S Books	Adjustment Necessary
Equipment	$88,000	$100,000	$12,000 credit
Accumulated depr.	80,000[a]	90,000[b]	10,000 debit

[a] Jan. 1, 20X1, balance ($8,000) + Years 1–9 (9 × $8,000) = $80,000
[b] Years 1–9 (9 × $10,000) = $90,000

2327.17 **Example 5:** Assume the same facts as in Example 4, except assume that Company S sold the equipment to Company P (instead of the reverse).

CW entries—20X1:
    Gain on Sale of Equipment $20,000
        Equipment $12,000
        Accumulated Depreciation   8,000
To eliminate unrealized gain and restore the equipment and accumulated depreciation accounts to their presale balances.

    Accumulated Depreciation $ 2,000
        Depreciation Expense $ 2,000
To eliminate excess depreciation recorded in 20X1 after the sale.

BSW entries—12/31/X1:
Retained Earnings—P (0.80($20,000 – $2,000))	$14,400	
Retained Earnings—S (0.20($20,000 – $2,000))	3,600	
Equipment		$12,000
Accumulated Depreciation		6,000

To eliminate remaining unconfirmed profit ($20,000 - $2,000) in ratio of 80% P and 20% S.

BSW entries—12/31/X2:
Retained Earnings—P (0.80($20,000 – $4,000))	$12,800	
Retained Earnings—S (0.20($20,000 – $4,000))	3,200	
Equipment		$12,000
Accumulated Depreciation		4,000

To eliminate remaining unconfirmed profit ($20,000 - $4,000) in ratio of 80% P and 20% S.

Intercompany Bond Investments

2327.18   The acquisition by one entity of another unrelated (unaffiliated) entity's outstanding bonds presents no special problems. The issuer must account for its bonds payable, whereas the acquiring entity must account for its investments in bonds. No gain or loss is recognized by the issuer when the bonds are sold nor by the acquirer when the outstanding bonds are purchased.

2327.19   The same is true from the standpoint of the separate entities if the two entities are affiliates of each other. However, from a consolidated entity standpoint the acquisition of an affiliate's outstanding bonds constitutes the consolidated entity's *reacquisition* of its own bonds. Accordingly, any difference between the carrying amount of the bonds and their acquisition price should be recognized as a gain or loss for consolidation purposes.

2327.20   Eliminations related to inventory and fixed assets involve the elimination of *recorded but unrealized* gains and losses. On the other hand, eliminations related to bonds involve the recognition of *realized but unrecorded* gains and losses.

2327.21   **Example 6:** On December 31, 20X0, the carrying value of Company P's outstanding 10% bonds is $110,000 (face amount $100,000, premium on bonds payable $10,000). The bonds pay interest annually on each December 31 and mature in 10 years. On December 31, 20X0, Company S acquired from existing bondholders all the outstanding bonds for $106,000 after interest had been paid for 20X0.

2327.22   The eliminating entry for purposes of consolidation on December 31, 20X0, is:

CW entries—20X0:
Bonds Payable (P)	$100,000	
Premium on Bonds Payable (P)	10,000	
Investment in P Bonds (S)		$106,000
Gain on Reacquisition of Bonds (P)		4,000

BSW entries—20X0:
Bonds Payable (P)	$100,000	
Premium on Bonds Payable (P)	10,000	
Investment in P Bonds (S)		$106,000
Retained Earnings (P)		4,000

2327.23 The gain on reacquisition is determined as follows:

Carrying value of bonds:		
Bonds payable	$100,000	
Premium on bonds payable	10,000	$110,000
Acquisition price		106,000
Gain on reacquisition of bonds		$ 4,000

2327.24 The gain or loss on reacquisition is identified with the *issuer* of the bonds (Company P in this case).

2327.25 Assuming that the straight-line amortization method is used, Company P and Company S would record the following transaction entries on their books during 20X1:

Company P:
  Interest Expense $10,000
    Cash (10% of $100,000) $10,000
  To record payment of contractual interest.

  Premium on Bonds Payable ($10,000 ÷ 10) $ 1,000
    Interest Expense $ 1,000
  To record amortization of premium.

Company S:
  Cash (10% of $100,000) $10,000
    Interest Income $10,000
  To record receipt of contractual interest.

  Interest Income $ 600
    Investment in P Bonds ($6,000 ÷ 10) $ 600
  To record amortization of premium.

2327.26 The 20X1 eliminating entries must, on the worksheet, zero-out all accounts related to the bonds. These accounts and their balances at December 3, 20X1, are:

On P books:
  Bonds payable $100,000
  Premium on bonds payable ($10,000 – $1,000)   9,000
  Interest expense ($10,000 – $1,000)   9,000

On S books:
  Investment in P bonds ($106,000 – $600) $105,400
  Interest income ($10,000 – $600)   9,400

2327.27 The eliminating entries on the 20X1 consolidated worksheet are:

CW entries—20X1:
(1) Bonds Payable $100,000
     Premium on Bonds Payable   10,000
       Investment in P Bonds $106,000
       Retained Earnings—P   4,000
To eliminate the related accounts as of January 1, 20X1, and to credit the 20X0 gain to retained earnings of P (the issuer).

(2) Interest Income $ 10,000
     Interest Expense $ 10,000
To eliminate the contractual interest recorded in 20X1.

(3) Interest Expense $ 1,000
     Premium on Bonds Payable $ 1,000
To eliminate the amortization of premium on bonds payable during 20X1.

	(4)	Investment in P Bonds	$ 600	
		Interest Income		$ 600

To eliminate the amortization of premium on the bond investment during 20X1.

2327.28 As a check on the eliminating entries, the balances in the accounts related to the bonds should be examined to see if they have zero balances after the eliminating entries:

Accounts	12/31/20X1 Balance per Trial Balance	Entry #	Effect of Worksheet Eliminating Entries	Balance Extended to Consolidated Column
Bonds payable	$100,000	(1)	$(100,000)	0
Premium on bonds payable	9,000	(1)	(10,000)	0
		(3)	1,000	
Interest expense	9,000	(2)	(10,000)	0
		(3)	1,000	
Investment in P bonds	105,400	(1)	(106,000)	0
		(4)	600	
Interest income	9,400	(2)	(10,000)	0
		(4)	600	

2327.29 The eliminating entry for a worksheet for a consolidated balance sheet at December 31, 20X1, is:

BSW entry—12/31/X1:
Bonds Payable	$100,000	
Premium on Bonds Payable ($10,000 – $1,000)	9,000	
Investment in P Bonds ($106,000 – $600)		$105,400
Retained Earnings—P ($4,000 – $1,000 + $600)		3,600

To eliminate balances in bond accounts at December 31, 20X1, and credit retained earnings of issuer with realized but unrecorded gain at this point in time, as shown:

Carrying amount of bonds, December 31, 20X0	$110,000	
Face amount of bonds	100,000	
Gain (loss) if bonds acquired at face		$ 10,000
Face amount of bonds	$100,000	
Acquisition price, Dec. 31, 20X0	106,000	
Gain (loss) if bonds issued at face		(6,000)
Net gain (loss) on reacquisition		$ 4,000
Gain recorded in retained earnings as a result of amortization of premium on bonds payable (reduction of interest expense) in 20X1		(1,000)
Loss recorded in retained earnings as a result of amortization of premium on bond investment (reduction of interest income) in 20X1		600
Realized but unrecorded gain, Dec. 31, 20X1		$ 3,600

2327.30 The eliminating entries for 20X2 are:

CW entries—20X2:
Bonds Payable	$100,000	
Premium on Bonds Payable	9,000	
Investment in P Bonds		$105,400
Retained Earnings—P		3,600

To eliminate balance in bond accounts as of January 1, 20X2, and credit retained earnings of issuer with realized but unrecognized gain as of January 1, 20X2.

Interest Income	$ 10,000	
Interest Expense		$ 10,000

To eliminate the contractual interest recorded in 20X2.

Interest Expense	$ 1,000	
Premium on Bonds Payable		$ 1,000

To eliminate the amortization of premium on bonds payable recorded in 20X2.

Investment in P Bonds	$ 600	
Interest Income		$ 600

To eliminate the amortization of premium on bond investment recorded in 20X2.

BSW entries—12/31/X2:

Bonds Payable	$100,000	
Premium on Bonds Payable ($10,000 − $2,000)	8,000	
Investment in P Bonds ($106,000 − $1,200)		$104,800
Retained Earnings—P ($4,000 − $2,000 + $1,200)		3,200

2327.31 Each year, $400 of the gain is being recognized in the accounts because of the amortization of the net premium ($1,000 − $600). Therefore, the amount of *realized but unrecognized* gain declines by $400 each year, as reflected in the decreasing amounts credited to the retained earnings of P each year.

2327.32 If S had been the issuer of the bonds (instead of P) and P had acquired the bonds, the only change in the eliminating entries illustrated would be that the credit to retained earnings would be allocated 80% to P and 20% to S instead of 100% to P. For example, the eliminating entry for a worksheet for a consolidated balance sheet at December 31, 20X2, would be (compare with the comparable entry shown in section **2327.30**):

Bonds Payable	$100,000	
Premium on Bonds Payable	8,000	
Investment in P Bonds		$104,800
Retained Earnings—P (0.80 × $3,200)		2,560
Retained Earnings—S (0.20 × $3,200)		640

2327.33 As mentioned previously, intercompany profits and losses affect the computation of the noncontrolling interest's share of net income only if the subsidiary is the seller of the asset or issuer of the bonds. The types of adjustments to be made to the reported net income of the subsidiary are summarized as follows:

	Computation of Noncontrolling Interest's Share of Sub's Net Income
$ XXX	Reported net income of subsidiary
	Intercompany profit in inventory (where sub is seller):
+ XXX	In beginning inventory
- XXX	In ending inventory
	Fixed assets sold by sub at a gain:
- XXX	Gain on sale (if sale in current year)
+ XXX	Excess depreciation (whether sale in current year or in a prior year)
	Fixed assets sold by sub at a loss:
+ XXX	Loss on sale (if sale in current year)
- XXX	Deficient depreciation (whether sale in current year or in a prior year)
	Intercompany bonds where sub is issuer:
+ XXX	Gain on reacquisition (if in current year)
- XXX	Amortization during current year of premium on bonds payable (by sub) and of discount on bond investment (by parent), whether bonds acquired in current year or in a prior year.
- XXX	Loss on reacquisition (if in current year)
+ XXX	Amortization during current year of discount on bonds payable (by sub) and of premium on bond investment (by parent), whether bonds acquired in current year or in a prior year.
$ XXX	Confirmed net income of subsidiary
MI%	Noncontrolling interest percentage
$ XXX	Noncontrolling interest's share of subsidiary's net income

2328 Miscellaneous Problem Areas

Subsidiary Has Both Preferred and Common Stock

2328.01 A subsidiary may have preferred stock outstanding as well as common stock. Careful consideration must be given to any preferred stock of the subsidiary, even if the parent company does not own any of the preferred shares.

2328.02 **Parent owns none of subsidiary's preferred stock.** Outstanding preferred stock of the subsidiary impacts the determination of the amount of net income of the subsidiary applicable to its common stock. The net income applicable to preferred stock (i.e., its stated dividend preference amount) is first deducted from the subsidiary's net income, with the remainder accruing to common stock.

Net income of subsidiary	$ XXX
Less: Preferred dividend	(XXX)
Net income applicable to common	$ XXX

2328.03 If the preferred stock is outstanding at the time the parent acquires its investment in the common stock of the subsidiary, retained earnings of the subsidiary at that date must be allocated between preferred and common as follows:

Total retained earnings of sub	$ XXX
Less: Amount applicable to preferred	(XXX)
Retained earnings applicable to common	$ XXX

2328.04 The amount of retained earnings determined to be applicable to the common stock then enters into the comparison of the cost of the parent's investment in common stock and the parent's share of the common stockholders' equity.

2328.05 **Parent invests in both preferred and common.** If the parent owns some of the subsidiary's preferred stock as well as common stock, the parent's investment in the preferred stock must be eliminated against the preferred stockholders' equity accounts when consolidated financial statements are prepared.

2328.06 **Example:** On December 31, 20X1, Company P acquired 30% of the outstanding preferred stock for $33,800 and 80% of the outstanding common stock of Company S for $225,000. The stockholders' equity of Company S on that date was as follows:

Preferred stock, 6%, $100 par (1,000 shares)	$100,000
Common stock, $10 par (20,000 shares)	200,000
Retained earnings	80,000
	$380,000

Preferred stock is cumulative; dividends are one year in arrears (6% per year).

2328.07 Retained earnings is allocated between preferred and common as follows:

Total retained earnings	$80,000
Less: RE applicable to preferred:	
Dividends in arrears (6% of $100,000)	(6,000)
RE applicable to common	$74,000

2328.08 The eliminating entries for a consolidated balance sheet at December 31, 20X1, are:

Preferred Stock—S (0.30 × $100,000)	$ 30,000	
Retained Earnings—S (0.30 × $6,000)	1,800	
Additional Paid-in Capital—P (or RE - P)	2,000	
Investment in S Preferred Stock		$ 33,800
Common Stock—S (0.80 × $200,000)	$160,000	
Retained Earnings—S (0.80 × $74,000)	59,200	
Goodwill	5,800	
Investment in S Common Stock		$225,000

Changes in Parent's Ownership Interest

2328.09 Changes in a parent company's ownership interest may occur if (a) the parent buys additional shares or sells shares it already owns or (b) the subsidiary sells additional shares or reacquires some of its outstanding shares. The various situations are depicted in the following illustration where the arrow indicates the possible direction of sale of shares of the subsidiary:

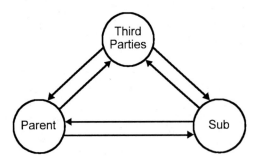

2328.10 **Parent/third-party transactions:** No particular problem arises where the parent purchases shares of the subsidiary from or sells to third parties (outsiders) if the parent-subsidiary relationship holds both before and after the purchase or sale.

2328.11 FASB ASC 810-10-45-23 adopts the economic unit concept to account for the parent's purchase or sale of a controlled subsidiary's stock. If the parent with control of a subsidiary buys or sells shares of stock but retains control, FASB ASC 810-10-45-23 requires that the change in ownership be accounted for as an equity transaction. No gain or loss is recognized. The carrying amount of the noncontrolling interest is adjusted to reflect the change in its ownership interest in the subsidiary. Any difference in the consideration paid or received and the amount by which the noncontrolling interest is adjusted is recognized in equity attributable to the parent. FASB ASC 810-10-55-4C includes the following examples:

Example 1

Subsidiary A has 10,000 shares of common stock outstanding, all of which are owned by its parent, ABC Co. The carrying amount of Subsidiary A's equity is $200,000. ABC Co. sells 2,000 of its shares in Subsidiary A to an unrelated entity for $50,000 in cash, reducing its ownership interest from 100% to 80%. That transaction is accounted for by recognizing a noncontrolling interest in the amount of $40,000 ($200,000 × 20%). The $10,000 excess of the cash received ($50,000) over the adjustment to the carrying amount of the noncontrolling interest ($40,000) is recognized as an increase in additional paid-in capital attributable to ABC Co.

Example 2

Subsidiary A has 10,000 shares of common stock outstanding. Of those shares, 9,000 are owned by its parent, ABC Co., and 1,000 are owned by other shareholders (a noncontrolling interest in Subsidiary A). The carrying amount of Subsidiary A's equity is $300,000. Of that amount, $270,000 is attributable to ABC Co., and $30,000 is a noncontrolling interest in Subsidiary A. Subsidiary A issues 2,000 previously unissued shares to a third party for $120,000 in cash, reducing ABC Co.'s ownership interest in Subsidiary A from 90% to 75% (9,000 shares owned by ABC Co. ÷ 12,000 issued shares).

Even though the percentage of ABC Co.'s ownership interest in Subsidiary A is reduced when Subsidiary A issues shares to the third party, ABC Co.'s investment in Subsidiary A increases to $315,000, calculated as 75% of Subsidiary A's equity of $420,000 ($300,000 + $120,000). Therefore, ABC Co. recognizes a $45,000 increase in its investment in Subsidiary A ($315,000 − $270,000) and a corresponding increase in its additional paid-in capital (that is, the additional paid-in capital attributable to ABC Co.). In addition, the noncontrolling interest is increased to $105,000, calculated as 25% of $420,000.

If the parent is no longer in control of the subsidiary, it would include any resulting gain or loss in consolidated net income. The gain or loss is measured using the fair value of any noncontrolling investment in the subsidiary retained by the parent (FASB ASC 810-10-40-5). The gain or loss is measured as the difference between the following:

a. The aggregate of:

(1) the fair value of any consideration received

(2) the fair value of any retained noncontrolling investment in the former subsidiary at the date the subsidiary is deconsolidated

(3) the carrying amount of any noncontrolling interest in the former subsidiary at the date the subsidiary is deconsolidated

b. The carrying amount of the former subsidiary's assets and liabilities

FASB ASC 810-10-50-1B

The result is that the retained investment is remeasured to fair value on the date control is lost.

2328.12 The parent would record the acquisition of additional shares at cost. It would also compare the portion of the subsidiary's stockholders' equity corresponding to the incremental percentage of shares acquired with the cost of those shares to determine if any goodwill (or other appropriate excess) is associated.

2328.13 The acquisition of additional shares by a company (investor) that previously has been using the cost method to account for the investment will necessitate a retroactive adjustment if the new shares result in the required use of the equity method.

2328.14 **Example:** Company P acquired 10% of the outstanding stock of Company S on January 1, 20X1, for $19,000. The stockholders' equity of S consisted of common stock, $100,000, and retained earnings, $50,000. Company S paid a dividend of $10,000 to its shareholders during the year.

2328.15 The following entries were recorded by Company P during 20X1 under the cost method:

Jan. 1, 20X1:
Investment in S $19,000
   Cash $19,000
To record investment.

May 1, 20X1:
Cash $ 1,000
   Dividend Income (0.10 × $10,000) $ 1,000
To record P's share of dividend of S.

2328.16 Company S reported net income in 20X1 of $30,000. However, no entry was recorded on P's books since Company P is using the cost method.

2328.17 On January 1, 20X2, Company P acquired an additional 70% of the outstanding stock of Company S for $139,000. Company P should record the following entry on January 1, 20X2, to record the acquisition:

Investment in S	$139,000	
Cash		$139,000
To record acquisition of additional 70% of S stock.		

2328.18 FASB ASC 810-10-25-10 requires that the acquiring corporation remeasure its previously held equity interest in the subsidiary at its acquisition-date fair value and recognize the resulting gain or loss in earnings. The acquisition date for this purpose is January 1, 20X2, the date that sufficient stock is acquired to give the acquiring corporation control. The 10% interest must be adjusted to 10% of the company's value. The company's inferred value is $139,000 ÷ .70 (70%), or $198,570 (rounded). Ten percent (10%) of that value is $19,857. The entry to record this gain would be:

Investment in S	$857	
Gain on revaluation of S		$857

Fair value of 10% at acquisition date	$19,857
Investment in S	19,000
Gain on revaluation of S to fair value	$ 857

2328.19 At this point, P Company's "Investment in S" account should be equal to the value of the stock. P Company owns 80% of S. The value of that stock is $158,857 ($198,570 × .80, rounded). The amount in the investment account is:

Jan. 1, 20X1, acquisition	$ 19,000
Jan. 1, 20X2, gain	857
Jan. 1, 20X2, acquisition	139,000
	$158,857

2328.20 Additional computations and eliminating entries are required for the preparation of consolidated financial statements. Goodwill associated with the shares acquired (70%) on January 1, 20X2, would be computed as follows:

Cost of shares acquired Jan. 1, 20X2 (70%)	$139,000
Value of other 30% (($139,000 ÷ .70) – $139,000)	59,570
Total acquisition-date fair value of S Company	$198,570
Less: Net assets at Jan. 1, 20X2	170,000
Goodwill (Jan. 1, 20X2, acquisition)	$ 28,570

2328.21 The eliminating entry for a consolidated balance sheet on January 1, 20X2, after the 70% acquisition, would be:

Common Stock—S	$100,000	
Retained Earnings	70,000	
Goodwill	28,570	
Investment in S		$158,857
Noncontrolling interest in S (20%)		39,713

2328.22 The proof of this entry is:

Jan. 1, 20X1, acquisition	$ 19,000
Jan. 1, 20X2, retroactive adjustment	857
Jan. 1, 20X2, acquisition	139,000
Stock owned by P Company—80%	$158,857
Noncontrolling interest—20%	39,713
Fair value of S Company	$198,570

2328.23 **Parent-subsidiary transactions:** The purchase or sale of shares of the subsidiary between the parent and subsidiary changes the parent's ownership percentage and its equity in the underlying net assets of the subsidiary.

2328.24 **Example:** On December 31, 20X1, Company P owns 60% of the outstanding common stock of Company S; the investment account shows a balance of $114,000. The stockholders' equity of Company S is:

Common stock, $10 par (10,000 shares)	$100,000
Retained earnings	50,000
	$150,000

Book value = $150,000 ÷ 10,000 shares = $15 per share

Eliminating entry 12/31/20X1:

Common stock—S (0.60 × $100,000)	$ 60,000	
Retained earnings—S (0.60 × $50,000)	30,000	
Goodwill	24,000	
Investment in S		$114,000

2328.25 Now assume that on January 1, 20X2, Company S issues 6,000 new shares, all of which are acquired by Company P for $106,000. The stockholders' equity of Company S now is:

Common stock, $10 par (16,000 shares)	$160,000
Capital in excess of par	46,000
Retained earnings	50,000
	$256,000

2328.26 The equity of Company P in the net assets of Company S increased as a result of the transaction as follows:

After transaction:		
Stockholders' equity of S	$256,000	
P's ownership percentage	× .75	
P's equity in net assets of S		$192,000
Before transaction:		
Stockholders' equity of S	$150,000	
P's ownership percentage	× .60	
P's equity in net assets of S		90,000
Increase in P's equity in net assets of S		$102,000

2328.27 The difference between the increase in P's equity in the net assets of S ($102,000) and the cost of the new shares ($106,000) is the amount of additional goodwill ($4,000). The goodwill arose because the new shares were sold at a price in excess of book value. If the sale price had been less than book value, a reduction in existing goodwill would have resulted.

2328.28 The eliminating entry immediately after the January 1, 20X2, transaction would be:

Common Stock—S (0.75 × $160,000)	$120,000	
Capital in Excess of Par—S (0.75 × $46,000)	34,500	
Retained Earnings—S (0.75 × $50,000)	37,500	
Goodwill ($24,000 + $4,000)	28,000	
Investment in S ($114,000 + $106,000)		$220,000

2328.29 Similar computations would have to be made if the parent sold shares it owns back to the subsidiary.

2328.30 **Subsidiary/third-party transactions:** The sale of shares (whether treasury stock or new shares) by the subsidiary to third parties increases the net assets of the subsidiary but decreases the parent's ownership percentage. The decrease in the parent's ownership percentage is analogous to a sale of a portion of the parent's investment; accordingly, the investment account and the amount of any existing goodwill must be adjusted.

2328.31 **Example:** Assume the same facts as in the example presented in sections **2328.24** and **2328.25**, except assume that the subsidiary sold the 6,000 additional shares to third parties instead of to the parent. The situation is summarized as follows:

	Shares O/S	Subsidiary (S) Net Assets	P's Ownership Percentage	P's Equity in Net Assets of S
(Before)	1,000	$150,000	60.0%	$90,000
(After)	1,600	$256,000	37.5%[a]	96,000
				$ 6,000

[a] 6,000/16,000 = 37.5

2328.32 P's equity in the net assets of S increased $6,000. However, the goodwill associated with the shares "sold" by P (i.e., the decline in P's ownership percentage) must also be adjusted. The adjustment would be determined as follows:

Ownership percentage:		
Retained	37.5%	5/8
Sold (60.0% - 37.5%)	22.5%	3/8[a]
Before sale	60.0%	8/8
Goodwill associated with shares sold:		
(3/8 × $24,000)	$9,000	

[a] It is merely coincidental in this case that the fraction representing the shares "sold" when expressed as a percentage (3/8 = 37.5%) is the same as the ownership percentage after the transaction (37.5%).

Increase in P's equity in net assets	$ 6,000
Goodwill associated with shares "sold"	9,000
Net adjustment to investment account	$(3,000)

2328.33 Company P should record the following entries on its own books:

Investment in S	$6,000	
Additional paid-in capital—P		$6,000
To record increase in P's equity in net assets.		
Additional paid-in capital—P	$9,000	
Investment in S		$9,000
Goodwill associated with shares "sold."		

2328.34 The eliminating entry for a consolidated[1] balance sheet at January 1, 20X1, immediately after the transaction would be:

Common Stock—S (0.375 × $160,000)	$60,000	
Capital in Excess of Par—S (0.375 × $46,000)	17,250	
Retained Earnings—S (0.375 × $50,000)	18,750	
Goodwill ($24,000 − $9,000)	15,000	
Investment in S ($114,000 − $3,000)		$111,000

[1] Technically, the ownership percentage of P (37.5%) no longer justifies the preparation of consolidated statements. The percentages used in this and the preceding example allow whole number results, and the candidate can contrast the same set of facts in two types of purchase-sale transactions (parent-subsidiary and subsidiary-third party).

Indirect and Reciprocal Shareholding

2328.35 In all the parent-subsidiary relationships illustrated thus far, the parent had a direct controlling interest. In some situations, the parent may have an indirect controlling interest, as shown in the following illustration:

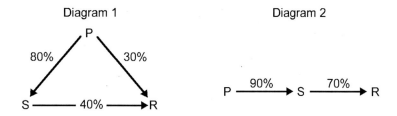

2328.36 In each diagram, P has a direct controlling interest in S and an indirect controlling interest in R. The calculation of consolidated net income must take into account the various holdings illustrated. For example, assume that P, S, and R report net income from their own operations (i.e., excluding their equity in the earnings of any subsidiaries or other investees) as follows:

P	$ 50,000
S	40,000
R	100,000

2328.37 Consolidated net income in Diagram 1 would be determined as follows:

P's income from own operations		$ 50,000
P's equity in earnings of R from shares owned directly by P		
(0.30 × $100,000)		30,000
P's equity in earnings of S:		
S's income from own operation	$40,000	
S's equity in earnings of R: (0.40 × $100,000)	40,000	
S's net income	$80,000	
P's ownership percentage of S	× .80	64,000
Consolidated net income		$144,000

2328.38 Consolidated net income under Diagram 2 is:

P's income from own operations		$ 50,000
P's equity in earnings of S:		
S's income from own operations	$ 40,000	
S's equity in earnings of R: (0.70 × $100,000)	70,000	
S's net income	$110,000	
P's ownership percentage of S	× .90	99,000
Consolidated net income		$149,000

2328.39 A parent company also may have a reciprocal relationship with a subsidiary, illustrated as follows:

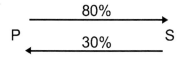

2328.40 Assume that P and S each report net income of $100,000 from their own operations. The traditional algebraic method of calculating consolidated net income is as follows:

- C = Consolidated net income
- P = Net income of P on an equity basis
- S = Net income of S on an equity basis
- C = 0.80P
- P = $100,000 + 0.80S
- ST = $100,000 + 0.30P

Solving the last two simultaneous equations gives:

P = $236,842

Therefore,

C = 0.80($236,842)
C = $189,474

2328.41 An alternate approach is to view the P shares held by S as treasury stock from a consolidation standpoint. Accordingly, consolidated net income is computed as follows:

- C = Net income of P from its own operations + 80% of net income of S from its own operations
- C = $100,000 + 0.80($100,000)
- C = $180,000

2328.42 Investment Elimination for a Pooling of Interests

Assume that P Company issued 10,000 shares of its own $5 par stock in exchange for 100% of the outstanding stock of S Company on January 1, 20X1, in a combination accounted for as a pooling of interests. P and S both continue to exist as separate legal entities. The stockholders' equity of S Company on January 1, 20X1, is as follows:

Common stock, $10 par	$100,000
Retained earnings	40,000
	$140,000

2328.43 P Company recorded the following entry on its own books on January 1, 20X1:

Investment in S (at book value)	$140,000	
Common Stock—P (10,000 × $5)		$50,000
Retained Earnings—P (from S)		40,000
Capital in Excess of Par—P		50,000

2328.44 The eliminating entry for a consolidated balance sheet on January 1, 20X1, would be:

Common Stock—S	$100,000	
Retained Earnings—S	40,000	
Investment in S		$140,000

2328.45 Assuming that S Company reported net income of $44,000 and declared no dividends in 20X1, the eliminating entries for a comprehensive worksheet for 20X1 would be:

Sub Income	$ 44,000	
Investment in Sub		$ 44,000
Common Stock—S	$100,000	
Retained Earnings—S (Jan. 1)	40,000	
Investment in S		$140,000

2328.46 The eliminating entries for a consolidated balance sheet at December 31, 20X1, would be:

Common Stock—S	$100,000	
Retained Earnings—S	84,000	
Investment in S		$184,000

Consolidation of Variable Interest Entities

2328.47 Under U.S. GAAP, consolidated financial statements are required when one of the entities in the group directly or indirectly has a controlling *financial* interest in the other entities. FASB ASC 810-10-15-8 specifies that the usual condition for a controlling financial interest is ownership of a majority *voting* interest. However, the FASB is concerned that strict application of the majority voting interest rule could result in a particular entity not being consolidated because the controlling entity does not own more than 50% of the voting interests but, nevertheless, maintains a controlling financial interest through arrangements that do not involve voting interests. That concern led the FASB to issue FASB ASC 810-10-05-8, in which it specifies the conditions under which an entity should consolidate another entity (the variable interest entity) even though it does not own a majority of the voting interests.

2328.48 An entity is known as a *variable interest entity* and is subject to consolidation under FASB ASC 810-10-05-8 if, by design, either of the following conditions (a. or b.) exists:

    a. The total equity investment at risk is not sufficient to permit the entity to finance its activities without additional subordinated financial support from other parties. For this purpose, the total equity investment at risk:

        (1) Includes only equity investments in the entity that might participate significantly in profits and losses even if those investments do not carry voting rights.

        (2) Does not include equity interests that the entity issued in exchange for subordinated interests in other variable interest entities.

        (3) Does not include amounts provided to the equity investor directly or indirectly by the entity or by other parties involved with the entity unless the provider is a parent, subsidiary, or affiliate of the investor that is required to be included in the same set of consolidated financial statements as the investor.

        (4) Does not include amounts financed for the equity investor unless that party is a parent, subsidiary, or affiliate of the investor that is required to be included in the same set of consolidated financial statements as the investor.

    b. As a group the holders of the equity investment at risk lack any one or more of the following three characteristics of a controlling financial interest:

        (1) The power, through voting rights or similar rights, to direct the activities of an entity that most significantly impact the entity's economic performance.

        (2) The obligation to absorb the expected losses if the entity if they occur.

        (3) The right to receive the expected residual returns of the entity if they occur.

    c. The reporting entity with a variable interest or interests that provide the reporting entity with a controlling financial interest in a variable interest entity (VIE) will have both of the following characteristics (FASB ASC 810-10-05-8A):

        (1) The power to direct the activities of a VIE that most significantly impact the VIE's economic performance

        (2) The obligation to absorb losses of the VIE that could potentially be significant to the VIE or the right to receive benefits from the VIE that could potentially be significant to the VIE

2328.49 Equity investments in an entity are interests that are required to be reported as equity in that entity's financial statements. Thus, investments in an entity's common stock are equity investments, whereas investments in its bonds are not.

2328.50 The fundamental notion is that if neither of the conditions in section **2328.48** is met, the entity is not under FASB ASC 810-10-05-8 and thus the consolidation issue would be based on the majority voting interest requirement of FASB ASC 810-10-15-8. However, if either of the conditions in **2328.48** is met, the entity is a variable interest entity and is subject to the consolidation rules of FASB ASC 810-10-05-8. Thus, the entity might be required to be included in another entity's consolidated financial statements because that entity has a controlling *financial* interest even though it does not have a controlling *voting* interest.

2328.51 The FASB provided a quantitative guideline for purposes of applying the "equity investment at risk" condition described in section **2328.48(a)** by specifying that generally an equity investment of less than 10% of an entity's total assets is not sufficient to permit the entity to finance its activities without subordinated support in addition to the equity investment. Thus, the entity would be subject to the consolidation rules of FASB ASC 810-10-05-8 unless the equity investment can be demonstrated to be sufficient in at least one of the following ways identified in FASB ASC 810-10-25-45:

   a. The entity has demonstrated that it can finance its activities without additional subordinated financial support.

   b. The entity has at least as much equity invested as other entities that hold only similar assets of similar quality in similar amounts and operated with no additional subordinated financial support.

   c. The amount of equity invested in the entity exceeds the estimate of the entity's expected losses based on reasonable quantitative evidence.

2328.52 However, the FASB points out that meeting the "10% guideline" may not be sufficient if the entity engages in high-risk activities, hold high-risk assets, or has exposure to risks that are not reflected in the reported amounts of the entity's assets or liabilities. In these cases, the entity has the burden of determining, without regard to the 10% guideline, if its equity investment is sufficient to permit it to finance its activities without subordinated financial support in addition to the equity investment.

2328.53 FASB ASC 810-10-65-2 eliminates the quantitative approach previously required for determining the primary beneficiary of a variable interest entity that was based on determining which enterprise absorbs the majority of the entity's expected losses, receives a majority of the entity's expected residual returns, or both.

2328.54 FASB ASC 810-10-65-2 requires an analysis to determine whether the enterprise's variable interest or interests give it a controlling financial interest in a variable interest entity. This analysis identifies the primary beneficiary (the entity that consolidates a variable interest entity) of a variable interest as the enterprise that has both of the following characteristics:

   a. The power to direct the activities of a variable interest entity that most significantly impact the entity's economic performance (FASB ASC 810-10-05-8A)

   b. The obligation to absorb losses of the entity that could be significant to the variable interest entity or the right to receive benefits from the entity that could potentially be significant to the variable interest entity

Additionally, an enterprise is required to assess whether it has an implicit financial responsibility to ensure that a variable interest entity operates as designed when determining whether it has the power to direct the activities of the variable interest entity that most significantly impact the entity's economic performance.

2330 Contingencies, Commitments, and Guarantees (Provisions)

Contingencies

2330.01 A *contingency* is an existing condition, situation, or set of circumstances involving uncertainty as to possible gain (*gain contingency*) or loss (*loss contingency*) to an enterprise that will ultimately be resolved when one or more future events occur or fail to occur.

2330.02 Examples of loss contingencies include the following:

    a. Collectibility of receivables

    b. Obligations related to product warranties

    c. Risk of loss due to damage of enterprise property due to fire, explosion, or other hazard

    d. Threat of expropriation of assets

    e. Pending or threatened litigation

    f. Guarantees of indebtedness of others

2330.03 Proper accounting for *loss contingencies* requires an assessment of the probability that a future event or events will confirm a loss or asset impairment or the incurrence of a liability as of the date of the financial statements (FASB ASC 450-20-25-2). Three ranges of probability exist:

1. **Probable:** The future events are likely to occur.
2. **Reasonably possible:** The chance of the future events is more than remote but less than likely.
3. **Remote:** The chance of the future events occurring is slight.

The assessment of the probability of occurrence must be made before the proper accounting and disclosure standards can be determined.

2330.04 Accounting and disclosure standards for contingencies in each of the three ranges of probability are described in the following table:

Probability of Occurrence	Accrual Requirement	Disclosure Requirements
Probable	Accrue if reasonably estimable (if not reasonably estimable, disclose only)	Nature of accrual and amount, if necessary, to make financial statements not misleading
Reasonably possible	None	Nature of contingency and an estimate of the loss or range of loss (or statement that no estimate is possible)
Remote	None	None (except that guarantees, normally with a right to proceed against an outside party, must be disclosed)

2330.05 Additional important considerations in accounting for loss contingencies are as follows:

    a. Losses that occur or are expected to have occurred after the balance sheet date may require disclosure to keep the financial statements from being misleading. In such cases, disclosure includes the nature of the loss or loss contingency, an estimate of the amount or range of loss, or a statement that such an estimate cannot be made.

    b. Accruals for general risk contingencies do not meet the conditions for accrual and should not be made.

    c. Appropriations of retained earnings for loss contingencies are acceptable provided they are shown within stockholders' equity and are clearly identified as appropriations of retained earnings. Appropriations or their elimination should not affect net income.

    d. The absence of insurance does not mean that an asset has been impaired or a liability incurred. The lack of insurance does not meet the conditions for accrual of a loss, and no accrual should be made until such time that a diminution of value takes place. Disclosure of the lack of insurance is not required but may be appropriate based on the specific circumstances.

2330.06 A prerequisite for accrual of a loss contingency is that the amount can be reasonably estimated. This does not require, however, that a single amount can be estimated. If a range of loss can be estimated, the best estimate within the range is accrued. If no amount within the range is a better estimate than any other amount, the minimum amount in the range is accrued and the estimated range of potential loss disclosed (FASB ASC 450-20-30-1).

2330.07 **Gain contingencies** are usually not reflected in the accounts, since to do so would be to recognize revenue prior to its realization. Adequate disclosure is made of gain contingencies but care must be taken to avoid misleading implications.

2330.08 **IFRS:** Under GAAP, provisions (estimated liabilities) are measured by reference to low end of range of amounts needed to settle, sometimes but not always discounted to present value. Under IFRS, provisions are measured by reference to best estimate to settle, discounted to present value.

2330.09 **IFRS:** Under GAAP, contingent gains are not recognized. IFRS provides for some recognition of contingent gains.

Guarantor's Accounting and Disclosure Requirements for Guarantees

2330.10 The FASB issued FASB ASC 460-10-10-1 because there was a diversity in practice about what disclosures were required to be made by the issuers of guarantees (guarantors) and about the need for the guarantor to recognize an initial liability for its obligations under the guarantee.

2330.11 The accounting and disclosure requirements specified in FASB ASC 460-10-15-4 apply to guarantee contracts that have any of the following characteristics:

    a. Contracts that contingently require the guarantor to make payments (either in cash, financial instruments, other assets, shares of stock, or provision of services) to the guaranteed party based on changes in an underlying (as defined in FASB ASC 815-10-20, a specified interest rate, security price, commodity price, foreign exchange rate, index of prices or rates, or other variable) that is related to an asset, a liability or an equity security of the guaranteed party. Examples of such contracts are:

        (1) A financial standby letter of credit of a financial institution to guarantee payment of a specified financial obligation

(2) A market value guarantee on either a financial asset or a nonfinancial asset owned by the guaranteed party

(3) A guarantee of the market price of the common stock of the guaranteed party

(4) A guarantee of the collection of the scheduled cash flows from individual financial assets held by a special-purpose entity

    b. Contracts that contingently require the guarantor to make payments to the guaranteed party based on another entity's failure to perform under an obligating agreement (performance agreement)

    c. Indemnification agreements that contingently require the guarantor to make payments to the guaranteed party based on changes in an underlying that is related to an asset, a liability, or an equity security of the indemnified party (such as an adverse judgment in a lawsuit or the imposition of additional taxes due to a change in the tax law)

    d. Indirect guarantees of the indebtedness of others. (An indirect guarantee of the indebtedness of another arises under an agreement that obligates one entity to transfer funds to a second entity upon the occurrence of specified events, under conditions whereby (a) the funds become legally available to creditors of the second entity and (b) those creditors may enforce the second entity's claims against the first entity under the agreement. Examples include agreements to advance funds if a second entity's net income or working capital falls below a specified minimum.)

2330.12 Commercial letters of credit and other loan commitments are not included in the scope of FASB ASC 460-10-55-16.

2330.13 FASB ASC 460-10-15-7 does not apply to the following guarantee contracts:

    a. A guarantee of an indemnification that is excluded from the scope of FASB ASC 450-20-15-2

    b. A lessee's guarantee of the residual value of the leased property if the lessee accounts for the lease as a capital lease

    c. A contract that is accounted for as contingent rent under FASB ASC 840-30

    d. A guarantee that is issued by either an insurance company or a reinsurance company that is appropriately accounted for under other FASB codification (such as FASB ASC 944-10 or FASB ASC 944-310-05-1) specifically related to those types of entities

    e. A contract that constitutes a vendor rebate (by the guarantor) based on sales (units or dollars) of the guaranteed party

    f. A guarantee whose existence prevents the guarantor from being able to either account for a transaction as the sale of an asset that is related to the guarantee's underlying or recognize in earnings the profit from that sale transaction

2330.14 The following types of guarantees are subject to the disclosure requirements of FASB ASC 460-10 but are excluded from its recognition and measurement requirements:

    a. A guarantee that is accounted for as a derivative instrument

    b. A guarantee for which the underlying is related to the performance of nonfinancial assets that are owned by the guaranteed party (e.g., product warranties issued by the guarantor)

    c. A guarantee issued in a business combination that represents contingent consideration

    d. A guarantee for which the guarantor's obligation would be reported as an equity item rather than as a liability

e. A guarantee by an original lessee that has become secondarily liable under a new lease that relieved the original lessee from being the primary obligor under the original lease

f. A guarantee issued either between parents and their subsidiaries or between corporations under common control

g. A parent's guarantee of its subsidiary's debt to a third party

h. A subsidiary's guarantee of the debt owed to a third party by either its parent or another subsidiary of that parent

Recognition and Measurement of the Liability for a Guarantor's Obligations

2330.15 A guarantee obligates the guarantor in two respects, a noncontingent aspect and a contingent aspect. The noncontingent aspect is that related to the guarantor's undertaking an obligation to stand ready to perform over the term of the guarantee in the event that the specified triggering events or conditions occur. The contingent aspect relates to the guarantor's contingent obligation to make future payments if those triggering events or conditions occur.

2330.16 FASB ASC 460-10-25-3 specifies that because of the noncontingent aspect of the guarantee, at the inception of a guarantee, the guarantor should recognize a liability for that guarantee even though it is not probable that payments will be required under that guarantee. (FASB ASC 450-25 generally requires for other types of contingent liabilities that a liability be recognized only if the triggering event is probable.) The liability should be measured at the fair value of the guarantee at its inception.

2330.17 It is possible that at the inception of a guarantee, the guarantor is required to recognize a liability under FASB ASC 450-20-25 for the related contingent loss (the contingent aspect of the guarantee, as defined in section **2330.06** above). In that case, the liability to be initially recognized related to the guarantee should be the greater of (a) the fair value of the guarantee at its inception or (b) the contingent liability required by FASB ASC 450-20-30. Normally, (b) will be less than (a).

2330.18 If the guarantor is required to recognize a liability at the inception of a guarantee, the offsetting account debited (the liability would be credited) depends on the circumstances in which the guarantee was issued. For example, if the guarantee were issued in conjunction with the sale of assets (e.g., inventory or a plant asset), the overall proceeds would be allocated between the consideration being remitted to the guarantor for issuing the guarantee and the proceeds from the sale.

2330.19 FASB ASC 460-10-35-1 does not describe in detail how the guarantor's liability under a guarantee should be measured subsequent to its initial recognition. However, it does indicate that if the liability is measured initially at its fair value (item (a) in section **2330.08** above), the liability should be reduced by a credit to earnings as the guarantor is released from risk under the guarantee.

Guarantor's Required Disclosures

2330.20 A guarantor must disclose the following information about each guarantee, or each group of similar guarantees, even if the likelihood of the guarantor's having to make any payments is remote:

a. Nature of the guarantee, including the term of the guarantee, how it arose, and the events or circumstances that would require the guarantor to perform under the guarantee.

b. Maximum potential amount of future payments (undiscounted) the guarantor could be required to make under the guarantee.

c. The current carrying amount of the liability.

       d. The nature of (1) any recourse provisions that would enable the guarantor to recover from third parties any of the amounts paid under the guarantee and (2) any assets held either as collateral or by third parties that, upon the occurrence of any triggering event or condition under the guarantee, the guarantor can obtain and liquidate to recover all of a portion of the amounts paid under the guarantee.

2330.21   **IFRS:** The issuer of a financial guarantee would account for it initially at fair value under IAS 39, and subsequently at the higher of that amount initially recognized less cumulative amortization recognized in accordance with IAS 18 or the amount determined in accordance with IAS 37. Guarantees based on an underlying price or index are derivatives within the scope of IAS 39.

2335 Earnings per Share

Fundamental Earnings-per-Share Concepts

2335.01   Earnings per share (EPS) is a comparison of the earnings applicable to common stock with the number of shares of common stock of that enterprise. The concept relates only to common stock and should be thought of as "earnings per common share."

2335.02   Assuming that there is no preferred stock outstanding, the fundamental EPS computation is:

$$EPS = \frac{\text{Net income}}{\text{Weighted-average common shares outstanding}}$$

2335.03   If the enterprise has preferred stock outstanding, the fundamental EPS computation is:

$$EPS = \frac{\text{Net income} - \text{Preferred dividends}}{\text{Weighted-average common shares outstanding}}$$

2335.04   All EPS computations involve the division of a dollar amount of earnings (earnings applicable to common stock) by a number of common shares. The resulting fraction or index represents the pro rata share of earnings (the numerator) allocated to each share of common stock (the denominator).

2335.05   Conceptually, earnings per share is a very simple notion. There are, however, securities that, because of their conversion feature (e.g., convertible preferred, convertible debt), right to acquire common stock (e.g., stock options, stock warrants), or capability of sharing in earnings in a manner similar to common stock (e.g., contingent issuance of common shares in conjunction with a business combination), create the potential for earnings per share to be less than if it is based solely on the number of outstanding shares of common stock. The existence of these other *potential* common shares makes it important to show their possible dilutive effect on earnings per share.

2335.06   The objective is to show (a) basic EPS—an earnings per share based only on the *actual* outstanding common stock and (b) diluted EPS—an earnings per share after giving consideration to these *potential* common shares. In the latter case, the earnings per share calculation takes into consideration the impact that the assumed conversion or exercise of the securities that constitute potential common stock would have on both the numerator earnings and the denominator shares. All earnings-per-share computations are based on a weighted-average number of common shares outstanding or assumed to be outstanding.

2335.07 Earnings per share (EPS) must be presented on the face of the income statement of publicly held enterprises as follows:

Type of Capital Structure	EPS Presentation
SIMPLE (only common stock outstanding, with no potential common stock)	BASIC EPS (based on weighted-average number of actual common shares outstanding)
COMPLEX (common stock outstanding and one or more types of potential common stock)	DUAL EPS: BASIC EPS (based on weighted-average number of actual common shares outstanding during the period) DILUTED EPS (based on weighted-average number of actual common shares outstanding during the period plus the weighted-average number of common shares that would result from the assumed conversion or exercise of all dilutive potential common stock)

2335.08 Because simple capital structures include no potential common stock, earnings per share is computed based only on the weighted-average number of common shares outstanding during the period. Complex capital structures, on the other hand, include the potential for dilution, and a dual presentation of EPS is required. Basic EPS is based on the weighted-average number of actual common shares outstanding during the period. Diluted EPS is based on the weighted-average number of actual common shares outstanding plus the weighted-average number of common shares that would result from the assumed conversion or exercise of all dilutive potential common stock.

2335.09 In certain circumstances, potential common stock may actually increase rather than decrease EPS. In that case, the potential common stock is said to be antidilutive. Since the objective of the dual presentation of EPS is to show the potential dilution of EPS by the assumed conversion or exercise of potential common stock, EPS calculations should include only those potential common shares whose inclusion would *decrease* EPS (i.e., those that are dilutive).

2335.10 Several definitions are important in an understanding of the dual presentation of EPS for enterprises with a complex capital structure.

   a. **Dilution (dilutive):** A reduction in EPS resulting from the assumption that convertible securities were converted, that options or warrants were exercised, or that other shares were issued on the satisfaction of certain conditions (FASB ASC 260-10-20).

   b. **Antidilution (antidilutive):** An increase in earnings-per-share amounts or a decrease in loss-per-share amounts (FASB ASC 260-10-20).

   c. **Potential common stock (PCS):** A security or other contract that may entitle its holder to obtain common stock during the reporting period or after the end of the reporting period (FASB ASC 260-10-20).

   d. **Weighted-average common shares (WACS):** The number of shares determined by relating (a) the portion of time within a reporting period that common shares have been outstanding to (b) the total time in that period (FASB ASC 260-10-20). In computing WACS, retroactive application is given to stock splits, stock dividends, and shares of common stock issued in a business combination accounted for as a pooling of interests (i.e., they are treated as if they were outstanding for all of any periods presented).

   e. **Basic EPS:** The amount of earnings for the period available to each share of common stock outstanding during the reporting period (FASB ASC 260-10-20).

        f. Diluted EPS: The amount of earnings for the period available to each share of common stock outstanding during the reporting period and to each share that would have been outstanding assuming the issuance of common shares for all dilutive potential common shares outstanding during the reporting period (FASB ASC 260-10-20).

2335.11 The most common types of potential common stock are convertible securities, stock options and warrants, and other contingent issuances (i.e., arrangements whereby the enterprise is required to issue common stock on the satisfaction of certain conditions). Each potential common stock must be evaluated to determine if it is dilutive.

EPS Computational Guidelines

2335.12 The basic EPS and diluted EPS computations can be generalized as follows:

$$\text{Basic EPS} = \frac{\text{Net income - Dividends on preferred stock}}{\text{WACS}}$$

$$\text{Diluted EPS} = \frac{\text{Net income - Dividends on preferred stock + PCS adjustments}}{\text{WACS + WPCS}}$$

WACS is the weighted-average number of **actual** common shares outstanding. WPCS is the weighted-average number of common shares that would result from the assumed conversion or exercise of dilutive **potential** common shares outstanding.

Preferred Stock Dividends

2335.13 In computing EPS, dividends on preferred stock are subtracted from net income for all EPS computations for which the preferred stock is assumed to be outstanding. If the preferred stock is **cumulative,** the amount to be deducted is the total dividend for the period whether it is declared or not. If the preferred stock is **noncumulative,** the amount to be deducted is the amount actually declared during the current period. This adjustment (deduction) is made to convert net income to the amount of earnings applicable to common stock only.

2335.14 In making the EPS computations for any given period, dividends in arrears are ignored. The preferred dividends applicable to those prior periods (i.e., the dividends in arrears with respect to the current period) should have been taken into consideration for the EPS computations for those prior periods.

2335.15 If there are preferred dividends and a net loss occurs, the preferred dividends are added to the net loss for purposes of computing the loss per share.

2335.16 Treasury Stock Method (for Stock Options and Warrants) - Stock options and warrants outstanding (whether or not presently exercisable) should be included in EPS calculations unless they are antidilutive.

2335.17 The dilutive effect of stock options and warrants is computed by the treasury stock method. This method is based on the assumption that the options or warrants are exercised at the beginning of the period (or date of issuance if later) and the proceeds from the exercise used to purchase outstanding common stock that would then become treasury stock. (Hence, the name "treasury-stock" method.) The dilutive effect is the net increase in outstanding shares from the assumed sale of the shares (arising from the exercise of the options or warrants) and the reacquisition of outstanding shares with the proceeds from the exercise of the options or warrants.

2335.18 If the average market price for the period (e.g., for the year) of the enterprise's common stock exceeds the exercise price of the options or warrants, the proceeds from the assumed exercise are not sufficient to buy back as many shares as were issued on the assumed exercise of the options or warrants. The net result is an increase in the number of shares outstanding. Assuming a net income (as opposed to a net loss), this increase in the number of shares outstanding would reduce EPS and, thus, the options or warrants would be dilutive for EPS purposes.

2335.19 If the average market price of the enterprise's common stock is less than the exercise price of the options or warrants, the proceeds from the assumed exercise are sufficient to buy back more shares than those issued on the assumed exercise of the options or warrants. The net result would be a decrease in the number of shares outstanding. Since a decrease in the number of shares assumed outstanding (the denominator shares) would cause EPS to increase, the options or warrants would be antidilutive. In that case, one would not assume the exercise of the options or warrants in calculating EPS.

2335.20 In summary, options or warrants are assumed exercised only if the average market price of the stock exceeds the exercise price of the options or warrants.

2335.21 **Example:** An enterprise has outstanding 10,000 options to acquire common stock at $20 and the average market price of the stock for the period is $25.

1. Shares assumed issued on exercise of the options
(Proceeds = 10,000 × $20 exercise price = $200,000)   10,000
2. Shares assumed reacquired with proceeds:
$200,000 ÷ $25 average market price   8,000
3. Incremental denominator shares   2,000

2335.22 Alternatively, the incremental denominator shares could be computed as follows:

$$\text{Incremental shares} = \frac{\text{Market price - Exercise price}}{\text{Market price}} \times \text{Number of options}$$

$$= \frac{\$25 - \$20}{\$25} \times 10,000$$

$$= 2,000 \text{ shares}$$

2335.23 Assuming net income of $100,000 and WACS of 50,000, basic EPS and diluted EPS are computed as follows:

$$\text{Basic EPS} = \frac{\$100,000}{50,000 \text{ shares}} = \frac{\$100,000}{50,000 \text{ shares}} = \$2.00$$

$$\text{Diluted EPS} = \frac{\$100,000}{50,000 + 2,000} = \frac{\$100,000}{50,000 + 2,000} = \$1.92$$

"If Converted" Method (for Convertible Securities)

2335.24 The "if converted" method assumes that convertible securities are converted into common stock for purposes of computing EPS. It requires that the numerator in the basic EPS computation be adjusted for the interest savings (net of the related tax effect) or the dividend savings that would be experienced if a convertible security is assumed to be converted into common stock for purposes of the diluted EPS computation. In other words, if one assumes that a convertible security is converted, it would be inconsistent to assume that interest or dividends would be paid on that security after it is assumed to be converted. Therefore, the numerator earnings must be adjusted for the effect that the assumed conversion of the security would have on the amount of interest or dividends.

2335.25 **Example:** A $200,000, 10% bond issue is convertible into 8,000 shares of common stock. Assuming net income of $100,000, WACS of 50,000, and a tax rate of 40%, basic EPS and diluted EPS are computed as follows:

$$\text{Basic EPS} = \frac{\text{Net income}}{\text{WACS}}$$

$$\text{Basic EPS} = \frac{\$100,000}{50,000 \text{ shares}} = \$2.00$$

$$\text{Diluted EPS} = \frac{\text{Net income + Interest (net of tax)}}{\text{WACS + Incremental common shares from assumed conversion of bonds}}$$

$$\text{Diluted EPS} = \frac{\$100,000 + \$12,000^a}{50,000 + 8,000^b} = \$1.93$$

^{a}Interest savings, after tax ($200,000 × 0.10) × (1-0.40 tax rate) = $12,000
^{b}Incremental common shares resulting from assumed conversion of bonds: 8,000

Computation of Weighted Average

2335.26 Both basic EPS and diluted EPS computations are based on a weighted-average shares concept. Under this concept, the computation of the denominator shares takes into consideration the portion of the period that the common shares were outstanding or assumed to be outstanding for purposes of EPS computations. To illustrate, assume that an enterprise had common stock outstanding as shown:

01/01/X1—15,000 common shares outstanding
05/01/X1—9,000 common shares issued
08/01/X1—6,000 outstanding common shares reacquired as treasury stock
WACS for 20X1:

15,000 × 4/12 =	5,000	(a total of 15,000 shares for 4 months)
24,000 × 3/12 =	6,000	(a total of 24,000 shares for 3 months)
18,000 × 5/12 =	7,500	(a total of 18,000 shares for 5 months)
	18,500	

2335.27 In like manner, if a potential common stock is outstanding for only part of a period for which EPS is computed, the computation of the number of common shares that would result from the assumed conversion or exercise of the potential common stock would be based on the portion of the period that the potential common stock was actually outstanding.

2335.28 **Example:** A $100,000, 6% bond issue was sold on April 1, 20X1, convertible into 10,000 shares of common stock. Assuming that net income is $200,000, WACS is 100,000, and the effective tax rate is 40%, earnings per share is as follows:

$$\text{Basic EPS} = \frac{\text{Net Income}}{\text{WACS}} = \frac{\$200,000}{100,000 \text{ shares}} = \$2.00$$

$$\text{Diluted EPS} = \frac{\text{Net Income} + \text{Interest (net of tax)}}{\text{WACS} + \text{WPCS}} = \frac{\$200,000 + \$2,700^a}{100,000 + 7,500^b} = \$1.89$$

^{a}[$100,000 × 0.06 × (1 - 0.40)] × 9/12 = $2,700
^{b}10,000 shares × 9/12 = 7,500 shares

2335.29 As the example illustrates, the computation of common shares resulting from the assumed conversion of the bonds takes into consideration that the bonds were not outstanding during the entire period. The incremental shares of common stock that would result from the assumed conversion of the bonds are weighted for the portion of the year (9/12) the bonds were outstanding. The numerator adjustment for the interest is similarly weighted for the portion of the year the bonds were outstanding.

Retroactive Application of Stock Splits and Stock Dividends

2335.30 Stock splits and stock dividends are treated retroactively in the computation of EPS, both for the current period and any prior periods presented for comparative purposes.

2335.31 **Example:** In 20X1, net income was $560,000 and WACS was 100,000 shares, giving an EPS figure of $5.60. In 20X2, a 10% stock dividend is issued on August 31 and net income for the year is $725,000. EPS for 20X2 is computed as follows:

$$\text{EPS} = \frac{\$725,000}{100,000 + 0.10(100,000)} = \$6.59$$

The 10,000 incremental shares issued as a stock dividend are treated as if they were outstanding for the entire year, even though the stock dividend was issued on August 31 and the resulting 10,000 shares were outstanding for only part of the year.

2335.32 EPS computations treat stock dividends and stock splits as if they occurred at the beginning of the earliest year presented in the current financial report.

2335.33 The EPS of $5.60 for 20X1 must be restated (in the 20X2 financial statements) to give effect to the 10% stock dividend declared in 20X2. The comparative years' presentation in the 20X2 financial statements would show EPS for the two years as follows:

	20X1	20X2
Earnings per share	$5.09	$6.59

2335.34 The $5.09 is determined by dividing the 20X1 net income of $560,000 by the equivalent share that would have been outstanding if the stock dividend were applied retroactively to the beginning of 20X1 ($560,000 ÷ 110,000 = $5.09).

2335.35 The retroactive application of a stock dividend applies to all shares issued or assumed to be issued prior to the stock dividend or split.

2335.36 **Example:** Assume the following events in 20X1 related to common stock:

01/01/X1 15,000 shares outstanding
05/01/X1 9,000 shares issued for cash
06/01/X1 4,800 shares issued as a 20% stock dividend (20% of 24,000 shares)
08/01/X1 6,000 outstanding shares reacquired as treasury stock

Dates Outstanding	Shares Outstanding	Restatement for 20% Stock Dividend	Fraction of Year	Weighted-Average Shares
Jan. 1 - May 1	15,000	1.20	4/12	6,000
May 1 - June 1	24,000	1.20	1/12	2,400
June 1 - Aug. 1	28,800		2/12	4,800
Aug. 1 - Dec. 31	22,800		5/12	9,500
			12/12	22,700

2335.37 Note that the shares outstanding prior to June 1 are retroactively restated to reflect the effect of the 20% stock dividend on June 1. Of course, the shares outstanding after June 1 already reflect the effect of the 20% stock dividend.

2335.38 If a stock dividend or split occurs after the end of the year but before the financial statements are issued, the weighted-average number of shares outstanding for the current year and any prior years presented in the current period in comparative form must be restated. For example, if in the example presented in section **2335.36**, a 2:1 stock split were issued on January 8, 20X2 (prior to the issuance of the 20X1 financial statements), the weighted-average common shares for 20X1 would be 45,400 (i.e., 22,700 × 2).

Inclusion of Only Dilutive Potential Common Stock

2335.39 The computation of diluted EPS includes only those potential common shares (PCS) that are dilutive. A convenient way to determine if all potential common shares are dilutive is to first calculate the per-share effect of each PCS and then include each PCS in the calculation of diluted EPS by starting with the PCS with the lowest per-share effect and continuing as long as the next lowest per-share effect is lower than the previously calculated diluted EPS. The per-share effect of a PCS is the ratio of (a) the change in the numerator earnings resulting from the assumed exercise or conversion of the PCS to (b) the change in the denominator shares resulting from the assumed exercise or conversion of that PCS.

2335.40 **Example:** In 20X1, Alpha Company reported net income of $200,000 and had 20,000 shares of common stock during the entire year. Alpha also had outstanding during all of 20X1 the following convertible securities:

a. Convertible preferred stock, 6%, $100 par, 1,000 shares, each share convertible into 15 shares of common stock

   b. Convertible bonds, 15%, $100,000 face amount, each $1,000 bond convertible into 10 shares of common stock

   Assume a tax rate of 40%.

2335.41 Basic EPS is:

$$\text{BEPS} = \frac{\text{Net Income}}{\text{WACS}} = \frac{\$200{,}000}{20{,}000} = \$10.00$$

2335.42 The per-share effect of each of the convertible securities is as follows:

Convertible preferred

$$\text{Per-Share Effect} = \frac{\text{Dividends}}{\text{Incremental Shares}} = \frac{\$6{,}000^a}{15{,}000 \text{ shares}^b} = \$0.40$$

^{a} Dividends = $100,000 x 0.06 = $6,000
^{b} Incremental shares = 1,000 preferred shares x 15 common shares per preferred share
= 15,000 common shares

Convertible bonds

$$\text{Per-Share Effect} = \frac{\text{Interest}(net\text{-}of\text{-}tax)}{\text{Incremental Shares}} = \frac{\$9{,}000^a}{1{,}000 \text{ shares}^b} = \$9.00$$

^{a} Interest = $100,000 x 0.15 x (1 – 0.40 tax rate) = $9,000
^{b} Incremental shares = $100,000 total face of bonds ÷ $1,000 face per bond = 100 bonds
= 100 bonds x 10 shares of common per $1,000 bond = 1,000 common shares

2335.43 Since the convertible preferred stock has the lowest per-share effect ($.40), it is the most dilutive and, therefore, should be assumed to be converted before the convertible bonds which have a higher per-share effect ($9.00). If only the preferred stock is assumed to be converted, the diluted EPS is:

$$\text{Diluted EPS} = \frac{\text{Net Income} + \text{Preferred Dividends}}{\text{WACS} + \text{WPCS}} = \frac{\$200{,}000 + \$6{,}000}{20{,}000 + 15{,}000} = \$5.89$$

2335.44 Note that even though the $9.00 per-share effect of the convertible bonds is less than basic EPS of $10.00, the convertible bonds are antidilutive because their per-share effect of $9.00 is greater than the $5.89 diluted EPS computed with only the convertible preferred stock assumed to be converted. Thus, by computing the per-share effect of each potential common stock and assuming their exercise or conversion in ascending order (smallest to largest per-share effects) and continuing until the next lowest per-share effect is greater than diluted EPS without including that next PCS (or until all PCS have been included in the computation of diluted EPS if all prove to be dilutive), one is assured that the final diluted EPS calculated is the lowest diluted EPS (and therefore the most dilutive diluted EPS) for that period.

Comprehensive EPS Illustration (Adapted from the Uniform CPA Examination)

2335.45 You are responsible for completing the income statement of the Mars Company at year end 20X2. Your workpapers disclose the following opening balances and transactions in the company's capital stock accounts during the year:

   a. Common stock (at October 1, 20X1, stated value $10, authorized 300,000 shares; effective December 1, 20X1, stated value $5, authorized 600,000 shares):

   Balance, October 1, 20X1 — issued and outstanding 60,000 shares
   December 1, 20X1 — 60,000 shares issued in a 2-for-1 stock split
   December 1, 20X1 — 280,000 shares (stated value $5) issued at $39 per share

b. Treasury stock—common:

    March 1, 20X2 — purchased 40,000 shares at $38 per share
    April 1, 20X2 — sold 40,000 shares at $40 per share

c. Stock purchase warrants, Series A (initially, each warrant was exchangeable with $60 for one common share; effective December 1, 20X1, each warrant became exchangeable for two common shares at $30 per-share):

    October 1, 20X1 — 25,000 warrants issued at $6 each

d. Stock purchase warrants, Series B (each warrant is exchangeable with $50 for one common share):

    April 1, 20X2 — warrants authorized and issued at $10 each

e. First mortgage bonds, 5½%, due 20X5 (nonconvertible; priced to yield 5% when issued):

    Balance October 1, 20X1 — authorized, issued, and outstanding—the face value of $1,400,000

f. Convertible debentures, 7%, due 20X9 (initially, each $1,000 bond was convertible at any time until maturity into 15 common shares; effective December 1, 20X1, the conversion rate became 30 shares for each bond):

    October 1, 20X1 — authorized and issued at their face value (no premium or discount) of $2,400,000

g. The market price for the company's common stock was as follows:

    10/01/X1 $66
    04/01/X2 $40
    09/30/X2 $43
    Average for year ended 09/30/X2—$37.50

h. Net income for the year ended September 30, 20X2, was $540,000. The appropriate tax rate is 40%.

i. **Required:**

(1) Compute WACS.

(2) Compute basic EPS.

(3) Determine the per-share effect of each potential common stock (PCS).

(4) Compute diluted EPS.

2335.46 **Requirement 1:** Compute WACS.

Dates Outstanding	Shares Outstanding	Restatement for 2:1 Stock Split	Fraction of Year	Weighted Average Shares (WACS)
Oct. 1 – Dec. 1	60,000	2.00	2/12	20,000
Dec. 1 – Mar. 1	400,000		3/12	100,000
Mar. 1 – Apr. 1	360,000		1/12	30,000
Apr. 1 – Sept. 30	400,000		6/12	200,000
			12/12	350,000

2335.47 **Requirement 2:** Compute basic EPS.

$$\text{Basic EPS} = \frac{\text{Net Income}}{\text{WAC}} = \frac{\$540,000}{350,000 \text{ shares}} = \$1.54$$

2335.48 **Requirement 3:** Determine the per-share effect of each potential common stock (PCS).

Series A warrants

Numerator effect = $0

Denominator effect:

Shares issued on exercise (25,000 × 2 shares per warrant)	50,000
Proceeds = 25,000 × 2 × $30 = $1,500,000	
Shares reacquired with proceeds ($1,500,000 ÷ $37.50 market price)	40,000
Incremental denominator shares	10,000

$$\text{Per-share effect} = \frac{\text{Numerator Effect}}{\text{Incremental Shares}} = \frac{\$0}{10,000 \text{ shares}} = \$0.00$$

Series B warrants: Antidilutive because the average market price of $37.50 is less than the exercise price of $50.

5.5% first-mortgage bonds: Not a potential common stock (PCS) because the bonds are not convertible.

7% convertible debentures:

Per Share Effect

$$\frac{\text{Numerator Effect}}{\text{Incremental Shares}} = \frac{\text{Interest(net-of-tax)}}{\text{Incremental Shares}} = \frac{\$100,800^a}{72,000 \text{ shares}^b} = \$1.40$$

^{a} Interest net of tax = $2,400,000 × 0.07 × (1 − 0.40) = $100,800
^{b} Incremental shares = $2,400,000 total face ÷ $1,000 face per bond = 2,400 bonds
2,400 bonds × 30 common shares per bond = 72,000 shares

2335.49 The per-share effects of the relevant potential common stocks arranged in ascending order are:

Series A stock purchase warrants	$0.00
7% convertible debentures	1.40

2335.50 Since the per-share effect of the Series A warrants is the lowest, one would assume exercise of these warrants provided that the per-share effect of the warrants ($0.00) is also less than the basic EPS of $1.54 (see section **2335.47**). Since that is the case, the Series A warrants are dilutive. Assuming the Series A warrants are exercised, the diluted EPS is:

$$\text{Diluted EPS} = \frac{\text{Net income} + \text{Numerator effect of warrants}}{\text{WACS} + \text{Denominator effect of warrants}}$$

$$= \frac{\$540,000 + \$0.00}{350,000 + 10,000} = \frac{\$540,000}{360,000 \text{ shares}} = \$1.50$$

2335.51 Since the per-share effect of the 7% convertible debentures ($1.40) is lower than the diluted EPS calculated in section **2335.47** assuming exercise of the warrants only, the assumed conversion of the debentures would reduce diluted EPS. Therefore, the debentures are dilutive and their conversion should be assumed. In that case, the diluted EPS is:

$$\text{Diluted EPS} = \frac{\$540,000 + \$0 + \text{Numerator effect of warrants}}{350,000 + 10,000 + \text{Denominator effect of debentures}}$$

$$= \frac{\$540,000 + \$0 + \$100,800}{350,000 + 10,000 + 72,000} = \frac{\$640,800}{432,000 \text{ shares}} = \$1.48$$

2335.52 Thus, earnings per share would be presented for the year ended September 30, 20X2, as follows:

Basic earnings per share	$1.54
Diluted earnings per share	1.48

Additional EPS Considerations

2335.53 This section contains discussion of several additional considerations with respect to the calculation and presentation of earnings per share.

2335.54 **Periods for Which EPS Must Be Presented**

Earnings per share must be presented for all periods for which an income statement or summary of earnings is presented. If diluted EPS is presented for any period included in the current financial report, it must be presented for all periods included in that financial report. In other words, if dual EPS is presented for any period, it must be presented for all periods presented.

2335.55 **Income Captions for Which EPS Are Presented**

EPS (if applicable, both basic EPS and diluted EPS) must be presented on the face of the income statement for each of the following income captions if they appear on the income statement:

a. Income from continuing operations

b. Income before extraordinary items (and/or cumulative effect of a change in accounting principle)

c. Net income

2335.56 EPS must also be presented for each of the following, either on the face of the income statement or in the notes to the financial statements:

a. Discontinued operations

b. Extraordinary items

c. Cumulative effect of a change in accounting principle (see section **2305.04–.23**)

2335.57 **Income from Continuing Operations Used as the "Control Number"**

If an enterprise reports a discontinued operation, an extraordinary item, or the cumulative effect of an accounting change in a period, it must use income from continuing operations as the "control number" in determining whether potential common shares are dilutive or antidilutive. If the entity has no discontinued operations, it must use income before extraordinary items and the cumulative effect of a change in accounting principle as the control number. If it has no discontinued operations, extraordinary items, or accounting changes, it must use net income as the control number.

2335.58 The importance of the control number is that the same number of potential common shares used in computing the diluted per-share amount for the control number must be used in computing all other reported per-share amounts, even if those amounts are antidilutive to their respective basic per-share amounts.

2335.59 **Example:** Assume that an enterprise reports the following on its income statement:

Income from continuing operations	$ 100,000
Discontinued operations	(250,000)
Net income	$(150,000)

Assume that 10,000 shares of common stock were outstanding during the entire year. In addition, assume that the enterprise had outstanding all year stock options that would result in 2,000 incremental common shares if exercised.

2335.60 The stock options are dilutive with respect to income from continuing operations—the control number—because their assumed exercise would reduce EPS. In this case, EPS would be presented as follows:

For income from continuing operations:

$$\text{Basic} = \frac{\text{Income from continuing operations}}{\text{WACS}} = \frac{\$100{,}000}{10{,}000} = \$10.00$$

$$\text{Diluted} = \frac{\text{Income from continuing operations}}{\text{WACS} + \text{WPCS}} = \frac{\$100{,}000}{10{,}000 + 2{,}000} = \$8.33$$

For net income or loss:

$$\text{Basic} = \frac{\text{Net Income}}{\text{WACS}} = \frac{(\$150{,}000)}{10{,}000} = (\$15.00)$$

$$\text{Diluted} = \frac{\text{Net Income}}{\text{WACS} + \text{WPCS}} = \frac{(\$150{,}000)}{10{,}000 + 2{,}000} = (\$12.50)$$

2335.61 Note that the stock options are dilutive with respect to income from continuing operations; the diluted EPS of $8.33 is less than the basic EPS of $10.00. However, the stock options are antidilutive with respect to net income or loss; the diluted EPS of $(12.50) is greater than (rather than less than) the basic EPS of $(15.00). A smaller loss per share is "better than" a larger loss per share; therefore, a smaller loss per share is antidilutive.

2335.62 In this case, dual EPS (EPS and diluted EPS) would be required because income from continuing operations is the control number and the stock options are dilutive with respect to income from continuing operations. Therefore, the stock options are considered to be exercised with respect to all of the diluted earnings per share calculations (i.e., those for income from continuing operations, discontinued operations, and net income).

2335.63 In contrast, assume that the enterprise reported the following income statement information:

Income from continuing operations	$(100,000)
Discontinued operations	250,000
Net income	$ 150,000

2335.64 Since income from continuing operations is a loss amount, the assumed exercise of the stock options would increase the denominator shares and, therefore, reduce the loss per share. Thus, the stock options are antidilutive with respect to income from continuing operations. Therefore, the stock options would not be assumed to be exercised because they are antidilutive with respect to the control number (income from continuing operations), even though they are dilutive with respect to net income (which is a positive amount). In this case, if this is the only year presented in the current financial report, the earnings per share would be reported as follows:

$$\text{Income from continuing operations} = \frac{\$(100{,}000)}{10{,}000} = \$(10.00)$$

$$\text{Net income} = \frac{\$150{,}000}{10{,}000} = \$15.00$$

$$\text{Income from continuing operations} = \frac{\$(100{,}000)}{10{,}000} = \$(10.00)$$

$$\text{Net income} = \frac{\$150{,}000}{10{,}000} = \$15.00$$

2335.65 Note that, in this case, basic EPS and diluted EPS are the same. Even though they are the same, both must be presented because the enterprise has potential common stock (the stock options) outstanding.

Contingent Issuance of Common Stock

2335.66 In some circumstances, an enterprise may agree to issue additional shares of common stock if certain conditions are met. An example is in the case of a business combination in which the acquiring company agrees to issue additional shares of common stock (contingent shares) if certain conditions are met. These contingent shares should be considered outstanding and included in *diluted EPS* as follows:

  a. If all necessary conditions have been satisfied by the end of the period, they should be included as of the beginning of the period in which the conditions were satisfied (or as of the date of the contingent stock agreement, if later).

  b. If all necessary conditions have not been satisfied by the end of the period, the number of contingently issuable shares included in diluted EPS should be based on the number of shares, if any, that would be issuable if the end of the reporting period were the end of the contingency period (e.g., the number of shares that would be issuable based on current-period earnings or period-end market price) and if the result would be dilutive.

2335.67 **Example:** Assume that Beta Company purchased Delta Company and agreed to give the stockholders of Delta Company 10,000 additional shares of common stock in 20X3 if Delta's net income in 20X2 is at least $100,000. If in 20X1 Beta's net income is $120,000, the diluted EPS in 20X1 would include the 10,000 contingent shares in the outstanding shares computation because (see section **2335.66(b)**) the net income in 20X1 (the reporting period) equals or exceeds the earnings level specified for the contingency period (20X2). Thus, if 20X1 were the end of the contingency period, the contingency would be satisfied. Therefore, the 10,000 contingent shares should be included in diluted EPS in the current reporting period (20X1).

Nonpublic Enterprises

2335.68 Nonpublic enterprises are not required to present earnings per share information. However, if they chose to do so, they must follow FASB ASC 260-10, which is the official pronouncement that all publicly held enterprises must follow.

Stock-Based Compensation Arrangements

2335.69 Fixed awards and nonvested stock to be issued to employees under a stock-based compensation arrangement should be considered the same as options for purposes of computing diluted EPS. Such stock-based awards should be considered to be outstanding as of the grant date for purposes of computing diluted EPS, even though their exercise may be contingent on vesting.

Required Disclosures

2335.70 An enterprise should make the following disclosures for each period for which an income statement is presented:

  a. A reconciliation of the numerators and the denominators of the basic and diluted per-share computations for income from continuing operations (the reconciliation should include the individual income and share amount effects of all securities that affect earnings per share)

  b. The effect that has been given to preferred dividends in arriving at income available to common stockholders in computing basic EPS

  c. Securities that could potentially dilute basic EPS in the future that were not included in the computation of diluted EPS, because to do so would have been antidilutive for the period or periods presented

IFRS

2335.71 **IFRS:** The IFRS rules concerning earnings per share are similar to those for U.S. GAAP. However, calculation of year-to-date earnings per share (versus previously reported interim date) varies from U.S. GAAP.

2340 Exit or Disposal Activities and Discontinued Operations

2340.01 FASB ASC 205-20 addresses the presentation of discontinued operations on the income statement. The presentation of discontinued operations is discussed in section **2345.06**.

2340.02 FASB ASC 360-10-35 addresses the accounting for long-lived assets to be disposed of.

2340.03 FASB ASC 420-10-05-2 applies to costs associated with an exit activity, which includes but is not limited to restructuring costs. Such costs do not include costs associated with an entity newly acquired in a business combination or with a disposal activity covered by FASB ASC 360-10-15-3. They also do not include costs associated with the retirement of a long-lived asset covered by FASB ASC 410-20.

2340.04 Exit activities include, but are not limited to:

    a. Termination benefits provided to current employees that are involuntarily terminated under the terms of a benefit arrangement that, in substance, is not an ongoing benefit arrangement or an individual deferred compensation contract

    b. Costs to terminate a contract that is not a capital lease

    c. Costs to consolidate facilities or relocate employees.

Recognition and Measurement (Except for One-Time Termination Benefits)

2340.05 Except in the case of a liability for one-time termination benefits that is incurred over time, a liability for a cost associated with an exit or disposal activity under FASB ASC 420-10-25-1 should be recognized and measured initially at its fair value in the period in which the liability is incurred.

2340.06 The liability is incurred when the definition of a liability, as defined in SFAC 6, *Elements of Financial Statements*, is met. SFAC 6 specifies that only present obligations to others are liabilities. SFAC 6 further holds that an obligation becomes a present obligation when a transaction or event occurs that leaves an entity little or no discretion to avoid the future transfer or use of assets to settle the liability.

2340.07 An exit or disposal plan, by itself, does not create a present obligation to others for costs expected to be incurred under the plan. Therefore, an entity's commitment to an exit or disposal plan, by itself, is not the requisite past transaction or event for the recognition of a liability.

2340.08 Thus, a liability for a cost associated with an exit or disposal activity should be recognized initially when the entity has little or no discretion to avoid the future transfer or use of assets to settle the liability. At that point, the liability should be recognized at its fair value.

2340.09 In periods subsequent to initial measurement, changes in the liability related to an exit or disposal activity should be measured using the credit-adjusted risk-free rate that was used to measure the liability initially.

2340.10 The cumulative effect of a change resulting from a revision to either the timing or amount of estimated cash flows should be recognized as an adjustment to the liability in the period of change and reported in the same line item in the income statement used when the related costs were recognized initially. Changes due to the passage of time should be recognized as an increase in the carrying amount of the liability and as an expense.

Recognition and Measurement for One-time Termination Benefits

2340.11 One-time termination benefits are benefits provided to current employees that are involuntarily terminated under the terms of a one-time benefit arrangement. A one-time benefit arrangement exists at the date the plan of termination meets all of the following criteria and has been communicated to employees:

— Management, having the authority to approve the action, commits to a plan of termination.

— The plan identifies the number of employees to be terminated, their job classifications or functions and their locations, and the expected completion date.

— The plan establishes the term of the benefit arrangement, including the benefits that employees will receive upon termination.

— Actions required to complete the plan indicate that it is unlikely that significant changes to the plan will be made or that the plan will be withdrawn.

2340.12 If employees are entitled to receive termination benefits regardless of when they leave or if they will not be retained to render service beyond the minimum retention period, a liability for the termination benefits should be recognized at its fair value at the communication date. (The minimum retention period should not exceed the legal notification period, or in the absence of a legal notification requirement, 60 days.)

2340.13 In cases in which employees are required to render services until they are terminated in order to receive the termination benefits and will be retained to render services beyond the minimum retention period, a liability for the termination benefits should be measured initially at the communication date based on the fair value of the liability as of the termination date. The liability should be recognized ratably over the future service period. The historical credit-adjusted risk-free rate should be used to measure a change resulting from revisions in either the timing or the amount of estimated cash flows over the future service period. The cumulative effect of the change should be recognized as an adjustment of the liability in the period of the change.

2340.14 If a plan of termination that meets the criteria for a one-time benefit arrangement includes both involuntary termination benefits and termination benefits offered for a short period of time in exchange for employees' voluntary termination of service, a liability for the involuntary termination benefits should be recognized in accordance with FASB ASC 420-10-25-10. A liability for any "excess" above that amount should be recognized in accordance with FASB ASC 712-10-25-1.

Contract Termination Costs

2340.15 A liability for costs to terminate a contract before the end of its term should be recognized at its fair value when the entity terminates the contract in accordance with the contract terms. Conversely, a liability for costs that will continue to be incurred under a contract for its remaining term without economic benefit to the entity should be recognized at its fair value when the entity ceases using the right conveyed by the contract.

Reporting

2340.16 Unless associated with a discontinued operation, costs associated with an exit or disposal activity should be included in income from continuing operations.

2340.17 If an event or circumstance occurs that discharges an entity's responsibility to settle a liability for a cost associated with an exit or disposal activity recognized in a prior period, the liability should be reversed. The reversal should be reported in the same line item(s) in the income statement that were used when those costs were recognized initially.

2340.18 **IFRS:** GAAP and IFRS differ in the definition of a discontinued operation. Both have proposed a common definition.

2345 Extraordinary and Unusual Items

2345.01 As discussed in section **2132**, several types of special gains and losses require unique treatment in the income statement. The presentation of these items is the same regardless of whether the enterprise is using the single-step or the multiple-step income statement format. In a properly prepared income statement, these special gains and losses are presented in the order and manner outlined in FASB ASC 225-20-45-10. The reader should refer to the example income statement presented in section **2132.01** for Tiger Co. when reviewing the proper disclosure of the special gains and losses.

Type of Gain/Loss	Description	Placement in Income Statement[a]
Unusual or infrequent item	An event or transaction that is either unusual in nature or infrequent in occurrence, but not both (and therefore is not an extraordinary item).	In the income statement as a part of ICO. Not presented on net-of-tax basis.
Discontinued operations	The results of operations of a component of an entity that has been disposed of or is classified as held for sale.	Preceded by ICO; followed by IBE/CECAP. Presented on net-of-tax basis.
Extraordinary item (EX)	An event or transaction which is both unusual in nature and infrequent in occurrence, taking into consideration the environment in which the enterprise operates.	Preceded by IBE/CECAP; followed by CECAP. Presented on net-of-tax basis.
Cumulative effect of change in accounting principle (CECAP)	FASB ASC 250-10-2 requires that accounting changes be accounted for under the retrospective method unless the FASB specifies otherwise. However, accounting changes for which the FASB specifies that this approach must be used would still be recognized using the "cumulative effect in earnings" approach. (See section **2305** for a discussion of accounting changes.)	Preceded by EX; followed by NI. Presented on net-of-tax basis.

[a] ICO = *Income from continuing operations*
IBE/CECAP = *Income before extraordinary items and cumulative effect of change in accounting principle*
EX = *Extraordinary item*
CECAP = *Cumulative effect of change in accounting principle (see section 2305.04–.23)*
NI = *Net income*

2345.02 One would not expect to encounter all the special gains or losses in a single accounting period. (The inclusion of all of them in the income statement of Tiger Co. is done for illustrative purposes to demonstrate the placement of each item in relation to the others.) It is important to understand how the captions on the income statement would be changed as a result of the omission of one or more items. The following outline provides guidance in this regard:

If there is no:	The following changes are required:
Discontinued operations	ICO is eliminated and there is no discontinued operations section.
Extraordinary item	IBE/CECAP is eliminated (if there is no CECAP) or presented as "Income Before Cumulative Effect of Change in Accounting Principle" (if there is a CECAP).
Cumulative effect of accounting change	IBE/CECAP is eliminated (if there is no EX) or presented as "Income Before Extraordinary Item" (if there is an EX) (see section **2305.04–.23**).

In summary, the elimination of an item means not only that there will be an absence of that item in the income statement, but also that the caption *preceding* the item will be changed.

2345.03 Additional considerations relative to each of the various types of special gains and losses are presented in the following paragraphs.

2345.04 Unusual or Infrequently Occurring Items

Items that are unusual in nature or infrequent in occurrence (but not both) are not extraordinary items. They are presented as separate components of income from continuing operations.

2345.05 Such items are not presented net of tax or in any other manner which implies that they are extraordinary. Earnings per share on such items are *not* presented on the face of the income statement.

2345.06 Discontinued Operations

Discontinued operations are presented in a separate section of the income statement between income from continuing operations and income before extraordinary items and the cumulative effect of accounting changes (if applicable). The discontinued operations section reflects the results of operations of a *component* of an entity as defined in section **2345.11** that either (a) is classified as held for sale or (b) has actually been disposed of. It is important to note that to be included in the discontinued operations section of the income statement, the results of operations must relate to a component of an entity. For example, the gain or loss on the sale of a long-lived asset that does not meet the definition of a component of an entity would not be included in the discontinued operations section of the income statement.

2345.07 The discontinued operations amount must be presented net of any related income tax effect.

2345.08 The discontinued operations amount includes the following:

a. Any results of operations of the component during the period (differences between revenues and expenses)

b. Any impairment loss recognized in writing down the component to its fair value less cost to sell

    c. Any gain for any subsequent increase in the fair value less cost to sell (however, these gains cannot exceed the cumulative loss previously recognized for a write-down)

    d. A gain or loss not previously recognized that results from the sale of a component (this particular gain or loss must be separately disclosed, either on the face of the income statement or in the notes to the financial statements)

2345.09 The results of operations of a component of an entity that either has been disposed of or is classified as held for sale must be reported in discontinued operations if both of the following conditions are met:

    a. The operations and cash flows of the component have been (or will be) eliminated from the ongoing operations of the entity as a result of the disposal transaction.

    b. The entity will not have any significant continuing involvement in the operations of the component after the disposal transaction.

2345.10 If necessary, the results of operations of the component in any prior years presented must be reclassified and presented in discontinued operations so that the presentation will be comparable to that reported for the current period.

2345.11 A component of an entity comprises operations and cash flows that can be clearly distinguished, operationally and for financial reporting purposes, from the rest of the entity. It may be a reportable segment or an operating segment (as discussed in section **2390**), a reporting unit, a subsidiary, or a qualifying asset group.

2345.12 Adjustments to amounts previously reported in discontinued operations that are directly related to the disposal of a component of an entity in a period should be classified separately in the current period in discontinued operations.

2345.13 A long-lived asset classified as held for sale must be presented separately in the balance sheet. The assets and liabilities of a disposal group (i.e., a component of an entity that is comprised of a group of assets) must be presented separately in the asset and liability sections, respectively. Those assets and liabilities may not be offset and presented as a single amount.

2345.14 A gain or loss recognized for a long-lived asset classified as held for sale that is not a component of an entity must be included in income from continuing operations.

2345.15 Extraordinary Items

Gains and losses must meet both criteria of being *unusual in nature* and *infrequent in occurrence* to be classified as extraordinary. In identifying extraordinary items, the following considerations are important:

    a. The environment in which the enterprise operates provides the framework for evaluation.

    b. Absence of management control over the event is irrelevant.

    c. An event or transaction may be unusual for one enterprise but not for another.

    d. Separate presentation as an extraordinary item is reserved for *material* items that meet the other criterion.

2345.16 Extraordinary items are presented immediately below the "discontinued operations" section of the income statement. Descriptive captions are used, and the extraordinary items are presented net of the related tax effect.

2345.17 The following items are normally *not* extraordinary, due to their failure to meet the *dual criteria*:

   a. Write-down or write-off of receivables, inventories, equipment leased to others, or intangible assets

   b. Gains or losses from the exchange or translation of foreign currencies, including those relating to major devaluations and revaluations

   c. Gains or losses on the disposal of a segment of a business

   d. Other gains or losses from the sale or abandonment of property, plant, or equipment used in the business

   e. Effects of a strike, including those against competitors and major suppliers

   f. Adjustments of accruals on long-term contracts

2345.18 Gains and losses resulting from events such as those listed may be extraordinary in certain circumstances, depending primarily on the underlying cause. This may be the case where such gains and losses resulted from the following:

   a. A major casualty, such as an earthquake

   b. An expropriation

   c. A prohibition under a newly enacted law or legislation

2345.19 Prior to the issuance of FASB ASC 470-50-45-1, gains and losses on extinguishment of debt were to be presented as extraordinary items, regardless of whether they were judged to be unusual in nature and infrequent in occurrence. After the effective date of FASB ASC 470-50-45-1, such gains and losses on extinguishment of debt are to be classified on the same basis as other gains and losses, that is, depending on whether they meet the criteria established for extraordinary gains and losses (see section **2345.15**). If they meet those criteria, they should be classified as extraordinary items; otherwise, they should be classified as ordinary items and included in the determination of income from continuing operations.

2345.20 Cumulative Effect of a Change in Accounting Principle

The cumulative effect of a change in accounting principle is presented on a net-of-tax basis immediately after extraordinary items and prior to net income. Most changes in accounting principle are accounted for using the retroactive approach and do not appear on the income statement. The situation in which such an item exists and the method of determining the item is developed in greater depth in section **2305.04–.23**.

2345.21 Other Considerations

Earnings per share—both basic and diluted, if applicable—are presented on the face of the income statement of publicly held companies for the following items:

   a. Income from continuing operations

   b. Income before extraordinary items and/or cumulative effect of a change in accounting principle

   c. Net income

2345.22 Prior-period adjustments are rare events that are recorded as direct adjustments to retained earnings rather than being presented as income statement elements. They are few in number and are generally limited to the following:

   a. Corrections of errors in previously issued financial statements

b. Adjustments to the accounts required as part of the specified transition rules for implementing new authoritative pronouncements of the FASB (ASC 250-10-45-2)

2345.23 **IFRS:** IAS 1 requires additional line items on the income statement. It does not require discontinued operations or accounting changes to be reported as separate components of income. It does not allow the extraordinary classification.

2345.24 **IFRS:** IAS 8 defined the concepts on a GAAP income statement in a manner similar to GAAP, except that there is no extraordinary classification and there is not a category for accounting errors.

2350 Fair Value Measurements, Disclosures, and Reporting

2350.01 Various pronouncements of the FASB and its predecessor standard-setting bodies (Accounting Principles Board and Committee on Accounting Procedures) have either required or allowed the use of fair value in certain circumstances. Unfortunately, these various pronouncements did not always use the same definition of fair value. In addition, in some cases they provided limited guidance for applying those definitions of fair value.

2350.02 FASB ASC 820-10 defines fair value, establishes a framework for measuring fair value, and expands disclosures about fair value measurements. It does not require any new fair value measurements; rather, it applies under other accounting pronouncements that require or permit fair value measurements.

Fair Value Defined

2350.03 FASB ASC 820-10-20 defines fair value as "the price that would be received to sell an asset or paid to transfer a liability in an orderly transaction between market participants at the measurement date."

2350.04 The FASB points out in FASB ASC 820-10-30-3 that a fair value measurement is for a particular asset or liability. Thus, the fair value measurement should consider attributes specific to the particular asset or liability.

Principal or Most Advantageous Market

2350.05 Any fair value measurement should assume that the transaction to sell the asset or transfer the liability occurs in the principal market for the asset or liability. The principal market is defined in FASB ASC 820-10-20 as "the market in which the reporting entity would sell the asset or transfer the liability with the greatest volume and level of activity for the asset or liability."

2350.06 If there is no principal market for that type of asset or liability, the entity should use the most advantageous market for that asset or liability. FASB ASC 820-10-20 defines the most advantageous market as "the market in which the reporting entity would sell the asset or transfer the liability with the price that maximizes the amount that would be received for the asset or minimizes the amount that would be paid to transfer the liability, considering transaction costs in the respective market(s)."

2350.07 In either case, principal market or most advantageous market, the fair value measurement should be considered from the perspective of the reporting entity.

Issue of Transaction Costs

2350.08 The price used to measure fair value should not be adjusted for transaction costs, which are the incremental direct costs to sell the asset or transfer the liability. Note, however, that transaction costs do not include the costs that would be incurred to transport the asset or liability to or from its principal (or most advantageous) market. If location is an attribute of the asset or liability, the FASB takes the position in FASB ASC 820-10-35-8 that "the price in the principal (or most advantageous) market used to measure the fair value of the asset or liability shall be adjusted for the costs, if any, that would be incurred to transport the asset or liability to (or from) its principal (or most advantageous) market."

Market Participants

2350.09 Market participants are defined in FASB ASC 820-10-20 as "buyers and sellers in the principal (or most advantageous) market for the asset or liability that are:

   a. "Independent of the reporting entity; that is, they are not related parties

   b. "Knowledgeable, having a reasonable understanding about the asset or liability and the transaction based on all available information, including information that might be obtained through due diligence efforts that are usual and customary

   c. "Able to transact for the asset or liability

   d. "Willing to transact for the asset or liability; that is, they are motivated but not forced or otherwise compelled to do so."

2350.10 The concept of "market participants" is a core issue in determining the fair value because FASB ASC 820-10-35-9 specifies that the fair value of the asset or liability must be determined based on the assumptions that market participants would use in pricing the asset or liability.

Application to Assets

2350.11 In making a fair value measurement, an entity must assume the "highest and best use" of the asset by market participants.

In-Use vs. In-Exchange

2350.12 The highest and best use of the asset is **in-use** if the asset would provide maximum value to market participants principally through its use in combination with other assets as a group (as installed or otherwise configured for use). That might be the case, for example, in the case of certain nonfinancial assets.

2350.13 Conversely, the highest and best use of the asset is **in-exchange** if the asset would provide maximum value to market participants principally on a standalone basis. That might be the case, for example, in the case of a financial asset.

Application to Liabilities

2350.14 The FASB specifies in FASB ASC 820-10-35-16 that a fair value measurement of a liability "assumes that the liability is transferred to a market participant at the measurement date (the liability to the counterparty continues; it is not settled) and that the nonperformance risk relating to that liability is the same before and after its transfer." The nonperformance risk is the risk that the obligation will not be fulfilled. It includes but is not limited to the reporting entity's own credit risk. The fair value of a liability must reflect any nonperformance risk relating to that liability.

Valuation Techniques

2350.15 The determination of fair value may require the use of one or more valuation techniques. In that case, the valuation technique used should be consistent with the market approach, income approach, and/or cost approach, as appropriate. These approaches are defined in FASB ASC 820-10-35-28. The key aspects of those definitions are as follows:

a. **Market approach.** The market approach uses prices and other relevant information generated by market transactions involving identical or comparable assets or liabilities (including a business). An example of a market approach is matrix pricing, which is a mathematical technique used principally to value debt securities without relying exclusively on quoted prices for the specified securities, but rather by relying on the securities' relationship to other benchmark quoted securities.

b. **Income approach.** The income approach uses valuation techniques to convert future amounts (for example, cash flows or earnings) to a single present amount (discounted). These valuation techniques include present value techniques; option-pricing models, such as the Black-Sholes-Merton model (a closed-form model) and a binomial model (a lattice model); and the multiperiod excess earnings method, which is used to measure the fair value of certain intangible assets.

c. **Cost approach.** The cost approach is based on the amount that currently would be required to replace the service capacity of an asset (often referred to as current replacement cost).

2350.16 In some cases, a single valuation technique may be appropriate, whereas in other cases multiple valuation techniques may be necessary.

Inputs to Valuation Techniques

2350.17 Inputs may be observable or unobservable. **Observable inputs** are "inputs that reflect the assumptions market participants would use in pricing the asset or liability developed based on market data obtained from sources independent of the reporting entity." **Unobservable inputs** are "inputs that reflect the reporting entity's own assumptions about the assumptions that market participants would use in pricing the asset or liability developed based on the best information available" (FASB ASC 820-10-20). The valuation techniques an entity uses should maximize the use of observable inputs and minimize the use of unobservable inputs.

Fair Value Hierarchy

2350.18 FASB ASC 820-10-35-37 identifies a fair value hierarchy that prioritizes the inputs to valuation techniques used to measure fair value into three broad levels, as follows:

a. **Level 1 inputs.** These are quoted prices (unadjusted) in active markets for identical assets or liabilities that the reporting entity has the ability to access at the measurement date.

b. **Level 2 inputs.** These are inputs other than quoted prices included within Level 1 that are observable for the asset or liability, either directly or indirectly.

c. **Level 3 inputs.** These are unobservable inputs for the asset or liability.

2350.19 A reporting entity should use a valuation technique that is consistent with the type of inputs available. For example, if quoted market prices for identical assets are available (level 1 inputs), those prices should be used. This would be the typical situation in valuing marketable securities. On the other hand, if quoted market prices for identical assets are not available but quoted prices for similar assets are available (level 2 inputs), valuation techniques appropriate for those types of inputs should be used. The fair value hierarchy prioritizes the inputs to valuation techniques, not the valuation techniques.

Inputs Based on Bid and Ask Prices

2350.20 Notwithstanding the general guide that a reporting entity should use a valuation technique that is consistent with the type of inputs available, the FASB has taken the position that "if an input used to measure fair value is based on bid and ask prices (for example, in a dealer market), the price within the bid-ask spread that is most representative of fair value in the circumstances should be used to measure fair value, regardless of where in the fair value hierarchy the input falls (Level 1, 2, or 3)." (FASB ASC 820-10-35-56).

Fair Value Measurement of a Liability

2350.21 A fair value measurement assumes that a liability is exchanged in an orderly transaction between market participants. However, liabilities are rarely transferred in the marketplace because of contractual or other legal restrictions preventing the transfer of liabilities. Some liabilities (for example, debt obligations), however, are traded in the marketplace as assets. (FASB ASC 820-10-35-16A)

2350.22 If a quoted price in an active market for the identical liability is available, it represents a Level 1 measurement. In circumstances in which a quoted price in an active market for the identical liability is not available, a reporting entity must measure fair value using one or more of the following techniques (FASB ASC 820-10-35-16B):

    a. A valuation technique that uses:

        (1) The quoted price of the identical liability when traded as an asset

        (2) Quoted prices for similar liabilities or similar liabilities when traded as assets

    b. Another valuation technique that is consistent with the principles of FASB ASC 820-10. Two examples would be an income approach, such as a present value technique, or a market approach, such as a technique that is based on the amount at the measurement date that the reporting entity would pay to transfer the identical liability or would receive to enter into the identical liability.

2350.23 In all instances, the reporting entity must maximize the use of relevant observable inputs and minimize the use of unobservable inputs. Furthermore, a reporting entity must apply all applicable guidance in FASB ASC 820-10 in determining fair value when the volume and level of activity for an asset or liability have significantly decreased and in identifying transactions that are not orderly. (FASB ASC 820-10-35-16C)

2350.24 When measuring the fair value of a liability using the quoted price of the liability when traded as an asset, the reporting entity must not adjust the quoted price of the asset for the effect of a restriction preventing its sale. However, the quoted price of the liability when traded as an asset must be adjusted for factors specific to the asset that are not applicable to the fair value measurement of the liability. Some circumstances in which a reporting entity must consider whether the quoted price of the asset should be adjusted include the following (FASB ASC 820-10-35-16D):

    a. The quoted price for the asset relates to a similar (but not identical) liability traded as an asset

    b. The unit of account for the asset is not the same as for the liability (for example, the quoted price for the asset includes the effect of a third-party credit enhancement). See FASB ASC 820-10-35-18A for further guidance.

2350.25 When estimating the fair value of a liability, a reporting entity must not include a separate input or adjustment to other inputs relating to the existence of a restriction that prevents the transfer of the liability. The effect of a restriction that prevents the transfer of a liability is either implicitly or explicitly already included in the other inputs to the fair value measurement. For example, at the transaction date, both the creditor and the obligor are willing to accept the transaction price for the liability with full knowledge that the obligation includes a restriction that prevents its transfer. As a result of the restriction already being included in the transaction price, a separate input or adjustment to an existing input into the fair value measurement of a liability is not required at the transaction date to reflect the effect of the restriction on transfer. Additionally, a separate input or adjustment to other inputs into the fair value measurement of a liability is not required at subsequent measurement dates to reflect the effect of the restriction on transfer. (FASB ASC 820-10-35-16E)

2350.26 In addition, there are two fundamental differences between the fair value measurement of an asset and a liability that justify different treatments for asset restrictions and for liability restrictions. First, restrictions on the transfer of a liability relate to performance under the obligation (that is, the reporting entity is legally obligated to satisfy the obligation and needs to do something to be relieved of the obligation), whereas restrictions on the transfer of an asset relate to the marketability of the asset. Second, virtually all liabilities include a restriction preventing the transfer of the liability, whereas most assets do not include a similar restriction. As a result, the effect of a restriction preventing the transfer of a liability would, theoretically, be consistent for all liabilities. However, the inclusion of a restriction preventing the sale of the asset typically results in a lower fair value for the restricted asset versus the nonrestricted asset, all other factors being equal. (FASB ASC 820-10-35-16F)

2350.27 When measuring the fair value of a liability using a valuation technique, a reporting entity shall ensure that the fair value measurement is consistent with the principles of FASB ASC 820-10, that is, the price that would be paid to transfer a liability in an orderly transaction between market participants at the measurement date. For example, when using a technique based on the amount at the measurement date that the reporting entity would receive to enter into the identical liability (see FASB ASC 820-10-35-16B), the inputs shall reflect the assumptions that market participants would use (or the reporting entity's own assumption about the assumptions that market participants would use) in the principal or most advantageous market for issuance of a liability with the same contractual terms. (FASB ASC 820-10-35-16G)

Fair Value Option for Financial Assets and Liabilities

2350.28 As of an entity's first fiscal year beginning after November 15, 2007, companies may, at the option of the reporting entity, measure a wide range of financial assets and liabilities at fair value. The fair value option established by FASB ASC 825-10-01-5 permits all entities to choose to measure eligible items at fair value at specified election dates.

Items Eligible for the Fair Value Option

2350.29 The following are eligible items for the fair value option:

a. A recognized financial asset and financial liability, except any listed below in exceptions

b. A firm commitment that would otherwise not be recognized at inception and that involves only financial instruments (An example is a forward purchase contract for a loan that is not readily convertible to cash. That commitment involves only financial instruments—a loan and cash—and would not otherwise be recognized because it is not a derivative instrument.)

c. A written loan commitment

d. The rights and obligations under an insurance contract that is not a financial instrument (because it requires or permits the insurer to provide goods or services rather than a cash settlement) but whose terms permit the insurer to settle by paying a third party to provide those goods or services

e. The rights and obligations under a warranty that is not a financial instrument (because it requires or permits the warrantor to provide goods or services rather than a cash settlement) but whose terms permit the warrantor to settle by paying a third party to provide those goods or services

f. A host financial instrument resulting from the separation of an embedded nonfinancial derivative instrument from a nonfinancial hybrid instrument under FASB ASC 815-15-25-1, subject to the scope exceptions listed below in section **2350.30** (An example of such a nonfinancial hybrid instrument is an instrument in which the value of the bifurcated embedded derivative is payable in cash, services, or merchandise but the debt host is payable only in cash.)

Items Not Eligible for the Fair Value Option

2350.30 The following are recognized financial assets and financial liabilities that are not eligible items for the fair value option under FASB ASC 825-10-15-5:

   a. An investment in a subsidiary that the entity is required to consolidate

   b. An interest in a variable interest entity that the entity is required to consolidate

   c. Employers' and plans' obligations (or assets representing net overfunded positions) for pension benefits, other postretirement benefits (including health care and life insurance benefits), postemployment benefits, employee stock option and stock purchase plans, and other forms of deferred compensation arrangements, as defined in FASB ASC 420, 710, 712, and 715

   d. Financial assets and financial liabilities recognized under leases as defined in FASB ASC 840-10 (This exception does not apply to a guarantee of a third-party lease obligation or a contingent obligation arising from a canceled lease.)

   e. Deposit liabilities, withdrawable on demand, of banks, savings and loan associations, credit unions, and other similar depository institutions

   f. Financial instruments that are, in whole or in part, classified by the issuer as a component of shareholder's equity (including "temporary equity") (An example is a convertible debt security with a noncontingent beneficial conversion feature.)

Unrealized Gains and Losses

2350.31 A business entity must report unrealized gains and losses on items for which the fair value option has been elected in earnings (or another performance indicator if the business entity does not report earnings) at each subsequent reporting date. A not-for-profit organization must report unrealized gains and losses in its statement of activities or similar statement.

Application of FASB ASC 825-10-25-1

2350.32 FASB ASC 825-10-25-1 permits election of fair value measurement on a contract-by-contract basis if the election is supported by concurrent documentation or a preexisting documented policy. The reporting entity may adopt fair value elections at two times—at initial adoption of the standard and subsequent to the initial adoption:

   a. Initial adoption of the standard—The entity may reclassify any existing eligible asset or liability at its fair value. Any gain or loss resulting from reclassification is reported as a cumulative adjustment to retained earnings.

   b. Subsequent to initial adoption—The entity may elect fair value at the initial recognition of any eligible financial asset or liability, or upon any event that gives rise to a new accounting basis for that item.

Portions of financial holdings currently accounted for as held to maturity or available for sale may be reclassified to fair value at the initial adoption date.

The election is irrevocable. It is applied only to entire instruments and not to portions of instruments.

Required Disclosure

2350.33 FASB ASC 825-10-50 requires a great deal of disclosure. In annual periods only, an entity must disclose the methods and significant assumptions used to estimate the fair value of items for which the fair value option has been elected. The following items are required for both annual and interim reports.

   a. On the statement of financial position, FASB ASC 825-10-45-1 requires that entities report assets and liabilities that are measured at fair value pursuant to the fair value option in a manner that separates those reported fair values from the carrying amounts of similar assets and liabilities measured using another measurement attribute. To accomplish that, an entity must either:

(1) present the aggregate of fair value and non-fair-value amounts in the same line item in the statement of financial position and parenthetically disclose the amount measured at fair value included in the aggregate amount or

(2) present two separate line items to display the fair value and non-fair-value carrying amounts.

b. As of each date for which a statement of financial position is presented, FASB ASC 825-10-50-28 requires that entities disclose the following:

(1) Management's reasons for electing a fair value option for each eligible item or group of similar eligible items

(2) If the fair value option is elected for some but not all eligible items within a group of similar eligible items:

(a) A description of those similar items and the reasons for partial election

(b) Information to enable users to understand how the group of similar items relates to individual line items on the statement of financial position

(3) For each line item in the statement of financial position that includes an item or items for which the fair value option has been elected:

(a) Information to enable users to understand how each line item in the statement of financial position relates to major categories of assets and liabilities presented in accordance with the fair value disclosure requirements of FASB ASC 825-10-50-11

(b) The aggregate carrying amount of items included in each line item in the statement of financial position that are not eligible for the fair value option, if any

(4) The difference between the aggregate fair value and the aggregate unpaid principal balance of:

(a) loans and long-term receivables (other than securities subject to FASB ASC 320) that have contractual principal amounts and for which the fair value option has been elected

(b) long-term debt instruments that have contractual principal amounts and for which the fair value option has been elected

(5) For loans held as assets for which the fair value option has been elected:

(a) The aggregate fair value of loans that are 90 days or more past due

(b) If the entity's policy is to recognize interest income separately from other changes in fair value, the aggregate fair value of loans in nonaccrual status

(c) The difference between the aggregate fair value and the aggregate unpaid principal balance for loans that are 90 days or more past due, in nonaccrual status, or both

(6) For investments that would have been accounted for under the equity method if the entity had not chosen to apply the fair value option, the information required by FASB ASC 323-10-50-3 (excluding the disclosures in FASB ASC 323-10-50-2 and 323-10-50-3(a) and (c))

    c. For each period for which an income statement is presented, FASB ASC 825-10-50-30 requires that entities disclose the following about items for which the fair value option has been elected:

        (1) For each line item in the statement of financial position, the amounts of gains and losses from fair value changes included in earnings during the period and in which line in the income statement those gains and losses are reported (FASB ASC 825-10-50-30 does not preclude an entity from meeting this requirement by disclosing amounts of gains and losses that include amounts of gains and losses for other items measured at fair value, such as items required to be measured at fair value.)

        (2) A description of how interest and dividends are measured and where they are reported in the income statement (FASB ASC 825-10-50-30 does not address the methods used for recognizing and measuring the amount of dividend income, interest income, and interest expense for items for which the fair value option has been elected.)

        (3) For loans and other receivables held as assets:

            (a) The estimated amount of gains or losses included in earnings during the period attributable to changes in instrument-specific credit risk

            (b) How the gains or losses attributable to changes in instrument-specific credit risk were determined

        (4) For liabilities with fair values that have been significantly affected during the reporting period by changes in the instrument-specific credit risk:

            (a) The estimated amount of gains and losses from fair value changes included in earnings that are attributable to changes in the instrument-specific credit risk

            (b) Qualitative information about the reasons for those changes

            (c) How the gains and losses attributable to changes in instrument-specific credit risk were determined

Effective Date

2350.34 FASB ASC 825-10-01-5 is effective as of the beginning of an entity's first fiscal year that begins after November 15, 2007. Early adoption is permitted as of the beginning of a fiscal year that begins on or before November 15, 2007, provided the entity also elects to apply the provisions of FASB ASC 820-10. No entity is permitted to apply FASB ASC 825-10-01-5 retrospectively to fiscal years preceding the effective date unless the entity chooses early adoption. The choice to adopt early should be made after issuance of FASB ASC 825-10-01-5 but within 120 days of the beginning of the fiscal year of adoption, provided the entity has not yet issued financial statements, including required notes to those financial statements, for any interim period of the fiscal year of adoption. FASB ASC 825-10-01-5 permits application to eligible items existing at the effective date (or early adoption date).

IFRS

2350.35   **IFRS:** IFRS has no comprehensive guidance issued by IASB regarding fair value measurements, disclosures, and reporting, but a current project promises a standard very similar to U.S. GAAP. The proposed IFRS is based on FASB ASC 820-10 with some terminology differences, and will essentially converge with the U.S. GAAP approach.

2355 Derivatives and Hedge Accounting

2355.01 FASB ASC 815, "Derivatives and Hedging," provides a comprehensive standard for the recognition and measurement of derivatives and hedging activities. It eliminates the inconsistencies that previously existed with respect to accounting for derivatives and hedging activities.

Four Fundamental Decisions

2355.02 The FASB concluded that the following four fundamental decisions should serve as cornerstones of its standards on derivatives and hedging activities:

    a. Derivative instruments represent rights or obligations that meet the definitions of assets or liabilities and should be reported in financial statements.

    b. Fair value is the most relevant measure for financial instruments and the only relevant measure for derivative instruments.

    c. Only items that are assets or liabilities should be reported as such in financial statements.

    d. Special accounting for items designated as being hedged should be provided only for qualifying items.

Derivative Instrument Defined

2355.03 A **derivative instrument** is a financial instrument or other contract with all three of the following characteristics:

    a. It has (a) one or more underlyings, (b) one or more notional amounts or payment provisions, or (c) both.

    b. It requires little or *no initial net investment*.

    c. Its terms require or permit *net settlement,* it can readily be settled net by a means outside the contract, or it provides for delivery of an asset that puts the recipient in a position not substantially different from net settlement.

2355.04 An **underlying** is a specified interest rate, security price, commodity price, foreign exchange rate, index of prices or rates, or other variable (including the occurrence or nonoccurrence of a specified event such as a scheduled payment under a contract). The underlying may be the price or rate of an asset or liability but is not the asset or liability itself.

2355.05 A **notional amount** is a number of currency units, shares, bushels, pounds, or other units specified in a derivative instrument.

2355.06 **Selected Types of Derivative Instruments**

FASB ASC 815 addresses the recognition and measurement issues and specifies that any instrument that meets the definition in section **2355.03** is a derivative instrument.

2355.07 Even though FASB ASC 815 applies to any instrument that meets the definition in section **2355.03,** the most frequently used derivatives are swaps, options, futures, and forward contracts.

2355.08 **Swaps:** A contract between two or more parties, referred to as counterparties, to exchange sets of cash flows over a specified period in the future. The two most prevalent types of swaps are interest rate swaps and currency swaps. In the case of an interest rate swap, for example, entity A might have a fixed-rate loan while entity B has a variable-rate loan. The two parties could enter into a contract to swap interest rates. The result would be that entity A would wind up with, in substance, a variable-rate loan and entity B a fixed-rate loan.

2355.09 **Options:** Allows the holder of the contract to buy or sell a given item at a specific price during a specific period of time. There are two fundamental types of options—call options and put options. A call option gives its owner the right to buy (call) a specific item at a specific price during a specific period of time. A put option gives its owner the right to sell (put) a specific item at a specific price during a specific period of time.

For example, if an individual believes that the price of Beta Company's stock (which is currently selling for $100) will increase, the individual might consider purchasing a call option for 100 shares of Beta Company's stock at $100. As a result, if the price of Beta's stock increases, the individual can call (buy) 100 shares at the call price of $100 per share and sell the stock at the higher market price.

2355.10 **Futures:** An agreement between a buyer and a seller, executed through a clearinghouse, that calls for delivery of some commodity or financial instrument at a specified later date at a price established at the time of contracting. The two most prevalent financial futures are foreign currency futures and interest rate futures.

2355.11 **Forward contracts:** An agreement reached at a point in time that calls for the delivery of a financial instrument or commodity at a specified later date at a price established at the time of contracting. The most widely used forward contracts are those for foreign currency. These contracts are agreements to exchange, at a specified future date, currencies of different countries at a specified rate of exchange.

Fundamental Measurement and Recognition Requirements

2355.12 An entity must recognize all of its derivative instruments in its balance sheet as either assets or liabilities. Thus, merely disclosing derivative instruments in the notes to the financial statements is unacceptable. They must be measured and the dollar amount included in the column totals of the balance sheet.

2355.13 All derivatives must be recognized on the balance sheet at fair value. Fair value is the amount at which an asset (liability) could be bought (incurred) or sold (settled) in a current transaction between willing parties in other than a forced or liquidation sale.

2355.14 The accounting for changes in the fair value (i.e., gains or losses) of a derivative depends on whether it has been designated as and qualifies for hedge accounting.

Types of Hedges

2355.15 FASB ASC 815 allows "special accounting" for the following three categories of hedge transactions:

    a. Fair value hedges—hedges of changes in the fair value of assets, liabilities, or firm commitments

    b. Cash flow hedges—hedges of variable cash flows of recognized assets or liabilities, or of forecasted transactions

    c. Hedges of foreign currency exposures of net investments in foreign operations

2355.16 The special accounting afforded hedges applies only to the extent that the hedging instrument is "highly effective" in serving as a hedge. For example, if the hedging instrument has a notional amount of $1.5 million but the asset or liability hedged is only $1 million, only $1 million of the hedging instrument is effective in serving as a hedge. The "extra" $0.5 million is not effective as a hedge.

Instruments That Do Not Qualify for Hedge Accounting

2355.17 The gain or loss on a derivative instrument that does not qualify as a hedge must be recognized currently in net income.

2355.18 **Example:** Assume that the price of commodity X on December 1, 20X1, is $1.00 per pound. Alpha Company believes that the price of commodity X will rise, and on December 1, 20X1, purchases a call option to purchase 100,000 pounds of commodity X at any time within the next three months at $1.05 per pound. Alpha currently does not own any commodity X and does not anticipate the purchase or sale of commodity X in the future, except that which would result from the exercise of the call option if Alpha chooses to exercise the option. The market price per pound of commodity X is the underlying and the 100,000 pounds is the notional amount of the contract. Assuming that the price of the call option to Alpha is $2,000, the purchase of the option is recorded on December 1, 20X1, as follows:

Option	$2,000	
Cash		$2,000

2355.19 Assume further that as of December 31, 20X1, the balance sheet date, an increase in the price of commodity X has caused the fair value of Alpha's call option to be $6,500. The $4,500 increase in the fair value of Alpha's call option is recorded in 20X1 as follows:

Option ($6,500 - $2,000)	$4,500	
Unrealized Gain (included in net income)		$4,500

2355.20 FASB ASC 815 specifies that gains or losses associated with derivatives that do not qualify as hedges must be included in net income. Since Alpha does not own any commodity X and does not anticipate the purchase or sale of any commodity X in the future (except that associated with the call option), its investment in the call option would not qualify as a hedge. Therefore, the $4,500 unrealized gain resulting from the increase in the fair value of the option (the derivative instrument) must be included in net income. The option is reported on Alpha's December 31, 20X1, balance sheet as an asset at its *fair value* of $6,500.

2355.21 Assume that on March 1, 20X2, the expiration date of the call option, the price of commodity X is $1.40 per pound and Alpha elects to exercise the call option. Assume further that Alpha enters into a separate contract to sell 100,000 pounds of commodity X on March 1, 20X2, at the market price of $1.40 per pound. Since the call option expires on March 1, 20X2, the fair value of the option on that date would be equal to the excess of the $140,000 market price of the 100,000 pounds of commodity X over the $105,000 call price (also known as the strike price), or $35,000. The entries on March 1, 20X2, are as follows:

Option	$ 28,500	
($35,000 fair value 03/01/X2 - $6,500 fair value 12/31/X1)		
Unrealized Gain (included in net income)		$ 28,500
To record the increase in the fair value of the option in 20X2.		
Commodity X	$105,000	
Cash		$105,000
To record the exercise of the call option.		
Cash	$140,000	
Commodity X		$105,000
Option ($2,000 + $4,500 + $28,500)		35,000
To record the sale of commodity X received on exercise of the call option.		

2355.22 The increase in the fair value was recognized in net income in the periods in which the increase took place—$4,500 in 20X1 and $28,500 in 20X2.

Fair Value Hedges

2355.23 Fair value hedges protect against the changes in value caused by *fixed* terms, rates, or prices. In contrast, cash flow hedges protect against the risk caused by *variable* prices, costs, rates, or terms that cause future cash flows to be uncertain.

2355.24 For fair value hedges, FASB ASC 815-25-35-1 requires that gains or losses associated with changes in the fair value of the *hedging* instrument be recognized in net income in the period in which the change in fair value takes place. In addition, changes in the fair value of the *hedged* item (i.e., the asset, liability, or firm commitment) must be simultaneously recognized in net income and as an adjustment to the carrying amount of the hedged item.

2355.25 For hedged items that, absent the hedge, would be measured at fair value with changes in fair value reported in other comprehensive income (e.g., available-for-sale securities), the adjustment of the hedged item's carrying amount should be recognized in net income rather than in other comprehensive income while the hedge exists.

2355.26 For a hedge to qualify as a fair value hedge, certain criteria must be met. The following are perhaps the most important of these criteria:

   a. At the inception of the hedge, there is formal documentation of the hedging relationship and the entity's risk management objective and strategy for undertaking the hedge.

   b. Both at the inception of the hedge and on an ongoing basis, the hedging relationship is expected to be highly effective in achieving offsetting changes in fair value attributable to the hedged risk during the period that the hedge is designated.

   c. The hedged item is specifically identified as either all or a specific portion of a recognized asset or liability or of an unrecognized firm commitment.

   d. The hedged item is a single asset or liability (or a specific portion thereof) or is a portfolio of similar assets or liabilities.

   e. The hedged item presents an exposure to changes in fair value attributable to the hedged risk that could affect reported earnings.

2355.27 The hedge accounting specified in FASB ASC 815-25-40-1 for a fair value hedge should continue to be used unless one of the following occurs:

   a. Any criterion identified in section **2355.26** is not met.

   b. The derivative expires or is sold, terminated, or exercised.

   c. The entity removes the designation of the fair value hedge.

Illustrative Example of Fair Value Hedge

2355.28 On December 31, 20X0, Company D issues at face value a $1 million, 8% fixed-rate note payable due on December 31, 20X3, with semi-annual interest payments on each June 30 and December 31. On the same day, Company D enters into an interest rate swap with Company E for a notional amount of $1 million. Under the swap, Company D will receive payments based on an 8% fixed interest rate and will pay a variable interest rate based on the London Interbank Offered Rate (LIBOR). The swap calls for semi-annual settlement with the first settlement on June 30, 20X1, and the last on December 31, 20X3. Assume that on December 31, 20X0, LIBOR is 7%.

2355.29 Assume that on June 30, 20X1, LIBOR is 6.5%, the fair value of the swap increases to $22,000, and the fair value of the debt has increased $22,000. At June 30, 20X1, the following entries are necessary:

Interest Rate Swap (an asset)	$22,000	
Gain on Hedge Activity		$22,000
To record the change in the fair value of the swap.		
Loss on Hedge Activity	$22,000	
8% Notes Payable		$22,000
To record the change in the fair value of the debt.		

Interest Expense	$40,000	
Cash		$40,000

To record the semi-annual interest on the debt at a fixed rate of 8% (i.e., $1,000,000 × 0.08 × 6/12).

Cash	$ 5,000	
Interest Expense		$ 5,000

To record the settlement on the receive-fixed, pay-variable interest rate swap (receive $40,000, pay $35,000).

2355.30 Note that with the interest rate swap, Company D's net interest expense is $35,000 ($1,000,000 X .07 X 6/12), which is the amount associated with the variable interest rate (LIBOR), rather than the $40,000 amount that would have been incurred without the swap. The variable interest amount is based on the LIBOR during the period (7%). The variable amount during the second half of 20X1 will be based on 6.5%, the rate after the reset on June 30.

2355.31 The $22,000 change in the fair value of the interest rate swap (the hedging derivative instrument) is included in Company D's net income. In like manner, the change in the fair value of the outstanding debt (the hedged item) is also included in net income. In the case of a "perfect" hedge such as this one, the change in the fair value of the hedging instrument (the derivative) and the change in the fair value of the hedged item will exactly offset each other. Therefore, the net effect on net income of the changes in these two fair values is zero.

2355.32 The interest rate swap (the hedging derivative) is recognized on Company D's June 30, 20X1, balance sheet at its fair value of $22,000. The hedged item, the 8% note payable, is reported at what would otherwise be its carrying amount, $1 million in Company D's case, plus the $22,000 increase in the fair value of the debt.

Cash Flow Hedges

2355.33 As mentioned previously, cash flow hedges protect against the risk caused by *variable* prices, costs, rates, or terms that cause future cash flows to be uncertain, whereas fair value hedges protect against the changes in value caused by *fixed* terms, rates, or prices. A cash flow hedge is a hedge of an anticipated or forecasted transaction that is probable of occurring in the future, but the amount of the transaction has not been fixed.

2355.34 Derivatives designated as hedges of anticipated or forecasted transactions are carried at fair value. The gain or loss resulting from changes in the fair value of the derivative is recognized in *other comprehensive income* rather than in net income. The change in the fair value of the hedged item is *not* recognized in the financial statements.

2355.35 For a hedge to qualify as a cash flow hedge, certain criteria must be met. The following are perhaps the most important of these criteria:

    a. At the inception of the hedge, there is formal documentation of the hedging relationship and the entity's risk management objective and strategy for undertaking the hedge.

    b. Both at the inception of the hedge and on an ongoing basis, the hedging relationship is expected to be highly effective in achieving offsetting cash flows attributable to the hedged risk during the period that the hedge is designated.

    c. The forecasted transaction is probable and is specifically identified as a single transaction or a group of individual transactions.

    d. The forecasted transaction is a transaction with a party external to the reporting entity and presents an exposure to variations in cash flows for the hedged risk that could affect reported earnings.

    e. The forecasted transaction is not the acquisition of an asset or incurrence of a liability that will subsequently be remeasured with changes in fair value attributable to the hedged risk reported currently in earnings. The hedged item presents an exposure to changes in fair value attributable to the hedged risk that could affect reported earnings.

2355.36 The hedge accounting specified in FASB ASC 815-30-40 for a cash flow hedge should continue to be used unless one of the following occurs:

   a. Any criterion identified in section **2355.35** is not met.

   b. The derivative expires or is sold, terminated, or exercised.

   c. The entity removes the designation of the cash flow hedge.

Illustrative Example of Cash Flow Hedge

2355.37 The following illustration assumes the same facts as those introduced in section **2355.28** for a fair value hedge, except that the transaction is discussed from the standpoint of Company E rather than Company D. This use of the same set of facts emphasizes the similarities and differences between a cash flow hedge and a fair value hedge. Company E initially had a $1 million note payable, issued on December 31, 20X0. The note pays interest semi-annually on June 30 and December 31 based on LIBOR. On December 31, 20X0, Company E entered into an interest rate swap with Company D. Under the swap, Company E will receive payments based on LIBOR and will pay interest based on an 8% fixed rate. The swap calls for semi-annual settlement with the first settlement on June 30, 20X1, and the last on December 31, 20X3. Assume that on December 31, 20X0, LIBOR is 7%.

2355.38 Assume that on June 30, 20X1, LIBOR is 6.5%, the fair value of the swap decreases to $22,000, and the fair value of the debt has decreased by $22,000. At June 30, 20X1, the following entries are necessary:

Other Comprehensive Income	$22,000	
Interest Rate Swap (a liability)		$22,000
To record the change in the fair value of the swap.		
Interest Expense	$35,000	
Cash		$35,000
To record the semi-annual interest on the debt at LIBOR, $1,000,000 X 0.07 X 6/12		
Interest Expense	$5,000	
Cash		$5,000
To record the settlement on the receive-fixed, pay-variable interest rate swap (receive $35,000, pay $40,000).		

2355.39 The item being hedged by Company E is its variable interest cash flow that is based on LIBOR. Since LIBOR can vary, Company E's interest cash flow is a variable rather than a fixed amount. The anticipated cash flow is the amount of interest that Company E will pay during the term of the note. (Recall that from Company D's standpoint, the future interest cash flow was a fixed amount rather than variable.)

2355.40 With the interest rate swap, Company E's net interest expense is $40,000, which is the amount associated with the fixed interest rate of 8%, rather than the $35,000 amount that would have been incurred without the swap.

2355.41 The $22,000 change in the fair value of the interest rate swap (the hedging derivative instrument) is included in Company E's *other comprehensive income* rather than in net income. In addition, the change in the fair value of the note payable is not recognized in the financial statements.

2355.42 If the interest rate swap contract is allowed to remain in effect until the December 31, 20X3, maturity date of the note payable, the fair value of the swap at that date will be zero. The accumulated other comprehensive income associated with the interest rate swap will be zero at December 31, 20X3.

2355.43 The cash flow hedge illustration assumes that the interest rate swap is "perfectly effective" in hedging the risk associated with the anticipated future interest cash flows. If that is not the case, the gain or loss associated with the "ineffective" portion would be included in net income rather than in other comprehensive income. For example, if the notional amount of the interest rate swap had been $1.5 million rather than $1 million (the amount of the note payable), the portion of any gain or loss associated with the $500,000 "extra" notional amount would be included in net income.

Hedge of Foreign Currency Exposure of Net Investment in Foreign Operations

2355.44 A derivative instrument *or a nonderivative financial instrument* that may give rise to a foreign currency transaction gain or loss under FASB ASC 830-20-35 (see section **2366**) can be designated as hedging the foreign currency exposure of a net investment in a foreign operation. The gain or loss on a hedging instrument that is designated as, and is effective as, an economic hedge of the net investment in a foreign operation should be reported in the same manner as a change in the cumulative translation adjustment, which is a component of other comprehensive income. A hedge of the foreign currency exposure of a net investment in a foreign operation is reported in a manner similar to that of a cash flow hedge. See section **2366** for an illustration of the hedge of an investment in a foreign entity.

Embedded Derivatives

2355.45 When defining derivative instruments and determining the types of instruments that would be considered derivative instruments under FASB ASC 815, the FASB was concerned that entities would attempt to circumvent the requirements of FASB ASC 815 by embedding a derivative instrument into a nonderivative instrument. That concern caused the FASB to specify that the scope of FASB ASC 815 includes derivatives that are embedded in other contracts. These "embedded" derivatives are implicit or explicit terms that affect some or all of the cash flows or the value of other exchanges required by the contract in a manner similar to a derivative instrument.

2355.46 FASB ASC 815-15-30-2 requires that these embedded derivatives be bifurcated (separated out) from the nonderivative host and be accounted for as a derivative if certain conditions are met.

2355.47 FASB ASC 815-15-30-2 allows for a fair value election for certain hybrid financial instruments with embedded derivatives that otherwise would be bifurcated. Under this election, the entity would account for the nonderivative instrument (that contains the embedded derivative) at fair value and thus avoid having to bifurcate the derivative instrument from the nonderivative host contract.

Disclosure About Derivative Instruments and Hedging Activities

2355.48 FASB ASC 815-10-50 requires a great deal of disclosure concerning derivative instruments. FASB ASC 815-10-50-1 requires that an entity that holds or issues derivative instruments (or nonderivative instruments that are designated and qualify as hedging instruments) disclose its objectives for holding or issuing those instruments, the context needed to understand those objectives, and its strategies for achieving those objectives. The description shall distinguish between derivative instruments (and nonderivative instruments) designated as fair value hedging instruments, derivative instruments designated as cash flow hedging instruments, derivative instruments (and nonderivative instruments) designated as hedging instruments for hedges of the foreign currency exposure of a net investment in a foreign operation, and all other derivatives. The description also shall indicate the entity's risk management policy for each of those types of hedges, including a description of the items or transactions for which risks are hedged. For derivative instruments not designated as hedging instruments, the description shall indicate the purpose of the derivative activity.

2355.49 In each statement of financial position presented, an entity must report hybrid financial instruments measured at fair value under the election and under the practicability exception in FASB ASC 815-10-50 in a manner that separates those reported fair values from the carrying amounts of assets and liabilities subsequently measured using another measurement attribute on the face of the statement of financial position. To accomplish that separate reporting, an entity may either (a) display separate line items for the fair value and non-fair-value carrying amounts or (b) present the aggregate of those fair value and non-fair-value amounts and parenthetically disclose the amount of fair value included in the aggregate amount. For those hybrid financial instruments measured at fair value under the election and under the practicability exception in FASB ASC 815-15-50-1, an entity shall also disclose the information specified in paragraphs 50-28 through 50-32 of FASB ASC 825-10.

An entity must provide information that will allow users to understand the effect of changes in the fair value of hybrid financial instruments measured at fair value under the election and under the practicability exception in paragraph 16 on earnings (or other performance indicators for entities that do not report earnings).

2355.50 An entity's disclosures for every reporting period for which a complete set of financial statements is presented also shall include the following:

   a. **Fair value hedges:** For derivative instruments, as well as nonderivative instruments that may give rise to foreign currency transaction gains or losses under FASB ASC 830-20-35 that have been designated and have qualified as fair value hedging instruments and for the related hedged items:

   (1) The net gain or loss recognized in earnings during the reporting period representing (a) the amount of the hedges' ineffectiveness and (b) the component of the derivative instruments' gain or loss, if any, excluded from the assessment of hedge effectiveness, and a description of where the net gain or loss is reported in the statement of income or other statement of financial performance.

   (2) The amount of net gain or loss recognized in earnings when a hedged firm commitment no longer qualifies as a fair value hedge.

   b. **Cash flow hedges:** For derivative instruments that have been designated and have qualified as cash flow hedging instruments and for the related hedged transactions:

   (1) The net gain or loss recognized in earnings during the reporting period representing (a) the amount of the hedges' ineffectiveness and (b) the component of the derivative instruments' gain or loss, if any, excluded from the assessment of hedge effectiveness, and a description of where the net gain or loss is reported in the statement of income or other statement of financial performance.

   (2) A description of the transactions or other events that will result in the reclassification into earnings of gains and losses that are reported in accumulated other comprehensive income, and the estimated net amount of the existing gains or losses at the reporting date that is expected to be reclassified into earnings within the next 12 months.

   (3) The maximum length of time over which the entity is hedging its exposure to the variability in future cash flows for forecasted transactions excluding those forecasted transactions related to the payment of variable interest on existing financial instruments.

   (4) The amount of gains and losses reclassified into earnings as a result of the discontinuance of cash flow hedges because it is probable that the original forecasted transactions will not occur by the end of the originally specified time period or within the additional period of time discussed in FASB ASC 815-10-50.

c. **Hedges of the net investment in a foreign operation**: For derivative instruments, as well as nonderivative instruments that may give rise to foreign currency transaction gains or losses under FASB ASC 830-20-35, that have been designated and have qualified as hedging instruments for hedges of the foreign currency exposure of a net investment in a foreign operation, the net amount of gains or losses included in the cumulative translation adjustment during the reporting period. The quantitative disclosures about derivative instruments may be more useful, and less likely to be perceived to be out of context or otherwise misunderstood, if similar information is disclosed about other financial instruments or nonfinancial assets and liabilities to which the derivative instruments are related by activity. Accordingly, in those situations, an entity is encouraged, but not required, to present a more complete picture of its activities by disclosing that information.

2360 Foreign Currency Transactions and Translation

2361 General Concepts

2361.01 The involvement of domestic (United States) corporations in foreign operations results in the need to convert the results of events and transactions originally measured in a foreign currency into the domestic currency (U.S. dollar). The discussion in this section focuses on foreign currency transactions and translation of foreign currency financial statements.

2361.02 The following definitions are important in understanding accounting for foreign operations:

a. **Exchange rate**: The amount of one currency that can be exchanged for another at a particular point in time.

b. **Spot rate**: The exchange rate existing at the current date.

c. **Forward rate**: A specified exchange rate between currencies at some specified future date.

d. **Forward exchange contract**: A contract to buy or sell currency at a forward rate.

e. **Functional currency**: The currency of the primary economic environment in which the entity operates (i.e., the environment in which the entity generates and expends cash).

2361.03 In the examples in this section, items are converted from a hypothetical foreign currency, zags (Z), into U.S. dollars. Thus, exchange rates are stated in terms of the dollars represented by one zag. For example, an exchange rate of 1Z = $1.50 means that one zag (Z) can be exchanged for $1.50.

2362 Foreign Currency Transactions Other Than Forward Contracts

2362.01 Foreign currency transactions are transactions denominated in a currency other than the entity's functional currency. For example, if a U.S. company purchases goods on account from a company located in Japan and agrees to pay the amount owed in yen (the Japanese currency), the payable is denominated in a foreign currency (yen) and the transaction is a foreign currency transaction. Similarly, assume that a U.S. company has a subsidiary located in Mexico and that the functional currency of the subsidiary is the peso (the currency of Mexico). If the subsidiary purchases goods on account from a company located in Japan and agrees to pay the debt in yen, the payable is denominated in a foreign currency (yen) and the transaction is a foreign currency transaction from the standpoint of the subsidiary. However, if the payable were denominated in pesos, the transaction would not be a foreign currency transaction with respect to the subsidiary.

2362.02 Foreign currency transactions may produce receivables or payables that are fixed in terms of the amount of foreign currency that will be received or paid. A change in exchange rates between the functional currency and the currency in which a transaction is denominated increases or decreases the expected amount of functional currency cash flows on settlement of the transaction. The increase or decrease in expected functional currency cash flows is a foreign currency transaction gain or loss that should generally be included in determining net income for the period in which the exchange rate changes. Exceptions for which the transaction gain or loss should not be included in the determination of net income are discussed in section **2363.07**.

2362.03 For other than forward contracts, the following should apply to all foreign currency transactions of an enterprise and its investees:

    a. At the date the transaction is recognized, each asset, liability, revenue, expense, gain, or loss arising from the transaction should be measured and recorded in the functional currency of the recording entity by use of the exchange rate in effect at that date.

    b. At each balance sheet date, recorded balances that are denominated in a currency other than the functional currency of the recording entity should be adjusted to reflect the current exchange rate as of the balance sheet date.

2362.04 **Example:** Domestic Company, a U.S. company, acquires inventory on October 1, 20X1, from Foreign Company and agrees to pay 10,000 zags (Z) on March 1, 20X2. The exchange rates are as follows:

Date	Exchange Rate
10/01/X1	1Z = $1.50
12/31/X1	1Z = $1.58
03/01/X2	1Z = $1.56

2362.05 The following entry is necessary on Domestic's books on October 1, 20X1, to record the purchase of the inventory:

Inventory $15,000
    Accounts Payable (10,000Z × $1.50 = $15,000) $15,000

The inventory account is an asset arising from the foreign currency transaction and is accordingly measured at the current exchange rate as of October 1, 20X1, and recorded in U.S. dollars. However, the inventory account is not denominated in a foreign currency and thus will not be adjusted for changes in the exchange rate. The accounts payable account is a liability arising out of the foreign currency transaction and therefore is measured at the current exchange rate at October 1, 20X1, and is recorded in U.S. dollars. Since the accounts payable is denominated in a foreign currency (i.e., it must be settled in units of a foreign currency), it must be adjusted at the balance sheet date for changes in the exchange rate.

2362.06 Assuming that Domestic's fiscal year is the calendar year, the following entry is necessary on December 31, 20X1, the balance sheet date, to remeasure the payable denominated in a foreign currency at the exchange rate at the balance sheet date:

Exchange Loss $800
    Accounts Payable (10,000Z × ($1.58 - $1.50) = $800) $800

The exchange loss is included in the determination of net income. It is not an extraordinary item.

2362.07 On the settlement date, March 1, 20X2, the payable must be remeasured to reflect any exchange gain or loss arising from fluctuations in the exchange rate between the balance sheet date and the settlement date. In addition, entries are necessary to reflect the following:

a. The acquisition of units of the foreign currency (zags) needed to pay the debt

b. The payment of the debt with the units of foreign currency

Accounts Payable	$200	
Exchange Gain		$200

To record the remeasurement of the accounts payable at the exchange rate at March 1, 20X2, 10,000Z × ($1.58 - $1.56) = $200.

Foreign Currency (zags)	$15,600	
Cash (10,000Z × $1.56)		$15,600

To record acquisition of zags to pay the 10,000Z due.

Accounts Payable	$15,600	
Foreign Currency		$15,600

To record the payment of the 10,000Z due.

2362.08 The three entries in section **2362.07** can be summarized in the following single entry:

Accounts Payable (balance before remeasuring on March 1, 20X2)	$15,800	
Exchange Gain		$200
Cash		15,600

2362.09 One can see that as the exchange rate increases, the debtor incurs an exchange loss because a greater number of U.S. dollars is required to satisfy the payable denominated in units of a foreign currency. Conversely, the debtor experiences an exchange gain when the exchange rate declines.

2363 Hedges of Foreign Currency Exposures That Do Not Qualify for Hedge Accounting

2363.01 Foreign currency transactions may expose an entity to foreign currency exchange gains or losses if exchange rates change between the transaction date and the settlement date. There are a number of foreign currency financial instruments that an entity may use to control these foreign currency risk exposures. Most of these foreign currency financial instruments qualify as derivatives. (See section **2355** for a discussion of derivatives in general.) Among these instruments are foreign currency swaps, foreign currency futures, foreign currency options, and foreign currency forward contracts. The most widely used is the foreign currency forward contract. Accordingly, the discussion in this and the next three sections focuses on the use of forward contracts. However, the fundamental nature of the measurement and recognition standards for other types of derivative instruments are the same as those for forward contracts.

2363.02 A *foreign currency forward contract* is an agreement to exchange different currencies at a specified future date and at a specified rate (the forward rate). For example, a U.S. company might enter into a forward contract to receive a specified number of units of a foreign currency (e.g., yen) on a specified future date. In return, the U.S. company would agree to pay a specified number of U.S. dollars to the other entity (e.g., a broker) on that specified future date. In this case, the foreign currency (yen) receivable from the broker is denominated in a foreign currency, whereas the U.S. dollars payable to the broker are not denominated in a foreign currency.

2363.03 The accounting for instruments that are used as hedges depends on whether the hedge qualifies for hedge accounting. Just because the instrument may serve as an economic hedge does not necessarily mean that under FASB ASC 815, it qualifies for hedge accounting. Under hedge accounting, the foreign currency exchange gains and losses are accounted for according to the particular type of hedge.

2363.04 There are three types of foreign currency hedges that qualify for hedge accounting: foreign currency fair value hedges, foreign currency cash flow hedges, and hedges of a foreign currency net investment in a foreign entity. This section, 2363, focuses on hedges that do not qualify for hedge accounting. The three types of foreign currency hedges that qualify for hedge accounting are discussed in sections **2364**, **2365**, and **2366**.

Illustration of a Foreign Currency Hedge that Does Not Qualify for Hedge Accounting

2363.05 The most common use of forward contracts is to hedge an exposed asset or liability denominated in a foreign currency. For example, an entity may have a receivable or payable denominated in a foreign currency that is the result of some prior transaction. Under FASB ASC 815, the hedge of a recognized foreign-currency-denominated asset or liability would not have qualified for hedge accounting. However, FASB ASC 815 allows hedges of recognized foreign-currency-denominated assets or liabilities to qualify for hedge accounting if such hedges meet all of the other criteria required for hedge accounting. The following example assumes that the hedge of a foreign-currency-denominated payable fails to meet one or more of the other criteria that must be met to qualify for hedge accounting. The reason the hedge fails to qualify for hedge accounting is not because it is a hedge of a recognized foreign-currency-denominated liability, but because it fails to meet certain other criteria. (Actually, because FASB ASC 815 requires the hedged recognized liability to be measured at the spot rate rather than the forward rate, the entries for this particular example are the same whether it is deemed to qualify for hedge accounting or not.)

2363.06 **Example:** (For simplicity, income taxes are ignored.) Domestic Company, a U.S. company, acquires inventory on October 1, 20X1, from Foreign Company and agrees to pay 10,000 zags (Z) on March 1, 20X2. On October 1, 20X1, Domestic also enters into a forward contract to receive 10,000Z on March 1, 20X2. Under the forward contract, Domestic agrees to pay the broker $15,100 U.S. dollars based on the forward rate on October 1, 20X1, of $1.51, which is the market forward rate. The exchange rates and fair values of the forward contacts are as follows:

Date	Spot Rate	Forward Rate for 03/01/X2		Fair Value of Forward Contract
10/01/X1	1Z = $1.50	5-month forward rate: 1Z =	$1.51	0
12/31/X1	1Z = $1.58	2-month forward rate: 1Z =	$1.60	891
03/01/X2	1Z = $1.56			(500)

2363.07 Any exchange gains or losses associated with the forward contract or with the accounts payable denominated in a foreign currency must be recognized in the period in which the exchange rate changes and be included in the determination of net income.

2363.08 The following entries are made by Domestic Company on October 1, 20X1:

Related to the purchase of the inventory:
Inventory $15,000
    Accounts Payable in zags ($10,000 × $1.50) $15,000
To record the purchase of the inventory at the spot rate.

Related to the forward contract:
    No entry required.

2363.09 The accounts payable denominated in a foreign currency is recorded (measured) at the spot rate on the date of the acquisition of the inventory, October 1, 20X1.

2363.10 The forward contract is a derivative instrument and must be recorded at its fair value. At October 1, 20X1, the inception of the contract, its fair value is $0. (The fair value of any forward contract is zero at the inception of the contract if the forward rate in the contract is the market forward rate.) Therefore, no entry is required on October 1, 20X1. Some would prefer to record both the receivable and payable portions of the forward contract rather than record the fair value of the contract on a net basis. Under that approach, the forward contract would be recorded at the forward rate on October 1, 20X1, as follows:

FC (zags) Receivable from Broker	$15,100	
$ Payable to Broker (10,000Z × $1.51 forward rate)		$15,100
To record the forward contract at the forward rate.		

2363.11 Most enterprises record forward contracts at fair value on a net basis rather than record both the receivable and payable portions as shown in section **2363.10**. The author has chosen to use the method most used in practice and, therefore, records forward contracts at their fair value on a net basis.

2363.12 Exposed assets or liabilities that do not qualify as hedged items under FASB ASC 815 (i.e., the hedge failed to meet all of the criteria for hedge accounting) must be initially measured at the spot rate on the date the asset (receivable, for example) or liability (payable, for example) is initially recognized. In addition, these exposed assets or liabilities must be remeasured each balance sheet date and at the date of settlement. Thus, at December 31, 20X1, the balance sheet date, Domestic's accounts payable denominated in a foreign currency (zags) must be remeasured at the spot rate on December 31, 20X1, and any related exchange gain or loss recognized and included in net income. The entry to remeasure the accounts payable denominated in zags is:

Foreign Currency Transaction Loss	$800	
Accounts Payable in zags		$800
To remeasure accounts payable at the December 31, 20X1, spot rate 10,000Z × ($1.58 – $1.50) = $800.		

2363.13 As discussed in section **2355**, derivative instruments must be recognized on an entity's balance sheet at fair value. The gains or losses resulting from changes in a derivative's fair value during the period must be included in net income of the period unless the derivative is used as a hedge and the hedge qualifies for hedge accounting under FASB ASC 815.

2363.14 Since Domestic's forward contract does not qualify for hedge accounting, it must be recognized on Domestic's balance sheet at December 31, 20X1, at fair value and the change in fair value included in net income. Under FASB ASC 815, one acceptable approach to determine the fair value of the forward contract is to multiply the change in the forward rate (expressed as units of foreign currency per U.S. dollar) by the number of foreign currency units and discount this amount for the remaining time to the settlement date. Using this approach to measuring fair value, and assuming a 6% discount rate, the fair value of Domestic's forward contract and the change in the fair value from October 1, 20X1, to December 31, 20X1, is determined as follows:

Fair value of forward contract at 12/31/X1:	
10,000Z × $1.60 forward rate at 12/31/X1	$16,000
10,000Z × $1.51 forward rate at 10/01/X1	15,100
Fair value of forward contract at 12/31/X1 before discount	900
Discount for period 12/31/X1 - 03/01/X2 ($900 × 0.06 × 2/12)	9
Fair value of forward contract at 12/31/X1	891
Fair value of forward contract at 10/01/X1 (inception of contract)	0
Increase in fair value of forward contract 10/01/X1 - 12/31/X1	$ 891

The entry to record the increase in the fair value of the forward contract is as follows:
Forward Contract $891
    Foreign Currency Transaction Gain $891
To record the change in the fair value of the forward contract.

2363.15 The entries at March 1, 20X2, the (settlement date) are:

Accounts Payable in zags $200
    Exchange gain $200
To remeasure the liability denominated in a foreign currency at the spot rate on 03/01/X2 (10,000Z × ($1.56 - $1.58) = $200).

Loss on forward contract $391
    Forward contract $391
To remeasure the forward contract for the change in its fair value since 12/31/X1, computed as follows:

Fair value of forward contract at 03/01/X2:	
10,000Z × $1.56 forward rate at 03/01/X2 (same as spot rate)	$15,600
10,000Z × $1.51 forward rate at 10/01/X1	15,100
Fair value of forward contract at 03/01/X2 before discount	500
Discount for period to settlement date	0
Fair value of forward contract at 03/01/X2	500
Fair value of forward contract at 12/31/X1	891
Increase (decrease) in fair value of forward contract	$ (391)

Foreign Currency (10,000Z × $1.56 spot rate 03/01/X2) $15,600
    Cash (10,000Z × $1.51 forward rate 10/01/X1) $15,100
    Forward Contract 500
To record settlement of the forward contract with the broker with the foreign currency received recorded at the spot rate on the settlement date and the U.S. dollars paid recorded at the forward rate that existed at the inception of the contract on 10/01/X1.

Accounts Payable (10,000Z × $1.56 spot rate 03/01/X2) $15,600
    Foreign Currency (10,000Z × $1.56 spot rate 03/01/X2) $15,600
To record the payment of the accounts payable denominated in a foreign currency (zags).

2363.16 The net effect of the forward contract was to lock in an outward cash flow of $15,100, the forward rate at the October 1, 20X1, inception of the forward contract. The difference between the $15,100 forward amount and the $15,000 spot rate amount at October 1, 20X1, when the inventory was acquired and the accounts payable incurred is the "insurance premium" that Domestic is willing to pay to avoid possible exchange losses. Since the 10,000 zags received under the forward contract serve as the 10,000 zags needed to pay for the inventory, the $15,100 U.S. dollars paid to the broker represent the $15,000 cost of the inventory and the $100 "insurance premium" paid to hedge foreign currency exchange losses. The $100 "insurance premium" is reflected in the $100 net foreign currency transaction loss recognized in 20X1 and 20X2 (net $600 loss related to the remeasurement of the accounts payable and $500 gain related to measurement of the forward contract).

2363.17 The impact of the forward contract on Domestic's foreign currency transaction gains and losses can be summarized as follows:

	Without the Hedge	With the Hedge
Gain (loss) associated with accounts payable denominated in a foreign currency ($800 gain in 20X1 and $(200) loss in 20X2)	$(600)	$(600)
Gain (loss) associated with the forward contract ($891 gain in 20X1 and $(391) loss in 20X2)		500
Effect on net income	$(600)	$(100)

2363.18 In summary, since Domestic's use of the forward contract as an economic hedge of an exposed liability does not qualify for hedge accounting, the exposed liability must be measured initially and remeasured at any balance sheet or settlement date based on the spot rate at that time. In addition, since the forward contract is a derivative, it must be recognized at fair value and any changes in fair value included in net income in the period of the change in fair value.

2363.19 Thus, the forward contract is treated the same as if it were not used as a hedge. This type of forward contract (and, more generally, this type of derivative instrument) is known as a *speculative forward contract.* Just as in Domestic's case, FASB ASC 815 requires that the gains and losses associated with speculative forward contracts (derivatives) be included in net income in the period(s) in which the changes in fair value of the forward contracts (derivatives) take place.

2364 Foreign Currency Fair Value Hedges

2364.01 FASB ASC 815 specifies two important measurement requirements for fair value hedges in general. The first is that gains or losses associated with changes in the fair value of the hedging instrument (the derivative instrument) be recognized in net income in the period in which the change in fair value takes place. The second is that changes in the fair value of the hedged item must be recognized in net income and as an adjustment to the carrying amount of the hedged item.

2364.02 Prior to the issuance of FASB ASC 815, foreign currency fair value hedges were limited to hedges of unrecognized firm commitments and available-for-sale securities. However, FASB ASC 815 allows foreign currency fair value hedges to include those in which the hedged items are recognized foreign-currency-denominated assets (in addition to available-for-sale securities) or liabilities.

2364.03 If Domestic Company's hedge of its foreign-currency-denominated accounts payable in section **2363** had qualified for hedge accounting, it would have been a foreign currency fair value hedge and the entries would have been the same as those shown in section **2363**.

2364.04 A *firm commitment* is an agreement with an unrelated party, binding on both parties and usually legally enforceable, that specifies all significant terms and includes a disincentive for nonperformance that is sufficiently large to make performance probable. Firm commitments are generally not recognized (recorded) as assets or liabilities prior to performance of both parties. Therefore, in the case of a foreign currency firm commitment (such as a commitment to purchase units of inventory at a specified price payable in a foreign currency), there is no recognized asset or liability to remeasure. FASB ASC 830-20-35 did not require the gain or loss resulting from the change in the fair value of the hedged foreign currency firm commitment to be included in net income. Thus, the accounting for hedges of foreign currency firm commitments under FASB ASC 830-20-35 is different than that for fair value hedges under FASB ASC 815 and is inconsistent with the basic notion in FASB ASC 815 that gains and losses associated with changes in the fair value of the hedged item (the firm commitment) should be included in net income. Therefore, in FASB ASC 815, the FASB chose to change the accounting for hedges of foreign currency firm commitments and specifies that hedges of foreign currency firm commitments must be accounted for as fair value hedges.

2364.05 Unrealized gains and losses associated with available-for-sale securities are included in other comprehensive income rather than in net income. Therefore, under FASB ASC 320-10-15-10 and FASB ASC 830-20-35, if an available-for-sale security were the hedged item, changes in the fair value of the hedged item would not be included in net income. The exclusion from net income of the gain or loss resulting from changes in the fair value of the hedged available-for-sale security is inconsistent with the basic notion in FASB ASC 815 that gains and losses associated with changes in the fair value of the hedged item (the available-for-sale security) should be included in net income. Therefore, as in the case of hedges of firm commitments, the FASB chose to change the accounting for hedges of the foreign currency exposure of an available-for-sale security. Under FASB ASC 815, the FASB requires that hedges of available-for-sale securities be accounted for as fair value hedges rather than in the manner in which such hedges would have been accounted for prior to FASB ASC 815.

2364.06 A hedge of a firm commitment denominated in a foreign currency is used as follows to demonstrate the recognition and measurement issues associated with a fair value hedge.

2364.07 **Illustration of a hedge of a firm commitment denominated in a foreign currency.** (For simplicity, income taxes are ignored.) Assume that Domestic Company, a U.S. company, on October 1, 20X1, enters into a firm commitment to purchase inventory for 10,000 zags (Z), with delivery of the inventory and payment to take place on March 1, 20X2. On October 1, 20X1, Domestic also enters into a forward contract to receive 10,000Z on March 1, 20X2. Under the forward contract, Domestic agrees to pay the broker $15,100 U.S. dollars based on the forward rate on October 1, 20X1, of $1.51, which is the market forward rate. The exchange rates and fair values of the forward contract are as follows:

Date	Spot Rate	Forward Rate for 03/01/X2		Fair Value of Forward Contract
10/01/X1	1Z = $1.50	5-month forward rate: 1Z =	$1.51	0
12/31/X1	1Z = $1.58	2-month forward rate: 1Z =	$1.60	891
03/01/X2	1Z = $1.56			(500)

2364.08 Note that these are the same facts as those used in the illustration introduced in section **2363.06** (for a hedge of an exposed liability), except that in the illustration in section **2363.06** the inventory was purchased and delivery made on October 1, 20X1. In the illustration in this section, the inventory will not be received until March 1, 20X2. The forward contract is being used to hedge an unrecognized foreign currency firm commitment rather than a recognized liability (the accounts payable denominated in a foreign currency). The forward contract hedges the changes in the fair value of the firm commitment that are attributable to changes in the foreign currency exchange rate.

2364.09 The following entries are made by Domestic Company on October 1, 20X1:

Related to the firm commitment:
No entry required.

Related to the forward contract:
No entry required.

2364.10 In the case of fair value hedges, FASB ASC 815 requires that the hedging derivative instrument (the forward contract in Domestic's case) be recognized at fair value. Since the fair value of the forward contract at the inception of the contract is zero, no entry is required at October 1, 20X1, for the forward contract.

2364.11 FASB ASC 815 also requires that the gain or loss on the hedged item attributable to the hedged risk should adjust the carrying amount of the hedged item (the purchase commitment in Domestic's case) and be recognized currently in earnings. Since the fair value of the firm commitment at the inception of the commitment is zero, no entry is required at October 1, 20X1, for the firm commitment.

2364.12 At December 31, 20X1, it is necessary to record the change in the fair value of the forward contract *and* the change in the fair value of the firm commitment that is attributable to changes in the foreign currency forward rate. It is important to note that other factors may change the fair value of the firm commitment, such as supply and demand related to this particular type of inventory. However, the only portion of the change in the fair value of the firm commitment that is recorded under FASB ASC 815 is that attributable to the changes in the foreign currency forward rate.

2364.13 The entries at December 31, 20X1, are:

Related to the firm commitment:
Foreign Currency Transaction Loss	$891	
Firm Commitment		$891

To recognize the change in the fair value of the purchase commitment attributable to the change in the foreign currency forward rate.

Related to the forward contract:
Forward Contract	$891	
Foreign Currency Transaction Gain		$891

To recognize the change in the fair value of the forward contract.

2364.14 The fair value and the change in the fair value of the forward contract (and thus the firm commitment) are given in section **2364.07**.

2364.15 Since the fair value of the forward contract at March 1, 20X2, is $500, the fair value of the forward contract (and thus the firm commitment) decreased $391 ($891 fair value at December 31, 20X1 – $500 fair value at March 1, 20X2) from December 31, 20X1, to March 1, 20X2. Therefore, the following entries are required at March 1, 20X2:

Firm Commitment	$391	
Foreign Currency Transaction Gain		$391

To recognize the change in the fair value of the purchase commitment attributable to the change in the foreign currency forward rate.

Foreign Currency Transaction Loss	$391	
Forward Contract		$391

To recognize the change in the fair value of the forward contract.

Foreign Currency (10,000Z × $1.56 spot rate 03/01/X2)	$15,600	
Cash (10,000Z × $1.51 forward rate 10/01/X1)		$15,100
Forward Contract		500

To record settlement of the forward contract with the broker with the foreign currency received recorded at the spot rate on the settlement date and the U.S. dollars paid recorded at the forward rate that existed at the inception of the contract on 10/01/X1.

Inventory	$15,100	
Firm Commitment	500	
Foreign Currency (10,000Z × $1.56 spot rate 03/01/X2)		$15,600

To record purchase of the inventory.

2364.16 The net effect of the forward contract was to lock in an outward cash flow of $15,100, the forward rate at the October 1, 20X1, inception of the forward contract and inception of the firm commitment. The difference between the $15,100 forward amount and the $15,000 spot rate amount at October 1, 20X1, when the firm commitment was entered into is the "insurance premium" that Domestic is willing to pay to avoid possible exchange losses. Since the 10,000 zags received under the forward contract serves as the 10,000 zags needed to pay for the inventory, the 15,100 U.S. dollars paid to the broker represent the effective cost of the inventory. Under this approach, the $100 "insurance premium" is treated as a part of the cost of the inventory rather than being immediately charged against net income.

2364.17 In summary, since Domestic used the forward contract as a hedge of a foreign currency firm commitment, the hedge must be accounted for as a fair value hedge. The following summarizes the basic measurement requirements and Domestic's compliance with those requirements:

Requirement 1: The hedging derivative instrument (the forward contract) must be measured at fair value.

Domestic's compliance with requirement 1: Domestic's forward contract was initially measured at fair value of zero at the inception of the forward contract, remeasured at fair value of $891 at the balance sheet date, and at $500 at the settlement date.

Requirement 2: Changes in the fair value of the forward contract must be included in net income.

Domestic's compliance with requirement 2: Domestic included an $891 gain related to the hedging derivative instrument in net income in 20X1 and a $391 loss in net income in 20X2.

Requirement 3: Changes in the fair value of the hedged item that are attributable to changes in the foreign currency forward rates must be included in net income and serve as an adjustment of the hedged item.

Domestic's compliance with requirement 3: Domestic included an $891 loss related to the hedged item in net income in 20X1 and a $391 gain in net income in 20X2. The net $500 loss served as a decrease in the carrying amount of the firm commitment and, consequently, in the carrying amount of the inventory when it was purchased.

2365 Foreign Currency Cash Flow Hedges

2365.01 An entity may have exposure to variability in expected future cash flows. That exposure may be associated with an existing recognized asset or liability or a forecasted transaction. For example, as discussed in section **2355** on derivatives, an entity is exposed to variability in expected future cash flows if it has a variable-rate note payable. An entity also is exposed to variability if it has a forecasted transaction (as opposed to a firm commitment) at a price or exchange rate that is subject to variation.

2365.02 The accounting issues associated with cash flow hedges in general are discussed in section **2355**. The emphasis in this section is on foreign currency cash flow hedges.

2365.03 An entity may designate a derivative instrument as hedging the exposure to variability in expected future cash flows that is attributable to a particular risk. Provided that all other criteria are met and assuming that it is denominated in a foreign currency, the hedged item of a qualifying foreign currency cash flow hedge may be a forecasted transaction (e.g., a forecasted export sale), a recognized asset or liability, unrecognized firm commitment, or a forecasted intercompany transaction (e.g., a forecasted sale to a foreign subsidiary).

2365.04 FASB ASC 815 specifies, for cash flow hedges in general, that the hedging derivative installment should be carried at fair value with the "effective portion" of the derivative's gain or loss recognized in other comprehensive income rather than in net income. The *effective portion* is the extent to which the changes in the fair value of the hedging instrument actually serve to offset the particular risk exposure being hedged. These gains and losses recognized in other comprehensive income are subsequently recognized in net income in the same period or periods the hedged item affects net income.

2365.05 The change in the fair value of the hedged item is not recognized in the financial statements.

2365.06 **Illustration of a hedge of a forecasted transaction denominated in a foreign currency.** (For simplicity, income taxes are ignored.) Assume that Domestic Company, a U.S. company, on October 1, 20X1, budgets a purchase of 10,000 units of inventory from its principal supplier in a foreign country. The inventory would be acquired on March 1, 20X2, and payment would be made in zags (Z). Currently, the inventory would cost 10,000 zags (1Z per unit). Domestic does not enter into a formal firm commitment for this inventory; rather, it merely anticipates the purchase of the inventory. (Hence, this is a forecasted transaction rather than a firm commitment.) On October 1, 20X1, Domestic also enters into a forward contract to receive 10,000Z on March 1, 20X2. Under the forward contract, Domestic agrees to pay the broker 15,100 U.S. dollars based on the forward rate on October 1, 20X1, of $1.51, which is the market forward rate. The exchange rates and fair values of the forward contract are as follows:

Date	Spot Rate	Forward Rate for 03/01/X2		Fair Value of Forward Contract
10/01/X1	1Z = $1.50	5-month forward rate: 1Z =	$1.51	0
12/31/X1	1Z = $1.58	2-month forward rate: 1Z =	$1.60	891
03/01/X2	1Z = $1.56			(500)

2365.07 Note that these are the same facts as those used in the illustrations introduced in sections **2363.06** (hedge of an exposed liability) and **2364.07** (hedge of a firm commitment), except that the illustration in this section deals with the hedge of a forecasted transaction. The use of similar facts (except with respect to the nature of the hedged item) emphasizes the similarities and differences among the accounting requirements for foreign currency hedges of recognized assets and liabilities (that do not qualify for hedge accounting), foreign currency fair value hedges, and foreign currency cash flow hedges.

2365.08 Since Domestic's forward contract in this section is being used to hedge a forecasted transaction, the hedge is accounted for as a cash flow hedge (rather than as a fair value hedge). Recall that in section **2364.07**, Domestic entered into a formal firm commitment and, as a result, the hedge was accounted for under FASB ASC 815 as a fair value hedge.

2365.09 Because it anticipates the purchase of 10,000 units of inventory on March 1, 20X2, and the payment will be in zags (a foreign currency), Domestic is exposed to changes in the exchange rate between U.S. dollars and zags. Domestic's forward contract hedges this foreign currency exposure.

2365.10 Domestic also has the risk exposure that the cost of 10,000 units of inventory will change between October 1, 20X1, and March 1, 20X2, for reasons other than changes in the foreign currency exchange rates. However, the forward contract hedges only one type of risk—the foreign currency risk associated with changes in the exchange rate. The forward contract does not hedge the other types of risk.

2365.11 The following entries are made by Domestic Company on October 1, 20X1:

Related to the forecasted transaction:
No entry required.

Related to the forward contract:
No entry required.

2365.12 In the case of cash flow hedges, FASB ASC 815 requires that the hedging derivative instrument (the forward contract in Domestic's case) be recognized at fair value. Since the fair value of the forward contract at the inception of the contract is zero, no entry is required at October 1, 20X1, for the forward contract.

2365.13 FASB ASC 815 specifies that the gain or loss on the hedged item attributable to the hedged risk should not be recognized in the financial statements. Therefore, no entry is required on October 1, 20X1, with respect to the forecasted transaction (the budgeted purchase of the inventory).

2365.14 At December 31, 20X1, it is necessary to record the change in the fair value of the forward contract. Only the effective portion is recognized in other comprehensive income. Any ineffective portion is recognized in net income. For example, if the forward contract had been for 15,000Z (instead of 10,000Z), the gain or loss related to the "extra" 5,000Z of the forward contract would be included in net income rather than in other comprehensive income.

2365.15 Assume that Domestic assesses hedge effectiveness based on the entire change in fair value of the forward contract. This means that the $100 "premium" paid due to the difference between the spot rate and the forward rate on October 1, 20X1 (10,000Z ($1.51 - $1.50) = $100), is included in the measurement of the gain or loss recognized in other comprehensive income. In that case, the entries on December 31, 20X1, are:

Related to the forecasted transaction:
No entry required.

Related to the forward contract:
Forward Contract	$891	
Other Comprehensive Income		$891

To recognize the change in the fair value of the forward contract.

2365.16 The fair value and the change in the fair value of the forward contract are given in section **2365.06**.

2365.17 Note that the gain resulting from the increase in the fair value of the forward contract is credited to other comprehensive income. The other comprehensive income account is closed into an accumulated other comprehensive income account, which is a balance sheet account. Assuming that the 10,000 units of inventory are purchased on March 1, 20X2, the cumulative gain or loss from changes in the fair value of the forward contract will remain in the accumulated other comprehensive income account until those units of inventory are sold by Domestic.

2365.18 The fair value of the forward contract decreased $391 ($891 fair value at December 31, 20X1 – $500 fair value at March 1, 20X2) from December 31, 20X1, to March 1, 20X2. Therefore, the following entries are required at March 1, 20X2, with respect to the forward contract:

Other Comprehensive Income	$391	
Forward Contract		$391

To recognize the change in the fair value of the forward contract.

Foreign Currency (10,000Z × $1.56 spot rate 03/01/X2) $15,600
   Cash (10,000Z × $1.51 forward rate 10/01/X1) $15,100
   Forward Contract   500
To record settlement of the forward contract with the broker with the foreign currency received recorded at the spot rate on the settlement date and the U.S. dollars paid recorded at the forward rate that existed at the inception of the contract on 10/01/X1.

2365.19 The other comprehensive income account would be closed into the accumulated comprehensive income account. The accumulated other comprehensive income account then would have a $500 credit balance, as shown:

Accumulated other comprehensive income:

	Dr(Cr)
Gain recognized on 12/31/X1	$(891)
Loss recognized on 03/01/X2	391
Balance 03/01/X2	$(500)

2365.20 Recall that no firm commitment was made to purchase the 10,000 units of inventory. If Domestic purchases the 10,000 units on March 1, 20X2, there is no "locked-in" price (i.e., Domestic will have to pay the market price on March 1, 20X2). The forward contract hedged the exposure to risk due to changes in fair value of the inventory attributable to changes in the foreign currency exchange rate but did not hedge other risk exposures. If there have been no other influences on the price of the 10,000 units of inventory, they will cost Domestic 10,000Z on March 1, 20X2. (Recall from section **2365.06** that on October 1, 20X1, the inventory could have been acquired at a cost of 1Z per unit, or for a total cost of 10,000Z.) In that case, the entry to record the purchase of the inventory is:

Inventory (10,000Z × $1.56 spot rate) $15,600
   Foreign Currency $15,600
To record the purchase of the inventory at the spot rate.

2365.21 It is quite possible, if not probable, that the inventory will cost some amount other than 10,000Z. In that case, the inventory would be recorded at the number of zags paid times the spot rate on March 1, 20X2 (the date of acquisition).

2365.22 The net effect of the forward contract was to hedge the risk exposure associated with changes in the foreign currency exchange rate. Assuming the price of the inventory did not change (i.e., that it cost 10,000Z on March 1, 20X2), the forward contract locked in a purchase price of the inventory of $15,100, which was the forward rate at the October 1, 20X1, inception of the forward contract. But note in section **2365.20** that the inventory is currently recorded at $15,600, which is based on the spot rate on March 1, 20X2. However, recall also that the accumulated other comprehensive income has a $500 credit balance that arose from the changes in the fair value of the forward contract from October 1, 20X1, to March 1, 20X2. This $500 credit balance will be transferred to net income proportionately as the 10,000 units of inventory are sold. For example, if all of the units are sold at the same time for $20,000, the following entries will be recorded:

Cash (or Accounts Receivable) $20,000
   Sales $20,000
To record the sale of the units at sales price.

Cost of Goods Sold $15,600
   Inventory $15,600
To record the cost of goods sold.

Accumulated Other Comprehensive Income	$500	
Cost of Goods Sold		$500

To record the transfer of the net unrealized gain on the forward contract to net income in the period of sale of the related inventory.

2365.23 In summary, since Domestic used the forward contract as a hedge of a foreign currency forecasted transaction, the hedge must be accounted for as a cash flow hedge. The following summarizes the basic measurement requirements and Domestic's compliance with those requirements.

Requirement 1: The hedging derivative instrument (the forward contract) must be measured at fair value.

Domestic's compliance with requirement 1: Domestic's forward contract was initially measured at fair value of zero at the inception of the forward contract, remeasured at fair value of $891 at the balance sheet date, and at $500 at the settlement date.

Requirement 2: Changes in the fair value of the forward contract must be included in other comprehensive income (rather than net income).

Domestic's compliance with requirement 2: Domestic included an $891 gain in other comprehensive income in 20X1 and a $391 loss in other comprehensive income in 20X2.

Requirement 3: The accumulated other comprehensive income must not be transferred to net income until the hedged item affects net income.

Domestic's compliance with requirement 3: Domestic's net $500 credit balance remained in accumulated other comprehensive income (a balance sheet item) until the related 10,000 units of inventory were sold. When Domestic sold the goods, the $500 credit balance was transferred to net income as a reduction of cost of goods sold.

2366 Foreign Currency Net Investment in a Foreign Entity Hedge

2366.01 An entity may have foreign currency risk exposure from its investments in foreign operations. FASB ASC 815 allows an entity to hedge this foreign currency risk by using a derivative instrument or a foreign currency denominated nonderivative financial instrument (such as a foreign currency denominated debt).

2366.02 Under FASB ASC 320-10-15-10, the investment in the foreign operations (e.g., equity method investee or subsidiary) is translated into U.S. dollars at the current exchange rate at each balance sheet date (see section **2367**). The effects of changes in exchange rates are recognized in *other comprehensive income* and closed to the cumulative translation adjustment account (a specific component of the accumulated other comprehensive income balance sheet account).

2366.03 If a derivative instrument is used to hedge the foreign currency risk exposure associated with the net investment in the foreign entity, FASB ASC 815 requires that the derivative be measured at fair value with the effective portion of the derivative's gain or loss recognized in *other comprehensive income*. These changes in other comprehensive income are also closed to the cumulative translation adjustment account.

2366.04 **Illustration of a hedge of a net investment in a foreign entity.** (For simplicity, income taxes are ignored.) Domestic Company, a U.S. company, has an equity-method investee in a foreign country. The functional currency of the investee is the zag (Z). On October 1, 20X1, Domestic's investment in the investee is 10,000Z. On October 1, 20X1, Domestic also enters into a 5-month forward contract to sell 10,000Z on March 1, 20X2, at the forward rate on October 1, 20X1, of $1.51. (Note that the forward contracts in sections **2363–2365** were to purchase rather than sell foreign currency.) Domestic enters into the forward contract to hedge its foreign currency risk exposure associated with its investment in its equity-method investee. Each period the investee pays a dividend equal to its net income for the period. The exchange rates are as follows:

Date	Spot Rate	Forward Rate for 03/01/X2
10/01/X1	1Z = $1.50	5-month forward rate: 1Z = $1.51
12/31/X1	1Z = $1.58	2-month forward rate: 1Z = $1.60
03/01/X2	1Z = $1.56	

2366.05 No entries are necessary on October 1, 20X1, because the fair value of the forward contract at its inception on October 1, 20X1, is zero.

2366.06 The derivative (forward contract) and the investment in the foreign entity must both be remeasured at each balance sheet date and at the settlement date.

2366.07 The forward contract is remeasured based on the fair value of the forward contract. The fair value of the forward contract is determined by multiplying the change in the forward rate (expressed as units of foreign currency per U.S. dollar) times the number of foreign currency units and discounting this amount for the remaining time to the settlement date.

2366.08 Assuming a 6% discount rate, the fair value of the forward contract at December 31, 20X1 (balance sheet date), and the change in fair value from October 1, 20X1, to December 31, 20X1, are:

Fair value of forward contract at 12/31/X1:	
10,000Z × $1.60 forward rate at 12/31/X1	$(16,000)
10,000Z × $1.51 forward rate at 10/01/X1	(15,100)
Fair value of forward contract at 12/31/X1 before discount	(900)
Discount for period 12/31/X1 - 03/01/X2 ($900 × 0.06 × 2/12)	9
Fair value of forward contract at 12/31/X1	(891)
Fair value of forward contract at 10/01/X1 (inception of contract)	0
Increase in fair value of forward contract 10/01/X1 - 12/31/X1	$(891)

2366.09 The fair value of the forward contract at March 1, 20X2 (settlement date), and the change in fair value from December 31, 20X1, to March 1, 20X2, are:

Fair value of forward contract at 03/01/X2:	
10,000Z × $1.56 forward rate at 03/01/X2 (same as spot rate)	$(15,600)
10,000Z × $1.51 forward rate at 10/01/X1	(15,100)
Fair value of forward contract at 03/01/X2 before discount	(500)
Discount for period to settlement date	0
Fair value of forward contract at 03/01/X2	(500)
Fair value of forward contract at 12/31/X1	(891)
Increase (decrease) in fair value of forward contract	$ 391

2366.10 The investment in the foreign entity must be remeasured based on the change in the fair value of the investment in the investee that is attributable to the change in the foreign currency spot rates. The changes for Domestic's investment in its equity-method investee are as follows.

Change 10/01/X1 to 12/31/X1:
($1.58 spot rate 12/31/X1 - $1.50 spot rate 10/01/X1) × 10,000 zags = $800 gain

Change 12/31/X1 to 03/01/X2:
($1.56 spot rate 03/01/X2 - $1.58 spot rate 12/31/X1) × 10,000 zags = $200 loss

2366.11 These fair value changes are summarized as follows:

Change in Fair Value of Forward Contract Gain (Loss)	Change in Fair Value of Net Investment Attributable to Change in Spot Rates Gain (Loss)
$(891)	$800
391	(200)

2366.12 The entries at the December 31, 20X1, balance sheet date to remeasure the net investment and the forward contract are:

Related to net investment in investee:
    Investment in Investee $800
        Other Comprehensive Income (cumulative translation adjustment) $800
To remeasure the net investment in a foreign entity.

Related to the forward contract:
    Other Comprehensive Income (cumulative translation adjustment) $800
    Loss (net income)   91
        Forward Contract $891
To remeasure the forward contract.

2366.13 The investment in the foreign entity must be remeasured based on the change in the fair value of the investment in the investee that is attributable to the change in the foreign currency spot rates. Therefore, Domestic's investment in its investee is remeasured to reflect the exchange gain associated with the change in the spot rate from October 1, 20X1, to December 31, 20X1. Since Domestic's investment in the investee is an asset, if Domestic converted its 10,000Z asset into U.S. dollars at the spot rate on December 31, 20X1, it would receive 800 more U.S. dollars than if it had converted the 10,000 investment into dollars on October 1, 20X1. Thus, with respect to the investment in the investee, the change in currency rates is a gain.

2366.14 The change in the fair value of the forward contact was an $891 loss. However, FASB ASC 815 limits the amount recognized in other comprehensive income to, in absolute amount, the lesser of that amount ($891) or the amount recognized in the current period as an adjustment to the investment account ($800) (i.e., the amount debited to other comprehensive income in the second entry in section **2366.12** cannot exceed the amount debited or credited to other comprehensive income in the first entry in section **2366.12**). Any excess of the change in the fair value of the forward contract over the change in the fair value of the investment attributable to the change in the spot rates must be recognized in net income. This excess is summarized for Domestic:

Absolute amount of gain or loss in fair value of investment attributable to change in spot rates	$800
Absolute amount of gain or loss in fair value of forward contract	891
Excess of the largest over the smallest	91

2366.15 The purpose of the limitation discussed in sections **2366.13** and **2366.14** is that the "excess" reflects the extent to which the hedging instrument was ineffective in hedging the foreign currency risk of the investment in the investee. Under FASB ASC 815, the *ineffective* portion of any hedge must be recognized in net income.

2366.16 The entries on March 1, 20X2, the settlement date of the forward contract, are:

Related to net investment in investee:		
Other Comprehensive Income (cumulative translation adjustment)	$200	
Investment in Investee		$200
To remeasure the net investment in a foreign entity.		
Related to the forward contract:		
Forward Contract	$391	
Other Comprehensive Income (cumulative translation adjustment)		$200
Gain (net income)		191
To remeasure the forward contract.		

2366.17 On March 1, 20X2, the investment is remeasured for the change in the fair value of the investment attributable to the change in the spot rate. The $200 loss was calculated in section **2366.10**.

2366.18 The second entry in section **2366.16** remeasures the forward contract based on the change in the fair value of the forward contract. However, the offsetting entry to other comprehensive income cannot exceed the $200 gain or loss recorded in the first entry in section **2366.16** related to the investment. The $191 absolute amount difference between the change in the fair value of the forward contract ($391) and the change in the fair value of the investment attributable to the change in the spot rates ($200) is recognized in net income.

2366.19 The following summarizes the basic measurement and recognition requirements for a hedge of a net investment in a foreign entity and Domestic's compliance with those requirements.

Requirement 1: The hedging derivative instrument (the forward contract) must be measured at fair value.

Domestic's compliance with requirement 1: Domestic's forward contract was initially measured at fair value of zero at the inception of the forward contract, remeasured at fair value of $891 at the balance sheet date, and at $500 at the settlement date.

Requirement 2: Changes in the fair value of the forward contract must be included in other comprehensive income to the extent that the hedging instrument served as an effective hedge of the hedged item.

Domestic's compliance with requirement 2: In 20X1, Domestic recognized an $891 loss in the fair value of the forward contract. However, the amount included in other comprehensive income in 20X1 was limited to the $800 change in the fair value of the investment in a foreign entity attributable to the change in the foreign currency spot rates. The remaining $91 of the loss was recognized in net income. In 20X2, Domestic recognized a $391 gain in the fair value of the forward contract. The amount included in other comprehensive income in 20X2 was limited to the $200 change in the fair value of the investment in a foreign entity attributable to the change in the foreign currency spot rates. The remaining $191 of the gain was recognized in net income.

2366.20 **IFRS:** Derivatives are always deemed held for trading unless they are designated as hedging instruments. Hedge accounting is permitted under IAS 35, provided that the hedging relationship is clearly defined, measurable, and actually effective.

2367 Translation of Foreign Currency Financial Statements

2367.01 The need for translation of foreign currency financial statements arises, for example, when a U.S. corporation has a subsidiary or equity-method investee located in a foreign country. The discussion in this section focuses on the case of a U.S. parent corporation and its foreign subsidiary. It is assumed that the parent company's functional currency (as well as its reporting currency) is the U.S. dollar. The translation issue then revolves around translating the foreign subsidiary's financial statements into the reporting currency of the parent for purposes of preparing consolidated financial statements.

2367.02 First, the financial statements of the subsidiary must be stated in terms of U.S. GAAP if they are not already so stated.

2367.03 Logically, one would assume that the foreign subsidiary's books and records are maintained in its local currency. For convenience, the currency in which the subsidiary's books and records are maintained will be referred to as the "recording" currency. Further, it is assumed that the subsidiary's local currency is the zag.

2367.04 Assuming the subsidiary's financial statements are already stated in terms of U.S. GAAP, the overall translation process can be summarized as a two-step process.

Step 1: If necessary, *remeasure* the subsidiary's financial statements from its recording currency into its functional currency.

Step 2: If necessary, *translate* the subsidiary's financial statements from its functional currency into the reporting currency of the parent.

2367.05 If the subsidiary's functional currency is the same as its recording currency, remeasurement is not necessary (i.e., the accounts are already stated in terms of the functional currency). If this is the case, only step 2 (translation) is necessary. For example, if the subsidiary's functional currency is the zag, step 1 (remeasurement) is not necessary. The accounts of the subsidiary would be translated (step 2) from the functional currency (zags) into the reporting currency (U.S. dollars).

2367.06 On the other hand, if the subsidiary's functional currency is the U.S. dollar, step 1 (remeasurement) is necessary (i.e., the accounts first would have to be remeasured from the recording currency (zags) into the functional currency (U.S. dollars)). In this case, step 2 (translation) would not be necessary because after remeasurement the accounts are already stated in terms of the reporting currency (U.S. dollars). Stated differently, when the functional currency of a foreign subsidiary is the same as the reporting currency of the parent, remeasurement of the subsidiary's accounts from its recording currency into its functional currency obviates translation.

2367.07 The particular significance of which currency is the subsidiary's functional currency is that exchange gains and losses resulting from *remeasurement* must enter into the determination of net income, whereas exchange gains and losses resulting from *translation* do not. In the latter case, the exchange gains and losses are included in the cumulative translation adjustment that is reported as a separate component of stockholders' equity.

2367.08 The objectives of translation are the following:

a. To provide information that is generally compatible with the expected economic effects of a rate change on an enterprise's cash flows and equity

b. To reflect in consolidated statements the financial results and relationships of the individual consolidated entities as measured in their functional currencies in conformity with U.S. GAAP

2367.09 Under FASB ASC 320-10-15-10, all elements of financial statements should be translated by using a current exchange rate. For assets and liabilities, the exchange rate (i.e., the spot rate) at the balance sheet date should be used. For revenues, expenses, gains, and losses, the exchange rate at the dates on which those elements are recognized should be used. Because translation at the exchange rate at the dates the numerous revenues, expenses, gains, and losses are recognized is generally impractical, an appropriately weighted-average exchange rate for the period may be used to translate those items.

2367.10 The translated amounts of the subsidiary's assets and liabilities determine the total dollar amount of the subsidiary's stockholders' equity. However, in the financial statements, this total dollar amount of stockholders' equity must be allocated among paid-in capital, retained earnings, and the cumulative translation adjustment.

2367.11 The paid-in capital accounts (capital stock and additional paid-in capital) are translated using the relevant historical exchange rate—using the rate in existence when the paid-in capital arose (such as when the capital stock was issued). However, the historical rate used should not predate the rate in effect on the date the parent made its investment in the subsidiary.

2367.12 The beginning-of-period retained earnings and the beginning-of-period cumulative translation adjustment are entered into the translated trial balance (in U.S. dollars) at the dollar amounts determined for each at the end of the preceding period. Any direct charges or credits to retained earnings (such as dividends) should be translated at the exchange rate in effect on the date the transaction took place.

2367.13 Applying the procedures described in sections **2367.09–2367.12** to the subsidiary's trial balance produces a trial balance in dollars that usually does not balance. The difference (the debit or credit amount needed to balance) measures the translation gain or loss resulting from the change in the exchange rate. This translation gain or loss is not included in net income but is added to or deducted from the beginning-of-period cumulative translation adjustment.

2367.14 **Example:** On January 1, 20X1, Red Company, a U.S. company, acquired all of the stock of Blue Company. The operations of Blue Company began on this date. Blue Company maintains its books and records in its local currency, zags (Z). Blue Company's functional currency is the zag. The exchange rates are as follows:

Date	Exchange Rate
01/01/X1	1Z = $0.65
20X1 (average for 20X1)	1Z = $0.68
12/31/X1	1Z = $0.70

2367.15 Condensed financial statements that illustrate the translation from the functional currency (zags) to the reporting currency (U.S. dollars) are shown as follows:

	Amount in Z	Translated Exchange Rate	Amount in U.S. $	
Income statement				
Revenues	$85,000	$0.68	$57,800	
Expenses	80,000	0.68	54,400	
Net income	$ 5,000		$ 3,400	(Carried forward)
Retained earnings statement				
Balance of 01/01/X1	$ 0	Note A	$ 0	
Net income	5,000		3,400	(Brought forward)
Balance 12/31/X1	$ 5,000		$ 3,400	(Carried forward)
Balance sheet				
Assets				
Cash	$ 5,000	0.70	$ 3,500	
Accounts receivable	10,000	0.70	7,000	
Inventories	8,000	0.70	5,600	
Plant assets	15,000	0.70	10,500	
	$38,000	0.70	$26,600	
Equities				
Accounts payable	$ 9,000	0.70	$ 6,300	
Bonds payable	13,000	0.70	9,100	
Capital stock	11,000	0.65	7,150	
Retained earnings	5,000		3,400	(Brought forward)
Cum. translation adjustment 01/01/X1	0	Note A	0	
Cum. translation adjustment, current year change			650	(Balancing amount)
	$38,000		$26,600	

Note A: These amounts are the amounts determined at the end of the preceding year.

2367.16 Remeasurement into the Functional Currency

If the foreign subsidiary's functional currency is the U.S. dollar (instead of the zag), it is necessary to remeasure the subsidiary's financial statements from its recording currency (zags) into the functional currency (U.S. dollars). The remeasurement process should produce the same result as if the subsidiary's books of record had been initially recorded in the functional currency (U.S. dollars). It is similar to translation except for two major differences.

2367.17 The first major difference is that, instead of the accounts being translated at current rates, exchange rates are used that retain the accounting principles used to measure the item before remeasurement. This is essentially the temporal method previously required by FASB ASC 830-30-45. In general, *monetary* items are remeasured using current rates and *nonmonetary* items are remeasured using historical rates. For example, plant assets and the related depreciation expense would be translated at historical rates (i.e., the rates in existence when the plant assets were acquired). Similarly, inventory carried at cost and the related cost of goods sold would be remeasured at historical rates. A specific difference from the FASB ASC 830-30-45 temporal method is that deferred income taxes and deferred life insurance policy acquisition costs are to be remeasured at the current exchange rate rather than at historical rates.

2367.18 The second major difference between remeasurement and translation is that exchange gains and losses resulting from the remeasurement process must be included in the determination of net income.

2367.19 If the subsidiary is located in a country whose economy is highly inflationary, it must use the reporting currency of the parent (the U.S. dollar) as its functional currency. A highly inflationary economy is one that has cumulative inflation of approximately 100% or more over a 3-year period.

2370 Impairment

Impairment of Long-Lived Assets Other Than Goodwill

2370.01 Long-lived assets other than goodwill, such as plant and equipment and other intangible assets, are initially recorded at cost, which usually is the fair value at the date of acquisition. Under normal circumstances, the original cost less any estimated residual value is allocated to expense in the periods in which the asset is used. This allocation process (called *depreciation* in the case of plant and equipment and *amortization* in the case of intangible assets) should be modified when an asset has been determined to be impaired.

2370.02 When a long-lived asset is deemed to be impaired, the asset should be written down to a new carrying amount and the impairment loss recognized in the income statement in the period of the impairment. The measurement and recognition of the impairment losses associated with long-lived assets other than goodwill is specified in FASB ASC 360-10-05-05. The measurement and recognition of impairment losses associated with goodwill is described in FASB ASC 350-20-35-2.

2370.03 The accounting for impairment losses associated with a long-lived asset other than goodwill depends on whether the long-lived asset is to be held and used, disposed of other than by sale, or disposed of by sale.

Long-Lived Assets to Be Held and Used

2370.04 An entity must review long-lived assets and certain identifiable intangible assets whenever events or changes in circumstances indicate that the carrying amount of an asset may not be recoverable.

2370.05 Examples of such events or circumstances that may indicate that the carrying amount of an asset may not be recoverable include the following:

    a. A significant decrease in the market price of a long-lived asset

    b. A significant adverse change in the extent or manner in which a long-lived asset is being used or in its physical condition

    c. A significant adverse change in legal factors or in the business climate that could affect the value of a long-lived asset, including an adverse action or assessment by a regulator

    d. An accumulation of costs significantly in excess of the amount originally expected for the acquisition or construction of a long-lived asset

    e. A current-period operating or cash flow loss combined with a history of operating or cash flow losses or a projection or forecast that demonstrates continuing losses associated with the use of a long-lived asset

    f. A current expectation that, more likely than not, a long-lived asset will be sold or otherwise disposed of significantly before the end of its previously estimated useful life

2370.06 If these or other events or changes in circumstances indicate that the carrying amount of a long-lived asset other than goodwill that an entity expects to hold and use may not be recoverable, the entity should estimate the future cash flows expected to result from the use of the asset and its eventual disposition. The estimated future cash flows should include only the net cash flows (cash inflows less associated cash outflows) that are directly associated with and that are expected to arise as a direct result of the use and eventual disposition of the asset. (Those estimates should exclude interest charges that will be recognized as expensed when incurred.)

2370.07 If the sum of the estimated future cash flows (undiscounted and without interest charges) is less than the carrying amount of the asset, the entity may have to recognize an impairment loss. The impairment loss, if any, to be recognized is any excess of the asset's carrying amount over its fair value. Notice, however, that no impairment loss is to be recognized unless the asset's estimated future cash flows (ECF) are less than its carrying amount, even if the asset's carrying amount (CA) exceeds its fair value (FV).

2370.08 **Example: FV < CA but no impairment loss:** Assume that an event occurs (such as those listed in section **2370.05**) that suggests that the carrying amount (CA) of one of an entity's long-lived assets (other than goodwill) to be held for use may not be recoverable. Further assume that the following related to this asset:

Carrying amount (CA)	$100,000
Estimated future cash flows (ECF)	110,000
Estimated fair value (FV)	90,000

2370.09 Since the estimated future cash flows (ECF) are not less than the carrying amount (CA), no impairment loss is recognized even though the estimated fair value (FV) is less than the carrying amount of the asset. The estimated future cash flows must be less than the carrying amount for an impairment loss to be recognized.

2370.10 **Example: ECF < CA and impairment loss is recognized:** Assume than an event occurs that suggests that the carrying amount of one of an entity's long-lived assets (other than goodwill) to be held for use may not be recoverable. Further, assume that the following related to this asset:

Carrying amount (CA)	$100,000
Estimated future cash flows (ECF)	80,000
Estimated fair value (FV)	75,000

2370.11 Since the estimated future cash flows are less than the carrying amount of the asset, the entity should determine whether an impairment loss should be recognized. The impairment loss, if any, to be recognized is the excess of the asset's carrying amount (CA) over its fair value (FV). The impairment loss to be recognized in this case is $25,000, determined as shown:

Estimated fair value (FV)	$ 75,000
Carrying amount (CA)	100,000
Impairment loss	$(25,000)

2370.12 In estimating future cash flows for determining whether an asset has been impaired, assets should be grouped at the lowest level for which there are identifiable cash flows that are largely independent of the cash flows of other groups of assets.

2370.13 After an impairment loss is recognized, the reduced carrying amount of the asset should be accounted for as its new cost basis. The new cost basis should be depreciated or amortized over the asset's estimated remaining useful life. Restoration of previously recognized impairment losses is prohibited.

2370.14 The impairment loss associated with assets held for use should be included in income from continuing operations.

Long-Lived Assets to Be Disposed of Other than by Sale

2370.15 A long-lived asset to be disposed of other than by sale should continue to be classified as held and used until it is disposed of. Examples of such disposals are abandonment, exchange for a similar productive long-lived asset, and distribution to owners in a spinoff.

2370.16 A long-lived asset to be abandoned is considered to be disposed of when it ceases to be used. Thus, any impairment loss should be recognized in the period in which the asset to be abandoned ceases to be used. However, a long-lived asset that has been temporarily idled should not be accounted for as if abandoned.

2370.17 A long-lived asset to be disposed of by exchange for a similar productive long-lived asset is disposed of when it is exchanged. A long-lived asset to be disposed of by distribution to owners in a spinoff is disposed of when it is distributed. In either of these two cases, if the asset is tested for recoverability while it is still classified as held and used, the estimates of future cash flows used in that test should be based on the use of the asset for its remaining useful life assuming that the disposal transaction will not occur. An impairment loss, if any, must be recognized when the asset is disposed of (exchange or distribution) if the carrying amount of the asset exceeds its fair value.

Long-Lived Assets to Be Disposed of by Sale

2370.18 A long-lived asset to be sold should be classified as held for sale in the period in which all of the following criteria are met:

    a. Management, having the authority to approve the action, commits to a plan to sell the asset.

    b. The asset is available for immediate sale in its present condition subject only to terms that are usual and customary for sales of such assets.

    c. An active program to locate a buyer and other actions required to complete the plan to sell the asset have been initiated.

    d. The sale of the asset is probable, and transfer of the asset is expected to qualify for recognition as a completed sale, except in certain limited specified situations.

    e. The asset is being actively marketed for sale at a price that is reasonable in relation to its current fair value.

    f. Actions required to complete the plan indicate that it is unlikely that significant changes to the plan will be made or that the plan will be withdrawn.

2370.19 If at any time the criteria in section **2370.18** are no longer met, a long-lived asset classified as held for sale must be reclassified as held and used.

2370.20 If the criteria in section **2370.18** are met after the balance sheet date but before the financial statements are issued, a long-lived asset must continue to be classified as held and used for the period ending with that balance sheet date.

2370.21 A long-lived asset classified as held for sale must be measured at the lower of its carrying amount or fair value less cost to sell. Cost to sell includes the incremental direct costs to transact a sale. Such costs do not include expected future losses associated with the operations of the long-lived asset while it is classified as held for sale.

2370.22 A loss should be recognized for any initial or subsequent write-down to fair value less cost to sell. A gain should be recognized for any subsequent increase in fair value less cost to sell, but not in excess of the cumulative loss previously recognized for a write-down to fair value less cost to sell. For example, assume that in 20X1 an entity writes down a long-lived asset held for sale $20,000 because its carrying amount of $100,000 exceeded its fair value less cost to sell of $80,000. If the entity still has the asset in 20X2 but its fair value less cost to sell has increased to $105,000, in 20X2 the entity should recognized a gain of $20,000. Note that even though the fair value less cost to sell in 20X2 exceeds the asset's carrying amount of $80,000 (the new carrying amount after the write-down at the end of 20X1), the amount of the gain recognized in 20X2 is limited to $20,000, the cumulative net loss previously recognized for the write-down to fair value less cost to sell.

2370.23 A gain or loss not previously recognized that results from the sale of a long-lived asset should be recognized at the date of sale. For example, if the asset in section **2370.22** had been sold early in 20X2 for $75,000, an additional loss of $5,000 would have been recognized in 20X2. On the other hand, if it had been sold early in 20X2 for $85,000, a gain of $5,000 would have been recognized in 20X2.

2370.24 It is possible that circumstances may arise that previously were considered unlikely and cause an entity to change its mind and not sell an asset that it previously had classified as held for sale. In that case, the asset should be reclassified from held for sale to held and used. Any asset so reclassified should be measured at the lower of its carrying amount before the asset was classified as held for sale, adjusted for any depreciation (amortization) expense that would have been recognized had the asset been continuously classified as held and used, or fair value at the date of the subsequent decision not to sell.

2370.25 For example, assume that an entity reclassifies a long-lived asset on December 31, 20X1, from held and used to held for sale. On that date the carrying amount and the fair value of the asset was $40,000. The fair value of the asset (no cost to sell) was $38,000 on December 31, 20X2. Accordingly, a $2,000 loss ($40,000 carrying amount less $38,000 fair value at December 31, 20X2), was recognized in 20X2. A drastic, unexpected change in the market on January 1, 20X3, caused the entity to change its mind about selling the asset. Thus, on January 1, 20X3, the asset should be reclassified from held for sale to held and used. It should be measured at the lower of its carrying amount on December 31, 20X1 (the date it was reclassified from held and used to held for sale), adjusted for depreciation that would have been recorded in 20X2, *or* its fair value at January 1, 20X3.

2370.26 Recall that no depreciation is recorded for an asset after it is classified as held for sale. However, assume that the depreciation for 20X2 would have been $1,500 if the asset had continued to be classified as held and used. Assume also that the drastic change in the market caused the fair value of the asset to drop from $38,000 at the December 31, 20X2, balance sheet date to $30,000 at the close of business on January 1, 20X3. In that case, the asset should be measured at the lower of $38,500 ($40,000 carrying amount on December 31, 20X1, adjusted for the $1,500 depreciation that would have been recorded in 20X2 if the asset had continuously been classified as held and used) or $30,000, the asset's fair value on January 1, 20X3, the date the entity changed its mind and decided not to sell the asset. Thus, on January 1, 20X3, the asset would be written down from the $38,000 carrying amount on the December 31, 20X2, balance sheet (the fair value to which the asset was written down on December 31, 20X2, while it was classified as held for sale) to $30,000 (the fair value of January 1, 20X3, the date the entity decided not to sell the asset). The entry would be as follows:

Impairment Loss	$8,000	
Long-lived Asset		$8,000

2370.27 The loss recorded in section **2370.26** would be included in income from continuing operations in 20X3.

Impairment of Goodwill

2370.28 The accounting for the impairment of long-lived assets other than goodwill is specified in FASB ASC 360-10-05-05. The accounting for the impairment of goodwill is specified in FASB ASC 350-20-35-2.

2370.29 Goodwill is not to be amortized. It is to be tested for impairment at least annually.

Reporting Unit

2370.30 The testing of goodwill for impairment is to be done at a level of reporting known as a *reporting unit.* A reporting unit is an operating segment (as defined in FASB ASC 350-20-20) or one level below an operating segment. In the latter case, the reporting unit is referred to as a *component.*

2370.31 FASB ASC 350-20-20 specifies that a component of an operating segment is a reporting unit "if the component constitutes a business for which discrete financial information is available and segment management regularly reviews the operating results of that component."

2370.32 Nonpublic enterprises are required to test goodwill for impairment at the reporting unit level.

Two-Step Impairment Test

2370.33 Goodwill of a reporting unit is impaired when the carrying amount (book value) of goodwill associated with that reporting unit exceeds that goodwill's implied fair value. The impairment test is a two-step test.

2370.34 The first step compares the fair value of a reporting unit with its carrying amount, including goodwill. If the fair value of the reporting unit exceeds the carrying amount of the reporting unit, goodwill of the reporting unit is deemed not to be impaired. In that case, the second step is not necessary.

2370.35 If the fair value of the reporting unit is less than the carrying amount of the reporting unit, the second step is necessary to determine the amount of goodwill impairment loss, if any. The second step compares the implied fair value of goodwill of the reporting unit with the carrying amount of that goodwill.

2370.36 The implied fair value of goodwill of a reporting unit is calculated in the same manner that goodwill is calculated in a business combination. An entity will allocate the fair value of the reporting unit to all of the assets and liabilities of that unit as if the reporting unit had been acquired in a business combination. The excess "purchase price" over the amounts assigned to assets and liabilities is the implied fair value of the goodwill of that reporting unit. (The allocation is only for the purpose of testing goodwill for impairment. The entity may not record the "step-up" in value of net assets.)

Example 1 – No Impairment

2370.37 ABC Corporation has a reporting unit, XYZ. ABC determined that the fair value of XYZ, including goodwill associated with XYZ, is $400,000. The carrying value of XYZ is $300,000.

2370.38 The first step of the impairment test is to compare the fair value of the reporting unit to its carrying amount. Since the $400,000 fair value of XYZ, including goodwill, exceeds the $300,000 carrying amount, there is no impairment of goodwill, and the second step is not necessary.

Example 2 – Impairment with No Impairment Loss

2370.39 DEF Corporation has a reporting unit, RST that has goodwill with a carrying amount of $150,000. DEF determines that the fair value of RST, including goodwill of RST, is $1 million, of which $800,000 is assigned to the identifiable assets and liabilities of RST. The carrying amount of RST is $1.1 million.

2370.40 Since the fair value of RST ($1 million) is less than the carrying amount of RST ($1.1 million), impairment of goodwill associated with RST is indicated. Thus, the second step is necessary to determine the amount, if any, of goodwill impairment loss.

2370.41 The second step consists of a comparison of the implied fair value of the goodwill associated with RST with the carrying amount of that goodwill. The implied fair value of RST's goodwill is computed as follows:

Fair value of RST (including goodwill)	$1,000,000
Amounts assigned to identifiable assets and liabilities	800,000
Implied fair value of goodwill associated with RST	$ 200,000

2370.42 No goodwill impairment loss exists because the implied fair value of the goodwill associated with RST, $200,000, exceeds the $150,000 carrying amount of the goodwill associated with RST.

Example 3 – Impairment with Impairment Loss

2370.43 JKL Corporation has a reporting unit MNO that has goodwill with a carrying amount of $150,000. JKL determines that the fair value of MNO, including goodwill of MNO, is $500,000, of which $450,000 is assigned to the identifiable assets and liabilities of MNO. The carrying amount of MNO is $700,000.

2370.44 Since the fair value of MNO ($500,000) is less than the carrying amount of MNO ($700,000), impairment of goodwill associated with MNO is indicated. Thus, the second step is necessary to determine the amount, if any, of goodwill impairment loss.

2370.45 The second step consists of a comparison of the implied fair value of the goodwill associated with MNO with the carrying amount of that goodwill. The implied fair value of MNO's goodwill is computed as follows:

Fair value of MNO (including goodwill)	$500,000
Amounts assigned to identifiable assets and liabilities	450,000
Implied fair value of goodwill associated with MNO	$ 50,000

2370.46 A goodwill impairment loss must be recognized because the implied fair value of the goodwill associated with MNO is less than the carrying amount of the goodwill associated with MNO. The amount of the goodwill impairment loss is the excess of the carrying amount of the goodwill of MNO, over its implied fair value, as shown:

Implied fair value of goodwill associated with MNO	$ 50,000
Carrying amount of goodwill of MNO	150,000
Goodwill impairment loss	$(100,000)

Reporting Goodwill Impairment Loss

2370.47 The aggregate amount of goodwill impairment losses must be reported as a separate line item in the income statement before the subtotal income from continuing operations unless a goodwill impairment loss is associated with a discontinued operation.

When to Test for Goodwill Impairment

2370.48 Goodwill must be tested for impairment at least annually. However, it must be tested between annual tests if an event occurs or circumstances change that would more likely than not reduce the fair value of a reporting unit below its carrying amount. Examples of such events or circumstances include the following:

   a. A significant adverse change in legal factors or in the business climate

   b. An adverse action or assessment by a regulator

   c. Unanticipated competition

   d. A loss of key personnel

   e. A more-likely-than-not expectation that a reporting unit or a significant portion of a reporting unit will be sold or otherwise disposed of

   f. The testing for recoverability under FASB ASC 360-10-05-6 of a significant asset group within a reporting unit

   g. Recognition of a goodwill impairment loss in the financial statements of a subsidiary that is a component of a reporting unit

2370.49 FASB ASC 350-20-35-29 specifies that a detailed determination of the fair value of a reporting unit may be carried forward from one year to the next if all of the following criteria have been met:

   a. The assets and liabilities that make up the reporting unit have not changed significantly since the most recent fair value determination. (A recent significant acquisition or a reorganization of an entity's segment reporting structure is an example of an event that might significantly change the composition of a reporting unit.)

   b. The most recent fair value determination resulted in an amount that exceeded the carrying amount of the reporting unit by a substantial margin.

   c. Based on an analysis of events that have occurred and circumstances that have changed since the most recent fair value determination, the likelihood that a current fair value determination would be less than the current carrying amount of the reporting unit is remote.

2370.50 If any other assets are to be tested for impairment (e.g., long-lived assets tested under FASB ASC 630-10) at the same time as goodwill is to be tested, those assets must be tested for impairment before goodwill.

2370.51 The goodwill impairment test does not have to be performed at the end of the fiscal year. It may be performed any time during the year as long as that date is used consistently from year to year. In addition, all reporting units do not have to use the same testing date.

Assigning Assets and Liabilities to Reporting Units

2370.52 For goodwill impairment testing purposes, acquired assets and assumed liabilities (including corporate assets and liabilities) should be assigned to a reporting unit as of the acquisition date if both of the following criteria are met:

   a. The asset will be employed in or the liability relates to the operations of the reporting unit.

   b. The asset or liability will be considered in determining the fair value of the reporting unit.

Assigning Goodwill to Reporting Units

2370.53 All goodwill acquired in a business combination must be assigned to one or more reporting units as of the acquisition date. The methodology used to determine the amount of goodwill to assign to a reporting unit must be reasonable and supportable and applied in a consistent manner.

Disposal of All or a Portion of a Reporting Unit

2370.54 Whenever an entity disposes of a reporting unit or a portion of a reporting unit, the carrying value of the net assets of the portion disposed must include all or a portion of goodwill, depending on how much of the reporting unit was disposed of. If a reporting unit is to be disposed of in its entirety, goodwill of that reporting unit should be included in the carrying amount of the net assets to be disposed of to determine the gain or loss on disposal.

2370.55 For example, assume that Alpha Corporation is selling one of its reporting units, Beta. Beta's net assets have a carrying amount of $300,000, including $50,000 of goodwill. If Alpha sells Beta for $440,000, the gain on the sale of Beta is calculated as follows:

Sales price of Beta		$440,000
Carrying amount of net assets of Beta		
Identifiable net assets	$250,000	
Goodwill	50,000	300,000
Gain on sale of Beta		$140,000

2370.56 When a significant portion of a reporting unit is disposed of, goodwill must be allocated to the net assets disposed of *if those net assets constitute a business*. The amount to be allocated is based on the relative fair value of the business disposed of and the fair value of the remainder of the reporting unit. To illustrate, assume that Park Corporation is disposing of a portion of one of its reporting units, Gamma, and that the portion being disposed of constitutes a business. The carrying value of the assets being disposed of (excluding goodwill) is $400,000. The carrying amount of the goodwill associated with the reporting unit (Gamma) is $200,000. The fair value of the reporting unit is $1 million and the fair value of the portion being disposed of is $600,000. Therefore, 60% (i.e., $600,000 ÷ $1,000,000) of the reporting unit is being disposed of. The gain on the disposal of the portion of the reporting unit is $80,000, shown as follows:

Sale price of portion being disposed of		$600,000
Carrying amount of net assets disposed of:		
Identifiable net assets	$400,000	
Goodwill allocated to portion being disposed of ($200,000 × .60)	120,000	520,000
Gain on sale		$ 80,000

Equity Method Investments

2370.57 A portion of the excess of the cost of an equity method investee over the investor's share of the investee's underlying net assets may be attributable to goodwill. In that case, the portion of the "excess" attributable to goodwill should not be amortized. However, equity method investments, including any goodwill associated with such investments, are to be reviewed for impairment in accordance with FASB ASC 323-10-35-32 rather than FASB ASC 360-10.

Goodwill Impairment Testing by a Subsidiary

2370.58 Any goodwill recognized by a subsidiary in its separate financial statements should be accounted for in accordance with FASB ASC 350-20-35-47. The subsidiary goodwill should be tested for impairment at the subsidiary level using the subsidiary's reporting units.

2370.59 If a subsidiary recognizes goodwill impairment loss associated with one of its reporting units, goodwill of the reporting unit or units (at the higher consolidated level) in which the subsidiary's reporting unit with impaired goodwill resides must be tested for impairment if the event that gave rise to the loss at the subsidiary level would more likely than not reduce the fair value of the reporting unit (at the higher consolidated level) below its carrying amount. Only if goodwill of that higher-level reporting unit is impaired would a goodwill impairment loss be recognized at the consolidated level. Thus, the recognition of an impairment loss by a subsidiary in its separate financial statements does not necessarily mean that an impairment loss would be recognized at the consolidated level in the consolidated financial statements.

IFRS

2370.60 **IFRS:** Under GAAP, measurement of impairment is done with reference to fair value (often operationalized as discounted cash flows). Measurement of goodwill impairment uses a special method that requires first comparing the fair value of the cash generating unit to book value including goodwill, then comparing implied goodwill to carrying value. It is measured at the level of the business segment or one level below that. Impairment testing is at the segment or lower level, except that indefinite life intangibles are tested separately from the business unit.

Under IFRS, measurement of impairment is done with reference to the higher of value in use or fair value less costs to sell. The measurement of goodwill impairment is similar to other long-lived assets and requires only single-step computation. It is measured at the lowest level goodwill can be assigned (cash-generating unit). Impairments are tested at the cash-generating unit level.

2375 Interim Financial Reporting

2375.01 Interim reporting has increased greatly in importance in recent years. Most accounting principles, however, were developed with the 1-year period in mind. Few specific references are made in the FASB Accounting Standards Codification and other official pronouncements concerning the applicability of accounting principles to financial statements for periods shorter than one year. Thus, variety has existed in interim reports in terms of the information presented and the manner in which it is prepared.

2375.02 Two alternatives exist concerning the nature of a quarter or other period of time shorter than one year for purposes of financial reporting.

    a. **Independent period (discrete) concept:** Each interim period is viewed as a discrete period and financial statements intended to reflect the results of operations and financial position for such periods should be prepared in the same way as would be done for an annual accounting period. Deferrals, accruals, and estimations at the end of each interim period are determined on the same basis as the same judgments would be made for an annual period.

    b. Dependent period (integral) concept: Each period shorter than the annual period is viewed as an integral part of the annual period rather than an independent period itself. This approach requires certain changes to be made, particularly in determining results of operations in the income statement from the accounting treatment normally followed for the annual period. For example, an expense that might be considered as falling wholly within an annual accounting period could be allocated among interim periods on some reasonable basis, even though it was incurred in total in one individual interim period.

2375.03 FASB ASC 270-10-05-1 discusses three things relative to interim financial reporting:

    a. Take a position on the nature of the interim period.

    b. Establish standards for determining interim financial information.

    c. Establish minimum disclosure standards for interim reports.

2375.04 Basic Position on the Nature of Interim Reports

In general, interim financial reports should be based on the principles, practices, and policies used in the preparation of the last annual report. However, certain accounting principles and practices followed for annual reporting purposes may require modification at interim reporting dates so that the reported results for the interim period may better relate to the results of operations for the annual period.

2375.05 It appears that the Accounting Principles Board (APB) took a position between the strict dependent and independent concepts. A closer look at specific reporting standards, however, indicates that numerous exceptions to annual reporting practices are required. Accordingly, the position taken is closer to the dependent (integral) than the independent (discrete) alternative.

2375.06 Standards for Determining Interim Financial Information

Revenues should be recognized as earned during an interim period on the same basis as followed for the full year.

2375.07 Costs and expenses for interim reporting purposes may be classified as those directly associated with revenue and all other costs and expenses.

    a. Direct costs of products sold or services rendered are treated as such for interim periods. Examples are material costs, wages, salaries and related fringe benefits, manufacturing overhead, and warranties. Certain exceptions, however, are allowable in the case of inventories because of the problems of interim inventory determination.

        (1) Methods used for determining inventory amounts at interim periods may differ from those used at annual periods (e.g., use of estimation procedures at interim dates). Disclosure of the method used is necessary.

        (2) Companies that use LIFO may encounter a reduction of inventory levels resulting in a liquidation of the base-period inventories at interim dates with the expectation that the inventories will be replaced before year end. In such cases, inventory should not reflect such liquidations at interim dates. Cost of sales should be based on expected cost of replacing the liquidated LIFO base.

        (3) Inventory declines below market at interim periods may be offset by gains in later interim periods of the same year on a predictable basis. *Temporary* market declines in early interim periods may not be recognized if the loss is expected to be reversed by year end. If losses recognized in early interim periods are recovered in later interim periods of the same fiscal year, such recoveries are recognized as gains in the appropriate interim periods.

(4) Companies may use standard cost systems in determining inventory figures for interim reports. If variances are planned and expected to be absorbed by the end of the annual period, they need not be reflected in earnings of the interim period.

b. **Indirect costs:** All other costs and expenses (those *not* directly associated with revenues) are charged to income as follows:

(1) Costs and expenses other than product costs are charged to income for interim periods as incurred or allocated on the basis of the passage of time, benefits received, or activity associated with the period. Procedures for assigning costs to interim periods should be consistent with procedures used for the annual period.

(2) Costs and expenses incurred within an interim period not identified with the activities of other interim periods are charged to the period in which the cost was incurred.

(3) Arbitrary assignment of the amount of costs to an interim period should not be made.

(4) Gains and losses of interim periods similar to those that would not be deferred at year end should not be deferred beyond the interim period in which they are incurred.

2375.08 **Seasonal revenues, costs, or expenses:** Seasonal variations are specifically disclosed to avoid the possibility that interim reports for companies with material variations may be taken as fairly indicative of the estimated results for a full year. Interim reports are supplemented with information for 12-month periods ended at the interim date for the current and preceding years.

2375.09 **Income tax provisions:** An estimate of the effective tax rate expected for the annual period is made at the end of each interim period. This rate is used in providing for income taxes on a current year-to-date basis.

Example: Gordon Co. determines income before income tax for each quarter of 20X1 to be as follows: 1st quarter—$100,000; 2nd quarter—$80,000; 3rd quarter—$130,000; 4th quarter—$140,000.

At the end of each quarter, an estimate of the effective annual income tax rate is made, as follows: 1st quarter—40%; 2nd quarter—42%; 3rd quarter—42%; 4th quarter—38%. The income tax to be recognized in each quarter is determined as follows:

	1st Quarter	2nd Quarter	3rd Quarter	4th Quarter
Accumulated income to date	$100,000	$180,000[a]	$310,000[b]	$450,000[c]
Estimated annual income tax rate	x 0.40	x 0.42	x 0.42	x 0.38
	$ 40,000	$ 75,600	$130,200	$171,000
Income tax recognized in previous quarters	0	(40,000)	(75,600)	(130,200)
Income tax recognized this quarter	$ 40,000	$ 35,600	$ 54,600	$ 40,800

[a] *$100,000 + $ 80,000 = $180,000*
[b] *$180,000 + $130,000 = $310,000*
[c] *$310,000 + $140,000 = $450,000*

2375.10 **Extraordinary items** are disclosed separately on a net-of-tax basis and are included in the determination of net income for the interim period in which they occur. In judging the materiality of such items, estimated income for the whole year is used.

Discontinued Operations

2375.11 The effects of discontinued operations shall also be reported separately net of related income taxes.

Unusual or Infrequent Occurring Gains or Losses

2375.12 Gains or losses that meet the test of being unusual or occurring infrequently (but do not meet both tests) must also be disclosed separately as a component of pretax income from continuing operations.

Minimum Disclosure Standards for Interim Reports

2375.13 The following information is required to be disclosed when publicly traded companies report summarized financial information:

a. Sales and gross revenues, provision for income taxes, extraordinary items, cumulative effect of a change in accounting principles (see section **2305.26**), net income, and comprehensive income

b. Basic and diluted earnings per share for each period presented

c. Seasonal revenues, costs, or expenses

d. Significant changes in estimates or provisions for income taxes

e. Discontinued operations and extraordinary, unusual, or infrequently occurring items

f. Contingent items

g. Changes in accounting principles or estimates

h. Significant changes in financial position

i. The following information about reportable operating segments: (1) revenues from external customers, (2) intersegment revenues, (3) a measure of segment profit or loss, (4) total assets from which there has been a material change from the amount disclosed in the last annual report, (5) a description of differences from the last annual report in the basis of segmentation or in the measure of segment profit or loss, and (6) a reconciliation of the total of the reportable segments' measures of profit or loss to the enterprise's consolidated income before income taxes, extraordinary items, discontinued operations, and the cumulative effect of changes in accounting principles

2375.14 This information is presented for the following:

a. The current quarter

b. The current year-to-date, *or* last-12-months-to-date

c. Comparable figures (a and b) for the preceding year

Treatment of Accounting Changes in Interim Periods

2375.15 FASB ASC 270-10-45-12 specifies that "each report of interim financial information should indicate any change in accounting principles or practices from those applied in (a) the comparable interim period of the prior annual period, (b) the preceding interim periods in the current annual period, and (c) the prior annual report."

2375.16 A change in an accounting principle made in an interim period should be reported in the period in which the change is made in accordance with FASB ASC 270-10-45-12 and FASB ASC 250-10-45-14. (See also section **2305** on accounting changes.) Thus, if a change in accounting principle is made in other than the first interim period, all prior interim periods of the current year, as well as all interim periods of prior years presented should be adjusted to reflect the new accounting principle. Recall, as discussed in section **2305**, the cumulative effect of the change in accounting principle must be reported retrospectively with the cumulative effect being shown as an adjustment of the opening balance of retained earnings (or accumulated other comprehensive income, if appropriate) of the earliest year presented.

Treatment of a Correction of an Error in Interim Periods

2375.17 A correction of an error made in an interim period should be reported in the period in which the correction is made. A correction of an error qualifies as a prior-period adjustment under FASB ASC 270-10-45-12 and 250-10-45-22. (See section **2305** on accounting changes.) If a correction of an error is made in other than the first interim period, all prior interim periods of the current year, as well as all interim periods of prior years presented should be restated to reflect the correction. Recall, as discussed in section **2305.44–.56**, the cumulative effect of the error must be reported retroactively with the cumulative effect being shown as an adjustment of the opening balance of retained earnings (or accumulated other comprehensive income, if appropriate) of the earliest year presented.

Adjustments Related to Prior Interim Periods of the Current Fiscal Year

2375.18 Certain adjustments or settlements of litigation or similar claims, of income taxes, of renegotiation proceedings, or of utility revenue under rate-making processes are given special treatment in interim reports. This is true if the adjustment or settlement meets each of the following criteria:

   a. The effect of the item is material in relation to income from continuing operations of the current fiscal year or in relation to the trend of income from continuing operations or other appropriate criteria.

   b. All or part of the adjustment or settlement is directly related to specific prior interim periods of the current year.

   c. The amount of the adjustment or settlement could not be reasonably estimated prior to the current interim period.

2375.19 Items meeting the listed criteria in section **2375.18** that occur in other than the first interim period of a fiscal year are treated as follows:

   a. The portion of the item that is directly related to business activities of the enterprise during the current interim period is included in the determination of income for that period.

   b. Prior interim periods of the current fiscal year are restated to include that portion of the item that is directly related to business activities of those periods.

   c. The portion of the item that is directly related to activities of prior years is included in the restated income of the first interim period of the current year.

2375.20 FASB ASC 855-10-65-1 applies to interim reports. See section **2392.01** for a discussion of reportable subsequent events.

2375.21 **IFRS:** The IFRS approach to interim financial reporting is similar to GAAP, but there are some timing differences in recognition of interim revenues and expenses.

2380 Leases

2381 General Lease Accounting Concepts

2381.01 Some leases are executory contracts that transfer the right to use property in exchange for future rental payments. The rights and obligations under such contracts (i.e., *operating leases*) are not recognized as assets and liabilities in the financial statements of either the lessor or lessee under generally accepted accounting principles. Other leases are essentially installment sales or purchases. In these cases (i.e., *capital leases*), the substance of the arrangement and not the legal form determines the accounting treatment. The accounting methods for the treatment of operating and capital leases have been established for some time and are generally accepted. The specific circumstances in which leases should be capitalized, however, have been a subject of significant debate.

2381.02 Four basic lease capitalization criteria are established in FASB ASC 840-10-25-1. These are applied by both the lessor and lessee. For a lease to be treated as a capital lease and given formal recognition in the financial statements of the lessor and lessee, only one of these criteria must be met. These criteria, accompanied by important definitions related to them, are as follows:

Basic Lease Capitalization Criteria	Definitions
A. Transfer of ownership The lease transfers ownership of the property to the lessee by the end of the *lease term*.	**Lease term:** The fixed noncancelable terms of the lease plus: – Periods covered by *bargain renewal options*. – Periods for which failure to renew imposes a significant penalty. – Periods during which the lessee guarantees the debt of the lessor. – All periods prior to the date of a *bargain purchase option*. – Periods where lessor has the option of renewal. – Renewal periods during which there will be a loan outstanding from the lessee to the lessor. **Bargain renewal option:** The option to renew the lease at a rental so significantly below the fair rental that exercise may be assumed.
B. Bargain purchase option The lease contains a *bargain purchase option*.	**Bargain purchase option:** The option to purchase the property at a price so significantly below the fair market value (at the time of the purchase option) that purchase may be assumed.
C. 75% of life The lease term is equal to 75% or more of the *estimated economic life* of the asset.	**Estimated economic life:** The remaining period during which the asset is expected to be useful for its intended purpose, assuming normal repair and maintenance.
D. 90% of fair value The present value of the *minimum lease payments* (excluding that portion which represents executory costs) equals or exceeds 90% of the excess of the fair value of the leased property to the lessor at the inception of the lease over any related investment tax credit retained by the lessor	**Minimum lease payments:** Payments which the lessee is required to make under the lease agreement including: – Minimum rental payments. – Guarantee of the residual value of the property by the lessee. – Penalty for failure to renew. – Payment required in bargain purchase option. **Fair value of leased property:** Exchange price of the property in a bargained transaction between unrelated parties.

The last two criteria (C. and D.) cannot be the basis for capitalization if the inception of the lease is within the last 25% of the asset's life.

2381.03 Assuming that at least one of the previous criteria is met, the following two additional criteria must be applied by the lessor:

1. Collectibility of the minimum lease payments is reasonably assured.

2. No important uncertainties surround the amount of unreimbursable costs yet to be incurred by the lessor under the lease.

The lessor capitalizes any lease that meets *one* or more of the four basic capitalization criteria and *both* of these additional criteria.

2381.04 Lessee accounting is summarized as follows:

	Operating Lease	or	**Capital Lease**
Conditions	Four capitalization criteria unmet		At least one capitalization criteria met.
Recording of lease	None		Recorded as asset and liability at lower of present value of minimum lease payments or fair value of asset.
Recording of subsequent payments	Recognized as rent expense paid or accrued		Interest portion of payments recognized as such, remainder as reduction in liability. Leased asset amortized or depreciated.

2381.05 Lessor accounting is summarized as follows:

	Operating Lease	or	**Capital Lease***
Conditions	Four capitalization criteria unmet (or one or both of additional lessor-only criteria unmet)		At least one capitalization criteria met; both additional lessor-only criteria met.
Recording of lease	None		Asset removed from books and receivable recorded at lower of present value of minimum lease payments or fair value of asset. Gross profit or loss recognized if a sales-type lease.
Recording of subsequent receipts	Recognized as rent revenue received or accrued		Interest portion of payments recognized as such, remainder as reduction in receivable.

These general rules apply for direct-financing and sales-type leases. Leveraged leases are a special type of capital lease for which special accounting requirements apply.

2382 Cases—Treatment of Leases Under Varying Circumstances

Case 1: Lessor – Direct-Financing/Lessee - Capital

2382.01 Lessor Company enters into a lease agreement with Lessee Company for the lease of equipment. Both companies are to capitalize the lease. The lessor further classifies the lease as a direct-financing lease because the present value of the lease payments is equal to the $1,000 carrying value of the property on the lessor's books. The lessee takes possession of the equipment on January 1, 20X1, and makes equal lease payments on December 31 of years 20X1, 20X2, 20X3, and 20X4. The appropriate interest rate for capitalizing the lease is 7% on the lessor's books. The lease calls for the transfer of ownership of the property to the lessee at the end of 20X4, so the lessee amortizes the lease over the equipment's estimated 5-year life.

2382.02 A lease payment schedule for the lessor-lessee relationship is:

Date	Annual Rent[a]	Interest[b]	Principal Decrease[c]	Principal Balance[d]
01/01/20X1	$ 0	$ 0	$ 0	$1,000
12/31/20X1	295	70	225	775
12/31/20X2	295	54	241	534
12/31/20X3	295	37	258	276
12/31/20X4	295	19	276	0
	$1,180	$180	$1,000	

[a] *Annual rent: $1,000/3.38721 (present value of an annuity of $1 at 7% for 4 periods) = $295.*

[b] *Interest: 0.07 × principal balance for year (e.g., in 20X1 interest is 0.07 × $1,000 or $70).*

[c] *Principal decrease: Annual payment less amount of payment representing interest (e.g., in 20X1 principal decrease is the $295 annual rent less $70 = $225).*

[d] *Principal balance: Principal balance of former period less current year decrease (e.g., in 20X1 the principal balance is $1,000 less decrease of $225 = $775).*

2382.03 Lessor accounting:

Journal entries for the lessor for 20X1 are as follows:

01/01/20X1
  Minimum Lease Payments Receivable $1,180
      Equipment $1,000
      Unearned Income   180

12/31/20X1
  Cash $ 295
      Minimum Lease Payments Receivable $ 295
  Unearned Income $ 70
      Interest Income $ 70

Balance sheet presentation for Lessor Company at 12/31/20X1 is as follows:
  Current assets:
      Net investment in direct-financing lease $ 241
  Noncurrent assets:
      Net investment in direct-financing lease ($258 + $276)   534

Income statement presentation for the Lessor Company for 20X1 is as follows:
                  Interest income $ 70

The current asset is the December 31, 20X2, payment and the noncurrent asset is the total of the remaining payments. The interest income is the $70 interest in the December 31, 20X1, payment.

2382.04 Lessee accounting:

Journal entries for the lessee for 20X1 are as follows:
01/01/20X1

Leased Property	$1,000	
Obligation Under Capital Lease		$1,000

12/31/20X1

Obligation Under Capital Lease	$ 225	
Interest Expense	70	
Cash		$ 295
Depreciation (amortization) Expense	$ 200	
Accumulated Depreciation (amortization)—		$ 200
Leased Property ($1,000/5)		

Balance sheet presentation for Lessee Company at 12/31/20X1 is as follows:

Noncurrent asset:	
Leased property, net of $200 accumulated amortization	$ 800
Current liabilities:	
Obligation under capital lease	241
Noncurrent liabilities:	
Obligation under capital lease	534

Income statement presentation for the Lessee Company for 20X1 is as follows:

Depreciation (amortization) expense	$ 200
Interest expense	70

2382.05 These procedures are continued for the 4-year period for the lessor and the lessee. Each year the current receivable or payable is the next year's payment, and the noncurrent receivable or payable is the remaining payment or payments to be made in years subsequent to the immediate next year.

2382.06 In many leases, payment is made at the *beginning of the period* rather than at the end, as illustrated in the examples. While the process followed is similar, the present value factor used is different due to the difference in the timing of the payments, and the first payment contains no interest element because the payment is made in advance of any credit period. For the example presented in section **2382.02** a lease payment schedule based on payments being made at the beginning of the period is as follows:

Date	Annual Rent[a]	Interest[b]	Principal Decrease[c]	Principal Balance[d]
01/01/20X1	$ 0	$ 0	$ 0	$1,000
	276	0	276	724
01/01/20X2	276	51	225	499
01/01/20X3	276	35	241	258
01/01/20X4	276	18	258	0
	$1,104	$104	$1,000	

[a] Annual rent: $1,000 /(1.0 + 2.62432) (1.0 plus present value factor of an annuity of $1 at 7% for 3 periods) = $276.

[b] Interest: 0.07 × principal balance for year.

[c] Principal decrease: Annual rent less interest portion.

[d] Principal balance: Principal balance of previous period less current year decrease.

Case 2: Lessor – Sales-Type Lease

2382.07 In this case, we shall assume all the same facts as in Case 1 (section **2382.02**), except that the required lease payments include a manufacturer's profit of $300. This means that the present value of the lease payments ($1,000) exceeds the cost or other carrying value of the asset (assumed to be $700) by $300. The lease payment schedule developed is still applicable because the lease payments are still based on $1,000. In this case, however, the manufacturer receives a profit on the "sale" of the equipment as well as lease revenue (i.e., interest) throughout the lease period.

2382.08 On January 1, 20X1, the lessor makes the following entry:

01/01/20X1		
Minimum Lease Payments Receivable	$1,180	
Cost of Sales	700	
Sales		$1,000
Equipment (or inventory)		700
Unearned Income		180

The remaining entries and the financial statement presentation of the lessor are the same as in Case 1. The income statement of the lessor for the year 20X1, however, would also include the following:

Sales	$ 1,000
Cost of sales	(700)
Increase in gross profit	$ 300
Interest income	$ 70

Case 3: Lessor – Operating/Lessee-Operating

2382.09 Under an operating lease, the leased property remains on the balance sheet of the lessor. The lessor depreciates the asset and reports the receipt of rents as would be the case with any revenue. Assuming a $500 lease payment, the following entry is made by the lessor:

Cash (or Receivable)	$500	
Rental Revenue		$500

Revenue is recognized on a straight-line basis unless some other method is deemed to be more appropriate.

2382.10 The lessor may incur expenses related to the leased property and records these similar to other costs. Initial direct costs relative to the lease are capitalized and amortized over the life of the lease, if material.

2382.11 The lessee does not record the lease as an asset and liability and records lease payments similar to any expense:

Rent Expense	$500	
Cash (or Payable)		$500

Expenses are recognized on a straight-line basis (even though payments may vary from straight-line) unless some other method is deemed to be more appropriate.

2383 Miscellaneous Lease Considerations

2383.01 FASB ASC 840-10 covers numerous complexities concerning accounting for leases in addition to the basic principles reviewed. Several additional aspects of leases that are relevant to the CPA candidate are covered in the paragraphs that follow.

Guaranteed-Unguaranteed Residual Value

2383.02 Where the lessee guarantees the residual value of the leased asset at the end of the lease term, the gross value of the residual value is included in the minimum lease payments, which are capitalized as an asset by the lessor and as a liability by the lessee. Where the residual value is not guaranteed by the lessee, the residual value is excluded from the lessee's minimum lease payments, and the lessor has a separate asset in the form of the residual value. In the latter case, the lessor's sales and cost of goods sold are reduced by the present value of the residual.

2383.03 **Example:** Acme Company (lessor) enters into a sales-type lease of equipment in which five payments of $10,000 each are required, the first payment coming at the beginning of the lease and the remaining payments in annual intervals thereafter. The equipment cost Acme $37,500 to build. The appropriate interest rate is 10%, and the estimated residual value at the end of the 5-year lease term is $12,000. If this residual value is guaranteed by the lessee, the present value of the minimum lease payments is computed as follows:

Present value of five payments of $10,000:
$10,000 × 4.16987 $41,699
Present value of $12,000 residual:
$12,000 × 0.62092   7,451
                                          $49,150

The entry to record the capitalization of the lease is as follows:
Minimum Lease Payments Receivable $62,000*
Cost of Goods Sold   37,500
  Sales $49,150
  Unearned Income   12,850**
  Inventory   37,500
* ($10,000 × 5) + $12,000
** $62,000 - $49,150

If the residual value is not guaranteed, the present value of the minimum payments is $41,699, as computed, and the entry to record the capitalization of the lease is as follows:
Minimum Lease Payments Receivable $50,000
Estimated Residual Value   12,000
Cost of Goods Sold   30,049
  Sales $41,699
  Unearned Income   12,850
  Inventory   37,500

The cost of goods sold is the inventory cost of the equipment less the present value of the residual ($37,500 - $7,451 = $30,049). The sales figure represents only the present value of the five $10,000 payments (i.e., excludes the present value of the residual value).

Executory Costs

2383.04 Executory costs are costs of maintaining the property, such as taxes, maintenance, and insurance. These costs may be paid directly by the lessee, or they may be included in the lease payments, in which case they are then paid by the lessor.

2383.05 Executory costs are not included in the amount capitalized as minimum lease payments receivable by the lessor or obligation under capital lease by the lessee. If executory costs are included in the contracted payments that the lessee makes to the lessor, they are subtracted in determining the amount to be capitalized. Executory costs are treated as expenses as paid by the lessee or amortized over the appropriate periods.

Lessee Amortization Period

2383.06 The asset resulting from the capitalization of a lease by the lessee is amortized as follows:

Basis for Amortization	Amortization Period
Transfer of ownership or Bargain purchase option	Estimate life of asset
75% of life or 90% excess fair value	Lease term

If one of the first two criteria is met, the amortization is over the estimated life of the asset, even if one or both of the last two criteria are met.

Sale and Leaseback

2383.07 Sale-leaseback transactions involve the sale of property and the lease of the property back to the seller. Sale-leaseback transactions are treated as follows by the lessor and lessee:

Lessor: If the lease meets the criteria for capitalization, the purchaser-lessor accounts for the transaction as a purchase and a direct-financing lease. If the lease does not meet the criteria for capitalization, the purchaser-lessor accounts for the transaction as a purchase and an operating lease.

Lessee: If the lease meets one of the criteria for capitalization, the seller-lessee accounts for the lease as a capital lease; otherwise, the lease is accounted for as an operating lease. Any profit or loss on the sale is ordinarily deferred and amortized in proportion to the amortization of the leased asset (capital lease) or in proportion to the gross rentals (operating lease), subject to certain exceptions (see section **2384.04**).

Leases Between Related Parties

2383.08 Leases between related parties are generally treated as those between unrelated parties unless:

  a. the substance of the lease is not reflected in the legal form or

  b. the lease is between a subsidiary whose principal business is leasing to the parent, in which case consolidated financial statements are prepared.

Where it is clear that the terms of the transaction have been significantly affected by the fact that the parties are related, the accounting treatment is altered to reflect the economic substance of the transaction rather than the legal form. Leasing transactions with related parties should be adequately disclosed in the financial statements.

Accounting for Subleases

2383.09 The central concept related to subleases is that an original lessee (now a sublessor) cannot transfer to a sublessee a higher level of rights than were obtained in the original lease. The following generalizations govern the treatment of subleases in accordance with this general principle:

a. If the original lease was treated as an operating lease by the original lessee or sublessor, the sublease is treated as an operating lease.

b. If the original lease met either of the "purchase" criteria (i.e., transfer of ownership or bargain purchase option criteria), the sublease is classified in the same manner.

c. If the original lease was treated as a capital lease by the original lessee based on either the 75% of economic life or the 90% of fair value criteria, the sublease is classified as either capital or operating by applying only the 75% of life or the 90% of fair value criteria.

Real Estate Leases

2383.10   The major distinguishing characteristic of leases involving real estate is the unusual nature of land—unlimited life. Therefore, because land does not expire (i.e., is not depreciated), a capital lease will not arise unless the lease agreement meets the transfer of ownership or the bargain purchase option criteria.

2383.11   There are several other problems evident in accounting for leases of real estate. For example, leases of real estate frequently involve a lease of both land and buildings. In such circumstances, if the land is a small part of the total package (i.e., the land is less than 25% of the total fair value of the two assets in total), the land is ignored and the lease classified according to the lease capitalization criteria as usual. On the other hand, if the land is a significant portion of the lease (i.e., greater than or equal to 25% of the total fair value), the land and building are separated and only the transfer of ownership and the bargain purchase option criteria apply to the land. All four capitalization criteria are evaluated in determining the proper classification of the building portion of the lease, however.

Leveraged Leases

2383.12   **Leveraged leases** are leases meeting the definition of direct-financing leases and have the following additional characteristics:

a. Leveraged leases have three parties: a lessee, a long-term creditor, and a lessor (commonly called the equity participant).

b. The financing provided by the long-term creditors is nonrecourse as to the general credit of the lessor (although the creditor may have recourse to the specific property leased and the unremitted rentals relating to it). The amount of the financing is sufficient to provide the lessor with substantial leverage in the transaction.

c. The lessor's net investment (as defined following) declines during the early years once the investment has been completed and rises during the later years of the lease before its final elimination.

2383.13   The investment of the lessor includes the following three elements:

1. Rentals receivable, net of that portion of the rental applicable to principal and interest on the nonrecourse debt

2. A receivable for the amount of the investment tax credit, if any, to be realized on the transaction

3. Unearned and deferred income consisting of:

   (a) the estimated pretax lease income (or loss), after deducting initial direct costs, remaining to be allocated to income over the lease term and

   (b) the investment tax credit, if any, remaining to be allocated to income over the lease term.

2384 Other FASB Codification on Leases

2384.01 **Changes in the Provisions of Lease Agreements Resulting from Refundings of Tax-Exempt Debt:** FASB ASC 840-30-35-10 is designed to resolve an apparent inconsistency relative to the early extinguishment of debt. Gains or losses that arise from changes in lease agreements resulting from refunding of tax-free debt, in which the perceived economic advantages of the refunding are passed on to the lessee and the revised agreement is classified as either a capital lease by the lessee or a direct-financing lease by the lessor, are recognized in the period in which they occur rather than over the remaining term of the lease.

2384.02 **Inception of the Lease:** FASB ASC 840-10-20 defines the inception of the lease as the date of the lease agreement or commitment, if earlier. In applying this definition, a commitment must be in writing, signed by the parties to the lease, and must specifically set forth the principal provisions of the transaction. If any of the principal provisions are not yet negotiated, the preliminary agreement is not a commitment for purposes of applying this definition.

2384.03 **Classification of Renewals or Extensions of Existing Sales-Type or Direct-Financing Leases:** The lessor must classify a renewal or an extension of a sales-type lease or direct-financing lease as a sales-type if the other conditions of a sales-type lease are met and the renewal or extension occurs at or near the end of the lease term. A renewal or extension occurring at an earlier time, however, cannot be classified as a sales-type lease. (FASB ASC 840-10-25-51)

2384.04 **Accounting for Sales with Leasebacks:** FASB ASC 840-40 requires the recognition of some profit or loss on sales with leasebacks in the following circumstances:

    a. If the seller-lessee retains the use of only a minor part of the property or a minor part of the remaining life, the sale and the lease are accounted for on the basis of their separate terms. If the lease rentals are unreasonable, however, an appropriate amount is deferred or accrued by adjusting the gain or loss on the sale. The amount deferred or accrued is then amortized as an adjustment to the rentals.

    b. If the seller-lessee retains the use of a significant part, but less than substantially all of the property, and the profit on the sale exceeds the present value of the minimum lease payments in the leaseback in an operating lease or the recorded amount of the leased asset in a capital lease, the excess is recognized as profit on the date of the sale.

2384.05 **Determining Contingent Rentals:** FASB ASC 840-40-25-14 discusses the definition of contingent rentals. Contingent rentals are defined as the increases or decreases in lease payments resulting from changes occurring subsequent to the inception of the lease in factors on which lease payments are based. Lease payments that depend on a factor that both exists and is measurable at the inception of the lease are included in minimum lease payments based on the factor at the inception of the lease. Lease payments that depend on a factor that does not exist or is not measurable at the inception of the lease, however, are contingent rentals and are excluded from the computation of minimum lease payments. Contingent rentals are included in income as they are accrued.

2384.06 **Accounting for Nonrefundable Fees and Costs Associated with Originating or Acquiring Loans and Indirect Costs of Leases:** FASB ASC 310-20-30-1 establishes standards of accounting and reporting for nonrefundable fees and costs associated with lending activities, including leases. It specifies the following:

    a. Loan origination fees are recognized over the life of the related loan as an adjustment to yield.

      b. Direct loan origination costs are recognized over the life of the related loan as a reduction of the loan's yield.

      c. Loan commitment fees are generally deferred and recognized over the loan commitment period (certain specified fees) or over the related loan's life (all other fees).

      d. Loan fees, direct loan origination costs, and purchase premiums and discounts on loans are recognized as an adjustment of yield by the interest method.

2384.07 **Accounting for Leases:** FASB ASC 840-40 covers a variety of lease-related items, including the following:

      a. A *sale-leaseback transaction involving real estate,* including real estate with equipment, must qualify as a sale under the provisions of FASB ASC 840-40-15-9 before it is appropriate for the seller-lessee to account for the transaction as a sale. If the transaction does not qualify as a sale under FASB ASC 840-40-15-9, it is accounted for by the deposit method or as a financing.

      b. A *sale-leaseback transaction involving real estate,* including real estate with equipment, that includes any continuing involvement other than a normal leaseback in which the seller-lessee intends to actively use the property during the lease is accounted for by the deposit method or as a financing.

      c. The *definition of lease term* (FASB ASC 840-40-20) is amended to include all renewal periods during which there will be a loan outstanding from the lessee to the lessor.

      d. *Initial direct costs of direct-financing leases*: A lease involving real estate may not be classified as a sales-type lease unless the lease agreement provides for the transfer of title to the lessee at or shortly after the end of the lease term. Sales-type leases involving real estate are accounted for under the provisions of FASB ASC 840-40-15-9.

2384.08 **Lessee Guarantee of the Residual Value of Leased Property:** FASB ASC 840-10-25-6 clarifies the determination of the amount attributable to residual guarantees to be used in the calculation of the minimum rental payments as follows:

      a. The requirement that a lessee make up a residual value deficiency due to damage, extraordinary wear and tear, or excessive usage is not considered a residual guarantee.

      b. If the lessee's residual guarantee is less than the stipulated residual value of the property, the lesser amount is used in calculating the minimum rental payments.

      c. A residual guarantee obtained by a lessee from a third party for the benefit of the lessor does not affect the minimum rental calculation unless the lessee is released from their own residual guarantee.

2384.09 **Accounting for Leases in a Business Combination:** Leases that are acquired through a business combination retain their previous classification unless the provisions of the lease have changed, in which case the lease must be reevaluated in light of the lease classification criteria. (FASB ASC 840-10-35-5)

2384.10 **Leases of Certain Property Owned by a Governmental Unit or Authority:** FASB ASC 840-10-25-25 clarifies the exemption from the capital lease classification of certain types of property owned by government units or authorities. Exempt leases must meet all six of the following conditions:

      1. The leased property is owned by a government unit or authority.

      2. The leased property is part of a larger facility operated by or on behalf of the lessor.

      3. The property is a permanent structure or part of a permanent structure.

      4. The lessor has the explicit right to terminate the lease at any time during the lease term.

5. The lessee cannot acquire the property under the terms of the lease.

6. The leased property or comparable property cannot be purchased or leased from a nongovernmental unit or authority.

2384.11 **Leases Involving Only Part of a Building:** Determination of the fair value of a portion of a building (e.g., space in a shopping center), while necessary to apply the standards of FASB ASC 840-10, may be difficult to determine objectively. Reasonable estimates can usually be obtained from independent appraisals or estimated replacement cost information. (FASB ASC 840-10-25-23)

2384.12 **Accounting for Purchase of a Leased Asset by the Lessee During the Term of the Lease:** The purchase by the lessee of property under a capital lease and the related lease termination are accounted for as a single transaction. The difference between the purchase price and the carrying amount of the lease obligation is recorded as an adjustment of the carrying amount of the asset or assets. (FASB ASC 840-30-35-14)

2384.13 **Accounting for a Loss on a Sublease:** Recognition of a loss by an original lessee who disposes of leased property or enters into subleases to mitigate the cost of an existing lease commitment is not prohibited. The determination of a gain or loss on the disposal of a segment includes amounts related to an original lease and a sublease entered into as part of a decision to dispose of the segment. A gain or loss resulting from such a sublease is an indistinguishable part of the gain or loss on the disposal. (FASB ASC 840-30-35-13)

2384.14 **IFRS:** IFRS treatment of losses is similar to that of GAAP.

2385 Distinguishing Liabilities from Equity

2385.01 Some financial instruments have characteristics of both liabilities and equity. The classification of these financial instruments has been somewhat controversial. FASB ASC 840-10 reduces at least some of the controversy.

2385.02 FASB ASC 480-10-10 addresses the classification of the following three classes of freestanding financial instruments:

a. Mandatorily redeemable financial instruments

b. Obligations to repurchase the issuer's equity shares by transferring assets

c. Certain obligations to issue a variable number of shares.

2385.03 A mandatorily redeemable financial instrument, such as mandatorily redeemable preferred stock, must be classified as a liability unless the redemption is required to occur only upon the liquidation or termination of the reporting entity.

2385.04 An entity also must classify as a liability a financial instrument, other than an outstanding share, that, at inception, (a) embodies an obligation to repurchase the issuer's equity shares, or is indexed to such an obligation, and (b) requires or may require the issuer to settle the obligation by transferring assets. Examples of these financial instruments include forward purchase contracts or written put options on the issuer's equity shares that are to be physically settled or net cash settled.

2385.05 A financial instrument that embodies an unconditional obligation, or one other than an outstanding share that embodies a conditional obligation, that the issuer must or may settle by issuing a variable number of its equity shares must be classified as a liability if, at inception, the monetary value of the obligation is based solely or predominantly on any one of the following:

    a. A fixed monetary amount known at inception (for example, a payable settleable with a variable number of the issuer's equity shares).

    b. Variations in something other than the fair value of the issuer's equity shares (for example, a financial instrument indexed to the Standard and Poor's 500 and settleable with a variable number of the issuer's equity shares).

    c. Variations inversely related to changes in the fair value of the issuer's equity shares (for example, a written put option that could be net share settled).

2385.06 The three classes of financial instruments described in section **2221.15–.18** must be presented in the balance sheet as liabilities. They may not be presented between the liabilities section and the equity section.

2385.07 **IFRS:** Debt and equity classifications are found in IAS 32 and are similar to GAAP.

2386 Nonmonetary Transactions (Barter Transactions)

2386.01 An exchange is a reciprocal transfer between an enterprise and another entity. The transfer is not an exchange if the transferor retains a substantial continuing involvement in the transferred asset such that the usual risks and rewards of ownership of the asset are retained by the transferor.

Basic Principle

2386.02 In general, the accounting for nonmonetary exchanges should be based on fair value, which is the same basis as that used in monetary transactions. The asset received should be recorded at the fair value of the asset surrendered or the fair value of the asset received, whichever is more clearly evident. The difference between this fair value and the book value of the asset surrendered should be recognized as a gain or loss at the time of the exchange.

Modifications of the Basic Principle

2386.03 FASB ASC 845-10-30-3 provides three exceptions cases in which a nonmonetary exchange should be recorded based on the recorded amount (carryover amount) rather than fair value:

    a. Fair value is not determinable

    b. Exchange transaction to facilitate sales to customers

    c. Exchange transaction that lacks commercial substance

2386.04 If the fair value is not determinable within reasonable limits (exception case a), the transferor should record a nonmonetary exchange based on the book value of the asset transferred (given up). Fair value should be regarded as not determinable within reasonable limits if major uncertainties exist regarding the realizability of the value that would be assigned to an asset received in a nonmonetary transaction accounted for a fair value.

2386.05 Exception case b relates to an exchange of a product or property held for sale in the ordinary course of business for a product or property to be sold in the same line of business to facilitate sales to customers other than the parties to the sale. For example, Company A, a real estate dealer, has an acre of land (land A) on the south side of town and Company B, another real estate dealer, has an acre of land (land B) on the north side of town. Company has a client that wants to buy an acre of land on the south side of town. To accommodate their respective clients, Company A and Company B exchange the acre lots in question. Company A would record the land exchange based on the book value of the land it transferred to Company B (land). Thus, land B would be recorded on Company A's books at the book value of land A.

Commercial Substance

2386.06 In determining if a nonmonetary exchange has commercial substance, the key issue is to determine if the exchange is expected to significantly change the entity's future cash flows. FASB ASC 845-10-30-3 specifies that the entity's future cash flows are expected to significantly change if either of the following criteria is met:

    a. The configuration (risk, timing, and amount) of the future cash flows of the asset(s) received differs significantly from the configuration of the future cash flows of the asset(s) transferred.

    b. The entity-specific value of the asset(s) received differs from the entity-specific value of the asset(s) transferred, and the difference is significant in relation to the fair values of the assets exchanged.

2386.07 If either of these criteria is met, the transferor's economic position has changed. Accordingly, the nonmonetary exchange should be recorded based on fair value.

2386.08 **Example:** Assume that Company C exchanges land that it owns for a building of Company D. This nonmonetary exchange likely changed the timing of Company C's future cash flows as well as the risk associated with those cash flows. It also may have changed the amount of those future cash flows. If that is the case, the nonmonetary exchange qualifies as having commercial substance. Thus, the exchange should be recorded on Company C's books based on the fair value of the land transferred or the fair value of the building received, whichever is more clearly evident. Any implied gain or loss should be recognized at the time of the exchange.

2386.09 It may be necessary to recognize any impairment loss associated with the asset being transferred prior to recording a nonmonetary exchange. For example, in the preceding paragraph (section **2386.08**), it may be necessary for Company C to recognize impairment on the land before the nonmonetary exchange is recorded. Impairment of long-lived assets is discussed more fully in section **2370.01–.27**.

Recording at Fair Value (Nonmonetary Exchange Has Commercial Substance)

2386.10 Assume that Alpha Company exchanges a machine for land. The machine has a book value of $4,000 (cost $12,000 and accumulated depreciation $8,000) and a fair value of $6,000. Alpha Company determines that the configuration of its future cash flows will be significantly different as a result of the exchange.

2386.11 Since the exchange has commercial substance, it should be recorded on Alpha's books based on fair value. Unless the fair value of land is "more clearly evident," the fair value of the machine should be used as the basis for recording the exchange, as shown below:

Land (fair value of machine transferred	$6,000	
Accumulated depreciation	8,000	
Machine		$12,000
Gain		2,000

Recording at Book Value (Nonmonetary Exchange Does Not Have Commercial Substance)

2386.12 Assume the same facts as those shown for Alpha Company in section **2386.10** except assume that Alpha Company determined that the exchange does not have commercial substance. In that event, Alpha should record the exchange based on the book value of the asset transferred, as follows:

Land (book value of machine transferred	$4,000	
Accumulated depreciation	8,000	
Machine		$12,000

Nonreciprocal Transfers

2386.13 A nonreciprocal transfer is a transfer of assets or services in one direction, either from an enterprise to its owners or another entity or from owners or another entity to the enterprise.

2386.14 In general, nonmonetary transactions involving nonreciprocal transfers should also be based on the fair values of the assets involved.

2386.15 A nonmonetary asset received in a nonreciprocal transfer should be recorded at the fair value of the asset received. For example, as mentioned previously, donated assets should be recorded at fair value of the asset at time of transfer.

2386.16 A transfer of a nonmonetary asset to a stockholder or to another enterprise in a nonreciprocal transfer should be recorded at the fair value of the asset transferred, and a gain or loss should be recognized on the disposition of the asset.

Involuntary Conversions of Nonmonetary Assets

2386.17 Involuntary conversions of nonmonetary assets to monetary assets are monetary transactions for which gain or loss must be recognized even though an enterprise reinvests the monetary assets in replacement nonmonetary assets. However, this basic position (i.e., that the involuntary conversion is a monetary transaction) does not apply to an involuntary conversion of a LIFO inventory for which replacement:

    a. is made by year-end or

    b. is intended but not made by year-end, provided the enterprise does not recognize a gain on the involuntary conversion for income tax purposes.

2387 Related Parties and Related Party Transactions

2387.01 Related party transactions frequently occur between the following:

    a. A parent company and subsidiaries

    b. Subsidiaries of a common parent company

    c. An enterprise and trusts for the benefit of employees (e.g., a pension plan)

    d. An enterprise and its owners or management

    e. Affiliate companies

2387.02 Typical related party transactions are as follows:

    a. Sales, purchases, and transfers of real and personal property

    b. Services received or furnished

  c. Use of property and equipment by lease or otherwise

  d. Borrowings and lendings

  e. Guarantees

  f. Maintenance of bank balances as compensating balances for the benefit of another

2387.03 Financial statements must include disclosures of material related party transactions (other than compensation arrangements, expense allowances, and other similar items). Disclosure of transactions that are eliminated in the preparation of consolidated or combined financial statements is not required.

2387.04 Specific information items to be disclosed are as follows:

  a. The nature of the relationship between the related parties

  b. A description of the related party transaction

  c. The dollar amount of transactions for each of the periods for which an income statement is presented and the effects of any change in the method of establishing the terms from that used in the preceding period

  d. Amounts due from or to related parties as of the date of each balance sheet presented and, if not otherwise apparent, the terms and manner of settlement

2387.05 Transactions between related parties cannot be presumed to have been carried out on an arm's-length basis. Representations about transactions between related parties should not imply that they are equivalent to arm's-length transactions unless such representations can be substantiated.

2387.06 **IFRS:** Related party disclosures are discussed in IAS 24. These disclosures are similar to GAAP.

2388 Research and Development Costs

2388.01 *Research* is defined by the FASB as a planned search or critical investigation aimed at the discovery of new knowledge with the hope that such knowledge will be useful in developing a new product or service, a new process or technique, or in bringing about a significant improvement to an existing product or process. *Development* is the translation of research findings or other knowledge into a plan or design for a new product or process or for a significant improvement to an existing product or process whether intended for sale or use. Both of these definitions involve futuristic terms and imply that doubt exists as to the ultimate outcome of activities identified as research and development (R&D).

2388.02 A useful way to analyze activities to determine if their costs are research and development costs is to establish if they relate to activities identified with the period prior to the beginning of commercial production.

Preproduction Period Example R&D Costs	Production Period Example Non-R&D Costs
Laboratory research aimed at discovery of new knowledge	Engineering follow-through in an early phase of commercial production
Conceptual formulation and design of possible products or processes	Quality control during commercial productions including routine testing of products
Testing in search for or evaluation of product or process alternatives	Routine, ongoing efforts to refine, enrich, or otherwise improve on the qualities of an existing product
Design, construction, and operation of a pilot plant that is not of a scale economically feasible for commercial production	Seasonal or other periodic design changes to existing products

2388.03 Research and development costs are identified in five categories.

1. Materials, equipment, and facilities used in R&D activities
2. Personnel engaged in R&D activities
3. Intangibles purchased or developed for use in R&D activities
4. Contract services acquired and used in conjunction with R&D activities
5. Indirect costs reasonably allocable to R&D activities

2388.04 A particularly important aspect of determining whether items included in (1) and (3) are R&D is whether the item (e.g., machinery, equipment, patent) has an alternative use in other R&D projects or otherwise. If an alternative use exists, the cost is capitalized as a tangible or intangible asset and depreciated or amortized. The periodic depreciation or amortization is identified as R&D expense as long as the asset is used in R&D activity. If no alternative use exists, the expenditure is charged to R&D in the period of acquisition.

2388.05 No asset identified as R&D should appear on the balance sheet. Disclosure is made in the financial statements of the total R&D cost charged to expense in each period for which an income statement is presented.

2388.06 **Example:** The EZ Company engages in various R&D and manufacturing activities related to the development and sale of automobile parts. The proper accounting treatment of various costs incurred by the company is suggested in the schedule following:

| | | Expense as: | |
Activity	Capitalize as:	R&D	Other
a. Acquisition of major research facility to be used for all research activities	Building Equipment, etc.		
b. Depreciation on building, equipment in (a) above		X	
c. Research conducted to develop new automobile bumper		X	
d. Models of new bumper prepared and tested		X	
e. Legal fees paid to obtain patent on new bumper	Patent		
f. Quality control in early stages of commercial production of bumper			Manufacturing expense
g. Routine continued research aimed at refinement of bumper			Manufacturing expense
h. Amortization of patent cost (e)			Amortization expense
i. Legal costs of unsuccessful patent defense			Legal expense
j. Salaries and wages of R&D personnel		X	
k. Computer services acquired in conjunction with specific R&D project		X	
l. Salaries of salespersons selling bumper			Salary expense
m. Cost of patent acquired for use in ongoing R&D activities	Patent		
n. Amortization of patent cost (m) above		X	

2388.07 In FASB ASC 730-20-25-3, the FASB specifies how an enterprise is to account for its obligation under an arrangement for the funding of its research and development activities by others. Generally, such arrangements are accounted for as follows:

    a. To the extent that the enterprise is obligated to repay the other parties, it records a liability and charges the R&D costs to expense as incurred.

b. To the extent that the financial risk associated with R&D has been transferred because repayment of any of the funds provided depends solely on the results of the R&D having future economic benefit, the enterprise should account for its obligation as a contract to perform R&D for others. The terms of such arrangements and the amount of compensation earned and cost incurred for each period for which an income statement is presented is disclosed (FASB ASC 730-20-25-4).

2388.08 **IFRS:** IFRS treatment of R&D costs is similar to that of GAAP.

2389 Risks and Uncertainties

2389.01 One of the purposes of financial statements is to provide information to help users to predict the reporting entity's future cash flows and results of operations. This assessment depends, to some degree, on the users' knowledge and assessment of the risks and uncertainties involving the entity's operations. Disclosure of these risks and uncertainties is a critical component of the user's process of evaluating these variables. FASB ASC 275-10 addresses the disclosures required to facilitate a user's evaluation of an entity's risks and uncertainties.

2389.02 An important element of the topic of risks and uncertainties is selectivity. **Selectivity** involves the specified criteria that serve to screen the risks and uncertainties encountered by every entity. The objective is to restrict required disclosures to matters that are significant to that specific entity. (FASB ASC 275-10-05-2)

2389.03 The disclosures discussed in this section focus on risks and uncertainties that could significantly affect amounts reported in the near-term. Near-term is defined as a period not to exceed one year from the date of the financial statements. (FASB ASC 275-10-20)

2389.04 The types of risks and uncertainties discussed in this section are (FASB ASC 275-10-05-2):

   a. the nature of the entity's operations,

   b. the use of estimates in the preparation of the entity's financial statements, and

   c. significant concentrations in certain aspects of the entity's operations.

Nature of Operations

2389.05 Nature of operations requires that an entity disclose information related to the environments in which the entity operates. Knowing these environments helps users of financial statements to assess risks of national and world events. Knowing the nature of an entity's business and the principal markets for its product or service indirectly alerts the user about the risks common to that business. (FASB ASC 275-10-05-4)

2389.06 Consequently, an entity's financial statements must include a description of the major products or service the reporting entity sells or provides and its principal markets. The disclosure must also provide an indication of the relative importance of its operations in each business and the basis for this determination, i.e., assets, revenues, or earnings. Terms such as *predominately, about equally,* or *major* should be used rather than quantitative descriptions of the nature of operations. (FASB ASC 275-10-50-2)

Use of Estimate in the Preparation of Financial Statements

2389.07 **Estimates** are a necessary part of the preparation of financial statements. It is necessary to explicitly communicate to the users of the financial statements that estimates have been used and that many of the amounts reported are approximations rather than exact amounts. This understanding should help users to make better decisions. (FASB ASC 275-10-05-6)

2389.08 The financial statements must include an explanation that the preparation of the statements requires the use of management's estimates in conformity with GAAP. The statements must also disclose certain significant estimates. (FASB ASC 275-10-50-6)

2389.09 Certain significant estimates are those estimates involving a situation where it is reasonably possible that the estimate will change in the term and the effect of the change will be material.

2389.10 Disclosure of these significant estimates must be made when the following conditions are present (FASB ASC 275-10-50-8):

    a. It is at least reasonably possible that the estimate of the effect on the financial statements will change in the near term due to one or more future confirming events (*reasonably possible* is a chance more than remote but less than likely).

    b. The effect of the change would be material.

2389.11 The disclosure must include the nature of the uncertainty and an indication that it is at least reasonably possible that this change in the estimate will occur in the near term. (FASB ASC 275-10-50-10)

2389.12 Examples of items that might require disclosure under this topic include (FASB ASC 275-10-50-15):

    a. inventory subject to rapid technological obsolescence,

    b. specialized equipment subject to technological obsolescence,

    c. valuation allowances for deferred tax assets based on future taxable income,

    d. capitalized motion picture film production costs,

    e. capitalized computer software costs,

    f. deferred policy acquisition costs of insurance entities,

    g. valuation allowances for commercial and real estate loans,

    h. environmental remediation-related obligations,

    i. contingent liabilities for obligations of other entities,

    j. amounts reported for long-term obligations, such as amounts reported for pension and postemployment benefits,

    k. estimated net proceeds recoverable, the provisions for expected loss to be incurred, or both, on disposition of a business or assets, and

    l. amounts reported for long-term contracts.

2389.13 In determining whether disclosure is required about an estimate of useful life of an intangible asset, determination of whether the effect would be material is made based on either the individual asset or by major asset class as it refers to either a change in the useful life or a change in the expected likelihood of renewal or extension of an intangible asset. (FASB ASC 275-10-50-15A)

Current Vulnerability Due to Certain Concentrations

2389.14 **Vulnerability to concentrations** refers to risk due to a lack of diversification. Disclosure of such risk must be made if, based on management's information, the following criteria are met (FASB ASC 275-10-50-16):

    a. the concentration exists at the date of the financial statements,

        b. the concentration make the entity vulnerable to the risk of a near-term severe impact, and

        c. it is at least reasonably possible that the events that could cause the severe impact will occur in the near term.

2389.15 A severe impact is defined as a significant financially disruptive effect on the normal functioning of an entity. Severe impact matters are matters that are more than material but less than catastrophic. (FASB ASC 275-10-20)

2389.16 Disclosure must be made of concentrations known to management rather than based on knowledge of which management could reasonably be expected to know. (FASB ASC 275-10-50-17)

2389.17 Examples of categories of concentrations include (FASB ASC 275-10-50-18):

        a. concentrations in the volume of business transacted with a particular customer, supplier, lender, grantor, or contributor,

        b. concentrations in revenue from particular products, services, or fund-raising events,

        c. concentrations in the available sources of supply of materials, labor, or services or of licenses or other rights used in the entity's operations, and

        d. concentrations in the market or geographic area in which an entity conducts its operations.

2390 Segment Reporting

2390.01 FASB ASC 280-10 requires publicly held business enterprises to report certain information about their operating segments in their annual financial statements. It also requires them to report selected information about their operating segments in their interim financial reports.

2390.02 In addition, FASB ASC 280-10-05-2 requires publicly held enterprises to report certain information about the following:

        a. Their products and services

        b. The geographic areas in which they operate

        c. Their major customers

2390.03 According to FASB ASC 280-10-10-1, the objective of requiring disclosures about segments of an enterprise and related information is "to provide information about the different types of business activities in which an enterprise engages and the different economic environments in which it operates to help users of financial statements:

        a. "Better understand the enterprise's performance,

        b. "Better assess its prospects for future net cash flows, and

        c. "Make more informed judgments about the enterprise as a whole."

2390.04 The method the FASB chose for determining what information to report is referred to as the "management approach" because it is based on the way that management organizes the segments within the enterprise for making operating decisions and assessing performance. The management approach focuses on financial information that an enterprise's decision makers use to make decisions about the enterprise's operating matters. The components that management establishes for that purpose are identified as "operating segments."

Operating Segments

2390.05 An *operating segment* is a component of an enterprise:

   a. that engages in business activities from which it may earn revenues and incur expenses (including revenues and expenses relating to transactions with other components of the same enterprise),

   b. whose operating results are regularly reviewed by the enterprise's chief operating decision maker to make decisions about resources to be allocated to the segment and assess its performance, and

   c. for which discrete financial information is available.

2390.06 The term "chief operating decision maker" is intended to identify a *function* rather than a manager with a specific title. That function is to allocate resources to and assess the performance of the segments of an enterprise. The chief operating decision maker may be an individual, such as the enterprise's chief executive officer (CEO) or chief operating officer (COO), or it may be a group consisting of, for example, the enterprise's president, executive vice presidents, and others.

2390.07 An operating segment usually has a **segment manager** who is directly accountable to and maintains regular contact with the chief operating decision maker to discuss operating activities, financial results, forecasts, or plans for the segment. (The chief operating decision maker may also be the segment manager for certain operating segments.)

2390.08 Information about two or more operating segments may be aggregated into a single operating segment only if the segments have similar economic characteristics and are similar in each of the following areas:

   a. The nature of the products and services

   b. The nature of the production processes

   c. The type or class of customer for their products and services

   d. The methods used to distribute their products or provide their services

   e. If applicable, the nature of the regulator environment, for example, banking, insurance, or public utilities

Reportable Segments

2390.09 After an enterprise has identified its operating segments (including those that represent an aggregation of two or more separate segments), it must report separately information about each operating segment that meets any one or more of the following tests. Those segments that meet at least one of the tests represent **reportable segments** for which specified information must be reported.

   a. **Revenue test:** If its revenue is 10% or more of the combined revenue of all operating segments (for purposes of this test, revenue includes both sales to external customers and intersegmental sales or transfers)

   b. **Profitability test:** If the absolute amount of its reported profit or loss is 10% or more of the greater, in absolute amount, of:

   (1) the combined reported profit of all operating segments that did not report a loss or

   (2) the combined reported loss of all operating segments that did report a loss

   c. **Asset test:** If its assets are 10% or more of the combined assets of all operating segments

2390.10 The amount of an operating segment's profit or assets used for these tests should be the measure reported to the chief operating decision maker for purposes of making decisions about allocating resources to the segment and assessing its performance. This amount may not necessarily be the same measure as that used to prepare the consolidated financial statements.

2390.11 The profitability test is demonstrated as follows for XYZ Company:

Operating Segment	Profit (Loss)
A	$450
B	50
C	(350)
D	(40)
E	(210)

First, the operating segments are grouped according to whether they incurred a profit or loss, as follows:

Segments Incurring Profits		Segments Incurring Losses	
Segment	Profit	Segment	Loss
A	$450	C	$(350)
B	50	D	(40)
		E	(210)
	$500		$(600)

From this point on in the profitability test, only absolute amounts are used. The combined total of those segments incurring a loss is larger than the combined total of those segments incurring a profit. Therefore, any segment for which the absolute amount of its operating profit or loss equals or exceeds $60 (i.e., 10% of $600) meets the profitability test and is therefore a reportable segment. Segments A, C, and E meet the profitability test, summarized as follows:

Operating Segment	Absolute Amount of Profit or Loss	≥ $60	
A	$450	Yes	(reportable segment)
B	50	No	
C	350	Yes	(reportable segment)
D	40	No	
E	210	Yes	(reportable segment)

2390.12 If the total external revenue (i.e., sales to unaffiliated customers) of the reportable segments is less than 75% of total consolidated revenue, additional operating segments must be identified as reportable segments (even if they do not otherwise qualify as a reportable segment) until at least 75% of total consolidated revenue is included in reportable segments.

2390.13 Information about all operating segments that did not qualify as reportable segments must be combined and disclosed in an "all other" category.

2390.14 If an operating segment was identified in the immediately preceding prior period as a reportable segment and management deems that segment to be of continuing significance, information about that segment should continue to be reported separately in the current period even if that segment does not otherwise qualify as a reportable segment in the current period.

2390.15 If an operating segment qualifies in the current period as a reportable segment but did not qualify as a reportable segment in the prior period(s), prior-period segment data presented for comparative purposes should be restated as if the segment qualified as a reportable segment in the prior period(s).

2390.16 FASB ASC 280-10-50-8 specifies that there may be a practical limit to the number of reportable segments for which an enterprise separately discloses information. Although the FASB did not set a precise limit, it did indicate that as the number of reportable segments goes above 10, the enterprise should consider whether a practical limit has been reached.

Required Disclosures

2390.17 Segment information is required in the following areas:

a. General information

b. Information about segment profit or loss and assets

c. Reconciliations of segment information to aggregate enterprise amounts

d. Interim period information

General Information

2390.18 An enterprise must disclose the following general information:

a. Factors used to identify the enterprise's reportable segments

b. Types of products and services from which each reportable segment derives its revenues

Information About Profit or Loss

2390.19 An enterprise must disclose a measure of profit or loss and total assets for each reportable segment. In addition, an enterprise must disclose the following about each reportable segment if the specified amounts are included in the segment's measure of profit or loss:

a. Revenues from external customers

b. Revenues from transactions with other operating segments

c. Interest revenue

d. Interest expense

e. Depreciation, depletion, and amortization expense

f. Unusual gains and losses

g. Equity in the net income of equity method investees

h. Income tax expense or benefit

i. Extraordinary items

j. Significant noncash items other than depreciation, depletion, and amortization expense

Information About Assets

2390.20 An enterprise must disclose the following about each reportable segment if the specified amounts are included in the segment assets:

a. The amount of investment in equity method investees

b. Total expenditures for additions to long-lived assets other than financial instruments, long-term customer relationships of a financial institution, mortgage and other servicing rights, deferred policy acquisition costs, and deferred tax assets

2390.21 The following is an example of how the information about the segments profit or loss and assets might be disclosed:

	Segments			All Other	Consolidated Totals
	A	B	C		
Revenues from external customers	$250	$300	$400	$100	$1,050
Intersegment revenues		50			50
Interest revenue	20	10			30
Interest expense	15	5			20
Depreciation and amortization	40	30	55		125
Segment profit	80	85	100	35	300
Segment assets	420	510	630	80	1,640
Expenditures for segment assets	55	40	70		165

Measurement of Segment Profit or Loss and Segment Assets

2390.22 An enterprise must provide the following, at a minimum, about the measurement of segment profit or loss and segment assets:

a. The basis of accounting for any transactions between reportable segments

b. The nature of any differences between the measurements of the reportable segments' profits or losses and the enterprise's consolidated income from continuing operations

c. The nature of any differences between the measurements of the reportable segments' assets and the enterprise's consolidated assets

d. The nature of any changes from prior periods in the measurement methods used to determine reported segment profit or loss and the effect, if any, of those changes

e. The nature and effect of any asymmetrical allocations to segments (e.g., an enterprise might allocate depreciation expense to a segment without allocating the related depreciable assets to that segment)

Reconciliation

2390.23 An enterprise must provide reconciliations of all of the following:

a. The total of the reportable segments' revenues to consolidated revenues

b. The total of the reportable segments' measures of profit or loss to the consolidated income from continuing operations

c. The total of the reportable segments' assets to consolidated assets

d. The total of the reportable segments' amounts for every other significant item of information disclosed to the corresponding consolidated amount

2390.24 An example of a reconciliation of profit or loss is presented as follows:

Total profit or loss for reportable segments	$5,000
Other profit or loss	400
Elimination of intersegment profits	(600)
Unallocated amounts:	
Litigation settlement received	450
Other corporate expenses	(300)
Adjustment to pension expense in consolidation	(1,000)
Income from continuing operations	$3,950

Interim Period Information

2390.25 An enterprise must disclose the following about each reportable segment in condensed financial statements of interim periods:

   a. Revenues from external customers

   b. Intersegment revenues

   c. A measure of segment profit or loss

   d. Total assets for which there has been a material change from the amount disclosed in the last annual report

   e. A description of differences from the last annual report in the basis of segmentation or in the basis of measurement of segment profit or loss

   f. A reconciliation of the total of the reportable segments' measures of profit or loss to the enterprise's consolidated income from continuing operations

Enterprise-wide Disclosures

2390.26 An enterprise must report the revenues from external customers for each product and service or each group of similar products and services unless it is impracticable to do so.

2390.27 An enterprise must report the following geographic information unless it is impracticable to do so:

   a. Revenues from an external customer attributed to the enterprise's country of domicile and attributed to all foreign countries in total from which the enterprise derives revenues. If revenues from external customers attributed to an individual foreign country are material, those revenues must be disclosed separately.

   b. Long-lived assets other than financial instruments, long-term customer relationships of a financial institution, mortgage and other servicing rights, deferred policy acquisition costs, and deferred tax assets (1) located in the enterprise's country of domicile and (2) located in all foreign countries in total in which the enterprise holds assets. If assets in an individual foreign country are material, those assets must be disclosed separately.

2390.28 An example of geographic information disclosures is presented as follows:

	Revenues	**Assets**
United States	$15,000	$10,000
Canada	5,000	4,000
Japan	3,000	6,000
Other foreign countries	14,000	12,000
	$37,000	$32,000

Information About Major Customers

2390.29 If revenues from transactions with a single external customer amount to 10% or more of an enterprise's revenues, the enterprise must disclose that fact, the total amount of revenues from each such customer, and the identity of the segments reporting the revenues. (The enterprise need not disclose the identity of a major customer.) A major customer is a single customer or a group of entities known to a reporting enterprise to be under common control. The federal government, a state government, a local government, or a foreign government each should be considered as a single customer.

2390.30 **IFRS:** Similar to GAAP, IFRS defines segments based on components of the entity that are businesses, having operating results reviewed by the chief operating decision maker, and having discrete financial information. These are reportable if one of three threshold criteria—sales, profits, or assets—are met. IFRS also requires capital expenditures and liabilities segment disclosures, as well as entity-wide and some geographic analyses.

2391 Software Costs

2391.01 Computer software costs to be sold, leased, or otherwise marketed are charged to expense as research and development until technological feasibility has been established for the product. *Technological feasibility* is established on completion of a detailed program design or completion of a working model.

2391.02 After technological feasibility has been established, all software production costs are capitalized and subsequently reported at the lower of unamortized cost or net realizable value. Capitalized computer software costs are amortized on the basis of current and future revenue for each product with the minimum annual amortization equal to the straight-line amortization over the remaining estimated economic life of the product.

2392 Subsequent Events

2392.01 Subsequent events are events or transactions that occur after the balance sheet date but before financial statements are issued or are available to be issued. Under FASB ASC 855-10, there are two types of subsequent events (FASB ASC 855-10-20):

1. The first type consists of events or transactions that provide additional evidence about conditions that existed at the date of the balance sheet, including the estimates inherent in the process of preparing financial statements (that is, recognized subsequent events).

2. The second type consists of events that provide evidence about conditions that did not exist at the date of the balance sheet but arose after that date (that is, nonrecognized subsequent events).

2392.02 Under FASB ASC 855-10, financial statements are considered issued when they are widely distributed to shareholders and other financial statement users for general use and reliance in a form and format that complies with GAAP (FASB ASC 855-10-20).

2392.03 Financial statements are considered available to be issued when they are complete in a form and format that complies with GAAP and all approvals necessary for issuance have been obtained, for example, from management, the board of directors, and/or significant shareholders. An entity that has a current expectation of widely distributing its financial statements to its shareholders and other financial statement users (including a public entity, as defined in section **2392.04**) must evaluate subsequent events through the date that the financial statements are issued. All other entities must evaluate subsequent events through the date that the financial statements are available to be issued (FASB ASC 855-10-20).

2392.04 A public entity is any entity that meets any of the following conditions (FASB ASC 855-10 25-1A):

a. Its debt or equity securities trade in a public market either on a stock exchange (domestic or foreign) or in an over-the-counter market, including securities quoted only locally or regionally.

b. It is a conduit bond obligor for conduit debt securities that are traded in a public market (a domestic or foreign stock exchange or an over-the-counter market, including local or regional markets).

      c. It files with a regulatory agency in preparation for the sale of any class of debt or equity securities in a public market.

      d. It is required to file or furnish financial statements with the SEC.

      e. It is controlled by an entity covered by criteria (a) through (d).

2392.05 An entity must recognize in the financial statements the effects of all subsequent events that provide additional evidence about conditions that existed at the date of the balance sheet, including the estimates inherent in the process of preparing financial statements. The following are examples of recognized subsequent events listed in FASB ASC 855-10-55-1:

      a. If the events that gave rise to litigation had taken place before the balance sheet date and that litigation is settled, after the balance sheet date but before the financial statements are issued or are available to be issued, for an amount different from the liability recorded in the accounts, then the settlement amount should be considered in estimating the amount of liability recognized in the financial statements at the balance sheet date.

      b. Subsequent events affecting the realization of assets, such as receivables and inventories or the settlement of estimated liabilities, should be recognized in the financial statements when those events represent the culmination of conditions that existed over a relatively long period of time. For example, a loss on an uncollectible trade account receivable as a result of a customer's deteriorating financial condition leading to bankruptcy after the balance sheet date but before the financial statements are issued or are available to be issued ordinarily will be indicative of conditions existing at the balance sheet date. Thus, the effects of the customer's bankruptcy filing shall be considered in determining the amount of uncollectible trade accounts receivable recognized in the financial statements at the balance sheet date.

2392.06 An entity must not recognize subsequent events that provide evidence about conditions that did not exist at the date of the balance sheet but arose after the balance sheet date but before financial statements are issued or are available to be issued. Under FASB ASC 855-10, the following are examples of nonrecognized subsequent events (FASB ASC 855-10-55-2):

      a. Sale of a bond or capital stock issued after the balance sheet date but before financial statements are issued or are available to be issued

      b. A business combination that occurs after the balance sheet date but before financial statements are issued or are available to be issued (FASB ASC 805 requires specific disclosures in such cases.)

      c. Settlement of litigation when the event giving rise to the claim took place after the balance sheet date but before financial statements are issued or are available to be issued

      d. Loss of plant or inventories as a result of fire or natural disaster that occurred after the balance sheet date but before financial statements are issued or are available to be issued

      e. Losses on receivables resulting from conditions (such as a customer's major casualty) arising after the balance sheet date but before financial statements are issued or are available to be issued

      f. Changes in the fair value of assets or liabilities (financial or nonfinancial) or foreign exchange rates after the balance sheet date but before financial statements are issued or are available to be issued

      g. Entering into significant commitments or contingent liabilities, for example, by issuing significant guarantees after the balance sheet date but before financial statements are issued or are available to be issued

2392.07 An entity must disclose the date through which subsequent events have been evaluated, as well as whether that date is the date the financial statements were issued or the date the financial statements were available to be issued (FASB ASC 855-10-50-1).

2392.08 Under FASB ASC 855-10, some nonrecognized subsequent events may be of such a nature that they must be disclosed to keep the financial statements from being misleading. For such events, an entity shall disclose the following (FASB ASC 855-10-50-3):

    a. The nature of the event

    b. An estimate of its financial effect, or a statement that such an estimate cannot be made

2392.09 An entity shall consider supplementing the historical financial statements with pro forma financial data. Occasionally, a nonrecognized subsequent event may be so significant that disclosure can best be made by means of pro forma financial data. Such data shall give effect to the event as if it had occurred on the balance sheet date. In some situations, an entity also shall consider presenting pro forma statements, usually a balance sheet only, in columnar form on the face of the historical statements (FASB ASC 855-10-50-3).

2392.10 FASB ASC 855-10 may require that an entity reissue financial statements. After the original issuance of the financial statements, events or transactions may have occurred that require disclosure in the reissued financial statements to keep them from being misleading. An entity must not recognize events occurring between the time the financial statements were issued or available to be issued and the time the financial statements were reissued unless the adjustment is required by GAAP or regulatory requirements. Similarly, an entity shall not recognize events or transactions occurring after the financial statements were issued or were available to be issued in financial statements that are later reissued in comparative form along with financial statements of subsequent periods unless the adjustment meets the criteria stated in this paragraph. An entity must disclose the date through which subsequent events have been evaluated in both the originally issued financial statements and the reissued financial statements (FASB ASC 855-10-25-4).

2393 Transfers and Servicing of Financial Assets and Derecognition

Transfers of Financial Assets

2393.01 Transfers of receivables to third parties is merely a subset of the broader issue of transfers of financial assets. The measurement principle, stated in its most basic form, is that if the transferor surrenders control, the transfer should be accounted for as a *sale* of the financial asset with any related gain or loss recognized in net income. If control is not surrendered, the transfer should be accounted for as a *borrowing*.

2393.02 FASB ASC 860-10 specifies that a transferor has surrendered control over transferred assets if, and only if, all of the following conditions are met:

    a. The transferred financial assets have been isolated from the transferor—put presumptively beyond the reach of the transferor and its creditors, even in bankruptcy or other receivership. Transferred financial assets are isolated in bankruptcy or other receivership only if the transferred financial assets would be beyond the reach of the powers of a bankruptcy trustee or other receiver for the transferor or any of its consolidated affiliates included in the financial statements being presented. For multiple-step transfers, an entity that is designed to make remote the possibility that it would enter bankruptcy or other receivership (bankruptcy-remote entity) is not considered a consolidated affiliate for purposes of performing the isolation analysis. Notwithstanding the isolation analysis, each entity involved in the transfer is subject to the applicable guidance on whether it must be consolidated.

    b. Each transferee (or, if the transferee is an entity whose sole purpose is to engage in securitization or asset-backed financing activities and that entity is constrained from pledging or exchanging the assets it receives, each third-party holder of its beneficial interests) has the right to pledge or exchange the assets (or beneficial interests) it received, and no condition both constrains the transferee (or third-party holder of its beneficial interests) from taking advantage of its right to pledge or exchange and provides more than a trivial benefit to the transferor.

    c. The transferor, its consolidated affiliates included in the financial statements being presented, or its agents do not maintain effective control over the transferred financial assets of third-party beneficial interests related to those transferred assets. Examples of a transferor's effective control over the transferred financial assets include, but are not limited to, (1) an agreement that both entitles and obligates the transferor to repurchase or redeem them before their maturity, (2) an agreement that provides the transferor with both the unilateral ability to cause the holder to return specific financial assets and a more-than-trivial benefit attributable to that ability, other than through a cleanup call, or (3) an agreement that permits the transferee to require the transferor to repurchase the transferred financial assets at a price that is so favorable to the transferee that it is probable that the transferee will require the transferor to repurchase them. (A cleanup call is an option held by the servicer or its affiliate, which may be the transferor, to purchase the remaining transferred financial assets, or the remaining beneficial interests not held by the transferor, its affiliates, or its agents in an entity if the amount of outstanding financial assets or beneficial interests falls to a level at which the cost of servicing those assets or beneficial interests becomes burdensome in relation to the benefits of servicing.)

Transfers That Qualify As a Sale

2393.03 A transfer of an entire financial asset, a group of entire financial assets, or a participating interest in an entire financial asset that meets the conditions listed in section **2393.02** should be accounted for as a sale to the extent that consideration other than beneficial interests in the transferred assets is received in exchange. (A beneficial interest is the right to receive all or portions of specified cash inflows to a trust or other entity.)

2393.04 If the transfer qualifies as a sale, the transferor should (1) derecognize the transferred assets or a group of entire financial assets, (2) recognize and initially measure at fair value servicing assets, servicing liabilities, and any other assets obtained (including a transferor's beneficial interest in the transferred financial assets) and liabilities incurred in the sale, and (3) recognize in earnings any gain or loss on the sale.

2393.05 To illustrate, assume that XYZ Company transfers (sells) without recourse accounts receivable with a carrying amount of $400,000 (accounts receivable of $420,000 less a $20,000 credit balance in the allowance for uncollectible accounts) for $390,000 cash. Assume that the reason that XYZ Company is willing to sell the receivables at a discount is because of the benefits of having access to the cash proceeds now rather than because of any impairment of the receivables. Assuming that the criteria in section **2393.02** are met (i.e., that the transferor surrenders control), the entry to record the transfer (sale) of the accounts receivable is:

Cash	$390,000	
Allowance for Uncollectible Accounts	20,000	
Loss on Sale of Receivables	10,000	
Accounts Receivable		$420,000

2393.06 The $10,000 loss on sale of receivables is determined as follows:

Net proceeds		$390,000
Carrying amount of receivables sold:		
Accounts receivable	$420,000	
Less allowance for uncollectible accounts	(20,000)	400,000
Loss on sale of receivables		$(10,000)

2393.07 **Factoring:** A frequently occurring example of the sale of accounts receivable is that known as *factoring*. Under a factoring arrangement, the receivables in their entireties are sold outright on a nonrecourse basis to a transferee (the factor). The factor assumes the duties of billing and collecting; customers are notified to make their payments directly to the factor. The factor normally controls the granting of credit. As the seller of the product or service (transferor of the receivables) makes approved credit sales, the sales invoices are forwarded to the factor.

2393.08 Transfers of financial assets may involve various types of continuing involvement of the transferor. Any type of continuing involvement of the transferor has to be evaluated carefully since it may indicate that control has not been transferred, which would require that the transfer be accounted for as a borrowing rather than as a sale.

2393.09 One form of continuing involvement that has to be evaluated particularly carefully is that of "recourse." In a transfer of receivables with recourse, the transferor provides the transferee with full or limited recourse. The effect of a recourse provision on the application of the criteria in section **2393.02** may vary by jurisdiction. In some jurisdictions, transfers with full recourse may not place transferred assets beyond the reach of the transferor and its creditors but transfers with limited recourse may. FASB ASC 860-10-5-15 specifies that a transfer of receivables in their entireties with recourse shall be accounted for as a sale, with the proceeds of the sale reduced by the fair value of the recourse obligation, if the conditions in section **2393.02** are met. Otherwise, such a transfer should be accounted for as a borrowing.

2393.10 To illustrate, assume the same facts as those presented in section **2393.05** except also assume that (1) XYZ Company transfers the receivables with recourse, and (2) the estimated fair value of the recourse provision is $26,000 (i.e., the fair value of XYZ Company's agreement to repurchase any uncollectible receivables is $26,000). Stated differently, it is the estimated fair value of the total outlay that XYZ Company expects to have to make for uncollectible receivables.

2393.11 The gain or loss on sale would be computed as follows:

Net proceeds:		
Cash received		$390,000
Less fair value of recourse obligation		(26,000)
Carrying amount of receivables sold:		364,000
Accounts receivable	$420,000	
Less: Allowance for uncollectible accounts	(20,000)	400,000
Loss on sale of receivables		$(36,000)

2393.12 The entry to record the sale of the receivables is as follows:

Cash	$390,000	
Allowance for Uncollectible Accounts	20,000	
Loss on Sale of Receivables	36,000	
Accounts Receivable		$420,000
Estimated Recourse Obligation		26,000

2393.13 Notice that the loss on the sale of the receivables would be $56,000 (rather than $36,000) if XYZ Company had not previously recognized any uncollectible accounts expense related to these receivables. However, the loss on the transfer of the receivables is the difference between the net proceeds and the carrying amount of the receivables at the time of transfer. Assuming that XYZ Company does, in fact, have to pay the transferee $26,000 for uncollectible receivables, XYZ Company would have suffered a total loss or expense of $56,000, consisting of $20,000 of uncollectible accounts expense recognized up to the date of transfer of the receivables and $36,000 of loss on the sale of receivables recognized at the date of transfer of the receivables to the transferee.

Transfers That Qualify As Borrowings

2393.14 If the criteria in section **2393.02** are not met, a transfer of financial assets is to be accounted for as a borrowing. For example, assume that the recourse provision caused XYZ Company's transfer to fail to qualify as a sale. In that case, XYZ Company should account for the transfer as a borrowing, as reflected in the following entry:

Cash	$390,000	
Obligation to transferee		$390,000

2393.15 **Assignment:** A type of transfer of receivables that may fail to qualify as a sale and thus be accounted for as a borrowing is that of an *assignment*. The assignment of accounts receivable is similar to pledging but usually involves a more formal process. In an assignment, the transferor (assignor) assigns accounts receivable to a transferee (assignee) for cash. Assignments are usually made on a with-recourse basis. In assignments, the assignor (transferor) is usually not attempting to sell the receivables to the assignee (transferee); rather the essence of the arrangement is that the receivables represent collateral for the related loan. The assignor (transferor) usually collects the receivables and remits the collections to the assignee (transferee). The assignee advances (in the form of a loan) a certain percentage of the amount of the receivables assigned, with interest being charged on the loan.

Accounting for Servicing of Financial Assets

2393.16 Servicing assets arise, for example, in situations in which a loan originator transfers (sells) loans to another entity and retains the obligation and right to service those loans. Motivations for servicing financial assets range from the desire to generate revenue through the servicing function to the need to maintain a relationship with the borrower.

2393.17 An entity must record servicing assets or liabilities initially at fair value at the time that an obligation is accepted to service financial assets in any of the following circumstances:

    a. At the time a servicer transfers an entire financial asset, a group of entire financial assets, or a participating interest in an entire financial asset in a transaction meeting the requirements for sale accounting (i.e., rather than accounting for the transfer as a collateralized borrowing).

    b. At acquisition or acceptance of an obligation to service a financial asset that does not relate to financial assets of the servicer or its consolidated affiliates or subsidiaries included in the financial statements being presented (e.g., a situation in which the servicer accepts the obligation of servicing another organization's loans for compensation).

    c. An entity that transfers its financial assets to an unconsolidated entity in a transfer that qualifies as a sale in which the transferor obtains the resulting securities and classifies them as debt securities held-to-maturity may either separately recognize its servicing assets or servicing liabilities or report the servicing assets or servicing liabilities together with the asset being serviced.

2393.18 Once the aforementioned servicing assets or liabilities have been recognized at their individual fair values, servicers are permitted to subsequently value those rights using either of two different methods:

    1. Amortization method: Servicing assets or servicing liabilities may be amortized over the period of estimated net servicing income or net servicing loss with servicing assets or servicing liabilities assessed for impairment (assets) or augmentation (liabilities) based on fair value at each reporting date.

2. **Fair value method:** Servicing assets or servicing liabilities are measured at fair value each reporting period and changes in fair values are reported in earnings in the period in which the changes occur.

2393.19 Servicing assets and servicing liabilities measured at fair value should be presented separately in the balance sheet.

This page intentionally left blank.

Section 2400
Governmental Accounting and Reporting

2410 Governmental Accounting Concepts
- 2411 Measurement Focus and Basis of Accounting
- 2412 Fund Accounting Concepts and Application
- 2413 Budgetary Accounting

2420 Format and Content of Comprehensive Annual Financial Report (CAFR)
- 2421 Government-Wide Financial Statements
- 2422 Governmental Funds Financial Statements
- 2423 Proprietary Funds Financial Statements
- 2424 Fiduciary Funds Financial Statements
- 2425 Notes to Financial Statements
- 2426 Management's Discussion and Analysis
- 2427 Required Supplementary Information (RSI) Other Than Management's Discussion and Analysis
- 2428 Combining Statements and Individual Fund Statements and Schedules
- 2429 Deriving Government-Wide Financial Statements and Reconciliation Requirements

2430 Financial Reporting Entity, Including Blended and Discrete Component Units

2440 Typical Items and Specific Types of Transactions and Events: Recognition, Measurement, Valuation, Calculation, and Presentation in Governmental Entity Financial Statements
- 2441 Net Assets and Components Thereof
- 2442 Fund Balances and Components Thereof
- 2443 Capital Assets and Infrastructure Assets
- 2444 General Long-Term Liabilities
- 2445 Interfund Activity, Including Transfers
- 2446 Nonexchange Revenue Transactions
- 2447 Expenditures
- 2448 Special Items
- 2449 Encumbrances

2450 Accounting and Reporting for Governmental Not-for-Profit Organizations

2410 Governmental Accounting Concepts

2410.01 When the Financial Accounting Foundation (FAF) established the GASB in a brother-sister relationship with the FASB, the FAF established the following jurisdiction policy.

   a. The GASB is to establish accounting and reporting standards for activities and transactions of *state and local governmental entities*—which include states, counties, cities, and towns; independent school districts; state and local government educational institutions (colleges and universities); hospitals and other health care organizations; and charitable and other not-for-profit organizations that are government organizations.

   b. The FASB is to establish accounting and reporting standards for activities and transactions of *all other entities*.

2410.02 **Definition of governmental organizations.** The GASB and the FASB agreed that the term "state and local governmental entities" should be defined as follows.

   Governmental organizations are:

   a. public corporations and bodies corporate and politic and

   b. *other organizations* that have *one* or more of the following characteristics:

   (1) popular election of officers *or* appointment (or approval) of a controlling majority of the members of the organization's governing body *by officials of one or more state or local governments,*

   (2) the potential for unilateral dissolution by a government with the net assets reverting to a government,

   (3) the power to enact and enforce a tax levy, or

   (4) the ability to issue directly (rather than through a state or municipal authority) debt that pays interest exempt from federal taxation.

   Entities meeting either part **a.** or part **b.** of this definition are under the GASB's jurisdiction; those not meeting this definition are under the FASB's jurisdiction.

2410.03 Consistent with the FAF jurisdiction agreement, the GASB has established a separate *state and local government* GAAP hierarchy with respect to the relative authoritativeness of the various standards, pronouncements, and other literature on financial accounting and reporting principles and procedures.

2410.04 In 2009, the GASB issued GASB Statement 55, *The Hierarchy of Generally Accepted Accounting Principles for State and Local Governments.* As outlined in GASB Statement 55, the sources of accounting principles that are generally accepted are categorized in descending order of authority as follows:

   a. Officially established accounting principles—Governmental Accounting Standards Board (GASB) Statements and Interpretations. GASB Statements and Interpretations are periodically incorporated in the Codification of Governmental Accounting and Financial Reporting Standards. Any AICPA or FASB pronouncements that have been made applicable by a GASB Statement or Interpretation are also a part of this level.

   b. GASB Technical Bulletins and, if specifically made applicable to state and local governmental entities by the American Institute of Certified Public Accountants (AICPA) and cleared by the GASB, AICPA Industry Audit and Accounting Guides, and AICPA Statements of Position

  c. AICPA Practice Bulletins if specifically made applicable to state and local governmental entities and cleared by the GASB, as well as consensus positions of a group of accountants organized by the GASB that attempts to reach consensus positions on accounting issues applicable to state and local governmental entities

  d. Implementation Guides ("Q&As") published by the GASB staff, as well as practices that are widely recognized and prevalent in state and local government

2410.05 If the accounting treatment for a transaction or other event is not specified by a pronouncement in category a., a governmental entity should consider whether the accounting treatment is specified by an accounting principle from a source in another category. In such cases, if categories b.–d. contain accounting principles that specify accounting treatments for a transaction or other event, the governmental entity should follow the accounting treatment specified by the accounting principle from the source in the highest category—for example, follow category b. treatment over category c. treatment.

2410.06 If the accounting treatment for a transaction or other event is not specified by a pronouncement or established in practice as described in categories a.–d., a governmental entity should consider accounting principles for similar transactions or other events within categories a.–d. and may consider other accounting literature. A governmental entity should not follow the accounting treatment specified in accounting principles for similar transactions or other events in cases in which those accounting principles either prohibit the application of the accounting treatment to the particular transaction or other event or indicate that the accounting treatment should not be applied by analogy.

2410.07 Other accounting literature includes GASB Concepts Statements; the pronouncements referred to in categories a.–d. of the GAAP hierarchy for nongovernmental entities if not specifically made applicable to state and local governmental entities by the GASB; Financial Accounting Standards Board pronouncements; Federal Accounting Standards Advisory Board (FASAB) Statements, Interpretations, Technical Bulletins, and Concepts Statements; AICPA Issues Papers; International Public Sector Accounting Standards of the International Public Sector Accounting Standards Board or International Financial Reporting Standards of the International Accounting Standards Board, or pronouncements of other professional associations or regulatory agencies; Technical Information Service Inquiries and Replies included in AICPA Technical Practice Aids; and accounting textbooks, handbooks, and articles. The appropriateness of other accounting literature depends on its relevance to particular circumstances, the specificity of the guidance, and the general recognition of the issuer or author as an authority. For example, GASB Concepts Statements would normally be more influential than other sources in this category.

2410.08 The essence of this GAAP hierarchy for state and local governments is as follows:

  a. **GASB Statements and Interpretations are the most authoritative sources** of GAAP applicable to state and local government entities—and supersede any guidance at levels b.–e.

  b. If the GASB has not issued a statement or interpretation that addresses the issue directly or by recognizing an AICPA or FASB pronouncement that addresses the issue, the literature at levels b.–d. should be researched in sequential (hierarchical) order for guidance.

  c. Finally, if guidance is not available at levels a.–d., determine if the principles found at those levels are applicable by analogy (if not prohibited) to the transaction being researched and consider other accounting literature (level e.), such as GASB Concepts Statements, textbooks, professional organization position papers, and other publications, journal articles, and speeches.

2410.09 Some not-for-profit organizations are government entities, but others are nongovernment.

    a. *Government* not-for-profit organizations follow the SLG government GAAP hierarchy in determining applicable GAAP. *These not-for-profit organizations are prohibited by GASB Statement 29 from applying FASB not-for-profit standards.*

    b. *Nongovernment* not-for-profit organizations should follow the authoritative guidance in the FASB's Accounting Standards Codification.

There are significant differences in GAAP applicable to *government* and *nongovernment not-for-profit organizations.*

2411 Measurement Focus and Basis of Accounting

Nature, Environment, Report Users and Uses, and Reporting Objectives

2411.01 **Nature of governments.** State and local governments differ from business organizations—but are similar to other nonbusiness organizations—in several ways. For example:

— **Service objective:** Governmental entities are established by the citizenry to render services to those citizens.

— **Lack of profit motive:** Governmental entities typically *do not* seek to profit from the activities in which they engage.

Governments differ both from businesses and from other nonbusiness organizations in several important respects. Among these are the following:

    a. **Dependence on legislative authorities and municipal law:** Governmental entities usually receive their authority to act directly from the state or local legislature that limits and oversees their operations. Likewise, their actions are subject to *municipal law*—which provides that governments can do only what they are legally authorized to do.

    b. **Power to levy taxes, licenses, fines, etc.:** The principal revenue source of most governmental entities is taxes levied on the citizenry, and many also have the power to license various activities, levy fines, and otherwise require involuntary, nonexchange contributions of financial resources by the citizenry.

    c. **Other restrictions and controls:** In the absence of a profit motive, net income bottom line, or other performance indicator, governments are subjected to a variety of other restrictions and controls. The most important are:

        (1) overall restrictions on the use of their financial resources—which led to *fund accounting* and

        (2) exercise of expenditure control through the annual budget—which led to *budgetary accounting and budgetary reporting.*

    d. **Responsibility to citizens:** In financial reporting matters, governmental entities have the responsibility (accountability) of demonstrating good stewardship over financial resources provided and entrusted to them by the citizenry.

2411.02 **The government environment.** General purpose units of governments typically engage in both (a) general government or governmental-type activities that are financed largely by taxes and similar revenues and (b) business-type activities that are financed largely by charges for services rendered. The GASB (Codification Appendix B) notes several particularly significant characteristics of the governmental-type activities environment that affect governmental accounting and financial reporting.

a. **Primary characteristics**

(1) **Representative form of government and separation of powers.** In a representative democracy:

    (a) A government's powers ultimately rest with the citizenry (who delegate those powers to public officials through the election process).

    (b) Governments are organized so as to separate their powers among the executive, legislative, and judicial branches and to provide checks and balances among the branches.

    (c) The executive branch typically proposes annual budgets, whereas the legislative branch has the power to approve or modify the proposed budget.

    (d) The executive branch is accountable to the legislative branch for operating within the approved budget and laws, regulations, etc.—and both branches are accountable to the citizenry.

(2) **Federal system of government and prevalence of intergovernmental revenues.** The federal-state-local government structure has resulted in higher-level governments affecting the activities of lower-level governments through intergovernmental grants and subsidies. These grants and subsidies cause the lower levels of government to be accountable to the higher levels of government as well as to the citizenry.

(3) **Relationship of taxpayers to services received.**

    (a) The power to tax is unique to governments and causes taxpayers to be involuntary resource providers.

    (b) Taxation typically is based on income, sales, property values, or other factors not related to the services received by the taxpayers. There is no reciprocal exchange or other arm's-length transaction that directly relates the taxes paid to the services received from the government.

    (c) Governments often have powers similar to taxation to levy license and permit fees, fines, and other charges. Government services financed by taxes and similar charges are not dictated or controlled by what the citizens would be willing to pay in an arm's-length transaction.

    (d) The power to tax and levy similar charges, and the fact that governments often have a monopoly on their services, make it difficult to measure and evaluate the efficiency or effectiveness of governments in providing services.

    (e) Public accountability is a uniquely important aspect of governmental accounting and financial reporting.

b. **Control characteristics**

(1) **The budget as an expression of public policy and financial intent and as a means of providing control.**

    (a) The annual budget, which is both an expression of public policy and intent and a financial plan of the proposed expenditures for the year and how they are to be financed, is extremely important in the government environment.

    (b) Further, the adopted budget has the force of law that both authorizes and limits expenditures.

    (c) The annual budget is a form of control and is one basis for evaluation of performance. A government must demonstrate its budgetary accountability.

(2) **Use of fund accounting for control purposes.**

    (a) A government's assets and liabilities are segregated into, and accounted for in, various types of funds that are separate accounting entities.

    (b) Funds and fund accounting controls complement the annual budget and budgetary control processes in assuring compliance with external restrictions and the annual budget.

c. **Other characteristics**

    (1) **Dissimilarities between similarly designated governments.** Governments with similar designations (i.e., states, counties, cities) often do not perform identical functions or render identical services. This fact hinders comparisons among governments and government financial statements.

    (2) **Significant investment in nonrevenue-producing capital assets.** Many governments have significant investments in streets, bridges, storm drainage systems, and other nonrevenue-producing general government capital assets, which they have an implicit obligation to maintain.

    (3) **Nature of the political process.**

        (a) The budget process is used to reconcile the virtually unlimited (and often conflicting) wants of the citizenry with the limited financial resources available to the government.

        (b) The budget process is an extremely important part of the political process.

        (c) To balance the budget, elected officials may be tempted to:

            1. pay for increased levels of current services with nonrecurring revenues,

            2. defer payment for current services to future periods, or

            3. provide highly visible services but defer equally important but less visible services to future years.

2411.03 **Users of financial reports.** The GASB (Codification Appendix B) identifies three groups of *primary users* of a government's external financial reports.

a. **The citizenry:** To whom the government is primarily accountable, including citizens (taxpayers, voters, service recipients), the media, advocate groups, and public finance researchers.

b. **Legislative and oversight bodies:** Those who directly represent the citizens, including members of state legislatures, county commissions, city councils, boards of trustees and school boards, and executive branch officials with oversight responsibility over other levels of government.

c. **Investors and creditors:** Who lend or participate in the lending process, including individual and institutional investors and creditors, municipal security underwriters, bond rating agencies, bond insurers, and financial institutions.

If a government's internal executive branch managers do not have ready access to a government's internal information, they constitute a fourth primary user group for that government.

2411.04 **Uses of financial reports.** The GASB (Codification Appendix B) notes that financial reporting should provide information useful in making economic and political decisions and in assessing accountability by:

a. comparing actual *financial results* with the legally adopted budget,

b. assessing financial condition and results of operations,

c. assisting in determining *compliance* with finance-related laws, rules, and regulations, and

d. assisting in evaluating *efficiency* and *effectiveness*.

2411.05 **Objectives.** The GASB observes the following in its Concepts Statement 1, *Objectives of Financial Reporting,* (Cod. Appen. B):

— *Accountability* is the *paramount objective* of government financial reporting.

— *Interperiod equity* is an important element of accountability.

Moreover, the GASB concluded that governmental financial reporting should provide information to assist users in assessing accountability and making economic, social, and political decisions. Accordingly, the GASB reporting objectives say that state and local government (SLG) financial reporting should provide the following:

a. A means of demonstrating the SLG's *accountability* that enables users to assess that accountability. Specifically, the information provided should:

(1) permit users to determine *whether current-year revenues were sufficient* to pay for current year services and/or whether future years' citizens must assume burdens for services previously provided,

(2) demonstrate the SLG's *budgetary accountability and compliance* with other finance-related legal and contractual requirements, and

(3) assist users in assessing the SLG's service efforts, costs, and accomplishments.

b. Information necessary to evaluate the SLG's operating results for the period, including information:

(1) about the sources and uses of financial resources,

(2) on how the SLG financed its activities and met its cash requirements, and

(3) that is necessary to determine whether the SLG's financial condition improved or deteriorated during the year.

c. Information necessary to assess the level of SLG services and its ability to continue to finance its activities and meet its obligations, including:

(1) information about the SLG's financial position and condition,

(2) information about the SLG's physical and other nonfinancial resources having useful lives that extend beyond the current year, including information that can be used to assess their service potential, and

(3) disclosure of legal and contractual restrictions on the use of resources and risks of potential loss of resources.

2411.06 **CPA Examination requirements:** CPA Examinations often have emphasized governmental accounting and reporting topics. Accordingly, these topics should be emphasized by CPA Examination candidates. Particular attention should be paid to the basic concepts and terminology, the nature of the funds, unique transactions and events and the journal entries required to record them. Both the government-wide and the fund financial statements presented by state and local governments are apt to be covered extensively. In 2011 and 2012 there is apt to be coverage of the fund balance classifications and fund type definitions established by GASB Statement 54 as well as the net asset classifications used in proprietary fund and government-wide financial statements.

Governmental Accounting and Reporting Concepts and Terminology

2411.07 **Fund accounting.** A government is not accounted for through a single accounting entity. Rather, the accounts of a government are divided into several separate accounting entities, called funds, and general capital assets and general long-term liabilities accounts.

   a. The GASB defines a **fund** as *a fiscal and accounting entity with a self-balancing set of accounts recording cash and other financial resources, together with all related liabilities and residual equities and balances, and changes therein, which are segregated for the purpose of carrying on specific activities or attaining certain objectives in accordance with special regulations, restrictions, or limitations.*

   b. A fund thus has three distinct characteristics.

      (1) An independent entity:

         (a) Operating (fiscal)

         (b) Accounting (self-balancing set of accounts)

      (2) To account for:

         (a) Specific activities

         (b) Attaining certain objectives

      (3) In accordance with:

         (a) Regulations and laws

         (b) Restrictions

         (c) Limitations

2411.08 **Types of funds.** The GASB requires the following categories and types of funds.

   a. **Governmental funds:** To finance and account for general government activities, such as police and fire protection, courts, inspection, and general administration. Most of their financial resources are budgeted and appropriated annually for specific general government uses (expenditures) by the legislative body. Governmental funds include the following:

      (1) General fund

      (2) Special revenue funds

      (3) Capital projects funds

      (4) Debt service funds

      (5) Permanent funds

   The *accounting equation* for *governmental funds* is presented in the GASB authoritative literature as:

   Financial assets - Related liabilities = Fund balance

   The accounting equation of most governmental funds also can be thought of and perhaps more easily understood as:

   Current assets (CA) - Current liabilities (CL) = Fund balance (FB)

   Note that the governmental fund accounting equation typically approximates a working capital equation, and governmental fund operations are measured in terms of sources and uses of working capital (i.e., *changes in working capital or in net current financial resources*).

The accounting equation is not truly a working capital equation. For instance, "related liabilities" excludes many liabilities that affect working capital because liabilities for claims, judgments, compensated absences, pensions, and so on are included in governmental funds *only when due and payable*. However, many find it useful to understand the accounting for these funds by relating it to working capital reporting.

b. **Capital assets and long-term liabilities:** Because the governmental funds are primarily working capital (or net expendable financial assets) entities, general government capital (fixed) assets are not accounted for in these funds. Likewise, general government long-term liabilities (with the exception of long-term interfund liabilities) are not accounted for in governmental funds. Therefore, these capital assets and long-term liabilities must be accounted for separately. Indeed, as will be discussed later, these assets and liabilities are ***reported only in government-wide financial statements,*** not in the governmental fund financial statements. Although GAAP does not mandate a specific accounting entity, the accounting entity typically used to maintain accountability for general government capital assets (called general capital assets) and general government long-term liabilities (called general long-term liabilities) is some version of the General Capital Assets and General Long-Term Liabilities accounts. The accounting equation for these accounts when they are maintained using a single accounting entity is:

General capital assets (GCA) - Accumulated depreciation - General long-term liabilities (GLTL) = Net assets

Note: Accounting and reporting for the governmental funds for the "general government" (or governmental) activities are tested extensively on the CPA Examination.

c. **Proprietary funds:** To finance and account for a government's self-supporting business-type activities (e.g., utilities). Proprietary funds include the following:

(1) Enterprise funds

(2) Internal service funds

The *accounting equation of proprietary funds* is similar to that of a business corporation. Thus, the proprietary fund accounting equation includes accounts for *all* related assets and liabilities—not just for current assets and current liabilities. However, the net asset (or equity) classifications used are different. *Contributed capital and retained earnings* are *not* reported. The accounting equation is:

$$\begin{pmatrix} Current\ Assets \\ +Capital\ (Fixed)\ Assets \\ +Other\ Noncurrent\ Assets \end{pmatrix} - \begin{pmatrix} Current\ Liabilities \\ +Long\text{-}Term\ Liabilities \\ +Other\ Noncurrent\ Liabilities \end{pmatrix} = Net\ Assets$$

Proprietary fund operations are measured in terms of revenues earned and expenses incurred. However, net income or loss is *not* reported. Fund equity (or net assets) is reported in three categories (discussed at section **2412.16**):

(1) Invested in capital assets, net of related debt

(2) Restricted net assets

(3) Unrestricted net assets

d. **Fiduciary funds:** To account for resources (and any related liabilities) held by a government entity for the benefit of others (not to support the government's programs) either in a trustee capacity (trust funds) or as an agent for others (agency funds). Fiduciary funds include the following:

(1) Private-purpose trust funds

(2) Investment trust funds

(3) Pension (and other employee benefit) trust funds

(4) Agency funds

Fiduciary fund reporting focuses on fiduciary net assets and changes in fiduciary net assets. Agency funds are purely custodial (assets equal liabilities).

2411.09 **Number of funds.** A government should have only one *General Fund.* It may have one, none, or several of the other types of funds, depending on its activities. The GASB states that governments should use the minimum number of funds consistent with their laws (and contracts) and sound financial management.

2411.10 **Governmental fund annual budgets.** Annual budgets of *estimated* revenues and *estimated* expenditures are prepared for most *governmental funds.*

    a. Approval of the budget by the legislative branch provides the legal authority to the executive branch to proceed with fund activities within the limitations of the budget. (The estimated expenditures authorized by the legislative body are called **appropriations.**)

    b. The approved budgets of such funds are recorded in budgetary accounts in the accounting system to provide budgetary control over governmental fund revenues and expenditures.

If proprietary funds and fiduciary funds are not dependent on annual budgets and legislative appropriations, budgets are not incorporated into their accounts.

2411.11 **Governmental fund account terminology.** Both budgetary accounts and actual operating accounts are employed in most governmental fund accounting systems. Budgetary accounts are necessary because the legal constraints and accountability imposed upon a government through the budget laws and processes require careful monitoring to ensure budgetary control and compliance.

— **Budgetary accounts** are nominal accounts used to record the officially adopted budgetary estimates of revenues, expenditures (appropriations), and other changes in fund balance.

— **Actual accounts** are nominal accounts used to record the actual revenues, expenditures, and other changes in fund balance.

Although terminology varies, the following operating and fund equity accounts are usually employed in governmental funds.

    a. Budgetary accounts

        (1) **Estimated revenues:** Officially approved estimates of asset inflows—of estimated sources of fund net current financial resources (except from nonrevenue other financing sources and interfund reimbursement transactions). The Estimated Revenues account is debited to record the revenue budget and is closed at the end of the period.

        (2) **Appropriations:** Officially approved estimates of (and authorizations of) asset outflows—of estimated uses of fund net current financial resources (except for nonexpenditure other financing uses). The Appropriations account is credited to record the budgeted expenditures and is closed at the end of the period.

        (3) **Encumbrances and Reserve for Encumbrances:** Encumbrances (offset by an account known as Reserve for Encumbrances) are used to record charges of goods and services against appropriations for budgetary control purposes. The estimated cost of the goods and services are recorded in the Encumbrances account temporarily from the time an order is approved (or a contract is signed) until the goods or equipment ordered are received (or the contract is filled) and recorded as actual expenditures against the appropriations. Encumbrances and Reserve for

Encumbrances do not affect actual asset, liability, revenue, or expenditure accounts and are not reported in GAAP-based financial statements. Encumbrances may affect fund balance classifications reported, however.

b. **Actual accounts**

(1) **Revenues:** Additions to fund assets or decreases in fund liabilities (except for nonrevenue other financing sources and interfund reimbursements) that increase the net assets of the fund—net inflows (sources) of fund net current financial resources from revenue-type financing sources. Governmental fund revenues differ from the commercial concept of revenues in that:

(a) they often are levied (e.g., taxes) or result from other nonexchange transactions (e.g., grants) rather than earned per se and

(b) the related financial resources must be both legally and physically available for use in order for revenues (rather than a liability for deferred revenues) to be recognized.

(2) **Expenditures:** Increases in fund liabilities or decreases in fund assets (except for nonexpenditure other financing uses) that decrease the net assets of the fund—net outflows (uses) of fund net current financial resources. *Expenditures differ from expenses* (as defined in commercial accounting) because expenditures include not only current operating expenditures that benefit the current period, but also capital outlays for general capital assets and repayment of general long-term liability principal.

(3) **Other financing sources:** Nonrevenue increases in fund net assets (e.g., from interfund transfers from other funds, sales of general capital assets, and bond issue proceeds). The Other Financing Sources account may be accompanied by an Estimated Other Financing Sources budgetary account.

(4) **Other financing uses:** Nonexpenditure decreases in fund net assets (e.g., for interfund transfers to other funds). The Other Financing Uses account may be accompanied by an Estimated Other Financing Uses budgetary account.

c. **Equity accounts**

(1) **Fund balance:** This equity account balances the asset and liability accounts of a governmental fund.

(2) **Fund balance classifications:** Fund balance is reported in five classifications that communicate the types of constraints on the use of the net current financial resources of a governmental fund. Five fund balance classifications were established by GASB Statement 54, *Fund Balance Reporting and Governmental Fund Type Definitions*:

(a) Nonspendable—Equal to the amounts of inventory and prepaid items (and long-term receivables that are not restricted, committed, or assigned in the *General Fund only*). Equal to the nonexpendable corpus in a Permanent Fund.

(b) Restricted—Equal to assets restricted (*externally enforceable* restrictions based contracts and other agreements, enabling legislation, or constitutional provisions) to expenditure for a specific purpose less liabilities payable from those assets.

(c) Committed—Equal to assets committed (by *formal action of the governing body*) to expenditure for a specific purpose less liabilities payable from those assets. May include *encumbrances* of otherwise unassigned General Fund fund balance if *the same formal action* of the governing body is *required* to establish the encumbrance.

(d) Assigned—Equal to assets assigned (by governing body or committee or individual to whom the governing body delegated assignment authority) to *reflect intent to expend* the assets *for a specific purpose* less liabilities payable from those assets. Also, in the General Fund (1) includes encumbered portion of otherwise unassigned fund balance unless the commitment action is required to approve the encumbrance and (2) can include an amount equal to a budgeted excess of appropriations over revenues.

(e) Unassigned—The residual amount of fund balance in the General Fund. (In the other funds, this classification can only be used to reflect a negative amount.) Only unassigned fund balance can have a negative balance in any fund.

2411.12 **Encumbrance accounting.** An encumbrance system is used in most governmental funds (General, Special Revenue, and Capital Projects) to prevent overexpenditure of appropriations and to demonstrate compliance with legal requirements.

    a. When a purchase order is issued or a contract is approved, the estimated amount of the planned expenditure—the encumbrance—is recorded by debiting Encumbrances (a budgetary account) and crediting Reserve for Encumbrances.

    b. When the related goods or services are received:

        (1) the encumbrance entry is reversed and

        (2) the actual expenditure is recorded.

    c. The unencumbered balance of the Appropriations account is the amount of uncommitted appropriations available for expenditures:

    Unencumbered appropriations = Appropriations - (Encumbrances + Expenditures).

    As encumbrances serve a budgetary control function, the usual accounting treatment is to close the Encumbrances and Reserve for Encumbrances accounts at year-end.

    d. The Reserve for Encumbrances account is *not* reported in the financial statements as its role is strictly related to budgetary accounting and control.

    e. At the beginning of the next period, the Encumbrances closing entry is reversed if the government plans to complete the expenditure. This entry returns the Encumbrances and Reserve for Encumbrances accounts to their usual offsetting relationship and reduces the available appropriation authority as required for effective budgetary control.

2411.13 **Budgetary accounting overview.** The usual governmental fund general ledger-subsidiary ledger configuration is illustrated in Exhibit 1. If nonrevenue and nonexpenditure other financing sources and uses also must be accounted for:

    a. Estimated Other Financing Sources (budgetary) and Other Financing Sources (actual) accounts would be added parallel to the Estimated Revenues (budgetary) and Revenues (actual) accounts.

    b. Estimated Other Financing Uses (budgetary) and Other Financing Uses (actual) accounts would be added parallel to the Appropriations (budgetary) and Expenditures (actual) accounts.

Exhibit 1

Budgetary Accounting Overview
(Governmental Fund)
General Ledger and Subsidiary Ledgers

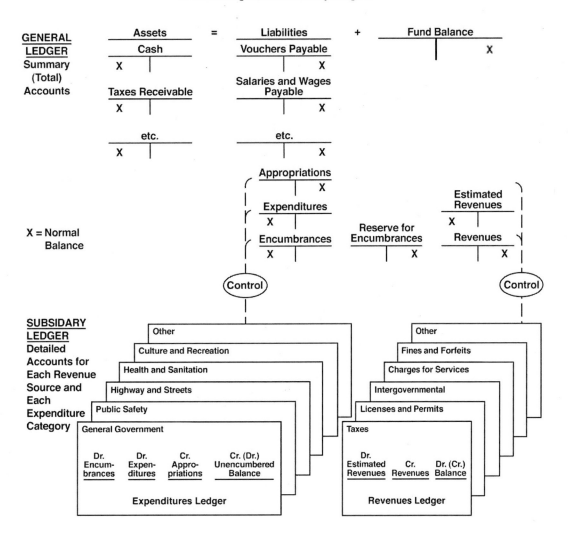

Source: Adapted from Freeman, Shoulders, and Allison, *Governmental and Nonprofit Accounting: Theory and Practice* (Prentice Hall, 2006), p. 89. Reprinted with permission.

2411.14 **Basis of accounting.** In governmental accounting, the measurement focus and basis of accounting used depend on the nature of the fund.

— The flow of economic resources measurement focus and the accrual basis are used in proprietary funds (Enterprise and Internal Service Funds)—where revenues and expenses are recorded.

— The flow of current financial resources measurement focus and the modified accrual basis are used in the governmental funds (General, Special Revenue, Capital Projects, Debt Service, and Permanent Funds)—where revenues and expenditures are recorded.

— Changes in net assets of trust funds are reported as additions and deductions, using the flow of economic resources measurement focus and the accrual basis of accounting.

The GASB Codification provides the following modified accrual basis guidelines:

a. **Revenues** should be recognized in the period that they become susceptible to accrual—both measurable and available to finance that period's expenditures.

Available to finance the period's expenditures means:

(1) the resources are *legally* available for use during the period and

(2) collected within the period or early enough in the next period to be used to pay the liabilities of the period. (Early enough in the next period cannot exceed 60 days for property taxes; therefore, most governments apply the same limits to other revenue sources.)

If revenue-related assets (i.e., taxes receivable) are not available, Deferred Revenues (a liability similar to Unearned Revenues) should be credited initially. When the assets are available, Deferred Revenues is debited and Revenues is credited to recognize the revenues.

b. **Expenditures** should be recorded as fund liabilities are incurred or assets are expended, *except*:

(1) *Inventory* items may be recorded as expenditures *either*:

(a) at the time of purchase (purchase method) or

(b) when the items are used (consumption or use method).

(2) Expenditures for prepayments (e.g., a 2-year insurance policy) may be recorded using either the purchase method or the consumption method.

(3) Payments made for interest and retirement of principal on general long-term liabilities, which usually are accounted for in Debt Service Funds, normally should be recorded as expenditures on their due date (when due) rather than being accrued prior to the due date.

(4) Unmatured noncurrent liabilities for vacation, sick leave, claims and judgments, landfill closure and postclosure costs, pollution remediation, and postretirement benefits such as pensions and health care are recorded as general long-term liabilities rather than as governmental fund expenditures and liabilities, and are recognized as fund expenditures in the year that the liabilities mature (become due).

In summary, expenditures are recognized at one of three points:

(1) *When goods/services are acquired*—Capital assets, salaries, contracted services, materials and supplies (purchases method), prepaid items (purchases method), etc. Indeed, this is the point at which a fund liability is incurred unless there is an expenditure recognition modification.

(2) *When goods/services are used or consumed*—Known as the consumption method, recognition at this point is permitted for materials and supplies and prepaid items such as insurance, but is never required in governmental funds.

(3) *When payment for goods/services is due*—Debt service on general long-term debt and the types of expenditures referred to in item b.(4) above—compensated absences, claims and judgments, special termination benefits, pensions, other postemployment benefits, pollution remediation, and so on.

2411.15 **Operating statements.** Two different types of fund-based operating statements are prepared by a government—one for its governmental funds and another for its proprietary funds. Comparative governmental fund and proprietary fund operating statement formats are illustrated in Exhibit 2 (section **2411.17**). A statement of changes in net assets is required for fiduciary funds.

2411.16 **Governmental fund statement of revenues, expenditures, and changes in fund balance.** This governmental fund operating statement must be presented on both:

— the GAAP basis as illustrated and

— the budgetary basis with original budget, final revised budget, actual, and variances (optional) columns. (If the budget is prepared on a non-GAAP budgetary basis, the differences between the budgetary basis and the GAAP basis must be explained and the statement amounts must be reconciled.) The budgetary statement, which is required only for the general fund and major special revenue funds in the basic financial statements, *may be presented as required supplementary information, as noted later.*

Observe the following in the governmental fund operating statement format illustrated in Exhibit 2 (section **2411.17**):

a. The statement is comprehensive (i.e., it explains all changes in fund balance).

b. Expenditures are reported by function or program and by character. Character classifications include operations (or current operating), capital outlay, and debt service (principal and interest). In addition, governments obviously classify expenditures by fund as that is required for fund financial statements to be presented. Because of their usefulness for various internal purposes, governments typically maintain three other expenditures classifications as well: organizational unit, activity, and object class. An activity classification identifies a specific line of work performed as part of a function or program. The object class is a grouping of expenditures based on the article purchased or service obtained.

c. Transfers of resources between and among funds (interfund transfers) are reported in the governmental fund operating statement as other financing sources or other financing uses. (Interfund transfers are discussed and illustrated later.)

d. Special items (a reporting category unique to governments) and extraordinary items both are reported in this statement.

e. The format shown is the required format.

2411.17 **Proprietary fund statement of revenues, expenses, and changes in net assets.** This proprietary fund operating statement has many similarities to a statement of net income and changes in equity of a business enterprise. Observe the following in the proprietary fund operating statement format illustrated in Exhibit 2:

a. The statement is comprehensive (i.e., it explains all changes in net assets or fund equity).

b. The distinction between operating and nonoperating revenues and expenses as in business enterprise operations reporting.

c. Net income is *not* reported.

d. Revenues from grants (and contributions) for capital asset acquisition or for endowment purposes and other similar amounts are reported after nonoperating revenues and expenses.

e. The presentation of special items (defined and discussed in section **2448**).

f. Interfund transfers are reported as the last item before the net increase or decrease in net assets.

g. The format shown in Exhibit 2 (following) is the required format.

Exhibit 2

"Operating Statement" Formats Governmental Funds and Proprietary Funds			
Governmental Fund Statement of Revenues, Expenditures, and Changes in Fund Balance For Year Ended (Date)		**Proprietary Fund** Statement of Revenues, Expenses, and Changes in Fund Equity For Year Ended (Date)	
Revenues (By Source):		**Operating Revenues:**	
Taxes	X	Sales of goods	X
Licenses and permits	X	Billings for services	X
Intergovernmental	X	Other	X
Charges for services	X		XX
Miscellaneous	X	**Operating Expenses:**	
Total Revenues	XX	Operations	X
		Depreciation	X
Expenditures:		Other	X
Operations (By Function)	X		XX
Capital Outlay	X	Operating Income	X
Debt Service			
Bond principal	X	Nonoperating Revenues (Expenses):	
Interest	X X	Investment income	X
Total Expenditures	XX	Interest expense	(X)
Excess of Revenues over (under) Expenditures	XX	Operating grants and contributions	X
		Other	X
Other Financing Sources (Uses):		Income (Loss) before contributions, special and extraordinary items, and transfers	X
Transfers *from* other funds	X		
Bonds (face value)*	X	Capital grants and contributions	X
Transfers *to* other funds	(X)	Contributions to endowments	X
Proceeds from general capital asset sales	X	Special items and extraordinary items	X
Total other financing sources and uses	X	Transfers out	(X)
Special items and extraordinary items	X	Transfers in	X
Net change in fund balance	XX	Increase (decrease) in net assets	XX
Fund balance, beginning	XX	Net assets, beginning	XX
Fund balance, ending	XX	Net assets, ending	XX

* A premium on bonds issued in a period is reported in other financing sources as a separate line item. A bond discount is reported as an other financing use.

Source: Adapted from Freeman, Shoulders, *et al, Governmental and Nonprofit Accounting: Theory and Practice* (Prentice Hall, 2011), p. 53. Reprinted with permission.

2411.18 **Investment accounting and reporting.** GASB Statement 31 requires that many government investments be reported at fair value—the amount at which they could be exchanged in a current transaction between willing parties, other than in a forced or liquidation sale. The investments usually reported at fair value are investments in the following:

a. Participating interest-earning investment contracts (such as negotiable certificates of deposit)

b. External investment pools

c. Open-end mutual funds

d. Debt securities (such as Treasury bills)

e. Equity securities (such as corporate common stock), option contracts, stock warrants, and stock rights

Participating interest-earning investment contracts are those whose value is affected by market (interest rate) changes—either under contract terms or because they are negotiable or transferable.

GASB Statement 31 permits other investments (and certain specifically exempted investments) to continue to be accounted for and reported using traditional amortized cost (including lower of cost or fair value) methods. The following types of investments are *exempt* from fair value reporting:

a. **Nonparticipating interest-earning investment contracts** such as most certificates of deposit (CDs), guaranteed investment contracts (GICs), and bank investment contracts (BICs)

b. Money market investments and participating interest-earning investment contracts that have a *remaining maturity when purchased* of one year or less

(GASB Statement 53, *Accounting and Financial Reporting for Derivative Instruments,* exempts governmental funds from the requirement of that statement to report derivatives at fair value.)

GASB Statement 31, *Accounting and Financial Reporting for Certain Investments and for External Investment Pools,* may result in some governments accounting for some investments at fair value and reporting other investments under amortized cost methods. Further, GASB Statement 31 requires reporting revenue currently for the change in fair value of investments that are reported at fair value. Both amortized cost and fair value investment accounting are illustrated in Exhibit 3.

Exhibit 3
Investment Accounting Methods—Interest-Bearing Debt Securities

	Amortized Cost		Fair Value	

When acquired ($500,000 par)	Investments
	  Cash
		$490,000
		$490,000
			Investments
			  Cash
				$490,000
				$490,000

Interest received (or accrued)	Cash
	  Revenues—Interest
		$ 30,000
		$ 30,000
			Cash
			  Revenues—Interest
				$ 30,000
				$ 30,000

Discount amortized	Investments Revenues—Interest	$ 2,000 $ 2,000	No Entry	
Change in fair value recognized	No entry—unless apparently permanent decline in fair value		Investments Revenues—Increase in Fair Value of Investments	$ 6,000 $ 6,000
Investment income reported	$32,000		$36,000	

2412 Fund Accounting Concepts and Application

Governmental Fund Accounting

2412.01 **Introduction to Governmental Fund Accounting.** Modified accrual accounting for governmental funds is the most unique aspect of state and local government accounting (and is tested extensively on the CPA Examination). Many common governmental fund transactions are discussed and illustrated briefly in this section. General capital assets and general long-term liabilities are discussed briefly at the end of this section and more extensively in sections **2443** and **2444**. Interfund activity and other transactions involving more than just one fund are discussed and illustrated in section **2445**.

The General Fund

2412.02 **The primary governmental fund.** The General Fund is the primary governmental fund and is used to account for most routine general government operations.

 a. All general government resources that are not required to be accounted for in another fund may be accounted for in the General Fund.

 b. General Fund revenues consist primarily of taxes (property, sales, income, and excise taxes), grants, licenses, fines, and investment income.

 c. General Fund expenditures are budgeted and appropriated typically by department or type of expenditure (e.g., salaries, supplies) by the legislative body.

 d. In its simplest form, the General Fund approximates a "working capital" entity. Its equation is current assets less current liabilities equals fund balance. Hence, all changes in General Fund working capital either increase or decrease fund balance and are reported in the General Fund statement of revenues, expenditures, and changes in fund balance. (Remember that the GASB literature uses the terms *financial assets and related liabilities,* not *current assets and current liabilities*.)

2412.03 **Illustrative entries.** A series of typical General Fund journal entries is presented as follows. *Note the format of the entries*—the general ledger entry appears first, followed by any subsidiary ledger entries, which are identified by subsidiary ledger account and column affected (see Exhibit 1 in section **2411.03**).

 a. **To record the budget adopted:**

Estimated Revenues	$8,000	
Appropriations		$7,400
Fund Balance (or Budgetary Fund Balance) (difference		600
= planned change in fund balance during year)		

Revenues Ledger (Estimated Revenues)

Property taxes	$5,000
Sales taxes	1,000
Licenses	1,500
Other	500
	$8,000

Expenditures Ledger (Appropriations)

Administration	$ 800
Police	3,100
Fire	2,900
Other	600
	$7,400

Notes:

(1) The budgetary entry causes the Fund Balance account to be carried at its planned year-end balance during the year (i.e., *if* actual revenues total $8,000 and if $7,400 of expenditures are incurred, the ending total fund balance will be $600 more than the beginning fund balance). Alternatively, the $600 planned change in fund balance may be recorded in a separate Budgetary Fund Balance account. Further, budgetary entries are reversed in the closing process and have no effect on amounts reported except that the budgeted amounts as well as actual amounts of revenues and expenditures are reported in the budgetary comparison statement.

(2) Subsidiary ledger entries do *not* balance, as do the general ledger entries, but sum to the amount of their related general ledger control accounts.

(3) The subsidiary ledger detail is assumed. However, the detail can be maintained by using detailed General Ledger accounts instead of using subsidiary ledgers. Detailed General Ledger accounts often are assumed on the CPA Exam questions and problems.

b. **To record property taxes levied:**

Taxes Receivable—Current	$5,400	
Allowance for Uncollectible Current Taxes		$ 300
Revenues		5,100

Revenues Ledger (Revenues)

Property Taxes	$5,100

Notes:

(1) Governmental fund revenues, including taxes, are recorded *net* of estimated uncollectible accounts. Therefore, estimated uncollectible accounts are recorded as direct deductions from revenues rather than as expenditures.

(2) Property tax receivables are identified as either current or delinquent or by year of levy. The receivables are recorded at the levy date, when the government's legal claim to the resources is established.

(3) If any of the taxes receivable were not *available* (i.e., were expected to be collected later than a specified period—not to exceed 60 days after year-end), that amount would be recorded initially as Deferred Revenues (a liability), and would be recognized as Revenues when they become available.

(4) Note that the previous recording of the budget in the accounts does not affect this GAAP-based entry for actual revenues. If a government did not maintain budgetary control directly through the accounting system, this and all other nonbudgetary entries would remain the same.

c. **To record cash receipts:**

Cash	$9,200	
Taxes Receivable—Current		$5,250
Notes Payable (short-term)		1,000
Revenues		2,950

Revenues Ledger (Revenues)

Sales taxes	$ 980
Licenses	1,550
Other	420
	$2,950

Notes:

(1) Short-term loans and other short-term liabilities are recorded as governmental fund liabilities (not as general long-term liabilities). Proceeds from short-term loans and retirement of short-term loan principal do *not* change fund balance and are *not* reported in the statement of revenues, expenditures, and changes in fund balance.

(2) Some governmental fund revenues are accrued prior to receipt (i.e., property taxes, other billed revenues, and interest earned), but other governmental fund revenues are not accruable (e.g., licenses and fees) and are recognized when received.

d. **To record:**

   (1) downward revision of allowance for uncollectible accounts,

   (2) reclassification of property taxes as delinquent when they become past due, and

   (3) write-off of uncollectible accounts:

(1) Allowance for Uncollectible Current Taxes	$150	
Revenues		$150

Revenues Ledger (Revenues)

Property taxes	<u>$150</u>

(2) Taxes Receivable—Delinquent	$150	
Allowance for Uncollectible Current Taxes	150	
Taxes Receivable—Current		$150
Allowance for Uncollectible Delinquent Taxes		150
(3) Allowance for Uncollectible Delinquent Taxes	$ 70	
Taxes Receivable—Delinquent		$ 70

Notes:

(1) Entry (1) reduces the Allowance for Uncollectible Current Taxes to equal the receivable amount because the government has collected more property taxes than anticipated. It is illogical for the allowance to exceed the receivable. Since the allowance amount was deducted directly from Revenues, the adjustment is credited to Revenues. (Essentially, this is treated as a change in estimate.)

(2) When property taxes become past due, both the receivable and the related allowance are reclassified as relating to delinquent taxes.

(3) Uncollectible accounts are written off against the related allowance, as in business accounting.

(4) Governments sometimes raise cash by selling receivables or by pledging them as collateral for loans. GASB Statement 48, *Sales and Pledges of Receivables and Future Revenues and Intra-Entity Transfers of Assets and Future Revenues,* provides criteria to distinguish sales of receivables from collateralized borrowings. To be accounted for as a sale of receivables, a transaction must effectively terminate a government's continuing involvement with the receivables. Continuing involvement is terminated if the government cannot prevent the transferee from subsequently selling or pledging the receivables to a third party, the government does not have the option or unilateral ability to substitute for or reacquire specific accounts from among those transferred, **and** neither party can cancel the agreement.

(5) Sales of receivables typically are recognized in a governmental fund by reducing related deferred revenues and recognizing revenues equal to the sale proceeds. A collateralized borrowing typically requires reporting other financing sources equal to the sale proceeds. In government-wide reporting (and proprietary funds), sales of

receivables result in recognition of a gain or loss for the difference between the carrying value of the receivables sold and the sale proceeds.

e. **To record purchase orders issued or other contractual commitments made:**

Encumbrances (expected cost)	$1,400	
Reserve for Encumbrances		$1,400

Expenditures Ledger (Encumbrances)

Administration	$ 200
Police	500
Fire	400
Other	300
	$1,400

Encumbrance accounting is unique to government accounting and is often tested on the CPA Examination. It was discussed in detail in section **2411.12**.

f. **To:**

(1) reverse encumbrances entry and

(2) record expenditures on receipt of goods or services (goods or services encumbered against Administration, for $200, were not yet received):

(1) Reserve for Encumbrances	$1,200	
Encumbrances		$1,200

Expenditures Ledger (Encumbrances)

Police	$ 500
Fire	400
Other	300
	$1,200

(2) Expenditures	$1,220	
Vouchers payable		$1,220

Expenditures Ledger (Expenditures)

Police	$ 490
Fire	400
Other	330
	$1,220

Notes:

(1) Entry (1) reverses the encumbrances entry for the goods and services received because its budgetary control role for this expenditure is complete. The balance remaining in the Encumbrances account are for the goods ordered, or services contracted, for Administration that were **not** received and are still outstanding.

(2) Entry (2) records the actual expenditure which may be the same as, more than, or less than anticipated in the encumbrance entry. The encumbrances entries are made to facilitate proper budgetary control over expenditures.

g. **To record unencumbered expenditures incurred:**

Expenditures	$5,900	
Vouchers Payable		$5,900

Expenditures Ledger (Expenditures)

Administration	$ 570
Police	2,590
Fire	2,495
Other	245
	$5,900

Note: Unfilled authorizations to acquire goods and services under purchase orders or other contracts are encumbered to help avoid overspending appropriations, but many other types of expenditures are controlled by other means and need not be encumbered. For example, salaries and wages usually are not encumbered since they are controlled by civil service boards and payroll procedures. Note that cash payment is **not** required prior to expenditure recognition.

h. **To record payment of invoices:**

Vouchers Payable	$6,700	
Cash		$6,700

i. **To record correction of a prior-year error:**

Accounts Receivable (previously understated)	$300	
Correction of Prior-Year Error (or Fund Balance)		$300

Note: Corrections of prior-year errors are reported as restatements of beginning fund balance.

j. **Routine accruals of revenues and expenditures are made at year end:**

(1)
Interest Receivable on Delinquent Property Taxes	$40	
Revenues		$40
Revenues Ledger (Revenues)		
Other		$40

(2)
Expenditures	$10	
Accrued Interest Payable (on short-term note)		$10
Expenditures Ledger (Expenditures)		
Other		$10

Note: Interest payable on *general long-term liabilities is not accrued* in the governmental funds until it is due to be paid unless specific criteria discussed later are met. Interest expenditures are accrued on all other liabilities.

k. **To record increase in supplies inventory during the year (supplies purchased were previously recorded as expenditures):**

Note: Inventory items may be charged to Expenditures in governmental fund accounting either (a) *when used* or consumed (the consumption or use method), or (b) *when purchased* (the purchases method). In either event, the inventory should be reported in the balance sheet of the governmental fund.

(1) If inventory is reported as expenditures when used (*consumption or use method*):

Supplies Inventory	$700	
Expenditures		$700

(2) If inventory is reported as expenditures when purchased (*purchases method*):

Supplies Inventory	$700	
Fund Balance		$700
(Nonspendable fund balance is reported for the inventory amount because inventory is required to be reported even under the purchases method.)		

Note: Under the purchases method, the amount of supplies purchased is reported as expenditures and the change in inventory during the year is reported as an other financing source (inventory increases) or use (inventory decreases).

Under the consumption method, expenditures equals supplies purchased less an inventory increase or plus an inventory decrease. No other financing source (use) is reported.

l. **To record general ledger closing entries at year end:**

Note: Three general ledger closing entry approaches may be encountered on the CPA Examination. Any reasonable approach that closes the budgetary and actual nominal accounts and updates the Unreserved Fund Balance account is acceptable. One common approach is illustrated here.

Reverse the Budget—Close the Actual Approach

(a) Appropriations $7,400
    Fund Balance (or Budgetary Fund Balance) 600
        Estimated Revenues $8,000

Reverses the budgetary entry in section **2412.03a** and returns the Fund Balance account to its actual preclosing balance.

(b) Revenues $8,240
        Expenditures $7,130
        Fund Balance 1,110

Closes actual revenues and expenditures and adjusts the Fund Balance account for its actual change during the year.

(c) Reserve for Encumbrances $ 200
        Encumbrances $ 200

(d) Correction of Prior-Year Error $ 300
        Unreserved Fund Balance $ 300

Closes correction of prior-year error to Fund Balance.

m. **To record subsidiary ledger closing entries at year end:**

Revenues Ledger (Balance)

Property taxes	$250	
Sales taxes		$ 20
Licenses	50	
Other		40
	$300	$60

Expenditures Ledger (Balance)

Administration	$30
Police	20
Fire	5
Other	15
	$70

Notes:

(1) The subsidiary ledger account balances represent the differences between estimated and actual revenues and appropriations less expenditures and encumbrances.

(2) The subsidiary ledger closing entries can be checked against the general ledger closing entries.

Revenues Ledger

Revenues—General Ledger	$8,240
Estimated Revenues—General Ledger	8,000
Difference—General Ledger Closing Entry	$ 240
Difference—Subsidiary Ledger Closing Entries ($300 - $60)	$ 240

Expenditures Ledger

Appropriations—General Ledger		$7,400
Expenditures—General Ledger	$7,130	
Encumbrances—General Ledger	200	7,330
Difference—General Ledger Closing Entry		$ 70
Difference—Subsidiary Ledger Closing Entries		$ 70

2412.04 **Encumbrances reversing entry.** For encumbrances that will be honored in the next year, the following encumbrances reversing entry, as well as any customary accrual reversing entries, should be made at the beginning of the following year:

Encumbrances	$200	
Reserve for Encumbrances		$200

Expenditures Ledger (Encumbrances)

Administration	$200

Note: This entry is the reverse of the encumbrances closing entry at the end of the prior year.

2412.05 **Recording special items and extraordinary items.** Extraordinary items and/or special items are sometimes reported in a governmental fund. Extraordinary items are transactions or events that are both *unusual in nature and infrequent in occurrence*. Special items are transactions or events that are *either unusual in nature or infrequent in occurrence* **and** *under the control of management*. The amounts to be reported in governmental funds are the gross increases or decreases in the net assets of the governmental fund, not the gain or loss on the transactions. For example, assume that a city sold its only undeveloped land to another party for $500,000 and the cost of the land was $75,000, the city would record in the General Fund a special item of $500,000 for the proceeds from the sale of the undeveloped land, *not* the gain of $425,000.

Cash	$500,000	
Special Item — Proceeds from Sale of Land		$500,000

Special Revenue Funds

2412.06 **Purpose and use.** Special revenue funds are used to account for resources raised from revenues that are either:

- **Restricted** (either by external parties through agreements and contracts such as grants agreements and bond indentures **or** by enabling legislation or constitutional provisions) or

- **Committed** (by formal action of the governing body that requires the same action to reverse)

…for expenditure for specific general government purposes other than capital outlay or debt service.

Note that restrictions in enabling legislation and constitutional provisions must be enforceable by parties outside the government to be considered restricted. Also, GASB Statement 54 requires the following:

a. Each Special Revenue Fund has a restricted or committed revenue source as a foundation both for initial use and for continued use of a Special Revenue Fund to report the restricted or committed resources raised and any other resources transferred to or earned by the Special Revenue Fund.

b. The restricted or committed revenues be reported as revenues of the Special Revenue Fund—not reported initially as revenues of another fund then transferred to the Special Revenue Fund.

Special Revenue Fund use is required if legally or contractually mandated for a restricted or committed revenue source. It is permitted in other instances meeting the definitional requirements. Examples of Special Revenue Funds include funds used to report:

   a. gasoline taxes that must be used to finance street maintenance.

   b. hotel and motel taxes that are restricted to expenditure for industrial development purposes.

   c. an expendable trust gift that is required to be used to benefit a specific general government program.

2412.07 **Interfund transfers.** Restricted revenues that may be used to finance current operations, capital outlay, and/or debt service expenditures related to the specified purposes are accounted for initially in a special revenue fund. Appropriate amounts are then transferred to capital projects funds and debt service funds to finance capital outlay and debt service expenditures, respectively. (Transfers are discussed and illustrated in section **2445**.)

Accounting and reporting. Special revenue fund accounting and reporting concepts and procedures are identical to those for the General Fund; thus, no example entries or illustrative financial statements are presented.

Capital Projects Funds

2412.08 **Nature, use, and termination.** Capital projects funds are used to account for and report financial resources that are restricted, committed, or assigned to expenditure for capital outlays, including the acquisition or construction of capital facilities and other capital assets. Capital projects funds exclude those types of capital-related outflows financed by proprietary funds or for assets that will be held in trust for individuals, private organizations, or other governments.

   a. Capital projects funds are often used to account for specific capital projects and constitute project financing and cost accounting entities.

   b. Fund resources are recorded as received or accrued (i.e., from transfer from the General Fund, issuing general obligation bonds, or federal grants) and are expended for authorized project expenditures, or other capital outlay if the fund is not used to account for a specific project.

   c. Capital projects funds typically have a limited life, which encompasses the construction or acquisition period, and are terminated on completion of the project.

   d. Neither the liabilities for any project-related bond issues or other long-term debt incurred nor the capital assets acquired or constructed are recorded in the governmental funds. As with other governmental funds, the CPF accounting equation is Financial Assets less Related Liabilities equals Fund Balance. Therefore, these long-term liabilities and capital assets do not fit the governmental fund model.

   e. On termination of a capital projects fund, the remaining assets typically are transferred to a debt service fund if project-related debt was incurred.

   f. Capital projects funds are required for projects financed with general obligation bond proceeds, but are used for most other major general government capital projects and many other major general government capital outlays.

   g. While all resources of a capital projects fund must be assigned, committed, restricted, or nonspendable, a restricted or committed *revenue source is not required* for a capital projects fund.

The construction-in-process (or the completed asset, if finished) and the bond liability or other long-term debt incurred are recorded in the General Capital Assets and General Long-Term Liabilities accounts. These items are *reported only in the government-wide financial statements.*

2412.09 **Budgetary accounting.** Capital projects fund accounting often does *not* require use of Estimated Revenues or Appropriations budgetary accounts, because its resources are determined and limited by the nature of the project. However, budgetary accounts *may* be used in the same manner as in the general and special revenue funds, particularly when two or more projects are accounted for in the same capital projects fund. In either case, encumbrances accounting is used to prevent overspending.

2412.10 **Illustrative entries.** Capital projects often are financed by general government bond issues and intergovernmental grants. Thus, the following types of Capital Projects Fund entries may be required in addition to those illustrated for the General Fund.

a. To record issuance of general obligation bonds, $5,000 par, at 104 less $350 bond issuance costs:

Cash ((1.04 × $5,000) - $350)	$4,850	
Expenditures—Bond Issue Costs	350	
Other Financing Sources—Bonds		$5,000
Other Financing Sources—Bond Premium		200

Note: Bond premiums or discounts are recognized separately as Other Financing Sources or Other Financing Uses. Bond issuance costs are reported as expenditures as illustrated here. (The Bonds Payable, Premium on Bonds, and Unamortized Bond Issue Costs are recorded in the General Capital Assets and General Long-Term Liabilities accounts and reported in the government-wide financial statements.)

b. To record award of a $1,000 state project grant (cash received) and a $4,000 federal grant (no cash received) for 80% of specified qualifying costs (not yet incurred) (Both grants are reimbursement grants):

Cash	$1,000	
Deferred Revenues—State Grant		$1,000

Note: This is an example of a reimbursement grant. Only the cash received is recorded—as is Deferred Revenues—since the GASB Codification states that:

(1) Reimbursement grant revenue is not recognized until earned by meeting all grant eligibility requirements, incurring qualifying expenditures, and

(2) Grants that have been awarded, but for which no reimbursable (eligible) costs have been incurred and no cash has been received, should *not* be recorded in the accounts, but may be disclosed in the notes.

c. To record grant expenditures incurred, $4,000, which include $1,000 that qualify for the state grant and $3,000 that qualify for the federal grant:

(1)	Expenditures—Capital Outlay	$4,000	
	Vouchers Payable		$4,000
(2)	Deferred Revenues—State Grant	$1,000	
	Revenues—State Grant		$1,000
(3)	Due from Federal Government (.8($3,000))	$2,400	
	Revenues—Federal Grant		$2,400

Note: If the grant cash has been received and recorded as Deferred Revenues, the entry required reclassifies the amount earned as Revenues (entry 2). If the amount earned has not been received, the receivable (and Revenues or Deferred Revenues) must be recorded. Grant revenues must be deferred, even if "earned," if the resources are not "available" at year end.

2412.11 **Bond anticipation notes (BANs).** Governments may issue bond anticipation notes (BANs) to provide interim financing of capital projects prior to issuing the bonds.

    a. If short-term BANs relate to an authorized (approved) bond issue and must be repaid from the bond issue proceeds, the BANs are usually considered general long-term liabilities, and the BAN proceeds are reported as an other financing source of the capital projects fund.

    b. The retirement of principal of BANs included as general long-term liabilities is reported as an other financing use (rather than as an expenditure).

    c. BANs with terms of a year or less are treated as long-term if (1) the SLG has taken all legal steps required to refinance the BANs with bonds *and* (2) this intent is accompanied by the demonstrated ability to refinance the BANs on a long-term basis.

2412.12 **Arbitrage.** Governments may issue tax-exempt bonds or notes and invest the proceeds in higher-yielding taxable investments. The Internal Revenue Code (IRC) requires that the *arbitrage* (the excess interest earned over the effective interest rate of the tax-exempt bonds or notes) be rebated to the U.S. Treasury. To illustrate:

    a. To record gross earnings (8%) on investment of proceeds of a 6% bond issue:

Cash or Accrued Interest Receivable	$1,000	
Revenues—Interest		$1,000

    b. To record rebate of arbitrage due to the federal government:

Revenues—Interest (or Expenditures—Arbitrage Rebate)	$ 250	
Due to Federal Government		$ 250

    Notes:

    (1) The arbitrage rebate may be recorded either as a deduction from revenues or as an expenditure.

    (2) These two entries may be compounded:

Cash or Accrued Interest Receivable	$1,000	
Due to Federal Government		$ 250
Revenues—Interest		750

    (3) Alternatively, the arbitrage rebate may be recorded as an expenditure (and interest revenues of $1,000 recorded).

2412.13 **Debt Service Funds**

Nature and when required. Debt service funds are used to account for and report payments of the (1) maturing principal of general government long-term debt and (2) related interest and fiscal agent charges. These liabilities are recorded in the General Capital Assets and General Long-Term Liabilities accounts, but are *reported only in the government-wide financial statements* (discussed later).

    a. Use of debt service funds is *required if*:

        (1) amounts are being accumulated for future general government debt service *or*

        (2) their use is required by law, bond indenture covenant, or other contractual agreement.

    Otherwise, their use is optional.

b. Most bond issues require use of debt service funds (and their use typically has been presumed in CPA Examination questions and problems), but capital leases and similar debt that do not require use of debt service funds may be serviced through the General Fund and/or special revenue funds.

c. All resources of a debt service fund are either restricted, committed, or assigned, but a restricted or committed *revenue source is not required*.

2412.14 **Nonaccrual illustrative entries.** Neither general government long-term debt principal nor related interest expenditures are accrued prior to their maturity (due date) as a rule, but only at maturity (when due). Thus, end-of-year accrual entries ordinarily are *not* required. To illustrate, assume that a calendar-year government paid $4,000 of bond principal and $9,000 interest on the bonds on July 15, 20X1, and must pay $3,000 of bond principal and $8,700 interest on the bonds on January 15, 20X2.

a. **To record accrual and payment of maturing bond principal and interest on its 07/15/X1 due date:**

(1)	Expenditures—Bond Principal		$4,000	
	Expenditures—Interest on Bonds		9,000	
	Matured Bonds Payable			$ 4,000
	Matured Interest Payable			9,000
(2)	Matured Bonds Payable		$4,000	
	Matured Interest Payable		9,000	
	Cash (or Cash with Fiscal Agent)			$13,000

b. Year-end adjusting entry—12/31/X1: None

This when-due, nonaccrual approach usually has been assumed in CPA Examination questions.

2412.15 **Accrual option illustrative entries.** Alternatively, the GASB Codification **permits** (but does not require) governments to accrue both principal and interest on general long-term debt that *matures within the first 30 days* of the following year if (1) dedicated resources are available in a debt service fund (and presumably are appropriated currently), and (2) such year-end accrual is done consistently each year so that 12 months of debt service are reported each year. Under this year-end accrual assumption, an accrual entry would be made at year end:

Year-end adjusting entry—12/31/X1 (accrual option):

Expenditures—Bond Principal	$3,000	
Expenditures—Interest on Bonds	8,700	
Bonds Payable		$3,000
Interest Payable		8,700

Note: This option is *not* the usual CPA Examination question assumption (though it may be encountered on the CPA Examination) and should not be assumed unless stated or implied in the question.

2412.16 **Funded reserves.** Bond covenants may require a government to maintain a specified level of net assets invested in a debt service fund as additional assurance against default. (Typically, the amount is equal to one year's debt service requirements, or the highest year's debt service requirements, though it may be a stated dollar amount.) Further, the covenants may require that the amount invested cannot be expended, except to meet debt service requirements during a financial emergency. Resources accumulated to meet such bond covenant requirements are reflected in the amount of restricted fund balance reported for the fund. The entries to establish a funded reserve are:

a. **To invest the amount required by the bond indenture:**

Investments	$3,000	
Cash		$3,000

b. **To reclassify fund balance (if desired):**

Assigned Fund Balance	$3,000	
Fund Balance Restricted for Financial Emergencies		$3,000

Note: While a government could choose to make entry (b.), most will maintain a single fund balance account during the year and classify fund balance only for reporting purposes at year-end.

2412.17 **Refundings.** In addition to their use for routine debt service purposes, debt service funds are also used to account for refundings of general government long-term debt. Refundings occur when the government:

a. issues new (refunding) bonds and

b. uses the proceeds to defease (extinguish) an old bond issue. The government may either call and retire the bond issue (a current refunding) or, more commonly, invest sufficient proceeds in an irrevocable trust to service the old debt during its remaining term or until an earlier call date (an advance refunding). A **legal defeasance** occurs when the advance refunding is done pursuant to a covenant in the old bond indenture. An **in-substance defeasance** occurs when the advance refunding complies with the conditions specified in GASB Statement 7, *Advance Refundings Resulting in Defeasance of Debt*. Governments refund existing bonds to obtain a lower effective interest rate, to refinance debt coming due soon, or to otherwise restructure their long-term debt.

2412.18 **Refunding illustrative entries.** To illustrate the accounting for legal and in-substance defeasances, assume that a government issues $8,000 par of 6% general government refunding bonds at 102, incurring $300 of issuance costs, and pays $8,200 into an irrevocable trust to in-substance defease an old 10%, $7,500 par bond issue.

a. **To record issuance of the 6% refunding bonds:**

Cash ((1.02 × $8,000) - $300)	$7,860	
Expenditures—Bond Issue Costs	300	
Other Financing Sources—Refunding Bonds		$8,000
Other Financing Sources—Premium on Refunding Bonds		160

b. **To record the refunding payment to the trustee:**

Other Financing Uses—Payment to Refunded Bond Trustee	$7,860	
Expenditures—Payment to Refunded Bond Trustee	340	
Cash		$8,200

Notes:

(1) The Refunding Bond Proceeds (net of the bond premium amount and issuance costs) and an equal portion of the Payment to Refunded Bond Trustee are reported as Other Financing Sources and Other Financing Uses, respectively, since the new debt is viewed as being substituted for the old debt and the net debt of the government is not changed.

(2) Amounts *paid from existing nondebt financial resources* are reported as expenditures. (The Other Financing Use cannot exceed the net borrowed resources.)

(3) The Refunding Bonds Payable and the Premium on Refunding Bonds, as well as the unamortized bond issue costs, are reported only in the government-wide statements.

(4) Proprietary fund debt refunding is discussed and illustrated in section **2412.32**.

2412.19 Special Assessment Projects

Nature of SA projects. Some capital projects are financed, entirely or partially, by special assessments levied against the benefited properties or property owners. (For example, subdivision street and/or water system improvements often are financed at least partly by special assessments.) In the typical special assessment project, the local government:

a. acts as the general contractor for the project, arranging for the necessary engineering studies, preparing construction specifications, awarding the construction contracts, etc.,

b. finances the construction either by issuing its own bonds or notes or by issuing special assessment bonds or notes, which typically are guaranteed by the government (called special assessment debt with governmental commitment),

c. when the construction has been completed and has been inspected and accepted, levies assessments against the property owners (or properties) benefited—permitting them to pay in installments (often for 10 years) and charging them interest on the unpaid balance, and

d. bills and collects the special assessments and related interest, which are used to service the debt issued to finance the construction.

2412.20 Special assessment project accounting. General government capital improvement projects financed by special assessments are accounted for like other general government capital improvement projects.

a. The *construction phase* is accounted for in a capital projects fund and the debt is recorded in the General Capital Assets and General Long-Term Liabilities accounts.

b. The *debt service phase* is accounted for in a debt service fund and the related capital assets are accounted for in the General Capital Assets and General Long-Term Liabilities accounts.

2412.21 Illustrative entries. The following entries illustrate selected aspects of accounting for a general government capital improvements project financed initially by special assessment notes guaranteed by the government.

a. **To record issuance of long-term special assessment notes (guaranteed by the government) to finance project construction:**

Capital Projects Fund

Cash	$10,000	
Other Financing Sources—Special Assessment Notes		$10,000

Notes:

(1) The liability for the notes is recorded as Special Assessment Debt with Government Commitment in the General Capital Assets and General Long-Term Liabilities accounts. It is *reported* in the government-wide statement of net assets.

(2) The special assessment note proceeds are reported as an other financing source of the capital projects fund.

b. **To record awarding of construction contract:**

Capital Projects Fund

Encumbrances	$10,000	
Reserve for Encumbrances		$10,000
(**Recall** that this entry is made for budgetary control purposes.)		

c. **To record acceptance of completed construction project and payment to contractor, less a 10% retained percentage pending final inspection:**

   Capital Projects Fund

(1)	Reserve for Encumbrances	$10,000	
	Encumbrances		$10,000
(2)	Expenditures—Capital Outlay	$10,000	
	Cash		$ 9,000
	Contracts Payable—Retained Percentage		1,000

d. **To record levy of assessments for project costs; assessments are payable equally over 10 years, beginning next year, with interest on the remaining balance:**

   Debt Service Fund

Assessments Receivable—Deferred	$10,000	
Deferred Revenues—Special Assessments		$10,000

   Note: Only current receivables are available and thus are recognized as revenues; deferred receivable amounts are recorded as deferred revenues until they become available.

e. **To record billing of property owners for the currently maturing assessments and interest to date:**

   Debt Service Fund

(1)	Assessments Receivable—Current	$1,000	
	Interest Receivable on Special Assessments	700	
	Assessments Receivable—Deferred		$1,000
	Revenues—Interest on Assessments		700
(2)	Deferred Revenues—Assessments	$1,000	
	Revenues—Assessments		$1,000

   Note: Interest receivable on special assessments is not accrued as earned, but when it is billed to property owners when due.

f. **To record collection of all currently maturing assessments and interest:**

   Debt Service Fund

Cash	$1,700	
Assessments Receivable—Current		$1,000
Interest Receivable on Special Assessments		700

g. **To record payment of maturing special assessment notes and interest due:**

Expenditures—Special Assessment Note Principal	$1,000	
Expenditures—Interest on Special Assessment Notes	600	
Cash		$1,600

   Note: Since the special assessment notes are general long-term liabilities, neither interest nor principal is accrued in the fund at year end; both are recorded as expenditures when due.

Permanent Funds

2412.22 **Nature and when required.** Permanent funds are used to account for and report resources that are restricted to the extent that only earnings, and not principal, may be used for purposes that support the reporting government's programs—that is, for the benefit of the government or its citizenry. Permanent funds are used only if the principal of the trust is required to be maintained intact. Expendable trusts are reported as special revenue funds if the government is the beneficiary and as private-purpose trust funds if other entities or individuals are the beneficiaries.

2412.23 **Accounting and reporting.** Accounting and reporting for permanent funds is virtually identical to accounting and reporting for other governmental funds. Therefore, it is not illustrated here. A permanent fund may have a balance of expendable earnings as well as the nonexpendable principal. In such cases, fund balance must be segregated into "Nonspendable Fund Balance" and "Restricted (or Committed or Assigned, if not restricted to expenditure for a specific purpose) Fund Balance."

The General Capital Assets and General Long-Term Liabilities Accounts

2412.24 **Nature and purpose.** Capital (fixed assets or intangible assets) assets of proprietary activities and of fiduciary activities are accounted for in appropriate proprietary funds or fiduciary funds. These assets are reported in proprietary funds and fiduciary funds financial statements, respectively, and proprietary fund capital assets are also reported in the government-wide financial statements. Capital assets of general government activities are reported only in the government-wide financial statements. They are not accounted for or reported in governmental funds, because those funds are essentially working capital entities, and these items are not part of working capital.

Similarly, long-term liabilities of proprietary activities and of fiduciary activities are accounted for and reported in appropriate proprietary funds or fiduciary funds. Unmatured long-term liabilities of general government activities are reported only in the government-wide financial statements. They are not accounted for or reported in governmental funds. These liabilities include debt such as notes payable and bonds payable as well as other liabilities, including unmatured liabilities for claims and judgments, compensated absences, pensions, other postemployment benefits, closure and postclosure liabilities for landfills, and termination benefits, for activities that are not reported in proprietary or fiduciary funds.

Proprietary Fund Accounting

2412.25 **Introduction and review of proprietary fund accounting.** The business-type activities of a state or local government are accounted for in proprietary funds in essentially the same manner as private sector profit-seeking business enterprises. Indeed, as noted earlier, the *proprietary fund accounting equation* is similar to the business accounting equation:

Current assets + Capital assets + Other assets = Current liabilities + Long-term debt + Net assets

Revenues and expenses (*not* expenditures) are measured on the accrual basis, as in business accounting, though the difference is reported as changes in net assets *not* as net income.

Note: GASB Statement 20, *Accounting and Financial Reporting for Proprietary Funds and Other Governmental Entities That Use Proprietary Fund Accounting,* requires government proprietary activities to apply all relevant GASB standards *and to either* (1) apply *only* FASB standards issued on or before November 30, 1989 (except those that conflict with GASB pronouncements), *unless* GASB has adopted newer FASB standards, *or* (2) apply all relevant FASB standards that do not conflict with GASB pronouncements.

2412.26 **Net asset classifications.** Proprietary fund net assets (which may be called fund equity) are reported in three classifications.

1. **Invested in capital (fixed) assets, net of related debt** equals the capital assets of the fund less accumulated depreciation less all capital-asset-related borrowings (whether current or long-term). Note that capital-asset-related "borrowings," not all capital-asset-related debt, affect this classification. For instance, accrued interest payable is not deducted here, even if capital debt.

2. **Restricted net assets,** or restricted equity, equals the difference between (1) assets externally restricted by creditors (perhaps through debt covenants), grantors, donors, or laws and regulations of other governments, or internally by constitutional provisions or enabling legislation and (2) liabilities payable from those restricted assets. The

restrictions must be more narrow than the purposes of the fund being reported. Internal restrictions based on enabling legislation must be *enforceable by parties outside* the government for assets to be included in restricted net assets.

3. **Unrestricted net assets** is the difference between the remaining assets and liabilities of the fund. Restricted net assets must be reclassified as unrestricted (or as invested in net assets, net of related debt) when the government satisfies the restriction.

Notes:

1. The familiar contributed capital and retained earnings classifications are *not* to be used.
2. There is no reason to maintain these net asset classifications in the accounts. The proper balances must be derived computationally at year end.

2412.27 **Financial statements.** Three proprietary fund financial statements are required.

1. Balance sheet (statement of net assets)
2. Statement of revenues, expenses, and changes in net assets
3. Statement of cash flows

2412.28 **CPA Examination requirements.** Exam questions often require the candidate to do the following:

a. Distinguish when proprietary fund accounting should be used, rather than general government accounting.

b. Distinguish between the use of enterprise funds and internal service funds.

c. Prepare basic proprietary fund entries and financial statements.

It is reasonable to expect some emphasis on the net asset classifications, the statement of revenues, expenses, and changes in net assets, and the statement of cash flows.

2412.29 **Enterprise Funds**

When required. Enterprise funds *may* (are permitted to) be used to report *any* activity for which a *fee* is *charged* to external users for goods or services. Such activities are *required* to be reported as enterprise funds *if any* one of the following *criteria* is *met*:

a. The activity is financed with debt that is secured *solely* by a pledge of the net revenues from fees and charges of the activity.

b. Laws or regulations require that the activity's costs of providing services, including capital costs (such as depreciation *or* debt service), be recovered with fees and charges rather than with taxes or similar revenues.

c. Although not required by law or regulation, the pricing policies of the activity establish fees and charges designed to recover its costs, including capital costs (such as depreciation *or* debt service).

Most government-owned public utilities (i.e., electricity, gas, water, and sewer systems) are required to be accounted for in enterprise funds. City bus lines or other mass transit systems are examples of government activities that often do not meet any of the three criteria requiring the use of enterprise funds, but which governments may choose to account for in enterprise funds. This option is permitted because fees to external users are a principal revenue source. Most major government colleges also apply the Enterprise Fund model under this option.

Enterprise Fund accounting is required to be used for government risk pools if the government's own agencies are not the predominant participants. Enterprise Fund accounting is permitted for municipal solid waste landfills by GASB Statement 18, which requires expenses and liabilities to include a pro rata share of the estimated closure and postclosure costs consistent with the percentage of landfill capacity used.

2412.30 **Subfunds.** If enterprise-related capital projects, debt service, trust, or agency funds are required by bond indentures, grant provisions, other contractual agreements, or laws, they are accounted for as enterprise fund subfunds within the enterprise fund rather than as separate funds.

   a. Such subfunds are accounted for by using restricted asset and related liability accounts (i.e., Cash—Construction, Contracts Payable—Construction, Investments—Debt Service, Accrued Interest Payable—Debt Service, and Cash—Customer Deposits).

   b. These subfunds need not balance, though all except agency subfunds may be balanced by net asset reserve accounts such as Reserve for Construction or Reserve for Debt Service.

   c. Any revenues and expenses related to the subfunds are recorded as enterprise revenues and expenses, not in separate subfund revenue and expense accounts.

2412.31 **Illustrative entries.** The following example entries illustrate the basics of enterprise fund accounting.

   a. **To record operating revenues:**

Cash	$3,000	
Accounts and Notes Receivable	6,000	
Revenues—Sale of Electricity		$5,000
Revenues—Sale of Appliances		2,500
Revenues—Other		1,500

   b. **To record (1) the provision for uncollectible accounts and (2) the write-off of uncollectible accounts:**

(1)	Revenues—Sale of Electricity	$500	
	Allowance for Uncollectible Accounts		$500
(2)	Allowance for Uncollectible Accounts	$375	
	Accounts and Notes Receivable		$375

   Note: Unlike business accounting, revenues are recorded net of expected uncollectible accounts. Hence, bad debts are not reported as expenses; they reduce revenues as illustrated next.

   c. **To record federal grants for operating and capital purposes:**

Cash	$6,000	
Cash—Construction	9,000	
Revenues—Federal Operating Grants		$6,000
Revenues—Federal Capital Grants		9,000

   Notes:

   (1) Operating grants, those which may be used for either operating or capital purposes or solely for operating purposes, are reported as *nonoperating revenues.*

   (2) Capital grants, which are restricted solely to capital outlay expenditures, are reported as capital contributions revenues after nonoperating revenues and expenses in the operating statement.

   (3) If, as is typical, restricted grants must be expended to be considered earned, they are initially credited to Deferred Revenues accounts, as appropriate, then credited to Revenues accounts when earned by being expended.

(4) This entry (and entry e as follows) assumes that a capital projects subfund is required by the federal capital grant or bond indenture provisions.

d. **To record operating expenses:**

Expenses—Cost of Electricity Purchased	$4,000	
Expenses—Depreciation	1,400	
Expenses—Salaries and Wages	2,700	
Expenses—Other	150	
Accumulated Depreciation		$1,400
Cash		2,700
Accounts and Notes Payable		4,150

Note: Depreciation expense and accumulated depreciation are recorded since expenses are being measured on the accrual basis.

e. **To record (1) issuance of enterprise revenue bonds to finance new electricity distribution lines and (2) acquisition of transmission equipment under capital lease:**

(1)	Cash—Construction	$8,000	
	Bonds Payable		$8,000
(2)	Transmission Equipment Under Capital Lease	$5,000	
	Liability Under Capital Lease		$5,000

f. **To record expenditure of revenue bond issue proceeds to build new electricity distribution lines:**

Transmission Lines	$8,000	
Cash—Construction (or Accounts Payable-Construction)		$8,000

g. **To record (1) payment of bond principal and interest and (2) capital lease principal and interest:**

(1)	Bonds Payable	$800	
	Expenses—Interest on Bonds	560	
	Cash—Debt Service		$1,360
(2)	Liability Under Capital Lease	$500	
	Expenses—Interest on Capital Lease	400	
	Cash		$ 900

Note: This entry assumes that a debt service subfund is used for bond debt service, but that the capital lease is serviced from enterprise fund operating cash.

h. **To record the sale of capital assets:**

Cash or Notes Receivable	$2,000	
Accumulated Depreciation	3,000	
Transmission Equipment		$4,000
Gain (or Loss) on Capital Asset Disposal		1,000

2412.32 **Proprietary fund debt refundings.** GASB Statement 23, *Accounting and Financial Reporting for Refundings of Debt Reported by Proprietary Activities,* requires deferral of the amount that would otherwise be reported as gain or loss on a proprietary debt refunding. This deferred amount is amortized in a systematic and rational manner as an adjustment to Interest Expense over the shorter of the term of the new debt or of the remaining term of the old debt being refunded. Accordingly, if the general government refunding illustrated in section **2412.18** were instead a proprietary fund refunding, it would be recorded:

a. **To record issuance of the 6% refunding bonds:**

Cash ((1.02 × $8,000) - $300)	$7,860	
Deferred Issuance Costs—Refunding Bonds	300	
Refunding Bonds Payable—6%		$8,000
Premium on Refunding Bonds		160

b. To record the refunding payment:

Bonds Payable—10%	$7,500	
Deferred Interest—Refunding	700	
Cash		$8,200

The Deferred Interest—Refunding would be amortized to future interest expense over the *shorter* of the life of the new refunding debt or of the remaining term of the old (refunded) debt, but the Premium on Refunding Bonds and Deferred Issuance Costs—Refunding Bonds would be amortized over the life of the *new* (refunding) issue. Also, the Deferred Interest-Refunding is deducted from Bonds Payable on the balance sheet if it has a debit balance (or added if it has a credit balance).

Note: General government refundings must be reported using this approach in the government-wide financial statements (but not in the fund statements).

Internal Service Funds

2412.33 **Nature and use.** Internal service funds are used to account for in-house business enterprise activities (i.e., to account for the financing of goods or services provided by one government department or agency to other departments or agencies of the government and perhaps to other governments also) on a cost-reimbursement basis. Common examples of internal service funds are those used to account for government motor pools, central repair shops and garages, data processing departments, and photocopy and printing shops.

2412.34 **Cost-reimbursement basis.** The GASB Codification cost-reimbursement basis criterion implies that internal service funds should break even annually or over a period of several years. The charges to other departments, which are accounted for as revenues of the internal service fund, are intended to recover internal service fund expenses. Internal service funds, thus, are cost accounting and cost distribution (to other funds) accounting entities and are accounted for in essentially the same manner as are enterprise funds.

2412.35 **Accounting differences.** There are two minor differences between enterprise fund and internal service fund accounting:

    a. Only those capital assets that are expected to be replaced through the internal service fund are recorded there and depreciated. Thus, the printing equipment for a central printing shop located in the basement of a county courthouse would be recorded in the print shop internal service fund and depreciated. The courthouse would be recorded in the General Capital Assets and General Long-Term Liabilities accounts (it will not be replaced from the internal service fund) and a portion of the courthouse cost would *not* be recorded in the internal service fund.

    b. An account such as Billings to Departments typically is used to record the internal service fund sales account rather than the usual Sales account.

2412.36 GASB Statement 53, *Accounting and Financial Reporting for Derivative Instruments,* provides guidance for reporting derivatives in proprietary funds, fiduciary funds, and government-wide financial statements. Statement 53 requires derivatives to be reported at fair value in the statements of net assets of these types of funds and in the government-wide statement of net assets. As noted in section **2411.18**, the scope of Statement 53 does not include governmental funds. Changes in the fair value of derivatives that are not used as hedges or that are not effective hedges should be reported as investment income or loss in the proprietary fund financial statements (or fiduciary fund financial statements) and in the government-wide statement of activities. Changes in fair values of effective hedging derivatives are not recognized in the operating statement. Instead, the cumulative changes are reported as deferred inflows or deferred outflows in the appropriate statement of net assets. When hedge accounting is terminated, the deferred inflow or deferred outflow balance is included in investment income in most situations. The statement omits a limited set of derivative instruments from these requirements.

Fiduciary Fund Accounting

2412.37 **Fiduciary funds defined.** Fiduciary funds are used to account for a government's fiduciary or stewardship responsibilities as an agent (agency funds) or trustee (trust funds) for other governments, organizations, and/or individuals. *Only resources held for the benefit of others are reported in fiduciary funds.*

    a. Agency funds are purely custodial (assets equal liabilities).

    b. Three types of trust funds are used. Two of these fund types are used to account for a specific type of activity. **Pension (or other postemployment benefit) trust funds** are used to account for pension plans or other postemployment benefit plans. **Investment trust funds** are used to account for the external portion (i.e., the investments of others) of investment pools administered by a government. All other trust assets held to benefit parties that are not part of the reporting government are accounted for in **private-purpose trust funds.** Although all trust funds are accounted for on the accrual basis, additions and deductions to net assets, not revenues and expenses, are reported.

2412.38 **Financial statements.** Two fiduciary fund financial statements are required in the basic financial statements.

    a. Statement of fiduciary net assets

    b. Statement of changes in fiduciary net assets (trust funds only)

2412.39 **CPA Examination requirements.** Normally, CPA Examination questions require only *general familiarity* with fiduciary fund accounting and financial reporting. Thus, the CPA Examination candidate will want to note the main points in this section, but need not study this section in the same depth as that on the governmental funds, GCA-GLTL accounts, and proprietary funds.

Agency Funds

2412.40 **Nature and accounting equation.** Agency funds are used to account for the custodial activities of a government that is serving as an agent for other governments, organizations, or individuals. The agency fund accounting equation is Assets = Liabilities.

The government has *no* equity in agency funds. Moreover, agency funds do *not* have operating accounts and are *not reported in the statement of changes in fiduciary net assets.*

2412.41 **Types of agency funds.** The most common type of agency fund is the tax agency fund, which is used when one government collects taxes for several governments (usually including itself). Some governments use a payroll withholding agency fund to accumulate the payroll taxes, insurance premiums, etc., withheld in its several funds, then remit them to the proper other governments, insurance companies, etc. Each of these common types of Agency Funds is illustrated briefly in the following paragraphs. *Recall that assets such as taxes receivable for the collecting government are not reported as agency fund assets.*

2412.42 **Payroll withholding agency fund.** Payroll withholding agency funds are simple conduit accounting entities used to account for the following:

    — The centralized accumulation of the various types of withholdings from the payrolls of the several funds of the government

    — The centralized payment of all amounts withheld in various fund payrolls to the proper recipients

The accounting entries for a payroll withholding agency fund are:

a. **To record receipt of payroll withholdings and employer matching amounts from other funds:**

Cash	$3,000		
Federal Income Tax Withholdings Payable		$	900
FICA Withholdings and Matching Share Payable			800
State Income Tax Withholdings Payable			600
Due to Insurance Companies			400
Due to Others			300

b. **To record payment of amounts withheld:**

Federal Income Tax Withholdings Payable	$ 900	
FICA Withholdings and Matching Share Payable	800	
State Income Tax Withholdings Payable	600	
Due to Insurance Companies	400	
Due to Others	300	
Cash (Paid to Proper Recipients)		$3,000

2412.43 **Property tax agency fund.** A property tax agency fund is established when one government (e.g., a county) bills and collects the property taxes for other governments in its geographic area (e.g., a city and a school district) as well as its own taxes. When such an agency fund is used:

— All governments record their property tax levies in the appropriate funds, as usual.

— The property tax receivables are also recorded in the property tax agency fund, both as assets and as liabilities to the governments levying the taxes.

— The taxes are billed and collected through the property tax agency fund, then paid to the levying governments.

— A billing and collection fee may be charged by the government administering the property tax agency fund. If so, it is recorded as a revenue in its General Fund or other appropriate fund and as an expenditure in the appropriate funds of the other governments.

The following example entries illustrate property tax agency fund accounting.

a. **To record property taxes levied by other governments and for other county funds which are to be collected through the county's property tax agency fund:**

Taxes Receivable—Other Funds	$ 3,000	
Taxes Receivable—Other Units	12,000	
Due to City (30%)		$4,500
Due to School District (50%)		7,500
Due to General Fund (of County) (20%)		3,000

Notes:

(1) The city, school district, and county record the taxes receivable, allowance for uncollectible taxes, and tax revenues (or deferred revenues) in their General Fund, Special Revenue Fund, or other funds when the taxes are levied. *Only the taxes receivable for and liabilities payable to other governments, organizations, or individuals are reported in the county's agency fund financial statements.* In this example, the $3,000 of taxes receivable for other funds of the county and the liability, Due to the General Fund, of $3,000 are *not reported* as agency fund assets and liabilities. The taxes receivable are reported in the General Fund. To report them in the agency fund financial statements would double count these assets.

(2) An allowance for uncollectible accounts is *not* recorded in the Property Tax Agency Fund.

(3) All property tax collections will be attributed to and paid to the several governments in the percentage their levy is of the total levy: city (30%), school district (50%), and county (20%).

b. To record tax collections:

Cash	$14,000	
Taxes Receivable—Other Units		$11,200
Taxes Receivable—Other Funds		2,800

Note: The $2,800 cash collected for county taxes will be reported as General Fund cash, not as tax agency fund assets.

To record payment of tax collections to other units and to the county General Fund:

Due to City (30%)	$4,200	
Due to School District (50%)	7,000	
Due to General Fund (20%)	2,800	
Cash		$14,000

Note: This entry is appropriate even if a tax collection fee is withheld from the payment to the city and school district and remitted to the county General Fund. If a 2% collection fee is charged, entries in the General Funds of the several units would be:

County General Fund

Cash ($2,800 + 0.02($11,200))	$3,024	
Taxes Receivable—Current		$2,800
Revenues—Property Tax Collection Fees		224

City General Fund

Cash	$4,116	
Expenditures—Property Tax Collection Fees (2%)	84	
Taxes Receivable—Current		$4,200

School District General Fund

Cash	$6,860	
Expenditures—Property Tax Collection Fees (2%)	140	
Taxes Receivable—Current		$7,000

Private-Purpose Trust Funds

2412.44 **Nature and accounting.** Private-purpose trusts are used to report trust arrangements under which principal and income (or just income) of the trust are to be used for the benefit of individuals, private organizations, or other governments. *Except for pension plans and similar retirement plans and the external portion of investment pools, all assets held in trust by a government for the benefit of others are reported in private-purpose trust funds.* The trust assets may be nonexpendable or expendable. A fund used to report escheat property is an example. In these trusts, the following apply:

a. Contributions or other increases (including investment earnings) are reported as additions.

b. All decreases in fund net assets are reported as deductions.

c. The difference between fund assets and fund liabilities is referred to as net assets held in trust.

Journal entries would be similar to those illustrated for pension trust funds at section **2412.49**.

Pension (and Other Postemployment Benefit) Trust Funds

2412.45 **Nature and use.** Pension trust funds are used to account for a government's fiduciary activities and responsibilities in managing pensions or other retirement trust funds for its retired, active, and former employees and their beneficiaries. Pension trust funds are needed only by governments that manage their own pension plans rather than participate in statewide or other group pension plans. *The reporting requirements for other postemployment benefit plans are virtually identical to those for pension plans.* The most common other postemployment benefits are retiree health care benefits.

2412.46 **Deferred compensation plans.** Some governments have deferred compensation plans that are qualified under Internal Revenue Code (IRC) Section 457.

Federal tax law requires assets of IRC Section 457 plans to be held in trust for the *exclusive benefit* of participants and their beneficiaries. Unless governments have fiduciary responsibility for the plan assets, these plans are *not* reported in government financial statements. In the relatively few governments which have fiduciary responsibility for such plans, the GASB requires that IRC Section 457 plans placed in trust should be *reported as pension trust funds.* The assets are reported at fair value.

2412.47 **Accounting.** The GASB Codification requires the following in accounting for and reporting a pension trust fund (PTF):

a. All contributions to and earnings of the plan are accounted for as PTF additions to net assets.

b. All benefit payments, refunds of contributions, and pension plan administrative costs are accounted for as PTF deductions from net assets.

c. Depreciation is recorded on depreciable capital assets used in administering the pension plan.

d. The actuarial present value of future benefits payable is *not* reported as a pension trust fund liability.

e. Although unique series of PTF fund balance reserve accounts may be employed to account for the equities of the several types of plan participants, PTF net assets are *reported* in a single amount.

f. The actuarial status of a defined benefit pension plan is disclosed in the *schedule of funding progress* and *schedule of employer contributions* that must be presented as required supplementary information.

g. Furthermore, GASB Statement 25, *Financial Reporting for Defined Benefit Pension Plans and Note Disclosures for Defined Contribution Plans*:

(1) sets forth specific parameters for actuarial methods to be acceptable as well as other guidance for defined benefit PTF and public employee retirement system (PERS) accounting and financial reporting and

(2) requires investments to be reported at fair value, and changes in the fair value of investments to be reported in PTF and PERS operating statements.

The primary PTF and PERS financial statements and actuarial schedules are presented in Exhibit 13 in section **2424.02**.

2412.48 **CPA Examination requirements.** CPA Examinations are *not* likely to require detailed knowledge of pension trust fund journal entries or financial statements. However, the CPA candidate should at least scan the following illustrative journal entries to obtain a general familiarity with pension trust fund accounting.

2412.49 **Illustrative entries.** The following entries illustrate the main points of pension trust fund accounting.

    a. **To record employer and employee contributions to the plan:**

Cash	$8,000	
Due from General Fund	1,000	
Additions—Employer Contributions		$4,500
Additions—Employee Contributions		4,500

    Note: Interfund employer contributions are recorded as additions—not as interfund transfers—because the pension trust fund is considered to be a trust separate from the government. Transactions between the other funds of the government and the pension trust fund are interfund transactions, called interfund services provided and used, which are defined and explained more fully in the next section of this chapter (section **2445**).

    b. **To record benefits paid to retirees and their beneficiaries and benefits accrued at year end:**

Deductions—Plan Benefits	$9,000	
Cash		$8,500
Plan Benefits Payable		500

    c. **To record investment earnings collected and accrued at year end, including change in fair value of investments:**

(1)	Cash	$4,500	
	Dividends Receivable	1,500	
	Additions—Dividends		$6,000
(2)	Cash	$5,000	
	Accrued Interest Receivable	200	
	Additions—Interest		$5,200
(3)	Investments	$8,000	
	Additions—Increase in Fair Value of Investments		$8,000

    d. **To record refunds to former employees (or their estates) who resigned, were terminated, or died before their plan benefits vested:**

Deductions—Refunds to Terminated Employees	$1,800	
Deductions—Refunds to Deceased Employees' Estates	2,200	
Cash		$3,300
Due to Terminated Employees		400
Due to Deceased Employees' Estates		300

    e. **To record closing entry at year end:**

Additions—Employer Contributions	$4,500	
Additions—Employee Contributions	4,500	
Additions—Dividends	6,000	
Additions—Interest	5,200	
Additions—Increase in Fair Value of Investments	8,000	
Deductions—Plan Benefits		$ 9,000
Deductions—Refunds to Terminated Employees		1,800
Deductions—Refunds to Deceased Employees Estates		2,200
Net Assets Held in Trust for Pension Benefits		15,200

2413 Budgetary Accounting

2413.01 Budgetary accounting and reporting are unique aspects of governmental accounting. Particularly because of the legal requirements associated with the legally adopted budgets of state and local governments, it is necessary that a government's accounting system is maintained in a manner that permits a government to ensure that it is not inadvertently overspending legal appropriation authority. The GASB describes the original legally adopted annual budget as including the expenditure authority created by the appropriation bills or ordinances that are signed into law as well as related estimated revenues. The original budget includes any automatic rolling forward of prior-year appropriations to provide for expenditures related to prior-year encumbrances as well as legally authorized changes to appropriations acts and ordinances that occur before the beginning of the budget year. The following discussion builds on the general fund transaction examples at section **2412.03**.

2413.02 **Alternative journal entry approaches.** The journal entries illustrated at section **2412.03** presume the use of a general ledger and separate revenues and expenditures subsidiary ledgers. Alternatively, many CPA Examination problems and questions may acceptably be completed using only a general ledger that includes a series of Revenues, Expenditures, and Encumbrances accounts. To illustrate, the budgetary entry under this assumption would be:

To record the budget adopted:

Estimated Revenues—Property Taxes	$5,000	
Estimated Revenues—Sales Taxes	1,000	
Estimated Revenues—Licenses	1,500	
Estimated Revenues—Other	500	
Appropriations—Administration		$ 800
Appropriations—Police		3,100
Appropriations—Fire		2,900
Appropriations—Other		600
Fund Balance (or Budgetary Fund Balance)		600

Indeed, CPA Examination problems and questions may require only summary general ledger control accounts (i.e., Revenues—Control, Expenditures—Control, Encumbrances—Control) and not require subsidiary ledger entries or a series of general ledger Revenues, Expenditures, and Encumbrances accounts. The budgetary entry in this case would be:

To record the budget adopted:

Estimated Revenues—Control	$8,000	
Appropriations—Control		$7,400
Fund Balance (or Budgetary Fund Balance)		600

The other entries also would be recast in this manner under this alternative approach.

2413.03 **Budgetary comparison statement.** A statement of revenues, expenditures, and changes in fund balance—budget and actual for the entries illustrated in section **2412.03** is presented as Exhibit 4. Note the following in Exhibit 4:

    a. Governmental fund statement headings include the name of the governmental unit and the name of the fund as well as the name of the statement and the period or date.

    b. The data columns are headed Original Budget, Revised Budget, Actual, and Variance—Actual Over (Under) Budget. The Variance—Actual Over (Under) Budget column is optional, but most governments present it.

    c. The revenues and expenditures data are presented both in detail and in total, and are derived from the budgetary entry (entry *a*) and closing entries (entries *l* and *m*) of the illustrative example.

        d. This simple example assumed no budget revisions after the budget was adopted. If the budget had been revised, the Original Budget would be the same as in Exhibit 4. The Revised Budget column would be changed to reflect the amendments of the budget during the year. The variances, if presented, always compare the *revised* budget amounts with actual amounts.

        e. The correction of a prior-year error is reported as a restatement of the beginning fund balance. Changes in beginning fund balance resulting from changes in accounting principles should be reported in the same manner. Also, note that fund balance means *total* fund balances.

        f. Both the budget and the actual amounts are presented using the budgetary basis of accounting even if it differs from GAAP.

        g. Budgetary comparisons that are required by GAAP (for the General Fund and for each major Special Revenue Fund, as discussed later) may be presented in the statement format required for the GAAP operating statement or in the format used for the budget.

        h. The budgetary comparison statement may be presented as part of the basic financial statements or as required supplementary information. CPA Examination questions may treat the budgetary comparison as "required supplementary information."

2413.04 Governments that adopt their budget based on using a budgetary fund structure (or organizational or program structure) that differs significantly from the GAAP fund structure may not be able to readily relate estimated revenues and appropriations to the revenue sources and expenditure functions reported in the General Fund and the major Special Revenue Funds. In the case of *significant* budgetary perspective differences, GASB Statement 41, *Budgetary Comparison Schedules-Perspective Differences*, requires a government to present its budgetary comparison schedule as required supplementary information using the fund, organization, or program structure used in the government's legally adopted annual budget.

2413.05 **Budgetary basis.** This illustrative statement presumes that the budget was prepared on the GAAP basis.

        a. If the budget is prepared on a non-GAAP basis—such as on the cash basis or on the encumbrances basis, under which encumbrances outstanding are considered to be equivalent to expenditures—the actual data must be presented on the non-GAAP budgetary basis to present a proper budget-actual comparison. Additionally, the GAAP basis change in fund balance or fund balance in the GAAP-based statement of revenues, expenditures, and changes in fund balance and the corresponding amount in this statement must be reconciled.

b. If the budget is prepared on the GAAP basis, as assumed in Exhibit 4, the statement of revenues, expenditures, and changes in fund balance (the GAAP-basis operating statement) would present the same actual data as the budgetary comparison statement in Exhibit 4. Non-GAAP budgetary bases are common in governments.

Exhibit 4
Budgetary Comparison Statement

Illustrative Government General Fund Statement of Revenues, Expenditures, and Changes in Fund Balance—Budget and Actual For Year Ended (Date)				
	Original Budget	Revised Budget	Actual*	Variance— Actual Over (Under) Budget
Revenues:				
Property taxes	$ 5,000	$ 5,000	$ 5,250	$ 250
Sales taxes	1,000	1,000	980	(20)
Licenses	1,500	1,500	1,550	50
Other	500	500	460	(40)
	$ 8,000	$ 8,000	$ 8,240	$ 240
Expenditures:				
Administration	$ 800	$ 800	$ 570	$ (230)
Police	3,100	3,100	3,080	(20)
Fire	2,900	2,900	2,895	(5)
Other	600	600	585	(15)
	$7,400	$7,400	$7,130	$ (270)
Excess of revenues over (under) expenditures	$ 600	$ 600	$1,110	$ 510
Fund balance—beginning of year**				
As originally reported	$ 1,000	$ 1,000	$ 1,000	$ 0
Correction of prior-year error	--	--	300	300
As restated	$ 1,000	$ 1,000	$ 1,300	(300)
Fund balance—end of year	$ 1,600	$ 1,600	$ 2,410	$ 810

* Only this data is presented in the statement of revenues, expenditures, and changes in fund balance.
** The $1,000 amount was assumed for illustrative purposes. A government may report only the restated beginning fund balance in the statement (with the restatement calculation disclosed in the notes to the financial statements) and the beginning fund balance presented as follows: Fund Balance—beginning of year—as restated (see Note X) $1,300

2420 Format and Content of Comprehensive Annual Financial Report (CAFR)

Financial Reporting

2420.01 **Introduction to financial reporting.** Governments prepare interim and annual financial statements for individual funds and, for annual reports, by major funds or fund type, and for the government in its entirety. GASB pronouncements primarily address annual financial statements, as do CPA Examination questions and problems. Indeed, the primary focus of the CPA Examination on financial reporting for governments is apt to be issues that affect the basic financial statements.

2420.02 **Interim financial statements.** Interim financial statements prepared monthly or quarterly by governments usually are of two distinct types:

  a. **Proprietary funds:** GAAP statements of fund operation, financial position, and cash flows that are similar to those prepared for commercial enterprises

  b. **Governmental funds:** Budgetary statements of fund operations and financial position on the budgetary basis

2420.03 **Annual financial statements and reports.** The major annual reporting considerations of concern to CPA Examination candidates are discussed and illustrated in this order:

  a. The comprehensive annual financial report (CAFR)

  b. Management's discussion and analysis

  c. The basic financial statements (BFS)

  d. Notes to the financial statements

  e. Combining and individual fund statements

  f. Statement headings and formats

  g. Reporting entity

  h. Joint ventures

  Note: The minimum external financial reporting requirements to satisfy GAAP are met by presenting items b, c, and d along with required supplementary information. A complete comprehensive annual financial report is presented either at the option of a government or because it is required by law.

The Comprehensive Annual Financial Report (CAFR)

2420.04 **The CAFR.** A comprehensive annual financial report (CAFR) prepared annually by state and local governments (see Exhibit 5) and includes three sections:

  a. Introductory

  b. Financial

  c. Statistical (Economic Condition Reporting, as required by GASB Statement 44)

Exhibit 5

INTRODUCTORY SECTION	
Components Required by the GASB	Other Items Commonly Included
1. Table of contents 2. Letter(s) of transmittal 3. Other materials deemed appropriate by management	* List of principal officials * Organization chart * GFOA Certificate of achievement for excellence in financial reporting (if awarded)

FINANCIAL SECTION
Auditor's Report

Basic Financial Statements and Required Supplementary Information	
* Management's Discussion and Analysis * Government-Wide Financial Statements * Governmental Fund Financial Statements * Proprietary Fund Financial Statements	* Fiduciary Fund Financial Statements * Notes to Financial Statements * Other required supplementary information (RSI)

Combining Financial Statements	
Funds Reported:	Combining Statement:
Nonmajor Governmental Funds	* Balance Sheet * Statement of Revenues, Expenditures, and Changes in Fund Balances
Nonmajor Enterprise Funds	* Statement of Net Assets * Statement of Revenues, Expenses, and Changes in Net Assets * Statement of Cash Flows
Internal Service Funds	* Statement of Net Assets * Statement of Revenues, Expenses, and Changes in Net Assets * Statement of Cash Flows
Trust Funds (for Fund Type)	* Statement of Net Assets * Statement of Changes in Net Assets
Agency Funds	* Statement of Changes in Agency Fund Assets and Liabilities

Individual Fund Financial Statements and Schedules
* Individual fund budgetary comparisons that are not part of the Basic Financial Statements or RSI * Individual fund statements with prior year comparative data * Individual fund statements with greater detail than combining or Basic Financial Statements * Schedules necessary to demonstrate compliance with finance-related legal and contractual provisions * Schedules to present information spread throughout the statements that can be brought together and shown in greater detail (e.g., taxes receivable, long-term debt, investments) * Schedules to present greater detail for information reported in the statements (e.g., additional revenue sources detail and object of expenditure data by departments)

Narrative Explanations
Notes useful in understanding combining and individual fund statements and schedules that are not included in the notes to the basic financial statements. They may be presented on divider pages, directly on the statements and schedules, or in a separate section.

continued

Exhibit 5 continued

STATISTICAL SECTION		
Statistical Section Categories	Statistical Tables Providing Information About	Periods Reported
Financial Trends Information	Net Assets	Last 10 Fiscal Years
	Changes in Net Assets	Last 10 Fiscal Years
	Governmental Funds	Last 10 Fiscal Years
Revenue Capacity Information	Revenue Base	Last 10 Fiscal Years
	Revenue Rates	Last 10 Fiscal Years
	Principal Revenue Payers	Current Year and Period Nine Years Prior
	Property Tax Levies and Collections	Last 10 Fiscal Years
Debt Capacity Information	Ratios of Outstanding Debt	Last 10 Fiscal Years
	Ratios of General Bonded Debt	Last 10 Fiscal Years
	Direct and Overlapping Debt	Current Fiscal Year
	Debt Limitations	Current Year Calculation for Legal Debt Margin; Last 10 Fiscal Years for all other Debt Limitation Information
Demographic and Economic Information	Demographic and Economic Indicators	Last 10 Fiscal Years
	Principal Employers	Current Year and Period Nine Years Prior
Operating Information	Government Employees	Last 10 Fiscal Years
	Operating Indicators	Last 10 Fiscal Years
	Capital Assets	Last 10 Fiscal Years

Source: Adapted from Freeman, et al., *Governmental and Nonprofit Accounting: Theory and Practice* (Prentice Hall, 2009), pp. 613–614. Reprinted with permission.

2420.05 **The CAFR financial section.** The financial section of the CAFR includes the following:

a. **Auditor's report**

b. **Management's discussion and analysis:** Required supplementary information that precedes the basic financial statements and in which management introduces those statements and provides an analytical overview of the government's financial activities.

c. **Basic financial statements:** The basic financial statements consist of four sets of financial statements (one set of government-wide financial statements and one set of fund financial statements for each of the three categories of funds) as illustrated in Exhibit 6. The government-wide financial statements present data for the governmental activities and business-type activities of the primary government, the primary government in its entirety, and its discretely presented component units. The fund financial statements present data for major governmental funds, for nonmajor governmental funds as a whole, for governmental funds (total), for major enterprise funds, for nonmajor enterprise funds as a whole, for enterprise funds (total), for the internal service fund type, and for each fiduciary fund type.

Exhibit 6 – Composition of Basic Financial Statements			
Basic Financial Statements *(Consists of Two Categories of Statements)*	**Government-wide Financial Statements** *(One set)*	Government-wide Statement of Net Assets	
		Government-wide Statement of Activities	
	Fund Financial Statements *(Three Sets)*	*Governmental Funds Financial Statements*	Governmental Funds Balance Sheet (Statement of Net Assets)
			Governmental Funds Statement of Revenues, Expenditures, and Changes in Fund Balances
			General Fund and major Special Revenue Funds Statement of Revenues, Expenditures, and Changes in Fund Balances – Budget and Actual (can be reported as RSI)
		Proprietary Funds Financial Statements	Proprietary Funds Statement of Net Assets
			Proprietary Funds Statement of Revenues, Expenses, and Changes in Net Assets
			Proprietary Funds Statement of Cash Flows
		Fiduciary Funds Financial Statements	Fiduciary Funds Statement of Net Assets
			Fiduciary Funds Statement of Changes in Net Assets

Source: Adapted from Freeman, et al, *Governmental and Nonprofit Accounting: Theory and Practice* (Prentice Hall, 2009), p. 55. Reprinted with permission.

d. **Notes to the financial statements:** These are notes to the basic financial statements. Any narrative explanations accompanying the combining statements, individual fund statements, and/or schedules are referred to simply as narrative explanations.

e. **Required supplementary information other than Management's Discussion and Analysis:** Certain historical trend information relating to pension plans must be presented after the notes by most governments with single-employer or agent multiple-employer PERS. Likewise, some must include similar information on other postemployment benefit plans. (Recall that governments that do not present the budgetary comparison statements for the general fund and major special revenue funds as basic financial statements must include them as required supplementary information.)

f. **Combining statements: by fund type and/or fund category:** In which separate columns present individual nonmajor fund data (grouped by fund type) for each nonmajor fund for the governmental fund category—if there are two or more nonmajor governmental funds; for each nonmajor enterprise fund where there are two or more nonmajor enterprise funds; for each individual internal service fund where there are two or more of these funds; or for each individual fiduciary fund for each fiduciary fund type of which there is more than one fund of that given type.

g. **Individual fund statements:** Where a government has only one nonmajor fund of a particular fund category or, if necessary, to present prior-year and budgetary comparisons not presented in the basic financial statements or required supplementary information.

h. **Schedules:** May be used to present data in the statements in greater detail, to report cash receipts and disbursements, to present detailed budgetary comparison data, or for other purposes deemed appropriate by management.

2421 Government-Wide Financial Statements

2421.01 **Basic financial statements.** As illustrated in Exhibit 6 (section **2420.05**), the required basic financial statements include the following statements.

a. Government-wide financial statements:

(1) Government-wide statement of net assets

(2) Government-wide statement of activities

b. Governmental funds financial statements:

(1) Statement of net assets (balance sheet)

(2) Statement of revenues, expenditures, and changes in fund balances

(3) General fund and major special revenue funds statement of revenues, expenditures, and changes in fund balances—budget and actual (alternatively, the budget comparisons may be presented as *required supplementary information*)

c. Proprietary funds financial statements:

(1) Statement of net assets (balance sheet)

(2) Statement of revenues, expenses, and changes in net assets

(3) Statement of cash flows (direct method required)

d. Fiduciary funds (and fiduciary component units) financial statements:

(1) Statement of net assets (balance sheet)

(2) Statement of changes in net assets

Notes:

1. The government-wide financial statements **report governmental activities, business-type activities, the primary government totals, and discretely presented component units.** All data in the government-wide statements are presented **on the accrual (revenue and expense) basis**—even for governmental activities. Fiduciary funds and fiduciary component units are *not* included in these statements.

2. The fund financial statements report on **major governmental funds and major enterprise funds,** rather than on governmental fund types and the enterprise fund type. Governmental funds, proprietary funds, and fiduciary funds are reported using three separate sets of financial statements. Finally, general capital assets, general long-term liabilities, and discretely presented component units (unless fiduciary in nature) are not reported in fund financial statements.

2421.02 **Illustrative financial statements.** The basic formats and content of these financial statements are illustrated in Exhibits 7–11 (sections **2421.03–.04, 2422.01,** and **2423.01**). The key features of each of these statements and their contents are noted as we review the statements.

2421.03 Government-wide statement of net assets. The government-wide statement of net assets is one of two required government-wide statements. The other is the government-wide statement of activities. Observe the following in reviewing the schematic of the government-wide statement of net assets in Exhibit 7:

    a. Governmental activities and business-type activities are reported separately.

    b. Governmental activities typically include:

        (1) all governmental fund assets and liabilities,

        (2) general capital assets (including infrastructure such as streets, roads, and bridges),

        (3) general long-term liabilities (using the effective interest method), and

        (4) the assets and liabilities of internal service activities that provide the majority of their services to general government departments.

    The information is aggregated. Appropriate eliminations and adjustments are made to convert the governmental funds data (Exhibit 9) to the revenues and expenses basis required to be used in the government-wide financial statements.

    c. Business-type activities normally include all:

        (1) enterprise activities and

        (2) any internal service activities that provide a majority of their services to enterprise activities.

    For some governments, this will simply be the same data reported in the total enterprise funds column of their proprietary funds balance sheet.

    d. General capital assets (including infrastructure capital assets) less accumulated depreciation are reported in the governmental activities.

    e. Current and noncurrent liabilities are distinguished. (Liabilities with average maturities of longer than a year must be reported in two components—those due within a year and those due in more than a year. This typically would affect the presentation of noncurrent liabilities.)

    f. The governmental activities column includes general long-term debt, measured using the flow of economic resources measurement focus and accrual basis of accounting (i.e., the revenue and expense-based approach of proprietary funds).

    g. The net assets are classified in the same three categories used for proprietary activities (see section **2412.26**). These classifications are as follows:

        (1) Net assets invested in capital assets, net of related debt

        (2) Restricted net assets

        (3) Unrestricted net assets

    h. Interfund payables and receivables between funds used to account for governmental activities are eliminated. Likewise, interfund payables and receivables between funds used to account for business-type activities are eliminated. **Payables and receivables between governmental activities and business-type activities** are reflected in the asset section of the governmental activities column and the business-type activities column as **internal balances.**

    i. The primary government total is presented after eliminating the internal balances.

    j. Discretely presented component units (other than those that are fiduciary in nature) are presented in the government-wide statements. They are not included in the fund-based statements.

Exhibit 7. Government-Wide Statement of Net Assets

Government-Wide Balance Sheet				
	Governmental Activities	Business-Type Activities	Primary Government (Total)	Component Units (that are not Fiduciary in nature)
Assets:				
Cash	XX	XX	XX	XX
.				
.				
Internal balances	(XX)	XX		
Capital assets (including general capital assets, including infrastructure, and net of accumulated depreciation)	<u>XX</u> <u>XX</u>	<u>XX</u> <u>XX</u>	<u>XX</u> <u>XX</u>	<u>XX</u> <u>XX</u>
Liabilities:				
Current liabilities	XX	XX	XX	XX
Noncurrent liabilities (including general long-term liabilities)	<u>XX</u> <u>XX</u>	<u>XX</u> <u>XX</u>	<u>XX</u> <u>XX</u>	<u>XX</u> <u>XX</u>
Net assets:				
Invested in capital assets, net of related debt	XX	XX	XX	XX
Restricted net assets	XX	XX	XX	XX
Unrestricted net assets	<u>XX</u> <u>XX</u>	<u>XX</u> <u>XX</u>	<u>XX</u> <u>XX</u>	<u>XX</u> <u>XX</u>

2421.04 **Government-wide statement of activities.** The format of the government-wide statement of activities—the most unique of the new statements—is illustrated in Exhibit 8. This statement should be viewed as having two distinct parts. The upper portion of the statement focuses on cost of services and reports both the total expenses and the net revenues or net expenses of the government by function. It is based on the formula:

Expenses – Program revenues = Net (expenses) revenues

The lower portion of the statement intends to report how the net program expenses incurred during the year compare with general revenues. It reports various types of general revenues, contributions to permanent funds, special items, extraordinary items, and transfers.

Observe the following in reviewing the government-wide statement of activities in Exhibit 8:

    a. Governmental activities and business-type activities are distinguished both in the presentation of functional classifications (the rows) and in the presentation of net revenues or expenses and changes in net assets (the right-hand columns).

    b. The primary government and discretely presented component units are distinguished in similar fashion.

    c. **Program revenues** raised for a function are deducted from the expenses incurred for that function to derive the net (expenses) revenues of that function.

        (1) Program revenues are described as revenues derived "directly from the program itself or from parties outside the reporting government's constituency."

        (2) Program revenues include the following:

            (a) Charges to users for services provided (*whether restricted or unrestricted*). Charges for services includes licenses and permits; fees, fines and forfeitures;

and revenues from other governments as a result of exchange transactions, in addition to more obvious charges for water and sewer services, swimming pool usage fees, purchases of lottery tickets, and so on.

    (b) Operating grants and contributions (including pass-through grants received and payments made by other governments on behalf of the reporting government) that are *restricted* to use for activities classified in a particular function but not restricted solely to capital asset construction, acquisition, or improvement

    (c) Capital grants and contributions that are *restricted* to use for activities classified in a particular function and restricted *solely to capital asset* construction, acquisition, or improvement

    (d) Investment income that is *legally or contractually restricted* to use for a particular program

(3) All charges for services are program revenues even if unrestricted. Other types of revenues must be *restricted* to a particular function or program to be program revenues. Grants, contributions, and investment income are program revenues *only* if restricted to a specific function or program. Multipurpose grants and contributions that specify the amounts restricted to use for each specific function are program revenues. Other multipurpose grants are not.

(4) Program revenues must be associated with functional reporting classifications. *Charges for services* typically are considered program revenues of the function that generates the revenues—even if the revenues are restricted for use for a different function. *Other types of program revenues* are assigned to the function for which their use is restricted. If the association of a program revenue with a function is unclear, the government should formulate a policy for its classification and apply it consistently.

d. All other revenues are *general revenues*.

  (1) All taxes of the reporting government, *even if restricted to a specific program*, are general revenues.

  (2) Unrestricted gifts, grants, and investment income are general revenues.

  (3) Restricted gifts, grants, and investment income that do not meet the requirements to be reported as program revenues are general revenues.

  (4) Contributions to endowments, special items, extraordinary items, and transfers are reported separate from and following general revenues.

  (5) *Special items* arise from *significant* transactions or other events that are (1) **within the control of management** and (2) **either** unusual in nature *or* infrequent in occurrence.

  (6) The amount reported as a special item or extraordinary item in the statement of activities will differ from the amount reported in the governmental funds statements, because different measurement focuses are used in the two statements.

e. The statement is not intended to report net income, and no net income number is presented. The final subtotal is simply net change in net assets.

f. Exhibit 8 presents only one column for expenses, which means that indirect costs such as those normally reported under the general government function have not been allocated. Alternatively, governments may choose not to report a general government function and allocate those costs to the other functional categories. If so, a second column showing the allocation of those indirect costs is required.

g. Depreciation on both general capital assets and business-type activities capital assets, including infrastructure capital assets, should be allocated to functions.

h. Interest on general long-term debt incurred for the benefit of a particular function should be reported as expenses of that function. Any other interest on general long-term debt should be reported as a separate line item.

i. As with interfund payables and receivables, interfund transfers between funds used to account for governmental activities are eliminated and those between funds that are used to account for business-type activities are also eliminated. The transfers reported here are transfers between governmental activities and business-type activities. For example, transfers from the general fund to capital projects funds would be eliminated. A transfer from the general fund to the airport enterprise fund would also be a transfer between governmental activities and business-type activities and would be reported as transfers in the government-wide statement of activities.

j. Internal service fund sales or service revenues from interfund sales (interfund services provided and used transactions) must be eliminated in the government-wide statements. Similar enterprise fund sales to other funds are *not* eliminated.

k. The statement explains changes in *total* net assets.

Exhibit 8
Government-Wide Statement of Activities Format

For most governments, the following format provides the most appropriate method for displaying the information required to be reported in the statement of activities:

		Program Revenues			Net (Expense) Revenue and Changes in Net Assets			
					Primary Government			
Functions	Expenses	Charges for Services	Operating Grants and Contributions	Capital Grants and Contributions	Governmental Activities	Business-Type Activites	Total	Component Units
Primary government								
Governmental activities								
Function #1	XXX	XX	X	X	(XX)	--	(XX)	--
Function #2	XXX	XX	X	--	(XX)	--	(XX)	--
Function #3	XXX	XX	X	X	(X)	--	(X)	--
Total governmental activities	XXXX	XXX	XX	XX	(XX)	--	(XX)	--
Business-type activities:								
BTA #1	XXXX	XXXX	--	X	--	XX	XX	--
BTA #2	XXXXX	XXXX	--	XX	--	XXX	XXX	--
Total Business-type activities	XXXXX	XXXX	--	XX	--	XXX	XXX	--
Total primary government	XXXXXX	XXXXX	XX	XXX	(XXX)	XXX	XX	--
Component units:								
CU #1	XXXX	XXXX	XX	XX	--	--	--	XX
General revenues--detailed					XXX	X	XXX	XX
Contributions to permanent funds					XX	--	XX	--
Special items and extraordinary items					X	--	X	--
Transfers (between governmental activities and business-type activities)					XX	(XX)	--	--
Total general revenues, contributions, special items, and transfers					XXX	X	XXX	XX
Change in net assets					X	XX	XX	XX
Net assets--beginning					XXXXX	XXXXX	XXXXXX	XXXXX
Net assets--ending					XXXXX	XXXXX	XXXXXX	XXXXX

Source: GASB 34, paragraph 54

2422 Governmental Funds Financial Statements

2422.01 **Governmental funds statements.** The governmental funds financial statements are illustrated briefly in Exhibit 9. Modified accrual accounting (revenues and expenditures reporting using the flow of current financial resources measurement focus) is used in the governmental funds.

    a. Key points to note relative to the governmental funds balance sheet in Exhibit 9 are as follows:

        (1) Presentation of a separate balance sheet for governmental funds

        (2) The balance sheet includes a separate column for each *major governmental* fund and a column with aggregated information for all other governmental funds as well as a total column for all governmental funds. Governmental funds are *not* reported by fund type.

        (3) *The general fund is always a major fund.* Other governmental funds (or enterprise funds) **must** be reported as major funds if they meet both of the following criteria:

            (a) Total assets, liabilities, revenues, or expenditures/expenses (excluding extraordinary items) of that individual governmental (or enterprise) fund are at least **10%** of the *corresponding* total (assets, liabilities, and so forth) for *all* funds of that *category or type* (i.e., total governmental or total enterprise funds).

            (b) The **same element** that met the 10% criterion in (a) is at least **5% of** the corresponding element total for **all governmental funds and all enterprise funds combined.**

        Individual governmental funds deemed important by management may be treated as major funds per management's judgment even if the criteria are not met.

        (4) A combining statement(s) must be presented in the CAFR to support the "other governmental funds" column. (This statement is *not* part of the basic financial statements.)

    b. The **governmental funds statement of revenues, expenditures, and changes in fund balances** in Exhibit 9 is also presented by major fund. The reporting format used in the exhibit is required. Several points should be noted:

        (1) The statement reconciles beginning and ending total fund balance. It is an all-inclusive statement.

        (2) The excess of revenues over (under) expenditures is a required subtotal.

        (3) All **transfers** are reported as other financing sources and uses.

        (4) **Special items** (see section **2421.04d(3)**) and extraordinary items, if any, are reported after other financing sources (uses).

        (5) The final subtotal is net change in fund balances.

c. A budgetary comparison statement is required only for the General Fund *and* for each major special revenue fund. (Budgetary comparisons for other funds are not to be included in the basic financial statements.) Additionally, this statement may be presented as a schedule in required supplementary information instead of as a basic financial statement. The statement must (1) be presented using the *budgetary basis* of accounting and (2) include columns for the original budget adopted, the final budget (after revisions made during the course of the year), and for actual amounts on the budgetary basis of accounting. The *variance column, based on actual versus the revised budget, is optional.* Hence, the statement of revenues, expenditures, and changes in fund balances, budget and actual, typically will have the following column headings:

Original Budget   Revised Budget   Actual (on budgetary basis)   Variance

Exhibit 9
Governmental Funds Balance Sheet

	General Fund	Major Fund #1	Major Fund #2	Major Fund #N	Other Governmental Funds	Total
Assets (list)	**Current Financial Resources**					
Liabilities (list)	Measurement Focus and Modified Accrual Basis					
Fund Balance Nonspendable Restricted Committed Assigned Unassigned	(Revenues and Expenditures)					

Governmental Funds Operating Statement
(Statement of Revenues, Expenditures, and Changes in Fund Balances)

	General Fund	Major Fund #1	Major Fund #2	Major Fund #N	Other Governmental Funds	Total
Revenues (list)						
Expenditures (list)						
Excess of revenues over expenditures						
Other financing sources (uses) (list)	**Current Financial Resources**					
Special items and extraordinary items	Measurement Focus and Modified Accrual Basis (Revenues and Expenditures)					
Net change in fund balance						
Fund balance—beginning						
Fund balance—ending						

2422.02 **Required reconciliations.** Governments are required to present a reconciliation between the governmental funds statements and the governmental activities column of the government-wide statements. Likewise, a reconciliation of the enterprise fund total columns from the proprietary fund statements (except the cash flow statement) and the business-type activities column in the government-wide statements must be prepared. The reconciliation may be presented either (1) on the face of the fund-based statements or (2) as separate schedules. Though not illustrated here, the concept is the same as the reconciliations required by current GAAP in a statement of cash flows or between the GAAP-basis statement of revenues, expenditures, and changes in fund balances and the budgetary comparison statement.

2423 Proprietary Funds Financial Statements

2423.01 **Proprietary fund statements.** The required proprietary funds financial statements—balance sheet (or statement of net assets), statement of revenues, expenses, and changes in net assets, and statement of cash flows—are illustrated in Exhibit 10. Accrual accounting on the economic resource (revenues and expenses) measurement focus is used for proprietary funds.

    a. In reviewing the exhibit, observe the following in the balance sheet:

        (1) The statements include a separate column for each major enterprise fund and a column with aggregate information for all other enterprise funds, as well as a total enterprise funds column for the fund type. (Note that major fund reporting is not used for internal service funds—only a single column for the fund type is presented.)

        (2) Fund equity, or fund net assets, is reported using the three classifications discussed in section **2412.26**: invested in capital assets, net of related debt, restricted net assets, and unrestricted net assets.

    b. Observe the following when reviewing the proprietary funds statement of revenues, expenses, and changes in net assets in Exhibit 10:

        (1) The statement focuses on major enterprise funds and on the internal service fund type rather than just on the fund types.

        (2) Operating and nonoperating revenues and expenses are distinguished.

        (3) The report format is the required format.

        (4) Revenues are reported *net* of uncollectibles and similar accounts (Therefore, bad debts is not reported as an expense).

        (5) Operating grants and contributions are reported as nonoperating revenues. Capital grants and contributions are reported after nonoperating revenues and expenses.

        (6) Items reported after nonoperating revenues and expenses are not distinguished between transactions affecting income and retained earnings and those affecting contributed capital. Indeed, contributed capital and retained earnings classifications are not used under GASB Statement 34 guidelines.

        (7) Net income is not reported.

        (8) Capital grants (and other capital contributions), special items, extraordinary items, and transfers are all reported after income before other revenues, expenses, and transfers and before "change in net assets."

        (9) Transfers are reported as the last item before change in net assets.

    c. The proprietary funds statement of cash flows in Exhibit 10 highlights three primary features:

        (1) The statement focuses on major enterprise funds and on the internal service fund type.

(2) The **direct method** of presenting cash flows from operating activities is **required.**

(3) The cash flow classifications differ from those for businesses and other nongovernment entities.

The cash flow statement for the Water and Sewer Fund in Exhibit 11 provides a more in-depth example of a cash flow statement. Note that the GASB-prescribed statement of cash flows differs from that required by the FASB in several respects. Most importantly, the cash flows statement required by the GASB:

a. classifies cash flows in four activities categories: (1) operating, (2) noncapital financing, (3) capital and related financing, and (4) investing, and

b. requires that all financing activities be classified as either noncapital or capital and related, depending on whether they are solely for capital asset construction, acquisition, or improvement.

(1) Debt proceeds received specifically for capital outlay and related debt service payments are classified as capital financing. All other debt proceeds and payments are noncapital financing activities.

(2) Operating grants are classified as noncapital financing, and capital grants are reported as capital and related financing. Likewise, transfers *in* are classified as capital and related financing if solely for capital asset purposes; otherwise, they are noncapital financing.

(3) All transfers *out* are reported as noncapital financing.

(4) *Purchases and sales* of capital assets are reported as capital and related financing activities.

(5) Only securities-related and similar investment transactions, and dividends and interest received, are classified as investing activities. *All* purchases of investments for cash, maturities and sales of investments for cash, and cash received from investment income are included here, regardless of whether the resources are ultimately to be used for capital asset purposes or not.

c. The cash balance includes both unrestricted cash and cash restricted for various purposes.

	Exhibit 10 Proprietary Funds Balance Sheet					
	Major Enterprise Fund #1	Major Enterprise Fund #2	Major Enterprise Fund #N	Other EFs	Total Enterprise Funds	Internal Service Funds
Assets (list)						
Liabilities (list)	**Economic Resources** Measurement Focus and Accrual Basis (Revenues and Expenses)					
Net Assets: Invested in capital assets, net of related debt Restricted net assets Unrestricted net assets						

Continued on next page

Exhibit 10 continued

Proprietary Funds Operating Statement
(Statement of Revenues, Expenses, and Changes in Net Assets)

	Major Enterprise Fund #1	Major Enterprise Fund #2	Major Enterprise Fund #N	Other EFs	Total Enterprise Funds	Internal Service Funds
Operating revenues (detailed)						
Operating expenses (detailed)						
Operating income						
Nonoperating revenues and expenses (detailed)						
Income before other revenues, expenses, and transfers	**Economic Resources** Measurement Focus and Accrual Basis (Revenues and Expenses)					
Capital contributions (grant, developer, and other), additions to permanent and term endowments, special and extraordinary items (detailed), and transfers						
Increase (decrease) in net assets						
Net assets/fund equity—beginning						
Net assets/fund equity—ending						

Proprietary Funds Statement of Cash Flows

	Major Enterprise Fund #1	Major Enterprise Fund #2	Major Enterprise Fund #N	Other EFs	Total Enterprise Funds	Internal Service Funds
Cash flows from operating activities, *direct method required* (detailed)						
Cash flows from noncapital financing activities (detailed)						
Cash flows from capital and related financing activities (detailed)						
Cash flows from investing activities (detailed)						
Net increase (decrease) in cash						
Cash—beginning						
Cash—ending						

Exhibit 11

(Name of Government)
Water and Sewer Fund
Statement of Cash Flows
for the Year Ended June 30, 20X1

Cash flows from operating activities:		
Cash received from customers	$ 912,000	
Cash payments to suppliers for goods and services	(450,000)	
Cash payments to employees for services	(300,575)	
Other operating expenses	(50,000)	
Other operating revenues	15,075	
Net cash provided by operating activities		$126,500
Cash flows from noncapital financing activities:		
Net borrowings (repayments) under revolving loan arrangement	$ (20,000)	
Interest paid on revolving loan	(1,500)	
Operating grants received	100,000	
Transfers to other funds	(75,000)	
Net cash provided by noncapital financing activities		3,500
Cash flows from capital and related financing activities:		
Proceeds from sale of revenue bonds	$ 250,000	
Acquisition and construction of capital assets	(350,000)	
Principal paid on revenue bond maturities and equipment contracts	(75,000)	
Interest paid on revenue bonds and equipment contracts	(33,500)	
Proceeds from sale of equipment	10,000	
Capital contributed by subdividers	60,000	
Net cash used for capital and related financing activities		(138,500)
Cash flows from investing activities:		
Purchases of investment securities	$(125,000)	
Proceeds from sale and maturities of investment securities	75,000	
Interest and dividends on investments	9,000	
Net cash used in investing activities		(41,000)
Net decrease in cash and cash equivalents		(49,500)
Cash and cash equivalents at beginning of year		175,600
Cash and cash equivalents at end of year		$ 126,100
Reconciliation of operating income to net cash provided by operating activities:		
Operating income (loss)		$ (110,500)
Adjustments to reconcile operating income to net cash provided by operating activities:		
Depreciation	$ 245,000	
Provision for uncollectible accounts	2,000	
Change in assets and liabilities:		
Increase in accounts receivable	(15,000)	
Decrease in inventory	2,000	
Decrease in prepaid expenses	500	
Increase in accounts payable	2,500	
Total adjustments		237,000
Net cash provided by operating activities		$ 126,500

Source: Adapted from GASB Statement 9, para. 75 (GASB Cod. Sec. 2450.901)

2424 Fiduciary Funds Financial Statements

2424.01 **Fiduciary fund statements.** Fiduciary fund reporting and the types of fiduciary funds are illustrated in Exhibit 12 (section **2424.02**).

Notes:

a. Fiduciary fund reporting is by fund type, not by major fund.

b. Note that fiduciary funds are used to *report only resources held by the reporting government for the benefit of parties other than the reporting government.*

c. The required fiduciary fund financial statements are the *statement of fiduciary fund net assets* and the *statement of changes in fiduciary fund net assets.* These statements are more fully illustrated for pension trust funds in Exhibit 13 (section **2424.02**).

d. Additions and deductions, not revenues and expenses, are reported in the statement of changes in net assets.

e. Agency funds are not reported in the statement of changes in net assets. Agency fund assets and liabilities are always equal.

f. Fiduciary component units are reported here, not in the government-wide statements. Only blended, not discretely presented, component units are included in other fund financial statements.

g. Fiduciary funds and fiduciary component units are reported only in the fund-based statements—they are not reported in the government-wide statements.

2424.02 **Pension (and other postemployment benefit) trust fund statements and schedules.** GASB Statement 25, *Financial Reporting for Defined Benefit Pension Plans and Note Disclosures for Defined Contribution Plans,* requires two statements and two schedules for pension trust funds (PTFs) and public employee retirement systems (PERS). The two primary PTF/PERS financial statements and one of two required supplemental information (RSI) schedules are illustrated in Exhibit 13. GASB Statement 45 requires the equivalent statements and schedules to report other postemployment benefit plans.

Exhibit 12

	Fiduciary Funds Balance Sheet (Statement of Net Assets)			
	Pension Trust	Private-Purpose Trust	Investment Trust	Agency
Assets				
Liabilities	**Not Presented in Government-Wide Statements**			
Net assets				

Continued on next page

Exhibit 12 continued

	Fiduciary Funds Statement of Changes in Net Assets		
	Pension Trust	Private-Purpose Trust	Investment Trust
Additions (detailed)			
Deductions (detailed)			
Net increase (decrease)	**Not Presented in Government-Wide Statements**		
Net assets—beginning			
Net assets—ending			

Note: Component units that are fiduciary in nature are added to the appropriate fiduciary fund type column, not presented in a separate column. For example, a component unit pension plan would be reported as if it were an additional pension trust fund by including it in the Pension Trust column.

Exhibit 13

(Name of Government)
Pension Trust Fund (PTF)

Statement of Plan Assets as of June 30, 20X2 (Dollar Amounts in Thousands)		Statement of Changes In Net Assets for the year ended June 30, 20X2 (Dollar Amounts in Thousands)	
Assets		Additions	
Cash and short-term investments	$66,129	Contributions	
		Employer	$137,916
Receivables		Plan members	90,971
Employer	16,451		
Interest and dividends	33,495	Total contributions	228,887
Total receivables	49,946		
Investments, at fair value			
U.S. government obligations	541,289	Investment income	
Municipal bonds	33,585	Net appreciation (depreciation) in fair value of investments	(241,408)
Domestic corporate bonds	892,295	Interest	157,371
Domestic stocks	1,276,533	Dividends	123,953
International stocks	461,350	Real estate operating income, net	10,733
			50,649
Mortgages	149,100		
Real estate	184,984	Less investment expense	54,081
Venture capital	26,795	Net investment income	(3,432)
Total investments	3,565,931	Total additions	225,455
Properties, at cost, net of accumulated depreciation of $5,164	6,351		
Total assets	3,688,357	**Deductions**	
		Benefits	170,434
		Refunds of contributions	15,750
		Administrative expense	4,984
Liabilities		Total deductions	191,168
Refunds payable and other	4,212	**Net increase**	34,287
		Net assets held in trust for pension benefits	
		Beginning of year	3,649,858
Net assets held in trust for pension benefits (A schedule of funding progress for each plan is presented on page___.)	$3,684,145	End of year	$3,684,145

Continued on next page

Exhibit 13 continued

Required Supplementary Information
Schedule of Funding Progress

Actuarial Valuation Date	Actuarial Value of Assets (a)	Actuarial Accrued Liability (AAL) – Entry Age (b)	Unfunded AAL (UAAL) (b–a)	Funded Ratio (a/b)	Covered Payroll (c)	UAAL as a Percentage of Covered Payroll ((b–a)/c)
12/31/X6	$2,005,238	$2,626,296	$621,058	76.4%	$ 901,566	68.9%
12/31/X7	2,411,610	2,902,399	490,789	83.1	956,525	51.3
12/31/X8	2,709,432	3,331,872	622,440	81.3	1,004,949	61.9
12/31/X9	3,001,314	3,604,297	602,983	83.3	1,049,138	57.5
12/31/X0	3,366,946	3,930,112	563,166	85.7	1,093,780	51.5
12/31/X1	3,658,323	4,284,961	626,638	85.4	1,156,346	54.2

*Source: Adapted from GASB Statement 25, par. 153. **Note:** A schedule of employer contributions also is required.*

GASB Statement 50, *Pension Disclosures—an Amendment of GASB Statements No. 25 and No. 27,* requires footnote disclosure of the Schedule of Funding Progress information for the most recent actuarial valuation. Consistent with this, several of the notes to the required supplementary information describing how the amounts are determined must be incorporated in the notes to the financial statements as well.

2424.03 **Special purpose governments.** The statements that must be presented by special purpose governments depend on whether the government is engaged solely in business-type activities, solely in governmental activities, in both governmental and business-type activities, or in fiduciary activities only. Note in Exhibit 14 that all governments must include management's discussion and analysis, notes to the financial statements, and other required supplementary information. *The financial statements that must be presented depend on the circumstances.* For instance, special purpose governments engaged solely in business-type activities only present proprietary fund financial statements. They do not present government-wide statements, governmental funds statements, or fiduciary funds statements.

Exhibit 14: Reporting Requirements for Special Purpose Governments

Special Purpose Governments Engaged In

Reporting Requirements	Business-Type and Governmental Activities	Governmental Activities Only	Business-Type Activities Only	Fiduciary Activities Only
Management's Discussion and Analysis	Required	Required	Required	Required
Government-wide statements	Required	Required		
Governmental funds statements	Required	Required		
Proprietary funds statements	Required		Required	
Fiduciary funds statements	Required*	Required*		Required
Notes to the financial statements	Required	Required	Required	Required
Required supplementary information other than MD&A	Required	Required	Required	Required

* Assumes there are fiduciary funds

2425 Notes to Financial Statements

2425.01 GASB Statement 38 indicates that certain information may be presented either on the face of the financial statements or in the notes. If information that is required to be disclosed is not presented on the face of the financial statements, that information is required to be presented in the notes to the financial statements.

The notes to the financial statements, which are notes to the basic financial statements, include many notes that are also in business financial statements as well as some that are unique to government financial statements. The GASB Codification summarizes most of the usual note disclosures, which include the following:

a. **Notes customarily included in business financial statements:** Such as the summary of significant accounting policies and notes on such matters as contingencies, leases, and subsequent events.

b. **Notes unique to government financial statements generally:** Including disclosures of the following:

   (1) Encumbrances outstanding

   (2) Material violations of finance-related legal and contractual provisions

   (3) Reporting entity (discussed in section **2430**)

   (4) Property taxes, including tax calendar and levy date, due dates, revenue recognition, etc.

   (5) The budgetary basis and its differences from the GAAP basis

   (6) Interfund transfers and receivables and payables (schedules of)

   (7) Pension plans (specific disclosures specified for various types of plans)

   (8) Deposit and investment risks including credit risk, concentration of credit risk, interest rate risk, and foreign currency risk

c. **Notes on individual funds unique to basic statements of governments** that result from the fact that nonmajor individual fund data are aggregated by fund category in the basic financial statements (which may bury relevant information) and include disclosure of:

   (1) deficit fund balances or net assets of individual funds and

   (2) material excess of expenditures over appropriations in individual, annually budgeted governmental (and similar fiduciary) funds.

2426 Management's Discussion and Analysis

2426.01 **Management's Discussion and Analysis (MD&A)** is presented *prior* to the basic financial statements both to introduce those statements and as an analytical overview of the government's financial activities. The MD&A differs from a transmittal letter in several ways. First, *it relates only to the basic financial statements (not to the CAFR as a whole)* and must always accompany those statements—even when issued separate from the CAFR. The MD&A must be *based only on currently known facts, conditions, or decisions*, whereas the transmittal letter can discuss the implications of events that might happen or decisions that are not yet made. The MD&A should do the following:

a. Focus on the primary government and distinguish information pertaining to the primary government from that of its discretely presented component units.

b. Present *both* a short-term and a long-term analysis of the SLG's activities and status.

c. Discuss the *current-year* results *compared with* the *prior year* with emphasis on the current year—discussing both positive and negative aspects of the comparisons.

d. Cover the following topic areas *(and no other topic areas)*:

(1) A brief discussion of the basic financial statements

(2) Presentation of condensed (government-wide) financial information

(3) An analysis of the SLG's overall (government-wide) financial position and results of operations

(4) An analysis of balances and transactions of individual funds

(5) An analysis of significant variations between (a) original and final budget amounts and (b) final budget amounts and actual budget results for the General Fund (or its equivalent)

(6) A description of capital asset activity and long-term debt activity during the year

(7) Information about the assessed conditions of and actual versus estimated maintenance/preservation expenditures for general infrastructure capital assets reported using the "modified approach" (discussed at section **2427.02**)

(8) A description of currently known facts, decisions, or conditions that are expected to have a material effect on financial position (net assets) or results of operations (revenues, expenses, and other changes in net assets)

2427 Required Supplementary Information (RSI) Other Than Management's Discussion and Analysis

2427.01 Required supplementary information for governments may include the following:

a. Budgetary comparison schedules for the general fund and major special revenue funds (if not presented as basic financial statements)

b. Information on infrastructure capital assets reported using the modified approach, described below

c. Schedules of funding progress and of employer contributions for pension plans and other postemployment benefit plans (discussed with fiduciary fund financial statements in section **2424.02**)

2427.02 Modified approach for infrastructure capital assets. Except for qualifying infrastructure capital assets, governments are required to depreciate all capital assets with limited lives.

Governments are permitted to use a modified approach for accounting for infrastructure capital assets that are part of a network or subsystem of a network that the government:

(1) manages using an asset management system with specified characteristics and

(2) documents is being preserved approximately at (or above) a target condition level determined by the reporting government.

All expenditures made for infrastructure capital assets accounted for under the *modified approach* are charged to expense when incurred. Only additions and improvements to those assets are capitalized. Depreciation and accumulated depreciation are not reported on those assets. Changes to and from the modified approach are treated prospectively.

Governments that used the modified approach are required to present the following in schedules, derived from the asset management system, in required supplementary information:

(1) The assessed condition for the three most recent condition assessments (with the assessment dates)

(2) The estimated annual amount at the beginning of the fiscal year to maintain and preserve the target condition level established versus amounts actually expensed for each of the past five reporting periods

2428 Combining Statements and Individual Fund Statements and Schedules

2428.01 **The combining and individual fund statements** are presented *only* in the comprehensive annual financial report (CAFR).

   a. **Combining statements** are, in essence, individual fund statements presented side-by-side in adjacent columns with a total column. The total column ties to and provides individual fund detail supporting a column reported in the fund financial statements that aggregates two or more funds of a fund type or fund category. For example, one set of combining statements—called combining statements for nonmajor governmental funds—would include a column for each nonmajor governmental fund. The overall total columns for these statements would include the same information presented in the "other (non-major) governmental funds" columns in the corresponding governmental funds financial statements in the basic financial statements. Similarly, there would be a set of combining financial statements for nonmajor enterprise funds, for internal service funds, and for each fiduciary fund type, if there is more than one of each of these nonmajor enterprise funds or other fund types.

   b. **Individual fund statements** present data for a single fund in more detail than is presented in the basic financial statements or combining statements. They are required only when such additional detail is considered necessary for fair disclosure in the CAFR at the individual fund materiality level, but they are also used to present prior-year and budgetary comparison data for individual funds.

2429 Deriving Government-Wide Financial Statements and Reconciliation Requirements

2429.01 **Developing Government-Wide Financial Statement Data** A key part of accounting practice for governments under GASB Statement 34 is developing government-wide financial statement data through a conversion (or consolidation and conversion) process at year end. As seen in earlier sections, fund data is captured in the accounts during the year. Government-wide data typically is not captured directly in the accounts and must be derived using the fund data and ancillary records. This derivation normally is achieved using a conversion worksheet at year end.

The starting point for the worksheet to derive governmental activities data is a trial balance comprised of the asset, liability, revenue, expenditure, and other financing source (use) data from the total columns of the governmental funds financial statements, as illustrated below. The fund balance used here to balance is essentially the beginning total fund balance for governmental funds.

Trial Balance
Year-end balances from Governmental Funds
Financial Statements

Total Column
Assets
Liabilities
Revenues
Expenses
Other Financing Sources
Other Financing Uses
Extraordinary Items and Special Items
Fund Balance (Preclosing)

The conversions necessary can be accomplished in varying orders or using different logic but will typically include the following:

a. Reclassify the fund balance as net assets (beginning), using the following worksheet adjustment:

Fund Balance	XXX	
Net Assets		XXX

b. Add the *beginning balances* of the GCA-GLTL accounts, including the beginning net assets balance.

This leaves the following as the starting point of the conversion worksheet.

Worksheet
Year-end balances from Governmental Funds Financial Statements
Total Columns and GCA-GLTL Beginning Balances

Assets
Liabilities
Revenues
Expenses
Other Financing Sources
Other Financing Uses
Extraordinary Items and Special Items
Fund Balance (Now with zero balance)

Land
Buildings
Accumulated Depreciation — Buildings
Other General Capital Assets
Bonds Payable
Premium on Bonds Payable
Long-Term Claims and Judgments Liabilities
Other General Long-Term Liabilities
Net Assets (Balance = the preclosing fund balance + the beginning balance in the GCA-GLTL accounts). *This balance is the beginning net assets for governmental activities except as noted below.*

c. As noted in the illustrative trial balance in item *b.*, the net asset balance—after renaming fund balance as net assets and adding the beginning balances from the GCA-GLTL records—approximates the ending net assets reported for governmental activities in the prior year's financial statements (i.e., this year's beginning total net assets). Only two general issues remain to adjust this number to the beginning governmental activities net assets balance:

— Eliminate governmental fund assets and liabilities that are not governmental activities assets or liabilities.

— Add governmental activities assets and liabilities that are not governmental fund assets or liabilities and that also are not included in the beginning GCA-GLTL account balances.

    (1) **Deferred Revenues.** The most common example of the first category of items is the deferred tax revenues (and similar deferred revenues) reported in governmental funds because of the available criterion of collected prior to the end of a certain cutoff period (often 60 days) after year end. Revenue recognition in the government-wide statements is not deferred because of the collection criterion. Therefore, this deferred revenues liability would not have been reported in the governmental activities balance sheet at the end of the last year and the net asset balance would have been increased by the additional revenues recognized over time. To adjust the net assets balance derived in the previous steps to the beginning net assets balance, one entry that would be required is to eliminate the beginning deferred revenues balance with the following entry:

Deferred Revenues (beginning balance)	XXX	
Net Assets (beginning)		XXX

    (2) **Accrued Interest Payable on GLTL.** A common example of the second category is the interest payable on GLTL that is not accrued in governmental funds, and typically not recorded in GCA-GLTL account records. This interest payable must be reported in the governmental activities liabilities in the government-wide statement of net assets. The beginning interest payable on GLTL is not included in the governmental funds assets and liabilities that we began this process with nor in the beginning GCA-GLTL trial balance that was added in the next step. Therefore, to get the correct beginning governmental activities net assets balance requires the following adjustment for the beginning balance of accrued interest payable on GLTL:

Net Assets (beginning)	XXX	
Accrued Interest Payable		XXX

  d. The most common items requiring conversion from the modified accrual basis in the governmental funds to the revenue and expense basis used in the government-wide financial statements include:

    (1) **Elimination of expenditures that do not have expense counterparts,** e.g., capital outlay expenditures and long-term debt principal retirement expenditures (These eliminations also result in recording the capital assets acquired and in reducing the long-term liability balance, as appropriate).

Equipment (or other Capital Asset)	XXX	
Expenditures — Capital Outlay		XXX
Bonds Payable (or other GLTL retired)	XXX	
Expenditures — Bond Principal Retirement		XXX

    (2) **Elimination of Other Financing Sources other than transfers** (These eliminations also result in recording the long-term liability incurred or in recording the gain or loss on capital asset disposition and removing the book value of the capital asset.)

Other Financing Sources — Bonds	XXX	
Other Financing Sources — Bond Premium	XXX	
Bonds Payable		XXX
Premium on Bonds Payable		XXX
Other Financing Sources — GCA Sale Proceeds	XXX	
Accumulated Depreciation	XXX	
Equipment (or other GCA disposed of)		XXX
Gain on Sale of Capital Assets		XXX

(3) **Elimination of Other Financing Uses other than transfers** (These eliminations also result in recording the reduction of the long-term liability principal balance and recording of a deferred interest credit or deferred interest debit from the refunding transaction as required in proprietary fund accounting for refundings of long-term debt, as appropriate.)

Bonds Payable	XXX	
Premium on Bonds Payable*	XXX	
Deferred Interest — Refunding*	XXX	
Discount on Bonds Payable*		XXX
Deferred Interest — Refunding*		XXX
Other Financing Uses — Payment to Refunded Bond Escrow Agent		XXX

* For a single refunding transaction, there will *not* be both a premium and a discount. Likewise, Deferred Interest — Refunding will either be debited or credited, not both.

(4) **Elimination of interfund transfers and interfund payables and receivables** to and from other governmental funds or internal service funds that are reported as part of governmental activities.

Other Financing Sources — Transfers from Other Governmental Funds	XXX	
Other Financing Uses — Transfers to Other Governmental Funds		XXX
Due to Other Governmental Funds	XXX	
Due from Other Governmental Funds		XXX

(5) **Recording expenses that do not have expenditure counterparts** (depreciation, for instance):

Depreciation Expense	XXX	
Accumulated Depreciation		XXX

(6) **Convert Expenditures that have Expense counterparts to expense measurements** (Interest, pensions, other postemployment benefits, claims and judgments, compensated absences). For example, the following entries related to interest might be required.

Interest Expense (for discount amortization)	XXX	
Discount on Bonds Payable		XXX
Premium on Bonds Payable	XXX	
Interest Expense		XXX
Interest Expense	XXX	
Accrued Interest Payable (on GLTL)		XXX *

* The amount is for the change in the amount of accrued interest payable during the year. This assumes that accrued interest has increased during the year and that the beginning balance was recorded in a separate entry. If the beginning balance were not recorded as illustrated earlier, this entry should be:

Net Assets	BB	
Interest Expense	Increase	
Accrued Interest Payable		EB

(BB = beginning balance; EB = ending balance)

Deferred Bond Issue Costs	XXX	
Expenditures — Bond Issue Costs		XXX

Bond Issue Costs Expense	XXX	
Deferred Bond Issue Costs (For the amortization of bond issue costs)		XXX

(7) **Compensated absences, pensions, other postemployment benefits, and claims and judgments** often require adjustment for a change in the related long-term liability.

Expenses — Compensated Absences	XXX	
Long-Term Liabilities for Compensated Absences		XXX

Expenses for compensated absences would equal the governmental funds expenditures for compensated absences plus this adjustment for the increase in the GLTL for compensated absences. A decrease in the liability would have the opposite effect. The same analysis and entries apply to pensions and claims and judgments.

(8) **Deferred revenues resulting from the 60-day rule must be eliminated.**

Deferred Tax Revenues (for the amount of an increase)	XXX	
Tax Revenues		XXX

This entry assumes that Deferred Tax Revenues was debited earlier for its beginning balance as illustrated, that the amount of these deferred revenues increased during the year, and that the revenues are deferred because they were not collected by the end of the revenue recognition cutoff period (usually 60 days). If the beginning balance has not been eliminated by an earlier entry, the following entry is required:

Deferred Tax Revenues	EB	
Tax Revenues		Increase
Net Assets		BB

(BB = Beginning Balance; EB = Ending Balance)

e. **Recording internal service fund assets and liabilities** of an internal service fund that provides the majority of its services to governmental activities (Simply record the ending balances of the internal service fund assets and liabilities as governmental activities assets and liabilities and increase or decrease net assets (ending) by the difference.)

f. **Other potential internal service fund adjustments** for funds that are part of governmental activities including:

(1) *Eliminating internal service fund profit from internal sales:*

Net Assets — Governmental Activities	XXX	
Expenses (of governmental activities, allocated by function)		XXX

(For profits associated with sales to governmental funds; losses would be the opposite)

Net Assets — Governmental Activities	XXX	
Internal Balances (or Transfers from Business-Type Activities		XXX

(For profits associated with sales to enterprise funds or other components of business-type activities; losses would be the opposite)

(2) *Eliminating internal profit associated with sales to governmental funds by internal service funds that are included in business-type activities:*

Internal Balances (or Transfers from Business-Type Activities	XXX	
Expenses (of governmental activities, allocated by function)		XXX

g. While other adjustments may be required for governmental activities, the ones above cover the vast majority of situations governments must deal with if their governmental activities do not include any enterprise fund activities. It is not typical for governmental activities to include enterprise fund activities, nor is it common for activities accounted for in governmental funds to be classified as part of business-type activities.

h. To derive business-type activities data, governments typically begin with the Enterprise Fund totals in the proprietary fund financial statements. Because this information already is presented using the same measurement focus and basis of accounting as required for business-type activities in the government-wide financial statements, few adjustments are required normally. The more likely ones are:

(1) **Elimination of interfund transfers and interfund payables and receivables** to and from other enterprise funds or internal service funds that are reported as part of business-type activities.

Transfers from Other Enterprise Funds	XXX	
Transfers to Other Enterprise Funds		XXX
Due to Other Enterprise Funds	XXX	
Due from Other Enterprise Funds		XXX

(2) **Recording internal service fund assets and liabilities** of an internal service fund that provides the majority of its services to business-type activities (Simply record the ending balances of the internal service fund assets and liabilities as business-type activities assets and liabilities and increase or decrease net assets (ending) by the difference.)

(3) **Other potential internal service fund adjustments** for funds that are part of business-type activities including:

Eliminating internal service fund profit from internal sales:

Net Assets — Business-Type Activities	XXX	
Expenses (of business-type activities, allocated by function)		XXX

(For profits associated with sales to enterprise funds; losses would be the opposite)

Net Assets — Business-Type Activities	XXX	
Internal Balances		XXX

(For profits associated with sales to governmental funds or other components of governmental activities; losses would be the opposite)

(4) *Eliminating internal profit associated with sales to enterprise funds by internal service funds that are included in governmental activities:*

Internal Balances	XXX	
Expenses (of business-type activities, allocated by function)		XXX

(5) *Recording revenues and expenses for internal service fund transactions with entities outside the government:*

Net Assets — Business-Type Activities	XXX	
Expenses — Business-Type Activities	XXX	
Revenues — Business-Type Activities — Charges for Services		XXX
Revenues — Business-Type Activities — Investment Income		XXX

i. **Computation of Net Assets.** Another significant step in deriving the government-wide statement data is to compute the amounts to be reported for each of the three required classifications of net assets. These net asset classifications and their computation are discussed at section **2441**.

2430 Financial Reporting Entity, Including Blended and Discrete Component Units

Financial Reporting Entity

2430.01 **Concept.** The government financial reporting entity is often the legal unit as defined by charter or by law. However, some governments are also accountable for other governmental units, quasi-governmental units, or not-for-profit corporations (some of which are in substance its departments or agencies while others are less integrally related) and must include these component units in their financial statements.

2430.02 **Basic definition.** The GASB defines the financial reporting entity of a state or local government as including the following:

    a. The primary government (PG)—(the legal entity)

    b. Organizations that are *fiscally dependent* on the PG, i.e., which must have the PG's approval to:

        (1) adopt a budget,

        (2) levy taxes or set rates or charges, *or*

        (3) issue bonded debt.

    c. Other organizations for which the PG is financially accountable because the PG appoints a voting majority of the governing board *and* either:

        (1) the PG can impose its will on the other organization (i.e., the PG can significantly influence its programs, projects, activities, and/or level of services), *or*

        (2) there is a potential for the other organization to provide specific financial benefits to (or to impose specific burdens on) the PG. Such a financial benefit or burden relationship exists *if*:

            (a) the PG is entitled to the other organization's resources (e.g., it is required to subsidize the PG),

            (b) the PG is legally or otherwise obligated to finance the deficits of the other organization or to provide it financial support, or

            (c) the PG is obligated in any manner for the debt of the other organization.

    d. Affiliated, tax-exempt entities whose resources are entirely (or almost entirely) for the benefit of the PG (or its constituency) if the PG is entitled to (or can otherwise access) over 50% of the organization's resources and that portion of the resources is significant to the PG (per GASB Statement 39 on affiliated organizations).

    e. Business entities of which the PG holds majority ownership for the purpose of facilitating delivery of government services.

    f. Organizations whose financial data must be included to assure that the reporting entity financial statements are not misleading.

Any organization that is included in the reporting entity (other than the primary government) is referred to as a *component unit*. Water and sewer districts, airport authorities, transit authorities, school districts, and recreation authorities are examples of the hundreds of types of special purpose governments that sometimes are component units of other governments.

The GASB states that each general purpose unit of government, e.g., state, county, city, town, and so on is a primary government. Legally separate special purpose units of governments such as school districts, airport authorities, etc. are primary governments if they meet all three of the following criteria:

— Has a popularly elected governing body

— Is a separate legal entity

— Is fiscally independent

2430.03 **Incorporating component unit data.** The GASB Codification provides specific guidance on how the data of a component unit (CU) should be included in the primary government's financial statements.

    a. **Blending.** If component units are in substance part of the primary government—*specifically, if the PG and CU governing bodies are substantively the same or the CU serves or benefits solely the PG*—the CU financial data is blended with the PG data in preparing the reporting entity financial statements. *Other CUs*, including all affiliated tax exempt entities whose resources are entirely for the benefit of the PG and that are CUs per Statement 39, are *discretely presented*. A PG and a CU have substantively the same governing body if a voting majority of the PG governing body serves on *and* constitutes a voting majority of the CU's governing body. Blending means the following:

        (1) **Proprietary-type** component unit data should be included just as if it were for another proprietary fund of the primary government.

        (2) **Governmental-type** component unit data should be included just as if the CU funds were funds of the same type of the PG—except that the component unit's General Fund should be reported as a special revenue fund of the PG.

    b. **Discrete presentation.** Discretely presented CUs are reported *only* in government-wide financial statements (except for CUs that are fiduciary in nature, which are reported in the fiduciary funds statements). The financial statements should allow users to distinguish between the PG and its component units. This is accomplished by reporting the CU data in a separate discrete column and row to the right of or below the PG data in the government-wide financial statements (see Exhibits 7 and 8 in sections **2421.03–.04**).

If major discretely presented CUs are not reported in separate columns in the government-wide financial statements, the reporting entity basic financial statements must also include:

    a. CU combining statements presenting major discretely presented component units or

    b. CU condensed summary statements.

2430.04 **Note disclosures.** The notes to the reporting entity's financial statements should:

    a. include a brief description of the CUs and their relationships to the PG as well as information on how to obtain the separate financial statements of individual CUs,

    b. distinguish between disclosures relating to the PG (including blended CUs) and those relating to discretely presented CUs, and

    c. include those CU disclosures that are essential to fair presentation of the reporting entity's basic financial statements.

Joint Ventures

2430.05 Certain accounting methods and disclosures are required by the GASB Codification for joint ventures between a government and other governments, private or nonprofit organizations, and individuals.

a. If the government has an explicit, measurable right to the net assets of the joint venture:

   (1) Joint venture investments made from the government's proprietary (or similar fiduciary) funds must be accounted for on the equity method.

   (2) Joint venture investments made from its governmental (or similar fiduciary) funds should be reported:

   (a) In the government-wide statement of net assets as a Net Investment in Joint Venture. Any portion meeting the definition of a financial resource (or fund debt, which is rare) would be reported in the appropriate governmental fund as well.

   (b) Expenditures would be recognized in the participant fund to the extent that any net investment in the joint venture reported in the fund is less than the amount contributed to the venture.

   (c) Subsequent changes in the government's equity interest in the joint venture would be recognized as fund revenues or expenditures only when the recognition criteria for governmental funds are met.

b. The primary facts of the joint venture should be disclosed in the notes to the financial statements, including a description of the joint venture, whether the joint venture is expected to provide a financial benefit to (or impose a financial burden on) the government, and the availability of separate joint venture financial statements.

2440 Typical Items and Specific Types of Transactions and Events: Recognition, Measurement, Valuation, Calculation, and Presentation in Governmental Entity Financial Statements

2441 Net Assets and Components Thereof

2441.01 Computation of the three categories of net assets reported in government-wide financial statements typically is accomplished in a year-end process. The same is true of proprietary fund net asset classifications. The three net asset classifications are invested in capital assets net of related debt, restricted net assets, and unrestricted net assets. Essentially, each asset and each liability balance at year end must be classified according to which net asset category it affects. The difference is the balance for that category. The categories are reviewed in detail below.

2441.02 Invested in Capital Assets, Net of Related Debt is defined as:

a. capital (fixed) assets, **less**

b. accumulated depreciation, **less**

c. the outstanding balances of any bonds, mortgages, notes, or other borrowings attributable to the acquisition, construction, or improvement of capital assets.

If there are unexpended proceeds of debt issued to finance construction of capital assets, this component does exclude a portion of the capital debt equal to those unexpended proceeds. (This amount of capital debt is included in the restricted net assets component to offset the unexpended proceeds, which are reported in the restricted net assets component.)

2441.03 Restricted Net Assets are reported when constraints placed on net asset use are narrower than the general limits of the activity. "Restricted" means the constraints are either:

   a. externally imposed by creditors (e.g., through debt covenants), grantors, contributors, or laws or regulations of other governments, or

   b. imposed by law through constitutional provisions or enabling legislation that:

   (1) authorizes the government to assess, levy, charge, or otherwise mandate payment of resources externally and

   (2) includes a legally enforceable requirement that those resources be used for a specific purpose(s).

   Any unexpended proceeds of capital debt are included in this component. An equal amount of the related capital debt is included, offsetting these proceeds. In essence, the "Restricted Net Assets" component equals:

   a. restricted assets **less**

   b. liabilities payable from restricted assets.

   If permanent endowments or other permanent fund principal amounts are included, "restricted net assets" should be presented in two subclassified components. The permanently restricted net assets amount should be reported as "Nonexpendable." The balance of the restricted net assets component should be classified as "Expendable."

2441.04 Unrestricted Net Assets is that portion of net assets that does not meet the definition of "restricted" or "invested in capital assets, net of related debt." It is equal to unrestricted financial assets less noncapital debt payable from those assets.

2442 Fund Balances and Components Thereof

2442.01 As seen in the governmental fund accounting equation in at section **2411.08,** fund balance is the difference between the financial assets of a governmental fund and the liabilities of that fund. Fund balance is required to be reported in five categories, which governments typically will determine at year-end based on an analysis of the assets and liabilities of a governmental fund's assets and liabilities. However, it should be noted that if a governmental fund has restricted, committed, assigned, and unassigned resources available to use for a particular expenditure, it is assumed that a government that has not established a policy on the order of the expenditure of resources will spend resources restricted for that purpose first, then those that are committed, then assigned, and finally unassigned resources will be used.

2442.02 The five fund balance classifications are listed below with the *most common source(s)* of the constraints on use that result in that classification. (These were also discussed in section **2411.11(c).**)

   a. Nonspendable fund balance—reflects balances of inventory and prepaid items held in a governmental fund at year-end.

   b. Restricted fund balance—reflects balances of restricted debt proceeds and of amounts raised from restricted taxes or other revenue sources (restricted by the enabling legislation authorizing the tax), contributions, shared revenues, etc. (Note that amounts of restricted assets held under restricted grant agreements typically are offset by deferred revenues and have no related fund balance.)

   c. Committed fund balance—resources with constraints on use imposed by a formal action (resolution or ordinance, for example) of the government's governing body that can be removed or modified only by the governing body taking the same level of action to do so.

d. Assigned fund balance—resources that an official or group based on authority delegated by the governing body has formally indicated the intent to constrain to use for a specific purpose.

e. Unassigned fund balance—the residual amount of fund balance of the general fund.

2442.03 Assume that a government's general fund has inventory of $50,000, unrestricted cash and receivables of $200,000, and restricted investments of $75,000. Further assume that liabilities payable from restricted resources amount to $23,000. Other liabilities of the fund were $20,000 and were not payable from restricted, committed, or assigned resources. The governing body adopted a resolution restricting $9,000 to development programs during future years and these resources must be used for this purpose unless modified by another resolution adopted by the board. Finally, the finance director, using authority given to her by the board, set aside $30,000 for establishing a park and recreation reserve.

The fund balance of the general fund of this government should be presented as follows:

Fund balance:	
Nonspendable	$ 50,000
Restricted	52,000
Committed	9,000
Assigned	30,000
Unassigned	141,000
Total	$282,000

2442.04 Other actions or circumstances can be the source of the constraints reflected in the fund balance classifications as well, however. For example:

a. Nonspendable fund balance is reported in the general fund when there is a long-term receivable (in excess of related deferred revenues, if any) if the proceeds are not restricted, committed, or assigned to a specific purpose. Nonspendable fund balance also must be reported for any resources received that must be maintained intact and not used up, such as endowment principal.

b. Encumbrances ultimately to be paid from unassigned resources are reported as assignments of fund balance unless the approval of the encumbrance required the same formal action as a commitment.

c. Budgeting to use part of otherwise unassigned fund balance to cover a deficit between next year's budgeted revenues and budgeted expenditures results in an equal amount being reported as assigned fund balance.

2442.05 Some limitations on reporting fund balance classifications also exist. For example:

a. Restricted fund balance for stabilization reserves established by a government or committed fund balance for stabilization reserves can be reported only if the circumstances under which the stabilization reserves (amounts accumulated for use during a fiscal hardship) can be used are both specific and nonroutine. Indicating that the resources can be used only for emergencies or only when there is a budget shortfall are not sufficient to be considered specific and nonrouting.

b. There cannot be a fund balance assignment for any reason if it causes or increases a deficit in unassigned fund balance.

2443 Capital Assets and Infrastructure Assets

2443.01 Capital assets (fixed assets and intangible assets) of proprietary funds are accounted for and reported in the proprietary funds and in the government-wide financial statements. Fiduciary fund capital assets are reported in the fiduciary funds, not in the government-wide financial statements. All other capital assets are general capital assets and are reported only in the governmental activities column of the government-wide statement of net assets.

2443.02 GASB Statement 51, *Accounting and Financial Reporting for Intangible Assets,* defines **intangible assets** as assets of a nonfinancial nature that lack physical substance and have initial useful lives extending beyond a single reporting period. The statement requires most intangible assets to be reported like other capital assets—including amortizing limited life intangibles. GASB Statement 51 permits capitalizing internally created intangible assets after several conditions are met, but excludes goodwill. The conditions for capitalization of internally generated intangible assets (including computer software) are as follows:

a. The project objective is to create a specific internally generated intangible asset.

b. The nature of the expected service capacity of the completed asset is determined.

c. The technical or technological feasibility of successful completion of the project is demonstrated.

d. The current intention, ability, and presence of effort to continue development of and complete the intangible asset is demonstrated (at least by including the project in the current budget).

Outlays related to creating internally generated capital assets (such as internally generated computer software) that are made after all four of these conditions are met are capitalized; any related outlays before that time are expensed.

Likewise, unmatured long-term liabilities of proprietary activities and of fiduciary activities are accounted for in appropriate proprietary funds or fiduciary funds, as discussed in section **2444**. These liabilities are reported in proprietary funds and fiduciary funds financial statements, respectively. The proprietary funds long-term liabilities are also reported in the government-wide financial statements. Long-term liabilities of general government activities are reported only in the government-wide financial statements. They are not accounted for or reported in governmental funds until they mature.

2443.03 The General Capital Assets and General Long-Term Liabilities accounts are used to account for general government capital assets and general government, unmatured long-term liabilities. These accounts are not reported in governmental fund financial statements. From a financial reporting standpoint, the purpose of these accounts is simply to capture most of the information needed to report general government capital asset and general government long-term liability related information appropriately in the government-wide financial statements. Some governments use a different mechanism to accumulate this information.

2443.04 Because the General Capital Assets and General Long-Term Liabilities accounting entity is not required directly by GAAP and are not reported separately in the financial statements, it is unlikely that the CPA Examination will test entries for these accounts directly. Understanding one method of recording general capital asset and general long-term liability information is useful both to complete your comprehension of accounting and reporting for general government activities and because the government-wide reporting of general government capital assets and general government long-term liabilities is likely to be tested on the CPA Examination. Reviewing the entries to see the effects of various transactions on these asset and liability accounts should enhance your understanding of the impact of these items on the government-wide financial statements. Further, conversion of governmental fund financial statement data to government-wide financial statements should be easier to understand as well.

2443.05 With the advent of GASB Statement 34, which prescribes both fund-based and government-wide reporting, these "self-balancing" accounts are no longer required for recording long-term assets and liabilities. Although general long-term assets and liabilities do not appear in the fund-based statements, they do appear in the government-wide statements. Capital assets reporting in the government-wide statements is discussed in GASB 1400.112. Per GASB 1400.119, information regarding capital assets can be derived from asset management systems. Per GASB 2300.111, note disclosures are required to provide detail about the capital assets and long-term liabilities of the primary government as shown in the statement of net assets.

2443.06 General Capital Assets Valuation. General capital assets purchased or constructed by a government usually are recorded at the purchase or construction cost. However, assets donated to the government are recorded at fair market value when donated, and capital assets may be recorded at estimated cost (when capital asset records are initially established) if the actual cost (or fair market value when donated) is not readily determinable.

2443.07 General Capital Assets and General Long-Term Liabilities (GCA-GLTL) accounting equation and procedures. Accounting procedures for general capital assets are relatively simple. As noted earlier, the accounting equation for the General Capital Assets and General Long-Term Liabilities accounts is:

General capital assets – Accumulated – General long-term = Net assets
    GCA   depreciation   liabilities (GLTL)

2443.08 General capital assets. Four primary types of capital asset transactions affect these accounts.

    a. Acquisition or construction. The general capital assets are recorded at cost in appropriately titled asset accounts (i.e., Land, Buildings, Other Improvements, Machinery and Equipment, and Construction-in-Progress). Net assets is credited to balance the accounting equation. These transactions will increase the amount reported in the government-wide financial statements as Net Assets—Invested in Capital Assets, Net of Related Debt.

    b. Depreciation. For most depreciable general capital assets, depreciation should be computed and recorded using standard depreciation approaches and entries. Depreciation expense is closed to Net Assets at year end. Both depreciation expense and accumulated depreciation are reported in the government-wide financial statements at year end. For infrastructure capital assets such as streets, roads, bridges, and other capital assets that are immovable in nature and of value only to the governmental unit, a modified approach is permitted in lieu of depreciation. Except for additions, both revenue expenditures and capital expenditures are expensed after an infrastructure asset is constructed if the modified approach is used.

c. **Disposal of capital assets.** When general capital assets are disposed of, the assets and the related accumulated depreciation are removed from the GCA-GLTL accounts. Any sale proceeds are recorded as other financing sources in the appropriate governmental fund, usually the General Fund. The gain or loss on the disposal should be kept up with in ancillary records so that the information will be available for presentation in the government-wide financial statements.

GASB Statement 48, *Sales and Pledges of Receivables and Future Revenues and Intra-Entity Transfers of Assets and Future Revenues,* requires that all sales and transfers of capital assets between components of a government reporting entity should be reported at book value. Therefore, no gain or loss on the transaction can be recognized. Any differential between the book value of the capital asset involved and other assets that change hands must be reported as a transfer if between components of the primary government entity.

d. **Capital Asset Impairment.** GASB Statement 42 requires evaluation of prominent events and changes in circumstances to determine if capital assets are impaired. If so, and the impairment is permanent, the impaired asset(s) must be written down and a loss recognized. *Impairment means that the service utility has declined both significantly and unexpectedly.* Assets no longer to be used are to be reported at the lower of their cost or fair value. Assets that will continue to be used should be written down by an amount that reflects the loss in service utility. For impairments caused by physical damage, the loss is measured using an estimate of the restoration cost (cost of restoring the lost service utility). Impairments resulting from enactment of laws or regulations, technological changes or obsolescence are measured using a service life approach that assigns a cost to the reduction of the service life of the asset. Certain other impairments are measured using a service units approach or deflated replacement cost.

2443.09 **Illustrative entries.** No financial statements are presented for the GCA-GLTL accounts. Example GCA-GLTL entries follow.

a. **To record general capital assets (e.g., police cars or fire trucks) acquired by expenditures from the General Fund:**

Machinery and Equipment (or Police Cars or Fire Trucks)	$4,000	
Net Assets		$4,000

b. **To record construction-in-process at the end of the first year of a 2-year capital projects fund project:**

Construction-in-Progress	$7,000	
Net Assets		$7,000

c. **To record completion of the 2-year capital projects fund project:**

Buildings	$6,500	
Other Improvements	3,500	
Construction-in-Progress		$7,000
Net Assets		3,000

Note: This entry (1) records the total costs of the completed general capital assets—here $10,000—resulting from expenditures of $7,000 in the first year and $3,000 in the second year, (2) removes the Construction-in-Progress account balance, and (3) adjusts the net assets account to indicate the amount of the total project cost.

d. **To record disposal of general capital assets (regardless of whether they are sold for more or less than book value):**

Net Assets	$17,000	
Accumulated Depreciation	21,000	
Land		$ 8,000
Buildings		30,000

Notes:

(1) This entry removes the book value of general capital assets disposed of from the GCA-GLTL accounts.

(2) Any sale proceeds are recorded as an Other Financing Source in the appropriate governmental fund, usually the General Fund. Any gain (loss) on general capital asset disposal is *not* recorded here, but must be maintained in supplemental records and be reported in the government-wide statement of activities.

2444 General Long-Term Liabilities

2444.01 **General long-term liabilities.** All *unmatured* long-term liabilities that are not liabilities of specific proprietary funds or specific fiduciary funds also are recorded in the General Capital Assets and General Long-Term Liabilities (GCA-GLTL) accounts. Like general capital assets, these liabilities are *reported only in the government-wide financial statements*, not in the fund financial statements.

    a. Specific fund long-term debt, which relates to and will be repaid from a specific proprietary fund or fiduciary fund, is recorded in the fund. Proprietary fund debt is reported in the proprietary fund financial statements and in the government-wide financial statements. Fiduciary fund long-term debt is reported only in the fiduciary fund financial statements. Fiduciary funds are not reported in the government-wide financial statements.

    b. General long-term liabilities should be recorded in the GCA-GLTL accounts at their present values (determined using the effective interest rate at issuance). Therefore, bonds payable are recorded at their face value and any related issuance premiums or discounts as well as unamortized bond issue costs should be recorded as well. Remember that the purpose of the GCA-GLTL accounts is to accumulate most of the information required to report these assets and liabilities in the government-wide financial statements. Discount and premium amortization and amortization of bond issue costs may be recorded as well. Interest accruals are not likely to be made in the accounts. Worksheet adjustments are usually made to update these accounts for accrued interest to determine the amounts reported in the government-wide financial statements.

    c. Four primary types of transactions and events affecting general long-term liabilities are accounted for in the GCA-GLTL accounts: (1) issuance or incurrence of new debt, (2) amortization of bond premiums or discounts, (3) amortization of bond issue costs, and (4) debt retirement. Recall that at issuance, other financing sources are recorded in a governmental fund—usually a capital projects fund or a debt service fund—for the bonds face value and for any premium received (other financing uses are recorded for any discount). Expenditures are recorded in the fund for any issuance costs. When general long-term liabilities mature, they are recorded as expenditures and a current liability of the governmental fund (typically a debt service fund) from which they are to be paid. The other two events affecting the GLTL accounts do not require corresponding entries in the governmental funds.

With the advent of GASB Statement 34, which prescribes both fund-based and government-wide reporting, these "self-balancing" accounts are no longer required for recording long-term assets and liabilities. Although general long-term assets and liabilities do not appear in the fund-based statements, they do appear in the government-wide statements. Capital assets reporting in the government-wide statements is discussed in GASB 1400.112. Per GASB 1400.119, information regarding capital assets can be derived from asset management systems. Per GASB 2300.111, note disclosures are required to provide detail about the capital assets and long-term liabilities of the primary government as shown in the statement of net assets.

2444.02 **Illustrative entries.** As noted earlier, no GCA-GLTL statements are required. GCA, GLTL, and the changes therein are reported only in the government-wide financial statements. Example GLTL-related entries follow.

a. **To record general long-term debt incurred:**

Net Assets	$10,050	
Unamortized Bond Issue Costs	150	
Bonds Payable		$5,000
Premium on Bonds Payable		200
Long-Term Notes Payable		3,000
Capital Lease Payable		2,000

Note: Most general long-term liabilities are capital-asset-related borrowings and reduce the balance of Net Assets—Invested in Capital Assets that is reported in the government-wide statement of net assets.

b. **To record discount and premium amortization:**

Premium on Bonds Payable	$ 20	
Interest Expense		$ 20
Interest Expense	$ 50	
Discount on Bonds Payable		$ 50

Note: Although governments are not permitted to accrue interest payable in the governmental funds on general long-term liabilities, this accrued interest payable must be reported in the government-wide statement of net assets because the government-wide statements are reported using the revenue and expense basis. The interest expense reported in the government-wide operating statement will be computed as follows:

```
         Interest expenditures (from the governmental funds)
    +    Discount amortization (from the GCA-GLTL records)
    -    Premium amortization (from the GCA-GLTL records)
 + or -  Change in accrued interest payable (from the government-wide information)
```

c. **To record amortization of bond issue costs:**

Bond Issue Costs Expense	$ 15	
Unamortized Bond Issue Costs		$ 15

d. **To record the removal (reversal) of matured general long-term debt principal from the GCA-GLTL accounts:**

Bonds Payable	$4,000	
Long-Term Notes Payable	2,000	
Capital Lease Payable	1,000	
Net Assets		$7,000

Note: The payment to retire the liabilities will be reported as expenditures in the appropriate governmental fund. For bonds, this typically will be a debt service fund, while the long-term notes and capital lease will be paid through the General Fund or perhaps a special revenue fund. The key point is that the liability account in the GCA-GLTL accounts is decreased and net assets are increased when the general long-term debt principal matures.

2445 Interfund Activity, Including Transfers

2445.01 **Introduction.** The discussions and illustrations to this point have focused primarily on accounting for each of the several types of funds and the GCA-GLTL accounts of state and local governments. This section of the chapter focuses on the following:

   a. **Interfund activity:** Where one transaction affects two or more funds

   b. **Interfund-GCA-GLTL accounts transactions:** Where one transaction affects one or more funds and the GCA-GLTL accounts

   Note: Interfund activity and interfund-GCA-GLTL accounts transactions and relationships are extremely important in state and local government accounting and reporting and have been *tested extensively* on CPA Examinations. The discussions and illustrations in this section also review and expand on those presented earlier.

2445.02 **Interfund activity** (i.e., interfund transactions) simultaneously affects two or more funds of the government. The GASB Codification provides specific reporting and guidance on four types of interfund activity:

The four types are categorized as either reciprocal interfund activity (interfund loans and interfund services provided and used) or nonreciprocal interfund activity (interfund reimbursements and interfund transfers).

   a. **Interfund loans** are transactions in which resources are provided by one fund to another fund and are required to be repaid. Interfund loans—whether short-term or long-term—should:

   (1) be reported as interfund receivables in lender funds and interfund payables in borrower funds,

   (2) *not* affect the fund balance or net assets of either fund involved, and

   (3) *not* be reported as "other financing sources or uses" in the governmental fund financial statements.

   Long-term interfund receivables for loans made from the General Fund to other funds result in reporting nonspendable fund balance in the General Fund if the proceeds from subsequent collection of the note are not restricted, committed, or assigned to a specific purpose.

   Note: If repayment of an interfund loan is not planned and expected within a reasonable time, the transaction should be reported as a *transfer* from the fund that made the "loan" to the fund that received the "loan."

   b. **Interfund services provided and used** includes sales and purchases of goods and services between funds for a price approximating their external exchange value. Interfund services provided and used:

   (1) include internal sales of goods and services of proprietary funds to other funds (or vice versa),

   (2) are reported by proprietary funds (at standard rates) even if the seller fund provides services for free to other departments (a corresponding transfer would be reported as well), and

   (3) should be reported as revenues in seller funds and expenditures or expenses in purchaser funds. (Unpaid amounts should be reported as interfund receivables and payables in the fund balance sheets or statements of fund net assets.)

c. **Reimbursements** are error-correction-like transactions that reimburse one fund for expenditures or expenses initially recorded there that are properly attributable to another fund. Reimbursements are recorded as:

(1) expenditures or expenses, as appropriate, in the reimbursing fund and

(2) reductions of the recorded expenditures or expenses in the fund that is reimbursed.

d. **Interfund transfers** are flows of assets (such as cash or goods or services) without a repayment requirement and without equivalent flows of assets or services in return. Interfund transfers:

(1) *of governmental funds* are reported as "other financing uses" in the funds making transfers and as "other financing sources" in the funds receiving transfers,

(2) *of proprietary funds* are reported as the last item before change in net assets,

(3) are reported as the last item before net change in net assets in the *government-wide statement of activities,* and

(4) include:

(a) interfund "payments in lieu of taxes" that are not payments for, and not reasonably equivalent in value to, services provided,

(b) the transfer of initial capital from the General Fund to establish an enterprise or internal service fund,

(c) return of all or part of initial capital to the General Fund on abolishing or reducing an enterprise or internal service fund,

(d) transfers of residual balances of terminated funds to the General Fund or to a debt service fund,

(e) routine transfers from the General Fund to debt service funds,

(f) transfers from the General Fund to capital projects funds,

(g) operating subsidy transfers from the General Fund or a special revenue fund to an enterprise or internal service fund, and

(h) transfers of bond issue premiums from capital projects funds to debt service funds.

Note: Transfers are *not* loans but are nonexchange (nonreciprocal) shifts of financial resources among funds that are *not* intended to be repaid.

2445.03 **Illustrative interfund entries.** The following example entries illustrate the accounting for these four types of interfund transactions and review and integrate some of the earlier illustrations.

a. **To record billings to departments financed by the General Fund for services rendered through enterprise fund and internal service fund departments:**

(1) General Fund

Expenditures—Services	$5,000	
Due to Enterprise Fund		$3,000
Due to Internal Service Fund		2,000

(2) Enterprise Fund

Due from General Fund	$3,000	
Revenues—Billings for Services		$3,000

(3) Internal Service Fund

Due from General Fund	$2,000	
Revenues—Billings for Services		$2,000

Note: These are interfund services provided and used transactions. A distinct revenues account, such as Billings for Services, is used in internal service fund accounting (instead of Sales or Service Revenues) to indicate that such revenues arose from interfund services provided and used transactions.

b. **To record employer contributions due from the General Fund and an enterprise fund to the pension trust fund:**

(1) General Fund

Expenditures—Pension Contributions	$3,500	
Due to Pension Trust Fund		$3,500

(2) Enterprise Fund

Expenses—Pension Contributions	$1,000	
Due to Pension Trust Fund		$1,000

(3) Pension Trust Fund

Due from General Fund	$3,500	
Due from Enterprise Fund	1,000	
Additions—Employer Contributions		$4,500

Note: These also are interfund services provided and used transactions.

c. **To record reimbursement of the General Fund for operating expenditures previously recorded there that are properly attributable to a special revenue fund and to an enterprise fund:**

(1) General Fund

Cash	$800	
Expenditures—Operating		$800

(2) Special Revenue Fund

Expenditures—Operating	$500	
Cash		$500

(3) Enterprise Fund

Expenses—Operating	$300	
Cash		$300

Note: These are interfund reimbursement transactions.

d. **To record transfers made from the General Fund to establish a new internal service fund and to increase the net assets of an enterprise fund:**

(1) General Fund

Transfer to Internal Service Fund	$6,000	
Transfer to Enterprise Fund	3,000	
Cash		$9,000

(2) Internal Service Fund

Cash	$6,000	
Transfer from General Fund		$6,000

(3) Enterprise Fund

Cash	$3,000	
Transfer from General Fund		$3,000

Notes:

(1) These are interfund transfers.

(2) In internal service funds and enterprise funds, the transfer accounts will be closed to the Net Assets account.

(3) The General Fund transfer accounts will be reported as "Other Financing Uses" and closed to Fund Balance.

e. **To record routine transfers from the General Fund to debt service and capital projects funds:**

(1) General Fund

Transfer to Debt Service Fund	$700	
Transfer to Capital Projects Fund	800	
Cash		$1,500

(2) Debt Service Fund

Cash	$700	
Transfer from General Fund		$700

(3) Capital Projects Fund

Cash	$800	
Transfer from General Fund		$800

f. **To record a short-term loan from the General Fund to a special revenue fund:**

(1) General Fund

Due from Special Revenue Fund	$1,750	
Cash		$1,750

(2) Special Revenue Fund

Cash	$1,750	
Due to General Fund		$1,750

Note: In governmental accounting, the terms *due to* and *due from* may indicate short-term interfund loans that are expected to be repaid during the current year or early in the next year.

g. **To record a long-term loan of unassigned resources from the General Fund to an enterprise fund:**

(1) General Fund

Advance to Enterprise Fund	$5,000	
Cash		$5,000

(2) Enterprise Fund

Cash	$5,000	
Advance from General Fund		$5,000

Notes:

(1) The terms *advance to* and *advance from* often denote noncurrent or long-term interfund loans. This terminology is not required, however.

(2) Nonspendable fund balance of $5,000 should be reported in the General Fund related to the advance because it is long-term and proceeds of the subsequent collection are not restricted, committed, or assigned (in which case the $5,000 would be reflected in the corresponding fund balance classification).

(3) Interfund loans, whether short-term or long-term, do not change total fund balance or total net assets.

h. **To record closing of selected transfer accounts in governmental funds (e.g., the General Fund) and proprietary funds (e.g., enterprise and internal service funds):**

(1) **General Fund**

Fund Balance	$6,000	
Transfer to Enterprise Fund		$2,000
Transfer to Internal Service Fund		4,000

(2) **Enterprise Fund**

Transfer from General Fund	$2,000	
Net Assets		$2,000

(3) **Internal Service Fund**

Transfer from General Fund	$4,000	
Net Assets		$4,000

Note: The amounts in entries h (1)–(3) are illustrative only (rather than being derived from entries a–g).

2445.04 **Interfund-GCA-GLTL transactions** simultaneously affect one or more funds and the General Capital Assets and General Long-Term Liabilities accounts. Interfund-GCA-GLTL transactions arise in general government capital outlay and long-term debt transactions.

2445.05 **Illustrative interfund-GCA-GLTL entries.** Example interfund-GCA-GLTL illustrative and review entries follow.

As noted in previous sections, the use of General Capital Assets and General Long-Term Liabilities accounts to maintain the required information to be reported in the government-wide financial statements and notes is only one available option for capturing this information. Therefore, the use of this entity will not be tested on the CPA Examination. It is presented here to help candidates visualize and track the impact of various transactions on these significant government-wide financial statement items. The fund entries are in accordance with GAAP requirements, not optional.

a. **To record issuing $5,000 par general obligation bonds at a premium for capital outlay purposes:**

(1) **Capital Projects Fund**

Cash	$5,280	
Other Financing Sources—Bonds		$5,000
Other Financing Sources—Bond Premium		280

(2) **General Capital Assets and General Long-Term Liabilities accounts**

Net Assets	$5,280	
Bonds Payable		$5,000
Premium on Bonds		280

Notes:

(1) The bond issue proceeds are recorded in the capital projects fund at the amount received, even if more or less than par.

(2) The liability is recorded at present value in the GCA-GLTL accounts.

(3) The same practices are followed in recording refunding bond proceeds in debt service funds and in any governmental fund in which bond issue proceeds are recorded (e.g., in the General Fund if bonds are issued to finance a General Fund deficit).

b. **To record the maturity of bonds and capital leases that are serviced through a debt service fund and the General Fund, respectively:**

   (1) Debt Service Fund

Expenditures—Bond Principal	$7,000	
Expenditures—Interest on Bonds	2,400	
Matured Bonds Payable (or Cash)		$7,000
Matured Interest Payable (or Cash)		2,400

   (2) General Fund

Expenditures—Capital Lease Principal	$1,400	
Expenditures—Interest on Capital Leases	800	
Matured Capital Lease Payments Payable (or Cash)		$2,200

   (3) General Capital Assets and General Long-Term Liabilities accounts

Bonds Payable	$7,000	
Capital Lease (Principal) Payable	1,400	
Net Assets		$8,400

   Recall that premium and discount amortization may be recorded in the GCA-GLTL accounts. Their effects must be reported in the government-wide financial statements regardless of whether they are recorded formally.

c. **To record capital outlay expenditures made from the (1) General Fund (equipment) and (2) a capital projects fund (land and buildings):**

   (1) General Fund

Expenditures—Capital Outlay	$2,000	
Cash or Vouchers Payable		$2,000

   (2) Capital Projects Fund

Expenditures—Capital Outlay	$9,000	
Cash or Vouchers Payable		$9,000

   (3) General Capital Assets and General Long-Term Liabilities accounts

Equipment	$2,000	
Land	3,000	
Buildings	6,000	
Net Assets		$11,000

   Note: Remember that depreciation expense and accumulated depreciation are recorded in the GCA-GLTL accounts as well. Depreciation of general capital assets does *not* affect any fund, however.

d. **To record the sale of land (general capital assets) originally acquired for $1,400, the sale proceeds were deposited in a debt service fund account and are to be used for bond retirement:**

   (1) Debt Service Fund

Cash	$3,700	
Other Financing Sources—Sale of General Capital Assets		$3,700

   (2) General Capital Assets and General Long-Term Liabilities accounts

Net Assets	$1,400	
Land		$1,400

Notes:

(1) If bonds or other debt incurred to finance the general capital assets sold are still outstanding, the sale proceeds usually are recorded in the related debt service fund; otherwise, they are typically recorded in the General Fund.

(2) The Gain on Sale of Land of $2,300 should be captured in ancillary records to be used to prepare the government-wide statement of activities.

e. **To record the transfer of equipment previously used in enterprise fund activities to the city Streets Department, which is financed from the General Fund:**

(1) Enterprise Fund

Accumulated Depreciation—Equipment	$5,800	
Net Assets (Contributions to Other Departments)	3,000	
Equipment		$8,800

(2) General Capital Assets and General Long-Term Liabilities accounts

Equipment	$8,800	
Net Assets		$3,000
Accumulated Depreciation		5,800

Notes:

(1) No interfund transfer is reported in the fund because the transaction involves a fund and the GCA-GLTL accounts, *not* two funds. In the government-wide statement of activities, this transaction will be reported as a transfer from business-type activities to governmental activities.

(2) The transaction is recorded at the book value of the equipment, as required by GASB Statement 48 and discussed in sections **2443.08** and **2443.09**.

f. **To record the increase in a county's liabilities for claims, judgments, and compensated absences (accrued vacation and sick leave) attributable to the general government (1 and 2) and to an enterprise fund (3):**

(1) General Fund

Expenditures—Claims and Judgments	$ 800	
Expenditures—Compensated Absences	900	
Current Liabilities—Claims and Judgments		$ 800
Current Liabilities—Compensated Absences		900

(2) General Capital Assets and General Long-Term Liabilities accounts

Net Assets	$7,300	
Claims and Judgments Payable (Noncurrent)		$3,200
Compensated Absences Payable (Noncurrent)		4,100

(3) Enterprise Fund

Expenses—Claims and Judgments	$4,000	
Expenses—Compensated Absences	5,000	
Current Liabilities—Claims, Judgments, and Compensated Absences		$1,700
Long-Term Liabilities—Claims, Judgments, and Compensated Absences		7,300

Notes:

(1) The GASB Codification states that the government's accrued liabilities for claims, judgments, and compensated absences are to be computed in accordance with GASB Statements 10, 16, and 17.

- In proprietary funds (and trust funds), the increases in these liabilities are recorded as fund expenses (or deductions) and liabilities immediately, as in commercial accounting.

- Increases in general government liabilities are recognized as governmental fund expenditures and current liabilities only to the extent they are normally to be paid from available expendable financial resources of the governmental funds. The remaining general government liabilities are recorded directly in the GCA-GLTL accounts—and are not recorded as governmental fund expenditures and liabilities until they are due.

- Changes in general government long-term liabilities will be reflected in the expenses reported for governmental activities in the government-wide statement of activities because revenues and expenses, not expenditures, are reported in that statement.

(2) The GASB Codification requires a similar pension (and other postemployment benefit) expenditure or expense and liability recognition approach. It states that any excess of the actuarial amount that should have been paid to the pension plan or fund over the amount actually paid should be recorded:

- in proprietary (and similar fiduciary) funds as expense and as current and/or noncurrent liabilities, as appropriate, and

- in governmental funds, only the amount that is reasonably expected to be paid from existing fund assets (i.e., amounts due and payable by year end) is recognized as a fund expenditure and current liability; the remainder is recorded in the GCA-GLTL accounts.

g. **To record consummating identical general government (1–2) and internal service fund (3) equipment capital lease agreements as lessee:**

(1) General Fund

Expenditures—Capital Outlay (Present Value of Minimum Lease Payments)	$6,000	
Cash (Initial Payment)		$ 800
Other Financing Sources—Increase in Capital Lease Liabilities (Difference—Liability Recorded as GCA-GLTL)		5,200

(2) General Capital Assets and General Long-Term Liabilities accounts

Equipment (Present Value of Minimum Lease Payments)	$6,000	
Liability Under Capital Lease		$5,200
Net Assets		800

(3) Internal Service Fund

Equipment Under Capital Lease (Present Value of Minimum Lease Payments)	$6,000	
Cash		$ 800
Liability Under Capital Lease		5,200

Note: The GASB Codification requires governments to apply the provisions of the FASB's lease accounting guidance that was in effect when the GASB's predecessor adopted its lease accounting standard. However, those provisions are applied somewhat differently in recording general government capital leases. The GASB Codification also requires general government capital leases to be recorded in governmental funds on the all financing and investing activities approach. Thus, General Fund entry g (1):

- records the fair market value of the property received as expenditures and

— records an other financing source for the difference between:

(a) the expenditures recognized and

(b) the cash paid and/or current liability recognized in the governmental fund. (This difference equals the long-term lease liability incurred, which is recorded at its present value in the GCA-GLTL accounts.)

2446 Nonexchange Revenue Transactions

2446.01 **Nonexchange transactions.** Taxes, fines, grants, and other nonexchange transactions—where a government does not give directly value equal to that received—are major revenue sources of many governments. GASB Statement 33, *Accounting and Financial Reporting for Nonexchange Transactions,* provides guidance for both asset recognition and revenue recognition for nonexchange transactions, which are classified as follows:

a. Derived tax revenues

b. Imposed nonexchange revenues

c. Government-mandated nonexchange transactions

d. Voluntary nonexchange transactions

The GASB Statement 33 guidance is summarized in Exhibit 15. A key point to recognize is that restrictions on use of resources for a particular purpose do **not** directly affect timing of revenue recognition.

\multicolumn{2}{c}{**Exhibit 15**}
\multicolumn{2}{c}{**Nonexchange Transactions**}
\multicolumn{2}{c}{**Classes and Timing of Recognition of Nonexchange Transactions**}
Class	Recognition
<u>Derived tax revenues</u> Examples: sales taxes, personal and corporate income taxes, motor fuel taxes, and similar taxes on earnings or consumption	<u>Assets*</u> Period when underlying exchange has occurred or when resources are received, whichever is first. <u>Revenues</u> Period when underlying exchange has occurred. (Report advance receipts as deferred revenues.) **When modified accrual accounting is used, resources also should be "available."**
Imposed nonexchange revenues (other than derived tax revenues) Examples: property taxes, most fines, and forfeitures	<u>Assets*</u> Period when an enforceable legal claim has arisen or when resources are received, whichever is first. <u>Revenues</u> Period when resources are required to be used or first period that use is permitted (e.g., for property taxes, the period for which levied). **When modified accrual accounting is used, resources also should be "available."**
Government-mandated nonexchange transactions Examples: federal government mandates on state and local governments Voluntary nonexchange transactions Examples: certain grants and entitlements, most donations	<u>Assets* and liabilities</u> Period when all eligibility requirements,** including time requirements, have been met or (for asset recognition) when resources are received, whichever is first. <u>Revenues and expenses or expenditures</u> Period when all eligibility requirements** including time requirements, have been met. (Report advance receipts or payments as deferred revenues or advances respectively. Permanent endowments, term endowments, and similar gifts should be reported as revenues when the resources are received.) **When modified accrual accounting is used for revenue recognition, resources also should be "available."**

* If there are purpose restrictions, report restricted net assets (or equity) or, for governmental funds, a reservation of fund balance.
** Eligibility requirements include the following:
(a) Required characteristics of recipients
(b) Time requirements—requirement in enabling legislation or imposed by provider that resources be used only during a certain time period or only after a certain date or that resources be maintained intact
(c) Resources were provided on an "expenditure-driven" (reimbursement) basis requiring the recipient to incur allowable costs under a certain program.
(d) Requirement that voluntary contributions are contingent on recipient taking specific actions. (An example is a requirement that the recipient raise matching amounts of resources.)

Source: Adapted from GASB Statement 33, *Accounting and Financial Reporting for Nonexchange Transactions* (GASB, 1998)

2447 Expenditures

2447.01 **Governmental funds** report expenditures, not expenses. Expenditures represent decreases in the net current financial resources of a governmental fund for operations, capital outlay, interest, and general long-term debt retirement. Expenditures are recognized in the period that the fund incurs a liability unless one of the expenditure modifications applies. Most capital outlay and many normal operating costs are recognized on this basis—when the fund incurs a liability.

However, debt service expenditures (principal retirement and interest) on general long-term liabilities and numerous operations-related expenditures are recognized in the period they mature (become due and payable). Examples of operating-cost-related expenditures that are recognized as they become due and payable include claims and judgments, compensated absences, pensions, other postemployment benefits, pollution remediation, and termination benefits.

Finally, two types of expenditures may be recognized either when purchased or as consumed. These are materials and supplies and prepayments (for rent, insurance, and so on).

At a minimum, expenditures must be reported by fund and by function or program in the governmental fund financial statements.

2447.02 For some, expenditures are understood best by relating them to expenses. In general, expenses relate to the costs of goods and services consumed during a period. Expenditures, by comparison, are more closely related to the cost of goods and services acquired during a period. For example, many operating "expenses" and "expenditures" occur simultaneously. Use of electricity results in an expense and an expenditure of equal amounts at the same point in time. The same is true for salaries and wages. In governmental funds, it is an expenditure, not an expense, that is reported.

For other items, the timing of recognition of expenditures and expenses differs dramatically. Purchase of a capital asset with a 5-year useful life results in a capital outlay expenditure in the year of acquisition and no additional expenditures in the next four years. The cost of this capital asset, however, is allocated to expense over the five years it is used through depreciation expense—in a proprietary fund and in the government-wide financial statements.

Finally, retirement of general long-term liability principal is reported as an expenditure. Debt principal retirement is not recognized as an expense at any point in time.

2447.03 The GASB permits an exception to the normal recognition timing for debt service expenditures on general long-term debt. Interest and principal expenditures on **general long-term liabilities** usually are recorded "when due," but may be accrued if:

a. due early in the next year and

b. debt service fund financial resources dedicated for their payment have been provided in the current year.

("Early in the next year" means not more than a month.)

2447.04 It may be useful to deal with a few other expenditure-related issues—accounting for capital leases and for certain estimated and/or actuarial liabilities. **Capital leases** of general capital assets by SLG "lessees" are required to be reported as *concurrent borrowing and capital expenditure transactions.* Accordingly, the inception of a "general government" capital lease with a present value of $200,000, assuming a reasonable lease interest rate, would be recorded as follows in an appropriate governmental fund:

Expenditures—Capital Outlay	$200,000	
Other Financing Sources—Capital Leases		$200,000
To record acquisition of general capital asset at inception of capital lease.		

The unmatured long-term liability and the capital asset would be reported in the government-wide financial statements.

2448 Special Items

2448.01 **Recording special items and extraordinary items.** Extraordinary items and/or special items are sometimes reported in a governmental fund. Extraordinary items are transactions or events that are both *unusual in nature and infrequent in occurrence*. Special items are transactions or events that are *either unusual in nature or infrequent in occurrence and under the control of management*. The amounts to be reported in governmental funds are the gross increases or decreases in the net assets of the governmental fund, not the gain or loss on the transactions. For example, assume that a city sold its only undeveloped land to another party for $500,000 and the cost of the land was $75,000, the city would record in the General Fund a special item of $500,000 for the proceeds from the sale of the undeveloped land, *not* the gain of $425,000.

Cash	$500,000	
Special Item—Proceeds from Sale of Land		$500,000

In the government-wide statement of activities, however, the special item reported would equal the gain. Similarly, if the special item related to a proprietary fund, the special item would equal the gain, not the proceeds from the sale.

2449 Encumbrances

2449.01 As discussed in section **2411.12**, governments record the estimated cost of orders and contracts for assets and services in a budgetary account called Encumbrances until the goods or services are received. Encumbrances are recorded at the estimated cost of the ultimate expenditures that will result upon receipt of the goods or services. The encumbrance decreases the available appropriations authority to reduce the possibility of inadvertent overexpenditure of appropriations. Once the order is filled or services are received, the estimated cost recorded in the Encumbrance account is removed and the expenditure is recorded at the actual cost.

2449.02 In the General Fund, outstanding year-end balances of encumbrances of otherwise unassigned fund balance cause an equal amount of fund balance to be reported as assigned fund balance instead of as unassigned fund balance. Encumbrances of restricted, committed, or assigned fund balance do not affect the classification of fund balance, either in the General Fund or any other fund.

2449.03 Major encumbrances are disclosed in the notes along with other commitments of the government.

2450 Accounting and Reporting for Governmental Not-for-Profit Organizations

Government Hospital Accounting and Reporting

2450.01 **Applicable GAAP.** The primary government "not-for-profit" organizations are government health care organizations and government colleges and universities. The GASB prohibits government entities from applying the primary FASB guidance related for nongovernment not-for-profit organizations. In large part, government not-for-profit organizations are to apply the same guidance applied to all other government entities.

Prior to GASB Statement 34, GAAP applicable to government hospitals had been determined largely by committees of the Healthcare Financial Management Association (HFMA) and the AICPA. The AICPA Audit and Accounting Guide, *Health Care Organizations,* was the primary guide to GAAP applicable to government hospitals. Under GASB Statement 34, most hospitals will be either enterprise (and business-type) activities of a primary government or special purpose governments engaged only in business-type activities. In this case, the basic financial statements required are the Enterprise Fund statements.

Reporting nongovernment, not-for-profit healthcare organizations is discussed briefly in section **2500**.

2450.02 **CPA Examination requirements.** CPA Examination questions often require knowledge of government hospital accounting concepts, journal entries, and financial statements. CPA Examination questions on government hospital and other government health care entity accounting typically have focused on its *major aspects* and have not been as detailed as those on governmental accounting.

Government Hospital Overview and Financial Statements

2450.03 Government hospitals and other government health care providers (hereafter *hospitals*) typically are treated as special purpose governments engaged only in business-type activities.

2450.04 The required financial statements for *government* hospitals using enterprise fund accounting are as follows:

    a. Statement of net assets

    b. Statement of revenues, expenses, and changes in net assets

    c. Statement of cash flows

Balance Sheet

2450.05 The government hospital balance sheet is illustrated in Exhibit 16. Note the similarity of this statement to the proprietary fund balance sheet discussed in section **2423.01**. Also note the following:

    a. The Assets Whose Use is Limited category is used to report assets whose use is limited to a specific purpose or purposes either by:

        (1) an internal management decision (often called board designations) or

        (2) external restrictions—other than those imposed by donors or grantors of the resources such as bond indenture provisions, third-party (Blue Cross, Medicare, Medicaid, etc.) reimbursement agreements, or other similar arrangements.

b. Assets restricted by donors or grantors for plant purposes or for endowment purposes are reported as separate line items.

Exhibit 16

Hospital Balance Sheet				
(Heading)				
Assets			**Liabilities and Net Assets**	
Current Assets:			Current Liabilities: (e.g., accounts and notes payable, contracts payable)	XX
			Long-term debt: (e.g., bonds payable, mortgages payable)	XX
Cash		XX		
Receivables		XX	Total Liabilities	XX
Assets whose use is limited—required for current liabilities		XX		
Other		XX	Net assets	
Total current assets			Invested in capital assets,	
		XX	net of related debt	XX
			Restricted	XX
Assets restricted to endowment		XX	Unrestricted	XX
Assets restricted to fixed asset acquisition		XX	Total net assets	XX
Assets whose use is limited				
By board for building additions		XX	Total liabilities and net assets	XX
By bond indenture		XX		
By third-party payor agreements		XX		
Total assets whose use is limited	XX			
Less assets whose use is limited and that are required for current liabilities		(XX)		
Noncurrent assets whose use is limited		XX		
Property, plant, and equipment		XX		
Other assets		XX		
Total assets		XX		

Statement of Revenues, Expenses, and Changes in Net Assets

2450.06 Government hospitals must, like other proprietary activities, present a single, comprehensive operating statement—the statement of revenues, expenses, and changes in net assets (Exhibit 17 in section **2450.10**). Nongovernment not-for-profit hospitals present a separate statement of operations and a statement of changes in net assets.

2450.07 **Unique income determination features.** Hospital accounting has several unique income determination conventions, which must be understood to comprehend the operating statement.

a. **Patient service revenues** of *government* hospitals are reported net of uncollectibles, charity services, and deductions from patient service revenues. (Charity services are excluded from the definition of gross services.) *Nongovernment not-for-profit hospitals* report uncollectibles as expenses; they are not deducted from patient service revenues.

b. **Charity services** are those services provided by a hospital for which no cash payment was expected because the services were provided to indigent patients.

c. **Deductions from patient service revenues:** The differences between gross patient service revenues at standard rates and the amounts intended to be collected are recorded in debit balance "deductions from revenue" accounts that describe the causes of the differences between the standard rates and collectible amounts. The most common deductions from revenue arise from the following:

(1) Contractual adjustments because of third-party insurer agreements or government regulations

(2) Discounts extended to doctors and nurses

(3) Bad debts (not deducted for nongovernment hospitals)

d. Government hospitals deduct bad debts from revenues rather than reporting them as expenses. Nongovernment hospitals report bad debts as expenses.

e. **Premium fee revenues** arise from contracts to provide patient services for a specific (usually monthly) fee per member of the covered group and are recognized in the period to which they relate.

f. Revenues and gains are classified separately and are reported in different sections of the statement of revenues, expenses, and changes in net assets. Likewise, expenses and losses are classified and reported separately.

g. **Revenues and expenses** are associated with the provision of services that comprise the ongoing, major, or central operations of a hospital. Gains and losses are associated with peripheral or incidental transactions or events. Thus, for example, contributions may be revenues or gains, depending on whether a significant fund-raising effort is an ongoing major source of financing that a hospital uses to fulfill its basic mission.

h. Government hospitals recognize revenues in accordance with the standards discussed throughout section **2400**.

(1) All unrestricted revenues are recognized immediately, including unrestricted earnings on investments.

(2) Grants and contributions with eligibility requirements are recorded as deferred revenues when received. Revenues are reported when the eligibility requirements are met.

(3) Net assets released from restrictions are not reported for government hospitals.

i. **Donated goods (commodities)** are recognized as both inventories and gains or revenues, as appropriate.

j. Recognition of donated services by government hospitals is optional.

k. **Donated services** of nongovernment not-for-profit hospitals are recognized as assets or operating expenses and, typically, as nonoperating revenues if:

(1) they enhance nonfinancial assets or

(2) they require specialized skills and are provided by individuals possessing these skills, and typically would need to be purchased if they had not been donated.

2450.08 The government hospital statement of revenues, expenses, and changes in net assets reports all changes in hospital net assets (see Exhibit 17 in section **2450.10**).

2450.09 The format of the government hospital operating statement (illustrated in Exhibit 17 in section **2450.10**) demonstrates many of the unique hospital income determination features as well as the types of accounts used in hospital accounting.

2450.10 Questions requiring knowledge of the format and content of this statement are likely on the CPA Examination.

Exhibit 17

Hospital Statement of Revenues, Expenses, and Changes in Net Assets (Heading)		
Net patient service revenues (Note 1)		$ 85,000
Premium fee revenues (Note 2)		50,000
Other revenues		
Cafeteria sales	$ 3,000	
Medical record transcript fees	1,000	
...	...	9,000
Total operating revenues		144,000
Operating expenses		
Nursing services	40,000	
Other professional services	20,000	
Administrative services	15,000	
...	...	
Depreciation expense	20,000	
Other	2,000	144,500
Operating income (Loss) (Note 3)		$(500)
Nonoperating gains (Losses)		
Unrestricted contributions	3,500	
Operating grants and contributions	1,500	
Donated commodities	1,000	
Income and gains (losses) from investments	2,800	
...	...	
		15,000
Income before capital grants and contributions		14,500
Capital grants and contributions		1,000
Change in net assets		15,500
Net assets, beginning		140,000
Net assets, ending		$155,500

(1) After deducting bad debts, charity services and deductions from revenues.
(2) Recognized in period covered by premium fee.
(3) Some items reported as gains here are reported as revenues by some hospitals.

2450.11 **Statement of Cash Flows:** Governmental hospitals are required to prepare a statement of cash flows per GASB Statement 9, *Reporting of Cash Flows of Proprietary and Nonexpendable Trust Funds and Governmental Entities That Use Proprietary Fund Accounting*. The statement of cash flows explains changes in both unrestricted and restricted cash and is prepared in the same manner as for similar municipal proprietary funds (government hospitals).

2450.12 Selected **illustrative entries** for government hospitals are presented here to emphasize hospital transactions. The key government hospital accounting journal entries are as follows.

    a. To record gross charges to patients at standard rates ($9,500), net of charity services ($600):

Accounts Receivable	$8,900	
Patient Service Revenues (Net of Charity Services)		$8,900

Note: CPA Examination questions assume that hospitals can identify charity patients immediately, so write off charity receivables directly rather than through an allowance account.

b. **To record deductions from revenue and bad debts:**

Deductions from Revenues—Contractual Adjustments	$700	
Deductions from Revenues—Bad Debts	800	
Allowance for Contractual Adjustments		$700
Allowance for Other Uncollectible Receivables		800

Conceptually, transactions *a* and *b* may be combined and recorded so that patient service revenues are reduced directly and separate deductions from revenue accounts are not maintained.

c. **To record write-offs for contractual adjustments (e.g., for Medicare, Medicaid, and insurance company third-party payors) and of other uncollectible patient receivables:**

Allowance for Contractual Adjustments	$180	
Allowance for Other Uncollectible Receivables	370	
Accounts Receivable		$550

d. **To record hospital operating expenses and other revenues (other than patient service revenues):**

Operating Expenses	$9,000	
Inventory		$1,500
Accumulated Depreciation		2,500
Cash or Payables		5,000
Cash or Receivables	$1,400	
Other Operating Revenues		$1,400

Notes:

(1) This illustrative example assumes that Operating Expenses and Other Revenues subsidiary ledgers are used to classify operating expenses and other operating revenues by type.

(2) CPA Examination questions and problems may require or imply that operating expenses and/or other revenues should be classified by appropriate category in the general ledger accounts (e.g., Operating Expenses—Nursing Services *or* Nursing Services Expense; Other Revenues—Cafeteria Sales or Cafeteria Sales Revenues) as illustrated for nonoperating gains and losses in later entries.

e. **To record gifts and donations received:**

Cash or Other Assets (e.g., Pharmacy Inventory)	$ 500	
Nonoperating Gains—Unrestricted Contributions		$ 500
Cash or Other Assets (e.g., Investments)	$7,500	
Deferred Revenues—Specified Operating Purpose(s)		$7,500

(This entry assumes restricted, reimbursement-type government grants or similar donations for which eligibility requirements are not met yet.)

Cash or Other Assets (e.g., Investments or Capital Assets)	$8,000	
Liabilities (if any are assumed)		$1,500
Revenues—Endowment X		6,500
Cash or Other Assets (e.g., Investments)	$9,000	
Deferred Revenues—Capital Purpose(s)		$9,000

(This entry assumes restricted, reimbursement-type government grants or similar donations for which eligibility requirements are not met yet.)

Note: Assets restricted for endowment and assets restricted for capital asset purposes are reported as separate line items.

f. **To record operating expenses incurred for specified purposes for which restricted grant monies are available and are used:**

Operating Expenses	$1,600	
Cash or Payables		$1,600
Deferred Revenues—Specified Operating Purposes	$1,600	
Nonoperating Revenues—Operating Contributions		$1,600

g. **To record capital outlays made from the capital gift or grant:**

Deferred Revenues—Capital Purpose(s)	$8,000	
Revenues—Capital Contributions		$8,000
Land	$1,500	
Buildings	4,000	
Equipment	2,500	
Cash or Payables		$8,000

h. **To record sales of hospital capital assets:**

Cash or Receivables	$3,700	
Accumulated Depreciation	6,000	
Land		$1,200
Equipment		7,800
Gain (loss) on Disposal of Capital Assets		700

i. **To record donations of pharmacy supplies:**

Inventory of Pharmacy Supplies	$300	
Gains—Donated Commodities		$300

j. **To record designation by the hospital board of directors of certain unrestricted assets for specified operating and capital purposes:**

Assets Whose Use is Limited—Cash—Designated	$750	
Cash		$750

Government College and University Accounting and Reporting

2450.13 The GASB issued Statement 35, *Basic Financial Statements—and Management's Discussion and Analysis—for Colleges and Universities,* in November 1999. GASB Statement 35 requires government colleges and universities to apply GASB Statement 34. This section discusses and illustrates the key aspects of government college and university reporting requirements. Section **2500** discusses accounting and reporting for nongovernment not-for-profit organizations, including colleges and universities.

2450.14 **Special purpose government guidance.** GASB Statement 35 treats government colleges and universities as special purpose governments. Most government colleges and universities will be treated as being engaged only in business-type activities. Because tuition and fees are essentially user charges and are a principal revenue source of most colleges and universities, most government colleges and universities will at least have the option of reporting as enterprise activities under the enterprise fund definition in GASB Statement 34. Special purpose governments engaged in only business-type (enterprise) activities are only required to present proprietary fund financial statements, MD&A, notes to the financial statements, and other required supplementary information.

Government colleges and universities that do not apply the business-type activity only model must present the government-wide financial statements and all applicable fund financial statements in their basic financial statements.

Some community colleges do not apply the enterprise fund model.

Institutions Engaged Only in Business-Type Activities

2450.15 **Reporting requirements.** Government colleges and universities engaged only in business-type activities should present only the proprietary fund financial statements. Most major four-year institutions use this reporting approach. These institutions are required to present the following:

   a. Management's discussion and analysis

   b. Balance sheet (or statement of net assets)

   c. Statement of revenues, expenses, and changes in net assets

   d. Statement of cash flows (direct method)

   e. Notes to the financial statements

   f. Required supplementary information

2450.16 **Key points** to be aware of for colleges and universities under this approach include the following:

   a. Tuition and fee revenues should be reported net of scholarship allowances and net of uncollectible amounts. This is true for all government colleges and universities.

   b. Operating revenues may include grants and contracts as a revenue source. Presumably, the substance of these amounts is better reflected by the term contract—implying an exchange or exchange-like transaction—than by the term grant. Many research grants fit this description. Operating grants (and gifts) are nonoperating revenues. Capital gifts and grants are reported after nonoperating revenues (expenses).

   c. Auxiliary enterprise revenues are separately identified under operating revenues.

   d. Revenues from state appropriations for other than capital-asset-related purposes are nonoperating revenues.

   e. Revenues from capital appropriations are reported as capital contributions, like capital gifts and grants.

   f. Additions to permanent endowments are reported after nonoperating revenues and expenses, like capital gifts and grants.

   g. Special items and extraordinary items should be reported as for other government proprietary funds.

   h. Endowments are reported as a separate line item in noncurrent assets. GASB Statement 52, *Land and Other Real Estate Held as Investments by Endowments,* requires real estate held by endowments to be reported at fair value and for changes in fair value to be reported in the changes in net assets. This statement makes the reporting of these assets consistent with their reporting when held in pension trusts and external investment pools.

i. Typical university revenues and expenses classifications are presented in the chart as follows.

Revenues	Expenses
Tuition and Fees Appropriations (by source, e.g., state) Grants and Contracts (by source, e.g., federal) Private Gifts, Grants, and Contracts Endowment Income Sales and Services of Educational Activities (e.g., testing services) Auxiliary Enterprises (e.g., residence halls, food service, athletic programs, hospitals) Other	Educational and General are classified by function (e.g., Instruction, Research, Public Services, Academic Support, Student Services, Institutional Support, Operation and Maintenance of Plant, Scholarships and Fellowships) Auxiliary Enterprises (e.g., as in Revenues classifications at left) Other

The statements required for institutions engaged only in business-type activities are outlined in Exhibit 18. Several of these key points can be observed in the exhibit on the following page.

Exhibit 18

College and University Balance Sheet		
	Primary Institution	**Component Units**

Assets (list)
  Current assets
  Noncurrent assets:
    Includes assets held in permanent endowments
Liabilities (list)
  Current liabilities
  Long-term liabilities:
Net assets:
  Invested in capital assets, net of related debt
  Restricted net assets
  Unrestricted net assets
	Economic Resources Measurement Focus and Accrual Basis (Revenues & Expenses)	

College and University Operating Statement		
	Primary Institution	**Component Units**

Operating revenues (detailed)
  Student tuition and fees (net of scholarship allowances and other tuition and fee waivers)
  Federal grants and contracts
  Auxiliary enterprises:
    Residential life (net of . . .)
    Bookstores (net of . . .)
Operating expenses (detailed)
 	
Operating income
 	
Nonoperating revenues and expenses (detailed)
  State appropriations
  Operating grants
  Gifts
  Investment income
  Interest expense
Income before other revenues, expenses, and transfers
  Capital appropriations
  Capital grants and gifts
  Additions to permanent endowments
  Special items
  Extraordinary items
Increase (decrease) in net assets
 	
Net assets—beginning
Net assets—ending
	Economic Resources Measurement Focus and Accrual Basis (Revenues & Expenses)	

(continued on next page)

Exhibit 18 continued

College and University Statement of Cash Flows		
	Primary Institution	Component Units
Cash flows from **operating activities** *Direct method required* (detailed)		
Cash flows from **noncapital financing activities** (detailed) Includes state appropriations other than for capital asset purposes		
Cash flows from **capital and related financing activities** (detailed) Includes state appropriations for capital asset purposes		
Cash flows from **investing activities** (detailed)		
Net increase (decrease) in cash		
Cash—beginning Cash—ending		

2450.17 **Institutions Engaged in Both Governmental and Business-Type Activities:** Applying the GASB Statement 34 model to colleges and universities engaged in both governmental activities and in business-type activities is more complex, as is applying the model to institutions engaged only in governmental activities. (The latter case is unusual and simply means there are no proprietary activities and therefore no proprietary fund financial statements as well as no business-type activities column in the government-wide statements.) In addition to the key facts pointed out in the previous section, these institutions will:

a. use the same fund structure as other governments and

b. prepare the same financial statements required for general purpose governments.

Because the same guidance applies to these universities as to other governments, we do not discuss this situation further. Many community colleges report as institutions engaged in both governmental and business-type activities.

2450.18 **Illustrative Entries:** The following transaction descriptions and entries illustrate the most important aspects of accounting for government universities.

a. **To record tuition and fee revenues earned during the year, tuition and fee waivers awarded, and tuition and fee collections that are applicable to the next fiscal year:**

Cash	$6,000	
Accounts Receivable	4,000	
Deductions from Revenues—Educational and General	700	
Revenues—Tuition and Fees		$9,700
Deferred Revenues—Educational and General		1,000

Notes:

(1) Tuition and fee revenues are reported net of scholarship allowances and net of uncollectible amounts. Tuition reductions or waivers provided as a benefit of employment—to faculty and staff or to graduate students performing teaching or research activities for pay—are reported as expenses. They are not treated as scholarship allowances.

(2) The Deferred Revenues will be recognized as revenues at the beginning of the next fiscal year.

b. **To record estimated uncollectible receivables:**

Deductions from Revenue—Educational and General	$800	
Allowance for Uncollectible Accounts		$800

Notes:

(1) Estimated uncollectible accounts (bad debts) are deducted from revenues.

(2) The uncollectible accounts written off are debited to the Allowance for Uncollectible Accounts.

c. **To record revenues earned during the year other than from tuition and fees:**

Cash	$4,200	
Accounts Receivable	3,300	
Due from State Government	2,500	
Revenues—Auxiliary Enterprises		$5,900
Revenues—State Appropriations		2,400
Revenues—Private Gifts, Grants, and Contracts		600
Revenues—Other		1,100

d. **To record expenses incurred during the year:**

Expenses—Educational and General	$9,200	
Expenses—Auxiliary Enterprises	5,000	
Expenses—Other	3,000	
Cash		$6,200
Accounts Payable		8,000
Inventories		3,000

e. **To record expenditures for capital outlay purposes:**

Equipment	$1,800	
Cash		$1,800

f. **To record unrestricted interest and endowment income:**

Cash (or Accrued Interest Receivable)	$6,000	
Revenues—Interest Income		$2,800
Revenues—Endowment Income		3,200

g. **To record financial resources restricted for operating purposes received and accrued during the year:**

Cash	$5,500	
Accounts Receivable	4,500	
Due from Federal Government	7,000	
Deferred Revenues—Operating Grants and Contributions*		$17,000

* Assumes that eligibility requirements for revenue recognition have not been met.

h. **To record expenses incurred for restricted operating purposes:**

Expenses—Auxiliary Enterprises	$8,000	
Expenses—Educational and General	9,500	
Cash		$7,700
Accounts Payable		9,800

i. **To recognize revenues earned by incurring expenses for restricted operating purposes:**

Deferred Revenues—Operating Grants and Contributions	$17,500	
Revenues—Auxiliary Enterprises		$8,000
Revenues—Private Gifts, Grants, and Contracts		900
Revenues—Federal Grants and Contracts		6,000
Revenues—Endowment Income		2,600

Section 2500
Not-for-Profit (Nongovernmental) Accounting and Reporting

2501 Not-for-Profit (Nongovernmental) Accounting and Reporting

2510 Financial Statements
- 2511 Statement of Financial Position
- 2512 Statement of Activities
- 2513 Statement of Cash Flows
- 2514 Statement of Functional Expenses

2520 Typical Items and Specific Types of Transactions and Events: Recognition, Measurement, Valuation, Calculation, and Presentation in the Financial Statements of Not-for-Profit Organizations
- 2521 Support, Revenues, and Contributions
- 2522 Types of Restrictions on Resources
- 2523 Types of Net Assets
- 2524 Expenses, Including Depreciation and Functional Expenses
- 2525 Investments
- 2526 Nongovernment Not-for-Profit Hospital and University Reporting

2501 Not-for-Profit (Nongovernmental) Accounting and Reporting

Nonbusiness Accounting Standards-Setting

2501.01 The FASB is the predominant accounting standards-setter for nonbusiness organizations *other than governments*.

2501.02 The effective not-for-profit organization-specific guidance is codified in Section 958 of the FASB's Accounting Standards Codification (ASC) and is discussed in the following material.

2501.03 While the FASB attempts to minimize the differences, GAAP applicable to nonbusiness organizations differ significantly from those applicable to business enterprises. Moreover, applicable GAAP differ significantly among the various types of nonbusiness organizations (e.g., between government hospitals—see sections **2450.01–.12**—and nongovernment hospitals, and between government educational institutions—see sections **2450.13–.18**—and nongovernment educational institutions).

Introduction to Nongovernment Not-for-Profit Accounting and Reporting

2501.04 The focus of reporting is on providing basic information for the organization as a whole, therefore, nongovernment VHWO/ONPO reporting, as well as reporting for not-for-profit hospitals, colleges and universities, etc., is based primarily on FASB ASC 958. Next to state and local government accounting and financial reporting, questions related to these requirements are the most likely for this part of the CPA Examination. The philosophy underlying the FASB NPO guidance is that accounting and reporting for these organizations should differ from that for businesses only when necessary. *The same basic requirements discussed and illustrated in this section apply also to nongovernment not-for-profit health care entities and nongovernment not-for-profit colleges and universities.* Some unique reporting options for nongovernment not-for-profit health care entities are discussed in section **2526**.

2501.05 Fund accounting is permitted, but not required. It seems doubtful that the VHWO/ONPO fund structure will be tested in the nongovernment not-for-profit organization context; therefore, it is not reviewed here.

Definitions and Examples

2501.06 **Voluntary health and welfare organizations (VHWOs)** provide services to the general public or to certain segments of society—for no fee or a low fee—and are supported primarily by public contributions. Examples include the United Way and similar community fund-raising organizations, YMCA and YWCA, Boy Scouts and Girl Scouts, Big Brothers-Big Sisters, and most other human services and social service organizations.

2501.07 **Other not-for-profit organizations (ONPOs)** include all other nonbusiness organizations, *except*:

    a. state and local governments, hospitals and other health care organizations, colleges and universities, and voluntary health and welfare organizations and

    b. entities that operate essentially as commercial businesses for the direct economic benefit of stockholders or members (e.g., mutual insurance companies or farm cooperatives).

The following types of organizations are among those classified as other not-for-profit organizations (ONPOs):

- Civic organizations
- Labor unions
- Political parties
- Fraternal organizations
- Religious organizations
- Libraries
- Museums
- Professional associations
- Cemetery organizations
- Performing arts organizations
- Other cultural institutions
- Private and community foundations
- Private elementary and secondary schools
- Public broadcasting stations
- Research and scientific organizations
- Zoological and botanical societies

2510 Financial Statements

2510.01 **Nongovernment VHWO/ONPO Financial Statements:** VHWO/ONPO accounting and reporting are best understood in the context of VHWO/ONPO financial statements.

Four primary financial statements are required for a nongovernment VHWO/ONPO:

1. Statement of Financial Position (Balance sheet)
2. Statement of activities
3. Statement of cash flows
4. Statement of functional expenses (optional for ONPOs)

Each of these statements is discussed and illustrated in the following sections.

2511 Statement of Financial Position

2511.01 Several key features should be noted with respect to the VHWO/ONPO statement of position (balance sheet), which is illustrated in Exhibit 1 (section **2511.02**).

2511.02 Observe the following in the illustrative statement of position in Exhibit 1.

a. Net assets are classified into three required categories (discussed at section **2523**).

b. An organization's assets and liabilities are not reported by net asset classes. Thus, the classifications in the net assets section are the primary means for communicating donor restrictions on resource use.

c. Most assets and liabilities are reported in the same manner they would be reported for a for-profit entity.

d. Cash, investments, and other assets restricted for plant asset purposes are reported as a separate line item (distinguished from other cash and investments, etc.). Likewise, cash, investments, and other assets restricted for endowment purposes are reported as a separate line item.

Exhibit 1

Not-for-Profit Organization **Statements of Financial Position** June 30, 20X1 and 20X0 (in thousands)		
	20X1	20X0
Assets:		
Cash and cash equivalents	$ 75	$ 460
Accounts and interest receivable	2,130	1,670
Inventories and prepaid expenses	610	1,000
Contributions receivable	3,025	2,700
Short-term investments	1,400	1,000
Assets restricted to investment in land, buildings, and equipment	5,210	4,560
Land, buildings, and equipment	61,700	63,590
Long-term investments	218,070	203,500
Total assets	$292,220	$278,480
Liabilities and net assets:		
Accounts payable	$ 2,570	$ 1,050
Refundable advance		650
Grants payable	875	1,300
Notes payable		1,140
Annuity obligations	1,685	1,700
Long-term debt	5,500	6,500
Total liabilities	$ 10,630	$ 12,340
Net assets:		
Unrestricted	$115,228	$103,670
Temporarily restricted	24,342	25,470
Permanently restricted	142,020	137,000
Total net assets	281,590	266,140
Total liabilities and net assets	$292,220	$278,480

Source: Financial Accounting Standards Board, Accounting Standards Codification, Section 958-205-55-7.

 e. The FASB guidance established in FASB ASC 320 provides that:

  (1) investments in debt securities are reported at market value,

  (2) investments in equity securities with readily determinable market values are reported at market value,

  (3) other investments may be reported at cost or at lower of cost or market, and

  (4) investment gains and losses are reported as changes in unrestricted net assets unless their use is temporarily or permanently restricted by explicit donor stipulations or by law.

 f. **Pledges receivable** are reported at the present value of the expected cash flows from pledges, except that those collectible within a year may be recorded at net realizable value. Pledges are *unconditional promises* to reduce liabilities of or to contribute assets to an organization. Conditional promises to give are *not* recorded as pledges until the conditions are met or the likelihood of their not being met becomes remote.

 g. Collections are works of art and historical treasures that meet three criteria:

  (1) Held for public exhibition, education, or research—not for financial gain

  (2) Protected, kept unencumbered, cared for, and preserved

(3) Policy requires sale proceeds to be used to acquire other collection items

    h. Three options for reporting collections (certain works of art and historical treasures) are permitted by the FASB:

        (1) Capitalize all collections purchased or donated (and recognize contributions revenue equal to the fair value of collections that are donated).

        (2) Capitalize collections purchased or donated after the effective date of the FASB's guidance on accounting for collections (and recognize contributions revenue equal to the fair value of such collections that are donated).

        (3) Do not capitalize collections. (No contributions would be reported for donated collections, and expenses would be reported for purchases of collections.)

    i. Unrestricted net assets may be subclassified. For example, the net amount invested in fixed assets may be reported and net assets to be used for specific purposes may be indicated using designations of unrestricted net assets.

    j. A merger of two not-for-profit entities (in which a new not-for-profit entity is established by the merger of the two previous entities) is accounted for by carrying forward the existing assets and liabilities of the merging entities to the books of the new entity. When a not-for-profit entity acquires another entity, acquisition accounting is used with limited variations from business guidance for an acquisition. The most significant difference is that the amount that normally should be reported as goodwill must be expensed *if* contributions are the primary source of support for the operations of the acquired entity as part of the combined entity.

2512 Statement of Activities

2512.01 The primary nongovernment VHWO/ONPO operating statement is the statement of activities. Alternatively, an organization can present a statement of operations, accompanied by a separate statement of changes in net assets. The statement of operations, which only includes changes in unrestricted net assets, reports (1) an operations subtotal such as operating income and/or excess of revenues over expenses and (2) other changes in unrestricted net assets. A statement of operations must be accompanied by a statement of changes in net assets (reporting all net asset classes). Since this alternative approach is required by an audit guide for nongovernment, not-for-profit hospitals, it is illustrated for a hospital in the next section (**2512.02**).

Several key features of accounting for not-for-profit organizations relate to this statement. (Several of these features can be observed easily in the illustrative statement of activities in Exhibit 2, section **2512.02**.)

2512.02 Key features to note in Exhibit 2 include the following:

    a. The statement is presented in three major sections, which could be reflected using three separate columns rather than the layered approach in the exhibit.

    b. Each section presents the changes in one of the net asset classes.

    c. To accommodate this presentation, each revenue, gain, and loss must be classified according to the net asset class affected.

    d. *All expenses* are reported as *changes in unrestricted net assets.*

        (1) Revenues and expenses must be reported at gross amounts.

        (2) Gains and losses may be reported at gross or at net amounts.

Exhibit 2, Part A: Layered Format for Statement of Activities

Not-for-Profit Organization
Statement of Activities
Year Ended June 30, 20X1
(in thousands)

Changes in unrestricted net assets:	
Revenues and gains:	
Contributions	$8,640
Fees	5,400
Income on long-term investments	5,600
Other investment income	850
Net unrealized and realized gains on long-term investments	8,228
Other	150
Total unrestricted revenues and gains	28,868
Net assets released from restrictions:	
Satisfaction of program restrictions	11,990
Satisfaction of equipment acquisition restrictions	1,500
Expiration of time restrictions	1,250
Total net assets released from restrictions	14,740
Total unrestricted revenues, gains, and other support	43,608
Expenses and losses:	
Program A	13,100
Program B	8,540
Program C	5,760
Management and general	2,420
Fund raising	2,150
Total expenses	31,970
Fire loss	80
Total expenses and losses	32,050
Increase in unrestricted net assets	11,558
Changes in temporarily restricted net assets:	
Contributions	8,110
Income on long-term investments	2,580
Net unrealized and realized gains on long-term investments	2,952
Actuarial loss on annuity obligations	(30)
Net assets released from restrictions	(14,740)
Decrease in temporarily restricted net assets	(1,128)
Changes in permanently restricted net assets:	
Contributions	280
Income on long-term investments	120
Net unrealized and realized gains on long-term investments	4,620
Increase in permanently restricted net assets	5,020
Increase in net assets	15,450
Net assets at beginning of year	266,140
Net assets at end of year	$281,590

Source: Financial Accounting Standards Board, Accounting Standards Codification, Section 958-205-55-13.

Exhibit 2, Part B: Columnar Format for Statement of Activities

THE AMERICAN RED CROSS
Consolidated Statement of Activities
Year Ended June 30, 2006
(with summarized information for the year ended June 30, 2005)
(in thousands)

	Unrestricted	Temporarily Restricted	Permanently Restricted	Totals 2006	Totals 2005
Operating revenues and gains:					
Contributions:					
Corporate, foundation and individual giving	$ 258,002	$2,387,042	$ -	$2,645,044	$ 976,674
United Way and other federated	60,025	102,275	-	162,300	158,990
Legacies and bequests	59,666	9,609	23,412	92,687	118,235
Services and materials	25,126	213,215	-	238,341	67,594
Grants	33,520	40,932	-	74,452	55,766
Products and services:					
Biomedical	2,165,172	-	-	2,165,172	2,137,209
Program materials	141,300	387	-	141,687	149,432
Contracts, including federal government:	311,435	-	-	311,435	83,307
Investment income	108,570	1,409	-	109,979	68,615
Other revenues	67,528	-	-	67,528	103,435
Net assets released from restrictions	2,517,098	(2,517,098)	-	-	-
Total operating revenues and gains	5,747,442	237,771	23,412	6,008,625	3,919,257
Operating expenses:					
Program services:					
Armed Forces Emergency Services	54,096	-	-	54,096	58,646
Biomedical services	2,103,572	-	-	2,103,572	2,161,078
Community services	133,467	-	-	133,467	128,548
Domestic disaster services	2,630,766	-	-	2,630,766	411,187
Health and safety services	224,594	-	-	224,594	220,385
International relief and development services	154,283	-	-	154,283	157,132
Total program services	5,300,778	-	-	5,300,778	3,136,976
Supporting services:					
Fund raising	140,082	-	-	140,082	118,568
Management and general	187,249	-	-	187,249	172,325
Total supporting services	327,331	-	-	327,331	290,893
Total operating expenses	5,628,109	-	-	5,628,109	3,427,869
Change in net assets from operations	119,333	237,771	23,412	380,516	491,388
Nonoperating gains	62,804	856	796	64,456	48,222
Additional minimum pension liability	94,470	-	-	94,470	(94,470)
Change in net assets	276,607	238,627	24,208	539,442	445,140
Net assets, beginning of year	1,319,460	856,594	470,067	2,646,121	2,200,981
Net assets, end of year	$1,596,067	$1,095,221	$494,275	$3,185,563	$2,646,121

Note: While the FASB illustrates the layered format, the columnar format is an equally acceptable alternative. It is included here because some of the key features of the report are more apparent—such as the fact that expenses are reported only in changes in unrestricted net assets and the equality of the increase in unrestricted net assets and decrease in temporarily restricted net assets resulting from satisfying temporary restrictions.

2513 Statement of Cash Flows

2513.01 The statement of cash flows is extremely similar to a business cash flow statement. The primary modifications are as follows:

   a. The indirect method of reporting cash flows from operating activities reconciles the change in net assets (rather than net income) to cash flows from operating activities.

   b. Cash flows for contributions and investment earnings that are restricted for either plant or endowment purposes are reported as financing activities.

2514 Statement of Functional Expenses

2514.01 Functional Expenses

   a. The statement of functional expenses represents the natural (or object class) detailed expense classification for the expenses incurred for each functional purpose. The statement is required for nongovernment VHWOs, but is optional for other nongovernment not-for-profit organizations.

   b. A skeleton statement of functional expenses is presented in Exhibit 3.

Exhibit 3

	VHWO Statement of Functional Expenses (Heading) (in $ thousands)							
	Program Services				**Supporting Services**			**Total**
	Research	Education	Community Services	Total	Management and General	Fund Raising	Total	
Salaries	XX	XX	XX	XX	XX	XX	XX	XX
Employee benefits	XX	XX	XX	XX	XX	XX	XX	XX
Payroll taxes	XX	XX	XX	XX	XX	XX	XX	XX
...	...	...	...	...	...	...	...	...
Total	XX	XX	XX	XX	XX	XX	XX	XX
Professional fees and contractual services	XX	XX	XX	XX	XX	XX	XX	XX
Supplies	XX	XX	XX	XX	XX	XX	XX	XX
Telephone	XX	XX	XX	XX	XX	XX	XX	XX
...	...	...	...	...	...	...	...	...
Misc.	XX	XX	XX	XX	XX	XX	XX	XX
Depreciation	XX	XX	XX	XX	XX	XX	XX	XX
Total expenses	765	320	160	1,245	50	115	165	1,410

2520 Typical Items and Specific Types of Transactions and Events: Recognition, Measurement, Valuation, Calculation, and Presentation in the Financial Statements of Not-for-Profit Organizations

2521 Support, Revenues, and Contributions

2521.01 Contribution revenues (support) from gifts, grants, bequests, and so on are reported in the period they are unconditionally promised or received, whichever is earlier. Revenues are measured at the present value (or net realizable value for any contributions expected to be received within a year after the unconditional promise was made).

2521.02 Recognition of contribution revenues is *not* deferred because donations are permanently restricted or temporarily restricted.

2521.03 Revenues are recognized in the period that unconditional pledges are made. Unrestricted pledges to be collected in the subsequent period or periods are reported as changes in temporarily restricted net assets because they are considered to have a time restriction. (This restriction is presumed unless the donor specified that the pledge was intended to finance current-period activities.)

2521.04 Contributions must be distinguished from exchange transactions since the revenue recognition criteria are different for the two. Some items (e.g., membership dues) are exchange transactions for some organizations, contributions for others, and part exchange transaction and part contribution for still other organizations. (Membership dues are exchange transactions to the extent that the organization provides benefits or services to the members.)

2521.05 VHWOs and ONPOs that report revenues for special fund-raising events must report those revenues at the gross amount raised. Direct costs of holding the event must be reported separately either as direct deductions from special event revenues or in the expenses section of the statement of activities.

2521.06 Contribution revenues should be reported for the fair value of donated materials and for free use of facilities or other assets. Expenses should be reported upon use of the materials or facilities.

2521.07 Contribution revenues and either assets or expenses should be reported for donated services that create or enhance nonfinancial assets *or* if the following three conditions are met:

    a. Specialized skills are required to perform the services.

    b. The individuals donating the services possess those skills.

    c. The organization would have to buy the services if they were not donated.

2521.08 Investment income, including unrealized gains and losses on investments reported at fair value, is reported as changes in unrestricted net assets unless there are donor restrictions on the use of the investment income.

2521.09 Some organizations receive cash or other financial assets as an intermediary for others. The FASB requires these contributions to be reported as contribution revenues by the intermediary organization if the intermediary is given the explicit, unilateral right to redirect the use of the transferred assets to parties other than the specified beneficiaries. If the intermediary and the beneficiary are financially interrelated, contribution revenues must be recognized also. The revenues equal the fair value of the assets received. If revenue is not to be reported, an agency liability should normally be reported.

2521.10 A temporary "time" restriction on a portion of net assets is satisfied by passage of time. A temporary "use" restriction on the purpose for which donated resources may be used is satisfied by expending resources for the restricted purpose. When temporary restrictions are satisfied, *"net assets released from restrictions"* are reported as an increase in the changes in unrestricted net assets section and as a decrease in the changes in temporarily restricted net assets section. (Nongovernment, not-for-profit health care entities report net assets released from restrictions as part of revenues, gains, and other support unless the restriction is for fixed asset purposes. Health care entities report net assets released from restrictions for fixed asset purposes as changes in unrestricted net assets, but after the excess of revenues over expenses.)

2522 Types of Restrictions on Resources

2522.01 Only restrictions imposed by donors or grantors are considered restrictions in accounting for not-for-profit organizations. Constraints on use of resources imposed by contracts with lenders, third-party payors, or others do not constitute restrictions in applying not-for-profit GAAP.

2522.02 Donor and grantor restrictions may be time restrictions or use restrictions. Restrictions that can be satisfied by the passage of time or by using the resources for a certain purpose (to finance expenses of a specific program or to construct a building, for example) are called temporary restrictions. Restrictions that cannot be fulfilled by either the passage of time or actions of the organization are known as permanent restrictions. The most common example of a permanent restriction is the requirement that the principal of an endowment gift be maintained intact in perpetuity.

2522.03 Revenues are classified into those that contribute to permanently restricted net assets, those that contribute to temporarily restricted net assets, and those that increase unrestricted net assets. Expenses are always reported as changes in unrestricted net assets.

2523 Types of Net Assets

2523.01 A not-for-profit organization classifies its net assets (and changes in net assets) into three categories. The three classes of net assets are:

1. **Permanently restricted net assets:** The portion of net assets whose use is limited by donor-imposed restrictions that are permanent in nature (i.e., the restrictions cannot be fulfilled by either passage of time or by actions of the not-for-profit organization)

2. **Temporarily restricted net assets:** The portion of net assets whose use is limited by donor-imposed restrictions on the *timing* of use *or purpose* of use of the donated resources

3. **Unrestricted net assets:** The portion of net assets *not* temporarily or permanently restricted

2523.02 Temporarily restricted net asset amounts are reclassified as unrestricted net assets when the related restriction is satisfied. Permanently restricted net assets are never reclassified because the restrictions cannot be fully satisfied.

2524 Expenses, Including Depreciation and Functional Expenses

2524.01 Expenses are recognized essentially as for business organizations. All expenses must be reported as changes in unrestricted net assets and classified as either program services expenses (by function) or supporting services expenses:

a. **Program services expenses:** Costs incurred in carrying out its primary missions, these expenses are subclassified by function.

b. **Supporting services expenses** are further clearly separated between:

(1) management and general expenses and

(2) fund-raising expenses.

The costs of benefits provided to donors may be reported as a separate line item under supporting services expenses.

2524.02 Fund-raising costs are incurred to induce individuals and organizations to contribute money, securities, real estate, or other properties, materials, or services to the organization. Identifying fund-raising costs can be controversial when fund-raising efforts are combined with efforts to provide educational materials or program services. Costs of such joint activities as fund-raising telethons and mailings are *required to be reported as fund raising activities unless three conditions are met*:

1. One or more of the *purposes* of the activity is to accomplish some program function or management and general responsibility of the organization.

2. The *audience* for the activity was chosen based on some criteria other than the ability to make contributions.

3. The activity motivates the audience to take specific *actions* other than making contributions and these actions support the program goals or fulfill a management and general responsibility of the organization.

Also, recall that direct costs of special fund-raising events are permitted to be reported as direct deductions to the special event revenues.

2525 Investments

2525.01 The FASB guidance on accounting for investments of not-for-profits provides that:

a. investments in debt securities are reported at market value,

b. investments in equity securities with readily determinable market values are reported at market value,

c. other investments may be reported at cost or at lower of cost or market, and

d. investment gains and losses are reported as changes in unrestricted net assets unless their use is temporarily or permanently restricted by explicit donor stipulations or by law.

2525.02 Not-for-profits that present a separate statement of operations may distinguish between investment income that is included in computing the operations total and that which is not using several approaches:

a. Based on the nature of the underlying transactions, realized amounts could qualify as operating and unrealized amounts as nonoperating.

b. The portion of investment income computed under a total return policy could be reported as operating and the remainder as nonoperating.

c. Changes in fair value of trading securities and other investment income amounts that affect net income of a business could be reported as operating and the remainder as nonoperating.

2526 Nongovernment Not-for-Profit Hospital and University Reporting

Nongovernment Not-for-Profit Hospital Reporting

2526.01 Nongovernment not-for-profit hospitals are reported in accordance with the guidance for other not-for-profit organizations presented in sections **2510–2525**. The primary uniquenesses are discussed next.

Balance sheet. The balance sheet for a not-for-profit hospital is very similar to the government hospital balance sheet in Exhibit 16 (section **2450.05**). The primary difference is that net assets are reported using the three net asset classes required by the FASB—unrestricted, temporarily restricted, and permanently restricted—rather than the government net asset classifications. The presentation of the assets whose use is limited classification is illustrated in Exhibit 16 and discussed in section **2450.05**.

2526.02 **The presentation of a separate statement of operations and a separate statement of changes in net assets instead of a statement of activities.** This alternative is permitted by the FASB for all nongovernment not-for-profits and is required for health care organizations by the AICPA's *Health Care Organizations* Audit and Accounting Guide.

2526.03 The not-for-profit hospital statement of operations is illustrated in Exhibit 4 (section **2526.05**). Note in particular that only changes in unrestricted net assets are reported in this statement. Also, net assets released from restrictions for the purchase of property, plant, and equipment are reported after the excess of revenues over expenses.

2526.04 The not-for-profit hospital statement of changes in net assets presents changes in all three net asset classes as illustrated in Exhibit 5 (section **2526.05**). The changes in unrestricted net assets are in summary form, beginning with the excess of revenues over expenses reported in the statement of operations. The total changes in unrestricted net assets are the same as reported in the statement of operations. The changes in temporarily restricted net assets and changes in permanently restricted net assets sections are exactly the same as they would have appeared in a statement of activities.

2526.05 The reporting of patient service revenues was discussed in a previous section, as noted in Exhibit 4.

Exhibit 4

Sample Not-For-Profit Hospital **Statement of Operations** Year Ended December 31, 20X0 (in thousands)	
	20X0
Unrestricted revenues, gains, and other support:	
Net patient service revenue*	XX
Premium revenue*	XX
Investment income	XX
Other revenue	XX
Net assets released from restrictions used for operations	300
Total revenues, gains, and other support	XX
Expenses:	
Operating expenses	XX
Depreciation and amortization	XX
Interest	XX
Provision for bad debts	XX
Other	XX
Total expenses	XX
Excess of revenues over expenses	XX
Change in net unrealized gains and losses on other than trading securities	XX
Net assets released from restrictions used for purchase of property and equipment	200
Increase in unrestricted net assets	XX

* Discussed in sections **2450.01–.12** and reported the same as for government hospitals, except that uncollectible accounts are not deducted. Bad debts are reported as expenses. A recent FASB Accounting Standards Update requires the disclosure of the level of charity care provided be based on cost and that the method of determining the cost must be disclosed. Cost must include both direct and indirect costs of providing charity care.

Exhibit 5

Sample Not-For-Profit Hospital
Statement of Changes in Net Assets
Year Ended December 31, 20X0
(in thousands)

	20X0
Unrestricted net assets:	
Excess of revenues over expenses*	XX
Net assets released from restrictions used for purchase of property and equipment	200
Increase in unrestricted net assets	XX
Temporarily restricted net assets:	
Contributions for charity care	XX
Contributions for cancer research	XX
Net realized and unrealized gains on investments	XX
Net assets released from restrictions	(500)
Increase (decrease) in temporarily restricted net assets	XX
Permanently restricted net assets:	
Contributions for endowment funds	XX
Net realized and unrealized gains on investments	XX
Increase in permanently restricted net assets	XX
Increase in net assets	XX
Net assets, beginning of year	XX
Net assets, end of year	XX

See accompanying notes to financial statements.
* Includes net assets released from restrictions for operations of $300.

Nongovernment Not-for-Profit University Reporting

2526.06 Accounting and reporting for nongovernment not-for-profit colleges and universities must follow the same guidance discussed for other nongovernment not-for-profit organizations (discussed earlier in section **2500**).

2526.07 Unlike hospitals, no differences in financial statement format and approach have been mandated for not-for-profit colleges and universities. A statement of activities may be presented. Alternatively, a statement of operations and a statement of changes in net assets may be presented. The balance sheet and the statement of cash flows follow the same guidelines discussed in sections **2511** and **2513**.

2526.08 Not-for-profit colleges and universities report tuition and fees revenues net of scholarship allowances—just as required for government institutions (section **2450.18(a), Note 1**).

2526.09 The functional classifications used to report expenses are the same as those discussed at section **2450.16(i)**.

2526.10 The statements are not illustrated here because of their similarity to the statements in sections **2511–2514** for other not-for-profit organizations.

Index

A

Accounting and reporting by defined benefit pension plans, 2264.44–.47
Accounting changes, 2305
    change in accounting estimate, 2305.27–.40
    change in accounting principle, 2305.04–.23
    change in reporting entity, 2305.41–.43
    corrections of errors, 2305.44–.56
    cumulative effect of, 2305.11, .13, .15, .17, & .24–.25
Accounting for costs at acquisition, 2230.23–.26
Accounting policy disclosure, 2136.04–.07
Accounting principles, 2100
Accounting Standards Codification (ASC), 2112.12–.17
Accounting standards, development of, 2112.18–.19
Accounting for uncertainty in income taxes, 2270.20–.21
Accounts receivable, 2211
    assignment, 2393.15
    factoring, 2393.07
    pledging, 2211.13
    sale of, 2393.01–.13
Accrual accounting, 2112.09, 2411.14
Accumulated benefit obligation, 2263.01–.03
Acquisition, 2315.04
Acquisition method, 2315.12–.32
Actuarial assumptions, 2264.05
Amortization
    of bond premium/discount, 2225.41
    of intangible assets, 2230.34–.40
Additional paid-in capital, 2250.04
Agency funds, 2412.40–.43
Application of judgment (GAAP), 2112.11
Appropriations, 2411.10–.13, 2412.03–.06
Arbitrage, 2412.12
Articulation of financial statements, 2121.17 & .20
Assets, 2121.15, 2131.09
    capital, 2443
    infrastructure, 2443
    net, 2441
Assignment, 2393.15
Available-for-sale securities, 2222.01–.02

B

Balance sheet
    format, 2131
    IFRS, 2131.07 & .12
    overview, 2131
Bank reconciliations, 2210.06–.13
Bankruptcy, 2224.34–.40
Basic earnings per share, 2335.10
Bond(s)
    convertible, 2225.67–.82, 2243.01
    discount/premium, 2242.03
    effective interest, 2242.02
    investment in, 2225.39–.48
    serial, 2242.09–.17
    warrants, 2243.02–.05
Bond anticipation notes, 2412.11
Book value method, 2225.69 & .73–.74
Book value per share, 2250.56–.59
Budget, governmental, 2411.02 & .10–.13
Budgetary accounts, 2411.11 & .13, 2412.09, 2413
Budgetary comparison statement, 2413.03–.05
Business combinations, 2315
    acquisition method, 2315.04 & .12–.14
    forms of, 2315.02–.07
    pooling of interests method, 2315.56–.68
    purchase method, 2315.33–.35

C

Capital assets, 2443
Capital projects funds, 2412.08–.21
Capital stock, 2250.03
Cash, 2210.04–.13
    proof of, 2210.11–.13
Cash basis, 2151
    modified, 2152
Cash discounts, 2213.11
Cash surrender value of life insurance, 2226.01–.02
Casualty insurance (coinsurance), 2230.04–.09
Changes in accounting estimates, 2305.27–.40
Changes in accounting principles
    current approach, 2305.24–.26
    retrospective approach, 2305.04–.23
Changes in reporting entity, 2305.41–.43
Classification and aggregation, 2121.20
Classification of stockholders' equity, 2250.01–.09
Colleges and university (government)
    accounting and reporting, 2450.13–.14
    business-type activities only, 2450.15–.16
    government and business-type activities, 2450.17
    illustrative entries, 2450.18
Common stock, 2250.12
Comparability, 2121.12
Compensated absences, 2261
Comprehensive annual financial report (CAFR), 2420
Comprehensive income, 2121.15, 2133
Conceptual framework, 2120
    cash flows and present value, using, 2121.29–.32
    elements of financial statements, 2121.14–.18
    IFRS, 2121.02, .08, .13 & .18,
    objectives, 2121.03–.08
    qualitative characteristics, 2121.09–.13

recognition and measurement, 2121.19–.28
Conservatism, 2112.11
Consignment sales, 2251.17–.18
Consistency, 2112.09
Consolidated financial statements, 2320
    adjusting and eliminating entries, 2323
    changes in parent's ownership interest, 2328.09–.34
    intercompany profits and losses, 2324, 2327
    miscellaneous problem areas, 2328
Consolidation, 2315.03
Consumption of benefit, 2121.27
Contingencies, 2330.01–.09
    accounting for, 2330.07
Convertible bonds, 2225.67
    conversion, 2225.69–.74
    issuance, 2225.68
Correction of errors, 2305
Cost(s), 2252
Cost-benefit, 2121.12
Cost method, 2225.08, 2250.27–.28
Cumulative effect of accounting change, 2345.01
Cumulative preferred stock, 2250.52 & .66, 2335.13
Current liabilities, 2231
    defined, 2231.01 & .07

D

Debt securities, 2220.06
Debt, modification of, 2244.01–.02
Debt service funds, 2412.13
Decision usefulness, 2121.12
Deferred compensation plan, 2412.46
Deferred payment contracts, 2213.12
Deferred tax, 2270.01–.10
Defined benefit pension plans, 2264.04–.05
Defined contribution plans, 2264.04
Dependent period (integral) concept, 2375.02
Depletion, 2230.10–.15
Depreciation, 2213.41–.58
    disclosure, 2213.59
    double-declining-balance, 2213.50
    group or composite, 2213.55
    straight-line, 2213.48
    sum-of-the-years'-digits, 2213.52
    units of production, 2213.54
Derivative instruments, 2363–66
Dilution, 2335.08–.10
Disclosure, 2112.09, 2136, 2155.04, 2213.59, 2225.83–.90, 2270.43, 2330.10–.14, 2387.04, 2390
    and IFRS, 2136.06–.07
Discounting, 2211.17–.23
Disposal of a segment, 2345.01 & .09–.17
Distribution(s) to owners, 2121.15
Distribution of partnership income/loss, 2224.09–.12

Dividends, 2250.33–.55
Donated assets, 2213.17
Donated capital, 2250.05

E

Earned, 2121.26
Earnings, 2121.22
Earnings per share, 2335
    antidilution, 2335.10
    basic EPS, 2335.07 & .10
    complex, 2335.07
    computational guidelines, 2335.12–.44
    concepts, fundamental, 2335
    dilution, 2335.10
    illustration, 2335.45–.52
Elimination of intercompany profits and losses, 2324, 2327
Embedded derivatives, 2355.45–.47
Emerging Issues Task Force (EITF) 94–3, 2112.16
Employee(s), 2264.02
Employee benefit plans/trusts, 2155
Employee stock options, 2265
Employer (sponsor), 2264.02
Encumbrances, 2411.12, 2412.03, 2449
Enterprise fund, 2412.29–.31
Entity, separate, 2112.09
Equity, 2131.02
Equity method, 2225.09 & .12–.17
Equity securities, 2210.08
Error correction, 2305
Estimated revenue, 2411.10–.11
Estimates, financial statements and, 2389.07–.13
Exchange of assets, 2386
Exchange rate, 2361.02
Expenditures, 2411.11, 2412.03, 2447
Expenses, 2121.15, 2132.05, 2252
Extinguishment of debt, 2244.03–.12
    gains and losses, 2244.12
Extraordinary items, 2345.01 & .15–.19, 2375.10

F

Factoring, 2393.07
Fair value measurements, 2350
Fair value option for financial assets and liabilities, 2350.28–.35
    disclosure, 2350.33
    and FASB ASC 825-10-25-1, 2350.32
    IFRS, 2350.35
    unrealized gains and losses, 2350.31
Fair value of plan assets, 2264.05
Fiduciary accounting, 2224.29–.40
    charge and discharge statement, 2224.32
    estates/trusts, 2224.30–.33

insolvency/bankruptcy, 2224.34–40
    statement of affairs, 2224.35–.37
    statement of realization and liquidation, 2224.38–.40
Fiduciary fund accounting, 2412.37–49
Financial Accounting & Reporting examination
    format, 2011
    readings and references, suggested, 2013
    purpose, 2010
Financial instruments, 2221.15–.27
Financial reporting
    by not-for profit (nongovernmental) entities, 2122
    by state and governmental entities, 2123
Financial statements, 2100, 2130, 2150
    balance sheet, 2131
    basic principles, 2112.02
    elements, 2121.14–.18
    employee benefit plans/trusts, 2155
    footnote and supplemental disclosure, 2136.04–.07
    full set, 2121.19
    IFRS and elements, 2121.18 & .28
    IFRS and footnote and supplemental disclosure, 2136.06–.07
    income statement, 2132
    modifying conventions, 2112.10–.17
    overview, 2131.01–.07
    recognition and measurement, 2121.19–.28
    statement of cash flows, 2135
    statement of stockholders' equity, 2134
Fixed assets, 2213
    cost at acquisition, 2213.06–.38
    depreciation, 2213.41–.59
    donated assets, 2213.17
    IFRS, 2213.60
    involuntary conversion, 2386.17
    nonmonetary exchanges, 2386
    nonreciprocal transfers, 2386.13–.16
    post-acquisition costs, 2213.39–.59
Fixed-percentage-of-declining-balance method, 2213.49
Footnotes, 2136
Foreign operations, 2360
    foreign currency transactions, 2362
    forward exchange contracts, 2361.02, 2363
    general concepts, 2361.01–.03
    translation of foreign currency financial statement, 2367
Forward rate, 2361.02
Franchise fee, 2251.19–.22
Functional currency, 2361.02
Fund balances, 2442
Fundamental earnings per share, 2335.01–.11
Funded reserves, 2412.16
Futures contracts, 2133.18

G

GAAP, nonbusiness organizations, 2122.09–.12
    colleges and universities, 2450.01
    hospitals, 2450.01
Gain(s), 2121.15, 2132.05
Gain contingency, 2330.07
GASB Concepts Statement 1, 2411.05
General fund, 2411.08, 2412.02–.05
General long-term liabilities group, 2412.24
General purpose financial statements, 2121.20
Generally accepted accounting principles (GAAP), 2112.02–.03 & .06
    hierarchy, 2114.08
Going concern, 2112.09, 2224.35
Goods in transit, 2212.13
Goodwill, 2224.17–.22
Governmental accounting, 2400
    actual accounts, 2411.11
    arbitrage, 2412.12
    budgetary accounts, 2411.11
    encumbrance accounting, 2411.12, 2449
    expenditures, 2447
    fiduciary fund, 2412.37
    financial reporting, 2420
    funds definition, 2411.11
    funds, types of, 2411.11
    general fund, 2412.02–.05
    governmental fund, 2411.11
    interfund transactions, 2445
    nature and objectives, 2411.01–.06
    proprietary fund, 2412.25–.32
    standards board, 2114
    reporting entity, 2420.03, 2425.01, 2430.01–.04
    revenue, 2411.14
    special items, 2448
    terminology, 2501.06–.07
Governmental Accounting Standards Board (GASB), 2114
Governmental entities, financial reporting by, 2123
Governmental fund, 2411.08 & .10, 2412
    capital projects fund, 2412.08–.12
    debt service fund, 2412.13–.18
    general capital assets account groups, 2411.08, 2443.03–.09
    general long-term liabilities account group, 2411.08, 2412.24
    operating statement, 2411.15
    special assessment projects, 2412.19–.21

H

Held-to-maturity securities, 2223
Historical cost, 2112.09
Holding gain, 2133.02
Hospital accounting, 2450.01–.12
    balance sheet, 2450.05

illustrative entries, 2450.12
statement of cash flows, 2450.11
statement of revenues, expenses, and changes in net assets, 2450.06–.12

I

If-converted method (EPS), 2335.24–.25
Impairment
    of loan, 2211.24, 2225.49–.66
    marketable securities, 2222.05
    notes receivable, 2211.15–.16
Impairment of long-lived assets, 2370.01–.27
Imputed interest on receivables and payables, 2252.05–.11
Income, 2132.05
Income statement, 2132
    cumulative effect of a change in accounting principle, 2345.20
    extraordinary items, 2345
    format, 2132
    IFRS, 2133.11
    multiple-step, 2132.07
    single-step, 2132.07
Income tax(es), 2270
    bad debt reserves of savings and loan, 2270.47–.48
    basis, 2153
    associations, 2270.47–48
    intraperiod allocation, 2270.11–.14
    investment tax credit, 2270.15–.19
    liability method, 2270.02 & .05
    surplus of life insurance companies, 2270.49
    temporary differences, 2270.02–.07 & .09–.10
    undistributed earnings of subsidiary, 2270.45–.46
Indirect guarantee, 2330.11
Industry (accounting) practices, 2112.10
Infrastructure assets, 2443
Insolvency, 2224.34–.38
Installment sales, 2251.10–.16
Insurance, 2230.04–.09
    coinsurance, 2230.04–.09
Intangible assets, 2230, 2443
    acquisition costs, 2230.23–.26
    amortization, 2230.27–.40
    impairment, 2230.31–.33, 2370
    nature of, 2230.16–.22
Interest, 2213.18
    capitalization, 2212.03–.04, 2213.19–.38
Interest imputed on receivables/payables, 2252.05–.11
Interfund transactions, 2445
Interim reporting, 2375
Internal service fund, 2412.33–.36
International Accounting Standards Board (IASB), 2113

International Financial Reporting Standards (IFRS), 2131.12, 2138
    business combinations, 2315.74
    financial statement presentation, 2230.43
    property, plant, and equipment, 2213.60
    segment reporting, 2390.29
Intraperiod income tax allocation, 2270.11–.14
Inventories, 2212
    basis of accounting, 2212.02
    comparison FIFO to LIFO, 2212.20
    consigned goods, 2212.14
    conventional retail, 2212.29
    cost flow methods, 2212.16–.20
    dollar-value LIFO, 2212.22–.23
    FIFO, 2212.16–.20
    gross profit method, 2212.31–.33
    LIFO, 2212.11, .16 & .18–.23
    lower of cost or market, 2212.09, .29 & .34–.41
    periodic inventory system, 2212.15 & .17–.18
    perpetual inventory system, 2212.15 & .17–.18
    retail method, 2212.24–.26
    systems, 2212.15
    weighted-average, 2212.18 & .21
Investment in stocks, 2225.01–.38
    cost method, 2225.08
    equity method, 2225.09
    stock dividends, 2225.19–.21
    stock dividends and splits, 2225.19–.21
    stock rights, 2225.22–..38
Investment tax credit
    accounting for, 2270.15–.19
Investments by owners, 2121.15
Investments in debt and equity securities, 2220.03–.08
Investments in debt securities, 2225.39–.48
    discount, 2225.41–.48
    premium, 2225.41–.48
Investments, long-term, 2220
    bonds, 2225.39–.48
    nature and classification, 2220.01–.02
    property, 2226
    stocks, 2225.02–.38
Involuntary conversions, 2386.17

J

Joint ventures, 2224

L

Large stock dividends, 2250.49
Leases, 2380
    amortization period, lessee, 2383.06
    capital lease, 2381.01–.02 & .04–.05
    capitalization criteria, 2381.02

cases, treatment of leases under varying circumstances, 2382
concepts, 2381
direct financing, 2381.05, 2382.01 & .03
executory costs, 2383.04–.05
lessor and lessee classification criteria, , 2381.04–.05
leveraged leases, 2381.05, 2383.12–.13
operating, 2381.01 & .04–.05, 2382.09–.11
real estate leases, 2383.10–.11
related parties, 2383.08
residual value, 2383.02–.03
sale and leaseback, 2383.07
subleases, 2383.09
Liabilities, 2121.15, 2131.08
Liabilities, current, 2210.03, 2231.07
Liabilities, long-term, 2240
asset retirement obligations, 2310
bonds, convertible, 2225.67–.82
bonds, nonconvertible, 2242
disclosure, 2225.83–.90
exit or disposal activities, 2340
statement presentation, 2240.01–.03
Life insurance
cash surrender value, 2226.01–.02
Long-term contracts revenue, 2251.05–.09
Long-term investments, 2220
cash surrender value of life insurance, 2226.01–.02
investment in debt securities, 2225.39–.48
investment in stocks, 2225.02–.38
nature, 2220.01–.02
special purpose funds, 2226.03–.05
Long-term obligations, 2240
disclosures, 2225.83–.90
unconditional purchase obligations, 2225.83–.89
Losses, 2121.15 & .18, 2132.05
Lower of cost or market
inventory, 2212.09, .29 & .34–.41
Lump-sum acquisitions, 2213.15, 2230.24–.25

M

Marketable securities, 2154.15, 2220
definitions, 2220.06–.07
disclosure requirements, 2220.08
financial statement presentation, 2220.08
Matching, 2112.09
Materiality, 2112.11, 2121.12 & .25
Measurability, 2121.25
Merger, 2315.02
Milestone method, 2251.32–.35
Modification of debt, 2244.01–.02
Modified accrual accounting, 2412.01
Modified cash basis, 2152

Modifying conventions, 2112.10–.11
Mutual agency, 2224.05

N

Natural resources, 2230.10–.15
Nature of operations, 2389.05–.06
Net assets, 2441
Net realizable value, 2211.02
Neutrality, 2121.12
Nonbusiness accounting standards-setting, 2122.09–.12, 2410
Nonbusiness organizations, 2410
government colleges and university, 2450
governmental accounting, 2400
hospital accounting, 2450
Nonconvertible bonds, 2242
debt issued with detachable stock purchase warrant, 2243.02–.05
extinguishment of debt, 2244.03–.11
gains and losses, 2244.12
serial bonds, 2242.09–.17
Nonmonetary exchange, 2386
Nonprofit entities, financial reporting by, 2122
Nonprofit organizations (NPO), 2450
expenses, 2524
hospital reporting, 2526.01–.05
investments, 2525
net assets, 2523
resources, restrictions on, 2522
support, revenues, and contributions, 2521
university reporting, 2526.06–.10
Nonreciprocal transfers, 2386.13–.16
Notes receivable, 2211.15–.16
discounting, 2211.17–.23
noninterest bearing, 2211.15
Notes to financial statements, 2425
Notional amount, 2355.05

O

Objectives of financial reporting, 2411.05
Objectivity, 2112.09
Offsetting, 2264.38, 2330.18
Operating segments, 2390
Other comprehensive bases of accounting (OCBOA), 2150
Overhead costs, 2213.13

P

Par value method, 2250.29
Partnership accounting, 2224.04–.28.
accounts, 2224.07–08
changes in partners, 2224.13–.22
distribution of income/loss, 2224.09–.12

general concepts, 2224.04–.06
liquidation, 2224.23–.28
Pension accounting, 2264
    accounting and reporting, 2263.04–.07
    basic concepts, 2264.01–.04
    defined benefit pension plan, 2264.05
    defined contribution plans, 2264.04
    gain or loss recognition, 2264.26–.41
    interest cost, 2264.07
    postemployment benefits, 2412.45–.49
    postretirement benefits, 2263.01–.03
    prior service cost amortization, 2264.07
    return on plan assets, 2264.07
    service cost, 2264.07
    settlement and curtailment, 2264.42–.43
Pension trust funds, 2412.49
Permanently restricted net assets, 2523.01
Periodicity, 2112.09
Personal financial statements, 2154
    GAAP, 2154.01–.02
    guidelines in determining estimated values, 2154.14–.15
    illustrative financial statements, 2154.22
    statement of changes in net worth, 2154.10–.13
    statement of financial condition, 2154.03–.09
Plant and equipment, 2213
    post-acquisition costs, 2213.39–.60
Pledging, 2211.13
Pooling of interest, 2315.08–.09 & .56–.74
Postemployment benefits, 2412.45–.49
Postretirement benefits, 2263.01–.03
Predictive value, 2121.12
Preferred stock, 2250.11
    conversion, 2250.60–.61
    dividends, 2250.51–.55
    and EPS, 2335.13–.14
    liquidation, 2250.65–.67
Prior period adjustment, 2225.14, 2270.11–.12, 2305.44, 2345.22, 2375.18
Prior service cost, 2264.05 & .07
Product financing arrangements, 2251.25–.27
Program services expenses, 2524.01
Projected benefit obligation, 2263.02
Proprietary fund, 2423
    enterprise fund, 2411.08
    internal service fund, 2411.08
Proof of cash, 2210.11
Purchase method, 2325–2327
Purchasing power, 2112.09, 2133.02

R

Ratio analysis, 2137
Real estate sales, 2251.28–.31
Realized, 2121.26
Receivables, 2154.15, 2211
Recognized, 2112.09, 2121.17, 2252.01
    IFRS, 2121.18
Refundings, 2412.17–.18
Related parties disclosures, 2387
Relevance, 2121.10, .12 & .25
Reliability, 2121.10, .12 & .25
Representational faithfulness, 2121.12
Required supplementary information (RSI), 2427
Research and development costs, 2388
Retained earnings, 2131.08, 2250.06
Revenue, 2121.15, 2132.05
Revenue recognition, 2112.09, 2251
    concepts, 2251
    consignment sales, 2251.17–.18
    franchise fee, 2251.19–.22
    installment sales, 2251.10–.16
    long-term contracts, 2251.05–.09
    product financing arrangements, 2251.25–.27
    revenue received in advance, 2232
    right of return exists, when, 2251.23–.24
    sales of real estate, 2251.28–.31
Risks and uncertainties, 2389

S

Sales
    discounts, 2211.05–.06
    returns and allowances, 2211.07
Seasonal revenues, costs, or expenses, 2375.08
Securities and Exchange Commission (SEC), 2111, 2140
Segment reporting, 2390
    asset information, 2390.20–.21
    asset test, 2390.09
    chief operating decision maker, 2390.06
    enterprise-wide disclosures, 2390.26–.28
    general information, 2390.18
    interim period information, 2390.25
    major customers, 2390.29
    measurement, 2390.22
    operating segments, 2390.05
    profit and loss, 2390.21
    profitability test, 2390.09 & .11
    reportable segments, 2390.09
    required disclosures, 2390.17
    revenue test, 2390.09
    segment manager, 2390.07
Separate entity, 2112.09
Serial bonds, 2242.09–.17
Significant influence, 2225.05–.07
Sinking fund, 2225.90, 2226.03, 2250.66
Small stock dividends, 2250.47
Software costs, 2391
Special assessment projects, 2412.19–.20
Special items (governmental), 2448
Special revenue fund, 2412.06–.07

Spot rate, 2361.02
State entities, financial reporting by, 2123
Statement of affairs, 2224.35–.36
Statement of cash flows, 2121.23, 2135
    financing activities, from, 2135.01–.05
    illustration, 2135.16–.19
    investing activities, from, 2135.01–.05
    objectives, 2135.06–.09
    operating activities, from, 2135.01–.05
    preparation tips, 2135.20–.24
    principles, 2135.10–.15
Statement(s) of Financial Accounting Concepts (SFAC)
    Statement 1, 2121
    Statement 2, 2121.09–.13
    Statement 4, 2122.02–.08
    Statement 6, 2121, 2131.08, 2132.05, 2133.02, 2231.01, 2340.06
    Statement 7, 2121.29–60
Statement(s) of the Governmental Accounting Standards Board (GASB)
    Statement 7, 2412.17
    Statement 9, 2450.11
    Statement 10, 2445.05
    Statement 16, 2445.05
    Statement 17, 2445.05
    Statement 20, 2412.25
    Statement 23, 2412.32
    Statement 25, 2412.47, 2424.02
    Statement 29, 2410.09
    Statement 31, 2411.18
    Statement 33, 2446.01
    Statement 34, 2429.01, 2443.05, 2444.01, 2450.01, .13–.14 & .17
    Statement 35, 2450.13–.14
    Statement 38, 2425.01
    Statement 39, 2430.02
    Statement 42, 2443.08
    Statement 44, 2420.04
    Statement 45, 2424.02
Statement of stockholders' equity, 2134
Stock
    appreciation rights, 2265.23–.25
    book value, 2250.01–.04
    dividends, 2225.19, 2250.43, 2335.13
    investment in, 2220
    issuance for fixed assets, 2213.16
    no par, 2250.16–.18
    par value, 2250.13
    preferred dividends, 2250.51–.55
    rights, 2225.22–.38
    stock splits, 2225.19
    subscription, 2250.19–.22
    treasury, 2250.23–.29
    warrants, 2225.22–.38, 2243.02–.05

Stock-based compensation plans, 2265
Stock option plans, 2265
Stock purchase warrants, 2243.02–.05
Stockholders' equity, 2250
    classification, 2250.01–.09
    dividends, 2250.33–.55
    IFRS, 2134.03
    issuance of stock, 2250.10–.22
    miscellaneous issues, 2250.56–.67
    statement of changes in, 2134
    stock splits, 2250.44
    treasury stock, 2250.23–.29
Subleases, 2383.09
Subsequent events, 2392
Subsidiary third-party transactions, 2328.30–.34
Substance over form, 2112.11
Supplemental disclosure, 2136

T

Temporarily restricted net assets, 2523.01
Temporary differences, 2270.02–.03
Timeliness, 2121.12
Trading securities, 2221.01–.14
Transfer of receivables, 2211.12–.14
Treasury stock, 2250.09 & .23–.29
    balance sheet presentation, 2250.26–.27
    cost method, 2250.24–.25
    in EPS, 2335.16–.17
    par value method, 2250.29
Treasury stock method, 2335.16–.17
Troubled debt restructuring, 2245.19
Trustee, 2264.02

U

Uncertainties, risks and, 2389
Underlying accounting principles, 2112.09
Understandability, 2121.12
Unit of measure, 2112.09
Unlimited liability, 2224.05
Unrealized capital, 2250.07
Usefulness, 2121.12 & .20
Users of financial reports, 2411.03

V

Variable interest entities (consolidation of), 2328.47–.54
Verifiability, 2121.12
Voluntary health and welfare organizations (VHWO), 2501.04 & .06, 2510.01, 2511.01

W

Warranty liability, 2231.03, 2270.03

Weighted-average common shares (WACS), 2335.02–.03, .06, .10, .12–.42 & .45–.52
With/without recourse, 2211
Working capital, 2210
    defined, 2210.01
Write-down
    discontinued operations, 2345.08
    extraordinary items, 2345.18
    fixed assets, 2213.05
    impairment of securities, 2222.05
    inventory, 2212.39
    long-lived assets, 2370.02, .22 & .26
    marketable securities, 2222.04–.05